Financing Residential Real Estate

14th Edition

Megan Dorsey
David Rockwell

Rockwell Publishing Company

13218 N.E. 20th Street
Bellevue, WA 98005
(425)747-7272 / 1-800-221-9347

ISBN-10: 1-887051-33-3
ISBN-13: 978-1-887051-33-0

PRINTED IN THE UNITED STATES OF AMERICA

Contents

Chapter 1
Finance and Investment

Borrowing Money to Buy a Home

- Mortgage financing and affordability
- How mortgage financing works
- Loans as investments

Investments and Returns

- Investment capital
- Return on investment vs. return of investment

Types of Investments

- Ownership investments
- Debt investments
- Securities

Investment Risk

- Safety, liquidity, and yield
- Diversification
- Lending risks
  - Risk of default
  - Risk of loss
  - Interest rate risk
  - Prepayment risk

Market Interest Rates

- Factors that affect mortgage rates
- How interest rates affect real estate activity

Introduction

Financing—lending and borrowing money—is fundamental to the real estate business. If mortgage financing weren't available, buyers would have to pay cash for their homes, something few people can afford to do.

This book has a practical focus; it explains the basic process of obtaining a loan to purchase a home and examines the wide variety of financing options that are currently being offered to home buyers. The opening chapters present background information about the financial system behind the mortgage business. This includes the sources of loan funds, the primary and secondary mortgage markets, the different types of mortgage lenders, and the effect of government fiscal and monetary policy on mortgage lending. All of these factors directly or indirectly affect whether home buyers can get the financing they need, and if so, on what terms.

Mortgage loans are a type of investment, one of many types that compete for a share of the available investment funds. This chapter provides an overview of investing and explains some of the underlying investment considerations that determine what kinds of loans mortgage lenders are (and are not) willing to make.

Borrowing Money to Buy a Home

In the United States, owning a home is considered an essential part of a middle-class lifestyle. It's seen as a mark of achievement, and also as part of the groundwork for future prosperity and security. Most Americans buy a home if they can afford to do so.

An individual or family's ability to afford a home depends on many factors, including housing prices, income level, tax considerations, and so on. Among the most important factors is the availability of mortgage financing. A home is the most expensive purchase most people ever make, and nearly everyone needs to borrow a large amount of money to do it.

Typical mortgage financing:
- Loan covers much of price
- Downpayment is from buyer's own resources
- Purchased property serves as collateral

In a typical mortgage loan transaction, the lender loans the home buyers a large portion of the purchase price and requires them to provide the rest out of their own resources, as a downpayment. In return for the loan, the buyers must execute a mortgage or deed of trust in the lender's favor. This creates a lien, giving the lender a security interest in the property being purchased, so that the property serves as collateral for the loan.

Principal: the original amount borrowed, or the part of the loan that remains to be repaid

The buyers agree to pay back the **principal** (the amount borrowed) by means of monthly payments over a specified period (the **loan term**). In addition, as long as part of the debt is outstanding, the buyers must pay the lender a specified percentage of the remaining principal balance as **interest**. From the buyers' point of view, the interest is the cost of borrowing money; it's the amount the lender charges them for the temporary use of the principal.

Interest: the cost of borrowing money

When the full amount borrowed and all of the interest owed have been repaid, the lender releases the property from its lien. This might not happen until the end of the loan term, when all of the scheduled monthly payments have been made. Or the loan could be paid off earlier—for example, out of the sale proceeds if the home is sold.

That summarizes the basic model of home financing. In the course of the book we'll be looking at dozens of variations on the basic model: adjustable-rate mortgages, zero-down mortgages, FHA-insured mortgages, loans with buydowns, loans with secondary financing, and so on. Especially in recent years, most of the innovations in mortgage financing have been specifically designed to help more people buy homes. There are so many options now that it's easy to take the availability of affordable mortgage financing for granted. After all, lenders want to make loans.

Loan is an investment; lender is an investor

Interest is lender's return on the loan/investment

But it's important to realize that from the lender's point of view, a loan is an investment. The interest paid by the borrower will be the lender's primary **return** (profit) on its investment. And regardless of innovations, trends, or other considerations, there's one key test that every mortgage loan has to meet: the lender must consider the loan a profitable investment under the economic conditions prevailing at the time the loan is made. Otherwise, the lender won't make the loan.

Because loans are investments, it will be helpful to look at mortgage lending in the broader context of investing and the economy as a whole.

Investments and Returns

The national economy—the system of businesses, industries, and trade that provides us with jobs, income, places to live, and goods and services—is driven in part by **investment capital**. Investment capital

Investment capital: accumulated wealth (savings) made available to fund enterprises

is simply money (accumulated wealth, or savings) that's used to fund business enterprises and other ventures, projects, and transactions.

An investor supplies capital for an enterprise or a project in the expectation that it will generate additional wealth for the investor—a return on the investment. Depending on the type of investment, the investor's return may take various forms, including interest, appreciation, rents, or dividends.

Return of investment: recapture of amount originally invested

Return on investment: investor's profit

A return *on* an investment is distinguished from a return *of* the investment. A return of the investment, also called **recapture**, refers to getting back the full amount originally invested. A return on the investment, by contrast, is a profit over and above the amount originally invested.

Sometimes an investor only breaks even, receiving a return of the investment without a return on the investment. And sometimes an investor runs the risk of losing part or even all of the money originally invested. In other words, if an investment turns out badly, the investor might not even receive a return of the investment, much less a return on the investment.

Types of Investments

There are two general categories of investments: ownership investments and debt investments.

Ownership Investments

Ownership investment: investor purchases an asset or a property interest in an asset

When an investor uses his investment funds to purchase an asset or a property interest in an asset, it's an ownership investment. If the asset is income-producing, the net income it generates during the investor's period of ownership is a return on the investment. And if the asset **appreciates** (increases in value over time), the appreciation is a return on the investment. An asset may appreciate because of inflation (a general increase in prices due to economic forces), because the demand for that type of asset increases, or as a result of both inflation and increased demand.

Real Estate Investment. The purchase of real estate is an example of an ownership investment. If the real estate is an income-producing property such as an apartment building, the net income from the property (rents paid by the tenants, minus the operating expenses) provides a return on the investment for the investor/owner. Whether or not the property is income-producing, when the property is sold the investor is likely to receive a higher price than she paid for it. The appreciation—the difference between the price paid (the amount invested) and the price received—is a return on the investment.

Return on ownership investment may be:
- Net income, and/or
- Appreciation

Corporate Stock. The purchase of shares of corporate stock is another example of an ownership investment. The shares represent an ownership interest in the corporation. The corporation uses its stockholders' invested funds to help its business grow and generate profits. If the corporation pays dividends (a share of its profits) to the stockholders, the dividends represent a return on their investment. They can also receive a return in the form of appreciation: if the corporation does well, the value of the corporation's stock goes up, and stockholders can sell their shares at a profit.

Ownership investment examples:
- Real estate purchases
- Stock purchases

Debt Investments

With a debt investment, the investor provides money to an individual or a company that will eventually repay it. In exchange for the temporary use of the funds, the investor/lender charges the borrower interest, a specified percentage of the amount owed, until the debt is repaid. The investor doesn't have an ownership interest in the property that the borrower is buying or improving, or the business or project that the borrower is undertaking. The investor is involved only as a creditor, and the return on the investment is the interest the borrower pays.

Debt investment: investor provides money to an entity that will eventually repay it

Loans. Any form of loan that will earn interest for the lender is a debt investment, including the residential mortgage loans we're concerned with in this book. When a bank loans a couple money so that they can buy a home, the loan represents a debt investment for the bank. The borrowers will repay the bank's invested capital in monthly installments over a period of years, and they'll also pay interest on the capital.

Debt investment examples:
- Loans
- Bonds
- Savings accounts

Note that at the same time the bank is making a debt investment, the home buyers are making an ownership investment. They're investing their own savings (the downpayment) plus the money they're borrowing, in order to purchase an asset (the home). Their primary reason for buying the home may be to have a place to live, but if the home appreciates while they own it, they'll get a return on their investment when they sell it.

Bonds. Another example of a debt investment is the purchase of bonds. A **bond** is a certificate of indebtedness issued by a governmental body or a corporation. An investor who buys bonds (a bondholder) is essentially loaning the price paid for the bonds to the entity that issued them. The issuer makes periodic payments of interest to the bondholder until the bond's maturity date, when the issuer repays the principal to the bondholder in a lump sum. The interest rate paid on a bond is called the coupon rate, and the principal is called the face amount of the bond.

Savings Accounts. An ordinary savings account is also a debt investment. A depositor puts his money into a savings account for safekeeping and so that it will earn interest. The financial institution uses its depositors' funds to make loans to home buyers and other borrowers. In effect, the depositors are loaning their money to the financial institution (and receiving interest as a return on their investment) to enable the financial institution to make debt investments of its own (loans to customers). To make a profit, the financial institution must charge a higher interest rate on the loans it makes than the rate it pays on its savings accounts.

A debt investment similar to a savings account is the **certificate of deposit**, or CD. With a CD, in return for interest payments the investor/depositor agrees to keep funds on deposit (and available for use by the financial institution) during a specified period, such as 6, 12, or 24 months. If the depositor withdraws the funds before the end of the commitment period, the financial institution charges a penalty. CDs with longer commitment periods have higher interest rates than shorter-term CDs.

Securities

Securities are investment instruments that:
- grant the holder an interest or right to payment
- do not grant the holder any direct managerial control

Certain types of investments are categorized as **securities**. A security is an investment instrument (a legal document such as a certificate) that grants the holder an interest or a right to payment, without giving the holder any direct managerial control over the enterprise in question. Securities may be either ownership investments or debt investments; stocks and bonds are the most prominent examples.

A key characteristic of securities is that they can be bought or sold easily in financial markets established for that purpose. Stocks may be traded on a stock exchange, bonds may be traded in the bond

Fig. 1.1 Types of investments

Ownership Investments
- Investment capital used to purchase an asset or a property interest in an asset or company
- Stocks, real estate, mutual funds
- Possible returns: appreciation, rental income, and/or dividends

Debt Investments
- Investment capital provided temporarily, subject to withdrawal or eventual repayment
- Loans, bonds, savings accounts, CDs
- Returns take the form of interest

Securities
- Investment instruments
- Ownership interest or right to repayment, without managerial control
- Traded in established financial markets
- Stocks and bonds

market, and so on. Thus, securities are **liquid assets**—assets that can quickly be converted into cash.

Securities: liquid assets that can be sold easily in established financial markets

Mutual Funds. A popular way for individuals to invest in securities is through a **mutual fund**. A mutual fund is a company that buys and sells stocks and bonds on behalf of its investors. The investors purchase shares in the company, which then uses the investor/owners' capital to invest in securities. The fund managers, who are investment professionals, choose which securities to buy and when to sell them. This makes it much simpler for an individual with limited knowledge of the financial markets to invest in a variety of securities and benefit from diversification (discussed later in this chapter).

Securities Regulation. To protect investors, both the issuance and trading of securities are regulated by the federal Securities and Exchange Commission (SEC). The SEC requires companies to disclose their financial information to the public, in order to help prospective investors judge which securities are likely to be good investments. The SEC also enforces the rules against insider trading. It's illegal

SEC regulates securities trading to protect investors
- Financial disclosures required
- No insider trading

for "insiders" such as company executives and stockbrokers to reap profits or avoid losses in the securities markets by taking advantage of information that isn't yet available to the public.

Securities and the Mortgage Industry. Securities trading affects mortgage lending in two main ways. First, it has an impact on mortgage interest rates and the availability of funds for home loans, since mortgage lending competes with other types of investments. Second, mortgages themselves can be pooled together and "securitized" for sale to investors. These **mortgage-backed securities** have come to play a crucial role in the mortgage industry. We'll look at mortgage-backed securities in the next chapter, when we discuss the secondary market.

Investment Risk

Investment opportunities compete for available investment funds

The pool of funds available for investment is large but not unlimited, and all of the different investment opportunities in the economy are in competition for those funds. When deciding where to put their money, investors have to weigh the benefits of particular investments against the risks they entail.

Key Investment Characteristics

Investors consider any investment opportunity in terms of three potential advantages: safety, liquidity, and yield.

Safety: low risk of losing amount originally invested

Safety. An investment is considered safe if there's little risk that the investor will actually lose money on it. Even if the investment doesn't generate the profit hoped for, the investor will at least be able to recover the money originally invested. In other words, the investor can probably count on a return *of* the investment, if not a return *on* the investment.

Liquidity: investment can quickly be converted to cash

Liquidity. An investment is liquid if it can be converted into cash (liquidated) quickly. Liquidity is important in case the investor suddenly needs cash for unexpected expenses, or perhaps for better investment opportunities. With an investment that's **illiquid** (not liquid), the investor's funds are effectively "locked up" and unavailable for other purposes.

Example: Two investors each have $20,000 to invest. Investor A uses his $20,000 to buy stock, a liquid asset. Investor B uses her $20,000 to buy real estate, an illiquid asset.

Six months later, both investors decide they want to use the funds they've invested for some other purpose. Investor A can sell his stock—cash in his investment—without delay. It will be much more complicated and time-consuming for Investor B to sell her real estate. Depending on B's situation, the delay may merely be an inconvenience, or it could result in financial difficulties or a missed opportunity.

While real estate and other illiquid assets can be excellent investments, their lack of liquidity has consequences that prospective investors should take into account.

Yield. An investment's yield is its rate of return. Investments that are both safe and liquid typically offer the lowest yields.

Yield: investor's rate of return

Example: Patterson deposits money in an ordinary savings account. This investment is very safe, because the deposited funds are federally insured against loss. It's also very liquid, because the funds can be withdrawn at any time without penalty. However, the investment's yield (the annual interest rate that the bank pays to Patterson) is only 1.15%.

In a sense, investors "pay" for safety and liquidity with low yields. For a high yield, an investor must be willing to take the risk of losing some (or possibly even all) of the original capital if the investment turns out badly. It may also be necessary to sacrifice liquidity, allowing the capital to be tied up for a while.

Safe, liquid investments offer comparatively low yields

As a general rule, the greater the risk, the higher the potential yield needs to be; otherwise, investors won't be willing to make the investment. The higher yield compensates the investors for the additional risk. Investors generally also expect higher yields for long-term investments, those that will take longer to achieve the desired yield.

Investors expect higher yields for greater risks

Of course, the yield from a particular investment isn't necessarily fixed at the time the investment is made. The yield may change with market conditions, such as a rise or fall in interest rates. In the case of ownership investments, the enterprise invested in may turn out to be either more or less successful than anticipated, making the actual yield higher or lower than the projected yield. In the case of debt investments, a bond default or loan default may result in a sharply reduced yield.

Yield isn't necessarily fixed when an investment is made

Diversification

Portfolio: investor's mix of investments plus cash reserves

Diversification: putting money into a variety of different investments to reduce the risk of loss

An investor's mix of investments, plus any cash reserves, is referred to as a **portfolio**. To reduce risk, investors are advised to **diversify** their portfolios, putting their money into a variety of different types of investments. An investor with a diversified portfolio is less likely to face a serious net loss; if one investment does poorly, there's a fair chance that the other investments will offset that loss with good returns. A diversified investment portfolio is more likely to match the growth of the economy overall, instead of being subject to fluctuations in one particular sector of the economy.

Lending Risks

The particular risks involved in mortgage lending, from the lender/investor's point of view, include the risk of default, the risk of foreclosure loss, interest rate risk, and prepayment risk.

Lenders face:

- risk of default (borrower)
- risk of loss (collateral)
- interest rate risk
- prepayment risk

Risk of Default. The degree of risk associated with a particular loan depends first of all on how likely it is that the borrower will default. A default occurs when the borrower fails to make the payments as scheduled. Naturally, the lender hopes to avoid this problem.

Through the underwriting process (see Chapter 8), lenders screen loan applicants to determine whether they are likely to pay off their loans on schedule. If a prospective borrower looks like a good risk—that is, if the risk of default is low—the lender will agree to make the loan. If the risk of default is somewhat higher, the lender might make the loan but charge a higher interest rate to compensate for the extra risk. If the risk of default is too great, the lender will decline to make the loan.

Risk of Loss. In addition to screening prospective borrowers to evaluate the risk of default, lenders take steps to limit the risk of loss in the event that a borrower eventually does default. These steps include appraising the property to make sure that it's worth enough to serve as collateral for the loan, in case foreclosure becomes necessary, and in some cases requiring mortgage insurance on the loan. (Appraisal is covered in Chapter 9; mortgage insurance in Chapter 10.)

Borrowers are also required to keep the collateral property adequately insured against fire and other natural hazards, to protect the lender from losses that might otherwise result from the impairment of the collateral.

Interest Rate Risk. Another type of risk that a lender may face in connection with a loan is interest rate risk. This is the risk that after the lender has loaned money to a borrower at a certain interest rate, market interest rates will rise.

> **Example:** A lender makes a $200,000 mortgage loan to a home buyer. Based on current market interest rates, the lender agrees to make the loan at a fixed interest rate of 5.5%. That interest rate represents the lender's return on its $200,000 investment.
>
> Shortly after the loan closes, market interest rates begin a steep climb. A year later, they've reached 7.25%. The lender would prefer to reinvest its $200,000 now, to get a 7.25% return instead of a 5.5% return. But the loan agreement allows the borrower to repay the lender over a 30-year term. The lender's money is tied up and can't be reinvested until it's repaid.

Interest rate risk increases with the length of the loan term. The longer the loan term, the longer the lender's funds could be tied up. This makes interest rate risk a particular concern for mortgage lenders, because home purchase mortgages have very long repayment periods compared to other types of loans. (In the U.S., 30-year repayment periods are common for mortgages. See Chapter 6.)

Mortgage lenders have devised a number of ways of dealing with interest rate risk, including adjustable-rate mortgages (see Chapter 6) and selling loans on the secondary market (see Chapter 2).

Prepayment Risk. It isn't only rising interest rates that can cause trouble for a mortgage lender. When market interest rates fall, a lender often has to worry about borrowers **prepaying** their loans—paying back all or part of the principal balance sooner than expected. This might not sound like a problem for the lender, but it can be one.

Prepayment: paying back all or part of the principal before it's due

> **Example:** The Henrys financed the purchase of their home when market interest rates were quite high. They got a 30-year mortgage from Acme Savings at 9% interest.
>
> Now it's four years later, and the outstanding balance on the mortgage is $192,400. Market interest rates have dropped to 6% since the Henrys bought their house, so they decide to refinance. They borrow $193,000 from Widget Mortgage at 6% interest and use the new loan to pay off their old 9% loan.
>
> When the Henrys prepay the old mortgage, Acme Savings has to reinvest the $192,400 they've paid back. It's unlikely that the new investment will provide Acme with a 9% return, like the Henrys' mortgage did. When the mortgage was prepaid, that effectively reduced Acme's yield on the investment.

Refinancing:
- home owners get new mortgage at lower rate
- use proceeds of new mortgage to pay off old mortgage

As in the example, a sharp decline in interest rates typically leads to a great deal of refinancing and loan prepayment.

Because prepayment can work to a lender's disadvantage, some loan agreements allow the lender to charge the borrower a penalty if the loan is prepaid. The penalty prevents the prepayment from reducing the lender's yield to the extent it otherwise could. (Prepayment penalties are discussed in more detail in Chapter 5.)

Market Interest Rates

Market interest rate: typical rate charged for a certain type of loan in the current market

We've referred more than once to "market interest rates," a concept that will come up repeatedly throughout the book. Market interest rates are the typical rates that lenders are currently charging borrowers for particular types of loans. The going rate for a residential mortgage may depend on the size of the loan, whether it has a fixed or adjustable interest rate, how long the loan term is, and certain other factors. A prospective borrower's credit score may also affect the rate lenders are willing to offer. A borrower with a poor credit score can generally expect to pay a higher interest rate than one with a good score. (Credit scoring is covered in Chapter 8.)

To attract business, some lenders offer borrowers an interest rate below the going market rate. But in most cases lenders with dramatically lower rates make up for it by charging higher loan fees (see Chapter 7). On the other hand, lenders won't charge much more than the market rate, to avoid losing customers to their competition.

At one time, market interest rates for mortgages varied significantly from one area of the country to another. That's no longer true; now the regional variations are usually slight. This is largely a result of the growth of the secondary market, as we'll discuss in Chapter 2.

Mortgage rates affect real estate activity:
- High rates cause a slowdown
- Low rates spur the market

Of course, market interest rates for mortgage loans have a considerable impact on real estate activity. If mortgage rates rise too high, as they did in the 1980s, it can bring real estate activity to a standstill. On the other hand, low rates, like those available in the past several years, stimulate home sales (and also spur lots of refinancing).

Mortgage "prices" (interest rates) respond to changes in supply and demand

The forces that cause market interest rates to rise and fall are very complex. But like other kinds of prices, market interest rates for mortgage loans are affected by supply and demand: if supply exceeds demand, prices (rates) go down; if demand exceeds supply, prices (rates) go up. We'll discuss some of the factors that affect the supply of and demand for mortgage funds in the next chapter.

Outline: Finance and Investment

I. Borrowing Money to Buy a Home
   A. Buyer's ability to afford a home depends in part on the availability of mortgage financing.
   B. From lender's point of view, a loan is an investment.
      1. Interest is lender's primary return on the investment.
      2. Lender will make a loan only if it appears to be a profitable investment under prevailing economic conditions.

II. What is an Investment?
   A. Investment capital: accumulated wealth (savings) made available to fund enterprises, projects, and transactions.
   B. Investor supplies capital in the expectation that it will generate additional wealth for the investor.
   C. Returns
      1. Return *on* investment: a profit over and above the amount originally invested.
      2. Return *of* investment: recapturing the amount originally invested (breaking even).

III. Types of Investments
   A. Ownership investments: investor buys a property interest in an asset.
      1. Ownership investments may generate net income, pay dividends, and/or appreciate.
      2. Examples: purchase of real estate, purchase of corporate stock.
   B. Debt investments: investor provides money that is to be paid back.
      1. Debt investments generate interest income.
      2. Examples: loans, bonds, savings accounts, certificates of deposit.
   C. Securities: may be either ownership investments or debt investments.
      1. Examples: stocks, bonds, mortgage-backed securities.
      2. Designed to be liquid investments, easily bought and sold in established markets.
      3. Mutual funds: investor purchases shares in a mutual fund company; fund managers use the capital to buy and sell securities.
      4. Federal Securities and Exchange Commission (SEC) regulates issuance and trading of securities to protect investors.

IV. Investment Risk

A. Key investment characteristics

1. Safety: low risk of losing part or all of original investment amount.
2. Liquidity
   a. Liquid asset can be converted into cash (sold) quickly.
   b. Liquidity tends to increase safety (reduce risk of loss).
3. Yield: rate of return.
   a. Investor usually pays for safety and liquidity with lower yield.
   b. Generally, the greater the risk, the higher the yield investors will demand.
   c. Investment's yield is not necessarily fixed at outset; may change with economy, success or failure of enterprise, etc.

B. Diversified investment portfolio reduces overall risk of loss.

C. Lending risks

1. Risk of default: borrower might not repay loan.
2. Risk of loss: property might be destroyed; foreclosure proceeds might not cover loan balance.
3. Interest rate risk: market rates may rise while loan funds are tied up at low rate.
4. Prepayment risk: loan may be paid off sooner than expected if market rates decline.

V. Market Interest Rates

A. Market rates are typical rates paid for a particular type of loan in the current market.

B. Factors that may affect market rates for mortgages include size of loan, fixed or adjustable rate, length of loan term, region of country, and/or borrower's credit score.

C. Real estate activity increases with low rates, decreases with high rates.

D. Market interest rates go up when demand for mortgage funds exceeds supply, and go down when supply exceeds demand.

Key Terms

Mortgage loan: A loan secured by a mortgage or deed of trust that creates a lien against real property; especially, a loan used to purchase real property when that same property serves as security for the loan.

Lien: A nonpossessory interest in real property, giving the lienholder the right to foreclose if the owner does not pay a debt owed to the lienholder.

Collateral: Property (personal or real) accepted by a lender as security for a loan. The lender has the right to keep or sell the collateral if the borrower fails to repay the loan as agreed.

Principal: The original amount of a loan, or the remainder of that amount after part of it has been repaid.

Interest: A periodic charge that a lender requires a borrower to pay in exchange for the temporary use of the borrowed funds, usually expressed as an annual percentage of the remaining principal balance. Sometimes referred to as the cost of borrowing money.

Investment: When someone (an investor) makes a sum of money (investment capital) available for use by another person or entity, in the expectation that this will generate a return (a profit) for the investor.

Investment capital: Accumulated wealth (savings) made available to fund business enterprises or other ventures, projects, or transactions.

Return on investment: A profit that an investment generates for an investor, over and above the amount of money that he or she originally invested in it.

Return of investment: When an investment generates enough money for an investor to replace the amount of money he or she originally invested in it. Also called recapture.

Ownership investment: An investment in which the investor's funds are used to purchase an asset or a property interest in an asset.

Debt investment: An investment in which temporary use of the investor's funds is exchanged for interest payments, pursuant to an agreement that requires repayment of the funds or allows withdrawal of the funds.

Appreciation: An increase in the value of an asset over time; the opposite of depreciation.

Dividend: A share of a company's profits paid to a stockholder as a return on the investment.

Certificate of deposit (CD): A savings arrangement in which a depositor agrees to leave money on deposit for the use of the financial institution for a specified period, or pay a penalty for earlier withdrawal.

Securities: Investment instruments that confer an interest or a right to payment, without allowing any direct managerial control over the enterprise invested in.

Stock: A share of a corporation's stock represents a fractional ownership interest in the corporation; a shareholder may receive a return on the investment in the form of dividends and/or appreciation of the share's value.

Bond: A certificate of indebtedness issued by a governmental body or a corporation; it will generate a return for the bondholder in the form of periodic payments of interest until the principal is repaid in a lump sum.

Mutual fund: A company that invests its capital in a diversified portfolio of securities on behalf of its investors, who own shares in the fund.

Liquid investment: An investment that can be quickly and easily converted into cash.

Yield: The rate of return that an investor receives on an investment, usually stated as an annual percentage of the amount invested.

Portfolio: The mix of investments and cash reserves held by an investor.

Diversification: The practice of investing in a variety of different ways and/or in a variety of different sectors of the economy, to make a portfolio safer.

Interest rate risk: The risk that, after a loan is made for a specified term at a fixed interest rate, market interest rates will rise and the lender will miss the opportunity to invest the loaned funds at a higher rate.

Prepayment risk: The risk that a loan will be paid off sooner than expected (often because market interest rates have dropped), reducing the lender's anticipated yield.

Market interest rates: The rates that, under current economic conditions, are paid on particular types of investments or charged for particular types of loans.

Chapter Quiz

1. In connection with a loan, the term "principal" refers to the:
   a. amount borrowed
   b. lender
   c. property purchased
   d. repayment period

2. Stocks and bonds are the primary examples of:
   a. ownership investments
   b. securities
   c. collateral
   d. All of the above

3. All of the following are debt investments, except:
   a. savings account
   b. government bond
   c. certificate of deposit
   d. purchase of real estate

4. A company that invests in a diversified portfolio of stocks and bonds on behalf of its investor/owners is called a:
   a. mutual fund
   b. security fund
   c. insider trading firm
   d. liquidity firm

5. Stevenson borrowed money from Acme Savings to buy a rental house. He paid 15% down. Which of the following is true?
   a. Acme has made a debt investment
   b. Stevenson has made an ownership investment
   c. Both of the above
   d. Neither of the above

6. The return that a mortgage lender receives on its typical investments takes the form of:
   a. appreciation
   b. dividends
   c. rental income
   d. interest

7. The phrase "return on an investment" refers to:
   a. recapture of the amount originally invested
   b. an annual yield of at least 10%
   c. an investor's profit over and above the amount originally invested
   d. net income after deducting dividends

8. As a general rule, the safer the investment:
   a. the less liquid the yield
   b. the less certain the yield
   c. the lower the yield
   d. the higher the yield

9. When market interest rates are rising, a lender making a 30-year loan at a fixed interest rate will probably be most concerned about:
   a. prepayment risk
   b. liquidity risk
   c. mutual fund risk
   d. interest rate risk

10. An investor who might need to cash in investments to cover unexpected expenses is likely to be especially concerned about:
    a. bond yields
    b. liquidity
    c. prepayment risk
    d. insider trading

Answer Key

1. a. A loan's principal is the money that was borrowed—the amount originally borrowed, and once repayment has begun, the amount that remains to be paid—as opposed to the interest that accrues on the principal.

2. b. Stocks and bonds are examples of securities, investment instruments that are traded in established financial markets. (Stocks are ownership investments, but bonds are debt investments.)

3. d. The purchase of real estate is an ownership investment, not a debt investment.

4. a. A mutual fund invests the capital provided by its shareholders in a diversified portfolio of securities; the fund managers who make the decisions are investment professionals.

5. c. Acme's loan to Stevenson was a debt investment, and Stevenson's real estate purchase was an ownership investment.

6. d. A mortgage lender's typical investments (mortgage loans) provide a return in the form of interest payments.

7. c. A return *on* an investment is a profit for the investor. (A return *of* the investment is the recapture of the amount originally invested.)

8. c. The safer the investment, the lower the yield. High-yield investments tend to be high-risk investments.

9. d. The lender will be most concerned about interest rate risk, the risk that market rates will rise significantly while the lender's funds are tied up in long term loans at lower rates.

10. b. If an investor might need to cash in an investment on short notice, it's better if the investment is a liquid one—one that's easily converted into cash.

Chapter 2
The Primary and Secondary Markets

The Two Mortgage Markets

- Primary market
  - Loan origination
  - Local financing
  - Real estate cycles
- Secondary market
  - Buying and selling loans
  - Mortgage-backed securities
  - Functions of the secondary market
  - Standardized underwriting

The Secondary Market Agencies

- Historical background
- Fannie Mae and Freddie Mac today
  - Restrictions and responsibilities
  - Financial oversight
  - Advantages of GSE status
  - Guaranties
  - Public benefits from the GSEs

Introduction

The residential mortgage industry is made up of the financial institutions, private companies, agencies, and other investors that make investment funds available to people who want to finance (or refinance) the purchase or construction of a home. The industry is divided into two "markets" that supply the funds for mortgage loans: the primary market and the secondary market.

In this chapter, we'll explain the two markets and the relationship between them. We'll also discuss the major secondary market agencies, Fannie Mae, Ginnie Mae, and Freddie Mac, and the mortgage-backed securities that are traded in the secondary market. (The different types of lenders in the primary market will be covered in Chapter 3.)

The Two Mortgage Markets

Primary market: where lenders make loans to home buyers

Secondary market: where lenders sell loans to investors

Home buyers borrow the money they need from banks and other mortgage lenders. Those loan transactions take place in the financial arena known in the mortgage industry as the **primary mortgage market**. To obtain money to make more loans, lenders often sell their loans to investors. These transactions take place in another arena, the **secondary mortgage market**. We'll look first at loan transactions in the primary market, and then at secondary market transactions. You'll see how the secondary market has come to play an extremely important role in making financing available to home buyers in the primary market.

The Primary Market

Loan origination:
- processing application
- approval decision
- funding the loan

In the primary mortgage market, home buyers apply for mortgage loans and residential mortgage lenders **originate** them. Loan origination includes processing the application, deciding to approve the loan, and then funding the loan.

Primary market was originally a local market, made up of local lending institutions

Local Market. At one time the primary market was purely a local market, consisting of the various financial institutions in a community—the local banks, savings and loan associations, and so on. Although the primary market is considerably more complicated than that today (as a result of interstate banking, Internet lenders, and other developments), it will be easier to explain the relationship between the primary market and the secondary market if we start with a simple example along traditional lines.

Example: The Browns live in a small city called Seacliff. When the Browns want to borrow money so that they can buy a house, they apply for a loan from one of the local financial institutions, Vault Savings Bank. Vault is a mortgage lender in the primary market.

Vault Savings Bank's original source of funds for making mortgage loans is the savings of its depositors, who are individuals and businesses in the Seacliff area. Vault uses the savings deposits to make loans to residents of that same community. It pays depositors 3% interest for the use of their savings, and it charges borrowers 7% interest on their mortgage loans. The difference between the interest rate charged to borrowers and the rate paid to depositors (less the bank's operational costs) is Vault's profit.

At times, the basic model of mortgage financing presented in the example works well: local lenders have an adequate supply of mortgage funds to meet the community's demand, enabling most people who want to finance the purchase of a home to do so. The residential real estate market is essentially local, so it's natural for mortgage financing to be a local matter, too.

Unfortunately, a local mortgage financing system doesn't always function smoothly; supply and demand aren't always in balance. Local real estate markets go through active periods followed by slumps. These periodic changes are called **real estate cycles**. They may be dramatic or more moderate, short-term or long-term. They may be affected by economic, political, or social factors, such as changes in employment levels, in tax policy, or in lifestyles.

Availability of funds for lending may be disrupted by local real estate cycles

Real estate cycles can create problems for local financial institutions and for potential home buyers.

Example: A new industry recently started up in Seacliff, and the local economy is booming. As a result of this new prosperity, the residents are saving somewhat more, but they're also spending more, and many people want to buy or build homes in the area.

Vault Savings Bank and the other local financial institutions don't have enough funds on deposit to meet the increased demand for mortgage loans. This may prevent some members of the community who want to finance the purchase of a home from doing so. It could also prevent local lenders from doing as much business as they otherwise could.

On the other hand, sometimes a community's demand for mortgage funds is weak. If the local economy goes into a slump, many people who might otherwise buy homes can't afford to. Local banks may have funds available for mortgage loans, but no one wants to borrow. This reduces the banks' main source of income (interest on loans), making the local economic slump that much worse.

Local conditions are not the only factor that affects a community's supply of and demand for mortgage funds. National economic and political forces and social trends may also have an impact on local real estate cycles.

Disintermediation: when depository institutions lose funds to higher-yielding investments

For example, a phenomenon known as **disintermediation** can reduce the supply of funds that local financial institutions have available for mortgage lending. Disintermediation occurs when depositors withdraw their funds from savings accounts and put them into competing investments that offer higher returns, such as stocks and bonds. The changes in interest rates and investment yields that lead to disintermediation take place on a national level.

Example: During most of the 1990s the stock market was soaring. Stock yields rose and remained high. As a result, public perception of the stock market changed; investing in the market seemed less risky than it once had.

At the same time, financial institutions were paying extremely low interest rates on savings accounts. The disparity between those rates and stock yields led many middle-class people who had never invested in the stock market before to withdraw part of their savings and invest the money in stock-based mutual funds. This disintermediation reduced financial institutions' supply of funds for mortgage lending.

Disintermediation affects the local supply of mortgage funds; other national factors can affect local demand. For example, if Congress changes the federal tax code in a way that favors home ownership, that encourages more people nationwide to purchase homes. The demand for mortgage financing in a local real estate market such as Seacliff's is likely to increase as a result. (We'll discuss the effect of government policy on interest rates and mortgage financing in more detail in Chapter 4.)

Correcting an Imbalance. At one time, there wasn't very much that local financial institutions—lenders in the primary market—could do about real estate cycles in their community. If the demand for mortgage funds exceeded the supply, some of the demand would go unmet; potential home buyers would have to wait, and the banks would miss out on opportunities to make money. If supply exceeded demand, the banks would have to make relatively unprofitable investments until demand picked up again, or they might even have to let funds on deposit sit uninvested.

What local financial institutions needed was a source of additional funds to lend when demand exceeded supply, and a place to invest their surplus funds when supply exceeded demand. The solution to their problems lay in the establishment and expansion of the secondary mortgage market.

The Secondary Market

The primary mortgage market is where lenders make mortgage loans; the secondary mortgage market is where lenders sell those loans to investors. The secondary market is a national market in which mortgages secured by residential real estate all over the country can be bought and sold.

Buying and Selling Loans. The idea of buying or selling a loan may be unfamiliar. But a loan is an investment, and like other investments (stocks, bonds, and so on) mortgage loans can be bought and sold.

Secondary market activities:
- Buying loans
- Issuing mortgage-backed securities

Valuing loans. The purchaser of a loan pays the lender the present value of the lender's right to receive payments from the borrower over the life of the loan. The present value is calculated by comparing the rate of return on the loan to the rate of return available on other investments.

> **Example:** A bank makes a home loan of $190,500 at 5.5% interest. One year later, approximately $187,900 of principal remains to be paid on the loan. But if market interest rates have gone up to 7% for investments of similar quality, then the present value of the loan is less than $187,900. The present value is the amount of money it would take to generate the same amount of income at a 7% rate of return. A 5.5% return on $187,900 would be $10,335 per year. This same return could be achieved by investing $147,640 at 7% interest. So (all other factors being equal) the present value of the loan is $147,640 rather than its face value of $187,900. If the bank decided to sell the loan at this point, the buyer would pay only $147,640.

Many factors affect the value of a loan; the degree of risk associated with it is especially important. In the example, the loan was being

Fig. 2.1 The two mortgage markets

Primary Market	Secondary Market
• Local market • Mortgage lenders such as banks and mortgage companies make loans to home buyers	• National market • Lenders from all over the country sell loans to the secondary market agencies and other investors

compared to "investments of similar quality," which means investments involving approximately the same degree of risk as the loan.

Who buys loans? A lender that decides to sell some of its mortgage loans may sell them directly to another lender in a different part of the country. For example, a bank in Arizona might get cash to make more loans by selling some of its loans to a bank in New York.

Loans are purchased on the secondary market by the secondary market agencies and other investors

More often, a lender sells mortgage loans to a **secondary market agency**. The secondary market agencies are the major purchasers of loans on the secondary market. They include:

- the Federal National Mortgage Association (FNMA or "Fannie Mae"),
- the Federal Home Loan Mortgage Corporation (FHLMC or "Freddie Mac"), and
- the Government National Mortgage Association (GNMA or "Ginnie Mae").

Ginnie Mae is a government agency within the U.S. Department of Housing and Urban Development (HUD). Fannie Mae and Freddie Mac are **government-sponsored enterprises**, chartered by Congress and supervised by HUD. By creating these agencies, the federal government established a strong secondary market for mortgage loans.

It's common for a lender to "package" a group of similar loans together for sale to one of the secondary market agencies. To be accepted for purchase, the packaged loans must meet standards of quality set by the agency that's going to buy them. We'll discuss the agencies and their standards in more detail later in the chapter.

Mortgage-backed Securities. In addition to buying mortgages from lenders around the country, the secondary market agencies also issue mortgage-backed securities. A mortgage-backed security (MBS) is an investment instrument that has mortgages as collateral. A secondary market agency creates mortgage-backed securities by buying a large number of mortgage loans, "pooling" them together, and pledging the pool as collateral for the securities.

Mortgage-backed securities: investment instruments with pools of mortgage loans as collateral

The investors who purchase mortgage-backed securities are purchasing ownership interests in the pool. They receive a return on their investment in the form of monthly payments from the secondary market agency that issued the securities. As the mortgage loans in the pool are repaid by the borrowers, the agency passes the payments of principal and interest on to the MBS investors.

Guaranties. Investors prefer to buy mortgage-backed securities instead of the actual mortgage loans for a number of reasons. The securities are more liquid than the mortgages, and they can be purchased in small denominations.

The biggest advantage of buying mortgage-backed securities instead of mortgages is that the securities are guaranteed by the issuing agency. Under the terms of the guaranty, the investor will receive the full monthly principal and interest payment from the secondary market agency whether or not payment has been collected from all of the pool's borrowers.

MBS guaranteed by secondary market agency

In exchange for this guaranty, the agency subtracts a **guaranty fee** before passing the payments along to the investor. In addition, a **servicing fee** is deducted for the lender that's servicing the loan. (Loan servicing includes tasks such as processing borrowers' payments, dealing with collection problems, and working with borrowers to prevent default. The lender that services a loan may or may not be the lender that originated it.)

Loan servicing:
- processing payments
- collections
- preventing default

MBS trading. Mortgage-backed securities can be purchased directly from Fannie Mae, Ginnie Mae, or Freddie Mac when the securities are first issued. These direct purchases tend to be made by large institutional investors such as life insurance companies, pension funds, commercial banks, thrifts, trust departments, and charitable endowments. Smaller companies and individual investors usually buy and sell the securities on Wall Street, through securities dealers.

MBS purchases may be made directly from secondary market agencies or on Wall Street

Private-label securities. Although most mortgage-backed securities are issued by the major secondary market agencies, there are also private firms that buy and pool mortgage loans and issue securities based on the pools. The firms that issue these "private-label" mortgage-backed securities are subsidiaries of investment banks, financial institutions, or, in some cases, home builders.

Secondary market functions:
- Promotes home ownership and investment
- Provides funds
- Stabilizes primary market

Functions of the Secondary Market. The secondary market serves two important functions for the real estate industry. First, it promotes home ownership and investment in real estate by making funds available for mortgage loans. Second, it provides a measure of stability in local markets by moderating the adverse effects of real estate cycles. Consider the following examples.

> **Example 1:** Acme Savings & Loan has a long list of prospective borrowers who need funds for the purchase of homes. Acme's problem is that all of its savings deposits are already tied up in mortgage loans. But by selling its existing mortgage loans on the secondary market, Acme can get the funds it needs to make new loans and satisfy its customers. The effects of a tight money market in Acme's local community are moderated because Acme can get funds in the national secondary market.

> **Example 2:** If Acme Savings & Loan had a surplus of deposits instead of a shortfall, it might have a difficult time finding enough local investments to absorb its funds. In this case, Acme could buy mortgages or mortgage-backed securities on the secondary market—in essence, investing in real estate located all over the country, without ever seeing the properties it is helping to finance or meeting the borrowers who are buying them.

Availability of funds in primary market depends on secondary market

Nowadays the availability of funds in the primary market depends to a great extent on the secondary market. Figure 2.2 shows how mortgage funds flow between the primary and secondary markets: first, mortgage funds are given to the home buyer by a lending institution in the primary market; then the mortgage is sold to a secondary market

Fig. 2.2 Mortgage funds flow from the secondary market, to lenders, to borrowers

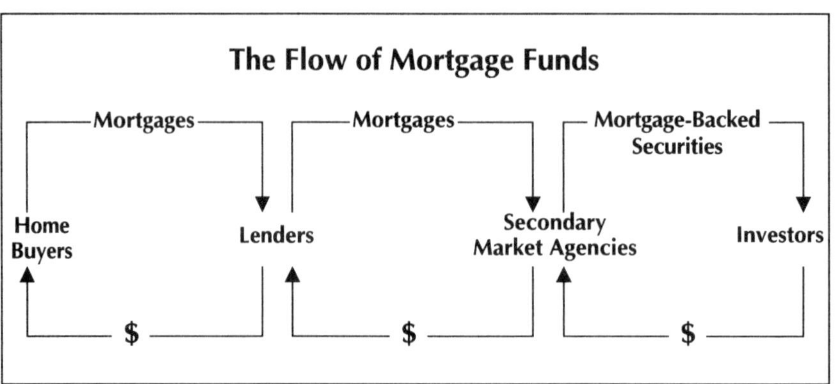

agency; finally, the agency may pool the mortgage with many others to create mortgage-backed securities, which it will sell to investors. As mortgage-backed securities are sold by the agency, more funds become available to the agency for the purchase of new mortgages from the primary market. As the agencies purchase more mortgages, more funds become available for primary market lenders to make loans to borrowers.

If a lender does not sell a loan on the secondary market (either by choice or because no one wants to buy it), the lender keeps the loan **in portfolio**—that is, it holds onto the loan and receives the principal and interest payments from the borrower. But the secondary market has become so important as a source of funds that many institutional lenders now keep only a small percentage of their residential mortgage loans in portfolio.

Many lenders keep very few mortgage loans in portfolio

Standardized Underwriting. The secondary market is able to function as it does because the major secondary market agencies have established their own underwriting guidelines. Underwriting guidelines are the rules lenders apply when they're qualifying loan applicants and deciding whether or not to make particular loans (see Chapter 8). Loans sold to a secondary market agency must meet the agency's underwriting rules, not just the lender's own rules.

Loans sold to a secondary market agency must comply with the agency's underwriting rules

The secondary market agencies have also developed uniform loan application forms, appraisal forms, and mortgage documents. As a general rule, if a lender makes a mortgage loan that doesn't conform to an agency's underwriting guidelines, or fails to use the uniform documents, the agency won't buy the loan from the lender. (Not only that, if one of the agencies buys a loan and later discovers the lender violated the guidelines, the lender can be required to buy the loan back.)

The underwriting guidelines and uniform documents are a quality control system, ensuring that the loans purchased by the secondary market agencies are of a certain quality. There is a risk that the borrower may default or the property may lose value, but the risk has been minimized. This inspires confidence in the investors who buy mortgage-backed securities. The investors know that the mortgages that back the securities do not involve an unreasonable degree of risk. Without this assurance, someone in New Jersey would be unlikely to invest in real estate in New Mexico (or vice versa) sight unseen.

Lenders want to have the option of selling their loans on the secondary market; otherwise they might end up without the funds to make more loans. As a result, the underwriting guidelines set by the secondary market agencies strongly influence lending activities in the primary market. For example, once the secondary market agencies began accepting adjustable-rate mortgages (ARMs), convertible ARMs, and 15-year fixed-rate mortgages, those types of financing became readily available in the primary market. Lenders were much more willing to make those types of loans after they were assured the loans could be sold on the secondary market.

The secondary market agencies expect lenders to carefully review property appraisals, origination documentation (the loan application, credit report, employment verification, and so on), and the ultimate decision on whether to approve a loan. By encouraging lenders to exercise care, the agencies exert their influence to increase the overall quality of loans made and decrease the rate of delinquency and foreclosure.

The Secondary Market Agencies

Now that you've seen how the secondary market works, we'll take a closer look at the major secondary market agencies: Fannie Mae, Ginnie Mae, and Freddie Mac.

Historical Background

The federal government created the three secondary market agencies at separate points during the course of the twentieth century.

Fannie Mae: Federal National Mortgage Association (FNMA)

Fannie Mae. The Federal National Mortgage Association, better known as Fannie Mae, was created in 1938. This was part of the response to the unprecedented credit problems caused by the Depression. The government had earlier established the Federal Housing Association and the FHA-insured loan program to help make home financing affordable again, and Fannie Mae's original purpose was to provide a secondary market for FHA-insured loans.

By 1948 the agency was purchasing FHA-insured loans on a large scale. That same year, Congress authorized Fannie Mae to start buying loans from the new VA-guaranteed loan program, which had been established in the wake of World War II.

Two decades later, Congress took steps to increase the size and scope of the secondary market, hoping to moderate the disruptive economic effects of local and regional real estate cycles. In 1968, Fannie Mae was reorganized as a private corporation owned by stockholders, although HUD retained limited authority over it as a government-sponsored enterprise (GSE).

Government-sponsored enterprise (GSE):
- created and supervised by the federal government,
- but owned by private stockholders

Ginnie Mae. At the same time that it turned Fannie Mae into a private corporation, Congress created a new wholly owned government corporation, the Government National Mortgage Association, or Ginnie Mae. Ginnie Mae managed and eventually liquidated mortgages that had been purchased by Fannie Mae before the change-over.

Ginnie Mae: Government National Mortgage Association (GNMA)

Today, Ginnie Mae buys FHA and VA loans. Ginnie Mae is also involved in a variety of other activities, such as helping to finance urban renewal and housing projects.

Freddie Mac. The Federal Home Loan Mortgage Corporation, nicknamed Freddie Mac, was created in 1970 by the Emergency Home Finance Act. Like Fannie Mae, Freddie Mac is a government-sponsored enterprise—a private corporation owned by its stockholders but chartered by Congress and supervised by HUD.

Freddie Mac: Federal Home Loan Mortgage Corporation (FHLMC)

Freddie Mac's original purpose was to assist savings and loan associations, which were hit particularly hard by a recession in 1969 and

Fig. 2.3 Secondary market agencies

Fannie Mae and Freddie Mac
- Government-sponsored enterprises (GSEs)
- Supervised by HUD
- Buy conventional, FHA, and VA loans from all types of lenders
- Issue mortgage-backed securities based on pools of conventional, FHA, or VA loans

Ginnie Mae
- Wholly owned government corporation
- Agency within HUD
- Buys FHA and VA loans (not conventional loans)
- Issues mortgage-backed securities based on FHA and VA loans

1970. Savings and loans (S&Ls) mostly made **conventional loans**—loans that aren't insured or guaranteed by the government—and there wasn't a dependable secondary market for conventional loans at that time. As a result, S&Ls had kept most of their loans in portfolio. By purchasing their conventional loans, Freddie Mac enabled S&Ls to acquire additional funds for lending.

The Emergency Home Finance Act also permitted Fannie Mae to start buying conventional loans as well as FHA and VA loans.

MBS Programs. Ginnie Mae started the first mortgage-backed securities program in 1970, offering investors guaranteed securities backed by pools of FHA and VA loans. Both Fannie Mae and Freddie Mac eventually followed in Ginnie Mae's footsteps. Fannie Mae and Freddie Mac issue securities backed by pools of conventional mortgages, as well as securities based on FHA and VA loans.

In the 1980s, Congress changed how mortgage-backed securities were taxed and removed certain statutory restrictions to make the securities more competitive with corporate bonds. This also contributed to the expansion of the secondary market.

Fannie Mae and Freddie Mac Today

In this section, we'll focus on the two government-sponsored enterprises, Fannie Mae and Freddie Mac. Because the GSEs buy conventional loans as well as FHA and VA loans, they have a greater impact on the mortgage industry than Ginnie Mae.

Fannie Mae and Freddie Mac are both now authorized to purchase conventional, FHA, and VA loans from any type of lender. Although they are private corporations, their status as government-sponsored enterprises chartered by Congress gives them certain advantages and imposes certain restrictions and responsibilities.

Restrictions and Responsibilities. Fannie Mae and Freddie Mac are restricted by charter to investment in residential mortgage assets (essentially, mortgage loans and mortgage-backed securities). They are also required to meet affordable housing goals that HUD sets annually.

GSEs must meet affordable housing goals set by HUD

HUD's goals require the GSEs to promote programs that help provide affordable home financing and affordable rental housing to low- and middle-income families and in neighborhoods that have been underserved by lenders (for example, low-income and inner city neighborhoods). These affordable housing programs are discussed in Chapter 10.

Financial oversight. The Office of Federal Housing Enterprise Oversight (OFHEO), an independent agency within HUD, was established in 1992. The agency is funded by assessments on Fannie Mae and Freddie Mac, not by the government.

The OFHEO conducts comprehensive examinations of the GSEs. It requires them to maintain sufficient capital so that they could weather even a severe economic crisis. It also prohibits the GSEs from paying excessive compensation to their corporate executives.

Advantages of GSE Status. By the terms of their charters, the GSEs are exempt from state and local taxes, although they are required to pay federal income taxes. They are also exempt from the registration and disclosure requirements of the Securities and Exchange Commission, but may voluntarily register their stock with the SEC.

While neither Fannie Mae nor Freddie Mac receives federal funding, each GSE has a limited back-up line of credit with the U.S. Treasury, which could be used in a financial emergency. (So far, these lines of credit have not been drawn upon.)

Guaranties. It's important to note that the mortgage-backed securities issued by Fannie Mae and Freddie Mac don't carry a government guaranty. Ginnie Mae's securities are backed up by "the full faith and credit" of the U.S. government; in the event of a financial crisis affecting the agency, Ginnie Mae's MBS investors won't lose their capital. Fannie Mae and Freddie Mac's private guaranties, on the other hand, only ensure that their investors will receive timely payments of principal and interest, even if borrowers fail to make their loan payments. They don't offer protection against a financial crisis affecting the GSEs themselves. If Fannie Mae or Freddie Mac were to fail, the government would not be required to intervene to protect the investors.

Mortgage-backed securities issued by Fannie Mae and Freddie Mac:

- are guaranteed by the GSEs themselves
- are not guaranteed by the federal government

Nonetheless, some investors believe that the government would have little choice but to intervene, to prevent serious and widespread economic repercussions. Based on that belief, they regard Fannie Mae and Freddie Mac securities as having an implicit government guaranty that is nearly equivalent to Ginnie Mae's explicit guaranty. This reputation allows the GSEs to borrow money at better rates than other private companies.

Secondary market agencies have successfully:
- stabilized the primary market
- increased home ownership rates
- produced other public benefits

Public Benefits from the GSEs. As we've discussed, the federal government created the secondary market agencies to increase the overall availability of mortgage funds throughout the country and limit the adverse effects of local economic conditions on real estate markets. On the whole, the agencies have been very successful in fulfilling those goals. In the process, they've produced some additional benefits for home buyers.

Many mortgage industry analysts give Fannie Mae and Freddie Mac credit for helping to:

- dramatically increase home ownership rates;
- reduce mortgage interest rates;
- enable lenders to offer a greater variety of mortgage loan products;
- cut down the time and cost involved in obtaining a mortgage loan;
- make underwriting practices in the industry sounder and fairer; and
- provide mortgage lenders access to global capital markets as a source of funds.

Fannie Mae and Freddie Mac have their critics, however. The critics argue that the GSEs have grown too large and wield too much power in the mortgage industry, limiting opportunities for other investors and enterprises. They objected, for example, when the GSEs began moving into the subprime market (see Chapter 3).

Critics also contend that claims about how much the GSEs have benefited the public tend to be exaggerated. For example, some industry analysts claim that the GSEs' programs and practices have reduced mortgage interest rates nationwide by as much as half a percentage point, or 0.5%. Other analysts, while agreeing that the GSEs have helped reduce interest rates, argue that the reduction has been 0.1%, or perhaps even less.

Fannie Mae's reputation was seriously tarnished by a massive accounting scandal that broke in late 2004, which eventually led to the resignation of top executives and payment of a $400 million fine. Critics point to the scandal as an additional reason to rein in the GSEs. But whatever changes at Fannie Mae and Freddie Mac result from the scandal or from industry criticism, both GSEs are likely to continue their dominance of the residential mortgage industry for some time to come.

Outline: The Primary and Secondary Markets

I. The Two Mortgage Markets
  A. Primary market: financial arena in which home buyers apply for loans and lenders originate them.
    1. Traditionally a local market, made up of local lending institutions.
    2. Problem: Local market is subject to real estate cycles.
      a. When business is booming, local community's demand for mortgage funds may exceed local lenders' supply.
      b. In an economic slump, local lenders' supply of mortgage funds may exceed local demand.
      c. Secondary market helps cure problem of real estate cycles.
  B. Secondary market: national market in which mortgage loans are bought and sold.
    1. Mortgage loans can be sold like other types of investments.
      a. Present value of loan based on yield currently available on investments of similar quality (same degree of risk).
      b. Lender may sell loans to other lenders or investors in another part of the country, or to a secondary market agency.
    2. Mortgage-backed securities
      a. Secondary market agency buys many mortgages and pools them together; pool is pledged as collateral for the securities.
      b. Investors who buy mortgage-backed securities:
        i. purchase ownership interests in the pool, and
        ii. receive monthly payments of principal and interest from agency as pooled loans are repaid.
      c. Agency guarantees full payment to investors, even if borrowers miss payments on underlying loans.
    3. Functions of the secondary market
      a. Makes funds available for mortgage loans nationwide.
      b. Promotes home ownership and real estate investment.
      c. Moderates adverse effects of local real estate cycles.
      d. Flow of mortgage funds
        i. Agency uses funds from sale of securities to buy more mortgage loans from primary market.
        ii. Primary market lender uses funds from sale of loans to make more loans to borrowers.

4. Loans sold to a GSE must meet the GSE's underwriting guidelines.
    a. GSEs have standardized underwriting and other aspects of the mortgage lending process across the country.
    b. GSEs' rules give MBS investors confidence in loan quality.
    c. Lenders are more willing to make specific types of loans once Fannie Mae and Freddie Mac have decided to purchase them.

II. Secondary Market Agencies
- A. Historical background
    1. Fannie Mae (Federal National Mortgage Association)
        a. U.S. government created Fannie Mae in 1938.
        b. Original purpose: buying FHA-insured loans from lenders.
        c. Reorganized as a private corporation in 1968, but remains a government-sponsored enterprise (GSE) supervised by HUD.
    2. Ginnie Mae (Government National Mortgage Association)
        a. Created in 1968 as a wholly owned government corporation to take Fannie Mae's place.
        b. Buys FHA and VA loans (not conventional loans).
        c. 1970: Started first mortgage-backed securities program, based on pools of FHA and VA loans.
    3. Freddie Mac (Federal National Mortgage Corporation): GSE created in 1970 to help savings and loans by buying conventional loans.
- B. Fannie Mae and Freddie Mac today
    1. Both GSEs now buy conventional, FHA, and VA loans from all types of lenders, and both issue mortgage-backed securities.
    2. Restrictions on and responsibilities of the GSEs
        a. Can invest only in residential mortgage assets.
        b. Must meet annual affordable housing goals set by HUD.
        c. Supervised by Office of Federal Housing Enterprise Oversight.
    3. Advantages of GSE status
        a. Exempt from state and local taxes and SEC registration.
        b. No federal funding, but back-up line of credit at Treasury.
    4. Fannie Mae and Freddie Mac's MBS guaranties aren't backed by full faith and credit of U.S. government. (Ginnie Mae's are.)
    5. Public benefits: GSEs have helped to increase homeownership rates, reduce loan processing times, make underwriting sounder and fairer, and reduce mortgage interest rates.

Key Terms

Primary mortgage market: The financial arena in which mortgage loans are originated, where lenders make loans to home buyers.

Secondary mortgage market: The financial arena in which investors buy mortgage loans from lenders throughout the country.

Loan origination: Processing a loan application, deciding whether to approve or reject the application, and funding the loan.

Real estate cycles: Ups and downs in the level of activity in a local real estate market, where a boom may be followed by a slump, or vice versa.

Law of supply and demand: A basic rule of economics which holds that prices (or interest rates) tend to rise when supply decreases or demand increases, and tend to fall when supply increases or demand decreases.

Disintermediation: When depositors withdraw their savings from financial institutions and put the money into other types of investments that have higher yields.

Secondary market agency: One of the three government-created entities that buy loans and issue mortgage-backed securities: Fannie Mae, Ginnie Mae, or Freddie Mac.

Government-sponsored enterprise (GSE): An entity that is privately owned but created, chartered, and supervised by the government. A GSE functions as a private corporation but must fulfill special legal responsibilities imposed by the government. The GSEs discussed in this chapter are Fannie Mae and Freddie Mac.

Mortgage-backed security (MBS): An investment instrument, issued by one of the secondary market agencies, that grants the investor an ownership interest in a pool of mortgage loans.

MBS guaranty: A guaranty offered by an issuer of mortgage-backed securities, which provides that the MBS investors will receive the expected payments of principal and interest from the issuer, even if borrowers fail to make their payments on some of the pooled mortgage loans.

Guaranty fee: A fee that an issuer of mortgage-backed securities deducts from payments to be made to an MBS investor, in exchange for the MBS guaranty.

Servicing fee: A fee paid by a secondary market agency or other investor to the lender that is servicing a mortgage loan.

Loan servicing: Processing loan payments, keeping payment records, and handling collection problems and defaults. The lender that services a loan is not necessarily the same lender that originated it.

Securities dealer: An investment professional who serves as an intermediary or middleman in investment transactions; for example, a stockbroker.

Private-label MBS: A mortgage-backed security issued by a company such as an investment bank, rather than by one of the secondary market agencies.

Portfolio loan: A mortgage loan that the lender keeps in its own investment portfolio until the loan is repaid (instead of selling the loan on the secondary market).

Conventional loan: A loan that is not insured or guaranteed by a government agency.

Chapter Quiz

1. The Cantors just borrowed money from Seacliff Savings to finance the purchase of a home. This transaction took place in the:
   a. national market
   b. primary market
   c. secondary market
   d. None of the above

2. The federal government created the secondary market agencies in order to:
   a. originate residential mortgage loans nationwide
   b. help moderate the adverse effects of real estate cycles
   c. bring inflation under control at the local level
   d. stimulate disintermediation

3. A lending institution with more mortgage loan applicants than available loan funds would be likely to:
   a. buy mortgage-backed securities from another lender
   b. buy mortgage-backed securities from a secondary market agency
   c. buy mortgages from a secondary market agency
   d. sell mortgages to a secondary market agency

4. A lender cannot sell a mortgage loan to Fannie Mae unless:
   a. it followed the agency's underwriting guidelines
   b. it is a federally certified primary market agency
   c. it is a federally insured savings and loan association
   d. the loan is either FHA-insured or VA-guaranteed

5. A mortgage-backed security is a type of:
   a. mortgage loan
   b. corporate debt certificate
   c. investment instrument
   d. guaranty

6. Taking a home buyer's loan application is a step in the:
   a. loan servicing process
   b. loan origination process
   c. loan guaranty process
   d. MBS process

7. Investors prefer to buy mortgage-backed securities instead of mortgages because the securities are:
   a. less liquid, and therefore safer
   b. serviced by the federal government
   c. guaranteed by the federal government
   d. guaranteed by the agency that issues them

8. Most residential mortgage loans are:
   a. kept in portfolio
   b. sold on the secondary market
   c. sold on the primary market
   d. None of the above

9. An investor's return on mortgage-backed securities usually takes the form of:
   a. monthly servicing fees
   b. annual dividends from the mortgage pool
   c. monthly payments of principal and interest
   d. annual installment bonds

10. As government-sponsored enterprises, Fannie Mae and Freddie Mac are:
    a. private corporations owned by stockholders
    b. private corporations financed with taxpayer dollars
    c. wholly owned government corporations
    d. separate agencies within the Department of Housing and Urban Development

Answer Key

1. b. Loan transactions take place in the primary market.

2. b. Moderating the negative effects of local real estate cycles and stabilizing the primary market were among the government's goals in creating Fannie Mae, Ginnie Mae, and Freddie Mac.

3. d. A mortgage lender with more loan applicants than funds could raise the money to make more loans by selling some of its existing loans to a secondary market agency.

4. a. A loan that's going to be sold to one of the secondary market agencies must comply with that agency's underwriting guidelines (not just the lender's own guidelines).

5. c. A mortgage-backed security is a type of investment instrument.

6. b. Loan origination refers to processing the loan application, making the decision to approve the loan, and funding the loan.

7. d. Mortgage-backed securities are usually guaranteed by the agency that issues them. Securities issued by Ginnie Mae can be considered government-guaranteed, but that's not true of mortgage-backed securities in general.

8. b. Nowadays, mortgage lenders tend to sell most of their loans on the secondary market.

9. c. MBS investors usually receive monthly payments of principal and interest from the agency that issued the securities.

10. a. The government-sponsored enterprises are private corporations owned by their stockholders, but supervised by the Office of Federal Housing Enterprise Oversight, an agency within HUD.

Chapter 3
Residential Mortgage Lenders

Types of Mortgage Lenders

- Commercial banks
- Savings banks
- Savings and loan associations
- Credit unions
- Mortgage companies
- Private lenders
- Comparing types of lenders

Government Intervention in Mortgage Lending

- The Depression and the mortgage industry
  - Foreclosure epidemic
  - Transforming home mortgages
- The S&L crisis
  - Dominating mortgage lending
  - Deregulation and disaster
  - Changing market shares

Mortgage Industry Trends

- Technological changes
- Nationwide lending
- Wholesale lending
- Subprime lending

Introduction

The previous chapter explained the relationship between the primary market and the secondary market; in this chapter, we'll take a closer look at the primary market. We'll start with an overview of the different types of residential mortgage lenders. Then we'll discuss how two historical events, the Depression and the savings and loan crisis, changed the mortgage industry. Finally, we'll describe some recent trends in the mortgage industry, including the dominance of giant nationwide lenders and the growth of subprime mortgage lending.

Types of Mortgage Lenders

There are five main sources of residential mortgage financing in the primary market. These are:

- commercial banks,
- savings banks,
- savings and loan associations,
- credit unions, and
- mortgage companies.

Nearly all prospective home buyers obtain financing from one of these five types of lenders. Their lending practices thus have the greatest impact on real estate transactions.

Commercial Banks

As their name suggests, commercial banks originally developed to serve commercial entities: merchants and other businesses. At first banks just provided a secure place for keeping money. Later they began paying interest on deposits and using deposited funds to make loans (see Chapter 1). Later still they began offering what are now called checking accounts, to facilitate commercial transactions.

Commercial banks have always emphasized commercial lending, supplying capital for business ventures and construction activities. Originally, residential mortgages weren't a significant part of their lending business. Various developments in the twentieth century, including regulatory changes and the expansion of the secondary

Traditionally, commercial banks didn't make many home mortgage loans market, helped make residential mortgage lending more attractive to commercial banks.

Even though commercial banks have increased their involvement in mortgage lending, it's still a comparatively small part of their business. A commercial bank might have 15% of its assets invested in residential mortgages, whereas a savings and loan typically has about half of its assets in mortgages. On the other hand, commercial banks control a large proportion of the total assets in the U.S., so even a 15% share of those assets represents a very large investment in residential lending. In recent years, commercial banks have made about one-fifth of the country's mortgage loans.

In the U.S., commercial banks are either national banks, chartered by the federal government, or state banks, chartered by a state government. (The other types of depository institutions we'll discuss—savings banks, savings and loans, and credit unions—may also have either a federal or a state charter.)

Commercial banks are distinguished from **investment banks**. Investment banks are securities firms. They raise capital for corporations, arrange for the issuance of government and corporate bonds, manage corporate finances, and handle mergers and acquisitions. Investment banking does not involve accepting deposits and making loans.

Commercial banks accept deposits and make loans

Investment banks: securities firms involved in corporate finance

The Glass-Steagall Act, a law adopted in 1933, required U.S. banks to choose between commercial banking services and investment banking services; a bank was prohibited from providing both. The act also made it illegal for banks to be involved in the insurance business. Intended to protect the public from conflicts of interest and prevent banks from becoming too powerful, these rules were gradually undermined over the course of several decades. The Glass-Steagall Act was finally repealed in 1999 by the Financial Services Modernization Act. It's now legal for a holding company to have a bank, a securities firm, and an insurance company as subsidiaries. (A holding company is basically a corporate entity created for the purpose of owning other companies.)

Savings Banks

Savings banks started out in the early nineteenth century by offering financial services to small depositors, especially immigrants and members of the new industrial working class. In addition to home mortgage loans, savings banks make consumer loans, providing financing for the purchase of furniture, appliances, and cars.

Savings banks make mortgage loans and other consumer loans

Savings banks are often called **mutual savings banks**, because they were originally organized as mutual companies, owned by and operated for the benefit of their depositors rather than stockholders. Only 16 states, most of them in the Northeast, had procedures for chartering mutual savings banks, and the federal government did not charter them. That changed in 1982 with the passage of the Garn–St. Germain Act, which gave savings banks the option of a federal charter. Federally chartered savings banks can be organized either as mutual companies or as stock companies.

Traditionally, savings banks provided only savings accounts, not checking accounts. Today they offer the same consumer services as commercial banks: checking accounts, savings accounts, and credit cards, as well as consumer loans and home mortgages.

Savings and Loan Associations

Like savings banks, savings and loan associations (S&Ls) developed in the nineteenth century. Originally called building and loan associations, S&Ls were formed in local communities to finance the construction of homes. An association was designed to serve only its members, who would pool their assets and then take turns using the money to build houses for themselves. After all the members had satisfied their financing needs, the association would be dissolved.

Over the years, however, savings and loan associations began to make some loans to nonmembers and to place more emphasis on soliciting and servicing deposits. Eventually they became permanent institutions, providing savings accounts to small depositors. For the most part, their lending activities continued to be limited to mortgage loans for single-family homes.

Savings and loan associations specialized in mortgage loans

Regulatory changes in the 1970s and early 1980s allowed savings and loans to become more like banks. They began offering checking accounts, and they got involved in other types of lending besides home mortgages. Deregulation was one of the factors that led to the savings and loan crisis, discussed later in this chapter.

Thrift industry: savings and loans and savings banks

Sometimes savings and loan associations and savings banks are grouped together and referred to as **thrifts** or "the thrift industry," because of their traditional emphasis on savings accounts for small depositors. In some contexts, credit unions are also considered part of the thrift industry.

Credit Unions

Credit unions got their start in the U.S. in the early twentieth century. They are nonprofit cooperative organizations designed to serve the members of a particular group, such as a labor union or a professional association, or the employees of a large company.

Credit union: a nonprofit depository institution that serves the members of a particular group

Originally, credit unions didn't make mortgage loans. They specialized instead in small, personal loans that were often unsecured. (In other words, no collateral was required.) This type of loan generally wasn't available from banks or savings and loans at that time, and small borrowers had previously turned to pawn shops and loan sharks. Credit unions provided an alternative.

Later on, many credit unions emphasized home equity loans. A home equity loan is a mortgage on the borrower's equity in the home he or she already owns. These are generally short-term loans. The legislation deregulating financial institutions in the early 1980s allowed credit unions to begin offering their members long-term home purchase loans. They still have a comparatively small share of the residential mortgage market, however.

As nonprofit organizations, credit unions are generally exempt from taxation. That advantage, along with certain others, enables credit unions to loan money to their members at interest rates that are slightly below market rates. They can also offer interest rates on deposits that are slightly higher than market rates.

Mortgage Companies

The residential lenders we've covered so far are all depository institutions. They offer checking and savings accounts and provide a variety of financial services in addition to mortgage loans. By contrast, mortgage companies are not depository institutions, and their business is completely focused on mortgage loans.

Mortgage companies (aka mortgage bankers) are not depository institutions

Mortgage companies are also called mortgage banking companies or **mortgage bankers**. The first of these companies in the U.S. were established in the 1930s. Mortgage companies make loans to borrowers in much the same way as a bank or savings and loan would. However, since they aren't depository institutions, mortgage companies can't use depositors' savings to fund loans; they have to raise the necessary capital in other ways.

How Mortgage Banking Works. In some cases, a mortgage company borrows money from a commercial bank, uses it to originate mortgages, and sells the mortgages to secondary market investors. The company then uses the proceeds of those sales to originate more mortgages and to repay its own bank loan.

Loan correspondents make loans on behalf of large investors

A mortgage company may also act as a **loan correspondent**. A loan correspondent makes loans to home buyers on an investor's behalf, then services the loans for the investor (collects and processes the payments). The investor pays the correspondent servicing fees, which can be a substantial source of income.

Loan correspondents usually work with large investors that operate on a national scale. For example, a mortgage company might be hired as a correspondent by a life insurance company or a pension fund. (Life insurance companies and pension funds control vast amounts of investment capital in the form of insurance premiums and employer contributions to employee pensions.) These large investors lack the time or the resources to understand the particular risks of local real estate markets or to deal with the day-to-day management of loans, so they hire local loan correspondents to make and service mortgage loans for them. Although banks and thrifts may also act as loan correspondents, mortgage companies specialized in this role early on.

Mortgage companies keep few loans in portfolio

Whether they're acting as loan correspondents or on their own, mortgage companies keep few, if any, loans in portfolio. The loans they originate are either made on behalf of a large investor or else immediately sold to a secondary market agency. When banks and thrifts began selling most of their loans on the secondary market, they were following in the footsteps of mortgage companies. In fact, many banks and thrifts established their own mortgage companies as subsidiaries, to facilitate their increased involvement in the secondary market.

Independent Mortgage Companies. Mortgage companies that aren't affiliated with a bank or thrift are called independent mortgage companies. It's worth noting that these lenders are not subject to the regulations and supervision that banks and thrifts are. Every depository institution is periodically required to undergo a governmental examination, to make sure its operations comply with the law. Independent mortgage companies aren't systematically examined in that way; their operations are investigated only if a complaint is filed with the Federal Trade Commission.

Mortgage Bankers vs. Mortgage Brokers. As mentioned above, mortgage companies are also known as mortgage bankers. The term "mortgage banker" is sometimes confused with "mortgage broker." The distinction between the two is fairly straightforward.

Mortgage bankers make and service loans

A **mortgage banker** originates a loan, either in its own name (with its own funds) or on behalf of an investor. The mortgage banker processes the borrower's application, makes the underwriting decision, and funds the loan. It then sells the loan or delivers it to the investor. After selling or delivering a loan, the mortgage banker often acts as the servicer, processing the payments from the borrower on behalf of the purchaser or investor.

Mortgage brokers: not lenders, but intermediaries that arrange loans

A **mortgage broker**, on the other hand, is not a lender but an intermediary who brings a borrower together with a lender in exchange for a commission. Borrowers go to a mortgage broker for help in finding a loan on the best possible terms. Once they've decided on a loan and filled out a loan application, the broker submits the application to the lender. After a loan is arranged, the mortgage broker's involvement ends. Mortgage brokers don't make loans out of their own funds, and they don't service loans. In some states, real estate agents often act as mortgage brokers, helping their buyers find suitable financing.

While mortgage banking and mortgage brokerage are distinct activities, some mortgage companies engage in both. A business called "Acme Mortgage" might be strictly a mortgage banker, strictly a mortgage broker, or a combination of the two.

Fig. 3.1 Mortgage companies usually act as mortgage bankers, not brokers

Mortgage Banker	Mortgage Broker
• A type of lender • Takes buyer's application, makes underwriting decision, and funds loan • May service loan after selling it	• An intermediary, not a lender • Helps buyer choose and apply for a loan • Doesn't underwrite, fund, or service loan

Private Lenders

Real estate limited partnerships, real estate investment trusts, and other types of private investment groups put a great deal of money into real estate. In addition to financing commercial ventures such as shopping centers, they often finance large residential developments. They do not offer loans to individual home buyers, however.

For home buyers, the most important type of private lender is the home seller. Sellers sometimes provide all of the financing necessary for the purchase of their homes, and it's even more common for sellers to supplement the financing that their buyers obtain from an institutional lender. Sellers have been an especially important source of financing in periods when institutional loans were hard to come by or market interest rates were high. Seller financing is covered in Chapter 13.

Sellers are an important source of financing when institutional loans are expensive

Comparing Types of Lenders

At one time the various types of lending institutions in the U.S. were quite distinct from one another. They offered different services, had different business practices, and were subject to different government regulations. In the last part of the twentieth century, however, economic and regulatory changes blurred the traditional distinctions between types of lenders. From a customer's point of view, lending institutions can now be regarded as "financial supermarkets" offering a wide range of services and loans.

The experience of applying for a mortgage can differ a great deal from one lender to another, but the differences depend on factors such as a lender's size, style, competence, and integrity. Whether a lender is a bank, a savings and loan, a credit union, or a mortgage company won't necessarily make much difference to a home buyer.

Government Intervention in Mortgage Lending

In addition to regulating lending institutions, from time to time the federal government has intervened in the mortgage industry more directly. The creation of the secondary market agencies, discussed in Chapter 2, is an example of this type of intervention. There are two other federal interventions that you should be aware of, because of their long-term effects on the industry. These occurred in response to the Depression in the 1930s and the savings and loan crisis in the 1980s.

The Depression and the Mortgage Industry

The nineteenth century was a period of tremendous and rapid growth in the United States, as the country expanded westward. Money was poured into investments that promised high returns, including real estate. In addition to depository institutions, many private investors got involved in mortgage lending. Home purchase loans were considered excellent investments, both safe and profitable. The loans were generally supposed to be repaid in five years, the value of the collateral (the home) was usually much greater than the loan amount, and property values were almost always going up. The mortgage business remained prosperous through the first decades of the twentieth century, up until the Depression.

A Foreclosure Epidemic. The economic collapse of the 1930s had a severe impact on housing and mortgage lending in the U.S. As unemployment rose to staggering levels, hundreds of thousands of home owners throughout the country defaulted on their mortgages. At the worst point, about half the outstanding home mortgage debt was in default. Foreclosures became commonplace; government officials estimated that in 1933 nearly one thousand homes were foreclosed on every day. Some states declared a moratorium on foreclosures, allowing defaulting borrowers to stay in their homes. Many financial institutions failed, and mortgage lending and home construction came to a standstill. As part of the New Deal, a broad plan to pull the nation out of the economic crisis, the federal government stepped in to try and revive the mortgage industry.

Mortgage lending and home construction virtually ceased during the Depression

New Deal Initiatives. Several of the agencies and programs that were instituted at this point long outlasted the Depression. These include the Federal Housing Administration (FHA), which encouraged residential lending by offering mortgage insurance to protect against foreclosure losses; the Federal Home Loan Bank Board (FHLBB), which assisted savings and loans; and, as we discussed in Chapter 2, the Federal National Mortgage Association (Fannie Mae), which provided a secondary market for FHA-insured loans.

Fig. 3.2 Mortgage loans changed dramatically after the Depression

Standard Loan, circa 1930	**Standard Loan, circa 1940**
• Five-year term • Renewable at lender's discretion, and interest rate may go up • Interest-only payments; full principal amount still owed at end of term	• Thirty-year term • Fixed interest rate • Amortized so that regular payments pay off all principal and interest by end of term

Depression foreclosures led to the introduction of long-term, fixed-rate, amortized mortgage loans

Transforming Home Mortgages. One important reaction to the Depression foreclosures was the introduction of long-term, fixed-rate, amortized home purchase loans. Earlier, home buyers had been expected to make interest-only payments for five years; at the end of the five-year term, the lender could renew the mortgage for another five years and raise the interest rate, or require the borrowers to pay off the entire amount originally borrowed (the principal) in one lump sum. By contrast, the mortgages offered through the FHA-insured loan program could be paid off over a 20- or 30-year term at an unchanging rate of interest. They were also fully amortized: each monthly payment included a share of the principal as well as interest, and the regular monthly payments were sufficient to pay off the principal in full by the end of the term. (Amortization is covered in Chapter 6.)

These features of FHA-insured mortgages made it much easier for home buyers to avoid default and foreclosure. Once that advantage was well established, lenders began to offer long-term, fixed-rate, fully amortized loans outside of the FHA program. By the early 1940s, these loans had become standard. They became even more prevalent after World War II, when many returning veterans bought homes with financing obtained through the Veterans Administration's new guaranteed loan program.

Today, many home buyers choose adjustable-rate mortgages over fixed-rate mortgages, and loans with terms shorter than 30 years have gained some popularity (see Chapter 6). Even unamortized loans (loans with interest-only payments) have made something of a comeback. Despite these alternatives, however, the 30-year, fixed-rate, fully amortized loan is still regarded as the standard mortgage in the

U.S. It may surprise you to learn that this type of loan isn't commonly available in other countries. The five-year renewable mortgage that the U.S. moved away from after the Depression has remained the standard in many places.

The Savings and Loan Crisis

Another chapter in the history of mortgage lending that had far-reaching effects was the savings and loan crisis in the 1980s. Savings and loans ruled the U.S. mortgage industry in the 1950s, yet three decades later many S&Ls faced insolvency.

Dominating Mortgage Lending. In the housing boom that followed World War II, savings and loan associations began to expand their mortgage business aggressively. Eventually they came to dominate local residential mortgage markets, becoming the nation's largest single source of funds for financing homes—even though commercial banks were much larger institutions with much more money to invest.

From the 1950s until the 1980s, savings and loans were the largest source of mortgage financing

A number of factors contributed to the dominance of savings and loans; one of the most important was that home purchase loans had become such long-term loans. The 30-year mortgage has a much longer repayment period than virtually any other common type of loan. (Most business and consumer loans must be paid off within five years.) From the lender's point of view, long-term loans pose some special problems. For example, as explained in Chapter 1, interest rate risk is a greater potential problem with long-term loans.

Government regulations limited the amount of long-term lending that commercial banks could engage in, but did not restrict savings and loans in the same way. The main reason for this distinction was that in those days S&Ls held only savings and time deposits, whereas commercial banks primarily held demand deposits.

S&Ls had long-term deposits well suited for making long-term loans

Demand deposits are kept in checking accounts for use in transactions such as bill paying. They can be withdrawn on demand, anytime the depositor wants the funds, so the amount on deposit may change frequently. In contrast, **time deposits** can be withdrawn without penalty only after giving notice to the financial institution, or after a specific period has elapsed; certificates of deposit are an example. **Savings deposits** may be withdrawn without notice, but are generally intended to remain on deposit for a long time (not to be used for transactions).

Because time and savings deposits are less susceptible to withdrawal than demand deposits, they're more stable and easier to use for long-term loans. So government regulations gave savings and loans, with their long-term deposits, free rein to make long-term mortgage loans.

Market interest rates skyrocketed in the late 1970s and early 1980s

Deregulation and Disaster. In response to changes in the national economy, market interest rates soared to unprecedented heights in the late 1970s and early 1980s. (In the early 1960s a typical mortgage rate was 4.5%; by the mid-1970s 10% was common, and by 1982 18% was not unusual.) Rates were also extremely volatile (unstable), changing by as much as 3% in the course of a single year.

As a result, lending institutions—especially savings and loan associations—began experiencing financial difficulties. Regulations imposed a decade earlier limited how much interest savings and loans could pay their depositors, so S&Ls now found themselves unable to offer attractive returns. They ended up losing a large portion of their deposits to competing investments such as money market funds and government bonds. (See the discussion of disintermediation in Chapter 1.) Making matters much worse, the S&Ls had most of their funds tied up in long-term mortgages at what were now considered very low interest rates.

Deregulation allowed S&Ls to pay depositors higher interest rates, charge higher rates on mortgage loans, and branch out from residential lending

Congress addressed these problems first in the Depository Institutions Deregulation and Monetary Control Act of 1980, and again in the Garn–St. Germain Depository Institutions Act of 1982. Among other things, this legislation loosened regulatory restrictions on savings and loan associations. It allowed S&Ls to pay higher interest rates than before, to attract depositors. It also preempted state usury laws so that S&Ls could charge higher interest rates on their loans. In addition, the legislation permitted S&Ls to make more consumer loans and nonresidential real estate loans than before, enabling them to branch out from their traditional role as residential lenders.

Deregulation is now seen as one of several factors that led the savings and loan industry into a much worse crisis. Some S&Ls tried new types of investments that were much riskier than single-family home loans, and often the risks didn't pay off. Due to economic slumps, mismanagement, and in some cases even fraud, many institutions found themselves in serious trouble. When insolvency loomed, the officers of some S&Ls took even greater risks, gambling to see if they could get back into black ink. Since the deposits were insured by the federal government, they felt they had little to lose.

The result was a sharp increase in the failure rate of savings and loans. Hundreds of federally insured S&Ls became insolvent, and eventually the Federal Savings and Loan Insurance Corporation could not meet all of the liabilities. Finally, to protect S&L depositors, the federal government stepped in. The bail-out of the savings and loan industry ultimately cost taxpayers about $124 billion.

Hundreds of S&Ls became insolvent, leading to a government bail-out of the industry

Reform. In response to the savings and loan crisis, Congress passed the Financial Institutions Reform, Recovery, and Enforcement Act, or FIRREA, in 1989. The act imposed new rules on the lending activities of savings and loans to prevent high-risk transactions, and it reorganized the federal agencies that supervise and insure financial institutions. The Federal Home Loan Bank Board was replaced by the Federal Housing Finance Board and the Office of Thrift Supervision. The Federal Savings and Loan Insurance Corporation was eliminated, and the Federal Deposit Insurance Corporation (FDIC) was reorganized to cover S&L deposits as well as bank deposits. FIRREA also formed the Resolution Trust Corporation to manage insolvent S&Ls, selling them or closing them and disposing of their assets.

The savings and loan industry recovered from its crisis. Because of insolvencies and mergers, there are far fewer savings and loan associations now than there were in the 1970s, but the industry is considered financially sound again.

Changing Market Shares. In the wake of the savings and loan crisis, the composition of the primary mortgage market changed. Where S&Ls had once dominated, mortgage companies now came to the forefront.

Between the 1930s and the 1970s, mortgage companies had grown into a significant force in residential lending, but that had been a fairly gradual process. In the 1980s, their share of the residential mortgage market began increasing rapidly and steadily. This dramatic growth continued through the end of the century.

HUD's Survey of Mortgage Lending Activity showed this trend very plainly. The survey, which was published annually until 1998, provided data about the origination of mortgages on properties with one to four dwelling units. In 1980, according to the HUD survey, 49.7% of the originations were made by thrifts (primarily savings and

Fig. 3.3 After the S&L crisis, mortgage companies took a larger share of the market

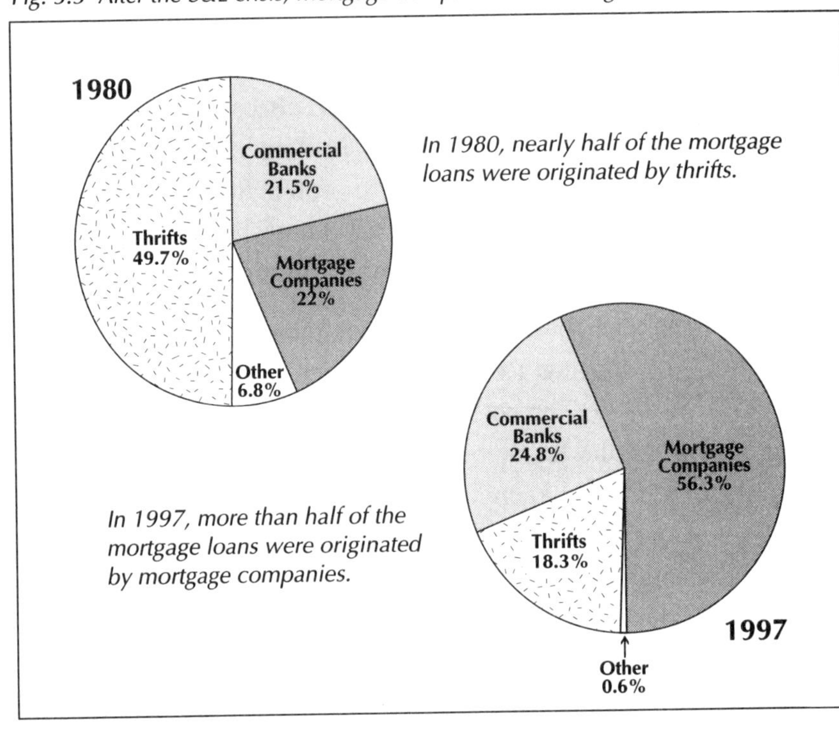

loans), 21.5% by commercial banks, and 22% by mortgage companies. In 1997, the last year before the survey was discontinued, only 18.3% of the originations were by thrifts, 24.8% were by commercial banks, and 56.3% were by mortgage companies. (See Figure 3.3.) In less than twenty years, mortgage companies became the dominant residential lenders, taking over the position that savings and loans once held.

A number of forces came together to cause this shift in the residential mortgage market. Clearly, one factor was the savings and loan crisis and the decline in the number of savings and loans. The growth of the secondary market (see Chapter 2) was another important factor, because it made much more capital available for mortgage companies to work with.

Mortgage Industry Trends

To close the chapter, we'll look at some recent developments and current trends in the primary market. These changes are affecting the way mortgage lenders do business and the financing choices available to prospective home buyers.

Technological Changes

Not surprisingly, computer technology has played an increasing role in mortgage lending since 1990. Loan origination software, automatic underwriting systems, and credit scoring have reduced the amount of time it takes to process mortgage loan applications. Some buyers can be qualified for a loan in minutes, and transactions that used to take weeks can often be handled in hours. The cost of loan processing has also been reduced, which has helped lower closing costs for borrowers. As you'll see in our discussion of automatic underwriting systems in Chapter 8, the new technology is also thought to have improved the accuracy of lending decisions.

Computerization has made loan processing faster and less expensive

Of course, it's now possible to apply for a mortgage online, over the Internet. A few major mortgage companies exist only in cyberspace, although most of the successful Internet lenders are divisions of well-established, brick-and-mortar companies. Internet lending has gained ground somewhat more slowly than expected, and as yet it represents only a small share of the market. But consumers are becoming increasingly comfortable making purchases and carrying out other transactions online, and it's possible that eventually most mortgage loans will be made over the Internet.

Internet mortgage lending is gradually gaining popularity with home buyers

Nationwide Lending

As we discussed in Chapter 2, primary market mortgage lenders used to have a local focus, linked to the local nature of residential real estate markets. This started changing as the secondary market expanded in the 1970s. Selling loans on the secondary market freed lenders from the economic conditions in their local markets, and Fannie Mae and Freddie Mac's uniform underwriting standards made it much easier for a lender based in one state to invest in mortgages secured by property in other states. This transformation of the primary market accelerated in the 1980s and 1990s, when federal regulations were loosened to allow interstate banking. A lender based in New York, Missouri, or Arizona now can have branch offices throughout the country.

One consequence of the trend toward nationwide lending has been remarkable consolidation in the mortgage industry. In recent years, the nation's 25 largest mortgage lenders have made between two-thirds and three-quarters of the mortgage loans. By contrast, in

Large nationwide lenders now dominate the mortgage industry

the early 1990s the mortgage lenders that were the 25 largest at that time made only about a third of the loans.

What effect this consolidation is having on consumers is subject to debate. On one hand, reduced competition among lenders could mean fewer options and higher financing costs for home buyers. On the other hand, the large lenders can take advantage of the economies of scale: a greater volume of business leads to greater efficiency and lower per-unit costs. In the mortgage industry, this could mean more options and lower costs for home buyers.

Wholesale Lending

With the rise of large nationwide mortgage lenders, the distinction between **retail lending** and **wholesale lending** has become important. In retail transactions, the lender works directly with customers (home buyers). In wholesale transactions, the lender is behind the scenes, as we'll describe shortly.

A particular lender might engage only in retail lending, only in wholesale lending, or in both. Whether they're banks, thrifts, or mortgage companies, lenders involved in wholesale lending tend to be large institutions. That doesn't mean that large lenders are always wholesale lenders, however. Many large institutions are still involved in retail lending.

Retail lender: deals directly with home buyers

Wholesale lender: makes loans through loan correspondents and mortgage brokers

Wholesale Originations. To explain how wholesale lending works, we need to take a closer look at the different ways in which mortgage loans are originated. In retail transactions, the lender handles the entire origination process, from the application through closing. In wholesale transactions, the lender makes a loan either through a loan correspondent or through a mortgage broker.

Correspondent originations. We described the role of a loan correspondent earlier in the chapter. A loan correspondent, sometimes called a **third party originator**, is a mortgage company, bank, or thrift that makes and services mortgage loans on behalf of a large investor. Nowadays, the investor is usually a wholesale lender. The correspondent is typically a smaller local lender that's knowledgeable about the real estate market in its community.

To a home buyer, a correspondent origination may seem just like a retail origination: the correspondent processes the loan application, decides whether to make the loan, and funds the loan, often in its own name. The difference is that the correspondent is making the loan in compliance with the underwriting standards of a particular wholesale lender, which has already arranged to purchase the loan on specified terms.

Broker originations. When a wholesale lender makes a loan through a mortgage broker, the broker isn't actually the originator of the loan. As explained earlier, mortgage brokers don't fund loans with their own money. The broker finds the customer, helps the customer choose a loan, takes the application, and then submits the application to the wholesale lender. It's the lender that makes the underwriting decision and funds the loan.

The Growth of Wholesale Lending. In the 1980s retail lending accounted for a large majority of mortgage originations. In recent years, however, only about 40% of all U.S. mortgage originations have been retail originations, and about 60% have been wholesale originations. As wholesale lending has expanded, mortgage brokers have taken on a more prominent role in the mortgage industry.

A majority of mortgage originations are now wholesale originations

Warehouse Lenders. You may come across the term "warehouse lenders" in some discussions of mortgage financing. Although it's easy to confuse "warehouse lenders" with "wholesale lenders," they aren't the same thing. A warehouse lender provides a retail lender or a correspondent with a line of credit it can use to borrow money on a short-term basis. For example, a mortgage company might use its line of credit with a warehouse lender to fund a loan before it arranges the sale of the loan to a secondary market agency. The warehouse lender treats the loan's promissory note as collateral until the mortgage company sells the loan and pays the warehouse lender back.

Warehouse lender: provides line of credit to a retail lender or loan correspondent

Subprime Lending

The last development in the primary market that we'll discuss is the remarkable boom in subprime mortgage lending that began in the 1990s. The subprime segment of the mortgage market is estimated to have increased from about $35 billion in 1994 to $332 billion in 2003.

What is Subprime Lending? Subprime lending involves making riskier loans than prime lending. Prime or standard financing is sometimes referred to as A credit; subprime ranges from A-minus credit to

Subprime lenders make riskier loans

B, C, and D credit. Subprime lenders can generally be distinguished from prime lenders by their advertisements. Subprime ads are aimed at potential home buyers who might have trouble getting a loan, and they often place special emphasis on their flexibility and personalized service. According to HUD, subprime lenders are more likely than prime lenders to have words such as "acceptance" or "consumer" in their names. Refinancing and home equity loans for debt consolidation make up a considerable part of the subprime market, along with home purchase loans.

A subprime loan may involve:
- poor credit rating,
- lack of documentation,
- high debt ratio,
- nonstandard property, or
- large loan amount

Who Needs Subprime Lending? While many of the home buyers who get subprime mortgages have blemished credit histories and mediocre credit scores, subprime lenders also deal with other categories of buyers. For example, subprime financing may be necessary for buyers who:

- can't (or would rather not have to) meet the income and asset documentation requirements of prime lenders;
- have good credit but carry more debt than prime lenders allow;
- want to purchase nonstandard properties that prime lenders don't regard as acceptable collateral; or
- need "super jumbo loans" in order to buy very expensive homes.

Loans to buyers in each of these categories involve greater risk for the lender, just as loans to buyers with poor credit histories do. If it weren't for the subprime market, these potential buyers might not be able to purchase the home they want—or, in some cases, any home at all.

Subprime lenders charge higher interest rates and higher loan fees

Subprime Rates and Fees. Subprime lenders can take on these riskier borrowers and riskier loans because they apply more flexible underwriting standards. In exchange, they typically charge much higher interest rates and fees than prime lenders charge.

> **Example:** The Gundersons want to buy a home. Because of some recent credit problems, they can't qualify for a prime loan. Their subprime lender classifies them as B-risk borrowers and charges them 9% interest for their loan, although the market rate for prime loans (A loans) is only 6%. If the Gundersons had an even worse credit history and were classified as C-risk borrowers, the lender would charge them 10.5% interest. And if they were D-risk borrowers, they'd have to pay 12%.

Fig. 3.4 Subprime financing is a growing part of the mortgage industry

Subprime Financing

- A-minus, B, C, D credit
- More flexible underwriting standards
- Higher rates and fees
- Risk-based pricing
- For nonstandard transactions, as well as borrowers with credit problems

Subprime lenders justify their higher rates and fees by pointing to their higher servicing costs. Subprime loans require more aggressive servicing because of higher delinquency and default rates. Charging more for riskier loans is called **risk-based pricing**, and it's a key aspect of subprime lending. We'll discuss it in more detail in Chapter 8.

Risk-based pricing: lender charges more for riskier loans

In addition to having high interest rates and fees, subprime loans are more likely than prime loans to have features such as prepayment penalties, balloon payments, and negative amortization (see Chapter 6). These features help subprime lenders counterbalance some of the extra risk involved in their loans, but they can also cause trouble for borrowers. The problem of **predatory lending**, discussed in Chapter 14, is generally associated with the subprime market. The majority of subprime lenders are legitimate, but there are some who profit by deliberately making loans on burdensome terms to home buyers who are likely to have great difficulty repaying them.

Some subprime lenders engage in predatory lending practices

Subprime and the Secondary Market. The secondary market for subprime loans grew in the 1990s, which helped fuel the subprime boom. Some Wall Street firms and large mortgage banking companies buy subprime loans and use them as the basis for issuing private label mortgage-backed securities.

Traditionally, Fannie Mae and Freddie Mac participated very little in the subprime market. In fact, their underwriting standards can almost be said to define prime mortgage lending. HUD encouraged Fannie Mae and Freddie Mac to enter the subprime market to help meet their affordable housing goals (see Chapter 2), and in the past few years both GSEs have started buying more subprime loans. This has drawn some protests from those already involved in the subprime market. For the most part, the GSEs are only purchasing the very top layer of the subprime market, A-minus loans, leaving other investors with the riskier subprime loans.

Dividing line between prime and subprime mortgage lending is beginning to blur

The GSEs' expansion into A-minus territory is one of several ways in which the line between prime and subprime mortgage lending is beginning to blur.

End of the Boom. Subprime lending ran into some trouble in the late 1990s. The default rate on subprime loans went up, and there were also economic changes that negatively affected subprime lenders. Some of them went out of business, while others were acquired by lenders that previously had engaged only in prime mortgage lending. Now many of the largest subprime lenders are owned by holding companies that also own prime lenders.

Even though the subprime market isn't increasing at the astonishing rate it did in the mid-1990s, it has continued to grow. Keep in mind, however, that subprime loans account for a minority of mortgage originations (less than 15%). Prime mortgage loans remain the standard in the mortgage industry.

Outline: Residential Mortgage Lenders

I. Types of Mortgage Lenders

   A. The five main types of residential lenders are commercial banks, savings banks, savings and loan associations, credit unions, and mortgage companies.

   B. Commercial banks

      1. Commercial banks were originally oriented toward commercial lending for activities like business ventures and construction; residential mortgages were a small part of their business.
      2. Regulatory changes have made residential lending more attractive to commercial banks, but commercial banks typically still have only a small minority of their assets invested in residential loans.
      3. Commercial banks are different from investment banks, which focus on securities and corporate finances, rather than accepting deposits and making loans.

   C. Savings banks

      1. Savings banks were oriented toward small depositors, offering savings accounts and making mortgage and consumer loans.
      2. Today, savings banks offer the same services as commercial banks.

   D. Savings and loan associations

      1. Savings and loan associations were originally started to provide financing for home construction, and their services were only available to members.
      2. S&Ls later began issuing loans to nonmembers and taking deposits from small depositors; deregulation in the 1970s allowed S&Ls to become more like banks.

   E. Credit unions

      1. Credit unions are nonprofit cooperatives that serve members of a particular group, such as a labor union or employees of a large company.
      2. Credit unions originally specialized in small, unsecured loans; they later began emphasizing home equity loans and issuing residential loans.

F. Mortgage companies

1. Mortgage companies, also known as mortgage bankers, are not depository institutions and focus entirely on mortgage loans.
2. Mortgage companies may borrow money from a commercial bank, use it to originate mortgages, and sell the mortgages to secondary market investors.
3. Mortgage companies may also act as loan correspondents, originating loans on an investor's behalf and servicing the loan in order to receive servicing fees.
4. Typical clients of a loan correspondent are national-scale investors such as life insurance companies and pension funds, which don't have the resources to deal with local real estate markets or day-to-day loan servicing.
5. Independent mortgage companies aren't subject to the same federal regulations as banks or S&Ls.
6. A mortgage banker originates loans, while a mortgage broker is an intermediary who brings a borrower and a lender together for a commission; some mortgage companies are strictly a broker or a banker, while others may do both.

G. Private lenders

1. Real estate investment trusts and real estate limited partnerships are the sources of financing capital, but generally to builders and not to individual home buyers.
2. Many home buyers receive financing from home sellers, either through primary or secondary financing.

II. Government Intervention in Mortgage Lending

A. The Depression

1. Prior to the Depression, many banks and private investors invested in home purchase loans, which usually were for five years with a large balloon payment.
2. The Depression brought about a wave of defaults and foreclosures; the government enacted a number of reforms during the Depression to fix the mortgage industry, including creation of the Federal Housing Administration.
3. The FHA provided insurance that protected lenders against default, so that lenders were more confident about issuing long-term (20 or 30 year) fully-amortized loans.

B. The savings and loan crisis
    1. Savings and loans came to dominate the residential lending market in post-World War II years.
    2. S&Ls were able to meet the need for deposit stability required for long-term residential lending, since they only accepted time deposits and savings deposits rather than demand deposits.
    3. Deregulation in the early 1980s allowed S&Ls to engage in new investments, many of which were risky and didn't pay off, causing many S&Ls to become insolvent.
    4. Congress reformed the S&L industry through the Financial Institutions Reform, Recovery and Enforcement Act, but fewer S&Ls remained and mortgage companies wound up with a much larger part of the residential lending market.

III. Mortgage Industry Trends
  A. Technological changes
    1. Loan origination software and automated underwriting systems have streamlined the loan application process and reduced loan processing costs.
    2. Internet-only lenders are a small share of the market, but are expected to gain in prominence.
  B. Nationwide lending
    1. Originally, most lending was focused on local markets, but this changed with the expansion of the secondary market in the 1970s and the use of uniform underwriting standards.
    2. With regulations allowing interstate banking, many lenders have consolidated.
  C. Wholesale lending
    1. In retail transactions, one lender originates and services a loan, while in wholesale transactions, a lender makes a loan through a loan correspondent.
    2. Most large investors are wholesale investors, while loan correspondents are usually smaller companies that understand a particular local real estate market.
    3. A "warehouse lender" provides retail lenders or short-term correspondents with a line of credit to fund loans until they can be sold to secondary market investors.

D. Subprime lending

1. Subprime lending involves riskier loans than prime lending, and is targeted toward buyers who might otherwise be unable to get a loan.
2. Subprime lenders apply more flexible underwriting standards, but typically charge higher interest rates and fees than other lenders to make up for the greater risk of default.
3. Since subprime lending often includes features such as prepayment penalties and balloon payments, predatory lending is often associated with the subprime market.
4. While Fannie Mae and Freddie Mac have made only small moves into the subprime secondary market, investment firms may purchase subprime loans and package them as private mortgage-backed securities.

Key Terms

Commercial bank: A type of financial institution that traditionally has emphasized commercial lending, but which also makes many residential mortgage loans.

Savings bank: A type of financial institution that has traditionally emphasized consumer loans and accounts for small depositors, and which also makes mortgage loans. Also called a mutual savings bank.

Savings and loan association: A type of financial institution that has traditionally specialized in home mortgage loans; also called a savings association or a thrift.

Thrift industry: Savings banks and savings and loan associations.

Credit union: A type of financial institution that serves only the members of a particular group, such as a professional organization or labor union. Credit unions have traditionally emphasized consumer loans, and now also make residential mortgage loans.

Mortgage company: A type of real estate lender that originates and services loans on behalf of large investors (acting as a mortgage banker) or for immediate resale on the secondary market; not a depository financial institution.

Mortgage banker: An intermediary who originates and services real estate loans on behalf of investors.

Mortgage broker: An intermediary who brings real estate lenders and borrowers together and negotiates loan arrangements between them.

Loan correspondent: An intermediary who arranges loans of an investor's money to borrowers and then services the loans.

Federal Housing Administration (FHA): An agency within the Department of Housing and Urban Development that provides mortgage insurance to encourage lenders to make more affordable home loans.

Time deposit: A deposit in a financial institution that is not supposed to be withdrawn until a certain period has elapsed, unless the depositor pays a penalty.

Demand deposit: A deposit in a financial institution that a depositor can withdraw at any time, without notice, such as a deposit in a checking account.

Financial Institutions Reform, Recovery and Enforcement Act (FIRREA): A federal law enacted in 1989 in response to the savings and loan crisis; it reorganized the federal agencies that oversee financial institutions.

Wholesale lending: Lending by a large investor through a loan correspondent who originates and services loans.

Subprime lending: Making riskier loans to persons who might otherwise be unable to qualify for a loan, often requiring higher interest rates and fees to make up for the increased risk of default.

Chapter Quiz

1. At one time, five-year home purchase mortgages were common. Today, however, the standard mortgage is a 30-year fully amortized loan. This change:
   a. was brought about in the Financial Institutions Reform, Recovery, and Enforcement Act (FIRREA) in 1989
   b. was imposed on lenders by the Garn–St. Germain Act in 1982
   c. occurred as a response to the large numbers of foreclosures that took place during the Depression
   d. happened as a result of the deregulation of financial institutions

2. As a general rule, mortgage companies do not:
   a. keep any loans in portfolio
   b. sell their loans on the secondary market
   c. service loans
   d. accept any type of deposits except demand deposits

3. FIRREA:
   a. deregulated financial institutions
   b. established the secondary market
   c. abolished the Federal Reserve System
   d. was enacted in response to the S&L crisis

4. A depository institution that limits its membership to members of a particular group, such as employees of a large company, is a:
   a. commercial bank
   b. credit union
   c. savings and loan association
   d. savings bank

5. An intermediary that brings together lenders and borrowers and arranges loans for a commission is a:
   a. mortgage banker
   b. mortgage broker
   c. loan correspondent
   d. subprime lender

6. In the 21st century, the majority of residential loans are made by:
   a. commercial banks
   b. credit unions
   c. mortgage companies
   d. savings and loan associations

7. A wholesale lender:
   a. originates and services loans
   b. issues loans to high-risk individuals
   c. issues short-term lines of credit to retail lenders
   d. makes loans through a loan correspondent

8. Which of the following borrowers would NOT use the services of a subprime lender?
   a. A person with a low credit rating
   b. A developer needing financing to build a subdivision
   c. A buyer of a nonstandard property that may not provide acceptable collateral
   d. A buyer of an expensive house needing a "jumbo" loan

9. A subprime lender is likely to:
   a. charge higher interest rates because of the greater risk
   b. charge higher interest rates because of the lower risk
   c. charge lower interest rates because of the greater risk
   d. charge lower interest rates because of the lower risk

10. Which type of lender is oriented toward short-term deposits and short-term loans to big business clients, although it may have significant investments in residential mortgages?
    a. Commercial bank
    b. Savings bank
    c. Credit union
    d. Savings and loan association

Answer Key

1. c. The 30-year, fully-amortized loan became standard after the Depression, in reaction to the high failure rate for the five-year loans that were common before the Depression.

2. a. Mortgage companies typically do not keep loans in portfolio, but sell them on the secondary market. Mortgage companies are not depository institutions.

3. d. FIRREA was a federal law passed in 1989 in response to the savings and loan crisis, which reformed the thrift industry to provide greater oversight and prevent high-risk transactions.

4. b. A credit union is a depository institution with membership limited to members of a particular group, such as a labor union or professional organization.

5. b. A mortgage broker is an intermediary who helps lender and brokers find each other, in exchange for a commission. By contrast, a mortgage banker originates and services loans, usually for the benefit of investors.

6. c. In the wake of the savings and loan crisis and the growth of the secondary market, the majority of residential loans today are made by mortgage companies.

7. d. A wholesale lender is a large investor that makes loans through many loan correspondents, who specialize in local real estate markets and originate and service loans on the investor's behalf.

8. b. A subprime lender may lend to a person with poor credit, a borrower with an unusual property, or a "jumbo loan" borrower. A real estate developer would probably seek financing from a private investment group, such as a real estate investment trust.

9. a. A subprime lender charges higher interest rates and fees because of the greater risk of default and more intensive servicing associated with such loans.

10. a. A commercial bank is oriented toward demand deposits and short-term commercial loans, although most commercial banks also have large investments in residential mortgages.

Chapter 4
Government Policy and Real Estate Finance

Fiscal Policy

- Spending and debt financing
- Taxation
  - Deduction of mortgage interest
  - Exclusion of gain on the sale of a home
  - Cost recovery deductions for investors

Monetary Policy

- Federal Reserve System
- Economic growth and inflation
- Tools for implementing monetary policy
  - Reserve requirements
  - Interest rates
  - Open market operations
- Changes in monetary policy

Introduction

As you saw in Chapters 2 and 3, the federal government has affected real estate finance by creating the secondary market agencies, by regulating lending institutions, and by intervening in the mortgage industry in times of crisis. The government also affects real estate finance by influencing the cost of mortgage funds.

The major cost of borrowing money to finance the purchase of a home is the interest rate charged by the lender. As we discussed in Chapter 1, market interest rates represent the current cost of money, the price that a borrower will have to pay to get a loan today. The cost of money, like the cost of other things in our society, is controlled primarily by the law of supply and demand. If the supply of money is large—if there is a large amount of money in circulation—interest rates tend to fall. The lower interest rates encourage more people to borrow money for both business and personal purposes, including borrowing to finance the purchase of homes. Then, as the money supply tightens, interest rates tend to rise, and fewer people can afford to borrow.

Government influences interest rates through:
- Fiscal policy
- Monetary policy

The cost of borrowing money is influenced by the federal government in two ways:

1. with **fiscal policy**, and
2. with **monetary policy**.

Fiscal policy refers to the government's actions in raising revenue (taxation), spending money, and managing its debt. These activities can indirectly affect the nation's money supply, and therefore the cost of money. Monetary policy refers to the government's direct efforts to control the money supply and the cost of money.

Fiscal Policy

Fiscal policy:
- Government spending
- Debt financing
- Taxation

Fiscal policy is determined by the government's executive branch (the president and the administration) and legislative branch (Congress). The two branches establish the federal tax laws, which generate the government's largest source of income, and the federal budget, which determines how the money will be spent. The U.S. Treasury Department carries out the fiscal policy; it is responsible for managing the federal government's finances, including the national debt.

Spending and Debt Financing

When the federal government spends more money than it takes in (through taxation and other income sources), a shortfall that's known as the **federal deficit** results. A deficit has occurred in most years since the Depression of the 1930s.

When there is a deficit, the Treasury obtains funds to cover the shortfall by issuing interest-bearing securities for sale to investors. Depending on their term, these securities are referred to as Treasury bills (less than one year), Treasury notes (one to five years), or Treasury certificates (five to ten years). In issuing these securities the federal government is actually borrowing from the private sector. And when the government borrows to cover the deficit, less money is available for private borrowers.

Federal deficit absorbs investment funds from private sector

As the graph in Figure 4.1 indicates, there were surpluses rather than deficits from 1998 through 2001. (The last surplus before that was in 1969.) The federal budget returned to a deficit in 2002, and in 2003 the deficit reached a record $377.6 billion ($87.2 billion over the previous record, $290.4 billion in 1992). The deficit was even higher in 2004 ($412.7 billion), but decreased to $318.3 billion in 2005.

Some economists believe the federal deficit has little, if any, effect on interest rates. Others believe large-scale federal borrowing pushes interest rates upward, as private borrowers are forced to compete for the limited funds remaining. It's true that not long after the deficit soared in 2003, interest rates began a gradual but steady climb. Yet during the recession in the early 1990s, when the deficit was setting previous records, interest rates dropped to their lowest levels in years. Whatever impact the deficit has on interest rates, it's clear that it is only one of several forces that affect them.

Taxation

The other element of fiscal policy is taxation. When taxes are low, taxpayers have more money to lend and invest. When taxes are high, taxpayers not only have less money to lend or invest, they are also more likely to invest what money they do have in tax-exempt securities instead of taxable investments. Since real estate and mortgage-backed securities are taxable investments, this has a significant impact on residential finance.

When taxes are high, taxpayers:
- have less money to lend or invest
- tend to prefer tax-free investments

Taxation also affects mortgage financing and the real estate industry in other ways. While the primary purpose of taxation is to raise

Fig. 4.1 When the federal government spends more money than it takes in, a deficit results

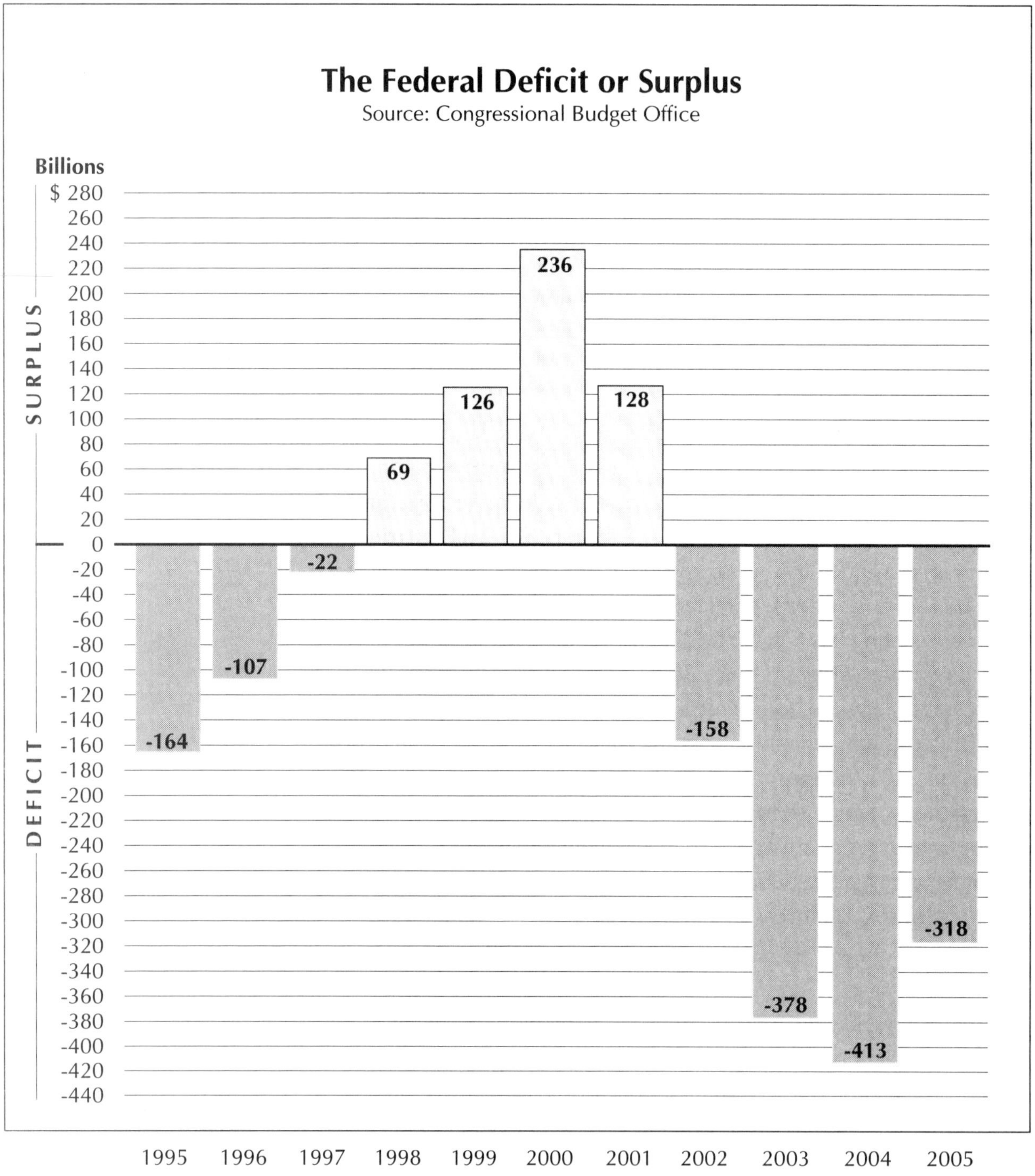

revenue, some provisions of the income tax laws are used to implement social policy. This is accomplished through tax exemptions, deductions, and exclusions. We'll take a brief look at some provisions in the federal tax code that affect the demand for real estate, and therefore have an indirect impact on the cost of mortgage funds.

Tax benefits for homeowners:
- Mortgage interest deduction
- Exclusion of gain on sale of principal residence

Deduction of Home Mortgage Interest. Taxpayers who own a home are allowed to deduct the interest they pay on their mortgage from their taxable income, which ultimately reduces the amount of taxes they have to pay. (Interest on other forms of consumer debt is not deductible.) By making it less expensive to own a home, the mortgage interest deduction implements the government's social policy of encouraging home ownership.

Limits on deductibility. There are some limits on the mortgage interest deduction. A taxpayer generally can deduct all of the interest paid on loans for buying, building, or improving first and second residences, as long as the loans don't add up to more than $1,000,000 ($500,000 for a married taxpayer filing separately). The same taxpayer can also deduct interest paid on home equity loans of up to $100,000 ($50,000 for a married taxpayer filing separately), without regard to the purpose of the loan.

If the taxpayer's mortgages exceed those limits, the interest paid on the excess is not deductible. For example, a married couple (filing jointly) with a $115,000 home equity loan could deduct the interest paid on the first $100,000, but not the interest paid on the remaining $15,000.

Exclusion of Gain on the Sale of a Home. Another tax code provision that benefits homeowners allows a gain or profit on the sale of a principal residence to be excluded from taxation. A taxpayer who sells his or her principal residence may exclude a gain of up to $250,000, or up to $500,000 if thc taxpayer is married and filing a joint return. If the gain on the sale exceeds the $250,000 or $500,000 limit, the excess is taxed at the capital gains rate. (The maximum capital gains tax rate is lower than the maximum tax rate on ordinary income.)

Eligibility. To qualify for this exclusion, the taxpayer must have both owned and used the property as a principal residence for at least two years during the five-year period before its sale. Because of this rule, the exclusion is available only once every two years.

If the sellers are married and filing a joint return, only one spouse has to meet the ownership test, but both spouses must meet the use test. If only one spouse meets both the ownership test and the use test, the maximum exclusion the married couple can claim is $250,000, even if they file a joint return.

In special circumstances, taxpayers who owned and used a principal residence for less than two years may be able to claim a reduced exclusion. For example, a reduced exclusion would be allowed if a home was sold after only a year because of a change in the taxpayer's health or place of employment, or because of some other unforeseen circumstances.

The deductibility of mortgage interest and the exclusion of gain on the sale of a principal residence both make a big difference to homeowners. Together, they are quite effective in helping to fulfill the government's social policy of encouraging homeownership.

Cost recovery (depreciation) deductions affect real estate investment

Cost Recovery Deductions for Investors. Many other provisions in the federal tax code also have an impact on real estate investment. To take one example, owners of income property, such as apartment buildings and rental homes, are allowed to take cost recovery deductions (also called depreciation deductions). In other words, they can deduct some of the cost of buildings and other property improvements that eventually will wear out and have to be replaced. The cost is spread out over a number of years (for residential rental properties, usually 27½ years), rather than deducted all at once. When the government changes the rules for these cost recovery deductions—for example, by requiring them to be stretched out over a greater number of years—it can affect the profitability of investing in real estate.

Thus, how the federal government raises revenue—how much it taxes income, how it taxes different kinds of income, and what tax deductions and exclusions it allows—can stimulate or dampen the demand for real estate and increase or decrease the availability of mortgage funds.

Monetary Policy

The federal government exercises considerable control over the nation's money supply—how much money is in circulation. Monetary policy refers to the government's efforts to use its control over the money supply to keep the national economy running smoothly.

Monetary policy is set and implemented by the Federal Reserve System, commonly called "the Fed."

The Fed:
- Regulates commercial banks
- Sets and implements monetary policy

The Federal Reserve System

The Federal Reserve System regulates commercial banks, and its responsibility for monetary policy grew out of that function.

Historical Background. In the early nineteenth century, there was very little government regulation of depository institutions in the United States. The security of bank deposits depended primarily on the integrity of bank managers. Not surprisingly, serious problems sometimes developed. For example, a bank might loan out nearly all of its deposits and keep almost no funds in reserve. When a depositor tried to make a withdrawal, the bank might not have enough cash on hand to fulfill the request. To protect the public against this kind of mismanagement, in 1863 Congress passed the National Bank Act, which established basic banking regulations and procedures for supervising commercial banks.

In spite of the 1863 law, certain problems persisted, and the public lacked confidence in the banking industry. Economic downturns periodically led to financial panics involving "a run on the bank," in which most of a bank's depositors would suddenly doubt the security of their money and withdraw it all at once. This could cause even a financially sound bank to fail, and the depositors who had not withdrawn their money would be left empty-handed.

Federal Reserve was established to strengthen the financial system and improve public confidence

To strengthen the financial system and improve public confidence, support grew for the creation of a central bank for the U.S., similar to the central banks of other countries. The American public had long resisted the idea of a central bank; average citizens tended to be hostile toward banks, Wall Street interests, and centralized authority in general. But huge losses suffered by depositors in a series of bank panics in 1907 finally overcame public resistance.

In the Federal Reserve Acts of 1913 and 1916, Congress created the Federal Reserve System and established the modern banking system. The Fed would regulate commercial banks, perform periodic bank examinations, and impose **reserve requirements**, specifying what proportion of a bank's deposits had to be held in reserve, available for immediate withdrawal on demand by depositors. In addition, the Federal Reserve would serve as a "lender of last resort," providing short-term backup loans to banks that ran low on funds.

Fig. 4.2 The organization of the Federal Reserve System

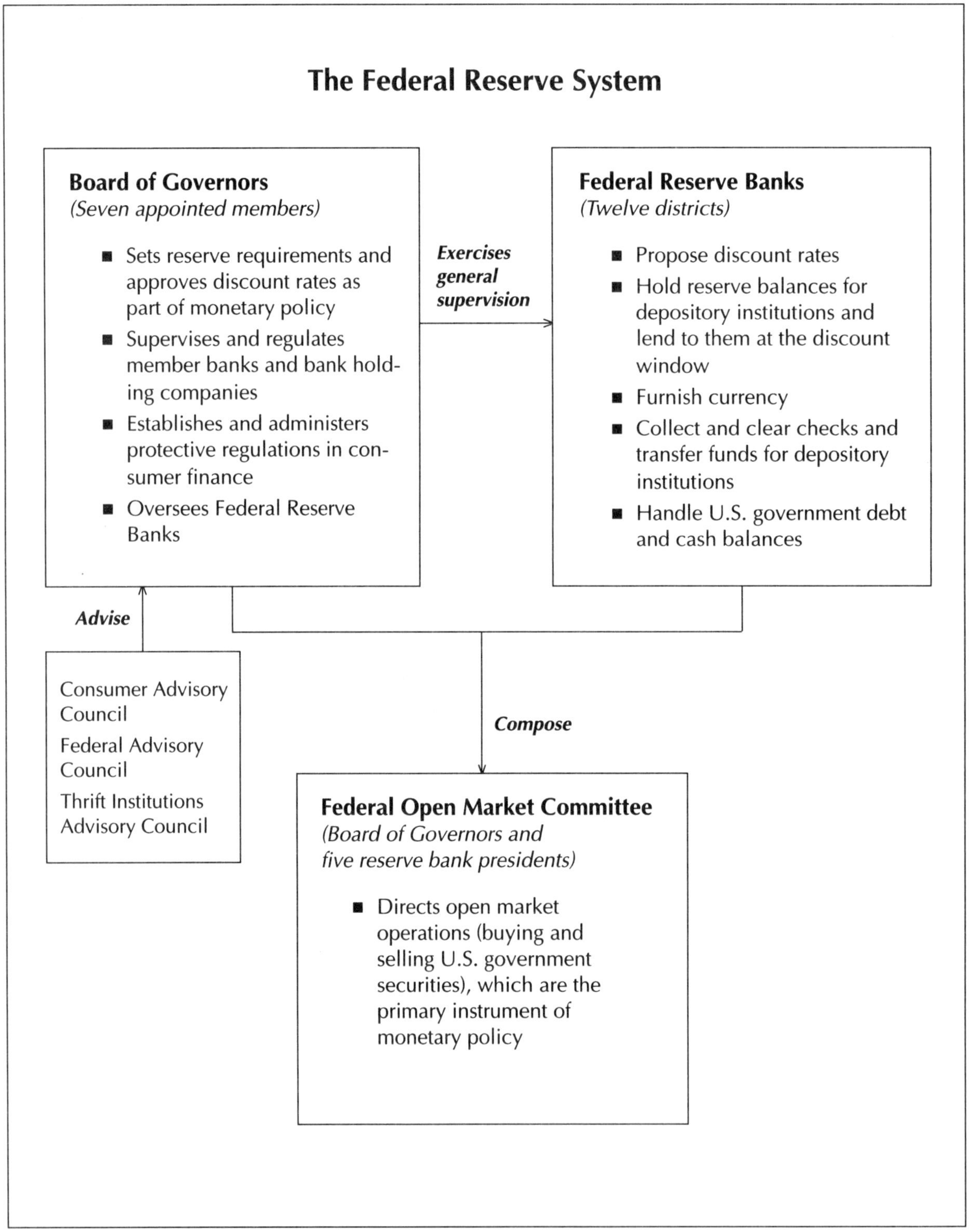

Source: The Federal Reserve

The creation of the Federal Reserve improved the financial system in many ways, but it did not entirely solve the problem of financial panics and bank runs. A more direct solution, federal deposit insurance, was developed in the 1930s, during the Depression. The Federal Deposit Insurance Corporation and the Federal Savings and Loan Insurance Corporation were created as part of the New Deal.

Organization. To prevent the centralization of too much power, Congress included checks and balances in the Federal Reserve System. Its structure was designed to spread power three different ways: geographically; between the private and government sectors; and among bankers, businesses, and the public. The Federal Reserve System is made up of:

- twelve regional Federal Reserve Banks in twelve Federal Reserve Districts,
- the Federal Reserve Board,
- the Federal Open Market Committee,
- the Federal Advisory Council, and
- over 5,000 member banks.

The system is controlled by the seven-member Board of Governors, known as the Federal Reserve Board (see Figure 4.2). The governors are appointed by the U.S. president and confirmed by the Senate for 14-year terms. To prevent one area of the country from having disproportionate power on the board, the governors must be chosen from different Federal Reserve Districts. The board's chairman is chosen from among the governors for a four-year term, and may be reappointed repeatedly. Some Fed chairmen have served under several presidents.

The Board of Governors controls the Fed's monetary policy. All seven governors are on the Federal Open Market Committee, which we'll discuss shortly. The governors set reserve requirements for commercial banks and, through the process of review and approval, effectively control the discount rate set by the Federal Reserve Banks. (We'll discuss the discount rate shortly, too.) The governors also have substantial control over regulations affecting the activities of commercial banks and bank holding companies.

Fed chairman and Federal Reserve Board make decisions concerning monetary policy

Each of the twelve Federal Reserve Districts has one main Federal Reserve Bank, and some districts have branch banks as well. Technically, each Federal Reserve Bank is an incorporated banking institution owned by the member commercial banks in the district. (The member banks are required to purchase stock in their reserve bank.) Each reserve bank has a nine-member board of directors. Six of the directors are elected by the stockholders and three are appointed by the Fed's Board of Governors. The nine directors appoint the president of their reserve bank, subject to the approval of the Board of Governors.

12 regional Federal Reserve Banks:
- Owned by member banks
- Make discount loans
- Set discount rates (with Board approval)
- Appoint bankers to Federal Advisory Council

All of the Federal Reserve Banks are involved to some degree in monetary policy. Each reserve bank has a staff that conducts research on economic conditions in its district, and each reserve bank selects one banker to be a member of the Federal Advisory Council. The Advisory Council meets and consults with the Board of Governors regarding monetary policy.

Economic Growth and Inflation

The Federal Reserve's ultimate goal in setting and implementing monetary policy is a healthy U.S. economy. The economy is considered healthy when there is sustainable economic growth with full employment, stable prices, and reasonable interest rates.

Inflation: prices increasing throughout the economy

Sustainable economic growth is neither too weak nor too strong, and neither too slow nor too fast. If growth is too strong and too fast, it's usually accompanied by **inflation**, a trend of general price increases throughout the economy. Uncontrolled inflation eventually chokes off economic growth. The ideal is for the economy to grow steadily, but at a moderate pace that won't trigger severe inflation.

Goal is sustainable growth with inflation in check

When the economy is stagnating, the Fed takes action to stimulate growth. But if the economy starts booming and inflation threatens to gain momentum, the Fed takes action to slow down growth and keep inflation in check.

Tools for Implementing Monetary Policy

The Fed relies on three main tools to implement its monetary policy and influence the economy:

Fed's tools for monetary policy:
- Reserve requirements
- Discount rate and federal funds rate target
- Open market operations

- reserve requirements,
- interest rates (the discount rate and federal funds rate), and
- open market operations.

Reserve Requirements. A commercial bank's reserve requirements are the percentages of its deposits the bank is required to maintain on reserve, either in its own vaults or on deposit at the Federal Reserve

Bank in its district. The requirements are set by the Federal Reserve Board, and they can vary from 3% to 12%. It used to be that only member banks were required to keep reserves at the reserve banks. But the Depository Institutions Deregulation and Monetary Control Act of 1980 subjected all commercial banks to the same reserve requirements as members of the Federal Reserve, and also imposed reserve requirements on savings banks, savings and loans, and credit unions. The same act also gave all commercial banks access to some Federal Reserve benefits such as check clearing and discount loans. As a result, there are now fewer differences between member and nonmember banks.

As explained earlier, the original purpose of reserve requirements was to help avert financial panics by giving depositors confidence that their deposits were safe and accessible. The requirements protect depositors by helping to ensure that their bank will always have enough funds available to meet unusual customer demand.

At the same time, reserve requirements also enable the Fed to exercise some control over the growth of credit. By increasing reserve requirements, the Fed can reduce the amount of money that banks have available to lend. On the other hand, a reduction in reserve requirements frees more money for investment or lending by banks. Thus, an increase in reserve requirements tends to decrease available loan funds and increase interest rates. Conversely, a decrease in reserve requirements tends to increase funds available for lending and decrease interest rates.

Reserve requirements:
- Increase — decreases funds available for investment and increases interest rates
- Decrease — increases supply of funds and decreases interest rates

Interest Rates. The Fed has control over two key interest rates: the federal discount rate and the federal funds rate.

The **discount rate** is the interest rate charged when a member of the Federal Reserve System borrows money from one of the Federal Reserve Banks, to cover a shortfall in funds. The discount rate is set by the Federal Reserve Banks with the approval of the Fed's Board of Governors.

Federal discount rate: interest rate charged banks that borrow from the Fed

The **federal funds rate** is the interest rate banks charge each other for overnight, unsecured loans. A bank that doesn't have enough funds to meet its reserve requirements may borrow the money needed from a bank that has excess reserves. Unlike the discount rate, the federal funds rate is not set directly by the Fed; the banks themselves can determine how much they'll charge each other for overnight loans. However, when the Federal Open Market Committee meets, it sets a

Federal funds rate: interest rate banks charge each other for overnight loans

Fig. 4.3 By changing the funds rate target, the Fed affects other interest rates and the economy as a whole

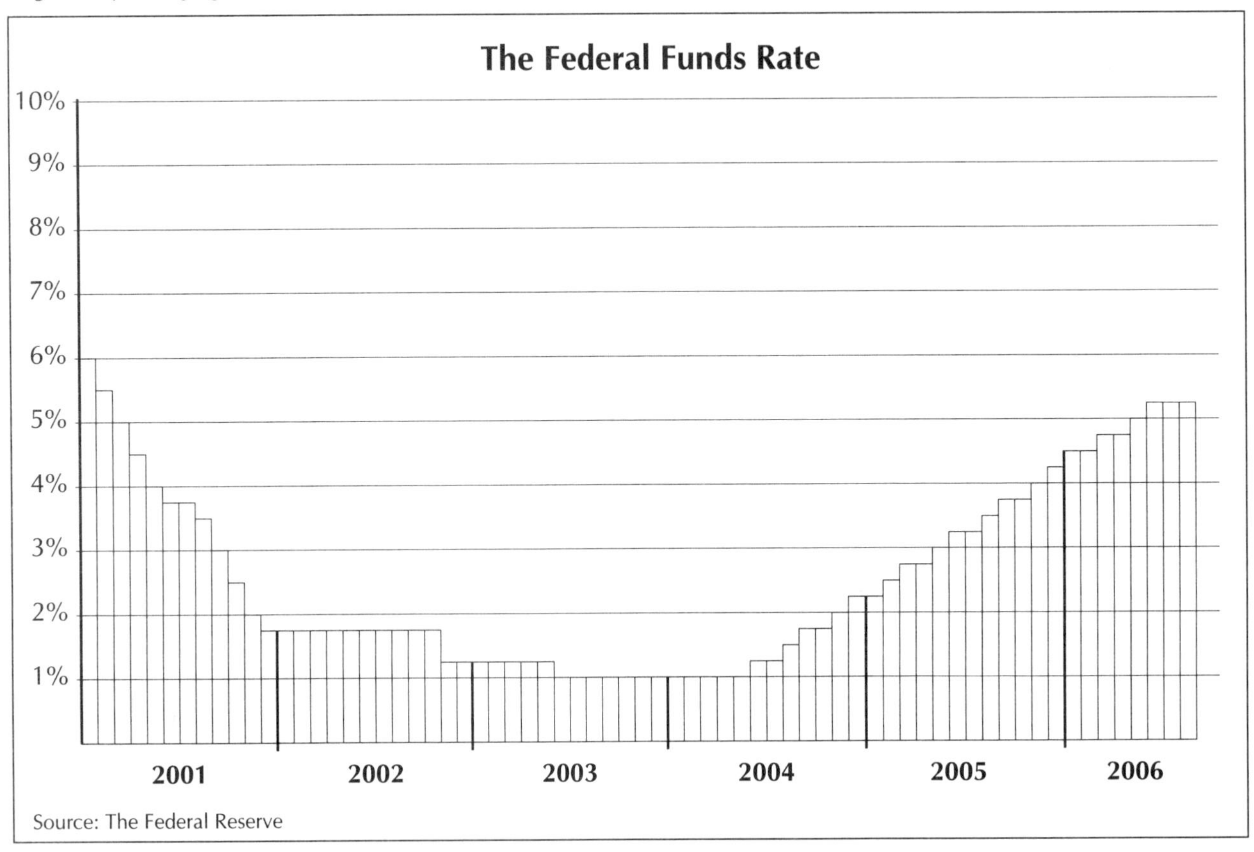

Source: The Federal Reserve

target for the federal funds rate. It also issues a directive indicating what open market operations will be conducted in an effort to achieve the target rate.

When the Federal Reserve raises or lowers the discount rate or the target for the federal funds rate, it's regarded as an indication of the Fed's overall view of the economy. For example, if either or both of these interest rates are lowered, that's seen as a signal that the Fed feels the economy needs a boost, since lower interest rates stimulate economic activity.

Lower interest rates stimulate economic activity

Lenders often respond to a change in the funds rate or the discount rate by making a corresponding change in the interest rates they charge on loans to their customers. For example, if the federal funds rate drops a quarter of a percentage point, market interest rates are likely to follow suit. However, this relationship is complicated by anticipation; sometimes lenders increase or decrease their rates in anticipation of an interest rate change by the Fed. In that case, the actual change in the federal funds rate or discount rate may have little impact.

Keep in mind that the market interest rates most affected by changes in the discount rate and federal funds rate are short-term interest rates. The Fed's interest rate adjustments don't have such a direct influence on long-term interest rates, which include the market interest rates for home purchase mortgages. Mortgage rates are, of course, affected by changes in the economy, but they generally don't go up or down in response to an increase or decrease in the discount rate or the target for the federal funds rate. When you hear that the Fed has raised or lowered interest rates, consider it an indication of the strength or weakness of the economy, but don't expect an immediate change in mortgage interest rates.

Long-term interest rates like mortgage rates don't respond directly to Fed's interest rate adjustments

Open Market Operations. The Fed also buys and sells government securities. These transactions are called open market operations. They are conducted by the Securities Department of the Federal Reserve Bank of New York (often referred to as "the Trading Desk," or just "the Desk"), following directives from the **Federal Open Market Committee** (FOMC). Open market operations are the most important tool for controlling the money supply, so the FOMC is the most important policy-making organization in the Fed.

Open market operations: the Fed buys and sells government securities

The FOMC meets approximately every six weeks. It consists of twelve members: the seven members of the Federal Reserve Board, the president of the New York Federal Reserve Bank, and four other Reserve Bank presidents (chosen on a rotating basis from the other eleven Reserve Banks). The seven Reserve Bank presidents who are not currently members of the FOMC usually attend and participate in the meetings, but they cannot vote on the committee's decisions.

Open market operations are the Fed's primary method of controlling the money supply (which also affects inflation and interest rates). Only money in circulation is considered part of the money supply, so actions by the Fed that put money into circulation increase the money supply, and actions that take money out of circulation decrease the money supply.

When the Fed buys government securities, it increases the money supply. The Fed may pay for the securities in cash, by check, or if purchasing from a bank, simply by crediting the bank's reserves with the Fed. Any of these actions puts more money into circulation. On the other hand, when the Fed sells government securities, the money the buyer uses to pay for the securities is taken out of circulation, decreasing the money supply.

Money supply:
- Increases when Fed buys government securities
- Decreases when Fed sells government securities

Other things being equal, an increase in the money supply is supposed to lead to lower interest rates. But other things are seldom equal, and several factors may apply upward pressure to interest rates at the same time that an increase in the money supply is exerting downward pressure. For example, an increase in the money supply is often associated with an increase in inflation, and when inflation is anticipated, interest rates tend to rise. The Fed uses open market operations and its other tools to balance these complicated forces. It tries to manage the money supply to adequately serve the growth of the economy at reasonable interest rates, without fueling inflation or fears of inflation that could lead to higher interest rates.

Changes in Monetary Policy

In the years since its creation, the Fed has frequently modified its monetary policy, both in terms of primary objectives and in the choice of tools employed to reach those objectives. Since the Fed really has no direct control over inflation or market interest rates, it works toward its goals by tracking certain economic indicators and by taking action to influence those indicators. At various times, the Fed has focused on the discount rate, reserve requirements, general money market conditions, the federal funds rate, and changes in one or more of its measures of the money supply. Its actions are more or less experimental, and when a particular experiment does not seem to be working, the Fed may try a different one.

Monetary policy is experimental, and Fed changes strategies from time to time

During the 1970s, the Fed's practice was to moderate interest rates by increasing the money supply whenever interest rates started to rise. Although this succeeded in keeping interest rates down, inflation got increasingly worse as money was pumped into the economy to satisfy the demands of borrowers.

In 1979, because of concern over inflation, the Fed adopted a different approach. It stopped its efforts to control interest rates by increasing the money supply, and instead tried to control inflation by restricting the growth of the money supply. In the months that followed, interest rates soared. (The high rates caused problems for savings and loans, which led to their deregulation. See Chapter 3.)

By 1982 the Fed had again shifted course. The inflation rate had fallen sharply, but interest rates remained high and variable. The Fed once again put more emphasis on preventing large fluctuations in interest rates. Since then, the inflation rate has been relatively moderate, and interest rates have been much lower and comparatively stable.

In the early years of the new century, the Fed tried to spur a slow economy by lowering interest rates to levels that hadn't been seen since the early 1960s. When the economy began improving, inflation once again became a concern. This led to a long series of incremental increases in the key interest rates. The Federal Open Market Committee met seventeen times between June 30, 2004 and June 29, 2006, and raised the target for the federal funds rate by a quarter point (0.25%) each time. Thus, over that two-year period, the federal funds rate target rose from 1.00% to 5.25%; the discount rate also went up steadily, from 2.00% to 6.25%. The Fed took a break from rate increases when it began to appear that economic growth was slowing down, even though inflation wasn't completely under control. As always, it isn't clear to what extent those conditions were the result of Fed policy or reflected other economic forces.

Outline: Government Policy and Real Estate Finance

I. Government Influences on Finance
   A. The federal government influences real estate finance by influencing the cost of mortgage funds.
   B. Market interest rates represent the cost of borrowing money, which is subject to the rules of supply and demand.
   C. The federal government affects the cost of borrowing through fiscal policy and monetary policy.

II. Spending and Debt Financing
   A. Federal government fiscal policy is determined by both the legislative and executive branches, and is carried out by the U.S. Treasury Department.
   B. If the federal government spends more money than it receives in a year, a deficit occurs.
   C. To finance the shortfall, the government sells interest-bearing securities to investors.
   D. When private investors lend money to the government to cover a deficit, less money is available to private borrowers.
      1. Some economists believe federal deficits have little effect on interest rates.
      2. Other economists believe deficit spending pushes interest rates up because government borrowing takes funds out of the money market and increases demand for funds.

III. Taxation
   A. Taxation affects mortgage rates by affecting how much money taxpayers have available to lend or invest.
   B. Taxation also affects mortgage rates through tax exemptions, deductions, and exclusions, which may affect demand for mortgages.
   C. Taxpayers are allowed to deduct home mortgage interest, which reduces the amount of taxes they pay.
      1. Limits on deductible mortgage interest are $1,000,000 for married couples filing jointly or $500,000 for individuals.
      2. Interest on home equity loans is also deductible.
   D. Taxpayers may exclude from taxation the gain received from selling a principal residence.

1. A gain of up to $250,000 for an individual or $500,000 for a married couple filing jointly may be excluded.
2. To qualify for this exclusion, the taxpayers must have owned the property and used it as a principal residence for at least two of the previous five years.

E. Investors may take deductions for cost recovery, meaning that depreciation of investment property may be deducted.

IV. Monetary Policy

A. Federal government monetary policy refers to the government's control over the money supply, which is implemented by the Federal Reserve System (or "Fed").

B. Historical background

1. Banks were first regulated in 1863 through the National Bank Act, which created basic procedures for supervising banks.
2. The Federal Reserve Acts of 1913 and 1916 created the modern banking system.
3. The Federal Reserve System imposes reserve requirements, specifying what amount of a bank's deposits must be kept in reserve to be available for withdrawal.
4. The Federal Reserve acts as a lender of last resort, providing short-term loans to banks running low on funds.
5. The stability of the banking industry was bolstered in the 1930s with the creation of the Federal Deposit Insurance Corporation.

C. Organization of the Federal Reserve

1. The Federal Reserve System is decentralized into twelve regional Federal Reserve Banks.
2. The system is controlled by the seven-member Board of Governors, each chosen for 14-year terms from different Federal Reserve Districts.
3. Each regional Federal Reserve Bank is an incorporated bank owned by the member commercial banks in its district.
4. Each regional bank is controlled by a nine-member board of directors.

D. Economic growth and inflation

1. If economic growth occurs too quickly, inflation results, causing price increases that hamper further growth.

2. If inflation appears to be a possibility, the Fed will take action to slow growth and limit inflation.

V. Tools for Implementing Monetary Policy

A. Reserve requirements: a percentage of deposits that each bank must maintain either in its own vaults or on deposit with the Federal Reserve Bank.

1. Reserve requirements were originally intended to avert financial panic by making sure that depositors were always able to withdraw deposits.
2. Reserve requirements also allow the Fed to control the money supply.
3. An increase in reserve requirements reduces the amount of money banks have available to lend and therefore increases interest rates.

B. Interest rates: the Fed controls two key interest rates, the federal discount rate and federal funds rate.

1. The discount rate is the rate charged to member banks when they borrow money from the Fed to cover a shortfall in funds.
2. The federal funds rate is the rate banks charge each other for loans to cover shortfalls.
3. Lenders' market interest rates will usually rise or fall in response to changes in the federal rates, although long-term rates (such as mortgages) are not immediately affected.

C. Open market operations: the Fed controls the money supply by buying and selling government securities.

1. If the Fed buys government securities, it puts more money into the money supply, which by itself will decrease interest rates.
2. If the Fed sells government securities, it takes money from investors out of the money supply, which will increase interest rates.

D. Changes in monetary policy

1. The Fed will modify its monetary policy in response to changing economic indicators.
2. In recent years, the Fed has tried to spur economic growth by lowering interest rates without allowing inflation to become a problem.

Key Terms

Fiscal policy: Government actions in raising revenue through taxation, spending money, and financing budget deficits.

Monetary policy: Government action in controlling the money supply and therefore the cost of borrowing money.

Federal deficit: A shortfall in funds that occurs when the federal government spends more money than it collects in a particular year.

Taxation: The federal government collects revenue through taxation. The rates at which people are taxed affects the amount of money taxpayers have available to invest.

Home mortgage interest deduction: Taxpayers may deduct from their taxable income all interest paid on home mortgages, up to a limit of $500,000 (or $1,000,000 for married couples filing jointly).

Exclusion of gain on sale of home: A taxpayer may exclude from taxation any gain on the sale of a principal residence, up to a limit of $250,000 (or $500,000 if filing jointly).

Cost recovery deductions: Real estate investors may take other deductions from their income taxes, such as deducting depreciation of investment property.

Federal Reserve System: The Federal Reserve System regulates commercial banks and implements the nation's monetary policy. Often referred to as "the Fed."

Reserve requirements: The Fed requires commercial banks to hold a certain portion of their deposits on reserve for immediate withdrawal by depositors.

Federal Reserve Bank: There are twelve Federal Reserve Banks, one for each Federal Reserve District, owned by the commercial banks within that district.

Federal Reserve Board: The Federal Reserve System is controlled by a seven-member Board of Governors, known as the Federal Reserve Board. Each of the seven members is appointed from a different district to a 14-year term.

Inflation: Inflation is a period of price increases which occurs as a result of too-rapid economic growth. The Fed seeks to limit inflation by using monetary policy to control growth.

Interest rates: The Fed has control over two key interest rates, the federal discount rate and the federal funds rate. Lenders tend to adjust their own short-term interest rates in response to changes in these rates.

Open market operations: The Fed adjusts the money supply by engaging in open market operations; as it buys and sells government securities it changes the amount of money available in circulation.

Federal Open Market Committee: The Federal Open Market Committee is a board that makes decisions regarding open market operations by the Fed.

Chapter Quiz

1. The government controls the money supply and cost of money through:
   a. fiscal policy
   b. monetary policy
   c. budgetary policy
   d. fiduciary policy

2. In a given year, the federal government spends more money than it receives as revenue. The result is a:
   a. federal deficit
   b. federal debt
   c. federal surplus
   d. federal default

3. Which item may be excluded from taxation, rather than simply taken as a deduction:
   a. Home mortgage interest
   b. Home equity loan interest
   c. Gain on the sale of a principal residence
   d. Depreciation of investment property

4. The gain from sale of which of the following properties would be excluded from taxation?
   a. A residential rental owned for the last ten years
   b. A residential property used as a primary residence from ten years ago until five years ago
   c. A vacation home owned for the last five years
   d. A residential property used as a primary residence from four years ago until one year ago

5. Which of the following is the best definition of reserve requirements?
   a. Buying and selling government securities on the open market
   b. Setting interest rates for loans to banks facing cash shortfalls
   c. Requiring banks to make a certain percentage of deposits available for immediate withdrawal
   d. Controlling inflation by raising interest rates in order to slow growth

6. How many Federal Reserve Districts and Federal Reserve Banks are there?
   a. 7
   b. 9
   c. 12
   d. 14

7. Inflation occurs when:
   a. rapid economic growth causes prices to increase
   b. the Fed raises interest rates
   c. the Fed decreases the pool of available funds by selling government securities
   d. economic stagnation causes higher unemployment

8. The interest rate charged by the Federal Reserve when a member bank borrows money to cover a shortfall in funds is the:
   a. federal funds rate
   b. federal discount rate
   c. federal key rate
   d. market interest rate

9. The Federal Reserve decides to decrease the supply of money available. It will:
   a. buy government securities and increase reserve requirements
   b. buy government securities and decrease reserve requirements
   c. sell government securities and increase reserve requirements
   d. sell government securities and decrease reserve requirements

10. In the early 1980s, the Fed tried to control inflation by restricting growth of the money supply. What happened?
    a. Interest rates shot up
    b. Interest rates plunged
    c. Inflation got worse
    d. The government bought back most of its government securities

Answer Key

1. b. Monetary policy refers to the government's efforts to control the money supply and thus the cost of borrowing money.

2. a. A federal deficit results if, in a particular year, the government spends more than it takes in.

3. c. Gain on the sale of a principal residence of up to $250,000 (or $500,000 for a married couple filing jointly) may be excluded from taxation.

4. d. To qualify for exclusion of gain, the taxpayer must have owned and used the property as a principal residence for at least two years during the five-year period before its sale.

5. c. Reserve requirements specify what percentage of a bank's deposits must be kept in reserve, available for immediate withdrawal by depositors.

6. c. There are twelve Federal Reserve Districts, each of which has its own Federal Reserve Bank.

7. a. Inflation occurs when economic growth is too rapid and prices throughout the economy shoot up. The Fed may take action to limit inflation—by raising interest rates, for example.

8. b. The federal discount rate is the interest rate charged by the Fed when a bank borrows funds to cover a shortfall in funds on deposit.

9. c. Both selling government securities on the open market and increasing reserve requirements take money that would otherwise be available to lend out of the money supply. A reduced money supply will increase the demand for funds and increase the cost of borrowing money.

10. a. The result of the Fed's efforts to decrease the money supply in the early 1980s was a decline in inflation, but also a sharp increase in interest rates.

Chapter 5
Finance Instruments

Promissory Notes

- Basic provisions
- Negotiability
- Types of notes

Security Instruments

- Purpose
- Historical background
- Mortgages
- Deeds of trust
- Foreclosure

Land Contracts

Finance Instrument Provisions

- Subordination clauses
- Late charge provisions
- Prepayment provisions
- Partial release clauses
- Acceleration clauses
- Alienation (due-on-sale) clauses

Types of Real Estate Loans

Introduction

Finance instruments:
- Promissory notes
- Mortgages
- Deeds of trust

The "instruments" discussed in this chapter are the legal documents used in real estate finance transactions: promissory notes, mortgages, and deeds of trust. We'll give an overview of how these instruments work, and also explain the provisions commonly found in them.

This chapter is only an introduction to finance instruments, to give you a basic understanding of their purpose and the differences between them. The information presented here should not be used as the basis for personal action or to advise clients or customers regarding particular documents. The laws governing creditor-debtor relations vary substantially from one state to another, and they are also subject to change by judicial or legislative action. As a result, it is important to consult an attorney for current, state-specific advice concerning the effect of these instruments in any particular transaction.

Promissory Notes

Promissory note:
- Maker is borrower
- Payee is lender
- Note is evidence of debt and promise to repay

A promissory note is a written promise to pay money. The one who makes the promise (the debtor) is called the **maker** of the note; the one to whom the promise is made (the creditor) is called the **payee**. In a typical real estate loan transaction, the maker is the buyer, who is borrowing money to finance the purchase of property, and the payee is the lender. (Or if the seller is extending credit to the buyer, the payee is the seller.) The promissory note is the basic evidence of the debt; it shows who owes how much money to whom.

Basic Provisions of a Note

A promissory note can be a very brief and simple document, as you can see from the example in Figure 5.1. The note states the names of the parties, the amount of the debt (the principal), the interest rate, and how and when the money is to be repaid. It may also specify the maturity date, which is the date by which the loan should be repaid in full.

In addition, the note may include provisions dealing with other rights held by the parties. For example, the note might address the maker's right to prepay the loan, or the payee's remedies if the money is not repaid according to the terms of the agreement. Real estate lenders often protect themselves with late charges, acceleration clauses, and

Fig. 5.1 Simple promissory note

PROMISSORY NOTE

FOR VALUE RECEIVED, Maker promises to pay to the order of ____________________, or to Bearer,

THE SUM OF $____________________

PAID AS FOLLOWS: $____________ OR MORE per month starting ____________, including interest at _____% per annum.

ACCELERATION: In the event of default, Payee or Bearer can declare all sums due and payable at once.

Maker/Borrower____________________

Date ____________________

similar provisions, which we'll discuss later in this chapter. Other provisions of the financing agreement between the borrower and lender are found in the mortgage or deed of trust instead of the note.

A promissory note must be signed by the maker, but the payee's signature isn't required. A legal description of the property also isn't required, because the note concerns only the debt, not the property. The legal description appears instead in the mortgage or deed of trust.

Negotiability

Promissory notes used in real estate financing are usually **negotiable instruments**. The Uniform Commercial Code (UCC), which every state has enacted into law in some form, sets forth the requirements for negotiable instruments. Under the UCC, a negotiable instrument is a written, unconditional promise to pay a certain sum of money, on demand or on a certain date; it must be payable "to the order of" a specified person or to the bearer, and it must be signed by the maker. An ordinary check is the most familiar example.

A negotiable instrument is freely transferable. That means the payee can transfer the instrument—and the right to payment that it represents—to a third party. For example, if the payee on a check

A negotiable instrument is freely transferable

endorses the check and gives it to someone else, the right to cash the check is transferred to that person. Real estate lenders use negotiable promissory notes so that they have the option of selling their notes (and their loans) on the secondary market to obtain immediate cash. (See Chapter 2.)

Without Recourse. If a promissory note or other negotiable instrument is endorsed "without recourse," it means that the issue of future payments is strictly between the maker and the third party the instrument is being endorsed to. The original payee will not be liable if the maker fails to pay as agreed.

Holder in Due Course. If a third party buys a negotiable promissory note from the payee for value, in good faith, and without notice of defenses against it, the third party purchaser is referred to as a holder in due course. The maker of a note is required to pay a holder in due course the amount owed even if there are certain defenses that the maker might have been able to raise against the original payee.

Types of Notes

Types of notes:
- Straight note
- Installment note

Promissory notes are sometimes classified according to the way in which the principal and interest are to be paid off. With a **straight note**, the required periodic payments are interest only, and the full amount of the principal is due in a lump sum on the maturity date. With an **installment note**, the periodic payments include part of the principal as well as the interest that has accrued. If an installment note is fully amortized, the periodic payments are enough to pay off all of the principal and interest by the maturity date. Amortization is explained in Chapter 6.

Whether the payments required by the promissory note are interest-only or amortized, the interest paid on a real estate loan is virtually always simple interest. This means that the interest is computed annually on the remaining principal balance. (By contrast, compound interest is computed on the principal amount plus the accrued interest.)

Security Instruments

Note is accompanied by security instrument

In a real estate loan transaction, the promissory note is accompanied by a security instrument—either a mortgage or a deed of trust against the borrower's property.

The Purpose of Security Instruments

While the note establishes the borrower's obligation to repay the loan, the security instrument makes the property the collateral (the security) for the loan. The security instrument gives the lender the right to foreclose on the property if the borrower doesn't repay the loan as agreed, or fails to fulfill any of the other obligations contained in the security instrument. In a foreclosure, the lender forces the sale of the property and collects the debt out of the sale proceeds.

Security instrument (mortgage or deed of trust) gives lender the right to foreclose

A lender can enforce a promissory note even if it is unsecured—in other words, even if the borrower has not executed a security instrument in the lender's favor. In that situation, if the borrower doesn't repay the loan as agreed in the note, the lender can file a lawsuit and obtain a judgment against the borrower. But without a security instrument, without collateral, the lender (now the judgment creditor) may have no way of collecting the judgment. The borrower might have already sold her property and spent the proceeds, leaving little or nothing for the lender.

A secured lender is in a much better position than an unsecured lender. Since a real estate loan involves a large amount of money, real estate lenders always require borrowers to sign a security instrument to back up the promissory note.

Historical Background

To understand how security instruments work, it may be helpful to know how they developed.

Possession of Collateral. In the earliest forms of secured lending, personal property was used as collateral. A borrower was expected to give the lender some form of valuable personal property (such as jewelry, or perhaps a herd of goats) to hold until the loan was repaid. The lender would actually take possession of the collateral pending repayment. If the loan was not repaid, the lender would keep the collateral. This type of secured lending is still with us; pawnshops provide the most common example.

Hypothecation. Transferring possession of personal property to a lender was a relatively straightforward matter. But when land was used as collateral, a transfer of possession to the lender could be complicated and inconvenient. It was also unnecessary, since the borrower could not move the land or conceal it from the lender. As a result, a practice called hypothecation developed. **Hypothecation** means pledging property as collateral without giving up possession of it. It became a standard arrangement for a borrower to remain in possession of his land and merely transfer the title to the lender. Once the loan had been repaid, the lender was required to return title to the borrower.

When title to property is transferred only as collateral, unaccompanied by possessory rights, the lender's interest in the property is referred to as **legal title**, or sometimes as naked title. The property rights the borrower retains (without legal title) are referred to as equitable rights or **equitable title**. The original function of mortgages and deeds of trust was to transfer legal title to land from borrower to lender.

Liens. Eventually, in many jurisdictions, a transfer of legal title was no longer considered necessary for the lender's protection. Instead, it became established that a mortgage or deed of trust simply created a **lien** against the borrower's property in favor of the lender. A lien is a financial encumbrance on a property owner's title that allows the lienholder to foreclose on the property to collect a debt.

In some states, referred to as "title theory" states, a security instrument is still considered to transfer legal title to the property to the lender until the loan is paid off. Most states, however, are "lien theory" states, where a security instrument creates a lien and doesn't transfer title. Nowadays, this theoretical distinction has little, if any, practical effect; either way, the security instrument enables the lender to foreclose.

The rights of the lender and the borrower under the terms of a security instrument vary according to the type of instrument used and according to the laws of the state where the property is located. We will look first at the difference between a mortgage and a deed of trust, and then at foreclosure procedures.

Mortgages

Mortgage:
- Mortgagor is borrower
- Mortgagee is lender
- Foreclosure by judicial process

A mortgage is a two-party security instrument in which the borrower (called the **mortgagor**) mortgages his property to the lender (the **mortgagee**). The document must include the names of the parties and an accurate legal description of the mortgaged property, and it must identify the promissory note that it secures.

Covenants. In the mortgage, the mortgagor promises to pay the property taxes, to keep the property insured against fire and other hazards, and to maintain any structures in good repair. These promises are intended to protect the property, so that the mortgagee's security does not lose its value. The mortgagee is allowed to inspect the property periodically to make sure that the mortgagor is maintaining it.

If the mortgagor fails to fulfill these or any other obligations imposed by the mortgage, or fails to pay as agreed in the promissory note, he is in default, and the mortgagee can foreclose.

Recording. After a mortgage is executed, the mortgagee has the document recorded in order to establish the priority of the mortgagee's security interest in the property. As we will discuss shortly, the priority of the mortgagee's security interest will become very important in the event of a foreclosure.

Satisfaction. When a mortgage has been paid off, the mortgagee is required to give the mortgagor a document that releases the property from the mortgage lien. This document is called a satisfaction of mortgage, or sometimes a "satisfaction piece." The mortgagor has the satisfaction document recorded, to provide public notice that the property is no longer encumbered by the mortgage.

Deeds of Trust

Deed of trust:
- Grantor is borrower
- Beneficiary is lender
- Trustee is independent third party with power of sale
- Nonjudicial foreclosure

The deed of trust (sometimes called a trust deed) is used for the same purpose as a mortgage: to secure the debtor's obligations under a loan agreement. The deed of trust involves three parties rather than two. The borrower is called the **grantor** or **trustor**; the lender is called the **beneficiary**; and there is an independent third party called the **trustee.** The trustee's role is to arrange for the property to be released from the deed of trust when the loan is paid off, or to arrange for foreclosure if necessary.

A deed of trust usually includes all of the same basic provisions that are found in a mortgage: the parties, the property, and the promissory note are identified; the grantor promises to pay the taxes and to insure and maintain the property; and the beneficiary has the right to inspect the property. Like a mortgage, a deed of trust should be recorded immediately to establish the priority of the lender's security interest.

When a deed of trust loan has been paid off, the trustee executes a **deed of reconveyance**, releasing the property from the lien. Like a satisfaction of mortgage, the deed of reconveyance is recorded to provide public notice that the property is no longer encumbered by the deed of trust.

Note that the terminology connected with a deed of trust—the fact that the instrument is called a deed, and that the trustee "reconveys" the property to the trustor—reflects its roots in title theory.

Foreclosure

The key difference between mortgages and deeds of trust concerns the procedures the lender is required to follow in order to foreclose. Since foreclosure procedures vary considerably from one state to another, this section will provide only a very general overview.

Traditionally, to foreclose on a mortgage, the lender was required to file a lawsuit against the borrower. If the lender proved that the borrower was in default, a court-ordered auction of the property (called a **sheriff's sale**) was held. The borrower's property was sold to the highest bidder at the auction, and the lender was entitled to the proceeds of the sale. This type of foreclosure process is called **judicial foreclosure**, and it is still used today.

Eventually, in many jurisdictions, an alternative to judicial foreclosure was developed. **Nonjudicial foreclosure** is generally associated with deeds of trust rather than mortgages. When the borrower defaults, the lender is not required to file a lawsuit and obtain a court order to foreclose. Instead, the trustee appointed in the deed of trust arranges for the property to be sold at a **trustee's sale**. Like a sheriff's sale, a trustee's sale is a public auction. The trustee sells the property to the highest bidder on the lender's behalf.

Power of Sale. Because court supervision is not required, nonjudicial foreclosure is generally less expensive and faster than judicial foreclosure. But nonjudicial foreclosure proceedings are permitted only if the security agreement contains a **power of sale** clause. This provision, which is standard in a deed of trust, authorizes the trustee to sell the property if the borrower defaults. In some states, a power of sale clause may also be included in a mortgage, enabling the mortgagee to foreclose nonjudicially.

A typical power of sale clause might read as follows:

> Upon default by Grantor in the payment of any indebtedness secured hereby or in the performance of any agreement contained herein, and upon written request of Beneficiary, Trustee shall sell the trust property, in accordance with the Deed of Trust Act of this state, at public auction to the highest bidder.

In many states, deeds of trust are now more widely used than mortgages, but in many other states mortgages remain the standard real estate security instrument. In some of the states that use mortgages, state law does not permit nonjudicial foreclosure.

In states that do allow nonjudicial foreclosure, a lender may choose to foreclose a deed of trust or mortgage judicially even though the instrument contains a power of sale clause. We'll explain why a lender might prefer judicial foreclosure under certain circumstances after we've discussed the procedures in more detail.

Judicial Foreclosure Procedures. In this section, for simplicity's sake, we'll describe the foreclosure of a mortgage. Keep in mind, however, that the same general procedures would be used for the judicial foreclosure of a deed of trust, if the lender chose judicial foreclosure.

Judicial foreclosure:
- Acceleration of debt
- Foreclosure lawsuit
- Equitable right of redemption
- Order of execution
- Public notice of sale
- Sheriff's sale
- Statutory right of redemption

Acceleration. When a mortgagor defaults—either by failing to repay the loan or by breaching covenants in the mortgage—the mortgagee notifies the mortgagor that the entire outstanding loan balance

Fig. 5.2 Security instruments and foreclosure procedures

Mortgage without power of sale clause
Judicial foreclosure only

Mortgage with power of sale clause
May be foreclosed either judicially or nonjudicially

Deed of Trust
Always includes power of sale clause
May be foreclosed either judicially or nonjudicially

(not merely any delinquent payments) must be paid off at once, or the mortgagee will foreclose. This is called **accelerating** the loan; in effect, the due date of the debt is moved up to the present, speeding up repayment. A provision in the mortgage known as an acceleration clause gives the mortgagee the right to demand immediate payment in full in the event of default.

Lawsuit. Not surprisingly, the defaulting mortgagor is usually unable to pay off the entire debt as demanded. The mortgagee's next step is to initiate a lawsuit, called a foreclosure action, in the county where the property is located. The purpose of this legal proceeding is to ask a judge to order the county sheriff to seize and sell the property. The defendants in the lawsuit are the mortgagor and any junior lienholders—other lenders who have mortgages against the property that have lower priority than the foreclosing lender's mortgage. The junior lienholders are included in the lawsuit because their security interests are likely to be affected by the foreclosure.

At the same time that the lawsuit is started, the mortgagee has a document called a **lis pendens** recorded. A lis pendens states that the property is subject to a foreclosure action. By recording the lis pendens, the mortgagee provides constructive notice to anyone who might consider buying the property from the mortgagor (or acquiring some other interest in it) that the title may be affected by the pending lawsuit.

Reinstatement vs. equitable redemption. Because court calendars are extremely crowded in many parts of the country, several months or even more than a year may elapse between the time the foreclosure action is filed and the time the case is heard by a judge. During this period when the lawsuit is pending, in some states the mortgagor has a right to "cure" the default. When the default was failure to make payments on the loan, the mortgagor can cure it by paying the delinquent amounts, plus interest and whatever costs have been incurred because of the foreclosure (such as court costs and attorneys' fees). If the mortgagor cures the default, the foreclosure is terminated and the loan is reinstated; the parties are back to where they were before the default.

Some states allow mortgagor to cure the default and reinstate the loan

In other states, however, a defaulting mortgagor doesn't have a right to cure and reinstate the loan. But the mortgagor does have an **equitable right of redemption.** This is the right to redeem the property by paying off the entire outstanding loan balance (not just

Equitable right of redemption: mortgagor can redeem the property before sheriff's sale

Fig. 5.3 Steps in a judicial foreclosure

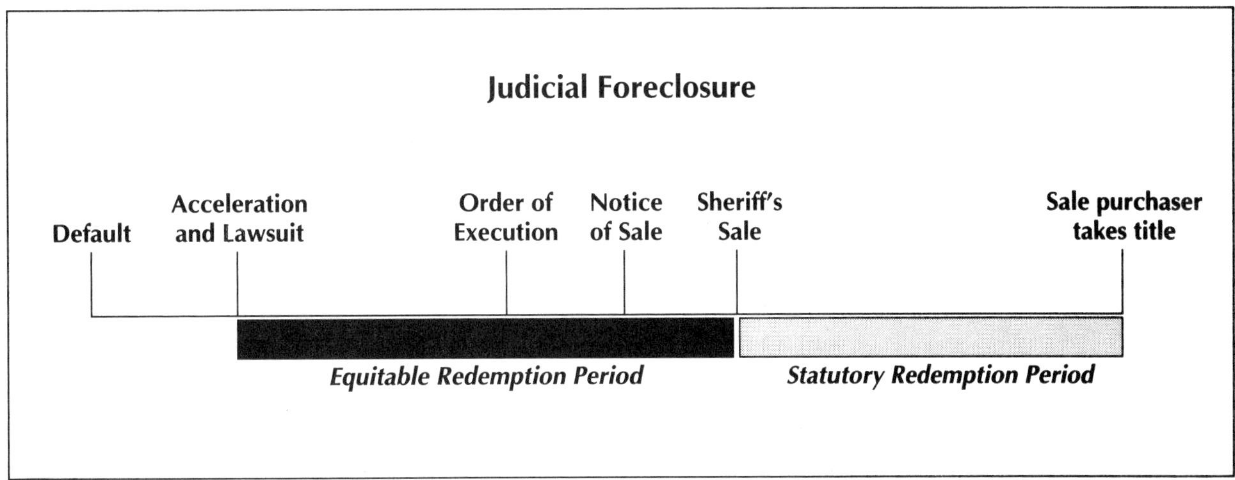

the delinquent payments), plus costs incurred as a result of the foreclosure. Redemption stops the foreclosure, satisfies the debt, and terminates the mortgagee's interest in the property.

Court order and notice of sale. Unless the mortgagor redeems the property (or in those states that allow it, cures and reinstates the loan) first, the scheduled court hearing in the foreclosure action is held. In most cases, after reviewing the note and mortgage and the facts concerning the default, the judge issues a court order directing the sheriff to seize the property and sell it. This type of court order is often called a **writ of execution**.

Acting under the court order, the sheriff notifies the public of the place and date of the sale. This usually requires posting notices at the property and the courthouse and running an advertisement of the sale in a newspaper circulated in the county. The number of times the ad must be published depends on state law, but the process generally takes several weeks.

In those states where the mortgagor has the right to cure the default and reinstate the loan, that right typically ends as soon as the judge orders the property sold. But the equitable right of redemption lasts until the sheriff's sale is held. The mortgagor can still prevent the sale and redeem the property by paying off the debt, plus costs.

Sheriff's sale. The sheriff's sale (sometimes called an execution sale) is a public auction. It is usually held at the county courthouse, and anyone who wants to bid on the property can attend. The property is sold to the highest bidder, who is given a **certificate of sale.**

Sheriff's sale:
- Public auction
- Foreclosed property sold to highest bidder
- Purchaser gets certificate of sale

The proceeds of the sale are used to pay for the costs of the sale, and then to pay off the mortgage and any other liens against the property. The mortgage and other liens are paid in order of their priority, which is usually established by their recording dates: the lien that was recorded first has the highest priority, and it is paid off first. The lien with the second highest priority is paid off only if there are sufficient funds left over—and so on, down the list. (This is why lien priority is so important to a lender: the difference between first and second lien position can be the difference between payment in full and no payment at all.) If the sale proceeds are enough to pay off all the liens, any surplus goes to the debtor.

If the property does not sell for enough to fully pay off the foreclosed mortgage (usually because the property's value has declined since the loan was made), the shortfall—the difference between the sale proceeds and the amount owed to the lender—is referred to as a deficiency. The court may award the lender a personal judgment against the debtor for the amount of the deficiency. This is called a **deficiency judgment.**

If sheriff's sale proceeds do not cover the debt, lender may be entitled to deficiency judgment

Many states place restrictions on the right of the mortgagee to obtain a deficiency judgment against the mortgagor. For example, some states prohibit a deficiency judgment if the mortgage secured a loan on homestead property (that is, the mortgagor's personal residence). And some states prohibit a deficiency judgment on a purchase money mortgage (a mortgage given by a buyer to a seller).

Post-sale redemption. Following the sale, the debtor (the former mortgagor) will have an additional period of time to save or redeem the property. To redeem it at this stage, the debtor usually must pay the sale purchaser the amount paid for the property plus accrued interest from the time of the sale. This right to redeem the property following the sheriff's sale is called the **statutory right of redemption**. It's called a statutory right because it was established by the state legislature in a statute. By contrast, the pre-sale right of redemption is referred to as an equitable right because it was originally created by the courts as a matter of equity (fairness).

Statutory right of redemption: mortgagor can redeem the property after the sheriff's sale

The length of the statutory redemption period varies from state to state, of course, but it is generally at least six months and sometimes as long as two years. In many states the length of the period may change according to such factors as whether the property is agricultural land, or whether the mortgagee is willing to waive the right to a deficiency judgment.

Rights of purchaser. The purchaser at the sheriff's sale may be entitled either to take possession of the property or to collect rent from the debtor during the statutory redemption period. However, in some states if the property is homestead property, the debtor is permitted to remain on the property without paying rent. At the end of the statutory redemption period, if the property has not been redeemed, the sheriff's sale purchaser receives a **sheriff's deed** to the property.

Depending on state law concerning notice requirements and redemption, and also on factors such as court congestion and the availability of the sheriff for foreclosures, judicial foreclosure of a mortgage may take anywhere from a few months to a few years from the time of default until a sheriff's deed is delivered to the purchaser, finally divesting the debtor of title.

Nonjudicial Foreclosure. In this section we'll describe the foreclosure of a deed of trust. But essentially the same procedures would apply to a mortgage with a power of sale clause, if the mortgagee chose nonjudicial foreclosure.

To foreclose a deed of trust nonjudicially, the trustee must follow steps similar to those taken by the sheriff in a judicial foreclosure. The trustee must give notice of the default to the trustor (and in some states must also record the notice of default), and then give notice of the impending sale to the public. As with judicial foreclosure, most states require that this notice of sale be posted at the property and published in a newspaper circulated in the county, so that the greatest number of potential buyers will have an opportunity to attend and bid at the trustee's sale.

Nonjudicial foreclosure:
- Notice of default
- Public notice of sale
- Cure & reinstatement
- Trustee's sale
- No post-sale redemption

After giving the trustor notice of default, the trustee must allow at least a certain length of time to expire before issuing the notice of sale (in most states, the minimum period is between three and six months). There is also a minimum period between the time the notice of sale is issued and the date of the sale (for example, one month). The grantor is allowed to cure the default and reinstate the loan by paying only the delinquent amounts plus costs. The right to cure and reinstate ends shortly before the trustee's sale is held (for example, five days before the sale).

The statutory right of redemption that follows the sheriff's sale in a judicial foreclosure does not apply to a trustee's sale. When the property is sold at the trustee's sale, a **trustee's deed** is given to the successful bidder. The debtor is immediately divested of title and may

Fig. 5.4 Steps in a nonjudicial foreclosure

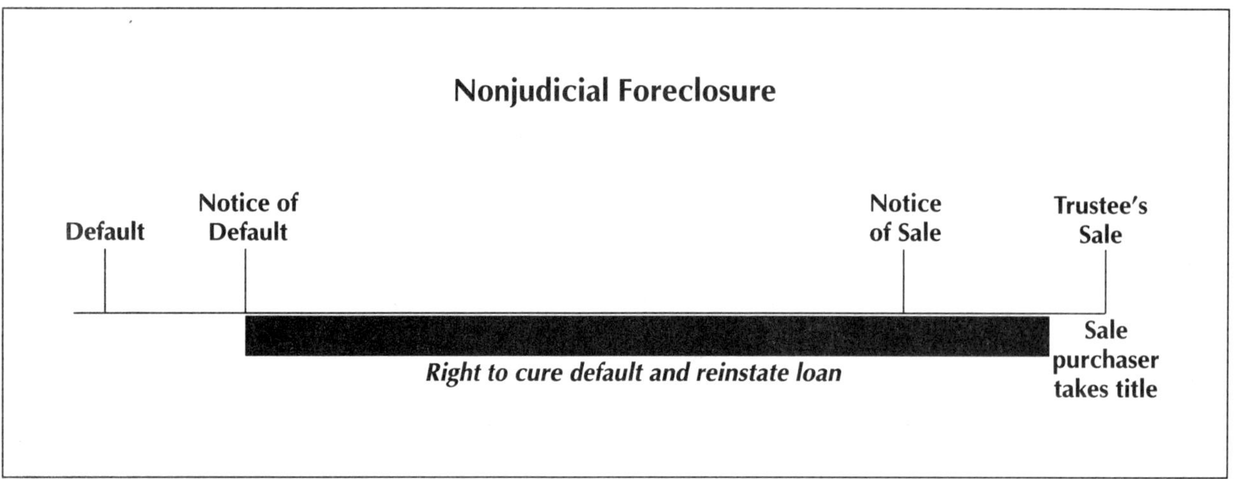

have only a short period of time (perhaps 20 or 30 days) to vacate the property. As in a sheriff's sale, the trustee's sale proceeds are first applied to the sale costs, then to the debt and other liens in order of priority, and any surplus is then given to the debtor.

The entire nonjudicial foreclosure process may be accomplished in most states in well under a year (usually around six or seven months) without many of the expenses involved in court proceedings. Naturally, there are expenses connected with a trustee's sale, but they tend to be substantially less than those connected with a court-ordered sheriff's sale.

No deficiency judgment after nonjudicial foreclosure

Restrictions. Even in states that allow it, a variety of restrictions may be placed on the use of nonjudicial foreclosure; for example, a post-sale redemption period might be required for agricultural property. One standard restriction is that the beneficiary is not allowed to obtain a deficiency judgment after a trustee's sale, even if the sale proceeds were far less than the amount of the debt. However, if the beneficiary chooses to foreclose the deed of trust judicially (just like a mortgage), then all of the procedures and rights relating to judicial foreclosure apply.

Comparing Judicial and Nonjudicial Foreclosure. From a lender's point of view, judicial foreclosure can have two main advantages over nonjudicial foreclosure. The first advantage concerns the difference between the equitable right of redemption and the right to cure and reinstate. In a nonjudicial foreclosure, the borrower generally has the right to cure the default and reinstate the loan even after the lender has accelerated it. But in a judicial foreclosure, some states do not give the borrower the right to cure and reinstate; the borrower can stop the foreclosure only by exercising the equitable right of redemption and paying off the entire debt. Thus, with judicial foreclosure the lender is not required to continue its relationship with a borrower who has proved unreliable.

Lender's point of view
- Advantages of judicial foreclosure:
  - Borrower can't reinstate loan
  - Right to deficiency judgment
- Advantages of nonjudicial foreclosure:
  - Quick and inexpensive

The second advantage of judicial foreclosure for the lender is the right to obtain a deficiency judgment against the borrower if the property does not bring enough at the sheriff's sale to satisfy the debt. In cases where the property has lost value since the loan was made, the lender is likely to protect itself by choosing judicial foreclosure.

The main advantage of nonjudicial foreclosure for the lender is that it is quick and inexpensive compared to judicial foreclosure. It is because of this advantage that deeds of trust have almost completely replaced mortgages in a number of states. And in many states where mortgages are still the predominant real estate security instrument, it's now common or even standard for a mortgage to have a power of sale clause.

Borrower's point of view
- Advantages of judicial foreclosure:
  - Slow process
  - Post-sale redemption
- Advantage of nonjudicial foreclosure:
  - Right to cure & reinstate

The advantages and disadvantages of the two forms of foreclosure for the borrower correspond to those for the lender, but in reverse. From the borrower's point of view, the right to cure the default and reinstate the loan is an important advantage of nonjudicial foreclosure. Without that right, a home buyer who misses just a couple of loan payments may be faced with the prospect of having to pay off the debt completely in order to save the home. On the other hand, in a judicial foreclosure the borrower usually has a long time to get the money together to pay off the debt, because of the slow court proceedings and the statutory redemption period. Another possible advantage for the borrower in a judicial foreclosure is the opportunity to present her side of the story to the judge. While it isn't likely that the judge will be persuaded to stop the foreclosure, that could happen in an unusual case.

Land Contracts

Land contract:
- Vendor is seller
- Vendee is buyer
- Vendor retains legal title until contract paid in full

An instrument that serves a purpose similar to that of a mortgage or deed of trust is the land contract, which is sometimes used in seller-financed transactions. With a land contract, the buyer (called the vendee) takes possession of the property right away, but the seller (the vendor) retains title until the contract has been paid off. At that point, the vendor delivers a deed to the buyer.

Because land contracts function very differently from mortgages or deeds of trust, we will discuss them separately in Chapter 13, which covers seller financing in detail.

Finance Instrument Provisions

This section of the chapter covers a variety of important provisions that may appear in real estate finance instruments. Some of them are used only in certain types of transactions; others are virtually always used. Depending on the transaction, the rights and responsibilities of the borrower and the lender may be affected by:

Clauses often found in finance instruments:
- Subordination
- Late charge
- Prepayment
- Partial release
- Acceleration
- Alienation

- a subordination clause,
- a late charge provision,
- a prepayment provision,
- a partial release clause,
- an acceleration clause, and/or
- an alienation (due-on-sale) clause.

Subordination Clauses

Ordinarily, the priority among mortgages and deeds of trust is determined by the date of recording: the first one recorded has first lien position, the highest priority. In some situations, however, the parties may want to give an instrument that was recorded later priority over one that was recorded earlier.

This is particularly common in construction financing. In many cases a developer who applies for a construction loan has already borrowed money to purchase the land that's going to be built on, so a mortgage or deed of trust against the property has already been recorded. But because construction loans involve some extra risk, lenders usually refuse to make a construction loan unless they can be assured of first lien position. In order for the later construction loan mortgage or deed of trust to take priority over the earlier instrument, the earlier instrument must contain a subordination clause.

Subordination clause gives mortgage recorded earlier lower priority than another mortgage that will be recorded later

A **subordination clause** states that the security instrument in which it appears will be **subordinate** (junior) to another security instrument that is to be recorded later.

> Lender agrees that this instrument shall be subordinate to a lien to be given by Borrower to secure funds for the construction of improvements on the Property, provided said lien is duly recorded and the amount secured by said lien does not exceed $125,000.

Inclusion of a subordination clause must be negotiated at the time of the earlier transaction (in our example, when the developer bought the land and the earlier security instrument was executed). If a subordination clause was not included in the earlier security instrument, the earlier lender might be willing to sign a separate subordination agreement later on. A prudent developer wouldn't count on that, however.

Subordination profoundly affects the strength of both lenders' security interests, so any subordination provision should be drafted or reviewed by a real estate lawyer.

Late Charge Provisions

In real estate loan transactions, the promissory note usually provides for late charges if the borrower doesn't make the payments on time. A lender typically allows for a grace period after the payment's actual due date, but if the payment hasn't reached the lender by the time the grace period expires, a late fee will be added to the amount overdue.

Many states have laws that protect borrowers against excessive late charges and unfair collection practices. For example, lenders generally aren't permitted to charge more than one late fee on a single overdue payment, even if the payment remains overdue for more than one month.

State laws protecting borrowers from excessive late charges and unfair collection practices may override provision in note

Prepayment Provisions

Some promissory notes have a provision that imposes a penalty on the borrower if she repays some or all of the principal before it is due. This is called **prepaying** the loan. Prepayment deprives the lender of some of the interest it expected to receive on its investment over the loan term. In effect, a prepayment penalty compensates the lender for the lost interest.

Prepayment charge imposed if loan repaid early, to compensate lender for lost interest

As an example, the following provision imposes a penalty if the borrower prepays more than 20% of the original loan amount in one of the first five years of the loan term. If the borrower's prepayment exceeds that limit, the borrower is required to pay the lender 3% of the original loan amount as a penalty.

> If, within five years from the date of this note, Borrower makes any prepayments of principal in excess of twenty percent of the original principal amount in any twelve-month period beginning with the date of this note or anniversary dates thereof ("loan year"), Borrower shall pay the Note Holder three percent of the original principal amount.

Prepayment penalties are no longer standard in residential loan agreements. The Fannie Mae/Freddie Mac promissory note used for most conventional loans specifically gives the borrower the right to prepay without penalty. Prepayment penalties are also prohibited in connection with FHA and VA loans.

Although prepayment penalties aren't standard, some lenders offer reduced loan fees or a lower interest rate in exchange for including a prepayment provision in the promissory note. While this can be a reasonable arrangement, the borrower should carefully consider the consequences before agreeing to a prepayment penalty.

In connection with a residential loan, a prepayment penalty is usually charged only if the loan is prepaid during the first few years of the loan term, as in the example above. The borrower should find out how many years the prepayment penalty provision will be in effect. He also needs to ask under what circumstances the penalty will be charged. Will he have to pay the penalty if the loan is paid off early because he has sold the property? What if he refinances? And how much will the penalty be?

Unreasonable prepayment penalities are considered predatory

Charging a heavy prepayment penalty with unreasonable terms is considered a predatory lending practice (see Chapter 14). Some states have laws limiting the amount of prepayment penalties and restricting how they can be imposed.

Partial Release Clauses

A partial release clause in a mortgage is often called a partial satisfaction clause; in a deed of trust, it's often called a partial reconveyance clause. This provision obligates the lender to release part of the property from the lien when part of the debt has been paid.

Partial release: part of the property is released from lien when part of debt is paid

Example: The Harveys borrowed money to purchase five acres of land. Their mortgage includes a partial satisfaction clause. The clause states that when the borrowers have repaid 25% of the loan amount, the lender will release one acre of their land from the mortgage lien.

A partial release clause is typically included in a mortgage or deed of trust covering a subdivision that is in the process of being developed and sold. When the developers find a buyer for a lot, they pay the lender a specified portion of the loan amount to have that lot released from the lien. The clause permits them to acquire clear title to that lot and convey it to the buyer, without having to pay off the whole loan.

> Upon payment of all sums due with respect to any lot subject to this lien, Lender shall release said lot from the lien at no cost to Borrower.

Acceleration Clauses

Almost all promissory notes, mortgages, and deeds of trust contain an acceleration clause. As we explained earlier, this provision allows the lender to accelerate the debt: that is, to declare the entire outstanding balance immediately due and payable in the event of a default.

Acceleration: upon default, lender may declare entire debt due immediately

This means that a borrower who misses even one payment might discover the next month that he owes not just two payments, but rather the entire remaining balance. In practice, though, most lenders wait until payments are at least 90 days delinquent before accelerating a loan.

Here is a typical acceleration clause:

> In case the Mortgagor [or Trustor] fails to pay any installment of principal or interest secured hereby when due or to keep or perform any covenant or agreement aforesaid, then the whole indebtedness hereby secured shall become due and payable, at the election of the Mortgagee [or Beneficiary].

Keep in mind that a lender's right to accelerate a loan is effectively limited when state law gives the borrower the right to cure the default and reinstate the loan.

Alienation Clauses and Assumptions

In the real estate context, **alienation** refers to transfer of ownership. An alienation clause (often called a **due-on-sale** clause) in a security instrument is designed to limit the borrower's right to transfer title to the property without the lender's permission, unless the loan is paid off first.

To understand the purpose of an alienation clause, let's look first at what happens if a borrower transfers the security property without paying off the loan. There are essentially three possibilities:

- the new owner may simply take title subject to the loan;
- there may be an assumption of the loan by the new owner without a release of the original borrower; or
- there may be an assumption and release.

Whenever ownership of real property is transferred, the new owner takes title **subject to** any existing liens, including an existing mortgage or deed of trust. The lender still has the power to foreclose on the property, in spite of the transfer of ownership.

Buyer who assumes loan takes on primary liability, but unreleased seller remains secondarily liable

The new owner may or may not agree to **assume** the loan. In an assumption, the new owner (the assumptor) takes on legal responsibility for repaying the loan. But unless the lender agrees to a release, the original borrower (the former owner) remains secondarily liable to the lender even after an assumption. If there is a foreclosure and the lender obtains a deficiency judgment, the original borrower can be forced to pay it if the assumptor does not.

Even though the original borrower is still liable to the lender after selling the property, the transfer of ownership may increase the lender's risk. The new owner could be a much worse credit risk than the original borrower, or might allow the security property to deteriorate. So the lender wants some control over transfer of the property, to ensure that any new owner is no more likely to default than the original borrower.

An alienation clause gives the lender that control. Most alienation clauses are triggered not only by a complete transfer of ownership, but also by the transfer of any significant interest in the property (including a long-term lease or any lease with an option to purchase). In the event of a transfer, the clause usually gives the lender the right to declare the entire loan balance due immediately—hence the name "due-on-sale" clause. This is acceleration of the loan triggered by transfer, instead of by default.

Alienation clause allows lender to call in the loan if borrower transfers an interest in the property

> If all or any part of the Property or an interest therein is sold or transferred by Borrower without Lender's prior written consent, Lender may, at Lender's option, declare all the sums secured by this instrument to be immediately due and payable.

If the lender is not satisfied with the person the borrower intends to sell the property to, the lender cannot forbid the sale; but it can require the borrower to pay off the loan rather than allowing the new owner to assume it.

If the proposed buyer is a good credit risk, the lender is likely to approve the assumption. The lender may reset the loan's interest rate, charging the buyer a rate between the loan's original rate and the current market rate. This is sometimes called a "blended rate." The lender will also charge an **assumption fee**, which may be as substantial as a loan origination fee—for example, 1.5% of the loan balance.

Lender that allows assumption may raise interest rate

Alienation clauses are now standard in residential security instruments. They appear in the security instruments used by Fannie Mae and Freddie Mac for conventional loans, and also in the security instruments used in FHA and VA loan transactions. However, some recent loans and many older loans do not have alienation clauses. To find out whether a seller's loan can be assumed without the lender's approval or whether it contains an alienation clause, contact the lender.

When the lender's consent to a sale is required, it should be obtained in the form of an **estoppel letter**. An estoppel letter acknowledges the transfer of ownership and waives the lender's right to accelerate the loan on account of the transfer. By writing the letter, the lender is estopped (legally prevented) from later trying to enforce the alienation clause based on this sale.

Estoppel letter:
- Acknowledges transfer and waives due-on-sale clause, or
- States balance and status of loan without any change in the existing loan's terms

An estoppel letter is often requested even in a transaction where the security instrument for the seller's existing loan does not contain an alienation clause. The lender is asked to state in the estoppel letter the amount of the outstanding principal balance, and also to acknowledge that the loan is not in default. The buyer then has written confirmation of the amount and the status of the obligation she is planning to assume or take title subject to.

When taking a listing, a real estate agent should ask the seller about the existing financing and consider whether offering assumption might be a good marketing tool. If the seller would like to offer assumption, the lender should be asked for an estoppel letter. (Note that many lenders charge a fee for preparation of an estoppel letter.) If an assumption of the seller's loan is eventually arranged, both parties—the seller and the buyer—should obtain legal advice, and the agreement should be drawn up by a lawyer.

Types of Real Estate Loans

Real estate finance terminology includes many terms for various types of mortgage loans—terms that describe the status, purpose, or function of different loans. We'll end this chapter with a review of some of the most common of these terms.

In accordance with general usage, we often use "mortgage" or "mortgage loan" to refer to any loan secured by real property, whether the security instrument actually used is a mortgage or a deed of trust. Keep in mind that in many states a deed of trust could be (and perhaps usually would be) used instead of a mortgage to make any of these types of loans.

Junior or Senior Mortgage. A **junior mortgage** is one that has lower lien priority than another mortgage (or deed of trust) against the same property. In relation to the junior mortgage, the mortgage with higher lien priority may be called a senior mortgage. A senior mortgage with first lien position is called a **first mortgage**; a junior mortgage may be referred to as a second mortgage or third mortgage, depending on its relative lien priority. And sometimes you'll hear a junior mortgage called a subordinate mortgage.

Senior mortgage has higher lien priority than junior mortgage

A property may become encumbered with two mortgages (or maybe even more than two) in a number of different situations. When property is purchased, a junior mortgage loan may provide secondary financing to supplement the primary loan that's secured by the first mortgage. (Secondary financing is discussed in Chapters 6 and 13.) A land purchase mortgage that has been subordinated to a construction mortgage is another example of a junior mortgage. And many junior mortgages secure home equity loans (see below).

As we discussed earlier, foreclosure of a mortgage affects any junior liens against the property. If a property has a senior mortgage and a junior mortgage against it and the senior lender forecloses, the foreclosure extinguishes the lien of the junior mortgage. The junior lender will be paid only after the senior lender has been paid in full. If the foreclosure sale proceeds aren't sufficient to pay off the senior lender and the other lienholders with higher priority, the junior lender receives no share of the proceeds. The junior lender could still sue the debtor, but the junior loan is now an unsecured loan.

If a junior mortgage is foreclosed on, the foreclosure sale purchaser takes title to the property subject to the lien of the senior mortgage. Foreclosure on the junior mortgage does not extinguish the senior mortgage.

Purchase Money Mortgage. This term is used in two ways. Sometimes it means any mortgage loan used to finance the purchase of the property that is the collateral for the loan. So when a buyer borrows money to buy property and gives the lender a mortgage on that same property to secure the loan, that may be referred to as a purchase money mortgage.

Purchase money mortgage:
- Any mortgage loan used to purchase the security property, or
- Seller financing

In other cases, "purchase money mortgage" is used more narrowly, to mean a mortgage that a buyer gives to a seller in a seller-financed transaction. Instead of paying the full price in cash at closing, the buyer gives the seller a mortgage on the property and pays the price off in installments.

> **Example:** The sales price is $180,000. The buyer makes a $20,000 downpayment and signs a promissory note and purchase money mortgage in favor of the seller for the remaining $160,000. The buyer will pay the seller in monthly installments at 7% interest over the next 15 years.

Purchase money mortgages used for seller financing are covered in Chapter 13.

Home Equity Loan. A property owner can obtain a mortgage loan using her equity in property that she already owns as collateral. This is called an **equity loan**; when the property is the borrower's residence, it's called a **home equity loan**.

Home equity loan: a loan secured by a mortgage against the borrower's equity in a home he or she already owns

A property owner's equity is the difference between the property's current market value and the liens against it. In other words, it's the portion of the property's value that the owner owns free and clear—the portion that is available to serve as collateral for another loan. With an equity loan, the lender agrees to loan a sum of money to the property owner in exchange for a second mortgage against the property.

> **Example:** The Hutchinsons bought their house six years ago for $260,000, making a $20,000 downpayment and borrowing $240,000 for the purchase. Naturally, the loan is secured with a mortgage against the house.
>
> The Hutchinsons' house has appreciated since they bought it, and it's worth about $280,000 in the current market. The balance due on the mortgage is now $223,000. So the Hutchinsons' equity is $57,000 ($280,000 – $223,000 = $57,000).
>
> When the Hutchinsons have some unexpected expenses, they apply to a lender for a $15,000 home equity loan. To provide security for the loan, they sign a deed of trust that gives the lender a junior lien against their property.

In some cases, a home equity loan is used to finance remodeling or other improvements to the property. In other cases, it's used for expenses unrelated to the property, such as a major purchase, college tuition, or medical bills. It's quite common for a home equity loan to be used to pay off credit cards. The interest rate on the home equity loan is often much lower than the rate on the credit cards, and the interest on the loan is usually deductible, whereas the credit card interest is not. (Mortgage interest is currently the only type of interest on consumer debt that is deductible.)

The interest rates charged on home equity loans are higher than the rates on home purchase loans. Since a home equity loan is a second mortgage, it represents a greater risk to the lender (see the discussion of junior mortgages, above). The higher interest rate compensates the lender for the additional risk.

Instead of having to apply for a home equity loan, some homeowners have a **home equity line of credit** (or **HELOC**) that they can draw on when the need arises. This works in much the same way as a credit card—with a credit limit and minimum monthly payments—except that the debt is automatically secured by the borrower's home. The line of credit is a revolving credit account, in contrast to the home equity loan, which is an installment loan with regular payments made over a certain term.

Refinance Mortgage. Borrowers who refinance their mortgage loan are actually obtaining an entirely new loan to replace the existing one. Funds from the refinance loan are used to pay off the existing loan. Depending on the situation, refinancing may be arranged with the same lender that made the existing loan, or with a different lender.

Refinancing: a new loan that's used to pay off an existing mortgage against the same property

Borrowers often choose to refinance when market interest rates drop; refinancing at a lower interest rate can result in substantial savings over the long run. However, they must take into account the loan fee, appraisal fee, and other expenses connected with the refinancing; these can add up to thousands of dollars. Refinancing to take advantage of lower interest rates may not make financial sense if it would take more than two or three years to recover the cost of the refinancing.

Another situation in which a borrower is likely to refinance is when the payoff date of the existing mortgage is approaching and a large balloon payment will be required. (See the discussion of partial amortization in Chapter 6.) Funds from the refinance loan will be used to make that balloon payment.

While a basic refinance loan is for no more than the amount needed to pay off the existing mortgage and cover the refinancing costs, borrowers who have a significant amount of equity when they refinance may have the option of a "cash-out" refinance loan. With cash-out refinancing, the loan amount is more than the amount of the existing mortgage balance plus the refinancing costs, so that the borrowers also receive some cash from the refinance lender. This is another way for homeowners to tap into their equity. As with a home equity loan, the cash from the refinancing may be used for remodeling or other improvements, or for expenses unrelated to the property.

Bridge Loan. It often happens that buyers are ready to purchase a new home before they've succeeded in selling their current home. They need funds for their downpayment and closing costs right away, without waiting for the proceeds from the eventual sale of the current home. In this situation, the buyers may be able to obtain a **bridge loan**. A bridge loan is secured by equity in the property that is for sale, and it will be paid off when that sale closes. In most cases, a bridge loan calls for interest-only payments (see Chapter 6), and the principal is due when the loan is paid off. A bridge loan may also be called a **swing loan** or a **gap loan**.

Bridge loan provides cash for purchase of a new home pending sale of the old home

Budget mortgage: monthly payments include property taxes and hazard insurance

Budget Mortgage. The monthly payment on a budget mortgage includes not just principal and interest on the loan, but one-twelfth of the year's property taxes and hazard insurance premiums as well. The lender keeps these tax and insurance payments in an **impound account** (also called a reserve account or escrow account) and pays the taxes and the insurance premiums out of the account when they come due. Most residential loans are secured by budget mortgages. This is the safest and most practical way for lenders to make sure the property taxes and insurance premiums are paid on time.

The payments on a budget mortgage are often referred to as PITI payments. PITI stands for principal, interest, taxes, and insurance.

Package mortgage is secured by personal property as well as real property

Package Mortgage. When personal property and real property are financed with a single mortgage loan, it's called a package mortgage.

> **Example:** A restaurant building on a city lot is being sold. The buyer also wants to purchase the restaurant equipment (ovens, freezers, and so on) that's in the building. The equipment is considered to be personal property, not fixtures. The buyer's purchase of this personal property along with the real property could be financed with a package mortgage.

Alternatively, a buyer may finance personal property separately from the real property, obtaining a separate loan either from the same lender or from a different lender. In that situation, in addition to executing a mortgage that creates a security interest in the real property, the buyer executes a **security agreement** that creates a security interest in the personal property. Under the Uniform Commercial Code, a lender with a security interest in personal property provides public notice and establishes the priority of that interest by filing a **financing statement** in the office of the Secretary of State in the state where the transaction takes place. The financing statement serves the same purpose in regard to personal property that a recorded mortgage or deed of trust serves for real property.

A key advantage of using a package mortgage, instead of financing the personal property separately, is that the mortgage term is usually much longer than the term of an ordinary loan for personal property. So the package mortgage allows the borrower to pay for the personal property over a longer period. In addition, the interest rate on the mortgage may be lower than the rate for a personal property loan, and the interest paid will be tax-deductible.

Blanket Mortgage. Sometimes a borrower mortgages two or more pieces of property as security for one loan. For example, a ten-acre parcel subdivided into twenty lots might be used to secure one loan made to the subdivider. Blanket mortgages usually have a partial release clause (also called a partial satisfaction clause, or in a deed of trust, a partial reconveyance clause). As we discussed earlier, this provision requires the lender to release some of the security property from the blanket lien when a specified portion of the overall debt has been paid off.

Blanket mortgage:
- Secured by more than one parcel of land
- Partial release clause

> **Example:** A ten-acre parcel subdivided into twenty lots secures a $500,000 loan. After selling one lot for $50,000, the subdivider pays the lender $45,000 and receives a release for the lot that is being sold. The blanket mortgage is no longer a lien against that lot, so the subdivider can convey clear title to the lot buyer.

The properties covered by a blanket mortgage do not have to be contiguous or neighboring parcels. A borrower who owns pieces of land in two different counties could offer both pieces of land as collateral for a single blanket mortgage loan. (To fully protect the lender's security interest, the blanket mortgage document would have to be recorded in both counties.)

Construction Loan. A construction loan (sometimes called an **interim loan**) is a short-term loan used to finance the construction of improvements on land already owned by the borrower. The mortgage for this type of loan creates a lien against both the land and the improvements under construction.

Construction loan: temporary financing that provides funds for construction until project is completed

Construction loans can be very profitable, but they are considered risky. Accordingly, lenders charge high interest rates and loan fees on construction loans, and they supervise the progress of the construction. There is always a danger that the borrower will overspend on the construction project and exhaust the loan proceeds before construction is completed. If the borrower cannot afford to finish, the lender is left with a security interest in a partially completed project.

Lenders have devised a number of plans for disbursement of construction loan proceeds that guard against overspending by the borrower. Perhaps the most common is the **fixed disbursement plan**.

This calls for a series of predetermined disbursements, called **obligatory advances**, at various stages of construction. Interest begins to accrue with the first disbursement.

> **Example:** The construction loan agreement stipulates that the lender will release 10% of the proceeds when the project is 20% complete, and thereafter 20% draws will be available whenever construction has progressed another 20% toward completion.

The lender will often hold back 10% or more of the loan proceeds until the period for claiming construction liens (mechanic's or materialmen's liens) has expired, to protect against unpaid liens that could affect the marketability of the property. The construction loan agreement usually states that if a valid construction lien is recorded, the lender may use the undisbursed portion of the loan to pay it off.

When the construction is completed, the construction loan is replaced by permanent financing that is called a **take-out loan**. The borrower then repays the amount borrowed, plus interest, over a specified term, as with an ordinary mortgage.

Nonrecourse mortgage
- Lender can't sue borrower
- Foreclosure is lender's only remedy

Nonrecourse Mortgage. A nonrecourse mortgage is one that gives the lender no recourse against the borrower. That means the lender's only remedy in the event of default is foreclosure on the collateral property; the borrower is not personally liable for repayment of the loan.

A loan may be a nonrecourse mortgage for one of two reasons. The loan contract itself may provide that the lender will have no recourse against the borrower in the event of default. Or, as we discussed earlier in this chapter, state law may prevent the lender from obtaining a deficiency judgment against the borrower. In either case, the loan may be considered a nonrecourse mortgage.

Participation mortgage entitles lender to a share of the property's earnings

Participation Mortgage. A participation mortgage allows the lender to participate in the earnings generated by the mortgaged property, usually in addition to collecting interest payments on the principal. In some cases the lender participates by becoming a part-owner of the property. Participation loans are most common on large commercial projects where the lender is an insurance company or other large investor.

Shared Appreciation Mortgage. Real property usually appreciates (increases in value) over time. Appreciation usually benefits only the

Fig. 5.5 Types of mortgage loans

- **Junior or Senior**
  Refers to lien priority
- **Purchase Money**
  Used to buy security property
- **Home Equity**
  Secured by equity in property already owned
- **Refinance**
  New loan used to pay off old
- **Bridge**
  Provides cash for purchase of new home pending sale of old
- **Budget**
  Payments include share of taxes and insurance
- **Package**
  Secured by both personal and real property
- **Blanket**
  Secured by multiple parcels
- **Construction**
  Temporary loan funds project until completed
- **Nonrecourse**
  Foreclosure is lender's only remedy
- **Participation**
  Lender receives share of property's earnings
- **Shared Appreciation**
  Lender receives share of equity
- **Wraparound**
  Underlying loan is still being paid off
- **Reverse Equity**
  Elderly owner receives payments from lender

property owner, by adding to her equity. With a shared appreciation mortgage, however, the lender is entitled to a specified share of the increase in the property's value.

Shared appreciation mortgage entitles lender to a share of increases in property's value

Wraparound Mortgage. A wraparound mortgage is a new mortgage that includes or "wraps around" an existing first mortgage on the property. Wraparounds are used almost exclusively in seller-financed transactions, and we will discuss them in detail in Chapter 13.

Wraparound mortgage is a form of seller financing

Reverse Equity Mortgage. A reverse equity mortgage, sometimes called a reverse annuity mortgage or simply a reverse mortgage, is designed to provide income to older homeowners. With this type of loan, a homeowner borrows against the home's equity but will receive a monthly check from the lender, rather than making monthly payments. This can make it possible for an elderly person who might otherwise have to sell his home (and invest the proceeds to obtain a source of income) to keep the home.

Reverse equity mortgage provides elderly homeowners with a source of income, without having to sell their home

Typically, a reverse equity borrower is required to be over a certain age (for example, 62 or 65) and must own the home with little or no outstanding mortgage balance. The home usually must be sold when the owner dies in order to pay back the mortgage. The amount of the monthly payment from the lender depends on the appraised value of the home, the age of the homeowner, the interest charged, and the terms of repayment.

Outline: Finance Instruments

I. Promissory Notes
   A. A promissory note is basic evidence of a borrower's legal obligation to pay a debt.
      1. The debtor (usually a buyer) is the maker of the note; the creditor (the lender) is the payee.
      2. The note will specify the names of the parties, the amount of debt, the interest rate, and how and when the money will be repaid.
   B. The promissory notes used in real estate loans are negotiable, to facilitate resale of the loans on the secondary market.
      1. A negotiable instrument is freely transferable by the payee to a third party.
      2. If a promissory note is endorsed "without recourse," the original payee will not be liable if the maker fails to make payments to the third party.
      3. A third party purchaser who buys a promissory note from a payee in good faith is known as a holder in due course.
   C. Types of notes
      1. Straight note: Required payments are interest only, with a balloon payment at the end of the term.
      2. Installment note: Payments include part of the principal as well as interest.

II. Security Instruments
   A. A security instrument makes the borrower's property collateral for the loan and gives the lender the right to foreclose in the event of default.
      1. Originally, under the theory of hypothecation, a borrower would transfer title to the property as security for the duration of the loan term.
      2. Now, in most jurisdictions, a mortgage simply creates a lien against the borrower's property in favor of the lender.
   B. Types of security instruments
      1. Mortgage: A two-party security instrument where a borrower (the mortgagor) mortgages his property to the lender (the mortgagee).
      2. Deed of trust: A three-party security instrument between the borrower (grantor) and the lender (beneficiary) where a third party (the trustee) holds the power of sale.

III. Foreclosure
  A. Types of foreclosure
    1. Judicial foreclosure: A mortgagee must file suit against a defaulting borrower in order for the court to order the property to be sold at a sheriff's sale to the highest bidder.
    2. Nonjudicial foreclosure: With a deed of trust, the lender does not need to file a lawsuit in the event of default; the trustee will arrange for the sale of the property through a trustee's sale.
  B. Judicial foreclosure process
    1. In a judicial foreclosure, in some states the borrower may repay the delinquent amount and reinstate the loan at any point before the court hearing occurs.
    2. In other states, the borrower can't reinstate the loan but may pay off the entire loan balance before the sheriff's sale in order to stop the foreclosure; this is known as the equitable right of redemption.
    3. If the foreclosure action goes to trial, in most cases the judge will issue a court order called a writ of execution, ordering the sheriff to seize and sell the property.
    4. Proceeds from the sheriff's sale will be used to pay off the mortgage and other liens, with any surplus going to the debtor.
    5. If the proceeds do not pay off the mortgage and other liens, the lender may also get a deficiency judgment against the borrower for the amount of the shortfall.
    6. The debtor has an additional period of time after the sheriff's sale to redeem the property, known as the statutory right of redemption.
    7. At the end of the statutory redemption period, the purchaser at the sheriff's sale receives a sheriff's deed to the property.
  C. Nonjudicial foreclosure process
    1. The trustee will provide notice of default to the borrower and then give notice of a trustee's sale.
    2. In the period before the sale, the borrower may reinstate the loan by paying the delinquent amount plus costs.
    3. A deed of trust borrower does not have the right of redemption; the lender is typically not able to receive a deficiency judgment.
    4. When the property is sold at the trustee's sale, title immediately passes to the winning bidder.

IV. Finance Instrument Provisions

- A. Subordination clause: Allows an instrument recorded later to take priority over an earlier recorded instrument.
- B. Late charge provisions: Adds a late fee to overdue payments.
- C. Prepayment provisions: May impose a penalty if the borrower repays some or all of the principal before it is due, in order to compensate the lender for lost interest.
- D. Partial release clause: In a security instrument covering multiple parcels, provides for the release of part of the security property when part of the debt has been paid.
- E. Acceleration clause: Declares the entire loan balance immediately due in the event of a default.
- F. Alienation clause: Limits the borrower's right to transfer the property without the lender's permission unless the loan is paid off first.
    1. If loan isn't paid off, the new owner may take title subject to existing liens; the lender will retain the power to foreclose on the property.
    2. Alternately, the new owner may assume the loan; the new owner will take on responsibility for paying the loan while the former owner retains secondary liability.
    3. The lender may charge an assumption fee if it approves an assumption.

V. Types of Real Estate Loans

- A. Junior or senior mortgage: A senior mortgage has first lien position, while a junior mortgage has lower lien priority.
- B. Purchase money mortgage: In its narrower sense, a mortgage that a buyer gives to a seller in a seller-financed transaction.
- C. Home equity loan: A loan using property that the borrower already owns as collateral.
- D. Refinance mortgage: A new mortgage used to replace an existing mortgage on the same property, often used by borrowers when interest rates drop.
- E. Bridge loan: A temporary loan used by buyers to purchase a new home before the sale of their old home closes.
- F. Budget mortgage: A mortgage where payments include not just principal and interest, but also property taxes and hazard insurance.
- G. Package mortgage: A mortgage that covers the purchase of both real property and personal property (such as fixtures or equipment).

H. Blanket mortgage: A mortgage which contains a partial release clause that uses multiple properties as collateral.

I. Construction loan: A short-term loan used to finance construction of improvements on land already owned by the borrower.

J. Nonrecourse mortgage: A mortgage that does not allow for a deficiency judgment against the borrower; the lender's only remedy is foreclosure.

K. Participation mortgage: A mortgage where the lender receives a percentage of earnings generated by the property as well as interest payments.

L. Shared appreciation mortgage: A mortgage where a lender is entitled to a portion of any increase in the property's value.

M. Reverse equity mortgage: A mortgage where a lender makes monthly payments to a homeowner (typically an older person); the home will typically be sold when the owner dies in order to pay back the mortgage.

Key Terms

Promissory note: A written, legally binding promise to repay a debt, which may or may not be a negotiable instrument.

Maker: In a promissory note, the party who promises to pay; the debtor or borrower.

Payee: In a promissory note, the party who is entitled to be paid; the creditor or lender.

Negotiable instrument: An instrument establishing a right to payment, which is freely transferable from one person to another, such as a promissory note or check.

Holder in due course: A third party purchaser of a promissory note who purchased the note for value and in good faith.

Straight note: A promissory note that calls for regular payments of interest only.

Installment note: A promissory note that calls for regular payments of principal and interest until the debt is paid off, as used in an amortized loan.

Security instrument: A document that creates a voluntary lien against real property to secure repayment of a loan.

Hypothecation: Making property security for a loan by transferring title to the lender, without surrendering possession.

Legal title: Title held as security, without the right to possess the property.

Equitable title: The property rights that a borrower retains while a lender or vendor holds legal title.

Lien: A nonpossessory interest in property giving the lienholder the right to foreclose if the owner does not pay a debt owed to the lienholder.

Mortgage: An instrument creating a voluntary lien on a property to secure repayment of a debt, consisting of two parties (a mortgagor/borrower and a mortgagee/lender).

Deed of trust: A security instrument similar to a mortgage giving power of sale to a third party; the parties are a grantor/borrower, a beneficiary/lender, and a trustee.

Judicial foreclosure: A court-supervised foreclosure, beginning with a lawsuit filed by a mortgagee (or beneficiary) to foreclose on property on which a borrower has defaulted.

Nonjudicial foreclosure: Foreclosure by a trustee under the power of sale contained in a deed of trust.

Power of sale: A clause in a deed of trust that gives the trustee the right to foreclose nonjudicially in the event of default.

Reinstatement: The right of a defaulting borrower to prevent foreclosure by curing the default plus costs.

Redemption: The right of a defaulting borrower to prevent foreclosure by paying off the entire loan balance plus costs.

Equitable right of redemption: A period prior to a sheriff's sale in which a mortgagor may avoid foreclosure by paying off the loan balance plus costs.

Statutory right of redemption: A period following the sheriff's sale in which a mortgagor may avoid foreclosure by paying off the loan balance plus costs.

Sheriff's sale: A public auction of property after a judicial foreclosure.

Deficiency judgment: A court judgment requiring the debtor to pay to the lender the difference between the amount of the debt and the proceeds of the foreclosure sale.

Trustee's sale: A nonjudicial foreclosure sale conducted by a trustee under the power of sale clause in a deed of trust.

Subordination clause: A provision in a security instrument that permits a later security instrument to have a higher lien priority than the instrument in which the clause appears.

Prepayment provision: A clause allowing a lender to charge borrowers for prepaying principal on a loan, to compensate for lost interest.

Partial release clause: A clause allowing one or more parcels under a blanket lien to be released from the lien while other parcels remain subject to it.

Acceleration clause: A provision in a security instrument allowing the lender to declare the entire debt due if the borrower breaches one or more provisions.

Alienation clause: A clause in a security instrument giving the lender the right to accelerate the loan if the borrower sells the property or transfers a significant interest in it without the lender's approval.

Assumption: When a buyer takes on responsibility for repaying an existing loan and becomes liable to the lender; the seller remains secondarily liable to the lender.

Estoppel letter: Letter from lender that either acknowledges transfer of ownership and waives due-on-sale clause, or states balance and loan status.

Junior mortgage: A mortgage that has lower lien priority than another mortgage against the same property (the senior mortgage).

Purchase money mortgage: Generally, any loan used to purchase the property that secures the loan; narrowly, a loan given to a buyer by a seller in a seller-financed transaction.

Home equity loan: A loan obtained by a borrower using property he already owns as collateral.

Refinance mortgage: A mortgage loan used to pay off an existing mortgage on the same property.

Budget mortgage: A mortgage where monthly payments include a share of the property taxes and insurance, in addition to principal and interest.

Package mortgage: A mortgage secured by items of personal property as well as real property.

Blanket mortgage: A mortgage that encumbers more than one parcel of property.

Construction loan: A loan used to finance the construction of a building, which remains in place only until construction is completed, at which point it is replaced with a take-out loan.

Reverse equity mortgage: An arrangement where a homeowner mortgages a home (usually owned free and clear) in exchange for a monthly payment from the lender.

Chapter Quiz

1. The purpose of a promissory note is to:
   a. give the lender the right to foreclose on the borrower's property in the event of default
   b. allow the lender to foreclose nonjudicially instead of judicially
   c. establish the borrower's legal obligation to repay the loan
   d. prevent the lender from accelerating the loan in the event of default

2. The equitable right of redemption:
   a. usually lasts until the sheriff's sale is held
   b. enables the mortgagor to redeem the property after the sheriff's sale
   c. allows the trustee to cure the default and reinstate the loan
   d. doesn't apply in a judicial foreclosure

3. If the proceeds of a foreclosure sale are not enough to pay off all the liens against the property:
   a. each lienholder receives a proportionate share of the proceeds
   b. the lien with the highest priority is paid off first, and the junior lienholders are paid only if there is money left over
   c. the sale is declared void, and the property is auctioned again
   d. clear title to the property will be transferred to the foreclosing lender

4. A deficiency judgment:
   a. usually must be paid off before the sheriff's sale is held
   b. is an alternative to foreclosure
   c. will be awarded to the borrower after foreclosure
   d. usually cannot be obtained after a trustee's sale

5. To redeem property after a sheriff's sale, the borrower is generally required to pay:
   a. only the amounts that were delinquent before the loan was accelerated, plus the costs of the sale
   b. the original principal amount of the loan, plus costs
   c. the amount paid for the property at the sheriff's sale, plus interest accrued from the time of the sale
   d. whatever the sheriff's sale purchaser asks for the property, as long as it is not more than the appraised value

6. In a deed of trust transaction, the lender is referred to as the:
    a. beneficiary
    b. trustor
    c. trustee
    d. grantor

7. The key difference between a mortgage and a deed of trust is that:
    a. the mortgage contains a power of sale clause
    b. the mortgage contains an acceleration clause
    c. the deed of trust contains an acceleration clause
    d. the deed of trust contains a power of sale clause

8. In a state where all of the following types of instruments are used, a lender who wants to be able to foreclose quickly and inexpensively probably should choose a:
    a. mortgage
    b. deed of trust
    c. bridge loan
    d. package mortgage

9. To give a mortgage that was recorded later higher lien priority than a mortgage that was recorded earlier:
    a. the earlier mortgage should contain a subordination clause
    b. the earlier mortgage should contain an acceleration clause
    c. the later mortgage should contain a subordination clause
    d. the later mortgage should contain an acceleration clause

10. A buyer can assume a seller's existing loan without the lender's permission only if the mortgage or deed of trust does not contain:
    a. a prepayment clause
    b. a subordination clause
    c. an acceleration clause
    d. an alienation clause

11. If the security instrument includes a due-on-sale clause, when the borrower sells the property, the lender may:
    a. agree to an assumption
    b. renegotiate the interest rate on the loan
    c. require the loan to be paid off immediately
    d. Any of the above

12. In an estoppel letter:
    a. the buyer assumes legal responsibility for repayment of the seller's loan
    b. the lender acknowledges the transfer and waives the right to exercise the due-on-sale clause
    c. the seller agrees to pay a prepayment penalty
    d. the seller accepts secondary liability for repayment of the loan assumed by the buyer

13. Which of the following types of loans calls for the lender to make monthly payments to the borrower?
    a. Purchase money mortgage
    b. Wraparound mortgage
    c. Reverse equity mortgage
    d. Participation mortgage

14. A refinance loan:
    a. enables the borrower to pay off an existing mortgage
    b. is a modification of the existing mortgage, not a new loan
    c. must be arranged with the same lender as the existing mortgage
    d. All of the above

Answer Key

1 c. A promissory note is written evidence of a borrower's legal obligation to repay a loan.

2. a. The equitable right of redemption will usually last until the sheriff's sale has been held.

3. b. If foreclosure sale proceeds are inadequate to pay all creditors, the lienholder with the highest priority is paid first, followed by each junior lienholder in order of priority.

4. d. A deficiency judgment is generally not allowed after a trustee's sale.

5. c. To redeem the property during the statutory redemption period, the debtor usually must pay the amount that was paid for the property at the sheriff's sale, plus any interest accrued since the time of the sale.

6. a. In a deed of trust, the lender is referred to as the beneficiary.

7. d. A deed of trust, unlike a mortgage, contains a power of sale clause that allows the trustee to foreclose nonjudicially.

8. b. A lender who wants quick, inexpensive foreclosure would prefer to use a deed of trust as a security instrument.

9. a. If an earlier mortgage contains a subordination clause, a later mortgage on the same property may take higher lien priority.

10. d. If a mortgage contains an alienation clause, the entire loan balance must be paid off if the property is sold without the lender's approval, preventing the possibility of assumption without permission.

11. d. If a property subject to a mortgage with a due-on-sale clause is sold, the lender may agree to an assumption, renegotiate the interest rate on the loan, or require the loan to be paid off immediately.

12. b. An estoppel letter is issued by a lender that wishes to acknowledge a transfer and waive a due-on-sale clause.

13. c. With a reverse equity mortgage, a lender makes monthly payments to a homeowner, typically an older homeowner who needs an income stream.

14. a. A refinance is a loan taken out to pay off an existing loan on the same property. It is a new loan, and does not need to be with the same lender.

Chapter 6
Basic Features of a Residential Loan

Introduction

The size of loan a home buyer can get depends on the buyer's income, net worth, and credit history, and on the value of the property in question. It also depends on the features of the loan and the way it's structured. How long does the buyer have to repay the loan? How much of a downpayment does the lender require? Is the interest rate fixed or adjustable? Lenders offer different financing options at different times, depending on the mortgage finance market and the cost of housing. They structure their loans to limit the risk of foreclosure loss while still enabling buyers to purchase homes.

To understand the financing options available to home buyers in your area at a given time, you first need to understand the basic features of a mortgage loan. It's variations in these features that distinguish one loan program from another and determine which type of loan is right for a particular buyer. The basic features of a mortgage loan include:

- how the loan is amortized,
- the length of the repayment period,
- the loan-to-value ratio,
- whether there is mortgage insurance or a guaranty,
- whether there is secondary financing, and
- whether the interest rate is fixed or adjustable.

Amortization

Loan amortization refers to how principal and interest are paid to the lender over the course of the repayment period. A loan is **amortized** if the borrower is required to make regular installment payments that include some of the principal (the money borrowed) as well as interest on the principal. The regular payments are usually made in monthly installments.

Fully amortized loan: level payments (including principal and interest) pay off loan by end of term

Most home purchase loans made by institutional lenders are **fully amortized**. With a fully amortized loan, the regular monthly payments are enough to pay off all of the principal and interest by the end of the loan term. Each payment includes both a principal portion and an interest portion. When a payment is made, the principal portion is applied to the debt, paying back some of the amount originally borrowed. The remainder of the payment, the interest portion, is retained by the lender as earnings or profit. With each payment, the amount of the debt is reduced and the interest due with the next payment is calculated based on the lower principal balance. The total monthly payment remains the same throughout the term of the loan, but every month the interest portion of the payment is smaller and the principal portion is correspondingly larger. The final payment pays off the loan completely; the principal balance is zero and no further interest is owed.

In the early years of a fully amortized loan, the principal portion of the payment is quite small, so it takes several years for the borrower's equity in the property to increase significantly through debt reduction. But toward the end of the loan term, the borrower's equity increases more rapidly.

> **Example:** A fully amortized, 30-year $100,000 loan at 6% interest calls for monthly payments of $599.55. Only $99.55 of the first payment is applied to the principal (see Figure 6.1). But by the twentieth year of the loan term, $327.89 of the $599.55 payment is applied to the principal.

There are two alternatives to a fully amortized loan: a partially amortized loan or an interest-only loan. Like a fully amortized loan, a **partially amortized** loan requires regular payments of both principal and interest. However, the regular payments are not enough to

Partially amortized loan: balloon payment required at end of term

Fig. 6.1 How an amortized loan's payments are applied to principal and interest

Example: $100,000 loan, 6%, 30-year term, monthly payments
(Figures approximate)

Payment Number	Principal Balance	Total Payment	Interest Portion	Principal Portion	Ending Balance
1	$100,000.00	$599.55	$500.00	$99.55	$99,900.45
2	$99,900.45	$599.55	$499.50	$100.05	$99,800.40
3	$99,800.40	$599.55	$499.00	$100.55	$99,699.85
4	$99,699.85	$599.55	$498.50	$101.05	$99,598.80
5	$99,598.80	$599.55	$497.99	$101.56	$99,497.24

completely pay off the debt by the end of the loan term. The regular payments have repaid only part of the principal, and the remaining balance must now be paid off. This final principal payment is called a **balloon payment**, because it is much larger than the regular payments made during the loan term.

> **Example:** A partially amortized $100,000 loan at 6% interest might require monthly payments of $599.55 for 15 years. At the end of that period, the remaining principal balance will be about $71,000. The borrower will have to make a balloon payment of $71,000 to pay off the loan.

In most cases, the borrower comes up with the funds for the balloon payment by refinancing. (Refinancing means using the funds from a new mortgage loan to pay off an existing mortgage.)

Interest-only loan requires no principal payments during the loan term, or for a specified period at the beginning of the term

With an **interest-only** loan, the regular payments the borrower is required to make during the loan term cover the interest accruing on the loan, without paying down the principal.

> **Example:** With a $100,000 interest-only loan at 6% interest, the borrower must pay the lender $500 in interest each month during the loan term. At the end of the term, the borrower will have to pay the lender the entire $100,000 originally borrowed.

Alternatively, an interest-only loan may allow the borrower to make interest-only payments for a specified period at the beginning of the loan term; at the end of this period, the borrower must begin making amortized payments that will pay off all principal and interest by the end of the term. This type of interest-only loan (sometimes called an "interest first mortgage") has become popular in some areas where housing prices are high.

Repayment Period

A loan's **repayment period** is the number of years the borrower has in which to repay the loan. The repayment period is often called the **loan term**.

As we discussed in Chapter 3, until the 1930s, the repayment period for a home purchase loan was ordinarily only five years, and a balloon payment of the full principal amount was required at the end of that period. When the Federal Housing Administration was established to help home buyers during the Depression, it made loans with a 30-year term available. With this longer repayment period, the loans could be fully amortized while keeping the monthly payments at an affordable level. Lenders realized that this dramatically decreased the risk of default, and thirty years soon became the standard repayment period for all home purchase loans.

30-year loan term:
- Standard
- Affordable payments

While 30-year loans are still regarded as standard and are still the most common, many lenders also offer 15-year and 20-year loans. In some cases a term as short as ten years or as long as forty years is allowed.

The length of the repayment period affects two important aspects of a mortgage loan:

1. the amount of the monthly payment, and
2. the total amount of interest paid over the life of the loan.

To see the impact that the repayment period has on the monthly payment and the total interest paid, let's compare a 30-year loan with a 15-year loan.

Monthly Payment Amount. As mentioned above, the main reason that thirty years became the standard term for a residential mortgage is that a longer repayment period reduces the amount of the monthly payment. Thus, a 30-year loan is more affordable than a 15-year loan.

> **Example:** The monthly payment on a $100,000 30-year loan at 7% interest is $665.30. The monthly payment on the same loan amortized over a 15-year period is $898.83.

The higher monthly payment required for a 15-year loan means that the borrower will build equity in the home much faster. But the higher payment also makes it much more difficult to qualify for a 15-year loan than for the same size of loan with a 30-year term. A buyer who wants a 15-year loan and has sufficient funds might decide to make a larger downpayment and borrow less money to make the monthly payment amount more affordable. Or the buyer might choose instead to buy a much less expensive home than he could afford with a 30-year loan.

Shorter loan term means higher payment amount:
- Equity builds faster
- But many buyers can't qualify for a loan as large as they could with a 30-year term

Total Interest. Probably the biggest advantage of a shorter repayment period is that it substantially decreases the amount of interest

Shorter term means total interest paid over loan term is much less

paid over the life of the loan. With a 15-year mortgage, a borrower will end up paying less than half as much interest over the life of the loan as a 30-year mortgage would require.

> **Example:** Let's look at the $100,000 loan at 7% interest again. By the end of a 30-year loan term, the borrower will pay a total of $239,508. But by the end of a 15-year term, the borrower will pay only $161,789. After deducting the original $100,000 principal amount, you can see that the 30-year loan will require $139,508 in interest, while the 15-year loan will require only $61,789 in interest.

Shorter term typically means a lower interest rate

Repayment Period and Interest Rate. To simplify our comparison of a 15-year loan and a 30-year loan, we applied the same interest rate (7%) to both loans. In fact, however, a lender is likely to charge a significantly lower interest rate on a 15-year loan than it charges on a comparable 30-year loan. Since the 15-year loan ties up the lender's capital for a shorter period, the lender's risk is reduced.

The interest rate on a 15-year loan might be half a percentage point lower than the rate on a 30-year loan. If the interest rate on the 15-year loan in our example were only 6.5% instead of 7%, the monthly payment would be $871.11. The total interest paid over the life of the loan would be $56,799.

Thus, the 30-year mortgage has affordable payments, but requires the borrower to pay much more interest over the life of the loan. On the other hand, the 15-year loan has higher monthly payments, but allows the borrower to pay far less interest over the life of the loan. Figure 6.2 compares $100,000, $150,000, and $200,000 mortgages at 6.5% interest for 15-year terms and 7% for 30-year terms.

As you can see, for a relatively small additional monthly payment, a 15-year loan offers substantial savings over its 30-year counterpart. A 15-year loan also provides the borrower with free and clear ownership of the home in half the time.

15-year loan term
- Advantages:
  1. Lower interest rate
  2. Total interest much less
  3. Clear ownership in half the time
- Disadvantages:
  1. Higher monthly payments
  2. Tax deduction lost sooner

On the other hand, the higher monthly payments make the 15-year loan more difficult to afford in the short run. A larger downpayment would make the payments more affordable, but that's not an option for many buyers, so a 15-year loan would sharply reduce their buying power. Another disadvantage of a shorter loan term is that the borrower loses the tax deduction on the mortgage interest payments sooner (because the mortgage is paid off sooner).

Fig. 6.2 Comparison of 15-year and 30-year loans (monthly payment amount and total payments)

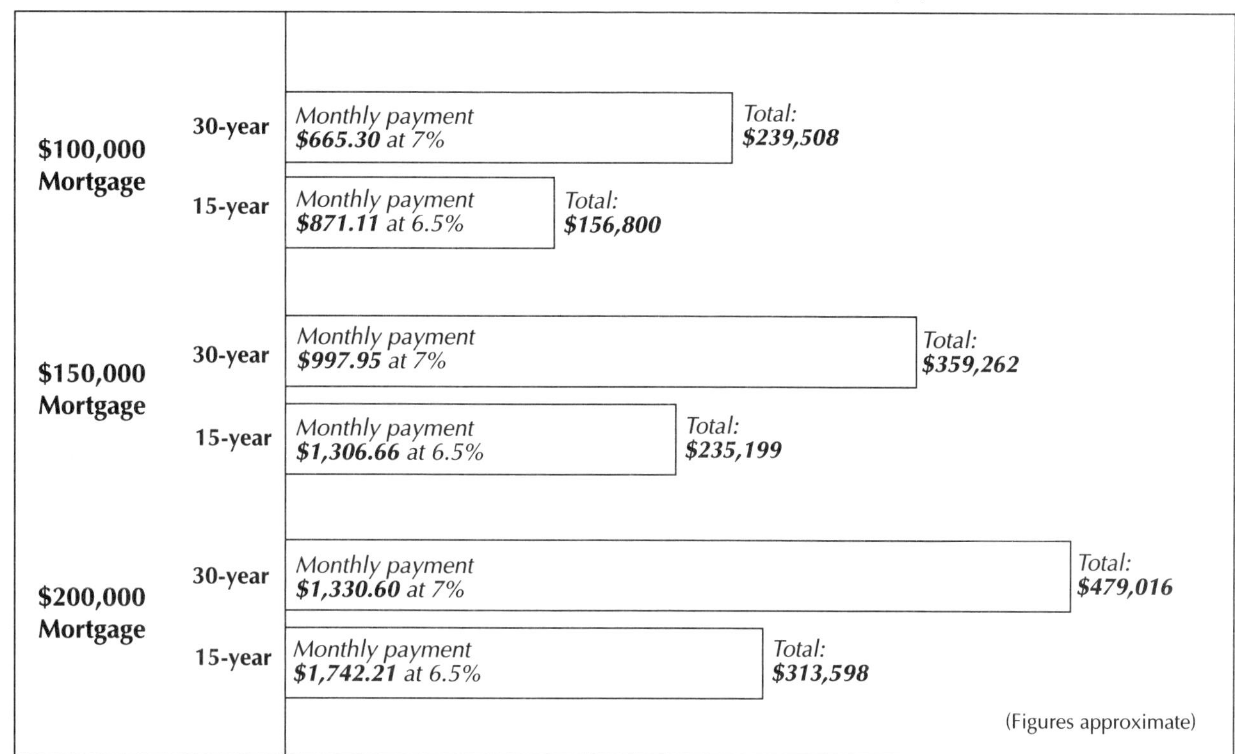

20-year loans. A 20-year loan represents a compromise between the standard 30-year loan and the 15-year loan. Although the monthly payments for a 20-year loan are higher than the payments for a 30-year loan, they aren't as high as the payments for a 15-year loan. And yet the 20-year loan still provides significant interest savings over the life of the loan.

20-year loan is a compromise between a 15-year loan and a 30-year loan

> **Example:** For purposes of comparison, suppose that a $200,000 loan at 7% interest is amortized over 15, 20, and 30 years (not even taking into account that 15-year and 20-year loans are offered at lower interest rates than 30-year loans).
>
> The monthly payment for the 30-year loan would be $1,330.60, and the borrower would have to pay about $479,016 over the life of the loan. The monthly payment for the 15-year loan would be $1,797.66 (35% more than the 30-year payment), but the total payments would be only $323,579 (32% less than the total payments on the 30-year loan). The monthly payment for the 20-year loan would be $1,550.60 (only 17% more than the 30-year payment), and the total payments would be $372,144 (still 22% less than the total payments on the 30-year loan).

Loan-to-Value Ratio

A loan-to-value ratio (LTV) expresses the relationship between the loan amount and the value of the home being purchased. If a buyer is purchasing a $100,000 home with an $80,000 loan and a $20,000 downpayment, the loan-to-value ratio is 80%. If the loan amount were $90,000 and the downpayment were $10,000, the loan-to-value ratio would be 90%. The higher the LTV, the larger the loan amount and the smaller the downpayment.

The higher the loan-to-value ratio, the smaller the downpayment

A loan with a low LTV is generally less risky than one with a high LTV. The borrower's investment in her home is greater, so she'll try harder to avoid defaulting on the loan and losing the home. And if the borrower does default, the outstanding loan balance is less, so it's more likely that the lender will be able to recoup the entire amount in a foreclosure sale.

Lenders use loan-to-value ratios to establish maximum loan amounts

Lenders use LTV limits to establish maximum loan amounts. For example, under the terms of a particular loan program, the maximum loan-to-value ratio might be 95% of the sales price or appraised value of the property, whichever is less. For a $100,000 home financed with a loan from that program, the maximum loan amount would be $95,000. The borrower would be required to make a downpayment of at least 5%, or $5,000.

As you can see, a loan program's maximum LTV determines not only the maximum loan amount for a transaction financed through that program, but also the minimum downpayment required. Thus, the maximum LTV is a key factor in determining how expensive a home a buyer can afford through a particular program.

> **Example:** The Allens have only $5,000 saved for a downpayment. They're hoping to buy a $100,000 house. If a particular loan program has a maximum LTV of 90%, the Allens won't be able to finance their purchase through that program unless they're able to come up with additional cash. Depending on the program's rules, they might be able to do that with gift funds (see Chapter 8) or secondary financing (discussed later in this chapter). Otherwise, they'll have to finance the purchase through a different loan program that has a higher LTV limit.

To protect themselves against foreclosure loss, residential lenders traditionally had low LTV limits. For example, many lenders allowed an LTV no higher than 80%, requiring borrowers to make a 20%

downpayment—a very substantial investment in the property. High-LTV home loans were available only through special programs such as the FHA and VA loan programs. In recent years, however, high-LTV loans have become widely available. This has made homeownership possible for considerably more people than it once was.

High-LTV loans help people buy homes when they don't have much money for a downpayment

There are various ways that lenders can reduce or compensate for the extra risk involved in making high-LTV loans. For instance, they can apply stricter qualifying standards or charge a higher interest rate. Probably the most effective way to minimize the risk of loss is with mortgage insurance or a loan guaranty. In fact, some form of mortgage insurance or guaranty is a requirement in almost all high-LTV home loan programs.

Mortgage Insurance or Loan Guaranty

Many home purchase loans are covered by a mortgage insurance policy or a loan guaranty. The purpose of the insurance or guaranty is to protect the lender from foreclosure loss. The coverage may be required by the lender or else offered as a feature of a particular loan program. (For example, the VA home loan program provides lenders with a guaranty on loans made to eligible veterans.) In either case, the insurance or guaranty serves as an incentive for lenders to make loans on terms that they would otherwise consider too risky. This may include not only high-LTV loans, as discussed above, but also loans to borrowers who represent extra risk (for example, a borrower with a high debt-to-income ratio or a mediocre credit score).

Mortgage insurance or loan guaranty often required for loan with high LTV or other increased risk factors

Mortgage Insurance. Mortgage insurance works basically like other types of insurance: in exchange for premiums, the insurer provides coverage for certain types of losses specified in the policy. Mortgage insurance premiums are ordinarily paid by the borrower. The policy protects the lender against losses that might result from the borrower's default on the mortgage and the subsequent foreclosure.

In the event that there is a default and foreclosure, the insurer will **indemnify** the lender. This means that if the proceeds of the foreclosure sale aren't enough to pay off the entire remaining amount that the borrower owes the lender, plus the lender's other expenses, the insurer will make up the shortfall. Depending on the policy, covered losses may include unpaid principal, interest, property taxes, and hazard insurance, attorney's fees, and the cost of preserving the property during the period of foreclosure and resale, as well as the cost of the foreclosure sale itself.

Because the mortgage insurer assumes most of the risk of loan default, the insurer also underwrites the loan. In other words, the borrower must meet the qualifying standards of the mortgage insurer as well as the standards of the lender.

We'll discuss mortgage insurance in more detail in Chapter 10 (private mortgage insurance policies for conventional loans) and Chapter 11 (the mutual mortgage insurance coverage offered through the FHA-insured loan program).

Loan Guaranty. With a loan guaranty, a third party (called the **guarantor**) agrees to take on secondary legal responsibility for a borrower's obligation to a lender. If the borrower defaults on the loan, the guarantor will reimburse the lender for resulting losses. Thus, although a loan guaranty is not technically a form of insurance, from a mortgage lender's point of view it serves the same purpose as mortgage insurance.

The guarantor for a mortgage loan might be a private party, a nonprofit organization, or a governmental agency. The guarantor's motive for providing the guaranty is usually to help the borrower, rather than to turn a profit. The guaranty encourages the lender to make a loan on special terms favorable to the borrower, making it easier for the borrower to purchase a home. For example, the VA-guaranteed loan program is intended to promote homeownership among veterans.

Like a mortgage insurer, a guarantor may be involved in underwriting the loan. This is true in the VA loan program, which we'll cover in Chapter 12.

Secondary Financing

Secondary financing: loan to pay part of downpayment or closing costs

Sometimes a home buyer obtains two mortgage loans at once: a primary loan for most of the purchase price, and a second loan to pay part of the downpayment or closing costs required for the first loan. This second loan is called **secondary financing**. Secondary financing may come from an institutional lender, from the seller, or from a private third party. When an institutional lender is the source of the secondary financing, it may be the same lender that is making the first mortgage loan, or it may be a different lender.

A lender making a primary loan will usually place restrictions on the type of secondary financing arrangement that the borrower may enter into. For example, the primary lender will make sure that the payments required for the second loan don't exceed the borrower's ability to pay. When qualifying ratios are applied to the borrower's stable monthly income, the payments for both the first loan and the second loan will be taken into account. Also, in most cases the primary lender will still require the borrower to make at least a minimum downpayment out of her own funds, even if the secondary lender would be willing to supply the entire downpayment needed for the first loan.

Buyer must qualify for combined payments on both loans

The basic point of these and other restrictions on secondary financing is to minimize the risk of default on the second loan, since both loans are going to be secured by the same property. A second mortgage with a high risk of default would impair the primary lender's security interest and make default on the first mortgage more likely.

The specific restrictions that a primary lender imposes depend in part on whether the primary loan is conventional, FHA-insured, or VA-guaranteed. We'll discuss the secondary financing rules for each of the major loan programs in Chapters 10, 11, and 12.

Fixed or Adjustable Interest Rate

The final basic loan feature that we're going to cover in this chapter is the interest rate. A loan's interest rate can be either fixed or adjustable (variable).

With a **fixed-rate loan**, the interest rate charged on the loan remains constant throughout the entire loan term. If a borrower obtains a 30-year mortgage loan with a 7% fixed interest rate, the interest rate remains 7% for the whole 30-year period, no matter what happens to market interest rates during that time. If market rates increase to 10%, or if they drop to 5%, the interest rate charged on the loan will still be 7%.

Fixed-rate mortgage: interest rate remains the same throughout loan term

The fixed-rate mortgage is regarded as the standard. It has been the cornerstone of residential financing since the Depression in the 1930s. In fact, through the end of the 1970s virtually all home purchase loans had fixed interest rates.

During the 1980s, however, market interest rates rose dramatically and also became more volatile—in other words, they changed more frequently. When mortgage interest rates are high, many potential home buyers can no longer afford financing. (Mortgage rates as high as 18% were not unheard of in the early 1980s.) And when rates are volatile, lenders are less willing to tie up their funds for a long period, such as 30 years, at a fixed rate.

For instance, suppose the current market rate for home mortgages is 10%, but economists are predicting much higher interest rates within the next year or so. A lender might hesitate to make a fixed-rate loan at 10% interest when it looks as though market rates might soon be up to 13%.

To address both of these issues—affordability and volatility—the **adjustable-rate mortgage (ARM)** was introduced. An ARM allows the lender to periodically adjust the loan's interest rate to reflect changes in the cost of money. This transfers the risk of interest rate fluctuations to the borrower. If market rates climb, the borrower's interest rate and payment amount go up; if market rates decline, the borrower's rate and payment amount go down. Because ARMs shift this risk to the borrower, lenders generally charge a lower interest rate on an ARM than on a fixed-rate loan. For example, if a borrower could get a fixed-rate mortgage at 7%, he might be able to get an adjustable-rate mortgage at an initial rate between 5.5% and 6.5%.

ARM: lender adjusts loan's interest rate from time to time to reflect changes in cost of money

Thus, in the 1980s, when mortgage interest rates were at record highs, ARMs became a popular way to afford the financing necessary to buy a home. More recently, when mortgage rates were at record lows, ARMs were considerably less popular. But even when rates are low, some buyers find ARMs attractive. For example, buyers who expect their incomes to rise sharply, or who plan to own the home they're buying for only a few years, may decide to take advantage of an ARM's extra-low initial rate.

Now let's look at how ARMs work and what their special features are. As you'll see, they're much more complicated than fixed-rate loans.

How ARMs Work

An ARM borrower's interest rate is determined initially by the cost of money (market interest rates) at the time the loan is made. Once the interest rate on the loan has been set, it is tied to one of several widely recognized indexes, and future interest rate adjustments are based on the upward and downward movements of the index. An **index** is a published statistical report that serves as a reliable indicator of changes in the cost of money.

ARM's interest rate tied to index that indicates changes in cost of money

At the time an ARM is made, the lender selects the index it prefers, and thereafter the loan's interest rate will be adjusted (increased or decreased) to reflect increases and decreases in the rates reported by that index. A change in the loan's interest rate will also result in an increase or decrease in the amount of the monthly payment the borrower is required to make.

ARM Features

To provide for interest rate and payment adjustments, adjustable-rate mortgages have a number of special features. Depending on the loan, an ARM may have all or only some of the following elements:

- a note rate,
- an index,
- a margin,
- a rate adjustment period,
- a mortgage payment adjustment period,
- a lookback period,
- an interest rate cap,
- a mortgage payment cap,
- a negative amortization cap, and
- a conversion option.

Note Rate. An ARM's initial interest rate is called the note rate because it is the rate stated in the promissory note. The note rate may also be referred to as the contract rate.

To attract borrowers, lenders sometimes offer ARMs with a discounted initial rate: an interest rate for the first year that is lower than the rate indicated by the index when the loan is made. This is often referred to as a "teaser rate."

Index. As we said above, an index is a statistical report that is used as an indicator of changes in the cost of money. There are several regularly published indexes that lenders use in connection with ARMs. Examples include the Treasury securities indexes (the weekly average yield on Treasury securities, adjusted to a constant maturity of one, three, or five years); the 11th District cost of funds index (an average of the interest rates paid by savings and loans for deposits and other borrowings with a certain range of maturities); and the LIBOR index (an international index based on the rate commercial banks pay for short-term loans from other commercial banks on the London market).

Some indexes are more responsive to changes in the cost of money than others. For example, the one-year Treasury securities index is very responsive to economic fluctuations, while the cost of funds index is more stable. Lenders tend to prefer the more responsive indexes. A borrower benefits from a more responsive index when interest rates are decreasing, but may prefer a more stable index if rates are increasing.

Index
+ Margin
Interest Rate

Margin. An ARM's margin is the difference between the index rate and the interest rate that the lender charges the borrower. Since the index is a reflection of the lender's cost of money, it's necessary to add a margin to the index to cover the lender's administrative expenses and provide a profit. In fact, between lenders who use the same index, it's the size of the margin that makes the difference in the interest rates they charge. Margins vary from 2% to 3%. The index plus the margin equals the interest rate on the loan.

Example:

3.25%	Current index value
+ 2.00%	Margin
5.25%	ARM interest rate

It is the index rate that fluctuates during the loan term and causes the borrower's interest rate to increase and decrease; the lender's margin remains constant.

ARM's interest rate adjusted only at specified intervals

Rate Adjustment Period. The interest rate on an ARM isn't adjusted every time the index rate changes. Instead, the ARM has a rate adjustment period that determines how often the lender will adjust the interest rate on the loan. It could provide for a rate adjustment every six months, once a year, or every three years, for example. A rate adjustment period of one year is the most common, and ARMs with one-year rate adjustment periods are referred to as one-year ARMs.

At the end of each rate adjustment period, the lender checks what the index rate was on a specified date. If the index has increased or decreased, the lender makes a corresponding change in the loan's interest rate and notifies the borrower in writing of the change.

Some ARMs have a two-tiered rate adjustment structure. These loans (often called **hybrid ARMs** because they're like a combination of an ARM and a fixed-rate loan) provide for a longer initial period before the first rate adjustment, with more frequent adjustments after that.

Hybrid ARMs have an initial fixed-rate period

> **Example:** The borrowers are financing their home with a 30-year ARM that has an initial rate adjustment period of three years, with annual rate adjustments from then on. The interest rate charged on their loan won't change during the first three years of the repayment period, but it will change each year after that.

The loan in the example would be called a 3/1 ARM. There are also 5/1 ARMs, 7/1 ARMs, and 10/1 ARMs. In each case, the first number is the number of years in the initial rate adjustment period, and the second number means that subsequent rate adjustments will occur once a year. Some borrowers who choose these types of loans intend to sell or refinance their home before the end of the initial adjustment period. As a general rule, the longer the initial adjustment period, the higher the initial interest rate. But the initial rate will still be lower than the rate for a comparable fixed-rate loan.

Mortgage Payment Adjustment Period. An ARM's mortgage payment adjustment period determines when the lender changes the amount of the borrower's monthly principal and interest payment to reflect a change in the interest rate charged on the loan. For most ARMs, the mortgage payment adjustment period is the same as the rate adjustment period. As soon as the interest rate is adjusted, the lender also adjusts the mortgage payment.

With some ARMs, however, the payment adjustment period doesn't coincide with the rate adjustment period. Instead, the lender adjusts the interest rate more frequently than the mortgage payment. For example, the loan agreement might call for interest rate adjustments every six months, but changes in the amount of the mortgage payment only every two years. This arrangement can have undesirable consequences for the borrower. (See the discussion of negative amortization later in this section.)

Payment amount not necessarily adjusted every time interest rate is adjusted

Lookback Period. As we've just explained, how often the lender changes an ARM borrower's interest rate and payment amount depends on the loan's rate and payment adjustment period(s). You may also hear reference to an ARM's "lookback period." A typical lookback period is 45 days. That means that the loan's rate and payment adjustments will actually be determined by where the index stood 45 days before the end of the adjustment period (not on the date the adjustment period ends).

> **Example:** A one-year ARM has a 45-day lookback period. At the end of the one-year rate adjustment period, on July 2, the index that the ARM is tied to has risen 0.75%. But 45 days earlier, on May 18, the index had risen only 0.50%. Therefore the lender can raise the interest rate on the borrower's loan only by 0.50%, not 0.75%.

Interest Rate Cap. Not long after adjustable-rate mortgages were introduced, some ARM borrowers encountered a problem that came to be known as **payment shock**. Payment shock occurred when market interest rates rose very rapidly. As market rates went up, so did ARM indexes, and that resulted in sharp increases in the interest rates lenders were charging ARM borrowers. Of course, a higher interest rate translated into higher monthly payments. In some cases the payments increased so dramatically that the borrowers could no longer afford them. Borrowers who fell victim to payment shock had to sell their homes or face foreclosure.

Payment shock: sharp increase in payment due to rate increase

To protect borrowers from payment shock (and protect themselves from default), lenders began including interest rate caps in their ARMs. An **interest rate cap** limits how much the interest rate on the loan can increase, regardless of what the index does. By limiting interest rate increases, the rate cap prevents the monthly payment from increasing too much.

Interest rate cap limits how much rate can increase:
- Per adjustment period
- Over the life of the loan

Most ARMs have two kinds of rate caps. One limits the amount that the interest rate can change in any single adjustment period. The other limits the amount that the interest rate can increase over the entire loan term. For example, a one-year ARM might have a 2% annual rate cap and a 5% life-of-the-loan cap. When the lender adjusts the loan's interest rate each year, the annual rate cap prevents the lender from increasing the rate more than 2% at one time. And because of the life-of-the-loan cap, the borrower knows from the outset that no matter how much the index increases over the course of the loan term, the interest rate charged on the loan can never be more than 5% higher than the note rate.

For most ARMs, the annual interest rate cap applies to rate reductions as well as rate increases.

> **Example:** A loan agreement provides that the loan's interest rate can't increase or decrease more than 2% per year. If the index rate rises 3% in one year, the lender can only raise the loan's interest rate by 2%; and if the index drops 3% in one year, the lender will only reduce the loan's rate by 2%.

In contrast, life-of-the-loan caps typically limit only rate increases, not decreases.

Mortgage Payment Cap. A second way of limiting payment increases is with a mortgage payment cap. A **payment cap** directly limits how much the lender can raise the monthly mortgage payment. Typically, payment caps limit mortgage payment (principal and interest) increases to 7.5% annually. (A 7.5% payment increase is considered to be approximately equivalent to a 1% interest rate increase.)

Payment cap directly limits how much mortgage payment can increase

Many ARMs have only an interest rate cap and no mortgage payment cap. Some have both an interest rate cap and a payment cap, and still others have only a payment cap. Any of these arrangements will protect the borrower from payment shock if interest rates skyrocket. However, if a loan has a payment cap and no rate cap, the borrower may encounter the problem of negative amortization (see below).

While protections against payment shock are important, keep in mind that steadily rising interest rates and sharp payment increases are the worst case scenario for an ARM. Over the course of a 30-year loan term, the borrower's interest rate and payment will probably decrease from time to time, offsetting the increases.

Over time, interest rate increases may be offset by rate decreases

Negative Amortization. When an adjustable-rate mortgage has certain features, changes in the loan's interest rate may result in negative amortization. Before we define negative amortization, let's look at an example.

> **Example:** The Walkers borrowed $190,000 to buy their home. Their mortgage is a one-year ARM with a 7.5% annual payment cap but no interest rate cap. Their initial interest rate was 4.5%, and their monthly payment during the first year has been $962.70. At the end of the first year, the index that the Walkers' ARM is

tied to has risen 2.75%. So the lender adjusts the loan's interest rate up by 2.75% (from 4.5% to 7.25%). Without a payment cap, this rate increase would increase the monthly payment by $325, to $1,287.70. Out of that payment amount, approximately $1,129.40 would be interest.

However, the payment cap limits the Walkers' payment increase to no more than 7.5% of the payment amount per year. In this case, that is $72.20:

$962.70	Year 1 payment amount
× 7.5%	Payment cap percentage
$72.20	Maximum payment increase for Year 2

As a result, the monthly payment during the second year of the Walkers' loan term can be no more than $1,034.90:

$962.70	Year 1 payment
+ 72.20	7.5% of the Year 1 payment
$1,034.90	Maximum Year 2 payment

In this situation, the payment cap has prevented the payment from increasing enough to cover all of the interest charged on the loan during the second year. Even if the Walkers' entire $1,034.90 monthly payment is applied only to interest (without paying down the principal balance at all), the interest accruing on the loan during the second year won't be fully covered. The shortfall will be about $94.50 per month, or $1,134 for the year.

Negative amortization: unpaid interest added to principal balance, increasing the amount owed

The lender will handle the situation in the example by adding the unpaid interest to the loan's principal balance. When unpaid interest is added to the loan balance, it is called **negative amortization**. Ordinarily, a loan's principal balance declines steadily, although gradually. But negative amortization causes the principal balance to go up instead of down. The borrower may owe the lender more than she originally borrowed.

ARM features that can lead to negative amortization:
- Payment cap but no rate cap; or
- Payments adjusted less often than interest rate

In the example, negative amortization occurred because there was a payment cap and no interest rate cap. Negative amortization can also occur when an ARM's interest rate adjustment period and mortgage payment adjustment period do not coincide. Suppose a borrower has an ARM with a six-month rate adjustment period and a three-year payment adjustment period. Over a three-year period, the loan's interest rate might increase five times while the payment amount stayed the same (see Figure 6.3). The borrower would be

Fig. 6.3 When an ARM's interest rate changes more often than the payment amount, negative amortization may result

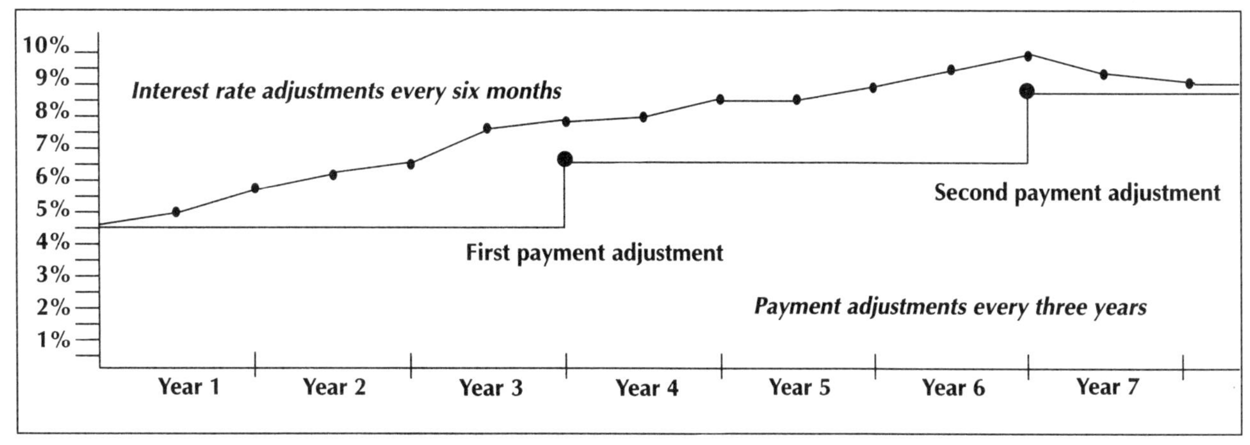

paying too little interest during that period, which would result in negative amortization.

Many adjustable-rate loans are structured to prevent negative amortization from occurring. But when negative amortization is a possibility, the loan usually has a negative amortization cap: a limit on the amount of unpaid interest that can be added to the principal balance.

A negative amortization cap typically limits the total amount a borrower can owe to 125% of the original loan amount. When that point is reached, the loan is recast and the monthly payment is set to fully repay the loan over the remainder of the term.

Conversion Option. Some borrowers feel uncomfortable continuing to bear the risk of rate and payment increases that an ARM involves. Many ARMs allow the borrower to convert the loan to a fixed-rate mortgage at designated times during the loan term.

Conversion option: opportunity to switch from adjustable to fixed interest rate

A conversion option ordinarily involves a limited time to convert, and the borrower is usually required to pay a conversion fee. For example, a borrower with a convertible ARM might have the option of converting from an adjustable interest rate to a fixed rate between the 13th and 59th month of the loan term (only on one of the annual rate adjustment dates), for a conversion fee of $250. If the borrower chooses to convert the loan, the fixed rate will be the current market rate at the time of conversion.

Explaining ARMs

Clearly, adjustable-rate mortgages are a lot more complicated than fixed-rate mortgages. It's not surprising that many buyers have trouble understanding ARMs. To address that problem, the Truth in Lending Act requires lenders to make special disclosures to ARM loan applicants (see Chapter 14).

When you're working with buyers who are considering an ARM, it can be helpful to go over the lender's required disclosures with them. You may also find the question and answer sheet shown in Figure 6.4 and the ARM comparison worksheet in Figure 6.5 useful.

Loan Features and Financing Options

As a real estate agent, in addition to helping home buyers evaluate their financing options, you may occasionally be called upon to help design a financing option to fit a special situation. The loan features that we've covered in this chapter—amortization, repayment period, loan-to-value ratio, a fixed or adjustable interest rate, and (in some cases) mortgage insurance or secondary financing—are the basic elements used to design financing. In combination with one another, they determine whether a particular loan will enable a particular buyer to buy a particular property. They determine how much money the buyer can borrow (the loan amount), how much money the buyer will need to close the loan (the downpayment), and how affordable the loan will be (the monthly payment amount). Those are the key issues that will come up again and again throughout the rest of the book.

Fig. 6.4 ARM questions and answers

What You Need to Know About ARMs

A real estate agent should be prepared to answer the following questions about adjustable-rate mortgages:

1. **What will my initial interest rate be?**
   It usually isn't necessary to break the rate down into index and margin. The buyer is concerned only with the total. The initial rate (note rate or contract rate) will be based on the cost of money when the loan is made.

2. **How often will my interest rate change?**
   The adjustment period will be stated in the loan agreement. Depending on the lender's preference, adjustments may occur every six months, annually, every three years, or every five years. Six-month and one-year intervals are most common.

3. **How often will my payment change?**
   Again, in order to give an accurate answer, you have to be familiar with the policies of the particular lender. Most lenders prefer simultaneous rate and payment changes.

4. **Is there any limit to how much my interest rate can be increased?**
   Most ARMs have interest rate caps. An annual cap is usually 1% or 2%; a life-of-the-loan cap is usually 5% or 6%.

5. **Is there any limit to how much my payment can be increased at any one time?**
   Some ARMs have payment caps, but most keep payment increases under control with interest rate caps. When there is a payment cap, payment increases are usually limited to 7.5% of the payment amount per year.

6. **Will my ARM involve negative amortization?**
   Most new ARMs don't allow negative amortization. However, it still is a possibility with some new ARMs, and also with some older ARMs (which a buyer might consider assuming). If negative amortization is a possibility, the loan should have a negative amortization cap.

7. **Can my ARM be converted to a fixed-rate loan?**
   Many ARMs contain a conversion option that permits the borrower to convert to a fixed interest rate at certain points in the loan term, for a fee. The fixed rate will usually be the market interest rate at the time of conversion.

Fig. 6.5 ARM comparison worksheet

ARM Comparison Worksheet

	Loan 1	Loan 2	Loan 3
Lender	____	____	____
Loan amount	$ ____	$ ____	$ ____
Discount fee	$ ____	$ ____	$ ____
Origination fee	$ ____	$ ____	$ ____
Index	____	____	____
Current index rate	____ %	____ %	____ %
Margin	____ %	____ %	____ %
Note rate	____ %	____ %	____ %
Initial payment	$ ____	$ ____	$ ____
Rate adjustment period	____	____	____
Payment adjustment period	____	____	____
Interest rate cap			
• periodic	____ %	____ %	____ %
• life of loan	____ %	____ %	____ %
Payment cap			
• periodic	____ %	____ %	____ %
• life of loan	____ %	____ %	____ %
Negative amortization			
• possible?	____	____	____
• cap	____ %	____ %	____ %
Conversion option			
• conversion fee	$ ____	$ ____	$ ____
• restrictions	____	____	____

Outline: Basic Features of a Residential Loan

I. Amortization
  A. An amortized loan involves regular payments of both principal and interest.
    1. Most home purchase loans are fully amortized.
    2. Alternatives to fully amortized loans are partially amortized loans and interest-only loans.

II. Repayment Period
  A. The repayment period or loan term is how long the borrower has to pay off the loan.
    1. A 30-year loan term is regarded as standard, but other terms such as 15 years and 20 years are available.
    2. A 30-year loan has a lower monthly payment than a 15-year loan, but a 15-year loan will require payment of much less interest over the life of the loan.
    3. A 15-year loan is likely to have a lower interest rate than a 30-year loan.

III. Loan-to-Value Ratio
  A. The loan-to-value ratio reflects the relationship between the loan amount and the value of the home being purchased.
  B. A loan with a lower LTV is less risky than one with a higher LTV.

IV. Mortgage Insurance or Loan Guaranty
  A. Mortgage insurance or a loan guaranty may be used to protect the lender from loss in the event of default.
  B. Mortgage insurance
    1. In exchange for mortgage insurance premiums, an insurer will indemnify a lender for any shortfall resulting from a foreclosure sale.
    2. Mortgage insurance is used in conventional and FHA loans.
  C. Loan guaranty
    1. In a loan guaranty (used in VA loans), a guarantor takes on secondary responsibility for a borrower's obligation.
    2. If the borrower defaults, the guarantor will reimburse the lender for any resulting losses.

V. Secondary Financing

A. A buyer may obtain, in addition to a primary loan, a secondary loan to cover part of the downpayment and closing costs.

B. Restrictions are placed on secondary financing, such as making sure that the borrower can afford payments on both loans.

VI. Fixed or Adjustable Interest Rate

A. A loan's interest rate can be fixed for the entire loan term, or adjustable.

B. Fixed rate loans are regarded as the standard, and were used almost exclusively until high interest rates in the 1980s encouraged use of ARMs.

C. An adjustable rate mortgage (or ARM) allows a lender to adjust the loan's interest rate periodically to reflect changes in the cost of borrowing money.

D. Adjustable rate mortgage features

1. Note rate: The initial rate stated in the promissory note is an ARM's note rate.
2. Index: A statistical report indicating changes in the cost of money, which the lender will use in order to adjust the ARM's interest rate.
3. Margin: The difference between an ARM's interest rate and the index rate, reflecting the lender's profit margin and administrative costs.
4. Rate adjustment period: The period that determines how often a lender will adjust the interest rate on an ARM.
5. Payment adjustment period: The period that determines how often a lender will adjust the payment amount on an ARM.
6. Interest rate cap: A limit on how high the interest rate for an ARM can go, either limiting how high it can go in one adjustment or a maximum rate for the entire loan.
7. Payment cap: A limit on how high the monthly payment for an ARM can go.
8. Negative amortization: When monthly payments on an ARM don't cover all of the monthly interest, thus adding to the principal balance instead of subtracting from it (which might occur if an ARM has a payment cap but no interest rate cap).
9. Conversion option: A feature allowing an ARM borrower to convert to a fixed-rate loan at certain points during the loan term.

Key Terms

Amortization: Gradually paying off a loan through installment payments that include both principal and interest.

Fully amortized loan: A loan with monthly payments that completely pay off the principal and interest by the end of the loan term.

Partially amortized loan: A loan with monthly payments that include both principal and interest, but don't pay off the entire principal amount by the end of the loan term; as a result, a balloon payment is necessary.

Interest-only loan: A loan that allows the borrower to pay only the interest due (with no principal) during the loan term, or during a specified period at the beginning of the term.

Repayment period: The number of years over which a borrower will make payments on a loan. Also called the loan term.

Loan-to-value ratio (LTV): The relationship between the loan amount and either the sales price or the appraised value of the property (whichever is less), expressed as a percentage.

Mortgage insurance: Insurance against losses resulting from mortgage default, in which an insurer will reimburse a lender for all or part of a loss.

Loan guaranty: An arrangement where a third party guarantor accepts secondary liability for a loan and will reimburse a lender for any losses from a borrower's default.

Secondary financing: Money borrowed to pay part of the required downpayment or closing costs for a first loan; this loan is secured by the same property as the first loan.

Fixed-rate loan: A mortgage loan in which the lender charges an unchanging interest rate throughout the loan term.

Adjustable-rate mortgage: A loan in which the interest rate is periodically increased or decreased to reflect changes in the cost of money; commonly called an ARM.

Note rate: The interest rate specified in a loan's promissory note; also called the coupon rate or contract rate.

Index: A published statistical report that indicates changes in the cost of money (market interest rates), used as the basis for the interest rate adjustments in an ARM.

Margin: The difference between the index rate and interest rate charged on an ARM.

Rate adjustment period: The minimum interval between adjustments of an ARM's interest rate.

Payment adjustment period: The minimum interval between adjustments of an ARM's monthly payment amount.

Interest rate cap: A provision in an ARM that limits the amount that the interest rate may be increased (or in some cases, decreased).

Mortgage payment cap: A provision in an ARM that limits the amount the monthly payment may be increased.

Negative amortization: When deferred interest on an adjustable-rate loan is added to the principal balance.

Conversion option: A provision in an adjustable rate mortgage allowing the borrower to convert the loan to a fixed rate at certain points in the loan term.

Chapter Quiz

1. Unpaid interest added to the loan balance is referred to as:
    a. payment shock
    b. a conversion option
    c. negative amortization
    d. positive amortization

2. A limit placed on the amount an ARM interest rate can increase in any given year is:
    a. an index cap
    b. a margin cap
    c. a negative amortization cap
    d. an interest rate cap

3. All of the following are disadvantages of a 15-year mortgage, except:
    a. The interest rate is higher
    b. The monthly payments are higher
    c. The mortgage interest deduction (for income tax purposes) is lost sooner
    d. A larger downpayment may be needed

4. An ARM with a conversion option:
    a. has graduated payments
    b. may be converted to a fixed-rate loan
    c. may be converted to a GEM
    d. has a negative amortization feature

5. A loan involves monthly payments of both interest and principal, but the borrower must still make a balloon payment at the end of the loan term. This is a/an:
    a. fully amortized loan
    b. partially amortized loan
    c. interest-only loan
    d. adjustable-rate loan

6. Which loan repayment period would involve paying the least amount of total interest over the life of the loan?
   a. 15 years
   b. 20 years
   c. 30 years
   d. 40 years

7. Which loan-to-value ratio would represent the greatest risk to a lender?
   a. 80%
   b. 90%
   c. 95%
   d. 97%

8. Which of the following will protect a lender against the risk of loss in the event of a borrower's default?
   a. Negative amortization
   b. Mortgage insurance
   c. Secondary financing
   d. A high loan-to-value ratio

9. When would secondary financing be used?
   a. The borrower wishes to purchase more than one property
   b. The borrower is using a VA loan
   c. The borrower has inadequate cash to make the downpayment and closing costs on the primary loan
   d. The borrower plans to finance the purchase of personal property as well as real property

10. An adjustable rate mortgage is structured so that its interest rate remains the same for the first five years, and then changes once every year for the remaining loan term. Five years and then one year would be the:
    a. payment adjustment period
    b. rate adjustment period
    c. monthly payment cap
    d. interest rate cap

Answer Key

1. c. If monthly payments for an ARM are insufficient to meet the interest charged in that particular month, the unpaid interest is added to the principal balance. This is known as negative amortization.

2. d. An interest rate cap prevents an ARM's interest rate from increasing over a particular limit, either in a given year or for the life of the loan.

3. a. The interest rate of a 15-year mortgage is typically lower, to reflect the lower risk to the lender.

4. b. An ARM with a conversion option may be converted to a fixed-rate loan at certain points in the loan term.

5. b. A partially amortized loan involves monthly payments of both principal and interest, but does not pay off the entire loan balance over the loan term, requiring a balloon payment at the end of the loan term.

6. a. Although it requires the highest monthly payments, a 15-year loan will require the lowest amount of total interest paid over the life of the loan.

7. d. The higher the loan-to-value ratio, the greater the risk to the lender. This is because a buyer who has made a larger downpayment will work harder to avoid default, and if default occurs, the lender is likelier to recover the entire loan amount in a foreclosure sale.

8. b. Mortgage insurance is used to protect a lender against the risk of loss in the event of a borrower's default, as it will reimburse a lender for some or all of a shortfall resulting from a foreclosure sale.

9. c. Secondary financing involves use of a second loan to cover some of the downpayment and closing costs associated with a first loan secured by the same property.

10. b. The rate adjustment period of an ARM dictates how frequently the interest rate may be increased or decreased.

Chapter 7
The Financing Process

Shopping for a Loan

- Assessing the buyers' circumstances
- Choosing a lender
- Loan costs
- Evaluating financing options

Applying for a Loan

- Loan interview
- Loan application form
- Disclosure statements
- Locking in the interest rate

Application Processing

- Verification
- Loan package
- Underwriting decision
  - Rejection
  - Conditional commitment
  - Preapproval letter
  - Firm commitment

Closing a Loan Transaction

- Closing agent
- Steps in the closing process

Introduction

Getting a mortgage loan can be a straightforward, painless experience, or it can turn into a complicated, time-consuming hassle that ends in disappointment. In most cases, of course, the process of getting a loan falls somewhere between those two extremes. How smoothly it goes depends on many factors, including the buyers' financial situation, how expensive a home they want, and the lender they choose. Helping buyers get through the process as easily as possible, given the circumstances, is part of a real estate agent's job.

The financing process can be broken down into these stages, and we'll look at each of them in turn:

1. shopping for a loan,
2. applying for a loan,
3. application processing, and
4. closing.

Shopping for a Loan

Home buyers should comparison shop for financing

There are more financing options available to home buyers than ever before. Buyers are encouraged to take advantage of this, to "comparison shop" and find the best type of loan for them, on the best possible terms. But so many choices can be overwhelming.

For home buyers, shopping for a mortgage loan involves:

- assessing their own wants, needs, and finances;
- choosing a lender;
- comparing rates and fees; and
- evaluating financing options.

Although we'll be treating these as separate topics, keep in mind that they aren't entirely separate steps that take place in order; instead, they overlap and influence one another. As a real estate agent, you can help buyers with all of these tasks, but they should also have the input of a financing expert: a mortgage lender.

Assessing the Buyers' Circumstances

For buyers, the starting point for mortgage shopping is really the same as the starting point for house hunting: considering what kind of home they want and need, and learning what kind of home they can afford. It's much better for the buyers if they have a realistic idea of their price range before they start house hunting in earnest.

Before shopping for a loan or a house, buyers need to assess their wants and needs and their financial situation

> **Example:** After talking about buying a home for a long time, the Morrisons have started driving through the neighborhood they like, keeping an eye out for "For Sale" signs. One day they find a house they love. It costs more than they planned to spend, but it's exactly what they want. They make a full-price offer, which the seller accepts.
>
> The Morrisons apply for a loan and start making arrangements to move into their new home. Then, to their surprise and embarrassment, their loan application is rejected. The sale, which was contingent on financing, terminates. The seller is inconvenienced and annoyed, and the Morrisons are so disappointed that they're reluctant to resume house hunting.

The events in the example could have been avoided if the buyers had known in advance how expensive a home they could afford—not just from their own point of view, but from a lender's point of view. The maximum monthly mortgage payment the buyers qualify for, together with how much money they have for a downpayment and closing costs, determines their maximum loan amount—the largest mortgage a lender will give them. The maximum loan amount plus their downpayment sets the upper limit of their price range.

Prequalifying vs. Preapproval. Home buyers can learn in advance how large a mortgage loan they'll qualify for. They can either get prequalified for a loan, or they can get preapproved for one.

Prequalifying is an informal process that can be performed either by a real estate agent or by a lender. The agent or lender asks the buyers questions about their income, assets, debts, and credit history, then uses that information to determine an affordable price range for them.

Prequalifying: informal process that may be done by a lender or a real estate agent

Preapproval, by contrast, is a formal process that can be done only by a lender. To get preapproved, buyers must complete a loan application and provide the required documentation of their income, assets, debts, and credit history, just as if they were applying for a loan after finding a house rather than beforehand. A lender evaluates an application for preapproval in the same way as an ordinary loan application, with this exception: there's no property appraisal or title report at this point, since the buyers haven't found the home they want

Preapproval: formal process that can only be done by a lender to buy yet. If the buyers are creditworthy, the lender sets a maximum loan amount based on their income and net worth. The lender gives the buyers a **preapproval letter**, agreeing to loan them up to the specified amount when they find the home they want to buy, as long as the property meets the lender's standards. (Preapproval letters are discussed in more detail later in this chapter.)

Preapproval letter states that lender will loan buyers up to a specified amount

The basic point of prequalifying and preapproval is the same. Both let the buyers know in advance how expensive a home they can afford. But preapproval has important advantages over prequalifying.

The first advantage is that a preapproval letter can be an extremely valuable tool in negotiations with a seller. It provides assurance that if the seller accepts the buyers' offer, the financing contingency won't be a problem; the buyers actually are ready, willing, and able to buy at the agreed price. (A financing contingency is a provision in a purchase and sale agreement that allows the buyers to withdraw from the contract without penalty if they can't obtain the specified financing.) At least in some parts of the country, many listing agents advise their sellers to accept offers only from preapproved buyers. Preapproval is especially important in an active real estate market, when lots of buyers are competing for desirable homes.

Advantages of preapproval:
- tool in negotiations
- streamlines the closing process

The second advantage of preapproval is that it helps streamline the closing process. The lender has already fully evaluated the buyers, and only the appraisal and title report remain to be done.

However, some buyers aren't ready to take the formal step of applying for a loan before they've even started to look for a house. They may want to get a better idea of what's available on the market and what they can afford before going any further. For these buyers, prequalifying can be a useful alternative to preapproval, at least at first. They can apply for preapproval later, after they've gotten their bearings. They shouldn't wait too long, though; it's generally advisable to get preapproved before starting to make offers.

How to Prequalify Buyers. Prequalifying buyers for financing was once a routine procedure for real estate agents. Now, in places where preapproval by a lender has become a standard practice, agents are no longer called upon to prequalify buyers very often, if at all. Even so, it's worthwhile for agents to know how prequalifying works, because it provides some practical insight into the financing process.

Prequalifying is essentially a simplified version of a mortgage lender's underwriting procedures.

Real estate agent uses simplified version of underwriting procedures to prequalify buyers

A real estate agent who's going to prequalify buyers should arrange to interview them in a quiet, private place. Most people consider their financial information confidential, and they're uncomfortable discussing it when strangers could overhear. For the same reason, the agent should make sure the buyers understand the purpose of prequalifying, so that they don't wonder why the agent is asking so many personal questions.

The agent should ask the buyers not only about their finances, but also about their motivations for buying a home, how ready to buy they feel, and their time frame for buying. Some of the questions an agent may want to ask are shown in Figure 7.1.

After getting the necessary information from the buyers, the agent's next step is to do the prequalifying calculations. A financial calculator or mortgage calculation software will be needed. If neither of these is available in the agent's office, many websites have mortgage calculators for online use.

Whatever calculation tool the real estate agent uses, this is the underlying process for prequalifying buyers:

1. Income ratios are applied to the buyers' monthly income to calculate the approximate maximum monthly mortgage payment they'll qualify for. The payment amount must cover principal, interest, taxes, and insurance, referred to as PITI. (Income ratios and PITI are covered in Chapter 8.)

PITI: Principal, interest, taxes, and insurance

2. A certain percentage representing property taxes and insurance is subtracted from the PITI figure, to arrive at an estimate of the maximum principal and interest payment.
3. This maximum principal and interest payment, along with the interest rate that would probably be charged in the current market, is used to calculate the maximum loan amount.

In prequalifying, buyers' maximum mortgage payment determines the maximum loan amount and price range ceiling

4. The maximum loan amount is divided by an appropriate loan-to-value ratio to determine the highest price the buyers should plan on paying for a home.

Fig. 7.1 Prequalifying interview questions

Prequalifying Questions

- Why do you want to buy a home?
- Have you owned a home before?
- How much thought and effort have you already put into planning to buy a new home?
- How soon would you like to move?
- Do you own your current home, or are you renting? How long have you lived there?
- Have you put your current home up for sale?
- Will you need the money from the sale of your current home to buy a new one?
- How much do you expect to get from the sale of your current home?
- Will you have to convert any other assets (such as stocks or bonds) into cash to buy a new home?
- What price range are you considering for your new home?
- For how long do you expect to own the new home?
- How much cash do you (or will you) have for a downpayment, closing costs, and reserves?
- How much do you feel you can spend for housing on a monthly basis?
- How much are your monthly expenses?
- Where are you employed? How long have you worked there?
- What is your monthly income from employment?
- Do you have any other sources of income?
- Do you expect your income to increase significantly in the near future?
- Have you had credit problems in the past?
- Have you reviewed your credit reports recently?

These steps are summarized in Figure 7.2. You'll understand them more fully after reading Chapter 8, which explains underwriting in detail. For now, here's an example to illustrate how prequalifying works:

> **Example:** Applying standard income ratios to the buyers' income and expenses, the agent calculates that they can qualify for a monthly mortgage payment of $1,941. The agent subtracts 15% as an estimate of the portion of the payment that will have to cover property taxes, hazard insurance, and mortgage insurance. The result is $1,650. That's the approximate principal and interest payment the buyers qualify for.
>
> The agent knows that in the current market they should be able to get a 30-year fixed-rate loan at 6.25% annual interest. By entering the payment amount, loan term, and interest rate into a financial calculator, the agent determines that the original principal amount of a 30-year mortgage at 6.25% interest with a monthly payment amount of $1,650 would be about $268,000. This is the buyers' maximum loan amount.
>
> The next step is to divide the loan amount by a loan-to-value ratio. The agent decides to use a 90% LTV in this case. The answer is approximately $298,000, and that's the buyers' maximum purchase price. They can qualify for a $268,000 loan to buy a $298,000 home, paying $30,000 down.

That example is just intended to give you a sense of the basic process. In real life, prequalifying is considerably more complicated. For instance, perhaps the buyers don't have $30,000 for a downpayment. In that case, they'll need to consider alternatives such as a smaller

Fig. 7.2 Steps in prequalifying a prospective home buyer

1. Apply income ratios to buyer's income and expenses to determine maximum monthly mortgage payment (PITI).
2. Subtract taxes and insurance to find maximum principal and interest payment.
3. Use current market interest rate to calculate maximum loan amount based on maximum principal and interest payment.
4. Divide maximum loan amount by loan-to-value ratio to determine ceiling of price range.

loan amount, a 95% loan-to-value ratio, or perhaps a special financing program. A lender's qualifying standards interact with factors such as the loan-to-value ratio, loan term, loan program, interest rate, and lenders' fees to create the financing options that particular buyers can afford. The more the agent knows about the alternatives, the better his or her prequalifying will be.

Remember that even though the informal prequalifying process may be useful for some buyers, formal preapproval is generally advisable as soon as the buyers feel ready to apply for it. Of course, before they can get preapproved for a loan, they'll have to choose a lender, which is our next topic.

Choosing a Lender

To choose a mortgage lender wisely, buyers first need to identify some good prospects and then use the right criteria to evaluate them.

Identifying Prospects. There are two main ways to decide which lenders to talk to: research and referrals.

Research tools for finding lenders:
- newspaper articles and ads
- yellow pages
- Internet

Research. For buyers who are willing to do some research, advertisements and articles in the business or real estate section of a local newspaper can provide leads. Looking under "Mortgages" in the yellow pages of the local telephone directory can also be useful.

An Internet search can be a good source of information about both local lenders and online lenders. Some websites allow buyers to quickly compare the interest rates and fees of several different lenders.

Of course, in print, online, or in other media, lenders' ads—like any ads—should be viewed with a skeptical eye. Even so, they're a reasonable starting point, to be followed up by making phone calls and talking to loan officers. A lender's **loan officers** are the employees who meet with loan applicants, discuss their financing needs, and help them submit their applications.

Lender referrals may come from family, friends, co-workers, real estate agents

Referrals. Referrals are often the best way to find a good lender, especially since many buyers don't have the time or inclination to do the kind of research suggested above. In addition to asking family members, friends, and co-workers who recently bought homes where they got their financing, many buyers ask their real estate agent for referrals. In fact, many rely entirely on the agent's advice. An experienced agent has typically worked with quite a few lenders and found some more knowledgeable and dependable than others. A less experienced agent should ask his or her broker or others in the office for the names of lenders to refer clients and customers to.

Mortgage brokers. A mortgage broker specializes in bringing buyers together with lenders (see Chapter 3). Deciding to consult a mortgage broker might seem to solve the problem of choosing a lender. But the buyers then have to rely on the same kind of research and referrals described above to find a good mortgage broker.

Research and referrals can help find a mortgage broker instead of a direct lender

For buyers working with a mortgage broker rather than directly with a lender, the broker performs most or all of the same tasks that loan officers do.

Buyer's own bank. When shopping for a mortgage, home buyers shouldn't overlook the financial institution where they do their banking. There may be special financing offers for established customers, and some people prefer to have one institution handle all of their financial transactions.

Interviewing Prospective Lenders. Whether buyers find prospective lenders through research or through referrals, mortgage financing experts generally think it's a good idea to talk to three or four lenders before deciding which one to submit an application to. Buyers should call each lender's office and arrange to talk to a loan officer, over the phone initially, and then in person if that lender still seems like a good prospect.

Buyers are encouraged to talk to three or four lenders, if possible

Unfortunately, many buyers don't talk to three or four lenders, often because they feel too busy, but sometimes simply because they feel too shy. Especially for unsophisticated buyers, talking to a loan officer can be intimidating. They may be embarrassed about their financial situation, or worried that they're asking stupid questions and taking up too much of the loan officer's time. Some buyers who are perfectly competent people in everyday life can become strangely passive in this context, accepting everything the loan officer says about their financing options as factual and not open to question. After meeting with a loan officer—even one who makes them uncomfortable—some buyers may feel obligated to go ahead and apply for a loan with that lender.

Of course, good loan officers won't let any of that happen. They're aware that many buyers feel intimidated, and they know how to put them at their ease. They don't take advantage of the situation and push buyers into submitting an application before they're ready.

Criteria for Choosing a Lender. Some buyers and even some real estate agents believe that one lender is much the same as another, and that the only real distinction between them is the interest rates and fees they charge. It's true that interest rates and fees are a very important consideration, and in the next section we'll discuss how to compare the rates and fees that different lenders are offering. But rates and fees shouldn't be the only consideration in choosing a lender.

Look for expertise, efficiency, and honesty, not just low interest rates and fees

Buyers should also be concerned with a lender's expertise, efficiency, and honesty. A lender might offer a low interest rate, but provide inaccurate information and slow, sloppy service. Loan officers who aren't really knowledgeable may not be aware of less common financing options that would be well suited to certain buyers. Mistakes in loan processing can delay the closing of a real estate transaction, or even derail it altogether. And if a closing cost estimate is carelessly or deceptively prepared, the buyers may be surprised by unexpected fees at closing, which can be very upsetting.

In the absence of a referral, it may be difficult to judge the competence and trustworthiness of a lender and its employees. Asking the loan officer for references from recent customers may be worthwhile. To a certain extent, however, buyers have to rely on their own impressions and instincts when they meet with a loan officer and other members of a lender's staff. Growing public awareness of predatory lending practices (see Chapter 14) may lead buyers to be more assertive and cautious when they're choosing a lender.

Loan Costs

For the majority of buyers, the primary consideration in choosing a lender is how much the loan they need is going to cost. The interest rate is the major charge for borrowing money, but it's by no means the only one. Mortgage lenders also impose a variety of other charges that can make a big difference in the cost of a loan.

Loan fees:
- Origination fee
- Discount points

One point = 1% of loan amount

Types of Loan Fees. Most significant among these other charges are origination fees and discount points, which are often grouped together and referred to as "loan fees" or as "points." The term "point" is short for "percentage point." One point is one percentage point (one percent) of the loan amount. For example, for a $100,000 loan, one point would be $1,000; six points would be $6,000.

Origination fee. An origination fee may also be called an administrative charge, a transaction fee, a service fee, or simply a loan fee. An origination fee is charged in almost every mortgage loan transaction, unless the loan is expressly designated as a "no fee" loan (discussed later in this section). Origination fees pay for the costs that a lender incurs in making loans, such as staff salaries, commissions, facilities costs, and other overhead expenses. A typical origination fee is anywhere from 1% to 3% of the loan amount. The fee is a closing cost, paid when the transaction closes, and it is usually paid by the buyer.

Origination fee covers lender's administrative costs

> **Example:** A home buyer is borrowing $325,000, and the lender is charging an origination fee of one point (one percentage point). That means the buyer must pay the lender a $3,250 origination fee at closing. ($325,000 × 1% = $3,250.)

Discount points. In some transactions, in addition to the origination fee, the lender charges discount points, also known as a loan discount, a discount fee, or simply as points. The term "points" may cause confusion. Some lenders use "points" to mean only discount points, but others use it to mean the discount points and the origination fee combined.

> **Example:** When Lender A says it's charging four points on a loan, that means four discount points. It doesn't include the origination fee that will be charged on top of the discount points.
>
> When Lender B says it's charging four points on a loan, that refers to the discount points and the origination fee combined. For instance, Lender B would refer to three discount points plus a 1% origination fee as four points. Lender B would also call two discount points plus a 2% origination fee four points.

Apparently either usage is considered correct. So when loan fees are discussed, it's important to make sure everyone involved is using "points" in the same way.

Discount points are designed to increase the lender's yield, or profit, on the loan. By charging discount points, the lender not only gets the interest on the loan throughout the life of the loan, but also collects a sum of money up front, right when the loan is funded. As a result, the lender is willing to make the loan at a lower interest rate than it would have without the points. In effect, the lender is paid a lump sum now so the borrower can avoid paying more interest later.

Discount fee increases lender's yield

Although discount points aren't charged in all transactions, they have become quite common. The number of points charged is usually directly related to how the lender's quoted interest rate compares to market interest rates; typically, lenders who offer below-market interest rates charge more points. One lender might quote an interest rate of 6.25% plus two points, while another lender quotes 6% interest with four points. Also, a given lender might offer different rates with different discounts (for example, 6% interest with four points, or 6.5% interest with no points). The choice is between paying more cash up front or more interest over the life of the loan.

Lenders with lower interest rates typically charge more points

You may come across this rule of thumb: it generally takes about six discount points to increase the lender's yield on a 30-year loan by 1%. In other words, a lender offering an interest rate 1% below market might charge six points to make up the difference. This rule of thumb provides only a very rough estimate, however. In fact, the rule of thumb is so imprecise that you may hear a different version—that it takes eight points, rather than six, to increase the yield by 1%. The actual relationship between points charged and the increase in the lender's yield is affected by several factors and varies with market conditions. Even so, the rule of thumb may help you understand how points work, and also help you explain them to buyers.

Relationship between number of points and increase in yield varies with market conditions

To determine how much a loan discount will cost, multiply the loan amount by the number of discount points.

Example: \$250,000 sales price; \$225,000 loan amount

\$225,000	Loan amount
× 3%	Discount of three points
\$6,750	Cost of loan discount

Either a buyer or a seller can pay the discount points that a lender is charging. In a buyer's market, a seller may agree to pay points to make his or her home more marketable. By paying the points, the seller makes it possible for the buyer to qualify for the loan with less cash for closing.

Points may be paid by buyer or seller

Even when the lender isn't charging points, a seller might offer to pay points to make the loan more affordable. This type of arrangement is called a **buydown**: the seller pays the lender points to "buy down" the buyer's interest rate, making the monthly loan payments smaller and easier to qualify for. (Buydowns are discussed in more detail in Chapter 10.)

When the buyer pays the points, the lump sum must be paid to the lender in cash at closing. In contrast, when the seller pays the points, the lender deducts the cost of the points from the loan amount.

> **Example:** The loan is for $170,000. The lender is charging four points, and the seller has agreed to pay the points on the buyer's behalf.
>
> When the loan is funded, the lender deducts 4% of the loan amount ($6,800) for the points. The remainder, $163,200, is delivered to the buyer to finance the purchase. The buyer signs a promissory note and mortgage agreeing to repay the entire $170,000 at the stipulated rate of interest. Thus, the lender is advancing only $163,200 but will eventually be repaid $170,000.
>
> At closing, the buyer transfers the loan funds ($163,200) to the seller without making up the difference, so the seller's net proceeds from the sale are reduced by the cost of the points. In effect, the seller paid the lender $6,800 so the buyer could get a loan at the lower quoted interest rate.

Other lender fees. In addition to interest, a loan origination fee, and discount points, mortgage lenders often charge a variety of minor fees. For example, a buyer might be required to pay the lender an application fee, a document preparation fee, or an underwriting fee.

Lenders charge a variety of minor fees in addition to main loan fees

These lender fees should be distinguished from other closing costs that relate to the loan but are paid to third parties instead of the lender. For instance, the appraisal fee and the credit report fee are paid to the appraiser and the credit reporting agency, not to the lender.

The minor fees that lenders charge vary considerably from one lender to another. Although the fees tend to be for comparatively small amounts, they may add up. If a buyer is unsure of the reason for certain fees, the loan officer should be able to provide an explanation. A buyer may also ask the loan officer if one or more fees can be reduced or waived altogether. Some lenders are quite willing to negotiate with buyers, and not just about miscellaneous fees, but also about the interest rate and points. Other lenders are not open to this type of negotiation, but there's no harm in asking.

Mortgage broker's fee. Buyers who are working with a mortgage broker are ordinarily charged a mortgage broker's fee or commission. This may be stated as a separate fee or included in the points quoted for the loan. Buyers should ask their broker about his or her compensation. (In some states, mortgage brokers are required by law to disclose this information to buyers.)

Mortgage broker's compensation doesn't necessarily make loan more expensive for buyer

As a general rule, the mortgage broker's compensation doesn't make a loan obtained through a mortgage broker more expensive than one obtained directly from a lender. Mortgage brokers deal with wholesale lenders (see Chapter 3) who offer their loans to brokers at wholesale prices. The brokers mark the loans up to retail prices and keep the markup as their compensation. The retail price that buyers pay is typically quite close to the market rate they'd be paying if they had gotten their loan directly from a retail lender, without a mortgage broker's help.

Comparing Loan Costs. Because different lenders charge different origination fees, loan discounts, and other fees, it becomes difficult to accurately compare the cost of two or more loans. For example, if one lender is quoting a 5.75% interest rate with four points, and another lender is quoting a 6% rate with two points, which loan is less expensive? The first loan (5.75% with four points) happens to be slightly less expensive, but it isn't easy to tell that just by looking at the lenders' quotes.

Truth in Lending Act requires loan costs to be disclosed to borrowers

A law that's intended to help loan applicants with this type of problem is the **Truth in Lending Act** (TILA), one of the federal consumer protection laws covered in Chapter 14. Under TILA, lenders must make certain disclosures to consumer loan applicants so that they'll understand exactly how much they're paying for credit. This information enables loan applicants to compare loan costs and shop around for the best terms.

Annual percentage rate (APR): relationship of total finance charge to loan amount

The most important disclosure required is the **annual percentage rate** (APR). The APR expresses the relationship of the **total finance charge** to the total amount financed (that is, the amount borrowed) as an annual percentage. In addition to interest, all of the following would be included in the total finance charge: the origination fee; any discount points paid by the buyer; a mortgage broker's fee, finder's fee, or service fee; and mortgage guaranty or insurance fees. (Title insurance costs, credit report charges, the appraisal fee, and points paid by the seller would not be included in the total finance charge.)

Because interest is rarely the only fee that a mortgage lender charges, the APR of a mortgage loan is almost always higher than the quoted interest rate. For example, a loan with an interest rate of 7% might have an APR of 7.32%, because the APR takes into account the origination fee and the mortgage insurance as well as the interest.

Fig. 7.3 Annual percentage rate chart

Annual Percentage Rates for 15-Year Mortgages with Points

Points	0	0.5	1.0	1.5	2.0	2.5	3.0	3.5	4.0	4.5
	5.00	5.08	5.15	5.23	5.31	5.39	5.47	5.55	5.63	5.71
	5.25	5.33	5.40	5.48	5.56	5.64	5.72	5.80	5.88	5.96
	5.50	5.58	5.66	5.73	5.81	5.89	5.97	6.05	6.13	6.22
	5.75	5.83	5.91	5.99	6.06	6.14	6.23	6.31	6.39	6.47
	6.00	6.08	6.16	6.24	6.32	6.40	6.48	6.56	6.64	6.73
	6.25	6.33	6.41	6.49	6.57	6.65	6.73	6.82	6.90	6.98
	6.50	6.58	6.66	6.74	6.82	6.90	6.99	7.07	7.15	7.24
	6.75	6.83	6.91	6.99	7.07	7.16	7.24	7.32	7.41	7.49
	7.00	7.08	7.16	7.24	7.33	7.41	7.49	7.58	7.66	7.75
	7.25	7.33	7.41	7.50	7.58	7.66	7.75	7.83	7.92	8.00
	7.50	7.58	7.66	7.75	7.83	7.92	8.00	8.09	8.17	8.26
	7.75	7.83	7.92	8.00	8.08	8.17	8.25	8.34	8.43	8.52
	8.00	8.08	8.17	8.25	8.34	8.42	8.51	8.59	8.68	8.77
	8.25	8.33	8.42	8.50	8.59	8.67	8.76	8.85	8.94	9.03
	8.50	8.58	8.67	8.75	8.84	8.93	9.02	9.10	9.19	9.28
	8.75	8.83	8.92	9.01	9.09	9.18	9.27	9.36	9.45	9.54
	9.00	9.09	9.17	9.26	9.35	9.43	9.52	9.61	9.70	9.79
	9.25	9.34	9.42	9.51	9.60	9.69	9.78	9.87	9.96	10.05
	9.50	9.59	9.67	9.76	9.85	9.94	10.03	10.12	10.21	10.31
	9.75	9.84	9.93	10.01	10.10	10.19	10.29	10.38	10.47	10.56
	10.00	10.09	10.18	10.27	10.36	10.45	10.54	10.63	10.72	10.82
	10.25	10.34	10.43	10.52	10.61	10.70	10.79	10.89	10.98	11.07
	10.50	10.59	10.68	10.77	10.86	10.95	11.05	11.14	11.24	11.33
	10.75	10.84	10.93	11.02	11.11	11.21	11.30	11.40	11.49	11.59

Annual Percentage Rates for 30-Year Mortgages with Points

Points	0	0.5	1.0	1.5	2.0	2.5	3.0	3.5	4.0	4.5
	5.00	5.04	5.09	5.13	5.18	5.22	5.27	5.32	5.36	5.41
	5.25	5.29	5.34	5.39	5.43	5.48	5.52	5.57	5.62	5.67
	5.50	5.55	5.59	5.64	5.68	5.73	5.78	5.83	5.87	5.92
	5.75	5.80	5.84	5.89	5.94	5.98	6.03	6.08	6.13	6.18
	6.00	6.05	6.09	6.14	6.19	6.24	6.29	6.34	6.39	6.44
	6.25	6.30	6.35	6.39	6.44	6.49	6.54	6.59	6.64	6.69
	6.50	6.55	6.60	6.65	6.70	6.75	6.80	6.85	6.90	6.95
	6.75	6.80	6.85	6.90	6.95	7.00	7.05	7.10	7.15	7.21
	7.00	7.05	7.10	7.15	7.20	7.25	7.30	7.36	7.41	7.46
	7.25	7.30	7.35	7.40	7.45	7.51	7.56	7.61	7.67	7.72
	7.50	7.55	7.60	7.66	7.71	7.76	7.81	7.87	7.92	7.98
	7.75	7.80	7.85	7.91	7.96	8.01	8.07	8.12	8.18	8.23
	8.00	8.05	8.11	8.16	8.21	8.27	8.32	8.38	8.44	8.49
	8.25	8.30	8.36	8.41	8.47	8.52	8.58	8.64	8.69	8.75
	8.50	8.55	8.61	8.66	8.72	8.78	8.83	8.89	8.95	9.01
	8.75	8.81	8.86	8.92	8.97	9.03	9.09	9.15	9.21	9.27
	9.00	9.06	9.11	9.17	9.23	9.29	9.34	9.40	9.46	9.52
	9.25	9.31	9.36	9.42	9.48	9.54	9.60	9.66	9.72	9.78
	9.50	9.56	9.62	9.68	9.73	9.79	9.85	9.92	9.98	10.04
	9.75	9.81	9.87	9.93	9.99	10.05	10.11	10.17	10.23	10.30
	10.00	10.06	10.12	10.18	10.24	10.30	10.37	10.43	10.49	10.56
	10.25	10.31	10.37	10.43	10.50	10.56	10.62	10.69	10.75	10.81
	10.50	10.56	10.62	10.69	10.75	10.81	10.88	10.94	11.01	11.07
	10.75	10.81	10.88	10.94	11.00	11.07	11.13	11.20	11.26	11.33

Compare APRs, not just interest rates

To determine which of two or more loans is the least expensive, it's necessary to compare the APRs quoted by the lenders. A buyer who compares only the quoted interest rates can easily be misled. A lender might quote a very low interest rate, but charge an unusually large origination fee or several discount points. In that case, the total cost of the loan may in fact be much greater than the cost of a loan from a competitor who is quoting a higher interest rate. The APRs of the two loans will reveal this difference in cost.

While a buyer won't get a Truth in Lending Act disclosure statement before actually applying for a loan, it's possible to get an estimate of a loan's APR by calling the lender. As long as the interest rate, origination fee, and discount fee are known, a chart like the one in Figure 7.3 can be used to estimate the APR. (Note that on this chart, "Points" refers to the origination fee and the discount fee combined.)

No-fee Loans. Some lenders offer no-fee loans. As the name suggests, the lender doesn't charge any of the loan fees a home buyer is typically expected to pay, such as an origination fee, discount points, or miscellaneous other lender fees. The interest is the only finance charge. As a result, the APR is the same as the interest rate.

No-fee loan reduces amount of money needed for closing

A no-fee loan can be very helpful for buyers who don't have much cash for closing. However, the interest rate on a no-fee loan is likely to be significantly higher than the rate on a comparable loan with typical fees. As a result, the two loans might have very similar APRs. Once again, the choice is between paying fees up front or paying additional interest over the long term.

The same is true with financed closing costs, another option for cash-strapped buyers. The lender charges loan fees, but the fees and certain other closing costs are added to the loan amount and paid as part of the mortgage payments rather than at closing. Of course, interest is charged on the financed costs as well as the loan principal.

Evaluating Financing Options

When it comes time for buyers to evaluate their financing options and choose the loan they want, loan costs—interest rates, origination fees, discount points, and other lender charges—will naturally be a key consideration. But the buyers also have to consider how each of the different financing options is structured, and how each would affect their overall financial situation in the short term and the long term. In addition, they need to consider what impact each option would have on the house they'll be able to buy. Would the financing enable them to buy a big enough house? Which neighborhoods would they be able to afford? Would they have enough money for furniture or necessary remodeling? All of these issues are part of choosing a loan.

Buyers should ask themselves the following questions in connection with any mortgage loan they consider:

- How much money would we have left in savings after the transaction closes?
- How much spending money would we have left over each month after paying the mortgage payment?
- At what pace do we anticipate that our income will grow?
- How long do we plan to stay in the home we're buying?
- How rapidly would our equity build?
- How soon would the mortgage be paid off?
- Are we more concerned with the short-term cost of financing or the long-term cost?
- What alternative investment opportunities are available for money we don't put into the house?

The answers to these questions can affect a buyer's financing decision in a variety of ways. For example, some buyers are only planning to live in the house they're purchasing for a few years. These buyers might be good candidates for a loan with an adjustable interest rate. They can take advantage of a low initial rate without worrying about how high the rate may rise ten years from now.

Length of time buyers expect to own their new house may affect financing choices

Also, when buyers don't expect to own the house they're buying for very long, it generally doesn't make sense to pay a lot of discount points to get a lower interest rate. Only a fairly long period of ownership will enable the buyers to recoup the money paid up front with interest savings over the long run.

Buyers who hope to retire early or reduce their workload may be most concerned with building equity and paying off their mortgage as soon as possible. They might prefer a loan with a 15-year or 20-year term, rather than the standard 30-year term, even though it means they will qualify for a smaller loan amount and have to buy a less expensive home than they otherwise could.

Many first-time buyers with limited buying power want to purchase the largest, most expensive home they can possibly afford. They are interested in any and all financing arrangements that can boost their price range: a downpayment assistance program, an adjustable interest rate, a high loan-to-value ratio, a 40-year loan term, secondary financing, and so on.

On the other hand, some buyers don't want to borrow as much money for a house as lenders would allow them to. They may want to invest their money differently, or they may simply prefer to avoid the financial stress that the maximum monthly mortgage payment would represent for them.

In short, buyers must evaluate every financing option in light of their own circumstances, goals, and preferences. Through qualifying standards, a lender takes certain aspects of the buyers' situation into account before agreeing to make a loan. But only the buyers themselves can decide which financing alternative is most comfortable for them and fits in best with their own financial plans.

Home Buyer Counseling Programs. Borrowing money to buy a house is such a complicated decision that it overwhelms many buyers, especially first-time buyers. In addition to asking real estate agents and loan officers for information and guidance, first-time buyers could benefit from participating in home buyer counseling before they decide what financing option will be best for them.

HUD-approved housing counseling may be helpful to first-time home buyers

The Department of Housing and Urban Development (HUD) has developed a Housing Counseling Assistance Program that's open to anyone who is going to be house hunting and applying for a mortgage. (It's also open to renters and people who already own a home.) The counseling is provided by HUD-approved housing counseling agencies around the country. It's intended to educate participants about the responsibilities of home ownership (or tenancy): making mortgage or rent payments, maintaining the home, avoiding foreclosure or eviction, and so on.

A buyer who enrolls in a counseling program starts off with a confidential interview with a housing counselor; additional services depend on the buyer's needs. As a general rule, participation in counseling is entirely voluntary, but eligibility for certain HUD programs may require a certificate from a housing counselor verifying that a counseling program has been completed.

Applying for a Loan

After shopping for a loan and choosing a lender, the next step is to fill out a loan application. The application isn't intended for people who are merely inquiring about mortgage loans, but for home buyers who plan to follow through and actually borrow the funds if the loan is approved.

The Loan Interview

To apply for a mortgage loan (or for preapproval), the home buyers or their real estate agent set up an appointment with a loan officer. This may be referred to as a loan interview or an application meeting. It's traditionally a face-to-face meeting between the buyers and the loan officer, but in some cases the interview may take place over the phone, by fax, or online.

In loan interview, buyers discuss financing options with loan officer and fill out application form

Prequalifying During the Interview. In the loan interview, the buyers and the loan officer will discuss the financing options the buyers have been considering and the loan programs that the lender offers. The loan officer will help the buyers decide which program best suits their needs.

While talking with the buyers, the loan officer may enter some key information about their finances into an automated underwriting system or other computer program. The system can provide a preliminary evaluation of what kind of loan the buyers are likely to qualify for. The loan officer can use it to try out alternatives: How large a loan could the buyers qualify for if they made a $20,000 downpayment? What if they put only $15,000 down? What if they chose an adjustable-rate mortgage instead of a fixed-rate loan? In effect, the loan officer is using the system to prequalify the buyers, before their application is formally submitted.

However, even if the system indicates at this stage that the buyers will qualify for the loan they want, that usually doesn't mean they've been preapproved for the loan. Preapproval won't take place until the buyers' application and the supporting documentation have been fully analyzed. Although automated underwriting systems have streamlined the approval process, it's still unusual for buyers to qualify for the loan they want so easily that it can be approved on the spot.

Deposit. At the loan interview, the buyers will be required to make a deposit to cover certain expenses that must be paid up front. Depending

Most lenders require buyers to make a deposit to cover initial costs when application is submitted

on the lender, these may include an application fee, a credit report fee, and other preliminary charges.

Loan officer reviews purchase and sale agreement for financing terms and closing date

Contract and Closing Date. If the buyers have already found the home they want to buy and have entered into a purchase and sale agreement with the sellers, the loan officer will ask for a copy of the agreement at the loan interview. In examining the agreement, the loan officer will pay particular attention to the terms of the financing contingency clause and the agreed-upon closing date. The agreement may set a closing date that's too soon to be realistic; the financing, inspections, or other arrangements may not be completed in time. If the loan officer feels the closing date should be changed, he or she will consult with the real estate agent, who will explain the problem to the parties. When everyone has agreed on a more suitable date, the agent will have the buyers and sellers sign an amendment to the purchase and sale agreement.

The Loan Application Form

Lenders want their loans to be repaid without collection problems, and they try to make loans only to borrowers who can be expected to repay on time, as agreed. The purpose of the loan application is to gather the information the lender needs to determine whether the applicants will be reliable borrowers. It focuses on employment stability, income, and net worth.

Some lenders prefer to have the loan officer review the buyers' loan application before the loan interview takes place. The buyers are asked to complete the form on their own and send it in by mail, e-mail, or fax before the interview appointment.

More commonly, the buyers are asked to come to the interview prepared to fill out the application form with the loan officer. If they don't bring all of the necessary information with them, the buyers will have to provide the missing information later, and that could delay the application process. The real estate agent working with the buyers should make sure they know in advance what information will be needed.

Uniform Residential Loan Application form is used by virtually all mortgage lenders

Virtually all mortgage lenders use the Uniform Residential Loan Application form shown in Figure 7.4. We'll go through the form to give you an overview of the information it requires.

Type and Terms of Loan. The application begins with questions about the loan being applied for: the type of loan, loan amount, loan term,

Fig. 7.4 Uniform Residential Loan Application form

Uniform Residential Loan Application

This application is designed to be completed by the applicant(s) with the Lender's assistance. Applicants should complete this form as "Borrower" or "Co-Borrower," as applicable. Co-Borrower information must also be provided (and the appropriate box checked) when ☐ the income or assets of a person other than the Borrower (including the Borrower's spouse) will be used as a basis for loan qualification or ☐ the income or assets of the Borrower's spouse or other person who has community property rights pursuant to state law will not be used as a basis for loan qualification, but his or her liabilities must be considered because the spouse or other person has community property rights pursuant to applicable law and Borrower resides in a community property state, the security property is located in a community property state, or the Borrower is relying on other property located in a community property state as a basis for repayment of the loan.

If this is an application for joint credit, Borrower and Co-Borrower each agree that we intend to apply for joint credit (sign below):

Borrower ______________________ Co-Borrower ______________________

I. TYPE OF MORTGAGE AND TERMS OF LOAN

Mortgage Applied for:	☐ VA ☐ FHA	☐ Conventional ☐ USDA/Rural Housing Service	☐ Other (explain):	Agency Case Number	Lender Case Number

Amount $	Interest Rate %	No. of Months	**Amortization Type:**	☐ Fixed Rate ☐ GPM	☐ Other (explain): ☐ ARM (type):

II. PROPERTY INFORMATION AND PURPOSE OF LOAN

Subject Property Address (street, city, state & ZIP)	No. of Units
Legal Description of Subject Property (attach description if necessary)	Year Built

Purpose of Loan	☐ Purchase ☐ Refinance	☐ Construction ☐ Construction-Permanent	☐ Other (explain):	Property will be: ☐ Primary Residence ☐ Secondary Residence ☐ Investment

Complete this line if construction or construction-permanent loan.

Year Lot Acquired	Original Cost	Amount Existing Liens	(a) Present Value of Lot	(b) Cost of Improvements	Total (a + b)
	$	$	$	$	$

Complete this line if this is a refinance loan.

Year Acquired	Original Cost	Amount Existing Liens	Purpose of Refinance	Describe Improvements ☐ made ☐ to be made
	$	$		Cost: $

Title will be held in what Name(s)	Manner in which Title will be held	Estate will be held in: ☐ Fee Simple ☐ Leasehold (show expiration date)
Source of Down Payment, Settlement Charges, and/or Subordinate Financing (explain)		

III. BORROWER INFORMATION

Borrower				Co-Borrower			
Borrower's Name (include Jr. or Sr. if applicable)				Co-Borrower's Name (include Jr. or Sr. if applicable)			
Social Security Number	Home Phone (incl. area code)	DOB (mm/dd/yyyy)	Yrs. School	Social Security Number	Home Phone (incl. area code)	DOB (mm/dd/yyyy)	Yrs. School
☐ Married ☐ Unmarried (include ☐ Separated single, divorced, widowed)	Dependents (not listed by Co-Borrower) no. ages			☐ Married ☐ Unmarried (include ☐ Separated single, divorced, widowed)	Dependents (not listed by Borrower) no. ages		
Present Address (street, city, state, ZIP) ☐ Own ☐ Rent ___No. Yrs.				Present Address (street, city, state, ZIP) ☐ Own ☐ Rent ___No. Yrs.			
Mailing Address, if different from Present Address				Mailing Address, if different from Present Address			

If residing at present address for less than two years, complete the following:

Former Address (street, city, state, ZIP) ☐ Own ☐ Rent ___No. Yrs.	Former Address (street, city, state, ZIP) ☐ Own ☐ Rent ___No. Yrs.

IV. EMPLOYMENT INFORMATION

Borrower			Co-Borrower		
Name & Address of Employer	☐ Self Employed	Yrs. on this job Yrs. employed in this line of work/profession	Name & Address of Employer	☐ Self Employed	Yrs. on this job Yrs. employed in this line of work/profession
Position/Title/Type of Business	Business Phone (incl. area code)		Position/Title/Type of Business	Business Phone (incl. area code)	

If employed in current position for less than two years or if currently employed in more than one position, complete the following:

Freddie Mac Form 65 7/05 **Page 1 of 5** **Fannie Mae Form 1003 7/05**

IV. EMPLOYMENT INFORMATION (cont'd)

Borrower			Co-Borrower		
Name & Address of Employer	☐ Self Employed	Dates (from – to) Monthly Income $	Name & Address of Employer	☐ Self Employed	Dates (from – to) Monthly Income $
Position/Title/Type of Business	Business Phone (incl. area code)		Position/Title/Type of Business	Business Phone (incl. area code)	
Name & Address of Employer	☐ Self Employed	Dates (from – to) Monthly Income $	Name & Address of Employer	☐ Self Employed	Dates (from – to) Monthly Income $
Position/Title/Type of Business	Business Phone (incl. area code)		Position/Title/Type of Business	Business Phone (incl. area code)	

V. MONTHLY INCOME AND COMBINED HOUSING EXPENSE INFORMATION

Gross Monthly Income	Borrower	Co-Borrower	Total	Combined Monthly Housing Expense	Present	Proposed
Base Empl. Income*	$	$	$	Rent	$	
Overtime				First Mortgage (P&I)		$
Bonuses				Other Financing (P&I)		
Commissions				Hazard Insurance		
Dividends/Interest				Real Estate Taxes		
Net Rental Income				Mortgage Insurance		
Other (before completing, see the notice in "describe other income," below)				Homeowner Assn. Dues		
				Other:		
Total	$	$	$	**Total**	$	$

* **Self Employed Borrower(s) may be required to provide additional documentation such as tax returns and financial statements.**

Describe Other Income

Notice: **Alimony, child support, or separate maintenance income need not be revealed if the Borrower (B) or Co-Borrower (C) does not choose to have it considered for repaying this loan.**

B/C		Monthly Amount
		$

VI. ASSETS AND LIABILITIES

This Statement and any applicable supporting schedules may be completed jointly by both married and unmarried Co-Borrowers if their assets and liabilities are sufficiently joined so that the Statement can be meaningfully and fairly presented on a combined basis; otherwise, separate Statements and Schedules are required. If the Co-Borrower section was completed about a non-applicant spouse or other person, this Statement and supporting schedules must be completed about that spouse or other person also.

Completed ☐ Jointly ☐ Not Jointly

ASSETS Description	Cash or Market Value
Cash deposit toward purchase held by:	$

Liabilities and Pledged Assets. List the creditor's name, address, and account number for all outstanding debts, including automobile loans, revolving charge accounts, real estate loans, alimony, child support, stock pledges, etc. Use continuation sheet, if necessary. Indicate by (*) those liabilities, which will be satisfied upon sale of real estate owned or upon refinancing of the subject property.

List checking and savings accounts below		LIABILITIES	Monthly Payment & Months Left to Pay	Unpaid Balance
Name and address of Bank, S&L, or Credit Union		Name and address of Company	$ Payment/Months	$
Acct. no.	$	Acct. no.		
Name and address of Bank, S&L, or Credit Union		Name and address of Company	$ Payment/Months	$
Acct. no.	$	Acct. no.		
Name and address of Bank, S&L, or Credit Union		Name and address of Company	$ Payment/Months	$
Acct. no.	$	Acct. no.		

Freddie Mac Form 65 7/05 **Page 2 of 5** **Fannie Mae Form 1003 7/05**

VI. ASSETS AND LIABILITIES (cont'd)

Name and address of Bank, S&L, or Credit Union		Name and address of Company	$ Payment/Months	$
Acct. no.	$	Acct. no.		
Stocks & Bonds (Company name/ number & description)	$	Name and address of Company	$ Payment/Months	$
		Acct. no.		
Life insurance net cash value Face amount: $	$	Name and address of Company	$ Payment/Months	$
Subtotal Liquid Assets	$			
Real estate owned (enter market value from schedule of real estate owned)	$			
Vested interest in retirement fund	$			
Net worth of business(es) owned (attach financial statement)	$	Acct. no.		
Automobiles owned (make and year)	$	Alimony/Child Support/Separate Maintenance Payments Owed to:	$	
Other Assets (itemize)	$	Job-Related Expense (child care, union dues, etc.)	$	
		Total Monthly Payments	$	
Total Assets a.	$	Net Worth (a minus b) ▶ $	**Total Liabilities b.**	$

Schedule of Real Estate Owned (If additional properties are owned, use continuation sheet.)

Property Address (enter S if sold, PS if pending sale or R if rental being held for income) ▼		Type of Property	Present Market Value	Amount of Mortgages & Liens	Gross Rental Income	Mortgage Payments	Insurance, Maintenance, Taxes & Misc.	Net Rental Income
			$	$	$	$	$	$
		Totals	$	$	$	$	$	$

List any additional names under which credit has previously been received and indicate appropriate creditor name(s) and account number(s):

Alternate Name	Creditor Name	Account Number

VII. DETAILS OF TRANSACTION

a.	Purchase price	$
b.	Alterations, improvements, repairs	
c.	Land (if acquired separately)	
d.	Refinance (incl. debts to be paid off)	
e.	Estimated prepaid items	
f.	Estimated closing costs	
g.	PMI, MIP, Funding Fee	
h.	Discount (if Borrower will pay)	
i.	Total costs (add items a through h)	

VIII. DECLARATIONS

If you answer "Yes" to any questions a through i, please use continuation sheet for explanation.	**Borrower** Yes	No	**Co-Borrower** Yes	No
a. Are there any outstanding judgments against you?	☐	☐	☐	☐
b. Have you been declared bankrupt within the past 7 years?	☐	☐	☐	☐
c. Have you had property foreclosed upon or given title or deed in lieu thereof in the last 7 years?	☐	☐	☐	☐
d. Are you a party to a lawsuit?	☐	☐	☐	☐
e. Have you directly or indirectly been obligated on any loan which resulted in foreclosure, transfer of title in lieu of foreclosure, or judgment? (This would include such loans as home mortgage loans, SBA loans, home improvement loans, educational loans, manufactured (mobile) home loans, any mortgage, financial obligation, bond, or loan guarantee. If "Yes," provide details, including date, name, and address of Lender, FHA or VA case number, if any, and reasons for the action.)	☐	☐	☐	☐

Freddie Mac Form 65 7/05 **Page 3 of 5** **Fannie Mae Form 1003 7/05**

VII. DETAILS OF TRANSACTION		
j.	Subordinate financing	
k.	Borrower's closing costs paid by Seller	
l.	Other Credits (explain)	
m.	Loan amount (exclude PMI, MIP, Funding Fee financed)	
n.	PMI, MIP, Funding Fee financed	
o.	Loan amount (add m & n)	
p.	Cash from/to Borrower (subtract j, k, l & o from i)	

VIII. DECLARATIONS	Borrower Yes	Borrower No	Co-Borrower Yes	Co-Borrower No
If you answer "Yes" to any questions a through i, please use continuation sheet for explanation.				
f. Are you presently delinquent or in default on any Federal debt or any other loan, mortgage, financial obligation, bond, or loan guarantee? If "Yes," give details as described in the preceding question.	☐	☐	☐	☐
g. Are you obligated to pay alimony, child support, or separate maintenance?	☐	☐	☐	☐
h. Is any part of the down payment borrowed?	☐	☐	☐	☐
i. Are you a co-maker or endorser on a note?	☐	☐	☐	☐
j. Are you a U.S. citizen?	☐	☐	☐	☐
k. Are you a permanent resident alien?	☐	☐	☐	☐
l. **Do you intend to occupy the property as your primary residence?** If "Yes," complete question m below.	☐	☐	☐	☐
m. Have you had an ownership interest in a property in the last three years?	☐	☐	☐	☐
(1) What type of property did you own—principal residence (PR), second home (SH), or investment property (IP)?	______		______	
(2) How did you hold title to the home—solely by yourself (S), jointly with your spouse (SP), or jointly with another person (O)?	______		______	

IX. ACKNOWLEDGEMENT AND AGREEMENT

Each of the undersigned specifically represents to Lender and to Lender's actual or potential agents, brokers, processors, attorneys, insurers, servicers, successors and assigns and agrees and acknowledges that: (1) the information provided in this application is true and correct as of the date set forth opposite my signature and that any intentional or negligent misrepresentation of this information contained in this application may result in civil liability, including monetary damages, to any person who may suffer any loss due to reliance upon any misrepresentation that I have made on this application, and/or in criminal penalties including, but not limited to, fine or imprisonment or both under the provisions of Title 18, United States Code, Sec. 1001, et seq.; (2) the loan requested pursuant to this application (the "Loan") will be secured by a mortgage or deed of trust on the property described in this application; (3) the property will not be used for any illegal or prohibited purpose or use; (4) all statements made in this application are made for the purpose of obtaining a residential mortgage loan; (5) the property will be occupied as indicated in this application; (6) the Lender, its servicers, successors or assigns may retain the original and/or an electronic record of this application, whether or not the Loan is approved; (7) the Lender and its agents, brokers, insurers, servicers, successors, and assigns may continuously rely on the information contained in the application, and I am obligated to amend and/or supplement the information provided in this application if any of the material facts that I have represented herein should change prior to closing of the Loan; (8) in the event that my payments on the Loan become delinquent, the Lender, its servicers, successors or assigns may, in addition to any other rights and remedies that it may have relating to such delinquency, report my name and account information to one or more consumer reporting agencies; (9) ownership of the Loan and/or administration of the Loan account may be transferred with such notice as may be required by law; (10) neither Lender nor its agents, brokers, insurers, servicers, successors or assigns has made any representation or warranty, express or implied, to me regarding the property or the condition or value of the property; and (11) my transmission of this application as an "electronic record" containing my "electronic signature," as those terms are defined in applicable federal and/or state laws (excluding audio and video recordings), or my facsimile transmission of this application containing a facsimile of my signature, shall be as effective, enforceable and valid as if a paper version of this application were delivered containing my original written signature.

Acknowledgement. Each of the undersigned hereby acknowledges that any owner of the Loan, its servicers, successors and assigns, may verify or reverify any information contained in this application or obtain any information or data relating to the Loan, for any legitimate business purpose through any source, including a source named in this application or a consumer reporting agency.

Borrower's Signature	Date	Co-Borrower's Signature	Date
X		X	

X. INFORMATION FOR GOVERNMENT MONITORING PURPOSES

The following information is requested by the Federal Government for certain types of loans related to a dwelling in order to monitor the lender's compliance with equal credit opportunity, fair housing and home mortgage disclosure laws. You are not required to furnish this information, but are encouraged to do so. The law provides that a lender may not discriminate either on the basis of this information, or on whether you choose to furnish it. If you furnish the information, please provide both ethnicity and race. For race, you may check more than one designation. If you do not furnish ethnicity, race, or sex, under Federal regulations, this lender is required to note the information on the basis of visual observation and surname if you have made this application in person. If you do not wish to furnish the information, please check the box below. (Lender must review the above material to assure that the disclosures satisfy all requirements to which the lender is subject under applicable state law for the particular type of loan applied for.)

BORROWER ☐ I do not wish to furnish this information	**CO-BORROWER** ☐ I do not wish to furnish this information
Ethnicity: ☐ Hispanic or Latino ☐ Not Hispanic or Latino	**Ethnicity:** ☐ Hispanic or Latino ☐ Not Hispanic or Latino
Race: ☐ American Indian or Alaska Native ☐ Asian ☐ Black or African American ☐ Native Hawaiian or Other Pacific Islander ☐ White	**Race:** ☐ American Indian or Alaska Native ☐ Asian ☐ Black or African American ☐ Native Hawaiian or Other Pacific Islander ☐ White
Sex: ☐ Female ☐ Male	**Sex:** ☐ Female ☐ Male

To be Completed by Interviewer	Interviewer's Name (print or type)	Name and Address of Interviewer's Employer
This application was taken by: ☐ Face-to-face interview ☐ Mail ☐ Telephone ☐ Internet	Interviewer's Signature — Date	
	Interviewer's Phone Number (incl. area code)	

Freddie Mac Form 65 7/05 **Page 4 of 5** **Fannie Mae Form 1003 7/05**

CONTINUATION SHEET/RESIDENTIAL LOAN APPLICATION

Use this continuation sheet if you need more space to complete the Residential Loan Application. Mark **B** f or Borrower or **C** for Co-Borrower.	Borrower:	Agency Case Number:
	Co-Borrower:	Lender Case Number:

I/We fully understand that it is a Federal crime punishable by fine or imprisonment, or both, to knowingly make any false statements concerning any of the above facts as applicable under the provisions of Title 18, United States Code, Section 1001, et seq.

Borrower's Signature **X**	Date	Co-Borrower's Signature **X**	Date

Freddie Mac Form 65 7/05 **Page 5 of 5** **Fannie Mae Form 1003 7/05**

interest rate, whether the rate will be fixed or adjustable, and whether the loan will involve any special amortization arrangement.

Property Information and Purpose of Loan. The next section of the application calls for the address and legal description of the property and when the house was built. (If the applicants are applying for preapproval and haven't found a house yet, this part of the form is left blank for now.) It also asks the purpose of the loan (purchase, construction, or refinance; primary residence, secondary residence, or investment property); the manner in which the buyers will take title (for example, as tenants in common); and the source of the downpayment, settlement charges (closing costs), and any secondary financing. This information will be used to order an appraisal of the property and to determine the maximum loan amount.

Borrower and Co-Borrower Information. The next section of the form requests the following information about each applicant: name, social security number, phone number, date of birth, years of schooling, marital status, and address. The lender also wants to know how many dependents the applicants must support, since children and other dependents may add considerably to their financial obligations. If the applicants have lived at their present address for less than two years, information about previous residences must also be provided.

Although it's legal for a lender to ask about a loan applicant's marital status and dependents, it's illegal for the lender to use that information in a discriminatory fashion. (See the discussion of the Equal Credit Opportunity Act, in Chapter 14.)

Lender uses application form to gather information about the applicant's employment stability, income, and net worth

Employment Information. Each applicant must fill in the name and address of his or her employer, the number of years employed at this job, and the number of years employed in this line of work. The position, title, type of business, and business phone number must also be included. If an applicant has been at his or her current job for less than two years, the same information must be given for previous employers.

Income and Monthly Housing Expense Information. This section requests information about primary employment income, overtime, bonuses, commissions, dividends and interest, net rental income, and income from any other sources. Each applicant must list his or her current monthly housing expense—either the rent or the house payment (including principal and interest, hazard insurance, property taxes, mortgage insurance, and homeowners association dues).

Assets and Liabilities. In the next section of the form, each loan applicant lists all of his or her assets and liabilities. Assets include the good faith deposit or earnest money given to the seller (if a purchase and sale agreement has been signed), money in checking and savings accounts, stocks and bonds, life insurance policies, retirement funds, automobiles, other personal property, and real estate already owned. (For real estate, a separate schedule on page 3 of the form must be filled out.) If the applicants own a business, they're supposed to list its net worth and attach a financial statement to the application form.

Assets may include:
- good faith deposit
- money in bank
- investments
- life insurance policy
- retirement account
- automobile
- personal property
- real property

The applicants' liabilities may include student loans, car loans, real estate loans, and other installment debts; revolving credit (charge accounts and credit cards); alimony and/or child support payments; child care expenses; and job-related expenses such as union dues. The applicants should also be prepared to list debts that have recently been paid off.

Liabilities may include:
- student loan
- car loan
- real estate loan
- other installment loan
- charge accounts
- credit cards
- alimony or child support owed
- job-related expenses

Details of Transaction. The next section asks for information on the real estate transaction itself. (Again, if the applicants are applying for preapproval and haven't found a house yet, this section will be left blank for the time being.) The applicants are to fill in the purchase price, the cost of alterations or improvements, the cost of the land (if the land is acquired separately), prepaid expenses, and closing costs. There are also blanks for the mortgage insurance or funding fee, discount fee, any secondary financing, any closing costs to be paid by the seller, and the loan amount. The lender will use these figures to calculate the cash the applicants will need to close the transaction.

Declarations. The loan applicants must answer several questions regarding outstanding judgments, bankruptcies, property foreclosures, lawsuits, loan defaults, and alimony or child support payments. Then the application asks whether any part of the downpayment is borrowed and whether each applicant is a co-maker or endorser on any promissory notes. Next, each applicant is asked whether he or she is a U.S. citizen or a permanent resident alien. Finally, the form asks if the applicants intend to occupy the property as a primary residence. If so, they are required to indicate whether they have owned any other property during the previous three years, what type of property it was (a principal residence, a second home, or an investment property), and how title was held. Applicants who haven't owned a home in the previous three years may be treated as first-time buyers for the purposes of certain loan programs.

Applicant agrees to correct or update information on the application if necessary

Acknowledgment and Agreement. By signing and dating the application form, the applicants are agreeing to several provisions regarding the application and the loan. Among other things, the applicants agree to inform the lender if any of the information provided in the application changes before closing.

Information for Government Monitoring. The last section on the third page of the application form sets forth optional questions regarding the applicants' ethnicity, race, and sex. If the applicants answer these questions, the federal government will use the information to evaluate the lender's compliance with fair lending laws.

Continuation Sheet. The fourth page of the loan application form is a continuation sheet, in case the applicants need more room to answer any of the questions on the previous pages. Note that the applicants must sign and date the continuation sheet in addition to the "Acknowledgment and Agreement" section on the previous page.

Agent should let buyer know information needed for loan application

Application Checklist. Real estate agents can help buyers prepare for the loan interview by going over a checklist of required information and documentation with them. See the sample checklist in Figure 7.5.

Disclosure Statements

In residential mortgage transactions, federal law requires lenders to give loan applicants two disclosure statements. The first is the Truth in Lending Act disclosure statement, which provides information about the overall cost of the loan applied for, including the annual percentage rate, the total finance charge, and the total amount financed. The second disclosure statement is the good faith estimate of closing costs, required under the Real Estate Settlement Procedures Act. It lists estimates of the loan-related charges and other costs that the buyers will be expected to pay at closing.

Lender must provide TILA and RESPA disclosure statements within 3 days after application

Lenders are required to provide these disclosure statements within three business days after the written loan application is submitted. Most lenders give them to loan applicants at the time of application. If any of the estimated figures change significantly over the course of

Fig. 7.5 Checklist of application information and documentation

Loan Application Checklist

Purchase and sale agreement (if the applicant has already entered into one)

Social security number for each applicant

Residence history:
- ✓ Addresses where the applicant has lived during the past few years
- ✓ Name and address of the applicant's current landlord

Employment history:
- ✓ Names and addresses of the employers the applicant has worked for in the last two years; positions held; whether employment was full- or part-time; and the wage or salary at time of departure
- ✓ If the applicant was recently in school or the military, a copy of the diploma or discharge papers

Income information:
- ✓ W-2 forms for the previous two years and payroll stubs for the previous 30 days (showing current and year-to-date earnings)
- ✓ If commissions are a significant part of the applicant's income, tax returns for the past two years
- ✓ If the applicant is self-employed, business and personal tax returns for the past two years, plus a year-to-date income and expense statement
- ✓ If the applicant is a major stockholder in a corporation (owns 25% or more of the stock), three years of corporate tax returns
- ✓ Amount and sources of income, including wages and secondary sources (such as a pension, social security, or child support)
- ✓ Documentation for all sources of income; child support or alimony requires a copy of the divorce decree

List of assets:
- ✓ Names, addresses, and account numbers for all bank accounts
- ✓ Bank statements for the past three months
- ✓ Investment statements for the past three months
- ✓ Value of household goods and other personal property
- ✓ Make, model, year, and market value of automobiles
- ✓ Cash and face value of insurance policies
- ✓ Address, description, and value of any real estate owned; any lease agreements
- ✓ Gift letter, if a gift is the source of part of the funds for closing (see Chapter 8)
- ✓ If the applicant's present home is to be sold, the net amount from the sale after deducting all selling expenses
- ✓ If the applicant is being relocated by an employer who is paying some of the closing costs, a letter from the employer stating which costs will be paid by the company

List of liabilities:
- ✓ For each debt, the name, address, and phone number of the creditor, and the balance, monthly payment, and account number
- ✓ Copy of divorce decree, for child support or alimony obligation

Current or estimated property taxes for the home being purchased (if the home has been chosen)

Certificate of Eligibility for VA loans

the transaction, new disclosures must be made before closing. (Both the Truth in Lending Act and the Real Estate Settlement Procedures Act are discussed in Chapter 14.)

Locking In the Interest Rate

Lock-in: lender guarantees certain interest rate for specified period

One other issue that should be addressed during the loan interview is whether the buyers want to have the interest rate on the loan they're applying for **locked in**, or guaranteed, for a certain period. If the rate isn't locked in, it will **float**, which means that it will move up or down with market interest rates until shortly before the transaction closes. Naturally, a change in the interest rate will also cause a change in the monthly payment for the loan.

> **Example:** When Jim Dawson applies for a loan, the loan officer says the interest rate will be 6.25%, and that's the figure filled in on the loan application form. Dawson doesn't ask to have the rate locked in, however.
>
> Market interest rates are going up, and by the time Dawson's loan closes (four weeks later) the rate on his loan has risen to 6.75%. Dawson is faced with the prospect of paying a higher interest rate and making a larger monthly mortgage payment than he anticipated. With the new interest rate, his monthly payment amount has increased from $1,231 to $1,297.

A situation like the one in the example could be a serious problem, especially for buyers who barely qualified for their loan in the first place. A sharp increase in the interest rate might increase the monthly payment so much that they no longer qualify. They could reduce the monthly payment back to an affordable level by putting more money down (to reduce the loan amount) or by paying discount points (to reduce the interest rate). Many buyers wouldn't be in a position to take either of those steps, however. If market interest rates are likely to rise, locking in the loan's rate can be extremely important.

Real estate agents should keep in mind that a buyer's failure to lock in the interest rate can affect the home seller as well as the buyer. If an increased interest rate forces the buyer to choose between an increase in the monthly payment amount, the downpayment amount, or the points, the transaction could be seriously delayed or even terminated.

Lock-in Period. When a loan officer quotes an interest rate, the buyers should ask whether the rate can be locked in, and if so, starting when and for how long. (Common lock-in periods are 30, 45, 60, or

90 days.) Some lenders are willing to lock in the interest rate when the application is submitted; others won't do it until the loan has been approved. Either way, the lock-in period should always extend beyond the expected loan processing time. A 30-day guarantee is worthless if there's little hope of closing the transaction in that time. The best arrangement is for the lock-in period to be extended automatically if the closing is delayed. Some lenders provide for a free automatic extension; others charge an extension fee.

Lock-in Fee. Buyers who want to lock in their interest rate will usually be required to pay a lock-in fee; for example, the lender might charge 1.5% of the loan amount. The fee is typically applied to the buyers' closing costs if the transaction closes. If the lender rejects the loan application, the lock-in fee is refunded; but if the buyers withdraw their application, the fee is forfeited to the lender.

Lock-in fee will be refunded if loan application is denied, but not if buyers withdraw application

Rate Decreases. If the buyers think market interest rates might drop in the next few weeks, it probably doesn't make sense to lock in the rate any sooner than necessary. (Lenders generally require the rate to be locked in 72 hours before closing, so that accurate settlement statements can be prepared.) A lender usually has the right to charge the locked-in rate even if market rates have gone down in the period before closing. In that situation, the lender might charge the buyers an additional fee to have the loan's interest rate reduced to the lower market rate.

Written Agreement. As you can see, the details of lock-ins—the fees, the duration, refunds and forfeitures, what happens if rates go down, and so on—can vary a lot from one lender to another. It's all just a matter of contract between the lender and the buyers. A real estate agent working with buyers should impress on them the importance of having their lender put all of the details of the lock-in agreement in writing. A spoken commitment from the loan officer is not enough to protect the buyers' interests.

Application Processing

Once a loan application has been filled out, the next step is to verify the information provided by the buyers. Verification forms are sent out to the buyers' employers, banks or other financial institutions, and previous mortgage lender, if any. Credit reports and credit scores are

Verification forms and other documentation are used to check information on application

obtained from the major credit reporting agencies (see Chapter 8). If the buyers have already entered into a contract for the purchase of a particular property, the lender orders a title report from a title insurance company and sends an appraiser to appraise the property.

When the completed verification forms, reports, and other documentation have been received, the loan officer or another member of the lender's staff puts together a loan package and sends it to the underwriting department.

The Underwriting Decision

Loan officer submits loan package to underwriter

The loan underwriter first looks over the loan package to make sure it's complete. If necessary, the underwriter will ask the loan officer to have the buyers submit additional documentation, such as investment account records, pension plan documents, or tax returns.

The underwriter carefully examines the application, verification forms, credit reports, and other documentation, and applies the appropriate qualifying standards to the buyers. These steps may be carried out with or without the help of an automated underwriting system (see Chapter 8). At the end of the evaluation process, the underwriter approves the loan, rejects it, or approves it subject to certain conditions.

Rejection. When a loan application is denied, the lender is required by federal law to provide the applicants with a written statement explaining why. Applicants are entitled to receive this statement within 30 days after submitting their completed application. Depending on the reasons for the denial, the buyers might want to apply to a different lender, apply for a smaller loan or a different type of loan, or decide to wait until they can pay off some of their debts or save additional money for a larger downpayment.

When an application is denied, some of the fees the applicants paid up front may be refunded, but others won't be. For example, a lock-in fee is typically refunded, while the application fee and credit report fee are not.

Conditional Commitment. A conditional approval, often called a conditional commitment, requires fulfillment of specified conditions and submission of additional documentation. For example, if approval is conditioned on the sale of the buyers' current home, final approval will require the settlement statement from that sale.

Preapproval Letter. Preapproval for a loan is a form of conditional commitment; the approval is contingent on a satisfactory appraisal and title report once the buyers have found the home they want to buy.

After an underwriter decides that buyers should be preapproved for the loan they're seeking, a **preapproval letter** is prepared. As explained earlier, the preapproval letter states that the lender will loan the buyers up to a specified amount of money to buy a house that meets the lender's standards.

The preapproval letter will expire at the end of a specified period, such as 90 days. If the buyers still haven't found the house they want to purchase, the lender may agree to an extension.

Some loan officers will prepare a **prequalification letter** for buyers at the loan interview, when their application for preapproval is still pending. Unlike a preapproval letter, a prequalification letter does not in any sense commit the lender to making a loan. The buyers' financial information still must be fully analyzed and verified before they will receive even a conditional approval.

Buyers and seller should beware of mislabeling. A loan officer might refer to a letter given to the buyers as a preapproval letter, when the text of the letter indicates that approval is subject to verification of the buyers' income and credit information. This is really only a prequalification letter, and it shouldn't carry the same weight in negotiations with sellers as a true preapproval letter.

Final Commitment. When all of the conditions for loan approval have been fulfilled, the lender will give the buyers a commitment letter, confirming the exact terms on which the loan will be made. This is sometimes called a firm commitment, in contrast to the earlier conditional commitment. The commitment letter will specify a date on which the lender's commitment will expire.

Firm commitment letter states exact terms on which loan will be made

Closing the Loan

The last stage of the financing process is coordinated with the closing of the real estate transaction as a whole. We'll look at some aspects of closing that concern the buyer's financing.

The Closing Agent

Real estate closing procedures vary from one part of the country to another. In many areas, closings are handled through escrow. **Escrow**

Escrow: neutral third party holds money and documents for buyer and seller

is an arrangement in which a neutral third party holds money and documents on behalf of the buyer and seller until their transaction is ready to close. When all of the conditions set forth in the purchase and sale agreement have been fulfilled, the third party—known as an **escrow agent** or **closing agent**—disburses the purchase price to the seller and delivers the deed to the buyer.

Depending on local practices, the closing agent may be an independent escrow agent, an employee of the buyer's lender or the title company, a lawyer, or a real estate broker.

Steps in the Closing Process

Lender's closing concerns:

- Clearing liens from title
- Establishing condition of title
- Inspections and repairs
- Buyer's funds for closing
- Document preparation and recording

The closing agent is usually responsible for handling all of the details that must be taken care of before the transaction can close. Some of these details involve requirements imposed by the lender.

Clearing and Insuring Title. Since the property being purchased is going to serve as collateral for the new loan, the lender wants to make sure that the title is free of encumbrances that could interfere with the lender's security interest. Except for property tax liens and special assessment liens, any liens that would have higher priority than the new mortgage or deed of trust must be removed. These older liens are the seller's responsibility, and the closing agent will usually arrange for them to be paid off out of the seller's proceeds at closing. The appropriate lien releases will be recorded along with the other documents (the new deed, the new mortgage or deed of trust, and so on).

The lender's security interest will also be protected by an extended coverage title insurance policy, usually paid for by the buyer. Under the terms of the policy, if it turns out that there are liens against the property that weren't listed as exceptions from coverage, the title insurance company will reimburse the lender for resulting losses.

Inspections and Corrective Action. Another way for a lender to protect the value of its collateral is by requiring certain inspections to be carried out. For example, a pest control inspection, a soil percolation test, or a flood hazard inspection might be considered necessary, depending on the type of property and the area it's located in. Inspection reports will be submitted to the lender for review, and the lender may decide that specific repairs must be made or other corrective action must be taken. The repairs or corrective action may or may not have to be completed before closing.

Loan Documents and Buyer's Funds. Once the buyer's loan has been approved, the lender forwards the loan documents (promissory note, mortgage or deed of trust, and—if necessary—an updated Truth in Lending Act disclosure statement) to the closing agent. At this point, the buyer can complete his or her part of the transaction by depositing funds for the downpayment and closing costs into escrow and signing the loan documents. The signed documents are then returned to the lender.

Impound Account. In most transactions, the buyer is required to make a deposit into an impound account at closing. An impound account, also called a reserve account or escrow account, is a trust account set up by the lender to ensure that the buyer's property taxes and hazard and mortgage insurance premiums are paid on time. The buyer will pay the lender a portion of these expenses each month along with the principal and interest payment on the loan. The lender will deposit the tax and insurance payments into the impound account, and when taxes or insurance premiums become due, pay them out of the impound account. At closing, the lender usually has the buyer make an initial deposit into the impound account.

Impound account ensures that taxes, hazard insurance, and mortgage insurance are paid on time

Interim Interest. In the course of this chapter we've already mentioned most of the fees and charges connected with the loan that the buyer will pay as closing costs. They may include an origination fee, discount points, a mortgage broker's commission, a document preparation fee, and so on. One charge the buyer will encounter at closing that we haven't explained yet is interim interest, also called prepaid interest.

Interim interest covers period from closing date to end of month in which closing occurs

Interim interest arises in part because of a custom concerning the due date of the buyer's initial loan payment. As a general rule, a buyer's first monthly mortgage payment is not due on the first day of the month immediately following closing, but on the first day of the next month after that.

Buyer's first payment is due on the first day of the second month following the month in which closing occurs

> **Example:** Closing takes place on January 23. The buyer is not required to make a mortgage payment on February 1. Instead, the first payment on the loan is due on March 1.

This practice gives the buyer a chance to recover from the financial strain of closing. But even though the first loan payment isn't due for an extra month, interest begins accruing on the loan as of the closing date.

Mortgage interest is paid in arrears

Interest on a mortgage loan is paid in arrears. In other words, the interest that accrues during a given month is paid at the end of that month. So, to return to the example above, the March 1 payment will cover the interest that accrues during February. However, that first payment won't cover the interest that accrued between January 23 (the closing date) and January 31. The lender requires the interest for those nine days to be paid in advance, when the transaction closes. This advance payment of interest, which is one of the buyer's closing costs, is the interim or prepaid interest.

Funding the Loan. When the loan documents have been executed and all of the lender's conditions have been satisfied, the lender releases the buyer's loan funds to the closing agent. This is referred to as funding the loan.

Settlement statement is a detailed listing of each party's credits and debits at closing

Settlement Statements. Once precise figures for all of the closing costs have been determined, the closing agent prepares final settlement statements for the buyer and the seller in compliance with the Real Estate Settlement Procedures Act (see Chapter 14). Each party's settlement statement provides a detailed list of all of the charges and credits that will be taken into account for that party in closing the transaction and disbursing funds.

Final Steps. The closing agent arranges for the deed, mortgage or deed of trust, lien releases, and other documents to be recorded, and disburses the appropriate funds to the seller, the real estate agent, and other parties entitled to payment. The title company issues the buyer's and lender's title insurance policies, the lender sends copies of the loan documents to the buyer, and the buyer provides a copy of the hazard insurance policy to the lender. The transaction has closed.

Outline: The Financing Process

I. Shopping for a Loan

   A. Loan consumers should engage in comparison shopping for a loan, which involves assessing their own needs and finances as well as comparing rates and fees.

   B. Prequalifying vs. preapproval

      1. Prequalifying: Informal process performed by either a lender or a real estate agent, used to determine an affordable price range for a buyer.

      2. Preapproval: Formal process performed by a lender, which results in a preapproval letter stating a maximum loan amount based on the buyer's income and net worth.

      3. Advantages of preapproval: Can make a buyer's offer more appealing to a seller, and streamlines the closing process.

   C. Prequalification process

      1. First step is to apply an income ratio to buyers' monthly income to calculate maximum monthly mortgage payment.

      2. Second step is to subtract a percentage representing taxes and insurance, to calculate the maximum principal and interest payment.

      3. Third step is to use market interest rates to calculate the maximum loan amount.

      4. Final step is to divide the maximum loan amount by the appropriate loan-to-value ratio to determine the appropriate price a buyer should pay for a home.

   D. Choosing a lender

      1. A buyer should research lenders by comparing interest rates and fees.

      2. A buyer also may rely on referrals to find a reputable and competent lender.

      3. Buyers should be concerned with a lender's expertise and efficiency as well as its interest rates and fees.

   E. Loan costs

      1. Loan fees: Usually described in terms of "points," where a point is one percentage point of the loan amount.

      2. Origination fee: A one-time service fee charged by the lender to cover administrative expenses associated with issuing and service the loan.

3. Discount points: An additional charge imposed by a lender upon issuing a loan in order to increase the lender's yield on the loan.
4. A lender may charge a lower interest rate in exchange for a buyer paying discount points upfront.
5. A seller may pay discount points on a buyer's behalf in order to "buy down" the buyer's interest rate.
6. Other fees: A lender may charge additional fees for application, underwriting, or document preparation.

F. Comparing loan costs

1. The Truth in Lending Act (TILA) is a federal consumer protection act requiring certain disclosures to help borrowers understand the true cost of credit.
2. TILA requires disclosure of the annual percentage rate (APR), which is the relationship of the total finance charge to the loan amount, expressed as an annual percentage.

G. Evaluating financing options

1. Home buyers need to weigh considerations other than the loan costs, such as financial priorities, how long they will live in the house, and other investment opportunities.
2. Home buyers may use a home buyer counseling program for assistance in deciding what financing option is most appropriate.

II. Applying for a Loan

A. Loan interview

1. Home buyers may interview with a loan officer, at which point they will prequalify and may need to deposit certain expenses that will be paid up front.

B. Loan application

1. At the loan interview, borrowers will fill out the loan application.
2. Borrowers will need to provide information regarding employment, income, current monthly housing expense, assets and liabilities.

C. Disclosure statements

1. The lender will provide a Truth in Lending disclosure, which discloses the overall cost of the loan, including annual percentage rate and total finance charge.
2. The lender will also provide the good faith estimate of closing costs required under the Real Estate Settlement Procedures Act.

D. Locking in the interest rate

1. Buyers may lock in the interest rate on the application date, rather than running the risk of interest rates going up between the application date and the closing date.
2. A lender will customarily charge a lock-in fee.

III. Application Processing

A. Underwriting decision

1. An underwriter will evaluate the loan application and decide whether to approve it, reject it, or approve it subject to conditions.
2. A conditional commitment may require additional documentation, such as proof of sale of the buyers' current home.
3. When all conditions for loan approval are met, the lender will issue a final commitment letter.

IV. Closing the Loan

A. Closing agent

1. A closing agent or escrow agent will act as a neutral third party who holds money and documents on behalf of the buyer and seller until the transaction is ready to close.

B. Steps in closing process

1. Clearing and insuring title: The lender will want to ensure that the property is free of encumbrances that could interfere with its security interest.
2. Inspections: A lender may require certain inspections of the property to be performed, to make sure that the property will continue to be adequate collateral.
3. Impound account: The buyer will make payments into an impound account as part of her monthly payments; property taxes and insurance will be paid out of the account.
4. Interim interest: Because mortgage interest is paid in arrears, but no payment is due in the month following closing, a buyer will need to pay interest up front to pay for the partial first month's interest.
5. Settlement statement: A closing agent will prepare settlement statements for both parties listing all charges and credits.

Key Terms

Prequalification: Informal approval from a lender or real estate agent suggesting the maximum amount a buyer could afford to spend on a home.

Preapproval: Formal loan approval from a lender stating a maximum loan amount that the lender is willing to issue, based on the borrower's income and assets.

PITI payment: The full monthly mortgage payment, including property taxes and hazard insurance as well as principal and interest.

Mortgage broker: An intermediary who brings lenders and borrowers together and negotiates loan agreements between them.

Loan fee: Any one-time fee that a lender charges at closing for a loan or an assumption, including origination fees and discount points.

Origination fee: A fee charged by a lender upon making a new loan, intended to cover the administrative cost of making the loan.

Discount points: A fee a lender may charge at closing to increase its profit on the loan above the interest rate.

Buydown: When a seller or third party pays the lender a lump sum at closing to lower the interest rate charged to the buyer.

Truth in Lending Act: A federal law that requires lender and credit arrangers to make disclosures concerning loan costs (including the total finance charge and annual percentage rate) to consumer loan applicants.

Annual Percentage Rate: Under the Truth in Lending Act, the relationship between a loan's total finance charge and the total amount financed, expressed as an annual percentage.

Total finance charge: All charges associated with a loan, including the interest, any discount points paid by the borrower, the loan origination fee, and mortgage insurance.

Real Estate Settlement Procedures Act: A federal law that requires lenders to disclose certain information about closing costs to loan applicants; also known as RESPA.

Lock-in: When a lender guarantees a loan applicant a particular interest rate if the transaction closes within a specified period.

Conditional commitment: A conditional approval of a loan that requires fulfillment of certain conditions.

Escrow agent: A third party who holds things of value (such as money and documents) on behalf of parties to a transaction until specified conditions are fulfilled.

Chapter Quiz

1. The best way to compare the cost of loans is by using the:
   a. lender's yield
   b. annual interest rate
   c. combination of the origination fee and the loan discount
   d. annual percentage rate

2. A lender will want to know a loan applicant's:
   a. current rent or house payment
   b. employment history for the past ten years
   c. tax bracket for the past three years
   d. All of the above

3. The Masons are buying a house. The sales price is $163,500, and they're borrowing $139,000. They've agreed to pay a loan discount fee of two points, which amounts to:
   a. $3,270
   b. $2,780
   c. $1,635
   d. $1,390

4. The fee that pays for the lender's overhead is the:
   a. loan discount
   b. APR
   c. origination fee
   d. interest rate

5. When a lender guarantees a particular interest rate for a certain period of time, it is called:
   a. a discount fee
   b. a lock-in
   c. a float
   d. an annualized percentage rate

6. The portion of a borrower's monthly payment that goes toward property taxes and insurance will be held in a/an:
   a. trust fund
   b. recovery account
   c. impound account
   d. balloon payment

7. The charges payable by or to a party in a real estate transaction show up on the:
   a. settlement statement
   b. good faith estimate of closing costs
   c. lender disclosure statement
   d. Uniform Land Cost Disclosure Statement

8. Which of the following costs are reflected in a loan's APR?
   a. Interest, points paid by borrower, loan origination fee, mortgage insurance
   b. Interest, appraisal fee, loan origination fee, points paid by either party
   c. Appraisal fee, credit report fee, loan origination fee
   d. Points paid by borrower, origination fee, appraisal fee, credit report fee

9. The purpose of discount points is to:
   a. cover the administrative costs associated with issuing and servicing the loan
   b. increase the lender's yield
   c. pay for costs associated with preparing the good faith estimate of costs
   d. increase the loan's interest rate in exchange for no loan fees

10. Formal approval by a lender, in the form of a letter stating the maximum loan amount the lender is willing to authorize, is:
    a. preapproval
    b. prequalification
    c. predetermination
    d. preauthorization

Answer Key

1. d. To compare loans costs, applicants should compare the various loans' annual percentage rates.

2. a. A lender will want to know a loan applicant's current housing expenses. The lender will not be concerned with the applicant's tax bracket, and will want to see employment information for only the previous two years.

3. b. The Masons' loan amount is $139,000 and two points of $139,000 is $2,780 ($139,000 × .02 = $2,780).

4. c. An origination fee pays for the lender's administrative costs.

5. b. With a lock-in, a lender guarantees a borrower's interest rate even if rates go up between the application date and the closing date.

6. c. An impound account is used to hold the portion of a borrower's monthly payments that are applied to property taxes and hazard insurance until those bills come due.

7. a. A settlement statement is used by a closing agent to show the charges and credits that will apply to each party during the closing process.

8. a. Interest, borrower-paid points, the origination fee, and mortgage insurance are all considered part of the total finance charge.

9. b. Discount points increase the lender's yield, or profit. A lender may be willing to charge a lower interest rate in exchange for payment of discount points.

10. a. Preapproval is a formal approval process performed by a lender, which results in the lender agreeing to loan the buyer up to a specified amount when he finds a home he wishes to buy.

Chapter 8
Qualifying the Buyer

The Underwriting Process
- Qualifying standards
- Automated underwriting

Evaluating Creditworthiness

Income Analysis
- Characteristics of income
- Stable monthly income
- Calculating stable monthly income
- Income ratios

Net Worth
- Funds for closing
- Assets
- Liabilities
- Gift funds

Credit Reputation
- Credit reports
- Length of credit history
- Payment record
- Major derogatory incidents
- Credit scores
- Explaining negative credit information

Other Factors in Underwriting

Risk-Based Loan Pricing

Introduction

Before agreeing to make a real estate loan, a lender will evaluate both the buyer and the property to determine whether they **qualify** for the loan—that is, whether they meet the lender's minimum standards. This evaluation process is called **loan underwriting**; the person who performs the evaluation is called a loan underwriter or credit underwriter.

Loan underwriter evaluates:
1. Loan applicant's overall financial situation
2. Value of property

The primary purpose of the evaluation is to determine the degree of risk that the loan would represent for the lender. This determination hinges on the answers to two fundamental questions:

1. Does the buyer's overall financial situation indicate that he or she can reasonably be expected to make the proposed monthly loan payments on time?
2. Is there sufficient value in the property pledged as collateral to ensure recovery of the loan amount in the event of default?

The underwriter tries to make sure the buyer is someone who can afford the loan and who is unlikely to default. But since default always remains a possibility, the underwriter also tries to make sure that the property is worth enough so that the proceeds of a foreclosure sale would cover the loan amount.

Our discussion of underwriting is divided into two main parts: qualifying the buyer, covered in this chapter, and qualifying the property, covered in the next one. This chapter explains the factors an underwriter takes into account in evaluating a home buyer's financial situation. The next chapter explains how a home is appraised and how an underwriter uses the appraised value to set the loan amount. First, however, let's begin with some general information about the underwriting process.

The Underwriting Process

Underwriting a mortgage loan involves these basic tasks: reviewing the loan application; obtaining additional information about the applicant from other sources; applying the lender's qualifying standards; verifying information provided by the applicant; evaluating the property appraisal; and making a recommendation in favor of or against loan approval. How these tasks are carried out varies from one lender to another, of course. And the underwriting process changes over time, as new practices become established in the lending industry. Over the past several years, the growing role of computer programs in underwriting has caused major changes, as we'll discuss below.

Qualifying Standards

The minimum standards used in underwriting—called **underwriting standards** or qualifying standards—draw a boundary line between acceptable risks and unacceptable risks. Loans that meet the standards are considered acceptable risks; loans that don't are considered unacceptable risks. Who sets those standards? In other words, who decides which loans are worth the risk of making them?

In theory, residential lenders are free to set their own qualifying standards. They can take virtually any risks they want to, as long as they don't violate the federal and state regulations that govern financial institutions. In practice, however, residential lenders usually apply qualifying standards set by the major secondary market agencies (Fannie Mae and Freddie Mac), by the FHA, or by the VA. If a conventional loan is going to be sold to Fannie Mae or Freddie Mac, their standards must be met. If the loan is going to be insured by the FHA or guaranteed by the VA, the FHA or VA standards must be met.

Underwriting standards:
- Most lenders use Fannie Mae/Freddie Mac standards for conventional loans
- FHA and VA standards must be used for FHA and VA loans

Each of these sets of qualifying standards (Fannie Mae, Freddie Mac, FHA, and VA) is different. The specific rules for the various loan programs are covered in Chapter 10 (*Conventional Financing*), Chapter 11 (*FHA-Insured Loans*), and Chapter 12 (*VA-Guaranteed Loans*). But all of the different rules are based on the underlying principles and concepts that we'll be discussing in this chapter.

Automated Underwriting

Within the limits set by the qualifying standards they apply, underwriters draw on their own experience and judgment in deciding whether to recommend that a particular loan be approved or denied. The qualifying standards guide them in evaluating various aspects of the loan application, but weighing the positive factors against the negative isn't always a simple matter. Underwriting has been described as an art, not a science.

Automated underwriting system: a computer program designed to analyze loan applications and recommend approval or rejection

However, the advent of **automated underwriting** (AU) has moved the underwriting process at least somewhat closer to the scientific end of the spectrum. An **automated underwriting system** (AUS) is a computer program designed to perform a preliminary analysis of loan applications and make a recommendation for or against approval. Introduced in the 1990s, these systems are now in widespread use. AU systems don't completely replace traditional underwriting (now referred to as **manual underwriting**). Instead, the two types of underwriting are used in conjunction with one another.

AU and the Secondary Market. Some large lenders have their own proprietary automated underwriting systems, but the predominant systems are the ones developed by Fannie Mae (Desktop Underwriter®) and Freddie Mac (Loan Prospector®). Both Desktop Underwriter and Loan Prospector can be used to underwrite conventional, FHA, or VA loans, applying the appropriate qualifying standards for each loan program.

The primary purpose of Desktop Underwriter and Loan Prospector is to make loan purchase decisions for Fannie Mae and Freddie Mac. (See Chapter 2 for a discussion of how lenders sell their loans to the secondary market agencies.) However, a lender who plans to sell a loan to either agency isn't required to use automated underwriting. Both Fannie Mae and Freddie Mac are still willing to purchase loans that have been underwritten manually, in the traditional way. Nonetheless, both agencies favor automated underwriting and encourage lenders to use their AU systems.

Also, a lender may choose to use Desktop Underwriter or Loan Prospector to underwrite loans that it plans to keep in portfolio. Even though these loans don't have to meet Fannie Mae or Freddie Mac standards, the AU analysis can still be very useful to the lender's underwriters.

Loan performance: whether loan payments are made as agreed

AU Programming. The programming of the secondary market agencies' AU systems is based on the performance of millions of mortgage loans. The term "loan performance" refers to whether the payments on a loan are made as agreed, or there are collection problems leading to default and foreclosure. Statistical analysis of the performance of millions of loans provides strong evidence of precisely which factors in a loan application make default more likely or less likely.

For instance, it's generally understood that a home buyer who has funds left over (cash reserves) after making the downpayment and paying the closing costs is less likely to default than one who doesn't have anything left over. Accordingly, some lenders require borrowers to have a specified amount in reserve after closing—for example, enough money to cover at least two months' mortgage payments, in case of emergency. What computerized statistical analysis of loan performance adds to this traditional, common-sense underwriting idea is greater precision. Exactly how much less likely to default is a borrower who has two months of reserves than one who has no reserves? What about a borrower with enough reserves for three months of payments, or six months? This type of information, along with computer analysis of all of the other factors that affect default risk, can be programmed into an automated underwriting system. The system will then be able to predict with considerable accuracy how likely it is that a particular loan applicant will default on the loan he or she is seeking.

The secondary market agencies' comprehensive computer analysis of loan performance is ongoing, and they use the latest information to adjust their automated underwriting systems and their qualifying standards. Because Fannie Mae and Freddie Mac are so influential in residential lending, these adjustments have a nationwide impact on underwriting.

How AU Works. To submit a loan application for automated underwriting, the underwriter enters specified information from the application into the AU system. (Some lenders have the loan officer or another employee perform this task.) The system then obtains the applicant's credit report directly from the major credit agencies. After analyzing all of this data using statistical models and the appropriate qualifying rules, the AU system provides the underwriter with a report.

The recommendations in an AU report fall into three categories:

- a risk classification,
- a documentation classification, and
- an appraisal classification.

Categories of AU recommendations:
- Risk
- Documentation
- Appraisal

Risk classification. The risk classification determines the level of underwriting scrutiny the loan application should receive. If the information submitted to the automated underwriting system meets all of the applicable qualifying standards, the AU system will give the application a risk classification of "Approve" or "Accept." (The exact terminology depends on the system.) On the other hand, an application that doesn't appear to meet all of the qualifying standards will receive a risk classification of "Refer" or "Caution." This doesn't necessarily mean that the loan should be denied, or that it can't be sold to Fannie Mae or Freddie Mac; instead, it indicates that further review of the application is needed.

This further review will take the form of manual underwriting. In other words, the underwriter will now examine the loan application in the traditional way, to see if it can be approved even though it didn't receive a "passing grade" from the automated underwriting system. The AU report provides the underwriter with guidance, listing the main factors that led to the Refer or Caution classification and pointing out where additional information might make a difference. The underwriter looks for favorable information about the loan applicant's situation that the AU system has not already taken into account.

Note that some lenders have a policy of rejecting Refer or Caution loans without underwriting them manually. These lenders don't consider this extra step—and the extra cost—to be worth their while. Other lenders are willing to manually underwrite Refer or Caution loans, in the expectation that the extra cost will be covered by profits from the additional loans that are ultimately approved. This policy difference is one reason why a loan applicant who's been rejected by one lender may be accepted by another.

Documentation classification. The AU report will also provide a documentation classification, indicating the level of documentation the underwriter should obtain in order to verify the information provided by the applicant. The basic documentation levels can be characterized as standard, streamlined ("low-doc"), and minimal ("no-doc"). The stronger the application, the lower the documentation requirement.

As the name suggests, standard documentation is the full verification process used in traditional underwriting. An automated underwriting system generally requires standard documentation for loans that have been given a risk classification of "Refer" or "Caution" (and therefore must be manually underwritten).

Loans given an "Approve" or "Accept" classification are eligible for either streamlined or minimal documentation, depending on the strength of the application. For example, if the applicant has a perfect credit reputation and is making a very large downpayment, the report might require no documentation of employment or income. Documentation will be discussed in more detail later in this chapter.

Appraisal classification. The third type of recommendation made in an AU report is the appraisal or inspection classification. For example, the report might tell the underwriter that a full appraisal is appropriate, or that a drive-by inspection would be sufficient, or even that no appraisal or inspection is necessary. The appraisal/inspection classification is based on the overall strength of the application and on information about the property that was submitted to the automated underwriting system.

Advantages of AU. Automated underwriting has a number of advantages over traditional underwriting, with benefits for both lenders and borrowers. First, it can streamline the underwriting process for many mortgage loans, requiring significantly less paperwork and enabling lenders to make approval decisions more quickly.

Second, AU makes the underwriting process more objective and consistent, since it generally reduces reliance on the underwriter's experience and subjective judgment. This helps ensure fair, unbiased lending decisions.

Advantages of AU:
- Streamlines process
- Increases objectivity
- Improves underwriting accuracy

Third, AU improves the accuracy of underwriting, because it can weigh all of the risk factors more precisely. Lenders (and the secondary market agencies) can have greater confidence in a loan approval decision reached with the help of AU. This allows them to accept more loan applications and extend financing to more home buyers, while still managing risk appropriately.

In spite of these advantages, automated underwriting by no means eliminates the need for human underwriters. Both Fannie Mae and Freddie Mac emphasize that an AU system is only a tool. The final decision on whether to approve or deny a loan is always made by the lender, not the computer.

Evaluating Creditworthiness

Now that you have some background information about the underwriting process, we'll look more closely at the factors that are taken into account in qualifying a buyer. As we said at the beginning of the chapter, a lender's fundamental question concerning a buyer is: "Does the buyer's overall financial situation indicate that he or she can reasonably be expected to make the proposed monthly loan payments on time?" If the answer is yes, the buyer is considered **creditworthy**.

Qualifying the buyer involves evaluation of:
- Income
- Net worth
- Credit history

To decide whether a buyer is creditworthy, the underwriter—with or without the aid of an automated underwriting system—must consider dozens of factors in the buyer's financial situation. These can be grouped into three main categories:

- income,
- net worth (assets), and
- credit reputation.

You can think of stable income, adequate net worth, and a good credit reputation as the basic components of creditworthiness. We'll be discussing each of these as separate topics, but you should keep in mind that underwriters don't look at any aspect of a loan application in isolation from the rest of it. Strength in one area may or may not be enough to offset weakness in another. The recommendation to approve or deny the loan is based on the buyer's financial situation as a whole.

Income Analysis

The buyer's income is usually the starting point in determining how large a loan the lender is willing to make, and therefore how expensive a home ("how much house") the buyer can afford.

Characteristics of Income

From an underwriter's point of view, income has three dimensions: quantity, quality, and durability.

Income analysis:
- Quantity
- Quality
- Durability

Quantity. A key consideration in underwriting is whether the loan applicant's monthly income is enough to cover the proposed monthly mortgage payment in addition to all of his or her other expenses. So the underwriter wants to know how much income the applicant has. Not all income is equal in an underwriter's eyes, however. Only income that meets the tests of quality and durability is taken into account in deciding whether the applicant has enough income to qualify for the loan.

Quality (Dependability). To evaluate the quality of a loan applicant's income, the underwriter looks at the sources from which it is derived. The income sources should be reasonably dependable, such as an established employer, a government agency, or an interest-yielding investment account.

> **Example:** Jeanne Ellington is applying for a mortgage. She works for a medium-sized company that manufactures machine parts. The company has been in business for 35 years and hasn't been subject to downsizing or periodic layoffs in recent memory. Because Ellington's employer is well-established and stable, the underwriter sees it as a very dependable source of income. Thus, Ellington's salary will be considered high-quality income.

The less dependable the source (a brand new company or a high-risk investment, for example), the lower the quality of the income.

> **Example:** Suppose instead that Jeanne Ellington works for a small graphic design company that was started less than a year ago. The underwriter might decide that the company isn't a very dependable source of income, and therefore conclude that Ellington's salary is relatively low-quality income. That will count as a weakness in her loan application, although by itself it won't lead to denial of the loan.

Durability (Probability of Continuance). Income is considered durable if it can be expected to continue in the future—preferably for at least the **next three years**. Wages from permanent employment (as opposed to a temporary job), permanent disability benefits, and interest on established investments are all examples of durable income. An underwriter will assume that these and similar types of income are going to continue, unless there is some evidence to the contrary.

> **Example:** The loan applicant is John Gifford. The company he works for has been one of the major employers in his town for many years, but recent news reports indicate that it's about to be taken over by a corporation based in another state. If that happens, many of the company's employees will lose their jobs. This information calls the durability of Gifford's income into question.

Stable Monthly Income

Income that meets the tests of quality and durability is generally referred to as the loan applicant's **stable monthly income**. Typically, stable monthly income is made up of earnings from one primary income source, such as a full-time job, plus earnings from acceptable secondary sources. Secondary income can take many forms, such as bonuses, commissions (over and above a base salary), social security payments, military disability and retirement income, interest on savings or other investments, and so on.

In addition to regular wages from a full-time job, stable monthly income may include:

- Bonuses
- Commissions
- Overtime
- Part-time earnings
- Self-employment income
- Retirement income
- Alimony or child support
- Public assistance
- Investment income

The following types of income generally meet the tests of quality and durability, so that lenders are willing to count them as part of the loan applicant's stable monthly income.

Employment Income. Permanent employment is the major income source for most home buyers. The underwriter will consider not only the loan applicant's current job and wage or salary level, but also his or her recent employment history. As you'd suppose, a history of steady, full-time employment is viewed favorably. Ideally, a loan applicant will have been employed by the same employer or in the same field continuously for **at least two years**.

Positive employment history:

- Consistency, usually 2 years in same job or field
- Job changes have been for advancement
- Special training or education

If the applicant has held his or her current position for two years or more, the underwriter usually won't consider it necessary to look at the applicant's previous employment. Otherwise, the underwriter may want to check into the applicant's two previous jobs.

Frequent changes in employment don't necessarily count against the applicant. While persistent job-hopping might indicate a problem, changing jobs for career advancement is usually a good sign. The key issue for the underwriter is whether the job changes have hurt the loan applicant's ability to pay his or her financial obligations.

On the whole, job continuity isn't as important as continuity of earnings. As long as the applicant has consistently been able to find work that brings in a certain level of income, it may not matter that he or she hasn't stayed in the same line of work. But if the loan application reveals a period longer than 60 days with no employment income, the applicant may be asked to explain it.

Note that in some cases loan approval may be warranted even without an established two-year work history. For example, the applicant may have recently graduated from college or a vocational school. Training or education that has prepared the applicant for a specific kind of work can strengthen the loan application. Also, even in the absence of special training, an unimpressive employment history could be counterbalanced by other factors in the loan application.

Commissions, overtime, and bonuses. These forms of employment income are considered durable if they can be shown to have been a consistent part of the loan applicant's overall earnings pattern, usually for at least two years. (Some lenders count bonuses as stable income only if the applicant has received them for three years or more.)

The underwriter will calculate the average amount of overtime, bonus, or commission income, but will also consider the trend: Have these earnings been steady, or have they been increasing or decreasing? If they're decreasing, the underwriter may count less than the average amount as stable income.

Part-time and seasonal work. Earnings from part-time work can be counted as stable income if the loan applicant has held the job for at least two years. Seasonal or periodic earnings—wages from agricultural work or a construction job, for instance—may also be treated as stable income if there is an established earnings pattern.

> **Example:** Harold Jensen has worked as a deckhand on a fishing boat every summer for the past three years, and he intends to continue doing that. Although his summer income alone isn't enough to qualify him for a mortgage loan, an underwriter would be willing to treat it as stable income and add it to his earnings from the rest of the year.

Self-employment income. When a loan applicant owns a business, the income received from that business is self-employment income. (It isn't necessary to be the sole owner of the business; lenders generally treat income from a business as self-employment income if the applicant has an ownership interest of 25% or more.) Income from freelance or consulting work is also considered to be self-employment income.

To lenders, self-employment adds an extra element of risk to a loan, because the borrower's income is often unpredictable, and many businesses fail. So a loan applicant should expect some extra scrutiny if self-employment is his or her main source of income. If the applicant hasn't been self-employed for very long, the underwriter may hesitate to approve the loan. Lenders are wary of new businesses and generally want to see that a self-employed applicant has operated his or her business profitably for at least two years. The underwriter will consider the trend of the applicant's earnings, his or her training and experience, and the nature of the business.

For some self-employed loan applicants, a lender may be willing to avoid the issue of self-employment income altogether and focus instead on the applicant's assets and credit reputation. As a general rule, this is only an option for applicants who have a substantial net worth and excellent credit.

Verifying employment income. As we discussed earlier, the information provided in the loan application must be verified—that is, confirmed and documented. Lenders generally require one of three levels of documentation (standard, streamlined, or minimal), depending on the strength of the application. For applications submitted to an automated underwriting system, the AU report tells the underwriter what level of documentation is needed; in manual underwriting, the underwriter usually follows the documentation rules for the loan program in question.

The standard method of verifying a loan applicant's employment income is to send a "Request for Verification of Employment" form (see Figure 8.1) directly to the applicant's employer. The employer fills out the form and sends it directly back to the lender. To eliminate the possibility that the applicant might tamper with the verification form, the applicant isn't allowed to return the form to the lender. Note that the form asks the employer about the probability of continued employment.

Employment verification:
- Verification form sent to employer, or
- W-2 forms for 2 years plus pay stubs for 30 days, with phone call to employer

For many mortgage loans, lenders now use a streamlined method of employment verification. The loan applicant can provide the lender with W-2 forms for the previous two years and payroll stubs or vouchers for the previous 30-day period. The pay stubs must identify the applicant, the employer, and the applicant's gross earnings for both the current pay period and the year to date. The lender may then confirm the employment and earnings information with a phone call to the employer.

When commissions, overtime, bonuses, or seasonal earnings are a significant part of the applicant's employment income, the lender typically requires copies of the applicant's federal income tax returns for the previous two years to verify these earnings. (The lender may want to obtain these directly from the IRS, rather than from the applicant. This requires the applicant's written permission.) The lender will ask the employer if overtime or bonus income is likely

Fig. 8.1 Request for Verification of Employment form

FannieMae

Request for Verification of Employment

Privacy Act Notice: This information is to be used by the agency collecting it or its assignees in determining whether you qualify as a prospective mortgagor under its program. It will not be disclosed outside the agency except as required and permitted by law. You do not have to provide this information, but if you do not your application for approval as a prospective mortgagor or borrower may be delayed or rejected. The information requested in this form is authorized by Title 38, USC, Chapter 37 (if VA); by 12 USC, Section 1701 et. seq. (if HUD/FHA); by 42 USC, Section 1452b (if HUD/CPD); and Title 42 USC, 1471 et. seq., or 7 USC, 1921 et. seq. (if USDA/FmHA).

Instructions: **Lender** – Complete items 1 through 7. Have applicant complete item 8. Forward directly to employer named in item 1.
Employer – Please complete either Part II or Part III as applicable. Complete Part IV and return directly to lender named in item 2.
The form is to be transmitted directly to the lender and is not to be transmitted through the applicant or any other party.

Part I – Request

1. To (Name and address of employer)	2. From (Name and address of lender)

I certify that this verification has been sent directly to the employer and has not passed through the hands of the applicant or any other interested party.

3. Signature of Lender	4. Title	5. Date	6. Lender's Number (Optional)

I have applied for a mortgage loan and stated that I am now or was formerly employed by you. My signature below authorizes verification of this information.

7. Name and Address of Applicant (include employee or badge number)	8. Signature of Applicant

Part II – Verification of Present Employment

9. Applicant's Date of Employment	10. Present Position	11. Probability of Continued Employment

12A. Current **Gross** Base Pay (Enter Amount and Check Period)
$ ________ ☐ Annual ☐ Hourly ☐ Monthly ☐ Other (Specify) ☐ Weekly

12B. **Gross** Earnings

Type	Year To Date Thru ____ 19__	Past Year 19___	Past Year 19___
Base Pay	$	$	$
Overtime	$	$	$
Commissions	$	$	$
Bonus	$	$	$
Total	$	$	$

13. For Military Personnel Only

Pay Grade	
Type	Monthly Amount
Base Pay	$
Rations	$
Flight or Hazard	$
Clothing	$
Quarters	$
Pro Pay	$
Overseas or Combat	$
Variable Housing Allowance	$

14. If Overtime or Bonus is Applicable, Is Its Continuance Likely?
Overtime ☐ Yes ☐ No
Bonus ☐ Yes ☐ No

15. If paid hourly – average hours per week

16. Date of applicant's next pay increase

17. Projected amount of next pay increase

18. Date of applicant's last pay increase

19. Amount of last pay increase

20. Remarks (If employee was off work for any length of time, please indicate time period and reason)

Part III – Verification of Previous Employment

21. Date Hired

22. Date Terminated

23. Salary/Wage at Termination Per (Year) (Month) (Week)
Base ________ Overtime ________ Commissions ________ Bonus ________

24. Reason for Leaving	25. Position Held

Part IV – Authorized Signature - Federal statutes provide severe penalties for any fraud, intentional misrepresentation, or criminal connivance or conspiracy purposed to influence the issuance of any guaranty or insurance by the VA Secretary, the U.S.D.A., FmHA/FHA Commissioner, or the HUD/CPD Assistant Secretary.

26. Signature of Employer	27. Title (Please print or type)	28. Date
29. Print or type name signed in Item 26	30. Phone No.	

Fannie Mae
Form 1005 July 96

to continue, and if the applicant has business expenses that will be deducted from commissions.

Self-employed applicant needs financial records and income tax returns for 2 years

Self-employed loan applicants should be prepared to provide business and personal income tax returns for the two years prior to the loan application. (If the business is well-established and the applicant won't be using any funds from the business to close the loan, the requirement for business tax returns may be waived.) If the business is a sole proprietorship, the underwriter may also want to see a balance sheet covering the previous one or two fiscal years and a year-to-date profit and loss statement. This additional documentation is especially likely to be requested if the stability or durability of the applicant's self-employment income is in doubt.

Retirement Income. Pension and social security payments received by retired persons are usually dependable and durable, so they can be included in stable monthly income.

The federal Equal Credit Opportunity Act (see Chapter 14) prohibits age discrimination in lending. Nonetheless, it is not illegal for an underwriter to consider an elderly loan applicant's life expectancy when deciding whether or not to approve a loan.

Investment Income. Dividends or interest on investments may be counted as part of stable monthly income. The underwriter will calculate an average of the investment income for the previous two years. Of course, if the loan applicant is going to cash in an investment to raise the funds needed for closing, then the underwriter will not regard that investment as a durable source of income.

Rental Income. A lender will count income from rental properties as stable monthly income if a stable pattern of rental income can be verified. The applicant should be prepared to submit authenticated copies of the property's books showing gross earnings and operating expenses for the previous two years, along with his or her income tax returns.

There are many unpredictable factors connected with rental income, such as emergency repairs, vacancies, and tenants who don't pay. To leave a margin for error, the underwriter usually includes only a certain percentage (for example, 75%) of the verified rental income in the loan applicant's stable monthly income. (The percentage allowed varies, depending on the type of loan applied for.)

If the loan applicant has negative rental income—if property expenses add up to more than the rent that the property generates—it will be treated as a liability when the underwriter calculates the applicant's monthly obligations.

Separate Maintenance, Alimony, and Child Support. These types of income are considered part of stable monthly income only if it appears that the payments will be made reliably. That determination depends on whether the payments are required by a court decree, how long the loan applicant has been receiving the payments, the overall financial and credit status of the estranged or ex-spouse, and the applicant's ability to legally compel payment if necessary.

Alimony & child support:
- Copy of court decree
- Proof of receipt
- Payments must be reliable
- Child support no longer counts when child reaches mid-teens

A copy of the court decree usually must be submitted to the lender. And unless the payments are made through the court, proof of receipt of payments is also required. Some lenders accept the loan applicant's bank statements (showing that the checks have been deposited) as proof of receipt; others require photocopies of the deposited checks.

The underwriter will examine the record of payment. If some payments in the preceding 12 months were missed or were significantly late, the underwriter will probably exclude the alimony, maintenance, or child support from the loan applicant's stable monthly income.

An ex-spouse's obligation to pay child support ordinarily ends when the child turns 18. As a result, whether an underwriter will include child support payments in a loan applicant's stable monthly income depends on the age of the applicant's child. The closer a child gets to age 18, the less durable child support becomes. If the child is over 15, it is unlikely that the underwriter will count the child support payments as stable monthly income.

In some situations, a loan applicant who receives (or is entitled to receive) alimony, maintenance, or child support might prefer not to list that income on the application. That might be the case, for example, if the ex-spouse is hostile or uncooperative. The Equal Credit Opportunity Act, which prohibits discrimination based on marital status in the underwriting process, prevents lenders from asking borrowers if they're divorced and from requiring them to disclose alimony or child support. Of course, if a particular source of income isn't listed on the loan application, the lender won't count it as part of the applicant's stable monthly income.

Public Assistance. The Equal Credit Opportunity Act prohibits lenders from discriminating against loan applicants because all or part of their income is derived from a public assistance program (such as welfare or food stamps). Public assistance payments will be counted as part of a loan applicant's stable monthly income only if they meet the test of durability. If the applicant's eligibility for the assistance program will terminate in the near future, the underwriter will not take the payments into account.

Unacceptable Types of Income. The following are some types of income that underwriters usually exclude from a loan applicant's stable monthly income.

Income that usually doesn't count as stable monthly income:
- Wages from temporary job
- Unemployment compensation
- Contributions from family members

Temporary employment. Income from any job (full- or part-time) that the employer classifies as temporary ordinarily does not count as stable monthly income. That's true even if there's no definite termination date.

> **Example:** A recent flood damaged a large section of an industrial complex. The property manager has hired several full-time workers to help clean up the debris and repair the damage. These jobs have no termination date, but they're temporary in nature. As a result, the workers' wages wouldn't be considered stable monthly income.

In some cases, however, when a loan applicant has supported him or herself through a particular type of temporary work for years, that income can be presented to the lender as income earned through self-employment.

Unemployment compensation. Unemployment compensation is rarely treated as stable monthly income because eligibility usually lasts only for a specified number of weeks (for example, 26 weeks). However, in some cases a worker receives unemployment compensation during a certain period each year, because of the seasonal nature of his or her work. For example, a farm worker or resort employee who can't find other work during the off-season might collect some unemployment benefits every year. If a loan applicant's tax returns for the preceding two years establish that unemployment benefits have been a regular part of his or her income, and this pattern appears likely to continue, an underwriter may be willing to count the benefits as stable monthly income.

Income from unobligated family members. An underwriter will ordinarily consider only the earnings of the head(s) of the household—the loan applicant(s)—when calculating stable monthly income. Contributions from other family members who are going to occupy the home, such as teenage children or an elderly parent, are usually voluntary rather than contractual. Since these other family members have no legal obligation to the lender or the borrower and may move out at any time, their contributions could stop without notice. As a result, they aren't regarded as durable.

However, if a primary borrower's family member is listed on the application as a co-borrower, that family member's income will be considered in the qualifying process. (See the discussion of cosigners later in this chapter.)

Calculating Stable Monthly Income

After deciding which of the loan applicant's forms of income meet the tests of quality and durability, the underwriter returns to the question of quantity. The income from all the acceptable sources is added up to determine the applicant's stable monthly income.

Many types of income are paid to the recipient once a month, but others are paid weekly, every two weeks, quarterly, or annually. Since what matters for the purposes of underwriting is stable *monthly* income, all payments are converted to monthly figures.

To convert hourly wages to monthly earnings, multiply the hourly wage by the number of hours the loan applicant works per week, then multiply by 52 (weeks in a year) and divide by 12 (months in a year).

Example:

Hourly wage: $14.50

Hours per week: 40

Weekly income: $14.50 × 40 = $580

Annual income: $580 × 52 = $30,160

Monthly income: $30,160 ÷ 12 = $2,513

There's a shortcut. You can reach the same result by multiplying the hourly wage by 173.33 (as long as the buyer is being paid for a 40-hour week).

Example:

Hourly wage: $14.50

Hours per week: 40

Monthly income: $14.50 × 173.33 = $2,513

Notice that being paid every two weeks (26 payments per year) is not the same as being paid twice a month (24 payments per year). If the buyer is paid every two weeks, multiply the payment amount by 26 to get the annual total, then divide that by 12 to get the monthly figure.

Nontaxable Income. To calculate a loan applicant's stable monthly income, an underwriter uses gross income figures—the full amount earned or received, without subtracting the taxes that have been withheld or that the applicant will have to pay. Qualifying standards have been set with the understanding that the applicant is required to pay taxes on most, if not all, of his or her stable monthly income, and only what's left over—the after-tax income—is actually available for personal use.

However, certain types of income, such as child support, disability payments, and some public assistance, are generally exempt from taxation. Since the recipient doesn't have to pay taxes on this income, 100% of it can be used for personal expenses, like paying the mortgage and other bills. An underwriter may take this into account when calculating a loan applicant's stable monthly income, by "grossing up" any nontaxable income. For instance, in the calculations, the underwriter might add 25% to the amount of child support a loan applicant actually receives, to approximate the equivalent amount of gross taxable income the child support payments represent.

Example: Each month, Cheryl Bowie earns $3,600 and receives $390 in child support from her ex-husband. When she applies for a mortgage, the underwriter grosses up the child support figure because Bowie won't have to pay income taxes on that part of her income. The underwriter estimates how much gross income the child support represents by adding 25% to it.

$390 + 25% = $487.50 (grossed up monthly child support)

$3,600	Employment income
+ 487.50	Child support
$4,087.50	Stable monthly income

Income Ratios

Once the underwriter has calculated the loan applicant's stable monthly income, the next step is to measure the adequacy of that income: Is it enough so that the applicant can afford the proposed monthly mortgage payment? To measure adequacy, underwriters use **income ratios**. The rationale behind the ratios is that if a borrower's expenses exceed a certain percentage of his or her monthly income, the borrower may have a difficult time making the payments on the loan.

There are basically two types of income ratios:

- A **debt to income ratio** (total obligations to income ratio) measures the proposed monthly mortgage payment plus any other regular installment debt payments against the monthly income.
- A **housing expense to income ratio** measures the monthly mortgage payment alone against the monthly income.

To measure adequacy of stable monthly income, underwriter uses income ratios:
- Total obligations to income ratio
- Housing expense to income ratio

For the purpose of income ratio calculations, the monthly mortgage payment includes principal, interest, property taxes, and hazard insurance—often abbreviated PITI. (When applicable, the monthly PITI payment will also include mortgage insurance and homeowners association or condominium association dues.) Each ratio is expressed as a percentage.

Example: Alice Cochrane's salary is $3,200 a month and her husband Eric's salary is $2,800, so their combined stable monthly income is $6,000. The mortgage they're applying for would require monthly PITI payments of $1,800. To calculate their housing expense to income ratio, divide the PITI payment by their monthly income:

$1,800 ÷ $6,000 = .30, or 30%

Their proposed housing expense represents 30% of their stable monthly income, so their housing expense to income ratio is 30%.

The Cochranes' other debt payments (credit cards, car loan, etc.) amount to $480 per month. To calculate their debt to income ratio, add the proposed housing expense and the other debt payments together, then divide by their monthly income:

$1,800 + $480 = $2,280 ÷ $6,000 = .38, or 38%

Their total monthly debt payments represent 38% of their stable monthly income, so their debt to income ratio is 38%.

Whether the income ratios in the example would be considered too high would depend on the lender and the type of loan the Cochranes were applying for. The specific income ratio limits used in each of the various financing programs—conventional, FHA, and VA—will be discussed in later chapters.

It's worth noting that in most loan programs, maximum income ratios are treated as guidelines rather than hard-and-fast limits. A loan may be approved in spite of a debt to income ratio or housing expense ratio that exceeds the recommended limit, as long as there are sufficient compensating factors—other strengths in the application that compensate for the weakness in income.

On the whole, lenders tend to be more concerned about the debt to income ratio than the housing expense to income ratio. The ratio that takes into account all of the monthly debt payments (including the housing expense) is a better predictor of default than the ratio that takes into account only the housing expense.

In recent years, some lenders have started considering a loan applicant's **debt-to-housing gap ratio**, in addition to the two traditional income ratios. The gap ratio measures the difference between a loan applicant's debt to income ratio and housing expense to income ratio. (Returning to the example, the Cochrane's debt to income ratio is 38% and their housing expense to income ratio is 30%, so the gap ratio is 8%.) A big gap may indicate that the applicant is carrying too much debt, even if the debt-to-income ratio doesn't exceed the lender's guidelines.

Cosigners. Sometimes a home buyer applies for a loan with a co-borrower who will not be occupying the property and will not have an ownership interest in it. This type of co-borrower is often referred to as a **cosigner**, because he or she will sign the promissory note along with the primary borrower. A primary borrower and a cosigner have **joint and several liability** for the loan, which means that a court can order either one of them to pay the entire loan balance, not just half of it. A cosigner may also be called a guarantor or surety.

Cosigner helps borrower qualify by sharing responsibility for loan

By sharing responsibility for repayment, a cosigner helps the primary borrower qualify for the loan. For example, parents may use their established income and financial status to help a son or daughter who otherwise would be unable to purchase a house. The lender is willing to make the loan because the borrower's parents will have to repay it if the borrower fails to do so.

Like a primary borrower, a cosigner must have income, assets, and a credit reputation that are acceptable to the lender. Marginal cosigners shouldn't be used; they may do more harm than good to the loan application.

To analyze an application involving a cosigner, the underwriter will combine the cosigner's stable monthly income with the primary borrower's, combine their housing expenses and other debts, and then calculate income ratios using these combined figures. In addition, the underwriter will calculate income ratios for the primary borrower alone, to make sure that they aren't too far over the standard limits. The primary borrower shouldn't be relying too heavily on the cosigner's income in order to qualify for the loan.

Exercise No. 1

Roy Cutter has recently been honorably discharged from the U.S. Air Force, where he received training as an airplane mechanic. After discharge, Roy and his wife Judy moved to a new city. Roy accepted a full-time job three months ago with an airline, with a starting position of apprentice mechanic; two weeks after that, Judy found a job with a local hospital as a vocational nurse. Roy's hourly wage is $26; Judy earns $685 a week.

1. What is the Cutters' stable monthly income?

2. Are there any special circumstances that might result in loan approval even though the Cutters have only been with their employers for a short time?

Net Worth

Net worth: assets minus liabilities
- Indicates ability to manage financial affairs
- Applicant must have enough liquid assets to close transaction

The second component of creditworthiness is net worth. An individual's net worth is determined by subtracting personal liabilities from total personal assets.

Someone who has built up a significant net worth from earnings, savings, and other investments clearly has the ability to manage financial affairs. Thus, lenders use net worth as a gauge of how well a loan applicant handles money.

Getting an idea of the applicant's financial management skills isn't the only reason for investigating his or her net worth, however. The underwriter also needs to make sure the applicant has sufficient liquid assets to close the purchase transaction.

Funds for Closing

Liquid assets: cash and other assets that can be easily converted into cash

Liquid assets include cash and any other assets that can be quickly converted to cash, such as stock. A loan applicant must have enough liquid assets to cover the cash downpayment, the closing costs, and other expenses incidental to the purchase of the property.

In addition, as we mentioned earlier in the chapter, the applicant may be required to have **reserves** left over after making the downpayment and paying the closing costs. The reserves generally must be enough cash on deposit, or enough other liquid assets, to cover a specified number of mortgage payments. This provides some assurance that the applicant could handle financial emergencies, such as unexpected bills or a temporary interruption of income, without defaulting on the mortgage.

Whether a loan applicant is required to have reserves—and if so, how many months of reserves—depends on the lender and the loan program. When reserves are required, the most common requirement is two or three months' worth of mortgage payments in reserve. Affordable housing programs (loan programs targeted at low-income and first-time buyers) often require only one month's payment in reserve. In any case, if the loan applicant will have more than the required amount in reserve after closing, that strengthens the application.

Assets

Almost any assets that a loan applicant has may help the application. Real estate, automobiles, furniture, jewelry, stocks, bonds, or cash value in a life insurance policy can all be listed on the application form, and the underwriter will take whatever steps are necessary to verify the information provided. Liquid assets tend to be more helpful than non-liquid ones, and the asset that underwriters usually regard most favorably is the most liquid one of all: money in the bank.

Bank Accounts. When standard documentation procedures are followed, a "Request for Verification of Deposit" form (Figure 8.2) is used to verify the loan applicant's funds. The verification form is sent directly to the bank where the account is, and returned to the underwriter without passing through the applicant's hands.

Verification of funds in bank accounts:
- Verification of deposit form sent to bank, or
- Bank statements for 2 or 3 months

In contrast, when streamlined documentation is allowed, the underwriter relies on bank statements to check how much money a loan applicant has in his or her bank account(s). The applicant is simply asked to submit original bank statements for the previous two or three months to show that there is sufficient cash for closing.

In reviewing either the applicant's bank statements or the completed Verification of Deposit form, the underwriter has these questions in mind:

1. Does the verified information conform to the statements in the loan application?
2. Does the applicant have enough money in the bank to meet the expenses of the purchase?
3. Has the bank account been opened only recently (within the last three months)?
4. Is the present balance notably higher than the average balance?
5. If the applicant claims that this account was the source of the good faith deposit (the earnest money), is the average balance high enough to confirm that?

Recently opened accounts or higher-than-normal balances must be explained, because these strongly suggest that the applicant has resorted to borrowed funds for the downpayment and closing costs. As a general rule, a home buyer is not allowed to borrow from relatives, friends, or other sources to come up with either the funds needed for closing or the reserves. Borrowing the money would defeat the purpose of the lender's requirements: the buyer would have an additional debt instead of an investment in the property.

Fig. 8.2 Request for Verification of Deposit form

FannieMae

Request for Verification of Deposit

Privacy Act Notice: This information is to be used by the agency collecting it or its assignees in determining whether you qualify as a prospective mortgagor under its program. It will not be disclosed outside the agency except as required and permitted by law. You do not have to provide this information, but if you do not your application for approval as a prospective mortgagor or borrower may be delayed or rejected. The information requested in this form is authorized by Title 38, USC, Chapter 37 (If VA); by 12 USC, Section 1701 et.seq. (If HUD/FHA); by 42 USC, Section 1452b (if HUD/CPD); and Title 42 USC, 1471 et.seq. or 7 USC, 1921 et.seq. (If USDA/FmHA).

Instructions: Lender – Complete Items 1 through 8. Have applicant(s) complete Item 9. Forward directly to depository named in Item 1.
Depository – Please complete Items 10 through 18 and return DIRECTLY to lender named in Item 2.
The form is to be transmitted directly to the lender and is not to be transmitted through the applicant(s) or any other party.

Part I – Request

1. To (Name and address of depository)	2. From (Name and address of lender)

I certify that this verification has been sent directly to the bank or depository and has not passed through the hands of the applicant or any other party.

3. Signature of lender	4. Title	5. Date	6. Lender's No. (Optional)

7. Information To Be Verified

Type of Account	Account in Name of	Account Number	Balance
			$
			$
			$

To Depository: I/We have applied for a mortgage loan and stated in my financial statement that the balance on deposit with you is as shown above. You are authorized to verify this information and to supply the lender identified above with the information requested in Items 10 through 13. Your response is solely a matter of courtesy for which no responsibility is attached to your institution or any of your officers.

8. Name and Address of Applicant(s)	9. Signature of Applicant(s)

To Be Completed by Depository

Part II – Verification of Depository

10. Deposit Accounts of Applicant(s)

Type of Account	Account Number	Current Balance	Average Balance For Previous Two Months	Date Opened
		$	$	
		$	$	
		$	$	

11. Loans Outstanding To Applicant(s)

Loan Number	Date of Loan	Original Amount	Current Balance	Installments (Monthly/Quarterly)		Secured By	Number of Late Payments
		$	$	$	per		
		$	$	$	per		
		$	$	$	per		

12. Please include any additional information which may be of assistance in determination of credit worthiness. (Please include information on loans paid-in-full in Item 11 above.)

13. If the name(s) on the account(s) differ from those listed in Item 7, please supply the name(s) on the account(s) as reflected by your records.

Part III – Authorized Signature - Federal statutes provide severe penalties for any fraud, intentional misrepresentation, or criminal connivance or conspiracy purposed to influence the issuance of any guaranty or insurance by the VA Secretary, the U.S.D.A., FmHA/FHA Commissioner, or the HUD/CPD Assistant Secretary.

14. Signature of Depository Representative	15. Title (Please print or type)	16. Date
17. Please print or type name signed in item 14	18. Phone No.	

Fannie Mae
Form 1006 July 96

There are exceptions to this rule, however. A buyer may be allowed to use funds from a loan secured by an asset such as a car, stock, a certificate of deposit, a life insurance policy, or real estate other than the home being purchased. Of course, the payments on such a secured loan would be counted as part of the buyer's total obligations when the debt to income ratio is calculated.

Also, affordable housing programs often have more flexible policies than standard programs. The buyer may be allowed to borrow part of the funds needed for closing from a relative or certain other sources. (See Chapter 10 for more information.)

Note, too, that a buyer may obtain the money needed for closing from a relative or another source if the buyer won't be required to repay it—in other words, if the money is a gift rather than a loan. We'll discuss the issue of gift funds later in this chapter.

Real Estate for Sale. If a loan applicant is selling another property to raise cash to buy the subject property, the net equity in the property that is for sale can be counted as a liquid asset, available to be applied to the downpayment, closing costs, and required reserves. The **net equity** is the difference between the market value of the property and the sum of the liens against the property plus the selling expenses:

Market value
− Liens and selling expenses
Net equity in real estate to be sold

Net Equity = Market Value – (Liens + Selling Expenses)

In other words, the loan applicant's net equity is the amount of money that he or she can expect to receive from the sale of the property.

Example: The Yamamotos put their home up for sale a month ago, and now they've found the home they want to buy. They've signed a purchase agreement for the new home that's contingent on the sale of the old home and also on their ability to obtain financing. When they apply for a loan to finance the purchase of their new home, the underwriter will count their net equity in the old home as a liquid asset.

$289,000	Market value of old home
–213,000	First mortgage (to be paid off)
– 10,000	Home improvement loan (to be paid off)
$66,000	Gross equity
– 29,000	Estimated cost of selling old home
$37,000	Net equity in old home
+ 13,000	In savings account
$50,000	Available for purchase of new home

The underwriter's calculation of net equity may begin with the appraised value or the listing price of the old home or, if the loan applicant has already found a buyer for the old home, with the price that buyer has agreed to pay. Selling costs vary from one area of the country to another, but 10% of the listing or sales price is often used as a rough estimate.

If equity is the exclusive source or one of the main sources of money for the purchase of the new home, the lender will not actually fund the loan until it has been given proof that the old home has been sold and the borrower has received the sale proceeds. A copy of the final settlement statement from the sale of the old home is usually required.

Of course, the purchase of the new home may be ready to close before the buyer has succeeded in selling the old home. In that case, the buyer may want to apply for a **swing loan** to obtain the cash needed for closing. The swing loan will be secured by the buyer's equity in the old home, and it will be paid off out of the proceeds from the eventual sale of the old home. (A swing loan may also be called a **bridge loan** or **gap loan**; it bridges the financial gap between the purchase of the new home and the sale of the old one.)

Other Real Estate. Often a loan applicant owns real estate that he or she is not planning to sell. Whether the real estate is income producing (e.g., rental property) or not (e.g., vacant land), it is an asset and should be considered in connection with the loan application.

Bear in mind, though, that it's the equity, not the value of the property, that contributes to net worth. Only the equity can be converted into cash in the event of need. When a loan applicant owns real estate with little or no equity in it, its impact as a liability cancels out its value as an asset.

Liabilities

All of the loan applicant's personal liabilities are subtracted from the total value of his or her assets to calculate net worth. The balances owing on credit cards, charge accounts, student loans, car loans, and other installment debts are subtracted; so are any other debts, such as income taxes that are currently payable. If the applicant owns real estate, the remaining balance on the mortgage will be subtracted, along with the amount of any other liens against the property.

Liabilities include:
- Credit card & charge account balances
- Installment debts
- Taxes owed
- Liens against real estate owned

Gift Funds

If a loan applicant lacks some of the funds needed to close a transaction, his or her relatives may be willing to make up the deficit. The underwriter will usually accept this arrangement, as long as the money is a gift to the applicant rather than a loan.

The rules concerning gift funds vary from one loan program to another (see Chapters 10, 11, and 12). Most programs have rules that limit how much of the downpayment and closing costs may be covered by gift funds; the loan applicant has to come up with the rest out of his or her own money, as a minimum investment. (A buyer who has made a significant investment of his or her own funds is less likely to default. See Chapter 6.) There are also different rules governing who can provide gift funds. For example, one program might permit gift funds only from close relatives, while another program might also accept gift funds from the applicant's employer or a nonprofit organization.

Whatever the source, the gift should be confirmed by means of a "gift letter" signed by the donor. The letter should clearly state that the money is a gift and does not have to be repaid. Most lenders have forms for gift letters, and some require that their form be used.

Gift funds
- Gift letter states funds do not have to be repaid
- Funds should be deposited in applicant's account

Since gift funds have to be verified, the donor should actually give them (not just promise them) to the loan applicant as soon as possible. The applicant should deposit the gift funds in the bank so that they can be verified along with the rest of the money in his or her account.

Exercise No. 2

Mr. Able wants to buy a home. The downpayment would be $17,000, and his closing costs are estimated at $3,400; he would also be required to have reserves of $2,615 (two months' mortgage payments) left over after closing.

Able has been working at a large, established company for three years. He is paid $1,400 every two weeks. He is selling his current home for $162,500; the mortgage on the property has a principal balance of $133,250, and the estimated selling expenses are $14,500. Able has checking and savings accounts with a local bank and plans to draw on those accounts to close the transaction (refer to the Verification of Deposit form in Figure 8.3).

1. What is Able's stable monthly income?

2. What is Able's net equity in the home that he is selling?

3. Will Able have any problems closing the transaction? Explain.

4. Do you see any problems with his verification of deposit? If so, explain what they are.

5. List some possible solutions to Able's problems.

Fig. 8.3 Verification of Deposit for Exercise No. 2

Request for Verification of Deposit

Privacy Act Notice: This information is to be used by the agency collecting it or its assignees in determining whether you qualify as a prospective mortgagor under its program. It will not be disclosed outside the agency except as required and permitted by law. You do not have to provide this information, but if you do not your application for approval as a prospective mortgagor or borrower may be delayed or rejected. The information requested in this form is authorized by Title 38, USC, Chapter 37 (If VA); by 12 USC, Section 1701 et.seq. (If HUD/FHA); by 42 USC, Section 1452b (if HUD/CPD); and Title 42 USC, 1471 et.seq. or 7 USC, 1921 et.seq. (If USDA/FmHA).

Instructions: Lender – Complete Items 1 through 8. Have applicant(s) complete Item 9. Forward directly to depository named in Item 1.
Depository – Please complete Items 10 through 18 and return DIRECTLY to lender named in Item 2.
The form is to be transmitted directly to the lender and is not to be transmitted through the applicant(s) or any other party.

Part I – Request

1. To (Name and address of depository)	2. From (Name and address of lender)
Seaside Savings 1919 Second Avenue Anytown, USA	Coastal Mortgage 332 Juniper Street Anytown, USA

I certify that this verification has been sent directly to the bank or depository and has not passed through the hands of the applicant or any other party.

3. Signature of lender	4. Title	5. Date	6. Lender's No. (Optional)
Warren Carter	Loan Officer	April 19	

7. Information To Be Verified

Type of Account	Account in Name of	Account Number	Balance
Checking	Carl B. Able	11616-6	$ 482.00
Saving	Carl B. Able	61161-1	$ 3,100.00
			$

To Depository: I/We have applied for a mortgage loan and stated in my financial statement that the balance on deposit with you is as shown above. You are authorized to verify this information and to supply the lender identified above with the information requested in Items 10 through 13. Your response is solely a matter of courtesy for which no responsibility is attached to your institution or any of your officers.

8. Name and Address of Applicant(s)	9. Signature of Applicant(s)
Carl B. Able 1800 Mill Street Anytown, USA	*Carl B Able*

To Be Completed by Depository

Part II – Verification of Depository

10. Deposit Accounts of Applicant(s)

Type of Account	Account Number	Current Balance	Average Balance For Previous Two Months	Date Opened
Checking	11616-6	$ 200.00	$ 215.00	2/20
Savings	61161-1	$ 3,600.00	$ 650.00	2/20
		$	$	

11. Loans Outstanding To Applicant(s)

Loan Number	Date of Loan	Original Amount	Current Balance	Installments (Monthly/Quarterly)	Secured By	Number of Late Payments
		$	$	$ per		
		$	$	$ per		
		$	$	$ per		

12. Please include any additional information which may be of assistance in determination of credit worthiness. (Please include information on loans paid-in-full in Item 11 above.)

none

13. If the name(s) on the account(s) differ from those listed in Item 7, please supply the name(s) on the account(s) as reflected by your records.

Part III – Authorized Signature - Federal statutes provide severe penalties for any fraud, intentional misrepresentation, or criminal connivance or conspiracy purposed to influence the issuance of any guaranty or insurance by the VA Secretary, the U.S.D.A., FmHA/FHA Commissioner, or the HUD/CPD Assistant Secretary.

14. Signature of Depository Representative	15. Title (Please print or type)	16. Date
Julia G. Hedges	Assistant Vice President	April 23
17. Please print or type name signed in item 14	**18. Phone No.**	
Julia G. Hedges	809-9696	

Fannie Mae
Form 1006 July 96

Credit Reputation

In addition to evaluating a loan applicant's income and net worth, an underwriter also analyzes the applicant's credit reputation, or credit history. A good credit reputation is the third major component of creditworthiness; some residential lending experts would say it's the most important.

Personal credit report: individual's debts and repayment record

To evaluate a loan applicant's credit reputation, lenders rely on credit reports obtained from credit reporting agencies. If a report reveals significant derogatory information, the loan application could be turned down for that reason alone. Or the loan could be approved on less favorable terms, at a higher interest rate. (See the discussion of risk-based pricing at the end of this chapter.)

Credit Reports

A personal credit report presents information about an individual's loans, credit purchases, and debt repayment for the previous **seven years**. It typically covers revolving credit accounts (credit cards and charge accounts), installment debts (such as car loans and student loans), and the mortgage, if the individual owns a home. Other bills, such as utility bills or medical bills, usually aren't listed unless they were turned over to a collection agency. A facsimile of a personal credit report is shown in Figure 8.4.

The credit reporting agencies (also called credit repositories or credit bureaus) are private companies, not government agencies. There are three major credit agencies in the U.S.: Equifax, Experian (formerly TRW), and TransUnion. Keeping track of credit information about millions of people is complicated, and the reports that these companies issue on a particular individual don't necessarily match perfectly. To underwrite a mortgage loan application, a lender may obtain reports from all three agencies, or else use a "tri-merge" report that combines the information provided by the three agencies.

The credit information that's important to an underwriter includes:

- the length of the credit history,
- the payment record,
- derogatory credit incidents, and
- credit scores.

Fig. 8.4 Personal credit report

Credit Report

Nobody, Helen L.
4525 Nowhere St.
Anytown, USA

PAGE	DATE	TIME	SOCIAL SECURITY NUMBER
1 of 2	9/3/2006	10:41 AM	63X-50-0004

EMPLOYER: NEVER COMPANY
64315 S.W. 40th
ANYTOWN, USA

YEAR OF BIRTH: 1970

Account Rating: Pos.	Non	Neg.	Creditor Name / Status Comment	Status Date	Date Opened	Type	Terms	Amount	Balance	Account Number / Balance Date	Amount Past Due	Payment History number of months prior to balance date: 1 2 3 4 5 6 7 8 9 10 11 12
	X		CHASE M/C CURR WAS 30	6-01	7-98	CRC	REV	LIMIT $5,400 MIN PYMT	 $2,096 $42	96X1236549X12 8-20-06		C C C C 1 C C C C C C C
X			COMERICA BANK VISA PAID SATIS	8-98	3-89	CRC	REV	LIMIT $1,000		2144X56232165		
X			STANDARD OIL CO. CURR		1-02	CRC	G	UNKN	$0	5521X3999		0 0 0 0 0 0 0 0 0 0 0 0
X			U OF M STU LOAN CURR 8-05		6-97	EDU	UNKN	ORIGL $10,000	$823	612300 8-25-06 LAST PYT 8-07		C C C C C C C C C C C C
	X		NORDSTROM CURR WAS 30	6-01	3-96	CHG	REV	HIBAL $500	$0	898923X4 8-01-06		0 0 1 C C 0 0 0 C 0 0 0
X			SEARS CURR 8-05		12-94	CHG	REV	LIMIT $1,000	$223	31510928 8-10-06		0 0 0 0 0 C C C C C C C
		X	CO SPR CT JUDGMENT	2-18-02				$2,500		7881009 BELL CORP.		

Payment History key: C = current; 0 = current/no balance reported; 1 = 30 days past due; 2 = 60 days past due; 3 = 90 days past due; 4 = 120 days past due.

Length of Credit History

The term "credit history" is generally used as a synonym for "credit reputation." In this broad sense, it refers to an individual's overall record of borrowing and debt repayment—how well he or she has handled credit. But "credit history" is also used in a narrower sense, to mean the length or duration of the applicant's experience with credit—how many years he or she has been borrowing money and paying it back.

As a general rule, a mortgage loan applicant should have at least a two-year history of credit use, with three or more active accounts (loans or credit cards). That doesn't present a problem for most applicants, but it is an obstacle for some. Young adults who are potential home buyers may not have had a chance to establish a credit history yet. A low-income head of household applying for an affordable housing program might never have been offered credit. And some people deliberately steer clear of credit, preferring to stay out of debt and manage their budgets strictly on a cash basis. While staying out of debt is a sensible course, it can backfire when it's time to borrow money to buy a home. If an applicant doesn't have an established credit history, a key set of data is missing, and it's harder for the lender to evaluate the risk of default.

In recent years, with the encouragement of Fannie Mae and Freddie Mac, lenders have become more willing to work with loan applicants who don't have an established credit history. To take the place of or supplement a traditional credit report, the applicant may provide records showing reliable, timely payment of rent, utility bills, insurance premiums, medical bills, school tuition, child care costs, and other regular non-credit payments.

Payment Record

For each account that appears on a credit report, there's a payment record showing whether the payments have been made on time. Late payments are shown as 30 days, 60 days, or 90 days overdue.

If a loan applicant is chronically late in making payments, the underwriter will interpret that as a sign that the applicant tends to be financially overextended or fails to take debt repayment seriously (or both). Late payments on a previous mortgage are particularly damaging. However, a spotless payment record generally isn't required, and late payments that occurred more than two years ago won't usually affect the underwriter's decision.

Major Derogatory Incidents

Serious credit problems that may show up on an individual's credit report include charge-offs, debt collection accounts, repossessions, judgments, foreclosures, and bankruptcy.

Negative information on credit report:
- Slow payment
- Charge-offs
- Collections
- Repossessions
- Judgments
- Foreclosures
- Bankruptcies

- **Charge-offs.** When there has been no payment on an account for six months, the chances that it will ever be collected are low. The tax code allows the creditor to write off or "charge off" such a debt, treating it as a loss for income tax purposes.

  However, the charge-off doesn't relieve the debtor of legal responsibility for repaying the debt. The creditor may continue to try and collect the debt after it has been charged off. If the debtor pays off the debt—or the creditor is willing to settle for partial payment—the charge-off can still appear on the debtor's credit report unless the creditor agrees to have it removed.
- **Collections.** After several attempts to get a debtor to pay a bill, a frustrated creditor may turn the bill over to a collection agency. Once this happens, the debt will show up on the debtor's credit report, even if the original bill did not.
- **Repossessions.** If someone purchases an item on credit and fails to make the payments, the creditor may be able to repossess the item.
- **Judgments.** When an individual is sued and loses the lawsuit, the court may order him or her to pay a sum of money (damages) to the person who sued. This order is called a judgment.
- **Foreclosures.** As you might expect, mortgage lenders regard a real estate foreclosure on a loan applicant's credit report as a matter of special concern.
- **Bankruptcy.** Not surprisingly, lenders also consider a bankruptcy on an applicant's credit report a very bad sign.

Under the federal Fair Credit Reporting Act, all of these incidents may remain on a credit report for no more than seven years, with the exception of bankruptcy, which may remain for ten years.

An underwriter won't necessarily be concerned about an incident that occurred more than two years before the loan application, unless it was a foreclosure or a bankruptcy. These are taken very seriously;

even after years have passed, a foreclosure or a bankruptcy will lead to an especially careful review of the application and may result in denial of the loan or less favorable terms.

Credit Scores

Credit scores:
- Predict likelihood of default
- Determine appropriate level of review

Most underwriters now use credit scores to help evaluate a loan applicant's credit history. A credit reporting agency calculates an individual's credit score using the information that appears in his or her credit report and a quantitative model developed by a national credit scoring company. Credit scoring models, which are based on statistical analysis of large numbers of mortgages, are designed to predict the likelihood of successful repayment or default on a mortgage. In general, someone with poor credit scores is much more likely to default than someone with good credit scores.

Types of Scores. The two most widely used types of credit scores are FICO bureau scores and MDS bankruptcy scores. FICO scores range from under 400 to over 800. A relatively high FICO score (for example, over 700) is a positive sign. MDS bankruptcy scores, which range from zero to over 1,000, work the opposite way: a high MDS score indicates an increased likelihood of bankruptcy, so it's a negative sign. In residential mortgage lending, MDS bankruptcy scores aren't used as often as FICO scores, which have become the industry standard. You may hear FICO scores referred to by other names; for example, Equifax calls the credit scores it bases on the FICO model Beacon scores.

Level of Review. An underwriter uses a loan applicant's credit scores to decide what level of review to apply to the applicant's credit history. For example, if the applicant has good credit scores, the underwriter might perform a basic review, simply confirming that the information in the credit report is complete and accurate without investigating further. Aside from a foreclosure or a bankruptcy, the underwriter probably won't question the applicant about derogatory information in the report, because it's already been taken into account in calculating the credit scores. On the other hand, if the applicant has mediocre or poor credit scores, the underwriter will perform a more complete review, looking into the circumstances that led to the credit problems.

Maintaining Good Credit Scores. Almost any information that appears on a person's credit report may affect the credit score he receives from the agency that prepared that report. Credit activity within the previous two years has the greatest impact, however.

While most people would expect chronically late payments and collection problems to hurt someone's credit scores, some of the other factors that can lower scores might come as a surprise. For example, with a credit card, maintaining a balance near the credit limit ("maxing out" the card) will have a negative impact on the cardholder's credit scores, even if he or she always makes the payment on time.

Applying for too much credit can also have a negative effect. Each time a person applies for credit (a store charge card, a car loan, and so on), the creditor makes a "credit inquiry" that becomes part of the applicant's credit history. Occasional inquiries are fine, but too many within the past year can detract from the applicant's credit scores. From a lender's point of view, a lot of inquiries may be an indication that the applicant is in danger of becoming overextended.

Special rules apply to credit inquiries for mortgages and car loans. Someone who wants to buy a home or a car often applies to several lenders, intending to compare financing offers and accept the best one. This will result in multiple credit inquiries, even though the consumer is looking for only one loan. To allow for that type of comparison shopping, when a credit score is calculated, mortgage and car loan credit inquiries in the previous 30 days are ignored. Also, multiple inquiries for a mortgage or a car loan within any 45-day period (a typical shopping period) are counted as a single inquiry.

Obtaining Credit Information

It's a good idea for prospective home buyers to obtain their credit reports and find out their credit scores well before they apply for a mortgage. (Obtaining a copy of your own credit report does not count as a credit inquiry.) A credit report may contain incorrect information, and the Fair Credit Reporting Act requires credit reporting agencies to investigate complaints and make corrections. This process can take a month or more.

Also, even if the negative information that appears on a buyer's credit reports is correct, reviewing the reports in advance will help prepare the buyer to explain his or her credit problems to potential lenders.

Explaining Credit Problems

In some cases, negative credit reports and poor credit scores do not prevent a home buyer from obtaining a loan. Credit problems can often be explained. If the underwriter is convinced that the past problems don't reflect the loan applicant's overall attitude toward credit and that the circumstances leading to the problems were temporary and are unlikely to recur, the loan application may well be approved.

Most people try to meet their credit obligations on time; when they don't, there's usually a good reason. Loss of a job, divorce, hospitalization, prolonged illness, or a death in the family can create extraordinary financial pressures and adversely affect bill paying habits. If a loan applicant has poor credit scores, it may be possible to show that the credit problems occurred during a specific period of time for an understandable reason, and that the applicant has handled credit well both before and since that period. The applicant should put this explanation in writing and provide supporting documentation from a third party (such as hospital records).

Letter explaining negative credit report:
- State reason for problem
- Problem occurred during specific period
- Problem no longer exists
- Good credit before and since
- Provide documentation from third party
- Don't blame creditors

When explaining credit problems to a lender, it's a mistake to blame the problems on misunderstandings or on the creditors. Underwriters hear too many explanations from loan applicants who refuse to accept responsibility for their own acts, insisting instead that the blame lies elsewhere. The reaction to these explanations is very predictable: skepticism, disbelief, and rejection. Underwriters reason that an applicant's reluctance to take responsibility for past credit problems is an indication of what can be expected from him or her in the future.

If a loan applicant's credit report is laced with problems over a period of years, there's little hope for approval of a prime loan, and even a subprime loan could be difficult to obtain. Perpetual credit problems are more likely to reflect an attitude than a circumstance, and it's reasonable to assume the pattern will continue in the future.

All credit problems can be resolved with time, however. When buyers tell you they have had some credit problems in the past, it would be a mistake to leap to the conclusion that they can't qualify for a loan. Refer them to a lender and get an expert's opinion.

Other Factors in Underwriting

In addition to the main components of creditworthiness we've discussed, certain other aspects of a proposed loan affect whether or not it will be approved. These include:

- the loan type,
- the repayment period,
- owner-occupancy, and
- the property type.

These factors may either add risk, making approval of the loan less likely, or compensate for risk, making approval more likely. In a case where income, net worth, or credit reputation is somewhat marginal, one of these other factors can make a difference, for better or worse.

Loan Type. Loan type refers to whether the proposed loan is a fixed-rate mortgage, an adjustable-rate mortgage, or some other type, such as a balloon mortgage. Borrowers tend to default more often on ARMs and other loans that involve changes in the payment amount than they do on fixed-rate mortgages. So an application for an ARM generally receives closer scrutiny, and this could tip the balance toward denial of the loan.

Repayment Period. The length of a proposed loan's repayment period affects the qualifying process because of its impact on the size of the monthly mortgage payments. A 15-year loan requires much bigger monthly payments than a 30-year loan for the same amount (see Chapter 6), and therefore is considerably more difficult to qualify for. But the repayment period also has another effect. A 15-year loan presents less risk for the lender (or a secondary market purchaser) than a 30-year loan, since the loan funds are committed for a shorter period. As a result, the fact that a buyer is applying for a 15-year loan often counts as a compensating factor in the qualifying process.

Owner-Occupancy. Most home buyers intend to occupy the property they're buying. If a loan applicant won't be occupying the home he or she wants to purchase, the loan is referred to as an **investor loan**. Investor loans have a much higher default rate than loans to owner-occupants, so an applicant's investor status is treated as an additional risk factor in the qualifying process.

Property Type. The type of home to be purchased can have an impact on the process of qualifying the buyer. Manufactured homes, condominium units, and some other types of residential property tend not to appreciate as much or as reliably as site-built single-family homes. If the home that the loan applicant wants to buy isn't a regular single-family home, that may be treated as an additional risk factor. That's true even when the appraisal shows that the home meets the lender's standards for the type of property in question.

Risk-Based Loan Pricing

To end the chapter, we'll take a brief look at risk-based loan pricing. **Risk-based pricing** refers to charging mortgage borrowers different interest rates and loan fees depending on whether they're good credit risks or poor credit risks. Poor credit risks are charged higher rates and fees than good risks. Only applicants with exceptionally bad credit histories are denied loans altogether.

Risk-based pricing has long been the standard practice in subprime lending, but it's only been used to a limited extent in prime lending. Instead, prime lenders have traditionally used what's known as **average cost pricing** or **par rate pricing**. With this type of pricing, all borrowers who are approved for a loan are charged the same interest rate and fees, without regard to whether they easily met the lender's underwriting standards or just barely squeaked over the approval threshold. Those who don't meet the lender's standards are denied a loan.

Prime lenders do charge higher rates and fees for certain types of loans that entail extra risk, such as loans with high loan-to-value ratios. But until recently, it was unusual for prime lenders to charge different rates based on the strength or weakness of a loan applicant's income, net worth, and credit reputation.

Now risk-based pricing is becoming established in prime lending. Automated underwriting is one of the main reasons for this change. It's comparatively easy for an AUS to draw distinctions between strong and weak borrowers and price their loans accordingly.

The advantage of risk-based pricing is that fewer loan applicants are denied financing. It also can be considered fairer than average cost pricing, since the best credit risks don't have to subsidize those who aren't quite as good.

On the other hand, with risk-based pricing, some buyers who no longer qualify for the best rates may be priced out of the market. Risk-based pricing can also make loan shopping more confusing, since lenders can't advertise one interest rate (or annual percentage rate) for all borrowers.

Whatever the advantages and disadvantages of risk-based pricing, it has taken hold in the prime market. This is a significant change for the industry, one that's blurring the distinction between prime and subprime mortgage lending.

Outline: Qualifying the Buyer

I. The Underwriting Process

  A. Underwriting is the process of evaluating a proposed loan to assess whether the buyer and the property meet the lender's minimum standards.

  B. Qualifying standards

    1. Underwriting standards establish what a lender considers to be acceptable and unacceptable risks.

    2. Because most loans will be sold on the secondary market, most lenders use underwriting standards established by Fannie Mae, Freddie Mac, the FHA, or the VA.

  C. Automated underwriting

    1. Today, most underwriting is done using software that makes a preliminary analysis of information provided on the loan application.

    2. Automated underwriting is based on the performance of millions of existing mortgage loans, which provides evidence of which factors make default more or less likely.

    3. An automated underwriting decision will take the form of a risk classification. An application classified as "Accept" can be approved, while one classified as "Refer" won't necessarily be denied but will require further scrutiny by an underwriter.

    4. The automated underwriting report will also state whether a "low-doc" or "no-doc" loan is possible, and whether a drive-by inspection is possible instead of a full appraisal.

II. Evaluating Creditworthiness

  A. Creditworthiness can be divided into three basic categories: income, net worth, and credit reputation.

  B. Strength in one area can offset weakness in another aspect of creditworthiness.

III. Income Analysis

  A. Characteristics of income

    1. Income has three dimensions: quantity, quality (how dependable the source of income is), and durability (the likelihood the income will continue in the future).

    2. Income that meets tests for quality and durability is considered stable monthly income.

B. Stable monthly income

1. If an applicant has held the same employment position for two years or more, it won't be necessary to investigate previous work history.
2. Continuity of earnings is more important than job continuity, and education or training that will enhance earning power can substitute for a two-year work history.
3. Commissions, overtime, bonuses, and part-time or seasonal work can be considered durable income if they have been earned consistently for two years or more.
4. Self-employment income adds an extra level of risk; lenders will expect to see that the business has been operated profitably for at least two years.
5. A lender may send a Request for Verification of Employment to the applicant's employer, or the applicant may be able to provide W-2 forms and payroll stubs.
6. Retirement income (such as pensions and social security) are dependable so they are considered stable monthly income.
7. Dividends or interest from investment income may be counted as stable monthly income if they are earned reliably.
8. Income from rental properties may be considered stable monthly income, although a percentage for bad debts and vacancies will be deducted.
9. Alimony, maintenance, and child support will be included as stable monthly income if it appears payments have been made reliably.
10. Unacceptable income includes income from temporary employment, unemployment benefits, and income from unobligated family members.

C. Calculating stable monthly income

1. All income payments paid on a weekly or biweekly basis must be converted to monthly income.
2. Qualifying standards assume that income will be taxed, so if some income is nontaxable (such as child support), it may be "grossed up."

D. Income ratios

1. Debt to income ratio: The relationship between the proposed monthly mortgage payment and all other regular installment debt payments, and the monthly income.

2. Housing expense to income ratio: The relationship between the proposed monthly mortgage payment alone, and the monthly income.
3. Debt to housing gap ratio: The difference between the applicant's debt to income ratio and housing expense to income ratio.
4. The income of a cosigner, who will accept joint liability for the debt but will not be occupying the property, may be added to the applicant's income to increase the likelihood a loan will be approved.

IV. Net Worth

A. Funds for closing

1. An applicant must have adequate liquid assets to cover the downpayment, closing costs, and other associated expenses.
2. The applicant may also be required to have two or three months' reserves left over after making the downpayment, to cover unexpected expenses without risk of default.

B. Assets

1. An underwriter will send a Request for Verification of Deposit to the applicant's bank to verify funds.
2. An underwriter will be suspicious of recently opened accounts or higher-than-normal balances, which may indicate funds for the downpayment borrowed from elsewhere.
3. If the borrower is selling property to generate cash to buy new property, the lender will be concerned with the equity in the property (market value minus liens and selling expenses) rather than the property's market value alone.
4. If a buyer is unable to sell an old home in time to use the funds for toward the new home, the buyer may use a temporary swing loan.

C. Gift funds

1. An underwriter will usually accept gift funds from friends or relatives, so long as it is specified that the money is a gift and not a loan.
2. The donor should give a gift letter stating that the funds given do not need to be repaid.

V. Credit Reputation

A. Credit report

1. A credit report will contain information about an individual's loans, credit purchases, and repayments for the previous seven years.
2. There are three credit reporting agencies, each of which can issue a separate credit report on an applicant.

B. Credit history
    1. Credit history, in its narrower sense, refers to how long an individual has been borrowing money and paying it back.
    2. While most applicants should have at least a two-year credit history, lending options are increasingly available for applicants without an established credit history.

C. Major derogatory incidents that will be listed on a credit report include charge-offs, collections, repossessions, judgments, foreclosures, and bankruptcies.

D. Credit scores
    1. Credit scores predict the likelihood that an individual will default on a loan, given her previous credit history.
    2. The most widely used credit scores are FICO scores.

VI. Other Factors in Underwriting

A. Loan type: An ARM is riskier than a fixed-rate loan, and may require closer scrutiny.

B. Loan term: A 15-year loan is less risky to a lender than a 30-year loan.

C. Owner-occupancy: If a borrower doesn't plan to live in the property being purchased, it is considered an investor loan and a higher risk.

D. Property type: Loans for certain property types that don't appreciate as fast, such as condos and mobile homes, might be considered riskier.

VII. Risk-based Pricing

A. Subprime lenders use risk-based pricing; they make loans to borrowers with poor credit histories and charge them higher rates and fees than they charge other borrowers.

B. Prime lenders have traditionally charged all borrowers who met their standards the same rates, and turned away loan applicants who didn't meet their standards.

C. Now prime lenders are beginning to use risk-based pricing, blurring the line between prime and subprime lending.

Key Terms

Underwriting: The process of evaluating the financial status of a loan applicant and the value of the property he or she hopes to buy, to determine the risk of default and risk of loss in the event of foreclosure.

Underwriter: The employee of an institutional lender who evaluates loan applications, deciding which loans to approve.

Qualifying standards: The rules (concerning income, net worth, credit history, loan-to-value ratios) that an underwriter applies in deciding whether or not to approve a loan application; also called underwriting standards.

Automated underwriting (AU): Underwriting using software that makes a preliminary analysis of a loan application and makes a recommendation for approval or additional scrutiny.

Automated underwriting system (AUS): A computer program designed to perform automated underwriting; widely used.

Stable monthly income: Gross monthly income (from primary and secondary sources) that meets the lender's tests of quality and durability.

Income ratio: A test applied in qualifying a buyer for a loan, to determine whether or not he has sufficient income; the buyer's proposed housing expense and other debt repayments should not exceed a specified percentage of his stable monthly income.

Debt to income ratio: A ratio describing the maximum percentage of total monthly income that may be taken up by the proposed housing expense plus all other installment debt payments.

Housing expense to income ratio: A ratio describing the maximum percentage of total monthly income that may be taken up by the proposed housing expense.

Debt to housing gap ratio: The difference between a loan applicant's debt to income ratio and housing expense to income ratio.

Cosigner: A co-borrower who agrees to share liability with a borrower but who will not be occupying the property or have an ownership interest, in order to help the borrower qualify for the loan.

Net worth: An individual's personal financial assets, minus total personal liabilities.

Asset: Anything of value an individual owns.

Net equity: The market value of a property, minus any liens against the property and all anticipated selling expenses.

Gift funds: Money given to a buyer who would otherwise not have enough cash to close the transaction.

Gift letter: A document in which a donor of gift funds states that money given is not a loan and does not have to be repaid; required by a lender when the borrower intends to use gift funds as part of the downpayment or closing costs.

Credit report: A report prepared by a credit reporting agency outlining the credit history of an individual, showing amounts of debt and record of repayment.

Credit score: A figure used in underwriting to evaluate a loan applicant's credit history, calculated by a credit reporting agency.

Chapter Quiz

1. To evaluate the quality of a loan applicant's income, an underwriter considers whether the income:
   a. is derived from a dependable source
   b. is taxable
   c. can be expected to continue for a sustained period
   d. can be treated as a liquid asset

2. As a general rule, a loan applicant should have been continuously employed in the same field for at least:
   a. one year
   b. two years
   c. three years
   d. five years

3. The loan applicant receives child support from her ex-husband. Their child is now 16 years old. Will the child support payments be counted as part of the applicant's stable monthly income?
   a. Yes
   b. Only if the ex-husband has made the payments reliably
   c. Only if the applicant can provide proof of receipt
   d. No

4. The Hendersons have applied for a mortgage loan. Which of these is the underwriter most likely to treat as part of their stable monthly income?
   a. Wages the Hendersons' teenage daughter earns at a part-time job
   b. Unemployment compensation the husband is collecting
   c. Overtime the wife has been earning at her permanent job
   d. Money the husband has earned through occasional freelance work

5. After determining the quantity of the loan applicant's stable monthly income, the underwriter measures the adequacy of the income using:
   a. the consumer price index
   b. income ratios
   c. gross multipliers
   d. federal income tax tables

6. One reason an underwriter looks at a loan applicant's net worth is to see how well the applicant manages his or her financial affairs. Another reason is to:
   a. determine if the applicant has enough liquid assets to cover the costs of purchase and the required reserves
   b. find out if the new mortgage will have first lien position
   c. verify the accuracy of the applicant's credit rating
   d. prevent the applicant from resorting to gift funds for part of the closing costs

7. The Stanleys are selling their old home, and they plan to use the sale proceeds as a downpayment in buying a new home. In adding up the Stanleys' liquid assets, an underwriter would be willing to include:
   a. the sales price of the old home
   b. the net equity of the old home
   c. the gross equity of the old home
   d. None of the above

8. Bronowski doesn't have enough money for closing, so his parents are going to give him $2,500. The underwriter will:
   a. reject the loan application
   b. deduct the amount of the gift from the maximum loan amount
   c. require the parents to sign the promissory note
   d. require the parents to sign a gift letter

9. A personal credit report generally includes information about an individual's debts and payment history for the preceding:
   a. fifteen years
   b. twelve years
   c. seven years
   d. five years

10. The Olsens have a proposed monthly housing expense of $1,800, a monthly student loan payment of $180, and a monthly credit card payment of $100. Their stable monthly income is $6,500. What is their debt to income ratio?
    a. 28%
    b. 32%
    c. 4%
    d. 312.5%

Answer Key

1. a. The quality of an applicant's income reflects the dependability of the source of the income.

2. b. An underwriter will prefer to see that an applicant has been employed in the same field for at least two years.

3. d. While child support is usually included as stable monthly income if it is regularly paid, if the child is 16 the child support isn't going to continue for three years, so it won't be counted as stable monthly income.

4. c. Overtime, commissions, or bonuses regularly earned for several years as part of a permanent job can be considered stable monthly income.

5. b. Income ratios are used to determine whether the applicant's income is adequate to support the proposed monthly mortgage payment.

6. a. Investigating an applicant's net worth is important because the applicant must not only be able to make the downpayment and closing costs, but may also be required to have reserves left over.

7. b. The loan applicants' net equity in the house they're selling (the property's market value, minus the amount of all liens and anticipated selling expenses) is considered to be a liquid asset.

8. d. If a loan applicant's parents are giving him funds for the downpayment or closing costs, the parents must provide a gift letter stating that the funds do not need to be repaid.

9. c. The information on a credit report generally covers the previous seven years.

10. b. To calculate the debt to income ratio, add the proposed housing expense and all other monthly debt payments. The total monthly payments the Olsens will make add up to $2,080, which divided by $6,500 is 32%.

Chapter 9
Qualifying the Property

The Lender's Perception of Value

- Appraisals and loan-to-value ratios

Appraisal Standards

The Appraisal Process

Appraisal Methods

- Sales comparison method
- Replacement cost method
- Income method
- Final value estimate

Dealing with Low Appraisals

- Preventing low appraisals
- Request for reconsideration of value

Introduction

Qualifying the property: Is it worth enough to serve as collateral for the loan?

After qualifying the buyer, the underwriter's second major task is qualifying the property. Qualifying a property involves an analysis of its features to determine whether it has sufficient value to serve as collateral for the proposed loan. An underwriter is concerned with both the present value of the property and whether it will maintain its value in the years to come.

Lenders make loans in anticipation of being repaid as agreed, not in anticipation of foreclosure. But regardless of the borrower's financial standing, it is the property that serves as security for the debt. Before approving the loan the underwriter makes certain that the property is worth enough to protect the lender's investment.

The Lender's Perception of Value

Underwriter relies on appraisal for estimate of market value

An underwriter's evaluation of a property is based on an appraisal prepared by a qualified appraiser. An appraisal is an *estimate* of the value of a piece of real estate. For a loan transaction, an appraiser is asked to analyze the property thoroughly and issue an objective estimate of its **market value**. Here is the most widely accepted definition of market value:

> The most probable price which a property should bring in a competitive and open market under all conditions requisite to a fair sale, the buyer and seller each acting prudently and knowledgeably, and assuming the price is not affected by undue stimulus.*

Notice that according to this definition, market value is the *most probable* price (not "the highest price") that the property *should* bring (not "will bring"). Appraisal is a matter of estimation and likelihood, not certainty.

An appraiser's estimate of market value will not necessarily coincide with the price agreed on by the buyer and seller. A purchase and sale agreement often reflects emotional or subjective considerations

*This definition is from the Uniform Standards of Professional Appraisal Practice (USPAP), guidelines adopted by the Appraisal Foundation, a nonprofit organization established in 1987 by several professional appraiser associations to enhance the quality of appraisals.

Fig. 9.1 Principles of value

Highest and Best Use: The use which, at the time of appraisal, is most likely to produce the greatest net return from the property over a given period of time.

Change: Property values are in a constant state of flux, increasing and decreasing in response to social, economic, and governmental forces.

Anticipation: Value is created by the expectation of benefits to be received in the future.

Supply and Demand: Value varies directly with demand and inversely with supply.

Substitution: The maximum value of property is set by how much it would cost to obtain another property that is equally desirable, assuming there would not be a long delay or significant incidental expenses involved in obtaining the substitute.

Conformity: The maximum value of property is realized when there is a reasonable degree of social and economic homogeneity in the neighborhood.

Contribution: The value of real property is greatest when the improvements produce the highest return commensurate with their cost (the investment).

Competition: Profits tends to encourage competition, and excess profits tend to result in ruinous competition.

that matter to the buyer and seller, but aren't pertinent to the property's market value. It's the true market value that the lender cares about.

To estimate market value, appraisers take into account the fundamental appraisal concepts known as the "principles of value." Figure 9.1 summarizes some of these principles.

Appraisals and Loan-to-Value Ratios

Lender uses appraised value to determine how much money to loan with property as security

A lender uses a property's appraised value to determine how much money it can safely loan with that property as security. The **loan-to-value ratio (LTV)** expresses the relationship between the loan amount and the property's value. For example, if a lender makes an $80,000 loan secured by a home appraised at $100,000, the loan-to-value ratio is 80%; the loan amount is 80% of the property's value, and the buyer makes a 20% downpayment. A $75,000 loan on the same property would have a 75% LTV and a 25% downpayment. The lower the LTV, the smaller the loan amount and the bigger the downpayment.

Loan-to-value ratio (LTV) affects:
- Risk of default
- Risk of loss if foreclosure required

LTVs and Risk. The loan-to-value ratio affects the degree of risk involved in the loan—both the risk of default and the risk of loss in the event of default. Borrowers are less likely to default on loans with low LTVs. A borrower who makes a large downpayment has a substantial investment in the property, and will therefore try harder to avoid foreclosure. And when foreclosure is necessary, the lender is more likely to recover the entire debt if the LTV is relatively low. Foreclosure sale proceeds are often less than the full market value of the property, but if the original loan amount was only 75% of the value (for example), it would be surprising if the sale proceeds were less than the loan balance.

Lower LTV = Lower Risk

Lenders use LTVs to set maximum loan amounts

The higher the LTV, the greater the lender's risk. So lenders use loan-to-value ratios to set maximum loan amounts. LTV rules limit the maximum loan that a lender is willing to make in relation to the appraised value of the property. For example, if a lender's maximum loan-to-value ratio for a particular type of loan is 80%, and the property has been appraised at $100,000, then $80,000 is the maximum loan amount.

As with other underwriting standards, the LTV rules that lenders apply depend on whether the loan is conventional, FHA-insured, or VA-guaranteed. They will be discussed in more detail in Chapters 10, 11, and 12.

Loan-to-value ratio based on:
- Sales price or
- Appraised value,
- Whichever is less

Loan Based on Sales Price or Appraised Value. Lenders actually base the maximum loan amount on the sales price or the appraised value, whichever is less. This is a universal policy.

Example: $100,000 sales price; $125,000 appraised value

$100,000	sales price
× 80%	loan-to-value ratio
$80,000	maximum loan amount

In the example, the maximum loan amount is based on the lower of the two figures, the sales price. If the lender were willing to base the loan amount on the higher of the two figures (the appraised value), an 80% loan-to-value ratio would result in a loan that is 100% of the sales price ($125,000 × 80% = $100,000). In that case the borrower would be making no downpayment, which would increase the risk of default to a level that lenders generally consider unacceptable.

Collateral vs. Creditworthiness. In recent years residential lenders have become more willing to make loans with high loan-to-value ratios—90%, 95%, and even higher. This trend is due to a variety of factors, such as the high cost of housing in large cities, which makes a 20% downpayment unaffordable for many homebuyers. It's worth noting that with a high-LTV loan, the lender is relying less on the value of the collateral (to prevent foreclosure loss) and more on the creditworthiness of the borrower (to avoid default in the first place).

As a result, some high-LTV loan programs require borrowers to meet stricter qualifying standards than they would have to for a low-LTV (large downpayment) loan. On the other hand, a borrower who is able to make a very large downpayment may be eligible for a "low-doc" loan, avoiding many of the usual qualifying rules (see Chapter 8). In effect, from the lender's point of view, there's a trade-off between collateral and creditworthiness. (Mortgage insurance, discussed in Chapter 6, also has an impact on this trade-off.)

Appraisal Standards

Because of the relationship between loan-to-value ratio and risk, an accurate appraisal is an essential element of the loan underwriting process. If the appraiser overvalues the property, the loan amount will be larger than it should be, and the lender's risk of loss in the event of foreclosure may be much greater.

> **Example:** An appraiser mistakenly estimates a house is worth $175,000, when its market value is really about $148,000. Based on the appraisal, the lender decides to loan the buyer $140,000. The lender believes the loan-to-value ratio is 80%, but in fact it is almost 95%. If foreclosure is necessary, the lender may take a substantial loss.

During the 1980s, there was a considerable increase in foreclosure losses, and that led to closer scrutiny of the appraisal field. Many analysts concluded that unreliable appraisals were a significant problem for the real estate lending industry.

Appraisals used for most mortgages must be prepared by licensed or certified appraiser

In 1989, Congress addressed this problem in the Financial Institutions Reform, Recovery, and Enforcement Act, which included provisions that prompted the states to begin licensing and certifying appraisers. The law does not require all appraisers to be licensed or certified. But only appraisals prepared by state-licensed or certified appraisers in accordance with the Uniform Standards of Professional Appraisal Practice can be used in "federally related" loan transactions. The majority of residential real estate loans are federally related, since the category includes loans made by any bank or savings and loan association that is regulated or insured by the federal government.

There's an exemption for loans for less than $250,000; the appraisals for these smaller loans may be prepared by an unlicensed appraiser, even if the lender is federally regulated or insured. But the major secondary market agencies generally require all the mortgages they purchase to be based on appraisals by licensed or certified appraisers, no matter what the loan amount.

Because of the federal law, every state has had to establish procedures to license and certify appraisers. Some states, going beyond the federal requirements, have made licensing or certification mandatory for all appraisers.

The Appraisal Process

It isn't necessary for real estate agents to be able to appraise real estate, at least not with the sophistication of a professional appraiser. It is helpful, however, to know something about the mechanics of the appraisal process and the reasoning that underlies many of the appraiser's conclusions. If an agent understands how appraisers estimate value, it makes writing and financing sales that will hold together much easier.

Performing a real estate appraisal generally involves the following steps:

1. **Define the problem.** This includes identifying the property to be appraised (referred to as the **subject property**), determining the purpose of the appraisal, and specifying the "as of" date. Since property values are constantly changing, an appraisal is only valid "as of" a particular date. For a standard residential appraisal, the "as of" date is the date the appraisal is performed. But property can also

be appraised as of a specified date in the past (estimating the past value of property involved in a lawsuit, for example) or even a specified date in the future (estimating the future value of property that is going to be developed, for example).

2. **Determine what data are needed.** The data needed will depend largely on the type of property being appraised. Appraisal data can be divided into two categories: general data and specific data.
3. **Gather and verify general data.** General data refers to information concerning factors outside the property itself that have a bearing on the property's value. In a residential appraisal, this includes information about the region's economy and information about the neighborhood the home is located in. (See the list of Neighborhood Considerations in Figure 9.2.)
4. **Gather and verify specific data.** Specific data refers to information concerning the property itself—the site, the house, and other improvements on the site. (See the list of Property Features in Figure 9.2.)
5. **Apply the appropriate methods of appraisal.** The three methods of appraisal are explained in the next section of this chapter. Each method that the appraiser applies results in a **value indicator**, a figure that the appraiser treats as an indication of the subject property's value.
6. **Reconcile the results to arrive at a final value estimate.** Taking into account the purpose of the appraisal, the type of property, and the reliability of the data gathered, the appraiser weighs the value indicators and decides on a final estimate of the subject property's market value.
7. **Issue the appraisal report.** The appraiser's last step is to prepare an appraisal report, presenting the value estimate and summarizing the underlying data for the client. When property is appraised to determine its value as collateral for a loan, the appraiser's client is the lender.

The steps in the appraisal process are:

- Define the problem
- Determine data needed
- Gather, verify general data
- Gather, verify specific data
- Apply appraisal method
- Reconciliation
- Issue appraisal report

Appraisers usually gather data about the subject property through an in-person inspection. In the case of a single-family home, the appraiser ordinarily walks through the rooms taking notes about the overall condition and about particular features, good and bad.

In certain cases, however, a residential lender may require only a "drive-by appraisal" instead of an inspection.

For a drive-by appraisal, the appraiser first collects information about the subject property from online sources (such as the website of the multiple listing service), then pays a very brief visit to the property to get an idea of its general condition. The appraiser simply looks at the exterior of the house, without going inside; in fact, she might not even get out of her car. If the house is well maintained on the outside, it's reasonably safe to assume that it's also well maintained on the inside. If the house doesn't meet this test, the appraiser may tell the lender that an actual inspection is needed, or possibly even that the loan application should be rejected. A drive-by appraisal is generally appropriate only if the property is typical for the area.

Appraisal Methods

Three methods of appraisal:
- Sales comparison
- Replacement cost
- Income

There are basically three ways to appraise real estate:

1. the sales comparison method,
2. the replacement cost method, and
3. the income method.

All three methods, or only one or two, may be applied in valuing a particular property, depending on the purpose of the appraisal and the type of property in question. As described above, each method that is used yields a value indicator. The appraiser will base the final estimate of value on these value indicators.

Sales Comparison Method

Sales comparison method: sales prices of comparables used to estimate market value of subject property

Of the three appraisal methods, the sales comparison method (also known as the market data method) is the one preferred by appraisers, especially for residential property. This technique involves comparing the subject property with similar properties in the same neighborhood that have sold recently (which are called **comparable sales** or **comparables**). Appraisers know that competitive forces influence prices. Under ordinary circumstances, an informed buyer will not pay more for a particular property than he would have to pay for an equally desirable substitute property, and an informed owner will not sell property for less than she could get for it. Thus, the sales prices of comparables give a good indication of their market values and can be used to estimate the probable market value of the subject property.

Sales Comparison Appraisal vs. CMA. Many real estate agents use a competitive market analysis (CMA) to help sellers set listing prices. A CMA is essentially a less formal version of the sales comparison method of appraisal, but it should not be referred to or treated as an appraisal. A real estate agent performing a CMA may make use of certain data that an appraiser would not rely on. In addition to using actual sales as comparables, the real estate agent might use properties that are listed for sale but have not sold yet. In an appraisal, although the appraiser may analyze current listings as supporting data, the main comparables must be actual sales.

CMA: informal version of sales comparison appraisal

Sales prices are excellent indicators of market value, because they represent actual agreements between buyers and sellers in a competitive marketplace. Listing prices, on the other hand, are less accurate indicators of market value. A home's listing price may be considerably higher than the price it eventually sells for.

CMA may use current and expired listings; appraisal is based on actual sales

Even so, current listings provide useful information about market conditions for a CMA. The seller's home will be competing with those other listings. Some CMAs also compare the subject property to homes that failed to sell before their listings expired; these homes apparently were priced too high.

Identifying Legitimate Comparable Sales. Sales make better comparables than listings, and some sales make better comparables than other sales. When evaluating a sale to see if it qualifies as a legitimate comparable, the appraiser is concerned with five issues:

- the date of the sale,
- the location of the property sold,
- the physical characteristics of the property,
- the terms of sale, and
- whether the sale was an arm's length transaction.

Choosing comparables:
- Date of sale
- Location
- Physical characteristics
- Terms of sale
- Arm's length transaction

1. Date of comparable sale. The sale should be recent, within the past six months if possible. Recent sales give a more accurate indication of what is happening in the marketplace today.

An appraiser ordinarily needs at least three comparables to apply the sales comparison method. If the market has been inactive and there are not enough legitimate comparable sales from the past six months, the appraiser can go back farther. Comparable sales over one year old are generally not acceptable, however.

Three comps needed for sales comparison approach

Comps should never be more than one year old

When using a comparable sale more than six months old, it's necessary to make adjustments for the time factor, allowing for inflationary or deflationary trends or any other forces that have affected prices in the area.

Example: A comparable residential property sold ten months ago for $277,000. In general, local property values have risen by 3% over the past ten months. The comparable property, then, should be worth approximately 3% more than it was ten months ago.

$277,000	value ten months ago
× 103%	inflation factor
$285,310	approximate present value

2. Location of comparable sale. Whenever possible, comparables should be selected from the neighborhood where the subject property is located. In the absence of any legitimate comparables in the neighborhood, the appraiser can look elsewhere, but the properties selected should at least come from comparable neighborhoods.

If a comparable selected from an inferior neighborhood is structurally identical to the subject property, it is probably less valuable; conversely, a structurally identical comparable in a superior neighborhood is probably more valuable than the subject property. It is generally conceded that location contributes more to the value of real estate than any other characteristic. A high-quality property cannot overcome the adverse effects on value that a low-quality neighborhood causes. On the other hand, the value of a relatively weak property is enhanced by a stable and desirable neighborhood.

Comp's price adjusted to indicate value of subject:

- Down if subject lacks feature;
- Up if subject has extra feature

3. Physical characteristics. To qualify as a comparable, a property should have physical characteristics (construction quality, design, amenities, etc.) that are similar to those of the subject property. When a comparable has a feature that the subject property lacks—or lacks a feature that the subject property has—the appraiser will adjust the comparable's price.

Example: One of the comparables the appraiser is using is quite similar to the subject property overall, but there are several significant differences. The subject property has a two-car garage, while the comparable has only a one-car garage. Based on experience, the appraiser estimates that space for a second car adds approximately $2,400 to the value of a home in this area. The comparable actually sold for $223,500. The appraiser will add

Fig. 9.2 Sales comparison considerations

Key Considerations in a Sales Comparison Appraisal

There are many things to consider during a residential appraisal; some of them are very important, others less so. Here's a list of some of the elements that matter most to appraisers in choosing comparables and valuing homes.

Neighborhood Considerations

Percentage of home ownership. Is there a high degree of owner-occupancy or do rental properties predominate? Owner-occupied neighborhoods are generally better maintained and less susceptible to deterioration.

Vacant homes and lots. An unusual number of vacant homes or lots suggests a low level of interest in the area, which has a negative effect on property values. On the other hand, significant construction activity in a neighborhood signals strong current interest in the area.

Conformity. The homes in a neighborhood should be reasonably similar to one another in style, age, size, and quality. Strictly enforced zoning and private restrictions promote conformity and protect property values.

Changing land use. Is the neighborhood in the midst of a transition from residential use to some other type of use? If so, the properties are probably losing their value as residences (even though the change promises higher values overall because of the potential for more productive use of the land in the future).

Contour of the land. Mildly rolling topography is preferred to terrain that is either monotonously flat or excessively hilly.

Streets. Wide, gently curving streets are more appealing than narrow or straight streets. Streets should be hard surfaced and well maintained.

Utilities. Is the neighborhood adequately serviced by electricity, water, gas, sewers, and telephones?

Nuisances. Nuisances in or near a neighborhood (odors, eyesores, industrial noises or pollutants, or exposure to unusual winds, smog, or fog) hurt property values.

Prestige. Is the neighborhood considered prestigious, in comparison to others in the community? If so, that will increase property values.

Proximity. How far is it to traffic arterials and to important points such as downtown, employment centers, and shopping centers?

Schools. What schools serve the neighborhood? Are they highly regarded? Are they nearby? The quality of a school or school district can make a major difference to property values in a residential neighborhood.

Public services. Is the neighborhood properly serviced by public transportation, police, and fire units?

Government influences. Does zoning in and around the neighborhood promote residential use and insulate the property owner from nuisances? How do the property tax rates compare with those of other neighborhoods nearby?

(continued)

Property Features

Site. The appraiser will note the lot's size, shape, and topography, and how much street frontage it has. Rectangular lots are more useful than lots with irregular shapes; unusually steep lots may have problems with soil instability. Drainage and landscaping are important, and a view can add substantially to value. An easement or encroachment will be taken into account, as well as zoning and private restrictions.

Design and appeal. Is the home's overall appeal good, average, or poor? There are dozens of house styles: ranch (rambler), colonial, Victorian, etc. The appraiser will try to find comparables in the same general style as the subject property. Comparisons between one- and two-story houses generally are not valid, but a one-story house can be compared to a split-level with certain adjustments.

Construction quality. Is the quality of materials and workmanship good, average, or poor?

Age/condition. When the subject property and comparables are in similar condition, a difference in age up to five years is generally inconsequential. Is the property's overall condition good, average, or poor?

Size of house (square footage). The appraiser is concerned with the gross living area (GLA), which is the improved living area, excluding the garage, basement, and porches.

Basement. A functional basement, especially a finished basement, contributes to value. (In many cases, however, the amount a finished basement contributes to value is not enough to recover the cost of the finish work.)

Interior layout. Is the floor plan functional and convenient? It should not be necessary to pass through a public room (such as the living room) to reach other rooms, or to pass through one of the bedrooms to reach another.

Number of rooms. The appraiser will add up the total number of rooms in the house, excluding bathrooms and (usually) basement rooms. Usually the appraiser will try to find comparables with the same number of rooms as the subject.

Number of bedrooms. Differences in the number of bedrooms have a major impact on value. For instance, if all else is equal, a two-bedroom comparable is worth considerably less than a three-bedroom subject.

Number of bathrooms. A full bath is a lavatory (wash basin), toilet, and bathtub, with or without a shower; a ¾ bath is a lavatory, toilet, and shower (no tub); a ½ bath is a lavatory and toilet only. The number of bathrooms can have a noticeable effect on value.

Air conditioning. The presence or absence of an air conditioning system is important in warm climates.

Energy efficiency. With spiraling energy costs, an energy-efficient home is more valuable than a comparable one that is not. Energy-efficient features include: double-paned windows; clock-controlled thermostats; insulated ducts and pipes in unheated areas; adequate insulation for floors, walls, and attic; weather stripping for doors and windows.

Garage/carport. An enclosed garage is generally better than a carport. How many cars can it accommodate? Is there work or storage space in addition to parking space? Is it possible to enter the home directly from the garage or carport, protected from the weather?

$2,400 to that price, to reflect the fact that the subject property has more garage space than the comparable.

On the other hand, the comparable has a fireplace and the subject property does not. The appraiser estimates a fireplace adds approximately $1,100 to the value of a home. She will subtract $1,100 from the comparable's price, to reflect the fact that the subject property has no fireplace.

After adjusting the comparable's price up or down for each difference in this way, the appraiser can use the resulting figure as an indication of the value of the subject property.

4. Terms of sale. The terms of sale can affect the price a buyer will pay for a property. Attractive financing concessions (such as seller-paid discount points or seller financing with an especially low interest rate) can make a buyer willing to pay a higher price than he would otherwise be willing to pay.

An appraiser has to take into account the influence the terms of sale may have had on the price paid for a comparable property. If the seller offered the property on very favorable terms, there's an excellent chance that the sales price did not represent the true market value of the comparable.

Special financing can make buyer willing to pay more, so appraiser takes terms of sale into account when evaluating a comparable

Under the Uniform Standards of Professional Appraisal Practice, an appraiser giving an estimate of market value must state whether it is the most probable price in terms of cash, in terms of financial arrangements equivalent to cash, or in other precisely defined terms.

If the estimate is based on financing with special conditions or incentives, those terms must be clearly set forth, and the appraiser must estimate their effect on the property's value. Market data supporting the value estimate (comparables) must be explained in the same way.

5. Arm's length transaction. Finally, a comparable sale can only be relied on as an indication of what the subject property is worth if it was an arm's length transaction. In an arm's length transaction, both the buyer and the seller are informed of the property's attributes and deficiencies; both of them are acting free of unusual pressure; and the property has been offered for sale on the open market for a reasonable length of time.

Arm's length transaction:
- Both parties fully informed
- No unusual pressure to act
- Property on open market for reasonable time

Adjustments. An appraiser can rarely find three ideal comparables: three homes exactly like the subject property, in the same neighborhood, that all sold for cash just within the last month or so. So, as you've seen, the appraiser has to make adjustments, taking into account differences in time, location, physical characteristics, or terms of sale.

It stands to reason that the more adjustments an appraiser has to make, the less reliable the resulting estimate of value will be. In fact, if the necessary adjustments add up to a significant percentage of a comparable's sales price (for example, 25% of the price), then that property isn't sufficiently similar to the subject to make a good comparable. Adjustments are an inevitable part of the sales comparison approach, but appraisers try to keep them to a minimum by selecting the best comparables available.

Replacement Cost Method

Replacement cost method: a property's value won't exceed the cost of replacing it

The replacement cost method of appraisal is based on the premise that the value of a house or other building is limited by the cost of building a new one just like it. (This is a version of the principle of substitution: a buyer won't pay more for a property than it would cost to obtain an equally desirable substitute. See Figure 9.1.) To use the cost method, appraisers must keep abreast of construction costs in their area. Here are the steps involved in the cost method:

Step 1: Estimate the cost of replacing the building(s) and any other improvements on the property.

Step 2: Estimate and deduct any accrued depreciation.

Step 3: Add the value of the lot to the depreciated value of the improvements.

Estimating Replacement Cost. A building's **replacement cost** is how much it would currently cost to construct a new building with equivalent utility—in other words, one that would have essentially the same features and could be used in essentially the same way. Replacement cost is not the same thing as **reproduction cost**, which is how much it would cost to construct an exact duplicate or replica of the building, at current prices. In most cases, the reproduction cost would be considerably higher than the replacement cost, and would not give an accurate indication of the property's current market value. For an ordinary appraisal, the appraiser is concerned with replacement cost, not reproduction cost.

There are a number of ways to estimate replacement cost. The simplest is the **square foot method**, also known as the comparative-unit method. By analyzing the average cost per square foot of construction for recently built improvements comparable to the subject property's, the appraiser can estimate what the square foot cost of replacing the improvements under appraisal would be.

Square foot method: using square foot cost of recently built comps to estimate cost of replacing subject

To calculate the cost of replacing the building on the subject property, the appraiser multiplies the estimated cost per square foot by the number of square feet in the building. The number of square feet in a house is determined by measuring the dimensions of each floor of the structure, including the outer wall surfaces. The square footage refers only to the improved living area; the garage, basement, and porches are excluded.

> **Example:** The subject property is a ranch-style house with a wooden exterior, containing 1,800 square feet. Based on an analysis of the construction costs of threc recently built homes of comparable size and quality, the appraiser estimates that it would cost $126.37 per square foot to replace the home.
>
> | | |
> |---:|---|
> | 1,800 | square feet |
> | × $126.37 | cost per square foot |
> | $227,466 | estimated cost of replacing improvements |

Of course, a comparable structure (or "benchmark" building) is unlikely to be exactly the same as the subject property. Variations in design, shape, and grade of construction will affect the square foot cost—moderately or substantially. The appraiser will make appropriate adjustments to take these differences into account.

When there aren't any recently built comparable homes available, the appraiser relies on current cost manuals to estimate the basic construction costs.

Estimating Depreciation. When the home being appraised is one that has been lived in, the presumption is that it is not as valuable as a comparable new home; it has depreciated in value. So, after estimating replacement cost, the appraiser's next step is to estimate the depreciation. This is the most difficult part of the replacement cost method of appraisal.

Depreciation is a loss in value due to any cause. Value can be lost as a result of:

- deferred maintenance,
- functional obsolescence, or
- external obsolescence.

Depreciation: loss in value from any cause
- Deferred maintenance
- Functional obsolescence
- External inadequacy

Deferred maintenance, also called physical depreciation, refers to physical wear and tear, damage, and structural defects that reduce the value of the property.

Functional obsolescence, also called functional depreciation, is a loss in value due to inadequacies such as poor design or outmoded features. In older homes, not enough bathrooms in relation to the number of bedrooms is a common example of functional obsolescence.

External obsolescence (also called external inadequacy, external depreciation, or economic obsolescence) is a loss in value due to factors outside the property, such as a deteriorating neighborhood, zoning changes, or poor access to schools, shopping, or employment centers.

Depreciation is considered **curable** if the cost of correcting it could be recovered in the sales price when the property is sold. Depreciation is **incurable** if it is impossible to correct, or if it would cost so much to correct that it would not make sense to do so. Deferred maintenance and functional obsolescence may be either curable or incurable. External obsolescence, on the other hand, is always incurable, because it is caused by factors beyond the property owner's control.

After estimating how much the depreciation in each of the three categories is reducing the subject property's value, the appraiser deducts the depreciation from the estimated replacement cost of the improvements.

Example:

$227,466	Estimated replacement cost
– 8,510	Deferred maintenance (roof in need of repair; garage door should be replaced)
– 7,050	Functional obsolescence (living room too small; family room too far from kitchen)
– 3,000	External obsolescence (odors from nearby factory)
$208,906	Depreciated value of improvements

Because estimating depreciation is difficult, the older the property, the less reliable the replacement cost method is. In many cases, an appraiser will decide not to use the cost method in an appraisal of an older home. The cost method also isn't used for appraising a unit in a condominium.

Deferred maintenance and underwriting. An appraisal is submitted to the underwriter in one of two ways: "as is" or "subject to." An "as is" appraisal reports deferred maintenance (broken windows, worn-out roof, drainage problems, damaged siding, etc.), but the final value estimate represents the market value of the property in its current condition. In a "subject to" appraisal, the final value estimate represents what the market value of the property would be if the deferred maintenance were corrected.

Appraisal may be "as is," or "subject to" repairs

In some cases the underwriter will make correction of the deferred maintenance a condition of loan approval. These "lender-required repairs" must be completed before the loan can be funded.

Adding Land Value. The last step in the replacement cost method is to add the value of the land to the depreciated value of the improvements, to arrive at an estimate of value for the property as a whole.

Example:

$208,906	Depreciated value of the improvements
+ 59,000	Land value
$267,906	Depreciated value of the property

The value of the land is estimated by the sales comparison method. Prices recently paid for vacant lots similar to the subject property's lot are compared and used as indications of what the subject property's lot is worth.

Income Method

The income method of appraisal is based on the idea that there is a relationship between the income that a property generates and its value to a potential investor (a potential buyer). To arrive at an estimate of the subject property's value, its annual net income is divided by a capitalization rate that represents the return an investor would expect from the property.

Residences generally aren't regarded as income-producing properties, so formal income analysis techniques don't apply when a home is being appraised. If a residential appraiser uses the income method at all, she will use a simplified version called the **gross income multiplier** method (also known as the gross rent multiplier method). As a rule, this is done only when the subject property is located in a neighborhood where most of the properties are rentals, not owner-occupied homes.

Gross income multiplier method: used to estimate value of rental home

In the gross income multiplier method, the appraiser looks at the relationship between a rental property's income and the price paid for the property.

Example:

Sales price: $246,000
Monthly rent: $2,000
Conclusion: Monthly rent is equal to 0.81% of the sales price; the sales price is approximately 123 times the monthly rent.

Monthly rents may run about one percent of selling prices in one market, and more or less in another. A market exists where specific rental properties compete with each other for tenants. For competitive reasons, rents charged for similar properties tend to be much alike within the same market. As a result, if one rental property has a monthly income that is one percent of its sales price, comparable properties will have similar income-to-price ratios.

A monthly multiplier is calculated by dividing the sales price by the monthly rental income. An annual multiplier is calculated by dividing the sales price by the annual rental income.

Example:

Sales Price		Monthly Rent		Monthly Multiplier
$246,000	÷	$2,000	=	123

Sales Price		Annual Income		Annual Multiplier
$246,000	÷	$24,000	=	10.25

After locating at least four comparable residential rental properties, the appraiser determines their monthly or annual gross income multipliers (either is acceptable—it's a matter of the appraiser's preference) by dividing the rents into their respective selling prices.

Example:

Comp.	Sales Price	Monthly Rent	Monthly Multiplier
1	$237,500	$1,950	121.79
2	$245,000	$1,975	124.05
3	$250,000	$2,025	123.46
4	$253,500	$2,100	120.71

The appraiser uses the multipliers of the comparables to determine an appropriate multiplier for the subject property, taking into account the similarities and differences between the properties. Then the appraiser multiplies the rent that the subject property is generating by the chosen gross income multiplier for a rough estimate of its value as an income-producing property.

The principal weakness of the gross income multiplier method is that it is based on gross income figures and does not take into account vacancies or operating expenses. If two rental homes have the same rental income, the gross income multiplier method would indicate they are worth the same amount; but if one is older and has higher maintenance costs, the net return to the owner would be less, and so would its actual value.

If possible, the appraiser should use the subject property's **economic rent** or **market rent** (the rent the property could command in the current marketplace if it were available for lease today) as opposed to the **contract rent** (the rent the owner is actually receiving).

> **Example:** The owner leased the home two years ago for $1,850 a month and the lease contract has another year to go. Market rents have risen sharply over the past two years, so that the property could now command a much higher rent—probably about $2,175 a month. If the appraiser were to use the $1,850 contract rent in the gross income multiplier method, it would distort the estimate of value.

Final Value Estimate

If the appraiser has applied all three appraisal methods (sales comparison, replacement cost, and income), he has to analyze and compare the three results in order to draw a conclusion about the property's value. That process of interpretation is known as **reconciliation** or **correlation**.

The appraiser's experience and judgment play a critical role in reconciliation. The final estimate of value is not simply the average of the results yielded by the three approaches. The appraiser weighs each result carefully, considering all the factors that affect its reliability for the type of property in question. From that analysis, the appraiser decides on a figure that represents his or her expert opinion of the subject property's market value.

Appraiser weighs results to arrive at final value estimate

For single-family homes not used as rental properties, the sales comparison method is far more reliable than the other methods. Appraisers frequently base the final value estimate for a single-family home on the result of the sales comparison method alone.

Sales comparison method most important for residential property

Dealing with Low Appraisals

Figure 9.3 is the Uniform Residential Appraisal Report form, which is used for nearly all residential loan transactions. Reviewing the form will give you a clearer idea of what the appraiser must do before she can issue a responsible estimate of value.

Understanding the appraisal process helps real estate agents eliminate or at least minimize the most common of all selling problems, the low appraisal. No one gets through an entire real estate career without facing the low appraisal problem at least a few times; some agents never seem to escape it.

Low appraisal: value estimate below the price agreed on

A low appraisal is an estimate of value that is below (perhaps way below) the price the buyer and seller agreed on. A sale is written, the parties are pleased, and then a week or so later the agent gets the bad news. A low appraisal puts the sale in serious jeopardy.

If the transaction is contingent on financing, the buyer does not have to complete the sale if the appraisal comes in low. Buyers are understandably reluctant to pay more for a property than a professional appraiser says it is worth. And even when a buyer would like to go ahead with the purchase in spite of the low appraisal, he may not be able to afford to. Since the purchase loan is based on the sales price or the appraised value, whichever is less, a low appraisal means a smaller loan—and a bigger downpayment.

Example:

1. Buyer is prepared to make a 10% downpayment and obtain a 90% loan.
2. Sales price is $300,000.
3. Appraisal is issued at $291,000.
4. Maximum loan amount is 90% of $291,000.

$291,000	appraised value
× 90%	loan-to-value ratio
$261,900	maximum loan amount

Because of the low appraisal ($9,000 less than the sales price), the loan amount is limited to $261,900. The buyer expected to make a $30,000 downpayment ($300,000 sales price × 90% = $270,000 loan). But the buyer would now have to make a $38,100 downpayment ($300,000 – $261,900 loan = $38,100) to pay the $300,000 price.

Fig. 9.3 Uniform Residential Appraisal Report form

Uniform Residential Appraisal Report

File #

The purpose of this summary appraisal report is to provide the lender/client with an accurate, and adequately supported, opinion of the market value of the subject property.

SUBJECT

Property Address | City | State | Zip Code
Borrower | Owner of Public Record | County
Legal Description
Assessor's Parcel # | Tax Year | R.E. Taxes $
Neighborhood Name | Map Reference | Census Tract
Occupant ☐ Owner ☐ Tenant ☐ Vacant | Special Assessments $ | ☐ PUD | HOA $ | ☐ per year ☐ per month
Property Rights Appraised ☐ Fee Simple ☐ Leasehold ☐ Other (describe)
Assignment Type ☐ Purchase Transaction ☐ Refinance Transaction ☐ Other (describe)
Lender/Client | Address
Is the subject property currently offered for sale or has it been offered for sale in the twelve months prior to the effective date of this appraisal? ☐ Yes ☐ No
Report data source(s) used, offering price(s), and date(s).

CONTRACT

I ☐ did ☐ did not analyze the contract for sale for the subject purchase transaction. Explain the results of the analysis of the contract for sale or why the analysis was not performed.
Contract Price $ | Date of Contract | Is the property seller the owner of public record? ☐Yes ☐No | Data Source(s)
Is there any financial assistance (loan charges, sale concessions, gift or downpayment assistance, etc.) to be paid by any party on behalf of the borrower? ☐ Yes ☐ No
If Yes, report the total dollar amount and describe the items to be paid.

NEIGHBORHOOD

Note: Race and the racial composition of the neighborhood are not appraisal factors.

Neighborhood Characteristics	One-Unit Housing Trends	One-Unit Housing		Present Land Use %	
Location ☐ Urban ☐ Suburban ☐ Rural	Property Values ☐ Increasing ☐ Stable ☐ Declining	PRICE	AGE	One-Unit	%
Built-Up ☐ Over 75% ☐ 25–75% ☐ Under 25%	Demand/Supply ☐ Shortage ☐ In Balance ☐ Over Supply	$ (000)	(yrs)	2-4 Unit	%
Growth ☐ Rapid ☐ Stable ☐ Slow	Marketing Time ☐ Under 3 mths ☐ 3–6 mths ☐ Over 6 mths	Low		Multi-Family	%
Neighborhood Boundaries		High		Commercial	%
		Pred.		Other	%

Neighborhood Description
Market Conditions (including support for the above conclusions)

SITE

Dimensions | Area | Shape | View
Specific Zoning Classification | Zoning Description
Zoning Compliance ☐ Legal ☐ Legal Nonconforming (Grandfathered Use) ☐ No Zoning ☐ Illegal (describe)
Is the highest and best use of the subject property as improved (or as proposed per plans and specifications) the present use? ☐ Yes ☐ No If No, describe

Utilities	Public	Other (describe)		Public	Other (describe)	Off-site Improvements—Type	Public	Private
Electricity	☐	☐	Water	☐	☐	Street	☐	☐
Gas	☐	☐	Sanitary Sewer	☐	☐	Alley	☐	☐

FEMA Special Flood Hazard Area ☐ Yes ☐ No | FEMA Flood Zone | FEMA Map # | FEMA Map Date
Are the utilities and off-site improvements typical for the market area? ☐ Yes ☐ No If No, describe
Are there any adverse site conditions or external factors (easements, encroachments, environmental conditions, land uses, etc.)? ☐ Yes ☐ No If Yes, describe

IMPROVEMENTS

General Description	Foundation	Exterior Description materials/condition	Interior materials/condition
Units ☐ One ☐ One with Accessory Unit	☐ Concrete Slab ☐ Crawl Space	Foundation Walls	Floors
# of Stories	☐ Full Basement ☐ Partial Basement	Exterior Walls	Walls
Type ☐ Det. ☐ Att. ☐ S-Det./End Unit	Basement Area sq. ft.	Roof Surface	Trim/Finish
☐ Existing ☐ Proposed ☐ Under Const.	Basement Finish %	Gutters & Downspouts	Bath Floor
Design (Style)	☐ Outside Entry/Exit ☐ Sump Pump	Window Type	Bath Wainscot
Year Built	Evidence of ☐ Infestation	Storm Sash/Insulated	Car Storage ☐ None
Effective Age (Yrs)	☐ Dampness ☐ Settlement	Screens	☐ Driveway # of Cars
Attic ☐ None	Heating ☐ FWA ☐ HWBB ☐ Radiant	Amenities ☐ Woodstove(s) #	Driveway Surface
☐ Drop Stair ☐ Stairs	☐ Other Fuel	☐ Fireplace(s) # ☐ Fence	☐ Garage # of Cars
☐ Floor ☐ Scuttle	Cooling ☐ Central Air Conditioning	☐ Patio/Deck ☐ Porch	☐ Carport # of Cars
☐ Finished ☐ Heated	☐ Individual ☐ Other	☐ Pool ☐ Other	☐ Att. ☐ Det. ☐ Built-in

Appliances ☐Refrigerator ☐Range/Oven ☐Dishwasher ☐Disposal ☐Microwave ☐Washer/Dryer ☐Other (describe)
Finished area **above** grade contains: | Rooms | Bedrooms | Bath(s) | Square Feet of Gross Living Area Above Grade
Additional features (special energy efficient items, etc.)
Describe the condition of the property (including needed repairs, deterioration, renovations, remodeling, etc.).
Are there any physical deficiencies or adverse conditions that affect the livability, soundness, or structural integrity of the property? ☐ Yes ☐ No If Yes, describe
Does the property generally conform to the neighborhood (functional utility, style, condition, use, construction, etc.)? ☐ Yes ☐ No If No, describe

Freddie Mac Form 70 March 2005 | Page 1 of 6 | Fannie Mae Form 1004 March 2005

Uniform Residential Appraisal Report

File #

There are comparable properties currently offered for sale in the subject neighborhood ranging in price from $ to $.

There are comparable sales in the subject neighborhood within the past twelve months ranging in sale price from $ to $.

SALES COMPARISON APPROACH

FEATURE	SUBJECT	COMPARABLE SALE # 1		COMPARABLE SALE # 2		COMPARABLE SALE # 3	
Address							
Proximity to Subject							
Sale Price	$		$		$		$
Sale Price/Gross Liv. Area	$ sq. ft.	$ sq. ft.		$ sq. ft.		$ sq. ft.	
Data Source(s)							
Verification Source(s)							
VALUE ADJUSTMENTS	DESCRIPTION	DESCRIPTION	+(-) $ Adjustment	DESCRIPTION	+(-) $ Adjustment	DESCRIPTION	+(-) $ Adjustment
Sale or Financing Concessions							
Date of Sale/Time							
Location							
Leasehold/Fee Simple							
Site							
View							
Design (Style)							
Quality of Construction							
Actual Age							
Condition							
Above Grade Room Count	Total Bdrms. Baths	Total Bdrms. Baths		Total Bdrms. Baths		Total Bdrms. Baths	
Gross Living Area	sq. ft.	sq. ft.		sq. ft.		sq. ft.	
Basement & Finished Rooms Below Grade							
Functional Utility							
Heating/Cooling							
Energy Efficient Items							
Garage/Carport							
Porch/Patio/Deck							
Net Adjustment (Total)		☐ + ☐ -	$	☐ + ☐ -	$	☐ + ☐ -	$
Adjusted Sale Price of Comparables		Net Adj. % Gross Adj. %	$	Net Adj. % Gross Adj. %	$	Net Adj. % Gross Adj. %	$

I ☐ did ☐ did not research the sale or transfer history of the subject property and comparable sales. If not, explain

My research ☐ did ☐ did not reveal any prior sales or transfers of the subject property for the three years prior to the effective date of this appraisal.

Data source(s)

My research ☐ did ☐ did not reveal any prior sales or transfers of the comparable sales for the year prior to the date of sale of the comparable sale.

Data source(s)

Report the results of the research and analysis of the prior sale or transfer history of the subject property and comparable sales (report additional prior sales on page 3).

ITEM	SUBJECT	COMPARABLE SALE # 1	COMPARABLE SALE # 2	COMPARABLE SALE # 3
Date of Prior Sale/Transfer				
Price of Prior Sale/Transfer				
Data Source(s)				
Effective Date of Data Source(s)				

Analysis of prior sale or transfer history of the subject property and comparable sales

Summary of Sales Comparison Approach

Indicated Value by Sales Comparison Approach $

RECONCILIATION

Indicated Value by: Sales Comparison Approach $ Cost Approach (if developed) $ Income Approach (if developed) $

This appraisal is made ☐ "as is", ☐ subject to completion per plans and specifications on the basis of a hypothetical condition that the improvements have been completed, ☐ subject to the following repairs or alterations on the basis of a hypothetical condition that the repairs or alterations have been completed, or ☐ subject to the following required inspection based on the extraordinary assumption that the condition or deficiency does not require alteration or repair:

Based on a complete visual inspection of the interior and exterior areas of the subject property, defined scope of work, statement of assumptions and limiting conditions, and appraiser's certification, my (our) opinion of the market value, as defined, of the real property that is the subject of this report is $, as of , which is the date of inspection and the effective date of this appraisal.

Freddie Mac Form 70 March 2005 Page 2 of 6 Fannie Mae Form 1004 March 2005

Uniform Residential Appraisal Report

File #

ADDITIONAL COMMENTS

COST APPROACH

COST APPROACH TO VALUE (not required by Fannie Mae)

Provide adequate information for the lender/client to replicate the below cost figures and calculations.

Support for the opinion of site value (summary of comparable land sales or other methods for estimating site value)

ESTIMATED ☐ REPRODUCTION OR ☐ REPLACEMENT COST NEW	OPINION OF SITE VALUE			= $
Source of cost data	Dwelling	Sq. Ft. @ $		=$
Quality rating from cost service Effective date of cost data		Sq. Ft. @ $		=$
Comments on Cost Approach (gross living area calculations, depreciation, etc.)				
	Garage/Carport	Sq. Ft. @ $		=$
	Total Estimate of Cost-New			= $
	Less Physical	Functional	External	
	Depreciation			=$( )
	Depreciated Cost of Improvements			=$
	"As-is" Value of Site Improvements			=$
Estimated Remaining Economic Life (HUD and VA only) Years	Indicated Value By Cost Approach			=$

INCOME

INCOME APPROACH TO VALUE (not required by Fannie Mae)

Estimated Monthly Market Rent $ X Gross Rent Multiplier   = $ Indicated Value by Income Approach

Summary of Income Approach (including support for market rent and GRM)

PUD INFORMATION

PROJECT INFORMATION FOR PUDs (if applicable)

Is the developer/builder in control of the Homeowners' Association (HOA)? ☐ Yes ☐ No   Unit type(s) ☐ Detached ☐ Attached

Provide the following information for PUDs ONLY if the developer/builder is in control of the HOA and the subject property is an attached dwelling unit.

Legal name of project

Total number of phases   Total number of units   Total number of units sold

Total number of units rented   Total number of units for sale   Data source(s)

Was the project created by the conversion of an existing building(s) into a PUD? ☐ Yes ☐ No   If Yes, date of conversion

Does the project contain any multi-dwelling units? ☐ Yes ☐ No   Data source(s)

Are the units, common elements, and recreation facilities complete? ☐ Yes ☐ No   If No, describe the status of completion.

Are the common elements leased to or by the Homeowners' Association? ☐ Yes ☐ No   If Yes, describe the rental terms and options.

Describe common elements and recreational facilities

Freddie Mac Form 70 March 2005   Page 3 of 6   Fannie Mae Form 1004 March 2005

Uniform Residential Appraisal Report

File #

This report form is designed to report an appraisal of a one-unit property or a one-unit property with an accessory unit; including a unit in a planned unit development (PUD). This report form is not designed to report an appraisal of a manufactured home or a unit in a condominium or cooperative project.

This appraisal report is subject to the following scope of work, intended use, intended user, definition of market value, statement of assumptions and limiting conditions, and certifications. Modifications, additions, or deletions to the intended use, intended user, definition of market value, or assumptions and limiting conditions are not permitted. The appraiser may expand the scope of work to include any additional research or analysis necessary based on the complexity of this appraisal assignment. Modifications or deletions to the certifications are also not permitted. However, additional certifications that do not constitute material alterations to this appraisal report, such as those required by law or those related to the appraiser's continuing education or membership in an appraisal organization, are permitted.

SCOPE OF WORK: The scope of work for this appraisal is defined by the complexity of this appraisal assignment and the reporting requirements of this appraisal report form, including the following definition of market value, statement of assumptions and limiting conditions, and certifications. The appraiser must, at a minimum: (1) perform a complete visual inspection of the interior and exterior areas of the subject property, (2) inspect the neighborhood, (3) inspect each of the comparable sales from at least the street, (4) research, verify, and analyze data from reliable public and/or private sources, and (5) report his or her analysis, opinions, and conclusions in this appraisal report.

INTENDED USE: The intended use of this appraisal report is for the lender/client to evaluate the property that is the subject of this appraisal for a mortgage finance transaction.

INTENDED USER: The intended user of this appraisal report is the lender/client.

DEFINITION OF MARKET VALUE: The most probable price which a property should bring in a competitive and open market under all conditions requisite to a fair sale, the buyer and seller, each acting prudently, knowledgeably and assuming the price is not affected by undue stimulus. Implicit in this definition is the consummation of a sale as of a specified date and the passing of title from seller to buyer under conditions whereby: (1) buyer and seller are typically motivated; (2) both parties are well informed or well advised, and each acting in what he or she considers his or her own best interest; (3) a reasonable time is allowed for exposure in the open market; (4) payment is made in terms of cash in U. S. dollars or in terms of financial arrangements comparable thereto; and (5) the price represents the normal consideration for the property sold unaffected by special or creative financing or sales concessions* granted by anyone associated with the sale.

*Adjustments to the comparables must be made for special or creative financing or sales concessions. No adjustments are necessary for those costs which are normally paid by sellers as a result of tradition or law in a market area; these costs are readily identifiable since the seller pays these costs in virtually all sales transactions. Special or creative financing adjustments can be made to the comparable property by comparisons to financing terms offered by a third party institutional lender that is not already involved in the property or transaction. Any adjustment should not be calculated on a mechanical dollar for dollar cost of the financing or concession but the dollar amount of any adjustment should approximate the market's reaction to the financing or concessions based on the appraiser's judgment.

STATEMENT OF ASSUMPTIONS AND LIMITING CONDITIONS: The appraiser's certification in this report is subject to the following assumptions and limiting conditions:

1. The appraiser will not be responsible for matters of a legal nature that affect either the property being appraised or the title to it, except for information that he or she became aware of during the research involved in performing this appraisal. The appraiser assumes that the title is good and marketable and will not render any opinions about the title.

2. The appraiser has provided a sketch in this appraisal report to show the approximate dimensions of the improvements. The sketch is included only to assist the reader in visualizing the property and understanding the appraiser's determination of its size.

3. The appraiser has examined the available flood maps that are provided by the Federal Emergency Management Agency (or other data sources) and has noted in this appraisal report whether any portion of the subject site is located in an identified Special Flood Hazard Area. Because the appraiser is not a surveyor, he or she makes no guarantees, express or implied, regarding this determination.

4. The appraiser will not give testimony or appear in court because he or she made an appraisal of the property in question, unless specific arrangements to do so have been made beforehand, or as otherwise required by law.

5. The appraiser has noted in this appraisal report any adverse conditions (such as needed repairs, deterioration, the presence of hazardous wastes, toxic substances, etc.) observed during the inspection of the subject property or that he or she became aware of during the research involved in performing this appraisal. Unless otherwise stated in this appraisal report, the appraiser has no knowledge of any hidden or unapparent physical deficiencies or adverse conditions of the property (such as, but not limited to, needed repairs, deterioration, the presence of hazardous wastes, toxic substances, adverse environmental conditions, etc.) that would make the property less valuable, and has assumed that there are no such conditions and makes no guarantees or warranties, express or implied. The appraiser will not be responsible for any such conditions that do exist or for any engineering or testing that might be required to discover whether such conditions exist. Because the appraiser is not an expert in the field of environmental hazards, this appraisal report must not be considered as an environmental assessment of the property.

6. The appraiser has based his or her appraisal report and valuation conclusion for an appraisal that is subject to satisfactory completion, repairs, or alterations on the assumption that the completion, repairs, or alterations of the subject property will be performed in a professional manner.

Freddie Mac Form 70 March 2005 Page 4 of 6 Fannie Mae Form 1004 March 2005

Uniform Residential Appraisal Report

File #

APPRAISER'S CERTIFICATION: The Appraiser certifies and agrees that:

1. I have, at a minimum, developed and reported this appraisal in accordance with the scope of work requirements stated in this appraisal report.

2. I performed a complete visual inspection of the interior and exterior areas of the subject property. I reported the condition of the improvements in factual, specific terms. I identified and reported the physical deficiencies that could affect the livability, soundness, or structural integrity of the property.

3. I performed this appraisal in accordance with the requirements of the Uniform Standards of Professional Appraisal Practice that were adopted and promulgated by the Appraisal Standards Board of The Appraisal Foundation and that were in place at the time this appraisal report was prepared.

4. I developed my opinion of the market value of the real property that is the subject of this report based on the sales comparison approach to value. I have adequate comparable market data to develop a reliable sales comparison approach for this appraisal assignment. I further certify that I considered the cost and income approaches to value but did not develop them, unless otherwise indicated in this report.

5. I researched, verified, analyzed, and reported on any current agreement for sale for the subject property, any offering for sale of the subject property in the twelve months prior to the effective date of this appraisal, and the prior sales of the subject property for a minimum of three years prior to the effective date of this appraisal, unless otherwise indicated in this report.

6. I researched, verified, analyzed, and reported on the prior sales of the comparable sales for a minimum of one year prior to the date of sale of the comparable sale, unless otherwise indicated in this report.

7. I selected and used comparable sales that are locationally, physically, and functionally the most similar to the subject property.

8. I have not used comparable sales that were the result of combining a land sale with the contract purchase price of a home that has been built or will be built on the land.

9. I have reported adjustments to the comparable sales that reflect the market's reaction to the differences between the subject property and the comparable sales.

10. I verified, from a disinterested source, all information in this report that was provided by parties who have a financial interest in the sale or financing of the subject property.

11. I have knowledge and experience in appraising this type of property in this market area.

12. I am aware of, and have access to, the necessary and appropriate public and private data sources, such as multiple listing services, tax assessment records, public land records and other such data sources for the area in which the property is located.

13. I obtained the information, estimates, and opinions furnished by other parties and expressed in this appraisal report from reliable sources that I believe to be true and correct.

14. I have taken into consideration the factors that have an impact on value with respect to the subject neighborhood, subject property, and the proximity of the subject property to adverse influences in the development of my opinion of market value. I have noted in this appraisal report any adverse conditions (such as, but not limited to, needed repairs, deterioration, the presence of hazardous wastes, toxic substances, adverse environmental conditions, etc.) observed during the inspection of the subject property or that I became aware of during the research involved in performing this appraisal. I have considered these adverse conditions in my analysis of the property value, and have reported on the effect of the conditions on the value and marketability of the subject property.

15. I have not knowingly withheld any significant information from this appraisal report and, to the best of my knowledge, all statements and information in this appraisal report are true and correct.

16. I stated in this appraisal report my own personal, unbiased, and professional analysis, opinions, and conclusions, which are subject only to the assumptions and limiting conditions in this appraisal report.

17. I have no present or prospective interest in the property that is the subject of this report, and I have no present or prospective personal interest or bias with respect to the participants in the transaction. I did not base, either partially or completely, my analysis and/or opinion of market value in this appraisal report on the race, color, religion, sex, age, marital status, handicap, familial status, or national origin of either the prospective owners or occupants of the subject property or of the present owners or occupants of the properties in the vicinity of the subject property or on any other basis prohibited by law.

18. My employment and/or compensation for performing this appraisal or any future or anticipated appraisals was not conditioned on any agreement or understanding, written or otherwise, that I would report (or present analysis supporting) a predetermined specific value, a predetermined minimum value, a range or direction in value, a value that favors the cause of any party, or the attainment of a specific result or occurrence of a specific subsequent event (such as approval of a pending mortgage loan application).

19. I personally prepared all conclusions and opinions about the real estate that were set forth in this appraisal report. If I relied on significant real property appraisal assistance from any individual or individuals in the performance of this appraisal or the preparation of this appraisal report, I have named such individual(s) and disclosed the specific tasks performed in this appraisal report. I certify that any individual so named is qualified to perform the tasks. I have not authorized anyone to make a change to any item in this appraisal report; therefore, any change made to this appraisal is unauthorized and I will take no responsibility for it.

20. I identified the lender/client in this appraisal report who is the individual, organization, or agent for the organization that ordered and will receive this appraisal report.

Freddie Mac Form 70 March 2005 | Page 5 of 6 | Fannie Mae Form 1004 March 2005

Uniform Residential Appraisal Report

File #

21. The lender/client may disclose or distribute this appraisal report to: the borrower; another lender at the request of the borrower; the mortgagee or its successors and assigns; mortgage insurers; government sponsored enterprises; other secondary market participants; data collection or reporting services; professional appraisal organizations; any department, agency, or instrumentality of the United States; and any state, the District of Columbia, or other jurisdictions; without having to obtain the appraiser's or supervisory appraiser's (if applicable) consent. Such consent must be obtained before this appraisal report may be disclosed or distributed to any other party (including, but not limited to, the public through advertising, public relations, news, sales, or other media).

22. I am aware that any disclosure or distribution of this appraisal report by me or the lender/client may be subject to certain laws and regulations. Further, I am also subject to the provisions of the Uniform Standards of Professional Appraisal Practice that pertain to disclosure or distribution by me.

23. The borrower, another lender at the request of the borrower, the mortgagee or its successors and assigns, mortgage insurers, government sponsored enterprises, and other secondary market participants may rely on this appraisal report as part of any mortgage finance transaction that involves any one or more of these parties.

24. If this appraisal report was transmitted as an "electronic record" containing my "electronic signature," as those terms are defined in applicable federal and/or state laws (excluding audio and video recordings), or a facsimile transmission of this appraisal report containing a copy or representation of my signature, the appraisal report shall be as effective, enforceable and valid as if a paper version of this appraisal report were delivered containing my original hand written signature.

25. Any intentional or negligent misrepresentation(s) contained in this appraisal report may result in civil liability and/or criminal penalties including, but not limited to, fine or imprisonment or both under the provisions of Title 18, United States Code, Section 1001, et seq., or similar state laws.

SUPERVISORY APPRAISER'S CERTIFICATION: The Supervisory Appraiser certifies and agrees that:

1. I directly supervised the appraiser for this appraisal assignment, have read the appraisal report, and agree with the appraiser's analysis, opinions, statements, conclusions, and the appraiser's certification.

2. I accept full responsibility for the contents of this appraisal report including, but not limited to, the appraiser's analysis, opinions, statements, conclusions, and the appraiser's certification.

3. The appraiser identified in this appraisal report is either a sub-contractor or an employee of the supervisory appraiser (or the appraisal firm), is qualified to perform this appraisal, and is acceptable to perform this appraisal under the applicable state law.

4. This appraisal report complies with the Uniform Standards of Professional Appraisal Practice that were adopted and promulgated by the Appraisal Standards Board of The Appraisal Foundation and that were in place at the time this appraisal report was prepared.

5. If this appraisal report was transmitted as an "electronic record" containing my "electronic signature," as those terms are defined in applicable federal and/or state laws (excluding audio and video recordings), or a facsimile transmission of this appraisal report containing a copy or representation of my signature, the appraisal report shall be as effective, enforceable and valid as if a paper version of this appraisal report were delivered containing my original hand written signature.

APPRAISER

Signature ______________________
Name ______________________
Company Name ______________________
Company Address ______________________
____
Telephone Number ______________________
Email Address ______________________
Date of Signature and Report ______________________
Effective Date of Appraisal ______________________
State Certification # ______________________
or State License # ______________________
or Other (describe) ____________ State # ____________
State ______________________
Expiration Date of Certification or License ______________________

ADDRESS OF PROPERTY APPRAISED
____
____

APPRAISED VALUE OF SUBJECT PROPERTY $ ____________

LENDER/CLIENT
Name ______________________
Company Name ______________________
Company Address ______________________
____
Email Address ______________________

SUPERVISORY APPRAISER (ONLY IF REQUIRED)

Signature ______________________
Name ______________________
Company Name ______________________
Company Address ______________________
____
Telephone Number ______________________
Email Address ______________________
Date of Signature ______________________
State Certification # ______________________
or State License # ______________________
State ______________________
Expiration Date of Certification or License ______________________

SUBJECT PROPERTY

☐ Did not inspect subject property
☐ Did inspect exterior of subject property from street
Date of Inspection ______________________
☐ Did inspect interior and exterior of subject property
Date of Inspection ______________________

COMPARABLE SALES

☐ Did not inspect exterior of comparable sales from street
☐ Did inspect exterior of comparable sales from street
Date of Inspection ______________________

Freddie Mac Form 70 March 2005 | Page 6 of 6 | Fannie Mae Form 1004 March 2005

The simplest solution to the problem of a low appraisal is for the seller to lower the sales price to the appraised value. But don't be surprised if your seller resists a price reduction. Once a seller has become accustomed to a certain sales price, she will be very reluctant to give it up.

Another possibility is a compromise price somewhere in between the appraised value and the original selling price. But this solution is likely to run up against both the seller's reluctance to lower the price and the buyer's reluctance (or inability) to pay any more than the appraised value.

Possible solutions after low appraisal:
- Buyer pays over value
- Seller lowers price to appraised value
- Compromise price
- Request for reconsideration of value

Because of these problems, when there's a significant gap between the sales price and the appraised value, the most likely result is termination of the sale. (According to some estimates, it happens more than two-thirds of the time.) But it's the real estate agent's job to help the parties avoid this outcome whenever possible.

In some cases the agent should ask the lender to reconsider the appraised value, in the hope that it will be increased to a figure more acceptable to the buyer and seller. This can work if it's handled properly. The correct way to request a reconsideration of value will be explained later in this chapter.

Of course, the best way to eliminate the problems that low appraisals create is to prevent them in the first place.

Preventing Low Appraisals

A real estate agent can prevent most low appraisals by helping sellers price properties realistically. A seller should not be given an unrealistic estimate of the property's worth; even if a buyer can be persuaded to pay the inflated price, the appraisal will come back low and the real struggle to keep the transaction together will begin.

Prevent low appraisal by helping seller price property correctly
- Perform careful CMA
- Price personal property separately
- Assist the appraiser

If for some reason the property is not priced realistically when it is listed, at least try to correct the problem when you write the sale. No case can be made for overstating the value when property is listed or sold; sooner or later every sale that is dependent on financing must yield to the conclusions of a professional appraiser.

CMA. The best way for an agent to help a seller price a home is to perform a competitive market analysis (CMA). As mentioned earlier in the chapter, a competitive market analysis is an informal version of a sales comparison appraisal. The agent suggests an appropriate price for the seller's home based on an evaluation of comparable homes that were recently sold or listed. Performing a reliable CMA takes patience and practice, but the results are worth the effort.

Sales comparison information can be obtained from a variety of sources, including real estate office files, multiple listing services, and appraisers' records. Acquaint yourself with the most comprehensive and accessible record systems in your area. If you're doing your job, you will refer to them often.

Personal Property. One pitfall to avoid when writing a sale concerns personal property (such as furniture) belonging to the seller that the buyer is interested in buying along with the home. In this situation, some real estate agents include the personal property in the real property transaction: the sale is written so the price covers both the real property (the land, the house, and other attachments) and the personal property that the buyer wants. This is always a mistake, and it can lead to a low appraisal.

Underwriting guidelines require residential appraisers to exclude the value of personal property from the final estimate of value for the real property. When the sales price includes personal property and the appraised value does not, the value estimate may be much lower than the price.

Thus, the sale of personal property to a home buyer should be treated as a separate transaction. The personal property should be priced and paid for separately from the home, and proper procedures for the transfer of title to personal property should be followed. (Those procedures vary from state to state, so you should be sure to check into local requirements.)

On the other hand, an appraiser will include the value of fixtures (such as built-in appliances) in the final estimate of value, because fixtures are considered part of the real property. So the sales price of the home should include all of the fixtures that are going to be transferred to the buyer.

If you're not certain whether a particular item will be treated as personal property or as a fixture in the appraisal, check with local sources. The distinction between personal property and fixtures sometimes depends on local custom.

Assisting the Appraiser. Another thing a real estate agent can do to help prevent a low appraisal is to offer assistance to the appraiser.

This should include accompanying the appraiser on his or her inspection of the home. Whenever possible, the appraiser's appointment to see the property should be arranged through the listing agent, not directly with the seller.

When meeting the appraiser, the agent should offer him an updated competitive market analysis with at least three good comparable sales (not current or expired listings). This can be extremely important; if the agent chose the comparables well, the appraiser might decide to use them instead of seeking out others. During the inspection, the agent can answer any questions the appraiser might have. The appraiser will have to verify all of the information provided by the agent, because the agent has a financial interest in the outcome of the appraisal. However, by offering information and assistance to the appraiser, the agent can make sure that none of the property's positive features get overlooked.

Request for Reconsideration of Value

Regardless of how objective an appraiser might try to be, subjective considerations and conclusions are a part of every appraisal. In the end the appraiser's findings can only be deemed an opinion of value. If you are affected by a low appraisal and sincerely believe the appraiser has made a mistake, there is a chance that you can appeal his decision and, with the proper documentation, get the appraisal increased—possibly to the figure the buyer and seller originally agreed on.

The sooner you find out about a low appraisal, the better. After the property has been inspected, ask the loan officer or the underwriter to call you with the results of the appraisal as soon as they are received. Don't try to get the results directly from the appraiser; the appraiser has a fiduciary relationship with the lender and is not allowed to disclose information about the appraisal to others without the lender's permission.

If the appraisal comes in low, ask the loan officer or underwriter for the following information:

1. the final value estimate,
2. the value indicated by the sales comparison method, and
3. the addresses of the three comparables the appraiser used.

When appraisal comes in low:
- Ask lender for information
- Evaluate appraisal
- Update CMA
- Submit request for reconsideration only if lender likely to grant it

This is the essential information, because the sales comparison analysis is the heart of a residential appraisal, the part that the lender really relies on in deciding whether to approve a loan.

Evaluate the appraiser's three comparables and update your competitive market analysis. Then decide if a request for reconsideration of value is a realistic option. You will have to support your request with at least three comparable sales that indicate a higher value estimate is in order. If you're going to persuade the lender to accept your comparables over the appraiser's, yours must be at least as similar to the subject property as the appraiser's are.

If you believe the lender is likely to grant a request for reconsideration, prepare the request and a cover letter as outlined below.

Preparing the Request. Some lenders have their own form for requests for reconsideration of value. If so, you should use their form (you may even be required to). Otherwise, you can prepare your own. It makes sense to present your information in the same format that's used in the "Sales Comparison Analysis" section of the Uniform Residential Appraisal Report form. Make four columns for the properties, with the subject in the first column and three comparables to the right, as in the example shown in Figure 9.4.

Write a cover letter making your request and attach your sales comparison analysis to it. The cover letter should be simple and very polite; do not criticize the appraiser.

Request for Reconsideration of Value

Mr. Arthur Jewel
Hillside Bank

Dear Mr. Jewel:

Attached is a sales comparison analysis that supports this request for reconsideration of the value estimate for 412 Acme Drive, dated November 14. I believe the market data presented indicate that an estimate of value in the amount of $235,000 is justified.

Thank you for your attention to this matter.

Sincerely,
Thomas M. Crane

Fig. 9.4 Data sheet supporting request for reconsideration of value

Sales Comparison Analysis
412 Acme Drive

Item	Subject Property	Comparable 1	Comparable 2	Comparable 3
Address	412 Acme Drive	131 Skip Road	221 Sutter Street	168 Bow Road
Sales price	$235,000	$238,000	$234,500	$229,500
Data source	sales contract	present owner	MLS	Selling broker
Date of sale		8/29/06	9/14/06	10/17/06
Location	high quality suburb	same	same	same
Site/view	corner lot	inside lot	corner lot	inside lot
Design	rambler	same	same	same
Appeal	excellent	same	same	same
Construction	good	same	same	same
Age	7 years	6 years	8 years	8 years
Condition	good	same	same	same
No. of rooms	8	7	7	6
No. of bedrooms	4	4	3	3
Living area	2,400 sq. ft.	2,500 sq. ft.	2,350 sq. ft.	2,150 sq. ft.
Garage/carport	2-car attached garage	same	same	same
Patio	15' × 21' patio	15' × 26' patio	18' × 16' patio	15' × 17' patio
Additional features	2 fireplaces, range, oven, D/W, disposal, central air	2 fireplaces, range, oven, D/W central air	1 fireplace, range, oven, D/W central air	1 fireplace, range, oven D/W, disposal, central air
Comments	Subject is more energy-efficient than Comps 2 and 3, and is at least equal in this respect to Comp 1.			

Sometimes appraisers don't use the best information available, and when they don't, their findings can be successfully challenged. If your request for reconsideration of value contains well-researched, properly documented information and is presented in a professional manner, your chances of success skyrocket. Make your request carelessly and the reverse is true.

Outline: Qualifying the Property

I. The Lender's Perception of Value

   A. An underwriter will evaluate the property based on an appraisal: an estimate of the value of a property, performed by a professional appraiser.

   B. An appraiser will focus on market value: the most probable price a property should bring in a competitive and open market where the parties act knowledgeably and without undue stimulus.

   C. The lender focuses on the loan-to-value ratio: the relationship between loan amount and the property's value.

      1. A higher LTV creates greater risk for a lender, since a buyer with a smaller downpayment is more likely to default.

      2. The LTV is based on either the sales price or the appraised value, whichever is lower.

      3. Lenders may be willing to make high-LTV loans but usually impose stricter qualifying standards to compensate for the higher risk.

II. Appraisal Standards

   A. To prevent unreliable appraisals, the federal government requires states to license and certify appraisers who perform appraisals for "federally related" loan transactions.

   B. Some states require that all appraisers be licensed or certified.

III. Appraisal Process

   A. There are seven steps in the appraisal process: defining the problem, determining what data are needed, gathering and verifying general data, gathering and verifying specific data, applying the appropriate methods of appraisal, reconciling the results to arrive at a final value estimate, and issuing the appraisal report.

   B. In some situations, an appraiser may be able to perform a "drive-by appraisal" rather than performing a full inspection of the property.

IV. Appraisal Methods

   A. Sales comparison method

      1. Appraisers using the sales comparison method rely on the sales prices of comparable properties to estimate the value of the subject property.

      2. The sales comparison method uses the same principles as a competitive market analysis, although a CMA can use data from current listings and expired listings.

3. To determine whether a recently sold property is comparable, an appraiser considers: the date of the sale, the location of the property, the physical characteristics of the property, the terms of sale, and whether the sale was an arm's length transaction.
4. The sale should have occurred within the previous six months, although the appraiser may adjust the sales price for changes in value if the property was sold in the last year.
5. Comparable properties should be located in the same neighborhood and have similar size, design, and quality as the subject property.
6. Comparable properties must have sold in an arm's length transaction: where the buyer and seller are fully informed and acting free of unusual pressure.
7. If there are differences between the subject property and comparables, the appraiser may adjust the sales price of the comparables to reflect what they would have sold for were they more similar to the subject property.

B. Replacement cost method

1. There are three steps in the replacement cost method: estimating the cost of replacing the improvements, deducting any depreciation, and adding the value of the land.
2. The appraiser usually relies on the replacement cost (the cost of constructing a new building with equivalent utility) rather than the reproduction cost (the cost of building an exact replica using the same materials and techniques).
3. The easiest way to estimate the construction cost is the square foot method, where the appraiser multiplies the estimate cost per square foot by square footage of the building.
4. There are three types of depreciation that must be estimated: deferred maintenance, functional obsolescence, and external obsolescence.
5. Depreciation may be considered curable or incurable, depending on whether correcting the problem adds more value than the cost of the repair.
6. An appraisal may be "as is," which evaluates the property in current condition, or "subject to," which values the property as if all deferred maintenance were repaired.

C. Income method

1. Value under the income method is calculated by dividing a property's annual net income by the rate of return an investor would expect from the property.

2. For residential rental properties, an appraiser will use a simplified version of the income method called the gross income multiplier method.
3. The appraiser finds value by multiplying the property's rent by a multiplier indicated by the relationship between other properties' rents and values.
4. An appraiser should use the property's economic rent (the rent the owner would receive if the property were currently available) rather than contract rent (the rent the owner currently receives).

D. Final value estimate

1. The appraiser will reconcile the values indicated by the various appraisal methods to arrive at a final estimate of value.
2. The result is not an average of the figures; the appraiser may give weight to certain methods based on the type of property.

V. Dealing with Low Appraisals

A. A low appraisal can terminate a transaction, since the lender will adjust its loan amount based on the property's appraised value, requiring the borrower to come up with a larger downpayment.

B. A real estate agent can seek to prevent low appraisals.

1. An agent should provide the appraiser with a copy of the agent's CMA.
2. The agent should avoid including personal property as part of the sales price.
3. The agent should accompany the appraiser during the inspection.

C. If a low appraisal occurs, an agent may request a reconsideration of value, by providing the lender with alternate comparables that suggest a higher value for the subject property.

Key Terms

Appraisal: An expert's estimate of the value of a piece of real estate as of a particular date, based on a documented analysis of the property's features.

Appraiser: One who estimates the value of property, especially an expert qualified to do so by training and experience.

Market value: The most probable price a property should bring if sold in an arm's length transaction.

Loan-to-value ratio (LTV): The relationship between the loan amount and either the sales price or the appraised value of the property (whichever is less), expressed as a percentage.

Sales comparison approach: Method of appraisal in which the sales prices of comparable properties are used to estimate the value of the subject property.

Subject property: In an appraisal, the property being appraised.

Comparables: In the sales comparison approach, properties similar to the subject property that have recently been sold; the appraiser uses the sales prices of the comparables as an indication of the value of the subject property.

Competitive market analysis (CMA): A real estate agent's estimate of the value of a listed home, based on the sales prices or listing prices of comparable homes.

Arm's length transaction: A sale in which both the buyer and seller are fully informed of the property's attributes and deficiencies, neither is acting under unusual pressure, and the property has been offered on the open market for a reasonable period of time.

Replacement cost method: Method of appraisal in which an estimate of the subject property's value is arrived at by estimating the cost of replacing the improvements, then deducting estimated depreciation, and adding the estimated market value of the land.

Replacement cost: The current cost of constructing a building with the same utility as the subject property, using modern materials and construction methods.

Reproduction cost: The current cost of constructing a replica of the subject property, using the same materials and methods as originally used but at current prices.

Depreciation: Loss in value due to any cause.

Deferred maintenance: Depreciation resulting from physical wear and tear.

Functional obsolescence: Depreciation resulting from functional inadequacies, such as poor or outmoded design.

External obsolescence: Depreciation resulting from factors outside the property itself and outside the owner's control.

Income method: A method of appraisal in which an estimate of the subject property's value is based on the net income it produces.

Gross income multiplier method: A method of appraisal used for residential rental property, in which an estimate of the subject property's value is based on the relationship between the sales prices and the rental income of comparable properties.

Economic rent: The rent a property could command in the current marketplace if it were available for lease today.

Contract rent: The rent an owner is currently receiving from a property.

Reconciliation: The final step in an appraisal, when the appraiser assembles and interprets the data in order to arrive at a final value estimate.

Low appraisal: An appraisal where the appraised value is lower than the agreed-upon sales price, which may affect financing and terminate the transaction.

Reconsideration of value: A request by an agent to a lender to increase the appraised value of a property, based on evidence provided by comparables other than those selected by the appraiser.

Chapter Quiz

1. A lender asks a residential appraiser to:
   a. estimate the book value of the home
   b. determine the assessed value of the home
   c. determine the subjective value of the home
   d. estimate the market value of the home

2. From the lender's point of view, a low-risk loan would be one that has:
   a. no downpayment
   b. a high loan-to-value ratio
   c. a low loan-to-value ratio
   d. a 100% loan-to-value ratio

3. For residential property, the most important method of appraisal is the:
   a. sales comparison method
   b. replacement cost method
   c. income method
   d. gross income multiplier method

4. A sales comparison appraisal is mainly based on:
   a. listing prices
   b. expired listings
   c. sales prices
   d. assessed values

5. An appraiser should not use a sale as a comparable unless:
   a. it occurred within the past six months
   b. it was in the same neighborhood as the subject property
   c. it involved financing concessions
   d. it was an arm's length transaction

6. The most difficult step in the replacement cost method of appraisal is:
   a. finding benchmark buildings
   b. measuring square footage
   c. estimating depreciation
   d. calculating the gross income multiplier

7. If a home sold for $175,000 and rents for $1,150 per month, then its monthly gross income multiplier is:
   a. .079
   b. 12.68
   c. 66.0
   d. 152.17

8. A real estate agent is helping the Martins set a listing price for their home. The Martins have some furniture they would like to sell along with the home. The agent should advise the Martins:
   a. to include the value of the furniture in the price of the home
   b. to price the furniture separately from the home
   c. not to sell the furniture to the person who buys the home
   d. to treat the furniture as fixtures

9. In the event of a low appraisal, the listing agent should:
   a. always submit a request for a reconsideration of value
   b. submit a request for reconsideration only if the appraiser has made a significant mathematical error
   c. submit a request for reconsideration only if the loan officer recommends it
   d. evaluate the appraisal, update the CMA, and submit a request for reconsideration only if there is a good possibility that it will be granted

10. A property's value is diminished by its proximity to a paper mill. This would be considered:
    a. deferred maintenance
    b. functional obsolescence
    c. external obsolescence
    d. curable depreciation

Answer Key

1. d. An appraiser performing an appraisal for a residential lender is typically concerned with the property's market value.

2. c. A low loan-to-value ratio, such as 80% or lower, is considered a low-risk loan. A larger downpayment reduces the risk of default, and increases the likelihood the full loan amount can be recovered in a foreclosure sale.

3. a. The sales comparison method is the most relevant method in residential appraisal.

4. c. The sales comparison method relies on the recent sales prices of comparable properties. A CMA may include current and expired listings, but an appraisal may not.

5. d. An appraiser should not include a sale that was not an arm's length transaction. An appraiser may make adjustments for the date of sale, the location of the property, or financing terms.

6. c. The most difficult part of the cost approach to value is estimating depreciation.

7. d. To calculate the monthly gross income multiplier, divide the property's value by its monthly rent. In this case, the monthly multiplier is 152.17 ($175,000 ÷ $1,150 = 152.17).

8. b. Furniture and other personal property should be priced separately from the real estate. Including personal property can inflate the sales price and lead to a low appraisal.

9. d. If a low appraisal occurs, an agent should investigate the appraisal and see if other comparables can be found that indicate a higher value for the subject property. If that is the case, the agent should request a reconsideration of value.

10. c. Loss of value caused by factors outside of the property, such as a nearby nuisance like a paper mill, would be external obsolescence. External obsolescence is always incurable.

Chapter 10
Conventional Financing

Conforming and Nonconforming Loans

Conventional Loan Characteristics

- Property types and owner-occupancy
- Loan amounts
- Repayment periods
- Amortization
- Loan-to-value ratios
- Private mortgage insurance
- Secondary financing

Qualifying Standards

- Evaluating risk factors
- Income analysis
- Net worth
- Credit scores

Special Programs and Payment Plans

- Buydowns
- Loans with lower initial payments
- Low downpayment programs
- Accelerated repayment plans

Introduction

Loans made by institutional lenders (such as banks, savings and loans, and mortgage companies) can be divided into two main categories: conventional loans and government-sponsored loans.

Conventional loan: not insured or guaranteed by government

A **conventional loan** is any institutional loan that isn't insured or guaranteed by a government agency. For example, a loan that's made by a bank and insured by a private mortgage company is a conventional loan. A loan that's made by a bank and insured by the FHA (Federal Housing Administration) or guaranteed by the VA (Department of Veterans Affairs) is not a conventional loan, because it is backed by a government agency.

Government-sponsored loan programs are covered in Chapters 11 and 12. In this chapter, we'll examine conventional loans.

Conforming and Nonconforming Loans

Conforming loan complies with Fannie Mae and/or Freddie Mac's guidelines

Fannie Mae and Freddie Mac are the major secondary market agencies that purchase conventional loans, and most conventional loans are made in compliance with their underwriting guidelines. The guidelines of the two agencies are similar in many respects, although they aren't identical. Loans that comply with (conform to) their guidelines are called **conforming loans**.

Nonconforming loan:
- Doesn't comply with the agencies' standards
- Fannie Mae and Freddie Mac won't buy it

Lenders making conventional loans aren't required to follow the guidelines of the secondary market agencies; they're free to apply their own underwriting standards instead. But if a loan isn't made in compliance with Fannie Mae or Freddie Mac's guidelines, it's considered **nonconforming** and can't be sold to either agency, except by special arrangement.

You may be wondering about the relationship between nonconforming loans and subprime loans. The great majority of subprime loans are nonconforming loans. But nonconforming loans aren't necessarily subprime.

> **Example:** Acme Mortgage specializes in making subprime loans. It makes loans to high-risk borrowers (borrowers with B, C, and D credit) and charges them above-market interest rates and fees.
>
> Acme's subprime loans don't conform to the underwriting guidelines of Fannie Mae or Freddie Mac. Thus, Acme's loans

are nonconforming loans. When Acme sells its loans on the secondary market, they're sold to subprime investors, not to Fannie Mae or Freddie Mac.

In contrast to Acme Mortgage, Vault Savings is considered a prime lender, because it makes loans only to borrowers with A credit and charges them market rates and fees. For most of its loans, Vault follows Fannie Mae's underwriting guidelines, so that it can count on selling the loans to Fannie Mae.

However, Vault also makes some loans that fall outside of the guidelines of both Fannie Mae and Freddie Mac. These are nonconforming loans, but they're still prime loans. The borrowers have A credit and they're charged market interest rates and fees. Vault usually keeps its nonconforming loans in portfolio, although it might be able to sell them to an investor other than Fannie Mae or Freddie Mac.

As the example illustrates, a nonconforming loan may be either a prime loan or a subprime loan. Although there's considerable overlap between the category of nonconforming loans and the category of subprime loans, they aren't the same thing.

Conventional Loan Characteristics

Lenders like to have the option of selling their loans on the secondary market, and when they make conforming loans, they know that they'll be able to sell them to Fannie Mae or Freddie Mac at good prices. As a result, the two agencies' underwriting guidelines are widely followed and very influential in the mortgage industry. For that reason, our discussion of conventional loans generally focuses on those guidelines. It's important to keep in mind, however, that not all conventional loans conform to the guidelines or have the characteristics described here.

Property Types and Owner-Occupancy Rules

Fannie Mae and Freddie Mac buy loans secured by residential properties, including detached site-built houses, townhouses, condominium units, cooperative units, and manufactured homes.

Conventional loan may be secured by:
- Principal residence
- Second home
- Investment property

The borrowers may intend to occupy the security property either as their principal residence or as a second home. A principal residence is allowed to have up to four dwelling units, but a second home should have no more than one dwelling unit.

Fannie Mae and Freddie Mac are also willing to buy **investor loans** secured by property with up to four dwelling units. A loan is considered an investor loan if the borrower doesn't intend to occupy the property; in most cases, the borrower plans to rent it out to tenants instead. Investor loans are underwritten using different (and generally stricter) standards than loans for owner-occupied homes. We'll mainly be discussing owner-occupied homes, not investment properties.

Loan Amounts

Conforming loan limits are set annually

Every year Fannie Mae and Freddie Mac set new **conforming loan limits**, or maximum loan amounts (see Figure 10.1). The agencies won't purchase a loan if the original principal amount exceeds the applicable limit. The limits are increased annually to reflect the annual increase in the national average price for single-family homes.

Jumbo loan: loan amount exceeds conforming loan limit

Loans that exceed the conforming loan limits are called **jumbo loans**. Extra-large loans (from $650,000 on up into the millions) are sometimes called **super jumbos**.

As you can see in Figure 10.1, there are higher conforming loan limits for the parts of the United States that have the very highest housing prices—Alaska, Guam, Hawaii, and the Virgin Islands. But there are other high-cost areas in the country where the standard limits apply. For example, they apply even in the most expensive parts of California. In those areas, the conforming loan amount isn't enough to buy a median-priced home, so lots of buyers need jumbo loans. On the other hand, in many other parts of the country jumbo loans are relatively rare; they're needed only by buyers who are purchasing homes at the very top of the price range in their area.

Adjustable-rate mortgages play a prominent role in the jumbo loan market. For example, nearly 70% of all jumbo loans originated in late 2005 were ARMs, compared to less than 30% of conforming loans.

*Fig. 10.1 Fannie Mae and Freddie Mac's conforming loan limits for 2006**

Number of Dwelling Units	Maximum Loan Amount	Properties in Alaska, Guam, Hawaii, or the Virgin Islands
1	$417,000	$625,500
2	$533,850	$800,775
3	$645,300	$967,950
4	$801,950	$1,202,925

* The loan limits are increased annually.

Lenders generally charge higher interest rates for jumbo loans than they do for conforming loans. A lender's jumbo rate might be anywhere from one-eighth of a percentage point higher to nearly one percentage point higher than the conforming rate.

Lenders also tend to impose stricter standards on jumbo loan transactions. For example, the maximum loan-to-value ratio for a jumbo loan is likely to be lower, and the buyers may be required to have higher credit scores and more money in reserve than they would for a conforming loan.

Repayment Periods

Repayment periods for conventional loans can range from ten years to forty years. Thirty years is still the standard term, but fifteen-year loans are also popular. See the discussion of repayment periods in Chapter 6.

Amortization

The majority of conventional loans are fully amortized (see Chapter 6). However, partially amortized and interest-only loans are also available. We'll discuss those types of loans at the end of the chapter, when we cover special programs and payment plans for conventional loans.

Loan-to-Value Ratios

Traditionally, the standard conventional loan-to-value ratio (LTV) was 80%. Lenders feel confident that borrowers who make a 20% downpayment with their own funds are unlikely to default on their loan. The borrowers would have too much to lose if the lender were to foreclose on the property. And even if the borrowers did default, a foreclosure sale would probably generate at least 80% of the purchase price, enough to pay off the loan. (See Chapter 6 for a general discussion of loan-to-value ratios.)

Conventional loans with loan-to-value ratios over 80% became widely available in the 1980s, and eventually they became more common than 80% loans. Lenders now routinely make conventional purchase loans with 90% or 95% loan-to-value ratios, and 97% LTVs are no longer rare. It's even possible to get a conventional loan with a 100% LTV, with no downpayment required.

Common conventional LTVs:
- 80%
- 90%
- 95%

Less common conventional LTVs:
- 97%
- 100%

Fig. 10.2 Conventional loans are categorized by loan-to-value ratio

Category	Loan-to-Value Ratio
80% loans	LTV is 80% or less
90% loans	LTV is over 80% but not more than 90%
95% loans	LTV is over 90% but not more than 95%
97% loans	LTV is over 95% but not more than 97%
100% loans	LTV is over 97% but not more than 100%

Conventional loans are often categorized by their loan-to-value ratios, with different underwriting rules applied to the different categories. A conventional loan is categorized as an 80% loan if the loan-to-value ratio is 80% or less, as a 90% loan if the LTV is over 80% but not more than 90%, as a 95% loan if the LTV is over 90% but not more than 95%, and so on (see Figure 10.2).

> **Example:** Alicia Hernandez is borrowing $164,000 to buy a $200,000 house. The loan amount is 82% of the value of the property ($164,000 ÷ $200,000 = 82%). In other words, the loan has an 82% loan-to-value ratio. Because the LTV is over 80% but not more than 90%, the loan will be treated as a 90% loan for underwriting purposes.

Because a smaller downpayment from the borrower means more risk for the lender, Fannie Mae and Freddie Mac require private mortgage insurance for any conventional loans they purchase that have LTVs over 80%. (Private mortgage insurance is discussed in the next section of this chapter.)

High-LTV loans:
- Higher interest rates and fees
- Stricter underwriting

Lenders often charge higher interest rates and fees for high-LTV loans. And it's generally harder to qualify for a high-LTV conventional loan; the higher the LTV, the more strictly the underwriting guidelines will be applied. Marginal buyers who don't have much cash for a downpayment may not be able to qualify for a high-LTV conventional loan. They might want to consider alternatives such as an affordable housing program, a government-backed loan, or seller financing, or they may choose subprime financing.

ARM LTV Ratios. At one time Fannie Mae and Freddie Mac didn't buy adjustable-rate mortgages with loan-to-value ratios over 90%, because ARMs are riskier than fixed-rate loans. Both agencies are now willing to buy ARMs with LTVs up to 95% if certain conditions are met.

Exercise No. 1

Rita Maynard would like to buy the Chandlers' house, which she would use as her primary residence. The sales price is $318,750, and the appraisal came in at $321,000. Maynard wants to make a $25,500 downpayment and obtain a conventional loan for the rest of the price.

1. What would Maynard's exact loan-to-value ratio be?

2. Would her loan be treated as an 80% loan, a 90% loan, or a 95% loan?

Private Mortgage Insurance

Private mortgage insurance (PMI) is called "private" because it's obtained from private insurance companies, not through the FHA's mortgage insurance program. Like FHA mortgage insurance, PMI is designed to protect lenders from the greater risk of high-LTV loans; the insurance makes up for the reduced borrower equity. Both Fannie Mae and Freddie Mac require PMI on conventional loans if the downpayment is less than 20%.

PMI:
- Protects lender
- Premium(s) paid by borrower

How PMI Works. When insuring a loan, a private mortgage insurance company actually assumes only a portion of the risk of default. Instead of covering the entire loan amount, the insurance just covers the upper portion of the loan. The amount of coverage varies, but it is typically 25% to 30% of the loan amount.

PMI typically covers 25% or 30% of the loan amount

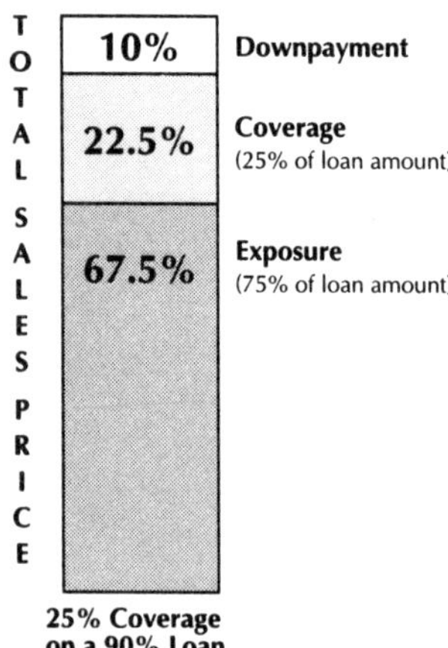

25% Coverage on a 90% Loan

Example: 25% coverage

$200,000	Sales price
× 90%	LTV
$180,000	90% loan
× 25%	Amount of coverage
$45,000	Amount of policy

In the event of default and foreclosure, the lender, at the insurer's option, will either sell the property and make a claim for reimbursement of actual losses (if any) up to the policy's coverage amount, or else relinquish the property to the insurer and make a claim for actual losses up to the coverage amount.

As explained in Chapter 6, private mortgage insurance companies have their own underwriting standards. A company will insure only loans that meet its standards, since it's the company that will bear most of the risk of default and foreclosure loss. Like the underwriting standards of Fannie Mae and Freddie Mac, the standards set by the largest private mortgage insurance companies have been influential throughout the mortgage industry.

PMI premiums:
- Initial premium at closing, plus renewal premiums, or
- Financed one-time premium

PMI Premiums. In return for insuring a loan, a mortgage insurance company charges insurance premiums, which are ordinarily paid by the borrower. Depending on the company, there are a variety of possible payment plans.

For example, the insurance company may charge an initial premium to be paid when the loan is made (at closing), plus annual renewal premiums. The amount of the initial premium depends on the amount of coverage requested and the LTV of the loan. For a 90% loan, the initial premium is usually less than 1% of the loan amount; for a 95% loan, it might be as much as 2% of the loan amount.

Example: $200,000 sales price; 90% loan

$180,000	Loan amount
× 0.65%	For 25% coverage
$1,170	Initial premium at closing

The annual renewal premium may be based on either the original loan amount or the declining loan balance. A typical renewal premium would be 0.34% of the loan amount for a 90% fixed-rate loan, or 0.49% of the loan amount for a 95% loan. The lender will usually require the borrower to pay one-twelfth of the renewal premium each month, as part of the monthly payment on the mortgage.

Example: \$200,000 sales price; 90% loan

\$180,000	Loan amount
× 0.34%	
\$612	Annual renewal premium
÷ 12	Months in a year
\$51	Monthly portion of renewal premium

An alternative to charging an initial premium plus renewal premiums is to charge a single life-of-the-loan premium that may be paid at closing, or else financed over the loan term. To finance the single premium, the lender adds the premium to the loan amount before calculating the monthly payment. An advantage of this plan is that the borrower doesn't have to come up with cash at closing for the PMI.

With some payment plans, the borrower may be entitled to a refund of part of the initial premium or financed premium if the borrower pays the loan off early or the lender cancels the mortgage insurance. Premiums are lower for plans that don't provide for refunds, however.

Cancellation of PMI. As a loan is paid off by the borrower, and as the value of the property serving as security for the loan increases, the loan-to-value ratio decreases. With a lower LTV, the risk of default and foreclosure loss is reduced, and eventually the private mortgage insurance has fulfilled its purpose.

Under the Homeowners Protection Act, a federal law passed in 1998, lenders are required to cancel a loan's PMI under certain conditions. The law requires the PMI to be canceled once the loan has been paid down to 80% of the property's original value, if the borrower formally requests the cancellation. Automatic cancellation of the PMI, without a request from the borrower, is required once the loan balance reaches 78% of the property's original value.

By law, lender must cancel PMI automatically when loan balance reaches 78% of property value

The Homeowners Protection Act applies only to loans on single-family dwellings (including condominium and cooperative units, townhouses, and manufactured homes) occupied as the borrower's principal residence.

If a borrower's mortgage insurance payment plan involved an initial premium and renewal premiums, canceling the PMI means that the monthly payment will be reduced by the amount attributable to the renewal premium. If the PMI was financed, the borrower may receive a refund of part of the premium, but the monthly payment usually won't change.

Secondary Financing

Lenders generally allow secondary financing, whatever the source, in conjunction with a conventional loan. However, most lenders impose some restrictions when secondary financing is used. Secondary financing increases the risk of default on the primary loan, and the primary lender wants to minimize that additional risk as much as possible.

Primary lender sets rules for secondary financing

Restrictions on Secondary Financing. Here are some examples of the types of rules that a lender might apply in a transaction that will involve secondary financing in addition to the lender's own loan:

1. **The borrower must be able to qualify for the payments on both the first and second mortgages.** For qualifying purposes, the primary lender will include the payments on the second loan in the borrower's housing expense.
2. **The borrower must make a 5% downpayment.** The primary lender might not allow the total of the first and second mortgages to exceed 95% of the appraised value or sales price, whichever is less. The borrower would be required to pay the remaining 5% of the purchase price out of his or her own funds. (Some lenders limit the combined LTV for the two loans to 90% and require a 10% downpayment.)
3. **Scheduled payments must be due on a regular basis.** The primary lender will almost certainly require the second loan to have regularly scheduled payments. In some cases, quarterly, semi-annual, or annual payments might be acceptable, but usually the primary lender will insist that the second loan have monthly payments. The scheduled payments can be designed to fully amortize the debt, or to partially amortize it or cover interest only, with a balloon payment due at the end of the term.
4. **The second mortgage can't require a balloon payment less than five years after closing.** If the second loan isn't fully amortized, the primary lender is likely to set a minimum term for it (often five years). This prevents the second lender from requiring a large balloon payment from the borrower early in the term of the primary loan, when the risk of default is greatest.

5. **If the first mortgage has variable payments, the second mortgage must have fixed payments.** In other words, the primary lender may require the second mortgage to be a fixed-rate loan if the first mortgage is an adjustable-rate loan, or if the first mortgage is subject to a temporary buydown. (Buydowns are discussed later in this chapter.) Conversely, if the first mortgage is a fixed-rate loan without a buydown, the primary lender will usually allow the second mortgage to be an ARM.
6. **No negative amortization.** The primary lender may specify that the regular payments on the second mortgage must at least equal the interest due on the second mortgage.
7. **No prepayment penalty.** The second mortgage usually must be payable in part or in full at any time without a prepayment penalty.

Again, these are just examples of secondary financing rules. If you're working with a buyer who plans to use secondary financing, ask the buyer's primary lender what rules will apply.

Piggyback Loans. You may hear lenders, mortgage brokers, and real estate agents refer to piggyback loans. That's basically just another term for secondary financing: a piggyback loan is a second loan "riding piggyback" on a first loan. But the term is typically applied when secondary financing is used either to avoid paying private mortgage insurance or to avoid jumbo loan treatment.

Piggyback loan enables borrower to avoid paying for PMI, or paying a higher interest rate for a jumbo loan

Avoiding PMI. Piggybacking is most often used in reference to the strategy of using secondary financing—a piggyback loan—to keep the loan-to-value ratio of the primary financing at 80% or less so that the borrower won't have to pay for mortgage insurance. This strategy works in some cases, but it can backfire. If the second loan has a high interest rate and steep fees, or requires expensive refinancing down the road, the borrower may end up spending more on the second loan than he or she saved by avoiding PMI.

Avoiding a jumbo loan. Piggybacking also comes up in connection with jumbo loans. In this context, it refers to getting a conforming primary loan (that is, one that doesn't exceed the conforming loan limits shown in Figure 10.1) along with a second loan to cover the rest of the financing needed to purchase an expensive home. Since conforming loans have lower interest rates than nonconforming loans, the piggyback combination will have a lower overall interest rate than a single jumbo loan would.

Example: The Marburys are buying a home for $530,000. They're going to make a $53,000 downpayment and use a piggyback arrangement to finance the remaining $477,000. Their first loan will be for $417,000 (the current maximum amount for a conforming loan), and they'll be charged the market interest rate for conforming loans, which is currently 6%. The interest rate on the second loan, for $60,000, will be 7%. With this piggyback combination, they'll pay $29,220 in interest during the first year they own the property. That's an effective interest rate of 6.13% on the total amount borrowed:

$$\$29{,}220 \div \$477{,}000 = 6.13\%$$

The Marburys' main alternative would be to get a single jumbo loan for the entire loan amount, $477,000. The current market rate for a loan that size is 6.75%, which means they'd pay $32,198 in interest the first year. That's $2,978 more than the first-year interest for the piggyback loan.

The Marburys' monthly payments would be smaller with the piggyback arrangement, too. The principal and interest payment for the jumbo loan would be $3,094 per month, compared to $2,899 for the piggyback combination.

Exercise No. 2

A buyer is seeking conventional fixed-rate financing in order to purchase a home. The sales price is $289,500 and the property has been appraised at $291,500. The buyer is planning to make a 5% cash downpayment and finance the balance with two loans: an 80% conventional first mortgage at 7% interest for 30 years and a 15% second mortgage from the seller at 6.5% interest. Payments on the second mortgage would be based on a 30-year amortization schedule, with a balloon payment of $40,650 due five years after closing. There would be a 1.5% loan origination fee on the first loan.

The first loan would require a monthly principal and interest payment of $1,540.84. The second loan would require a monthly principal and interest payment of $274.48. In addition, one-twelfth of the annual property taxes of $3,190 and one-twelfth of the annual hazard insurance premium of $720 would be included in the buyer's total monthly mortgage payment.

1. What would the loan amounts for the first and second loans be?

2. How much would the buyer pay at closing for the downpayment and the loan origination fee?

3. What would the buyer's total monthly payment for both loans come to, including principal, interest, taxes, and insurance (PITI)?

Qualifying Standards

Chapter 8 explained the general process of qualifying buyers for home purchase loans. Now we'll discuss the qualifying standards that apply to conventional loans. As explained earlier, the qualifying standards most lenders use for conventional loans are based on guidelines established by Fannie Mae and Freddie Mac.

Evaluating Risk Factors

Over the past few years, both Fannie Mae and Freddie Mac have made significant changes in how they evaluate the creditworthiness of loan applicants. They're still concerned with income, net worth, and credit history, but they have new methods for weighing that information in order to decide whether or not to make a loan.

These newer methods have been influenced by automated underwriting systems and computer analysis of data about mortgage borrowers (see Chapter 8). The secondary market agencies are using these data to revise their rules for manual underwriting—the underwriting that's still carried out by human underwriters, often in conjunction with an automated underwriting system.

Primary risk factors for comprehensive risk assessment:
- credit score
- loan-to-value ratio

Fannie Mae now uses a "comprehensive risk assessment" approach to evaluate the risk factors in a loan application. In this approach, there are two **primary risk factors**. The first is the applicant's credit history, as reflected in his or her credit score. The second is the cash investment the applicant will be making, measured by the loan-to-value ratio. Based on the credit score and the loan-to-value ratio, a proposed loan is ranked as having a low, moderate, or high primary risk, and that determines the level of review applied to the rest of the loan application.

Fannie Mae treats the other aspects of the application, such as the debt to income ratio and cash reserves, as **contributory risk factors** that may increase or decrease the risk of default. Each contributory risk factor is assigned a value depending on whether it "satisfies basic risk tolerances," increases risk, or decreases risk. The underwriter makes the decision to approve or reject the loan application based on the cumulative effect of the primary and contributory risk factors.

Underwriter may evaluate overall layering of risk

In Freddie Mac's approach, the underwriter first evaluates each of the main components of creditworthiness—capacity to repay (income and net worth), credit reputation, and collateral. Then the underwriter considers the "overall layering of risk." Weakness in one component of the application may be balanced by strength in the others. But even if each of the main components seems acceptable on its own, the combined risk factors from all of the components may amount to excessive layering of risk. In that case, the loan should be denied.

As we look at the rules generally used in qualifying buyers for conventional loans, keep in mind that Fannie Mae now uses these rules in the context of its primary risk and contributory risk analysis. Freddie Mac now uses them in the context of an evaluation of layering of risk.

Income Analysis

Stable monthly income is income that meets the lender's tests of quality and durability (see Chapter 8). Fannie Mae and Freddie Mac consider income durable if it is expected to continue for at least three years after the loan is made.

Once the lender determines how much stable monthly income the loan applicant has, the next step is to decide if the amount of stable monthly income is adequate to support the proposed monthly mortgage payment. This is where the income ratios come into play.

Total Obligations to Income Ratio. Lenders generally consider a loan applicant's income adequate for a conventional loan if the applicant's **total monthly obligations** do not exceed **36%** of his or her stable monthly income. Total monthly obligations include the proposed housing expense plus the applicant's other recurring obligations. The **housing expense** includes PITI: principal, interest, taxes, hazard insurance, and—if applicable—mortgage insurance and homeowners association dues.

Benchmark for total obligations ratio: 36%

A loan applicant's **recurring obligations** can be broken down into three categories: installment debts, revolving debts, and other obligations. **Installment debts** have a fixed beginning and ending date. The most common example is a car loan. The monthly payments are a fixed amount and continue for a fixed number of months. An installment debt will be included when calculating the loan applicant's total obligations to income ratio if there are more than ten months' worth of payments remaining. (A debt that will be paid off in ten months or less may also be included if the required payments are very large.)

Total obligations include:

- Housing expense
- Installment debts
- Revolving debts
- Other obligations

Revolving debts involve an open-ended line of credit, with minimum monthly payments. The most common examples are Visa, MasterCard, and department store charge accounts. In calculating a loan applicant's total obligations to income ratio, some lenders consider any revolving charge account if it is still open and there has been account activity in the previous six months—even if the account balance has been completely paid off. The lender will use the most recent required minimum payment in its calculations. To avoid having the lender consider a revolving charge account that has been paid off in the previous six months, the applicant may have to close the account (cancel the credit card). Ask the lender whether this step is necessary.

The "other" category of recurring obligations includes alimony, child support, and similar ongoing financial obligations. At present, neither Fannie Mae nor Freddie Mac considers child care expenses as part of a loan applicant's recurring obligations. However, some individual lenders do take child care expenses into account, especially if they are planning to keep the loan in portfolio.

Benchmark for housing expense to income ratio: 28%

Housing Expense to Income Ratio. The second ratio that lenders have traditionally used for conventional loans is the housing expense to income ratio. The proposed housing expense (PITI) generally should not exceed **28%** of the loan applicant's stable monthly income.

Applying the Ratios. Using income ratios, it's a simple matter to determine how large a mortgage payment a buyer is likely to qualify for. Take the buyer's stable monthly income and multiply it by the 36% total obligations to income ratio. The buyer's total monthly payments on all long-term obligations (including the proposed mortgage) should not exceed this amount. Take this figure and subtract the buyer's total monthly payments on long-term obligations other than the mortgage; the result is the largest mortgage payment allowed under the total obligations to income ratio. Next, multiply the stable monthly income by the 28% housing expense to income ratio. This answer is the largest mortgage payment allowed under the second ratio.

Example:

$425	Car payment (18 installments remaining)
+ 250	Credit card payments
$675	Monthly obligations
$6,100	Stable monthly income
× 36%	Total obligations to income ratio
$2,196	
− 675	Monthly obligations
$1,521	Maximum mortgage payment under the total obligations ratio
$6,100	Stable monthly income
× 28%	Housing expense to income ratio
$1,708	Maximum mortgage payment under the housing expense ratio

As in the example, the mortgage payment determined by the total obligations to income ratio is usually smaller than the payment determined by the housing expense to income ratio. This is because most buyers have significant recurring obligations besides the proposed mortgage payment. In any case, the smaller of the two results is the maximum allowable mortgage payment.

> **Example:** Marianne Smith has a stable monthly income of $4,200. She has four long-term monthly obligations: a $310 car payment, a $65 personal loan payment, a $40 Sears credit card payment, and a $45 MasterCard payment. What is the largest mortgage payment she can qualify for?
>
> Total obligations to income ratio:

$4,200	Stable monthly income
× 36%	Income ratio
$1,512	Maximum total obligations
– 310	Car payment
– 65	Personal loan payment
– 40	Sears credit card payment
– 45	MasterCard payment
$1,052	Maximum mortgage payment under the total obligations ratio

> Housing expense to income ratio:

$4,200	Stable monthly income
× 28%	Income ratio
$1,176	Maximum mortgage payment under the housing expense ratio

> The largest mortgage payment that Smith could probably qualify for is $1,052. Remember, after both ratios have been applied, the lower resulting figure is the one that counts. Of course, if Smith could pay off some of her debts and reduce her total obligations, she could qualify for a larger mortgage payment.

Lenders regard the housing expense ratio as less important than the total obligations ratio, which takes all of the loan applicant's other recurring obligations into account as well as the housing expense. In fact, Fannie Mae no longer applies a housing expense to income ratio; the agency now considers the monthly housing expense only as one of the components of the total obligations to income ratio. We'll continue to use both ratios in our examples, since many lenders still use both.

Housing expense ratio is less important than total obligations ratio

Debt-to-Housing Gap Ratio. In addition to the total obligations ratio and the housing expense ratio, Freddie Mac requires lenders to calculate a debt-to-housing gap ratio. The gap ratio is calculated by subtracting the housing expense ratio from the total obligations

Debt to housing gap ratio: total obligations ratio minus housing expense ratio

ratio. For example, if a loan applicant has a 40% total obligations ratio and a 28% housing expense ratio, the gap ratio is 12%. Freddie Mac's guideline concerning the gap ratio is that it generally should not exceed 15%.

Income ratios may exceed benchmarks if there are compensating factors

Higher Ratios and Compensating Factors. Although we've been referring to 36% and 28% as the "maximum" allowable income ratios for conventional loans, that isn't strictly accurate. Both Fannie Mae and Freddie Mac consider these income ratios to be benchmarks or guidelines rather than rigid limits. Both agencies will purchase a loan even though the borrower's ratios exceed 36% and/or 28%, as long as there are **compensating factors** that justify making the loan in spite of the higher ratios. The stronger the compensating factors, the higher the ratios are allowed to be. In this analysis, a lender could treat any of the following as a compensating factor:

- a large downpayment;
- substantial net worth;
- a demonstrated ability to incur few debts and accumulate savings;
- education, job training, or employment history that indicates strong potential for increased earnings;
- short-term income that doesn't count as stable monthly income (because it won't last for three years);
- a demonstrated ability to devote a greater portion of income to basic needs, such as the housing expense; or
- significant energy-efficient features in the home being purchased.

Let's look at an example to see how a lender might take some of these compensating factors into account.

Example: Walter Quinn and Lisa Porter have a stable monthly income of $5,200. Their only recurring obligation is a $342 monthly car payment. They've applied for a mortgage with monthly payments of $1,686 (including principal, interest, taxes, hazard insurance, and mortgage insurance).

When the underwriter calculates Quinn and Porter's income ratios, he finds that their total obligations ratio is 39% and their housing expense ratio is over 32%. So the underwriter reviews their application for compensating factors, to see if loan approval would be justified in spite of income ratios that exceed the benchmarks.

First, the underwriter checks Porter and Quinn's credit scores. Both have good scores, in the mid-700s. Next, the underwriter notes that Porter and Quinn have been paying $1,575 a month for rent on their current home, so the proposed housing expense wouldn't represent a dramatic increase for them. They've demonstrated that they can devote a greater portion of income to basic needs than most people.

Quinn also receives $400 per month from his first wife, for the support of their 15-year-old daughter. The child support wasn't included in stable monthly income, because the payments will end in two and a half years, when the daughter turns 18. It can count as a compensating factor, however.

Finally, the underwriter notes that Quinn and Porter have few debts and a fairly low debt-to-housing gap ratio (7%), and they will have $16,000 in savings left over after meeting all the expenses of purchasing their home. He decides that Quinn and Porter's application is supported by sufficient compensating factors to justify loan approval.

Compensating factors:
- Large downpayment
- Substantial net worth
- Savings and few debts
- Potential for increased earnings
- Short-term income
- More income devoted to basic needs
- Energy-efficient home

Keep in mind that even when there are compensating factors to justify income ratios higher than the 36% and 28% benchmarks, lenders won't accept ratios that are too far over those limits. Exactly how far is too far may vary from one lender to another, however.

Also, lenders who apply both ratios generally treat the housing expense to income ratio more flexibly than the total obligations to income ratio. That means there's a good chance that a lender will approve a loan if the applicant's total obligations ratio is the standard 36%, even though his or her housing expense to income ratio is high. The lender might require stronger compensating factors to approve the loan if the housing expense ratio was 28% but the total obligations ratio was high.

Factors that Increase Risk. Of course, instead of compensating factors, some loan applications present factors that represent increased risk for the lender, such as a mediocre credit score or an unsettled work history. In that situation, income ratios in excess of the benchmarks would generally be unacceptable.

Income Analysis for 95% Loans. For conventional loans that have loan-to-value ratios over 90%, lenders generally won't accept income ratios higher than 36% and 28% unless there are especially strong compensating factors.

Some lenders even apply a stricter test for these high-LTV loans; for example, they may require the applicant to have a total obligations to income ratio no higher than 33%, and will accept a ratio up to the standard 36% only if there are compensating factors. With a 33% ratio, the mortgage payment the applicant can qualify for is smaller, which reduces the risk of default.

Example: Miguel Diaz is applying for a loan at Seaside Savings. His stable monthly income is $4,000. His recurring obligations total $310. The underwriter at Seaside will apply the standard income ratios, because there aren't any compensating factors to justify higher income ratios for Diaz. If he applies for an 80% loan or a 90% loan, he could probably qualify for a monthly mortgage payment of $1,130.

$4,000	Stable monthly income
× 36%	Total obligations to income ratio
$1,440	
− 310	Monthly obligations
$1,130	Maximum mortgage payment

However, for 95% loans, Seaside Savings won't allow a total obligations ratio higher than 33%. So if Diaz applies for a 95% loan at Seaside, the largest mortgage payment he could qualify for is $1,010.

$4,000	Stable monthly income
× 33%	Total obligations to income ratio
$1,320	
− 310	Monthly obligations
$1,010	Maximum mortgage payment

It was once fairly common for lenders to use a 33% ratio for high-LTV loans, but now it's comparatively rare; the mortgage industry as a whole has become more comfortable with high-LTV loans. That's partly because lenders have gotten used to them, and partly because automated underwriting has made the evaluation process more accurate.

Loans with 95% LTV must be underwritten more carefully than 80% and 90% loans

Fannie Mae and Freddie Mac are willing to buy 95% loans underwritten using the standard 36% ratio. However, they require these loans to be evaluated very carefully. The lender is supposed to pay special attention to the applicant's credit history, reserves, ability to accumulate savings, and potential for increased earnings. The lender should also consider how much of an increase over the current housing expense (mortgage payment or rent) the proposed housing expense would represent. If an application for a 95% loan is weak in any of these respects, it may be rejected.

Income Analysis for ARMs. Lenders also evaluate applications for adjustable-rate mortgages very carefully, because the monthly payments for an ARM may increase sharply, often in the first few years of the loan term. Fannie Mae and Freddie Mac generally accept ARMs underwritten using the standard income ratios, but they expect the lender to consider whether the loan applicant will be able to handle payment increases. An ARM borrower should either have strong potential for increased earnings, significant liquid assets (reserves), or a demonstrated ability to manage finances and apply a greater portion of income to housing expenses.

ARMs must be underwritten more carefully than fixed-rate loans

ARMs are offered at lower interest rates than fixed-rate loans—sometimes much lower. For example, if fixed-rate loans are available at 7% interest, borrowers may be able to get an ARM with an initial interest rate of 5%. Since the interest rate affects the monthly payment amount, this can make it easier to qualify for an ARM than for a fixed-rate loan. However, that may be counteracted by the extra scrutiny an ARM application will receive. Also, in some cases a lender won't use the actual initial interest rate to qualify an ARM applicant. Instead, the applicant will be qualified using the maximum interest rate that could be in effect at the end of the first year of the loan term.

> **Example:** The Conrads have applied for a $210,000 ARM from a lender that's offering an initial interest rate of 5.5%. The loan would have an LTV of 90%, a 30-year term, a one-year rate adjustment period, and a 2% annual rate cap.
>
> The lender will apply the standard 36% and 28% income ratios to qualify the Conrads. But their income ratios will be calculated using a proposed housing expense based on 7.5% interest (the maximum rate possible at the end of the first year) rather than the 5.5% they'll actually have to pay during the first year if the loan is approved. This means the Conrads will qualify only if their income is sufficient to handle a $1,468 principal and interest payment, as opposed to the $1,192 principal and interest payment they would actually be making during the first year.
>
> In addition, the lender won't approve the loan unless there is reason to believe the Conrads will be able to handle future payment increases. They must have strong potential for increased earnings, significant liquid assets, or the ability to devote an extra share of their income to housing expenses, if necessary.

This method of qualifying is generally used only for ARMs with features that permit sharp payment increases, such as the 2% annual interest rate cap in the example. If the Conrads had applied for an ARM with a 1% rate cap, then the lender would probably have qualified them using the 5.5% interest rate.

Net Worth

As we discussed in Chapter 8, lenders want to know a loan applicant's net worth because it's an indication of the applicant's money management skills. They also need to determine whether the applicant has enough money for the downpayment and closing costs, and whether there will be any funds left in reserve after closing.

Gift funds
- Donor must be a relative, employer, city, or nonprofit organization
- Borrower usually still must make 5% downpayment from own funds

Gift Funds. In regard to the resources that a borrower has available for closing, Fannie Mae and Freddie Mac set limits on the use of gift funds. First of all, the donor must be:

- the borrower's relative, fiancé, or domestic partner;
- the borrower's employer;
- a municipality or public agency; or
- a nonprofit religious or community organization.

Also, as a general rule the borrower is required to make a downpayment of at least 5% of the sales price out of his or her own resources.

> **Example:** Grace Wessel has agreed to buy a house for $200,000; the appraised value is $201,000. Wessel hopes to qualify for a 90% loan. Her mother is willing to give her $14,000 to close the transaction. But Wessel can use only $10,000 in gift funds toward the downpayment; she will be required to come up with the remaining $10,000 out of her own resources. (Wessel may use the additional $4,000 gift from her mother for closing costs or reserves.)
>
> If Wessel were trying to obtain a 95% loan, she could not use any gift funds for the downpayment, but she could use them for closing costs or reserves.

When the loan-to-value ratio is 80% or less, the 5% requirement does not apply. For example, if Wessel's mother were to supply a 20% downpayment, Wessel would not have to contribute any of her own money toward the purchase.

Reserves. It's desirable for borrowers to have liquid assets in reserve after closing, because the more they have in reserve, the more likely it is that they'll be able to weather financial emergencies without defaulting on their mortgage.

Fannie Mae and Freddie Mac traditionally required conventional borrowers to have the equivalent of two months' mortgage payments left in reserve after making the downpayment and paying all their closing costs. However, the secondary market agencies no longer treat cash reserves as a strict requirement. If a loan applicant will have a significant amount of money in reserve after closing, that's a compensating factor that can offset some risk. If an applicant has little or no money in reserve after closing, that's an added risk factor.

Conventional borrower may be required to have 2 months' mortgage payments in reserve

In spite of this change in policy on the part of Fannie Mae and Freddie Mac, some lenders may continue to require loan applicants to have at least two months' mortgage payments in reserve. For a 95% loan, three months of reserves may be considered necessary.

Credit Reputation

Fannie Mae and Freddie Mac both strongly encourage lenders to use credit scores in evaluating loan applicants' credit histories. Indeed, as explained earlier, credit scores are one of Fannie Mae's two primary risk factors.

Credit scores have become a central factor in conventional underwriting

An excellent credit score can offset weaknesses in certain other aspects of the loan application, such as marginal income ratios, low reserves, or a high LTV.

When two people apply for a conventional loan together (as in the case of a married couple), the lender will obtain credit scores for both applicants. However, in most cases the lowest score is the one that the lender will use in qualifying the applicants. If the other applicant's score is very high, that might be treated as a compensating factor.

For couples, underwriter uses lowest credit score, not an average

Exercise No. 3

Mike and Barbara Tanaka want to buy a home. Mike makes $62,000 a year as a controller for a small electronics company. Barbara makes $4,750 a month as an administrator at a local community college. They have two car payments, one at $317 a month

(21 payments left) and the other at $375 a month (13 payments left). They have a personal loan with a remaining balance of $2,400, which requires monthly payments of $250. The Tanakas make three credit card payments every month, with the following minimum payments: $55 a month to a department store, $42 a month to Visa, and $54 a month to MasterCard.

1. Suppose the Tanakas would like a fixed-rate 90% loan. Applying the benchmark income ratios, how large a mortgage payment would the Tanakas qualify for?

2. List two or three compensating factors that might allow the Tanakas to qualify for a somewhat larger payment, if these factors were present in their financial situation.

3. Even if there aren't any compensating factors in the Tanakas' financial situation that would lead the lender to accept income ratios higher than the standard limits, what can the Tanakas do to qualify for a larger payment?

Special Programs and Payment Plans

The traditional conventional mortgage loan had a 30-year term, an 80% loan-to-value ratio, a fixed interest rate, and fully amortized monthly payments. We've already discussed some of the important alternatives to that traditional model that are now in widespread use, including loans with 15-year terms, with 90% and 95% loan-to-value ratios, and with adjustable interest rates. In this section of the chapter we'll discuss a variety of other alternatives available with conventional financing. Some of them involve specially structured payment plans, and others are programs that combine a number of special features. As you'll see, the point of most of these plans and programs is to make conventional financing more affordable.

Buydown Plans

One of the easiest ways to make a loan less expensive is a **buydown**. In a buydown arrangement, a property seller or a third party pays the lender a lump sum at closing to lower the interest rate on the buyer's loan. The lump sum payment increases the lender's yield on the loan, and in return the lender charges a lower interest rate, which lowers the amount of the borrower's monthly payment. The lender will evaluate the borrower on the basis of a reduced payment, making it easier to qualify for the loan.

Buydown:
- Seller or third party pays lump sum to lender at closing
- Increases lender's yield
- Lowers buyer's payment
- May make it easier to qualify

This is the equivalent of paying the lender discount points, but it's called a buydown when the seller or a third party pays the points on the buyer's behalf. Also, a buydown can be arranged even when the lender was quoting a specified interest rate without discount points.

> **Example:** Seaside Savings is offering fixed-rate 30-year loans at the market interest rate, 11%. In order to help buyers afford financing to purchase her home, Irene Glover is willing to pay for a 2% buydown, which would reduce the quoted interest rate to 9%.

Buydowns are generally used when interest rates are high, as in the example.

A buydown can be permanent or temporary. With a **permanent buydown**, the borrower pays the lower interest rate (and a lower payment) for the entire loan term. With a **temporary buydown**, the interest rate and monthly payment are reduced only during the first years of the loan term.

Permanent Buydowns. If a borrower's interest rate is bought down permanently (for the entire loan term), the buydown reduces the note rate—the interest rate stated in the promissory note.

> **Example:** Bowen needs to borrow $150,000 to buy Sanderson's property. The lender quoted a 12% interest rate for a 30-year fixed-rate loan, and Bowen can't quite afford the loan at that rate. Sanderson offers to buy down Bowen's interest rate to 11%. The

lender agrees to make the loan to the buyer at this lower rate if Sanderson pays the lender $9,000.

With this arrangement in place, the promissory note that Bowen signs sets the interest rate at 11%. The buyer will pay 11% interest for the life of the loan. At closing, the lender will withhold $9,000 from the loan funds, reducing Sanderson's proceeds from the sale.

By reducing the interest rate from 12% to 11%, the buydown will lower Bowen's mortgage payment by $115 per month and enable her to qualify for the loan.

$1,543	Payment at quoted 12% rate
− 1,428	Payment at 11% after buydown
$115	Monthly savings resulting from buydown

The cost of a permanent buydown is calculated in terms of points (percentage points) of the loan amount. The number of points required to increase the lender's yield by 1% (and decrease the borrower's interest rate by 1%) varies from one area to another. It's affected by current market conditions, including prevailing interest rates, and the average time that loans are outstanding before being paid off.

Permanent buydown rule of thumb: 6 points for 1% interest rate reduction

To know the exact cost of a permanent buydown, you should ask the lender. But when all you need is a rough estimate, you can use the rule of thumb explained in Chapter 7: It takes about six points to increase the lender's yield on a 30-year loan by 1%.*

Example: In the example above, the lender charged the seller six points for a 1% buydown.

$150,000	Loan amount
× 6%	Six points
$9,000	Cost of 1% buydown

Remember that this rule of thumb only estimates the cost of a buydown. The lender that the buyer expects to borrow from should be consulted before the buyer and seller sign an agreement.

Temporary Buydowns. A temporary buydown reduces the buyer's monthly payments in the early months or years of the loan term. Temporary buydowns appeal to buyers who feel they can grow into a larger payment, but need time to get established.

Temporary buydowns:
- Level payment
- Graduated payment

There are two types of temporary buydown plans: level payment plans and graduated payment plans.

* The six points rule of thumb is the most widely used. In some parts of the country, however, the rule of thumb is eight points for 1%.

Level payments. A level payment plan calls for an interest reduction that stays the same throughout the buydown period.

> **Example:** The lender agrees to make a 30-year loan of $185,000 at 13% interest. The property seller buys down the borrower's interest rate to 11% for three years by paying the lender $10,224 at closing.
>
> As shown in Figure 10.3, during the first three years of the loan term the buydown lowers the monthly payment on the loan by $284, from $2,046 to $1,762. At the beginning of the fourth year, the payment amount goes up to the unsubsidized level, $2,046, and stays at that level for the remaining 27 years of the loan term.

Fig. 10.3 Three-year temporary buydown with level payments

Year	Note Rate	Buydown	Effective Rate	Payment at 13%	Actual Payment	Monthly Subsidy	Annual Subsidy
1	13%	2%	11%	$2,046	$1,762	$284	$3,408
2	13%	2%	11%	$2,046	$1,762	$284	$3,408
3	13%	2%	11%	$2,046	$1,762	$284	$3,408
4	13%	- 0 -	13%	$2,046	$2,046	- 0 -	- 0 -
							Total Buydown: $10,224

Graduated payments. A graduated payment buydown plan calls for the largest payment reduction in the first year, with progressively smaller reductions in each of the remaining years of the buydown period.

> **Example:** The lender agrees to make a 30-year loan of $185,000 at 13% interest. By paying the lender $10,188 at closing, the seller buys down the borrower's interest rate by 3% the first year, 2% the second year, and 1% the third year. Figure 10.4 shows how the monthly payment will change.

Fig. 10.4 Three-year temporary buydown with graduated payments

Year	Note Rate	Buydown	Effective Rate	Payment at 13%	Actual Payment	Monthly Subsidy	Annual Subsidy
1	13%	3%	10%	$2,046	$1,624	$422	$5,064
2	13%	2%	11%	$2,046	$1,762	$284	$3,408
3	13%	1%	12%	$2,046	$1,903	$143	$1,716
4	13%	- 0 -	13%	$2,046	$2,046	- 0 -	- 0 -
							Total Buydown: $10,188

The graduated payment buydown in the example (in which the interest rate is bought down 3% the first year, 2% the second year, and 1% the third year) is called a 3-2-1 buydown. Probably the most common form of graduated payment buydown is the 2-1 buydown. In a 2-1 buydown, the interest rate is bought down 2% the first year and 1% the second year; the buyer starts paying the note rate in the third year.

Computing the cost of a temporary buydown. As with a permanent buydown, to get the exact cost of a temporary buydown, it's best to ask a lender for a quote. But the cost of a temporary buydown can be computed fairly accurately with a financial calculator.

Estimating cost of temporary buydown:
- Calculate difference between unsubsidized and subsidized payments
- Multiply by 12 for annual cost
- Add up annual costs for total cost

1. Calculate the buyer's monthly principal and interest payment without the buydown, at the full rate of interest the lender is charging.
2. Calculate the buyer's monthly payment with the bought-down interest rate.
3. Subtract the bought-down payment from the actual payment and multiply by twelve for the annual buydown amount.
4. For a level payment buydown, multiply the annual buydown amount by the number of years in the buydown plan.

Example: Three-year level payment buydown

$203,000	Loan amount
11.25%	Note rate
9.25%	Bought-down rate

1. Calculate the monthly principal and interest payment without the buydown: $1,971.66.
2. Calculate the payment with the buydown: $1,670.03.
3. Subtract the bought-down payment from the actual payment and multiply by twelve (months).

$1,971.66	Actual payment
– 1,670.03	Bought-down payment
$301.63	Monthly buydown amount
× 12	Months
$3,619.56	Annual buydown amount

4. Multiply the annual buydown amount by the number of years in the buydown plan.

$3,619.56	Annual buydown amount
× 3	Years in buydown plan
$10,858.68	Total buydown: lump sum required by lender

A graduated payment buydown is calculated in the same way, except that the amount of each year's buydown has to be calculated separately and then all the annual figures are added together. The sum is the total cost of the graduated payment buydown.

Buydowns and Qualifying Rules. As we said earlier, by lowering the monthly payment, a buydown can make it easier for the buyer to qualify for a loan. With a permanent buydown, the lender uses the bought-down interest rate to calculate the payment, and then determines if the buyer can qualify for that reduced payment. If the seller permanently buys down the loan's interest rate from 12% to 10%, the buyer only has to qualify for a payment at 10% interest.

With permanent buydown, lender qualifies buyer at bought-down interest rate

It isn't that simple with a temporary buydown. Since the buydown is only going to last a few years, the buyer will eventually have to afford the larger payment based on the full note rate. So in some cases, instead of qualifying the buyer at the bought-down rate, the lender uses a higher rate for the qualifying calculations; for instance, the lender might use a rate only 1% below the note rate to qualify the buyer.

With temporary buydown, lender may qualify buyer at:
- the bought-down rate,
- the note rate, or
- an intermediate rate

> **Example:** Refer back to the 3-2-1 graduated payment buydown shown in Figure 10.4. The note rate is 13%. In the first year, the interest rate will be bought down 3%—from 13% to 10%. Even so, the lender qualifies the buyer at 12%, only one percentage point below the note rate. The buyer has to qualify for a $1,903 payment (the payment calculated using 12% interest), even though the actual payments will be lower than that in the first two years of the loan term. This gives the lender some assurance the buyer will be able to handle the payment increases when the time comes.

Fannie Mae will allow a buyer with a temporary buydown to be qualified using the bought-down rate, as long as the loan has a fixed interest rate or, if it is an ARM, an initial period of three years or more; in addition, the buyer's credit score should be 660 or higher.

Freddie Mac has its own rules for temporary buydowns. The buyer can usually be qualified using the bought-down interest rate if the property will be the buyer's principal residence. (If the property is a second home, the note rate must be used.) For a 3-2-1 buydown, if the loan-to-value ratio is over 80%, the buyer must be qualified using the second year's interest rate.

Both Fannie Mae and Freddie Mac expect lenders to evaluate loans subject to temporary buydowns with special care. As with an ARM, the buyer should have strong potential for increased income, or significant liquid assets, or the ability to apply an extra share of his or her income to the housing expense, if necessary.

Many lenders follow other policies of their own in regard to temporary buydowns. When you're handling a transaction in which the parties would like to arrange a temporary buydown, always ask the lender what interest rate and what income ratios will be used for qualifying, and what other rules apply.

Limits on Buydowns and Other Contributions. Fannie Mae and Freddie Mac limit the amount of a buydown to a percentage of the property's sales price or appraised value, whichever is less, as shown in Figure 10.5. The limits also apply to most other contributions the buyer accepts from the seller, or from another interested party, such as the builder or a real estate agent involved in the transaction. For example, if the seller agreed to pay closing costs that would ordinarily be paid by the buyer, these limits would apply.

If seller's contributions exceed limits, excess deducted from sales price in loan amount calculations

If the seller's contributions exceed these guidelines, the excess contribution must be deducted from the sales price before determining the maximum loan amount.

Example:

$300,000 sales price; $302,000 appraised value; 90% loan
Maximum contribution: $18,000 (6% of the sales price)

For this transaction, any contribution in excess of $18,000 would be deducted from the sales price, which would result in a lower loan amount. For instance, if the seller were to contribute $19,000, the extra $1,000 would be subtracted from the sales

Fig. 10.5 Limits on contributions from sellers or other interested parties

Contribution Limits for Owner-Occupied Homes	
Loan-to-Value Ratio	*Maximum Contribution*
Over 90%	3%
90% or less	6%
75% or less	9%

price, and the maximum loan amount would be only $269,100 instead of $270,000.

$300,000	Sales price
– 1,000	Excess contribution
$299,000	
× 90%	LTV
$269,100	Loan amount

These limits on contributions from interested parties generally don't apply to contributions from someone who isn't participating in the transaction—for example, the buyer's employer, or a family member.

Exercise No. 4

Dan Johnson agrees to purchase Morris Callahan's home for $110,000, on the condition that Johnson is able to obtain a 90%, 30-year conventional loan at 10.75% interest. Johnson locates a lender who is willing to make the loan but insists on 11.75% interest. Callahan offers to pay for a permanent buydown so Johnson can afford the loan and go through with the purchase.

1. Approximately how much would the buydown cost Callahan?

2. With the buydown, Johnson's monthly principal and interest payment would be $924.15, compared to $999.32 without the buydown. How much could the buydown save Johnson over the life of the loan?

Loans with Lower Initial Payments

Many first-time home buyers are just starting out in their careers. They expect their incomes to increase steadily, so that they'll eventually be able to afford a higher mortgage payment than they can now. These buyers may be able to buy a more expensive home without waiting if they get a loan that has lower payments at first and higher payments later on.

As we just discussed, a temporary buydown is one way of making a loan more affordable in the first years of the repayment period. In Chapter 6, we also discussed hybrid ARMs: adjustable-rate mortgages with two-tiered rate adjustment schedules. One example is the 5/1 ARM: the interest rate and payment amount start out lower than the rate and payment for a fixed-rate loan, and they don't change during the first five years; the lender makes annual adjustments after that. Other types of two-tiered conventional loans that offer lower payments in the initial years than a comparable fixed-rate loan include:

Loans with lower initial payments:
- Hybrid ARMs
- Two-step mortgages
- Balloon/reset mortgages
- Interest first mortgages

- two-step mortgages,
- balloon/reset mortgages, and
- interest first mortgages.

Two-step Mortgages. A two-step mortgage provides some of the advantages of an ARM, but less uncertainty for the borrower. A two-step mortgage is a 30-year loan that allows the lender to adjust the loan's interest rate at only one point during the loan term. The most common two-step programs are the 5/25 plan and the 7/23 plan.

The interest rate of a 5/25 loan is automatically adjusted after five years to the current market rate (but no higher than 6% above the initial rate), and the monthly payment is adjusted accordingly. The interest rate and payment then stay at that level for the remaining 25 years of the loan term.

> **Example:** When Paul Jacoby obtained a loan, the current fixed interest rate was 6%. Jacoby was able to get a 5/25 two-step loan at a 5.5% initial interest rate. Five years later, the market rate has increased by 2%, so Jacoby's rate increases to 7.5%. He will continue to pay 7.5% interest for the remainder of the loan term, 25 years.

A 7/23 loan automatically adjusts after seven years to the current market rate (up to 6% above the initial rate), and then stays at that rate for the remaining 23 years of the loan term.

Because the lender will have an opportunity to adjust the loan's interest rate to reflect changes in the market rate, two-step mortgages are offered at a lower initial rate than fixed-rate loans. And while the borrower assumes the risk that interest rates will increase in the next five or seven years, he also gets to take advantage of lower rates without refinancing if market rates decrease during that five- or seven-year period. Because the interest rate on a two-step loan changes only once, many borrowers feel more comfortable with this type of loan than with an ARM.

Balloon/Reset Mortgages. Balloon/reset mortgages are similar to two-step mortgages, with some key differences. Like two-step mortgages, balloon/reset mortgages come in two versions, 5/25 and 7/23. With a balloon/reset mortgage, however, the initial five- or seven-year period is actually the term of the loan. Although the payment amount is based on a 30-year amortization schedule, the entire mortgage balance becomes due at the end of the five- or seven-year term. In other words, a balloon/reset mortgage is a partially amortized loan.

Two-step or balloon/reset mortgage: interest rate adjusted only once (5 or 7 years into loan term)

At the end of the five- or seven-year term, the borrowers may have to refinance in order to make the balloon payment. Alternatively, they may be allowed to "reset" the loan. Under the reset option, the loan stays in place and the interest rate is adjusted to the current market rate (up to 5% above the initial rate). The rate and payment are then level for 25 or 23 years.

By exercising the reset option, the borrowers can avoid refinancing charges. To be entitled to reset the loan, the borrowers have to meet certain conditions. For example, they must not have been delinquent on the mortgage payments during the preceding year, and they must not have placed other liens against the property.

Interest First Mortgages. With an interest first mortgage, the monthly payments are lower in the earlier years of the loan because they are interest-only payments. The borrower isn't required to start paying off the principal until later on. The loan has a 30-year term, and the interest-only period typically lasts 10 or 15 years, with principal repayment beginning in the 11th or 16th year. The interest rate may be either fixed or adjustable.

Interest first mortgage allows interest-only payments during first part of loan term, then is fully amortized for the remainder of the term

When it's time for the borrower to begin paying off the principal, the entire loan amount is fully amortized over the remainder of the loan term. As a result, the amount of the required monthly payment is likely to rise sharply at this point. However, the borrower is allowed to make prepayments of principal at any time during the initial interest-only period. Any prepayments will reduce the amount of the monthly payment later on.

Low-Downpayment Programs

Many home buyers have very little cash available for a downpayment

For many potential home buyers, especially first-time buyers, coming up with enough cash is the biggest challenge in buying a home. They have a steady, reliable income, but they don't have the savings to cover the downpayment and closing costs required for a standard conventional loan. Even the 5% downpayment required for a 95% loan may be beyond their means. Buyers in this situation may want to consider special programs that have reduced cash requirements and allow them to draw on alternative sources for the cash they need. At one time, the FHA-insured loan program would have been their only real choice, but now the secondary market agencies—with strong encouragement from the federal government—have developed some conventional loan programs to help make home ownership more affordable.

The details of these programs vary. But here are examples of the types of loans that buyers can look for:

- A loan with a 95% LTV that requires a 3% downpayment from the borrower's own funds, with 2% from alternative sources.
- A loan with a 97% LTV that requires a 3% downpayment from the borrower's own funds, plus a 3% contribution to closing costs that may come from alternative sources.
- A loan with a 100% LTV that requires no downpayment from the borrower's funds, but a 3% contribution to closing costs that may come from alternative sources.

Depending on the program, the allowable alternative sources of funds may include gifts, grants, or unsecured loans. The funds may come from a relative, an employer, a public agency, a nonprofit organization, or a private foundation. More than one source may be tapped to get the necessary funds together.

Some of these programs don't require the borrower to have any reserves after closing. Others require one month's mortgage payment in reserve.

Affordable Housing Programs. Although some conventional low-downpayment programs are open to any prospective home buyer, many are specifically targeted at low- and moderate-income buyers. These are called affordable housing programs. As a general rule, buyers can qualify for one of these programs if their stable monthly income does not exceed the median income in the metropolitan area in question. (Increased income limits apply in high-cost areas.) To make it even easier for low- and moderate-income buyers to get a mortgage, these programs often allow a maximum debt to income ratio of 38% or even 40% and have no maximum housing expense to income ratio. A 97% loan-to-value ratio is typically permitted, and in some cases the LTV can be 100%.

Affordable housing programs:
- Easier to qualify
- Cash requirements reduced
- Eligibility based on income or property location

To encourage neighborhood revitalization, some affordable housing programs waive their income limits for buyers who are purchasing homes in low-income or rundown neighborhoods. Thus, buyers whose income is well above the area median could still qualify for a low-downpayment program targeted at low-income buyers if they're buying a home in a neighborhood that meets the program's standards.

Other conventional low-downpayment programs are offered to specific groups such as teachers, police officers, and firefighters. These programs are intended to enable the borrowers to purchase homes in the urban communities they serve, instead of being priced out into the suburbs.

Accelerated Payment Plans

We'll end the chapter by describing two alternative payment plans that can be used to repay a conventional loan more quickly than its stated term. Some buyers might prefer to get a loan with a shorter stated term (for example, a 15-year mortgage instead of a 30-year mortgage), or else to pay their 30-year loan off more quickly by sending in extra payments at their own discretion, as they're able to afford them. But the two accelerated payment plans that we're going to discuss next—bi-weekly mortgages and growing equity mortgages—have been around for a long time and work well for certain buyers.

Fig. 10.6 Comparison of bi-weekly loan payments to ordinary monthly payments

Example: $90,000 loan, 8.5% fixed rate, 30-year amortization			
Schedule	Payments	No. of Payments	Total Paid
Monthly	$692.02	360	$249,130
Bi-weekly	$346.01	582	$201,365
The bi-weekly loan would be paid off in a little over 22 years, with total interest payments of approximately $47,765 less than the loan with monthly payments.			

Bi-Weekly Mortgages. With a bi-weekly mortgage, both the interest rate and the payment amount are fixed, but payments are made every two weeks instead of every month. Each payment is equal to half of what the monthly payment would be for a fully amortized, 30-year, fixed-rate loan of the same amount at the same interest rate.

Bi-weekly loan:
- 26 half payments per year, equivalent to 13 monthly payments
- Loan paid off in 20 to 22 years

The attraction of the bi-weekly loan is the amount of interest the borrower can save. For example, a $90,000 loan at 8.5% interest paid on a bi-weekly basis saves almost $48,000 in interest compared to the monthly payment plan (see Figure 10.6). By paying every two weeks (26 payments a year), the borrower makes the equivalent of 13 monthly payments a year. As a result, bi-weekly loans are usually paid off in 20 to 22 years, instead of 30 years.

The disadvantage of bi-weekly loans for lenders is that it costs more to service 26 payments per year instead of 12. Most lenders require a bi-weekly borrower to transfer his or her checking account to their institution, and to authorize the lender to deduct the payment directly from the checking account. The borrower may also be required to purchase overdraft protection. Since many people get paid on a bi-weekly basis, setting up the mortgage payment on the same basis has a certain logical appeal. However, the borrower must make sure the funds are available for payment every two weeks.

Growing Equity Mortgages. A growing equity mortgage (GEM) is designed to pay off the loan balance more quickly than its stated term. Though there are many variations, most GEMs share the following characteristics:

- The interest rate is fixed over the life of the loan.
- First-year payments of principal and interest are based on a 15- or 30-year term.
- The borrower's payments are increased at specified intervals (usually annually) for all or a portion of the loan term.

- Since the interest rate is fixed, 100% of the annual payment increases are used to reduce the principal balance.

Annual payment adjustments. There are a number of different ways of handling the annual payment adjustments for a GEM, but the most popular method is to increase the payments by a fixed percentage—typically 3% or 5% per year.

> **Example:** The Morenos are getting a 30-year growing equity mortgage at 8.25% interest. The loan amount is $137,000, and their initial monthly payment is $1,029.24.
>
> With this loan, the Morenos' payments will increase by 3% each year (see Figure 10.7), and the entire increase will always be applied to the loan balance. The annual payment increases will continue until the loan is paid off.

Equity builds up quickly. Because payment increases are used to reduce the principal balance, a borrower will pay off a GEM much sooner than a 30-year fixed-rate mortgage. If payments are increased 3% per year on a loan at 10% interest, the entire debt will be retired in 16 years and 2 months; with 5% annual increases, the same loan will be paid off in just 13 years and 6 months. A GEM's actual repayment period depends on the interest rate and the magnitude of the annual payment increases. Most GEMs with stated terms of 30 years pay off in 11 to 17 years. The graph in Figure 10.8 illustrates the difference between the repayment patterns of a GEM and a 30-year fixed-rate mortgage.

GEM:
- Fixed interest rate
- Initial payment based on 30-year amortization
- Annual payment increases
- Quick principal reduction
- Payoff in 11 to 17 years

As you can see in Figure 10.8, GEM payments become substantially higher than the level fixed-rate payments. In the 1980s, this annual rate of increase was well below the rate of inflation, and GEM payments did not rise as fast as borrowers' incomes. Borrowers could readily adjust to payment hikes, and to many borrowers it was worth

Fig. 10.7 The payments for this GEM loan will increase 3% per year until the loan is repaid

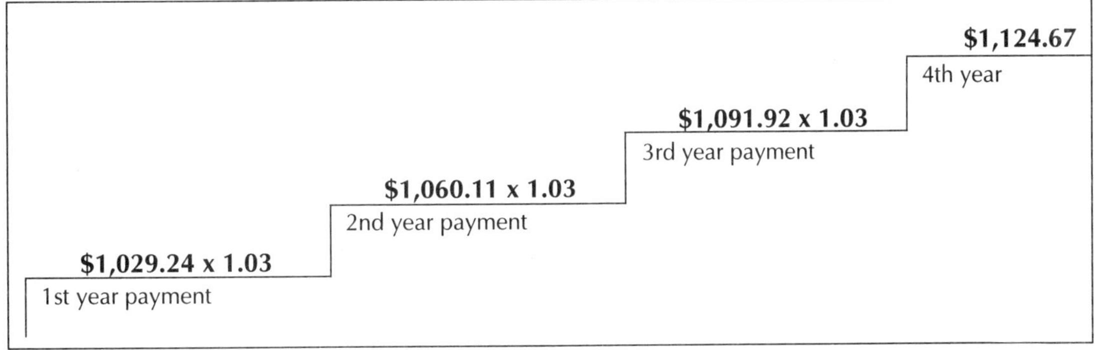

Fig. 10.8 Comparison of the repayment patterns of a GEM and an ordinary fixed-rate mortgage

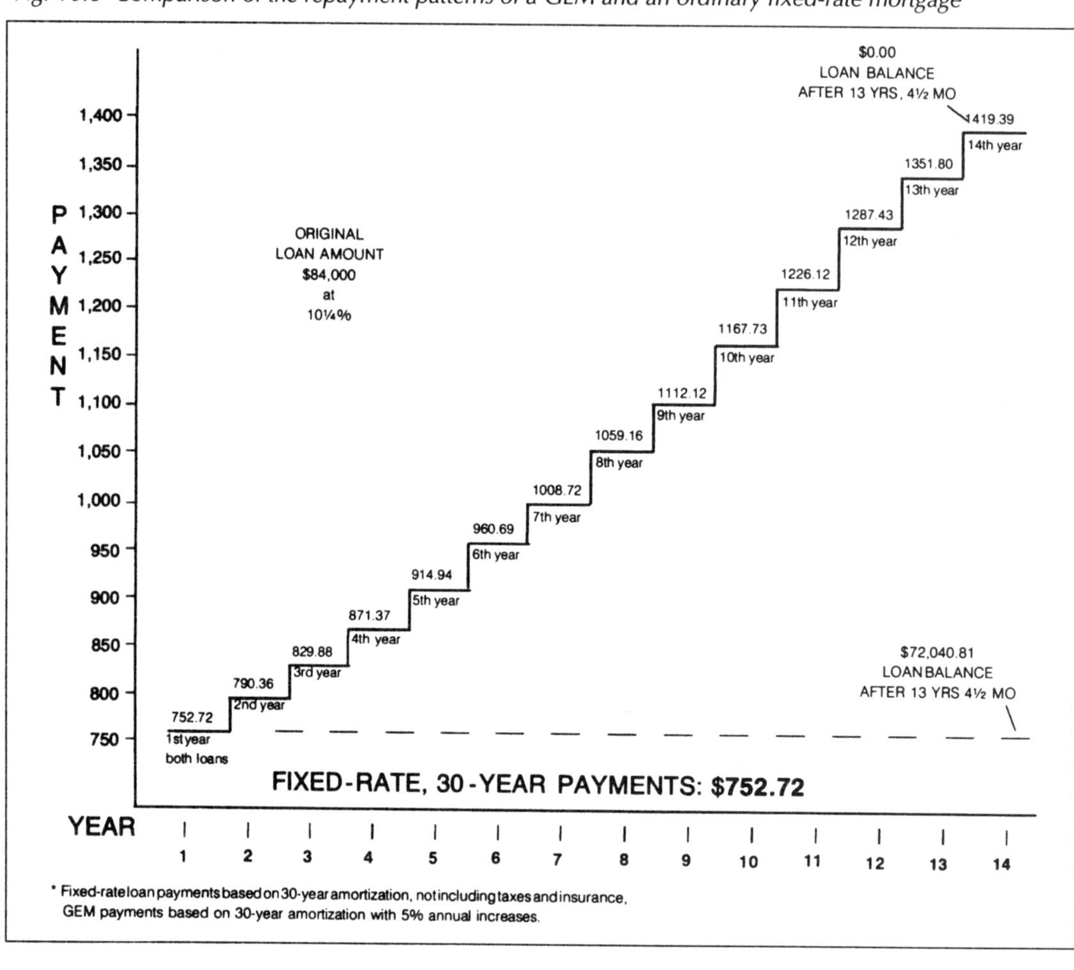

* Fixed-rate loan payments based on 30-year amortization, not including taxes and insurance, GEM payments based on 30-year amortization with 5% annual increases.

paying more every year to hasten the equity build-up. An $84,000, 30-year, fixed-rate mortgage shows a balance of $72,040.81 after 13 years and 4 months; at the end of the same period, the GEM loan is paid in full. When the inflation rate is low, however, the GEM payment increases do not look so attractive. The primary advantages of GEMs—fast amortization and predictable payments—are also available with the more popular level payments of fixed-rate 15-year loans.

Advantages of a GEM. Here are some other advantages of a growing equity mortgage, in addition to the rapid equity build-up and early loan payoff.

1. **Reduced interest costs.** A GEM borrower will pay less than half the interest that a traditional 30-year fixed-rate mortgage would require. Look again at Figure 10.8. You can see that after more than 13 years, the borrower has paid only $11,959

in principal on the 30-year fixed-rate mortgage. The balance of the $120,811 in payments has been applied to interest, and much more interest will be paid before the loan's 30-year term is over. Total interest on a GEM is much less, and the interest portion of each succeeding payment declines as rapidly as the loan balance itself.

2. **Lower interest rate.** Lenders are often willing to make GEMs at lower-than-market rates because they will recapture the principal so quickly. Recaptured principal can be reinvested at competitive market rates. A lower-than-market rate means additional interest savings for the borrower.
3. **Payments are predictable.** The borrower's payments will increase annually, but the amount of each annual increase is known at the outset of the loan. This is an advantage over an ARM, which has unpredictable payment changes.

Outline: Conventional Financing

I. Conforming and Nonconforming Loans
   A. Conforming loans: Loans that comply with Fannie Mae and Freddie Mac underwriting guidelines.
   B. Nonconforming loans: Loans that don't follow secondary market agency guidelines, which can't be sold to either agency; may be prime or subprime.

II. Conventional Loan Characteristics
   A. Property types and owner-occupancy
      1. Fannie Mae and Freddie Mac will purchase loans secured by residential properties, including site-built homes, manufactured homes, townhouses, condos, and co-ops.
      2. The loan may be for a principal residence (with up to four units) or a second home (with no more than one unit).
      3. Fannie Mae and Freddie Mac also buy investor loans, which are for properties that will be rented out to tenants; these loans are underwritten differently.
   B. Loan amounts
      1. Conforming loan limits are set annually; limits are higher in Alaska, Guam, Hawaii, and the Virgin Islands.
      2. Jumbo loans are loans that exceed conforming loan limits; they typically have higher interest rates and stricter qualifying standards.
   C. Repayment periods: can range from ten to forty years; thirty years is standard.
   D. Amortization: Most conventional loans are fully amortized, but partially-amortized and interest-only loans are also available.
   E. Loan-to-value ratios
      1. The traditional loan-to-value ratio (LTV) for conventional loans is 80%, but 90%, 95%, 97%, and even 100% loans are also available.

2. Fannie Mae and Freddie Mac require private mortgage insurance on loans over 80%.
3. Lenders usually charge higher interest rates and fees for high-LTV loans and impose stricter qualifying standards.

F. Private mortgage insurance (PMI)
   1. PMI is issued by private companies instead of a government agency. It protects lenders from the greater risk of high-LTV loans.
   2. PMI typically covers 25% to 30% of the loan amount rather than the whole amount.
   3. In the event of default, the lender may either foreclose on the property or relinquish it to the insurer, and then submit a claim for actual losses up to the policy amount.
   4. PMI premiums are paid by the buyer.
      a. There may be an initial premium (which is paid at closing) plus annual renewal premiums (which are usually paid on a monthly basis).
      b. Or there may be a one-time premium (which is paid at closing or financed over the loan term).
   5. Homeowners Protection Act requires lenders to cancel PMI at the borrower's request when the loan is paid down to 80% of the property's original value, or automatically when it reaches 78% of the original value.

G. Secondary financing
   1. Lenders typically allow secondary financing, regardless of the source, but impose a number of restrictions to reduce risk of default.
   2. Examples of rules concerning secondary financing:
      a. Borrower must be able to qualify for the payments on both the first and second mortgages.
      b. Borrower must make at least a 5% downpayment.
      c. Payments must be regularly scheduled.
      d. Second mortgage can't require a balloon payment until at least five years after closing.

e. If the first mortgage has variable payments, the second mortgage must have fixed payments.
f. Negative amortization and prepayment penalties are not allowed.

3. Piggyback loans: Using secondary financing to avoid having to pay private mortgage insurance or to avoid the loan being designated a jumbo loan.

III. Qualifying Standards

A. Evaluating risk factors

1. Fannie Mae's comprehensive risk assessment approach uses primary risk factors and contributing risk factors.
2. Two primary risk factors determine level of review applied to the rest of the application:
   a. credit score, and
   b. proposed loan-to-value ratio.
3. Contributory risk factors include the other aspects of the application, such as income ratios and cash reserves.

B. Income analysis

1. Total obligations to income ratio: Total monthly obligations generally should not exceed 36% of stable monthly income.
2. Recurring obligations include housing expense (PITI), installment debts (such as car loans), revolving debts (such as credit cards), and other debts (such as alimony and child support).
3. Housing expense to income ratio: Proposed housing expense (PITI) generally should not exceed 28% of stable monthly income.
4. The smaller of the two ratios is the maximum allowable mortgage payment.
5. 36% and 28% aren't strict maximums. Compensating factors such as a large downpayment or an excellent credit score may give the lender a reason to allow higher ratios.

6. For loans with an LTV over 90%, most lenders won't accept ratios higher than 36% or 28% without especially strong compensating factors; some may not allow a total obligations to income ratio higher than 33%.
7. ARM borrowers may receive greater scrutiny because of the risk of payment shock; lenders may require borrowers to qualify under the maximum interest rate that could be in effect at the end of the loan's first year.

C. Net worth and funds for closing
   1. Gift funds can be used for most of downpayment and closing costs, but borrowers generally must pay at least 5% of the sales price out of their own resources, unless LTV is 80% or less.
   2. Reserves
      a. Fannie Mae and Freddie Mac no longer have specific reserve requirements, although reserves can be an important compensating factor.
      b. Some lenders still require borrowers to have two months' payments in reserve after making the downpayment and closing costs; some lenders require three months' payments.

D. Credit reputation: An excellent credit score can offset other weaknesses, such as marginal income ratios.

IV. Special Programs and Payment Plans

A. Buydown lowers interest rate permanently or temporarily.
   1. Temporary buydown may have level or graduated payments.
   2. Fannie Mae and Freddie Mac limit how much a seller or other interested party can contribute for buyer.

B. Loans with lower initial payments: hybrid ARMs, two-step loans, balloon/reset loans, interest first loans.

C. Low downpayment programs: high-LTV conventional loans; affordable housing programs with eligibility based on income or property location.

D. Accelerated payment plans: bi-weekly mortgages and growing-equity mortgages (GEMs).

Key Terms

Conventional loan: An institutional loan that is not insured or guaranteed by a government agency.

Conforming loan: A loan made in accordance with the standardized underwriting criteria of the major secondary market agencies, Fannie Mae and Freddie Mac, and which therefore can be sold to those agencies.

Nonconforming loan: A loan that does not meet the underwriting guidelines set by Fannie Mae and Freddie Mac, and therefore can't be sold to those agencies except by special arrangement.

Investor loan: A loan issued for the purchase of property that will be rented to tenants rather than owner-occupied.

Jumbo loan: A loan that exceeds the conforming loan limits set annually by Fannie Mae and Freddie Mac based on national average housing prices.

Loan-to-value ratio (LTV): The relationship between the loan amount and either the sales price or the appraised value of the property (whichever is less), expressed as a percentage.

Private mortgage insurance (PMI): Insurance used to diminish the risk of high-LTV conventional loans; provided by a private insurance company (instead of a government agency).

Homeowners Protection Act: A federal law that requires lenders to eliminate private mortgage insurance payments on the borrower's request when the loan balance reaches 80% of the original property value, or to automatically cancel the PMI when the loan balance reaches 78% of the original property value.

Secondary financing: Money borrowed to pay part of the required downpayment or closing costs for a first loan, when the second loan is secured by the same property that secures the first loan.

Piggyback loan: Secondary financing used to avoid the payment of private mortgage insurance by keeping the primary loan's loan-to-value ratio at 80% or less, or used to avoid the higher interest rate a jumbo loan would require.

Total obligations to income ratio: A figure used in loan underwriting to measure the adequacy of the applicant's income; states in percentage terms how much of the applicant's stable monthly income would be required to make all the monthly payments on the applicant's debts and other liabilities plus the proposed housing expense. Also called a debt to income ratio.

Recurring obligations: Financial obligations that a borrower must meet each month, including housing expense, installment debts, revolving debts, and other obligations.

Buydown: When the seller or a third party pays the lender a lump sum at closing to lower the interest rate charged on the buyer's loan.

Permanent buydown: A buydown that lowers the loan's interest rate for the entire term.

Temporary buydown: A buydown that lowers the loan's interest rate for only the first few years of the term; the monthly payments during the buydown period may be level or graduated.

Two-step mortgage: A loan that allows the lender to adjust the loan's interest rate to the market level at one point during the loan term, such as a 5/25 plan where the interest rate is adjusted once after five years.

Balloon/reset mortgage: A loan with an initial term of only five or seven years; at the end of the term, the loan term may be reset, or a balloon payment will be required.

Interest first mortgage: A loan that allows the buyer to make interest-only payments during the first part of the loan term.

Affordable housing program: A loan program that features easier qualifying standards and lower downpayment requirements, with eligibility limited to buyers who have low or moderate incomes or are purchasing property in a targeted neighborhood.

Bi-weekly mortgage: A loan that requires a payment every two weeks instead of once a month; the borrower makes the equivalent of 13 payments per year, and thus pays the loan off early and saves a considerable amount in interest.

Growing equity mortgage (GEM): A fixed-rate loan with annual payment increases that are used to reduce the principal balance, so that the loan is paid off much more quickly than it would be with ordinary level payments.

Chapter Quiz

1. A buydown plan:
   a. helps lower the buyer's initial monthly mortgage payments
   b. may help the buyer qualify for the loan
   c. is a plan in which a party pays a lump sum to the lender up front to reduce the loan's interest rate
   d. All of the above

2. One major advantage of a bi-weekly loan is that:
   a. the interest rate is usually higher
   b. equity builds more quickly
   c. payments are lower during the first two years
   d. interest costs are the same as for a fixed-rate loan

3. Private mortgage insurance is ordinarily required only if the loan-to-value ratio is:
   a. 75% or higher
   b. 90% or higher
   c. over 95%
   d. over 80%

4. As a general rule, a buyer who is seeking a 90% loan:
   a. must make a 10% downpayment from his or her own funds
   b. must make a 5% downpayment from his or her own funds
   c. may use secondary financing to come up with the additional 10% of the purchase price
   d. can expect to pay a higher interest rate than he or she would for a 95% loan

5. The Turinos are applying for an 80% loan. Unless there are compensating factors, their total obligations to income ratio should not exceed:
   a. 25%
   b. 28%
   c. 36%
   d. 33%

6. Jamison is applying for a 90% conventional loan. Which of the following is a compensating factor that might justify loan approval in spite of income ratios that are slightly higher than the standard limits?
   a. Jamison will have one month's mortgage payment in reserve after closing.
   b. Her parents are providing gift funds for 5% of the downpayment.
   c. She is a first-time home buyer.
   d. She has strong potential for increased earnings and advancement at work.

7. Shaw is applying for a 90% conventional loan. His stable monthly income is $2,950. His recurring monthly obligations total $375. In the absence of any compensating factors, what is the maximum monthly mortgage payment he will qualify for?
   a. $826
   b. $687
   c. $784
   d. $912

8. A 2-1 buydown plan calls for:
   a. the interest rate to be bought down by 1% for two years
   b. the seller and the broker to buy down the interest rate by 1%
   c. the interest rate to be bought down by 2% the first year and 1% the second year
   d. the interest rate to be bought down by 1% the first year and 2% the second year

9. A conventional lender will take an installment debt into consideration when calculating income ratios:
   a. only if it has more than twelve payments remaining
   b. only if it has more than ten payments remaining
   c. no matter how many payments remain to be made
   d. only if the borrower has a poor credit history

10. Secondary financing used in conjunction with a conventional loan may be:

    a. partially amortized with a balloon payment
    b. fully amortized
    c. interest-only
    d. Any of the above

Answer Key

1. d. In a buydown, a seller or third party pays a lump sum to a lender to reduce the borrower's interest rate. This lowers the borrower's initial payment amount and makes it easier for the borrower to qualify.

2. b. A bi-weekly loan allows equity to build more quickly, since the borrower makes the equivalent of 13 monthly payments per year.

3. d. Private mortgage insurance is usually required for loans with an LTV over 80%.

4. b. A borrower seeking a 90% loan generally must make a downpayment of at least 5% out of her own funds, even if using gift funds.

5. c. For most conventional 80% loans, the maximum total obligations to income ratio will be 36%, absent any compensating factors.

6. d. A potential compensating factor for a person whose income ratio is slightly higher than allowable limits would be the potential for increased future earnings.

7. b. To calculate the maximum monthly mortgage payment, multiply the stable monthly income by the total obligations to income ratio ($2,950 × .36 = $1,062) and then subtract any recurring monthly obligations ($1,062 – $375 = $687).

8. c. The 2-1 buydown plan is a temporary buydown where the interest rate is reduced 2% in the first year and 1% in the second year.

9. b. An installment debt will be considered when calculating income ratios only if more than ten months' payments remain.

10. d. Secondary financing used in conjunction with a conventional loan may be fully or partially amortized, or interest-only. Certain restrictions may apply, such as requiring scheduled payments and not allowing a balloon payment within the first five years.

Case Study: Qualifying the Buyer Conventional Financing

Rick and Teresa Cortina are thinking of buying their first home. Based on the financial information shown below, answer the questions that follow. There are worksheets at the end of the case study that you can use for the calculations.

Employment:

Rick has been employed as a salesperson by Acme Tire, Inc. for four years. Teresa has been an administrative assistant at Tarman & Andrews (a law firm) for two and a half years.

Income:

Rick earns the following income:

- Monthly salary: $1,300
- Commission: $1,465 per month (average for the previous two years)
- Bonus: $1,500 bonus last year (for the first time)

Teresa earns the following income:

- Full-time hourly wage: $18.50

Taxes (monthly figures):

Rick's taxes:

- Federal income taxes: $259
- State income taxes: $73
- Social security: $185

Teresa's taxes:

- Federal income taxes: $223
- State income taxes: $65
- Social security: $166

Credit scores:

Rick and Teresa both have FICO credit scores around 700.

Assets:

- Savings account: $39,500
- Vacation property (unimproved lot): $3,700 equity
- Miscellaneous (cars, furniture, etc.): $19,000

Liabilities (monthly payments):

- Car loan: $265 (30 payments remaining)
- Car loan: $215 (8 payments remaining)
- Installment contract (on vacation property): $142 (85 payments remaining)
- Credit cards: $105 (minimum payments)
- Student loan: $50 (23 payments remaining)

Interest rates:

Through your contacts in the mortgage market, you know that current interest rates for 30-year conventional loans are approximately as follows:

Fixed rate, 90% LTV: 6.75% interest, 2% origination fee, no discount fee

One-year ARM (1% rate cap), 90% LTV: 5.5% interest, 1.75% origination fee, no discount fee

Fixed rate, 95% LTV: 6.875% interest, 2% origination fee, no discount fee

1. What is the Cortinas' stable monthly income?

2. What is the maximum monthly principal and interest payment the Cortinas could qualify for in each of the following cases? Assume that 15% of the Cortinas' total mortgage payment will go toward property taxes, hazard insurance, and mortgage insurance. (This is only an approximation. Use it for the purposes of this exercise, but in practice, choose a percentage that reflects the costs in your area.)

   a) They apply for a conventional loan with a 90% LTV.

   b) They apply for a conventional loan with a 95% LTV, and the lender uses the standard total obligations to income ratio to qualify them.

c) They apply for a conventional loan with a 95% LTV, and the lender won't accept a total obligations ratio over 33%.

3. The PITI payments you arrived at in question 2 indicate that the Cortinas could qualify for the maximum loan amounts listed below if they applied for the following types of loans. For each of these loans, use the loan-to-value ratio to estimate the sales price of a home that could be purchased with the maximum loan amount plus the corresponding minimum downpayment.

   a) 90% fixed-rate loan at 6.75% interest; maximum loan amount: approximately $212,871.

   b) 90% ARM at 5.5% (initial interest rate); maximum loan amount: approximately $243,168.

   c) 95% fixed-rate loan at 6.875% interest (if the standard total obligations ratio is used for qualifying); maximum loan amount: approximately $210,172.

d) 95% fixed-rate loan at 6.875% interest (if the 33% total obligations ratio is used for qualifying); maximum loan amount: approximately $186,459.

4. Now calculate how much cash would be needed at closing for each of the transactions in question 3. Add the minimum downpayment and the origination fee. Use 3% of the sales price as an estimate of the rest of the closing costs. Also add in two months' mortgage payments (PITI) as reserves. Do the Cortinas have enough cash to qualify for any of these transactions?

   a) A 90% fixed-rate loan.

   b) A 90% ARM.

   c) A 95% fixed-rate loan, if the standard total obligations ratio is used for qualifying.

   d) A 95% fixed-rate loan, if the 33% total obligations ratio is used for qualifying.

5. Based on this analysis, what general price range of homes do you think the Cortinas should look at?

Income Qualifying—Conventional Loans
FIXED RATE, LTV 90%

Stable Monthly Income

Base salary	
Wage earner 1	________
Wage earner 2	________
Overtime	________
Commissions	________
Bonuses	________
Other	+ ________
Total	________

Recurring Liabilities

Car loans	________
Credit cards	________
Student loans	________
Other loans	________
Child support	________
Alimony	________
Other	+ ________
Total	________

Total Obligations to Income Ratio

________	Stable monthly income
x 36%	Maximum ratio
________	Maximum obligations
– ________	Recurring liabilities
________	Maximum mortgage payment (PITI) under total obligations ratio

Housing Expense to Income Ratio

________	Stable monthly income
x 28%	Maximum ratio
________	Maximum mortgage payment (PITI) under housing expense ratio

Maximum Mortgage Payment (PITI) ________

________	Maximum PITI payment
÷ 115%	(less 15% for taxes and insurance)
________	Maximum principal and interest payment

Interest rate ________

Maximum Loan Amount ________

________	Maximum loan amount
÷ 90%	Loan-to-value ratio
________	Sales price

Sales Price ________

Income Qualifying—Conventional Loans
ADJUSTABLE RATE, LTV 90%

Stable Monthly Income

Base salary	
Wage earner 1	______
Wage earner 2	______
Overtime	______
Commissions	______
Bonuses	______
Other	+ ______
Total	______

Recurring Liabilities

Car loans	______
Credit cards	______
Student loans	______
Other loans	______
Child support	______
Alimony	______
Other	+ ______
Total	______

Total Obligations to Income Ratio

______	Stable monthly income
x 36%	Maximum ratio
______	Maximum obligations
– ______	Recurring liabilities
______	Maximum mortgage payment (PITI) under total obligations ratio

Housing Expense to Income Ratio

______	Stable monthly income
x 28%	Maximum ratio
______	Maximum mortgage payment (PITI) under housing expense ratio

Maximum Mortgage Payment (PITI) ______

______	Maximum PITI payment
÷ 115%	(less 15% for taxes and insurance)
______	Maximum principal and interest payment

Interest rate ______

Maximum Loan Amount ______

______	Maximum loan amount
÷ 90%	Loan-to-value ratio
______	Sales price

Sales Price ______

Income Qualifying—Conventional Loans
FIXED RATE, LTV 95%
Using 36% total obligations to income ratio

Stable Monthly Income

Base salary	
Wage earner 1	________
Wage earner 2	________
Overtime	________
Commissions	________
Bonuses	________
Other	+ ________
Total	________

Recurring Liabilities

Car loans	________
Credit cards	________
Student loans	________
Other loans	________
Child support	________
Alimony	________
Other	+ ________
Total	________

Total Obligations to Income Ratio

________	Stable monthly income
x 36%	Maximum ratio
________	Maximum obligations
– ________	Recurring liabilities
________	Maximum mortgage payment (PITI) under total obligations ratio

Housing Expense to Income Ratio

________	Stable monthly income
x 28%	Maximum ratio
________	Maximum mortgage payment (PITI) under housing expense ratio

Maximum Mortgage Payment (PITI) ________

________	Maximum PITI payment
÷ 115%	(less 15% for taxes and insurance)
________	Maximum principal and interest payment

Interest rate ________

Maximum Loan Amount ________

________	Maximum loan amount
÷ 95%	Loan-to-value ratio
________	Sales price

Sales Price ________

Income Qualifying—Conventional Loans
FIXED RATE, LTV 95%
Using 33% total obligations to income ratio

Stable Monthly Income

Base salary	
Wage earner 1	______
Wage earner 2	______
Overtime	______
Commissions	______
Bonuses	______
Other	+ ______
Total	______

Recurring Liabilities

Car loans	______
Credit cards	______
Student loans	______
Other loans	______
Child support	______
Alimony	______
Other	+ ______
Total	______

Total Obligations to Income Ratio

______	Stable monthly income
x 33%	Maximum ratio
______	Maximum obligations
– ______	Recurring liabilities
______	Maximum mortgage payment (PITI) under total obligations ratio

Housing Expense to Income Ratio

______	Stable monthly income
x 28%	Maximum ratio
______	Maximum mortgage payment (PITI) under housing expense ratio

Maximum Mortgage Payment (PITI) ______

______	Maximum PITI payment
÷ 115%	(less 15% for taxes and insurance)
______	Maximum principal and interest payment

Interest rate ______

Maximum Loan Amount ______

______	Maximum loan amount
÷ 95%	Loan-to-value ratio
______	Sales price

Sales Price ______

Chapter 11
FHA-Insured Loans

FHA Mortgage Insurance

Characteristics of FHA Loans

FHA Loan Programs

- Section 203(b): Standard loans
- Section 203(k): Rehabilitation loans
- Section 223(e): Loans in declining areas
- Section 234(c): Condominium unit loans
- Section 245(a): GPMs and GEMs
- Section 251: ARMs
- Section 255: HECMs

Maximum Loan Amounts

- Local loan ceilings
- Loan-to-value ratios

Minimum Cash Investment

FHA Insurance Premiums

- Upfront MIP
- Annual MIP

Sales Concessions and FHA Loans

Secondary Financing with FHA Loans

- Secondary financing for the cash investment
- Secondary financing for the base loan

Assumption of FHA Loans

FHA Underwriting

Introduction

In Chapter 10 we discussed conventional loans: institutional loans that are not insured or guaranteed by a government agency. Now we'll look at institutional loans that have government backing.

The federal government has two main home financing programs: the FHA-insured loan program and the VA-guaranteed loan program. These programs were established to encourage residential lending and make housing more affordable; they are available to eligible home buyers throughout the United States. Many state, county, and city governments offer similar programs for their own residents. These are commonly called "bond programs." Although the state and local bond programs sometimes resemble FHA or VA financing, each one has rules of its own. We're going to focus on the two federal programs, discussing FHA-insured loans in this chapter and VA-guaranteed loans in Chapter 12.

FHA Mortgage Insurance

The Federal Housing Administration (FHA) was created by Congress in 1934 as part of the National Housing Act. The purpose of the act, and of the FHA, was to generate new jobs through increased construction activity, to exert a stabilizing influence on the mortgage market, and to promote the financing, repair, improvement, and sale of residential real estate nationwide.

FHA:
- Insures loans
- Does not make loans itself

Today the FHA is part of the Department of Housing and Urban Development (HUD). Its primary function is insuring mortgage loans; the FHA compensates lenders who make loans through its programs for any losses that result from borrower default. The FHA does not build homes or make loans.

In effect, the FHA is a giant mortgage insurance agency. Its insurance program, known as the Mutual Mortgage Insurance Plan, is funded with premiums paid by FHA borrowers.

Under the plan, lenders who have been approved by the FHA to make insured loans either submit applications from prospective borrowers to the local FHA office for approval or, if authorized by the FHA to do so, perform the underwriting functions themselves. (Note that prospective borrowers always apply to an FHA-approved lender, not to the FHA itself.)

Lenders who are authorized to underwrite their own FHA loan applications are called **direct endorsers**. Direct endorsers are responsible for the entire lending process, from application through closing. When a direct endorser has approved and closed a loan, the application for mortgage insurance is submitted to the FHA.

Direct endorsers: lenders authorized to handle entire underwriting process for FHA loans

As the insurer, the FHA is liable to the lender for the full amount of any losses resulting from default and foreclosure. After the FHA has compensated the lender, however, the borrower is liable to the federal government for the amount paid. This liability is considered a delinquent federal debt, which means that the government can collect it out of any federal income tax refund owed to the borrower, or garnish any pay the borrower receives from the federal government. Unless the borrower enters into an agreement to repay the debt, he or she is not eligible for another FHA-insured loan (or for a VA-guaranteed loan).

If FHA borrower defaults:
- FHA reimburses lender for full amount of loss
- Borrower required to repay FHA

In exchange for insuring the loan, the FHA regulates many of its terms and conditions. The lender must comply with FHA regulations, which have the force and effect of law. These regulations and FHA procedures have influenced the real estate lending industry as a whole.

Characteristics of FHA Loans

The FHA-insured loan program was designed to help people with low or moderate incomes buy homes. Although the program doesn't have income restrictions—eligibility isn't limited to borrowers whose incomes are under a certain limit—it does have restrictions on loan amounts. The FHA sets maximum loan amounts based on median housing prices, so FHA loans can't be used to buy expensive properties. In addition, the program has always had low downpayment requirements and lenient underwriting standards. Because of these features, for many years FHA loans were considered the main financing option for home buyers who didn't have a lot of savings or a substantial income. It was significantly easier to qualify for an FHA loan than for a conventional loan.

FHA-insured loans are designed for low- and moderate-income buyers

But in the last decade or so, changes throughout the mortgage industry have made conventional financing much more accessible than it used to be. Now even buyers with very little cash for closing can get a conventional loan, and conventional underwriting standards are considerably looser than they once were, even among prime lenders. (See Chapter 10.) At the same time, housing prices have soared so high in some parts of the country that FHA maximum loan amounts have become a serious drawback, making the program practically useless for buyers in very high-priced areas. In California, for example, the FHA insured approximately 109,000 loans in 2000, but only about 5,000 in 2005—a 95% drop.

Substantial reforms have been proposed to breathe new life into the FHA program. In June 2006, the U.S. House of Representatives passed a bill that would reduce FHA downpayment requirements and increase loan limits. A corresponding bill was under consideration in the Senate, but had not yet been voted on, when this book went to press in early September 2006. The legislation, known as the Expanding American Homeownership Act of 2006, is expected to become law; until it does, however, the details of the new rules are uncertain and the current rules remain in force. We will discuss the current rules, and also mention anticipated changes.

Here's an overview of the characteristics of FHA loans. We will cover some of these in more detail later in the chapter.

1. **Loan term.** The typical term for an FHA loan is 30 years, although the borrower usually has the option of a shorter term. The Expanding American Homeownership Act would increase the maximum term for FHA loans to 40 years.
2. **First lien.** The FHA requires the loans it insures to have first lien position.
3. **Interest rate.** At one time the FHA used to set a maximum interest rate for FHA loans, but now the rate for each loan is freely negotiable between the borrower and the lender. As a result, interest rates for FHA loans are determined by market forces, in the same way that the rates for conventional loans are determined. The lender must give the borrower a HUD interest rate disclosure statement, which explains that the loan terms are negotiable.
4. **Loan fees.** A lender will charge a 1% origination fee on an FHA loan, and may also charge a discount fee (points). The points can be paid by the borrower or by another party, such as the seller.

5. **Local loan ceilings.** Maximum loan amounts for FHA loans vary from one area to another, with larger loan amounts allowed in areas where housing prices are high. The loan ceilings change annually; we'll look at the rules used to set these limits later in the chapter.

6. **LTV and borrower's investment.** The maximum FHA loan amount for the purchase of a particular property is determined not only by the local limit but also by rules concerning the loan-to-value ratio. Current LTV rules require the borrower to make a small downpayment (ranging from 1.25% to 2.85%, depending on the value of the property and other factors we'll explain later in the chapter).

   Another requirement is that the borrower must make a minimum cash investment of at least 3% of the property's sales price. The downpayment and the closing costs paid by the borrower count toward the required investment. Secondary financing from the seller or a lender cannot be used to make up any part of the minimum cash investment. Under certain circumstances, however, secondary financing from a family member, government agency, charitable organization, employer, or close friend may be used for the minimum cash investment.

   The Expanding American Homeownership Act would eliminate the 3% minimum cash investment requirement and authorize the FHA to give borrowers a variety of downpayment options.

7. **Mortgage insurance.** Regardless of the size of the downpayment, mortgage insurance is required on all FHA loans. In most cases, there is a premium due at closing, plus annual renewal premiums that are paid as part of the monthly payment on the loan. The premiums will be explained in more detail later in the chapter.

8. **Prepayment.** Some conventional loans provide that the lender may impose a substantial penalty if the borrower pays off the loan within the first few years of its term. In contrast, FHA loans may be paid off at any time without additional charges. (Lenders may require FHA borrowers to make any prepayment on a regular installment due date, and for loans

Distinguishing features of FHA loans:

- Maximum loan amount determined by local limit and also by LTV rules
- Minimum cash investment is 3% of sales price
- Mortgage insurance always required
- No prepayment charges
- Property must be owner-occupied primary residence
- Lenient qualifying standards

made before August 1985, to give 30 days' written notice of their intention to prepay.)

9. **Owner-occupancy.** FHA borrowers must intend to occupy the property they're buying. As a general rule, the property must be used as the borrower's primary residence.

   At one time, the FHA insured investor loans (allowing the borrower to buy the property only as an investment, without intending to occupy it). Investor loans were eliminated from most FHA programs at the end of 1989.

   The FHA also used to insure loans for secondary residences. A secondary residence is a home the borrower occupies less than 50% of the time. Since 1991, the FHA has insured loans for secondary residences only if denial of the loan would cause undue hardship for the applicant. The secondary residence must be needed for employment-related reasons; it can't be a vacation home.

10. **Less stringent qualifying standards.** It's easier to qualify for an FHA loan than for a conventional loan. The FHA qualifying standards are explained at the end of this chapter.

Almost every new FHA-insured loan has the characteristics listed above. Other features of the loan are determined by the particular FHA program through which it's insured.

FHA Loan Programs

The FHA has many different programs to address specific financing needs. The programs are commonly referred to by their section numbers, which are taken from the numbered provisions in the law that established them. We'll look at the programs that are of most interest to the average home buyer or owner.

Section 203(b): Standard FHA-Insured Loans

Most FHA loans are 203(b) loans

The 203(b) program is the standard FHA mortgage insurance program, accounting for a substantial majority of all FHA-insured loans. A loan made through the 203(b) program can be used to purchase or refinance a residential property with up to four dwelling units, if the borrower occupies one of the units as a primary residence.

The other FHA programs are largely based on the 203(b) program. We'll describe them briefly here before going on to discuss the rules for 203(b) loans in depth.

FHA loan programs:
- 203(b) – standard FHA loans
- 203(k) – rehab loans
- 223(e) – declining areas
- 234(c) – condo units
- 245(a) – GPMs and GEMs
- 251 – ARMs
- 255 – reverse mortgages

Section 203(k): Rehabilitation Loans

The 203(k) program insures mortgages used to purchase (or refinance) and rehabilitate residences with up to four units. A portion of the loan proceeds are used to purchase the property or refinance an existing mortgage, and the remaining funds are deposited into a Rehabilitation Escrow Account to be released as the work progresses.

A home financed under this program must be at least a year old, and the FHA imposes certain structural and energy-efficiency standards on all rehabilitation work. The range of improvements that qualify as rehabilitation is fairly wide, although the costs of upgrade work must total at least $5,000 to be eligible for 203(k) financing. Luxury or temporary improvements are not eligible.

The basic rules of 203(b) (such as those governing minimum investment, loan term, and loan limits) apply to mortgages insured under Section 203(k). In some cases, however, lenders may charge a supplemental origination fee, and 203(k) borrowers do not pay an upfront mortgage premium (mortgage premiums are discussed later in the chapter). The property's value (for determining the maximum loan amount) is the least of:

1. the property's current value, plus the costs of rehabilitation;
2. the existing debt to be refinanced, plus the costs of rehabilitation; or
3. 110% of the property's value after rehabilitation.

Section 223(e)—Loans in Declining Urban Areas

Section 223(e) authorizes insurance for mortgages used to purchase, rehabilitate, or build housing in older, declining urban areas, where it's often difficult to obtain financing.

The property financed with a loan insured under 223(e) must be located in a "reasonably viable" neighborhood that needs additional housing for low- and moderate-income families. Although the property must be an acceptable credit risk, 223(e) allows the FHA to waive considerations concerning the property's economic soundness and economic life that would otherwise prevent it from being financed through other FHA programs.

Mortgages eligible under Section 223(e) are insured through another FHA program (such as 203(b)), in accordance with the rules of the other program.

Section 234(c): FHA Loans for Condominium Units

234(c) loans for units in FHA-approved condos

The 234(c) program covers the purchase or refinancing of a unit in a condominium that has been approved by the FHA (or by the VA, the Department of Veterans Affairs). This program works in conjunction with the other FHA programs. For a purchase loan, the condominium buyer can get a fixed-rate loan through the standard 203(b) program, a Section 245(a) GPM or GEM, or a Section 251 ARM.

Spot loan: for unit in condo that isn't FHA-approved

A condominium developer who wants FHA approval ordinarily applies for it when the project is built or converted. If you are helping to sell a unit in an established condominium that has not been approved, it may be possible to arrange an FHA loan for that individual unit using the "spot loan" procedure. A spot loan will be approved only if the condominium meets certain criteria; for example, the condominium project must be completed, at least 90% of the units must have already been sold, and at least 51% must be owner-occupied.

Section 245(a): FHA GPMs and GEMs

The Section 245(a) program provides mortgage insurance for graduated payment mortgages and growing equity mortgages. The 245(a) program works in conjunction with the other FHA loan programs.

Graduated Payment Mortgage. A graduated payment mortgage (GPM) is a fixed-rate loan that has lower payments in the early years of the loan term, and provides for a specified payment increase each year until a maximum payment amount is reached. The payment then remains the same for the rest of the loan term. This mortgage structure is attractive to buyers who currently have lower incomes but expect their incomes to rise significantly in the near future.

Five different GPM plans may be insured under Section 245(a). Each plan calls for payments to increase annually over the first five or ten years of the loan term.

The property financed with a GPM must be a one-family dwelling (either a house or a condominium unit). GPM loans must otherwise conform to the requirements of 203(b) or 234(c).

Growing Equity Mortgage. A growing equity mortgage (GEM) is similar to a GPM in that it also has lower initial payments that increase over time. However, the payment increases in a GEM are directly applied to reduce the principal, resulting in a shorter loan term.

The FHA accepts five different GEM plans. Each plan has payments that increase annually, at varying rates, over a ten-year period. GEM payment plans may be used in conjunction with loans insured under 203(b) (one- to four-unit homes), 203(k) (rehabilitation), or 234(c) (condominium units).

Section 251: FHA ARMs

FHA ARM:
- 30-year term required
- One-year Treasury index
- May have initial fixed-rate period
- 1%-2% annual rate cap
- 5%-6% life-of-loan cap

Section 251 provides FHA mortgage insurance for adjustable-rate mortgages. The ARM program is administered in conjunction with Section 203(b), 203(k), or 234(c), so the loan may be for the purchase, refinancing, or rehabilitation of a one- to four-unit residence or a condominium unit. The loan term of an FHA ARM must be 30 years; a shorter term is not permitted.

FHA ARMs are tied to the one-year Treasury securities index. The initial interest rate (contract rate), discount points, and the margin are negotiable between the lender and the borrower.

An FHA ARM may provide for annual interest rate adjustments from the outset, or there may be an initial period during which the interest rate is fixed; this may be three, five, seven, or ten years. After the initial period, interest rate adjustments (both increases and decreases) occur on an annual basis.

Like most ARMs, an FHA ARM has a limit on annual rate adjustments and a life-of-the-loan rate cap. These depend on the length of the initial fixed-rate period.

For 1-year, 3-year, and 5-year ARMs:
- annual interest rate adjustments are limited to 1%;
- the interest rate can't increase more than 5% over the life of the loan.

For 7- and 10-year ARMs:
- annual interest rate adjustments are limited to 2%;
- the interest rate can't increase more than 6% over the life of the loan.

The lender must notify the borrower at least 25 days before any change in the monthly payment amount. The notice must state the new interest rate, the new payment amount, the current index interest rate value, and how the payment adjustment was calculated.

Note that there's a limit on the number of ARMs that the FHA is authorized to insure each fiscal year. Specifically, the number of ARMs can't exceed 30% of the total number of FHA loans insured during the previous fiscal year.

Section 255: HECMs

Section 255 provides FHA insurance for **home equity conversion mortgages** (HECMs), also known as reverse equity mortgages (see Chapter 5). This program allows older homeowners to convert the equity in their homes into either a source of monthly income or a line of credit. Repayment is not required as long as the property remains the owner's principal residence.

HECM (reverse mortgage):
- Borrower 62 or older
- Free and clear ownership
- Repayment not required while home is borrower's primary residence

To qualify for an FHA HECM, a homeowner must be at least 62 years old. The property may have up to four dwelling units or be a condominium unit; it must be owned free and clear, or have only a small balance remaining on the mortgage. Homeowners are required to consult a HUD-approved HECM counselor to help decide if this type of mortgage would suit their needs.

The loan amount will depend on the local FHA loan ceiling, the appraised value of the home, the current interest rate, and the age of the borrower. (If there's more than one borrower, the age of the youngest is the one that counts.) The more valuable the property, the lower the interest rate, and the older the borrower, the larger the loan amount can be, up to the FHA ceiling. There are no income requirements or credit qualifications.

The lender recovers the amount borrowed, plus interest, when the property is sold. If the sale proceeds exceed the amount owed, the excess goes to the owner (the seller) or his heirs. If the proceeds don't cover the amount owed, the FHA will make up the difference.

Maximum Loan Amounts

As we explained earlier, the FHA-insured loan program is intended to help low- and moderate-income home buyers. To prevent FHA loans from being used to purchase expensive properties, the FHA limits the size of loans that can be insured under Section 203(b) and the related programs we've discussed.

Fig. 11.1 Maximum loan amounts vary, based on local median housing costs

2006 FHA Maximum Loan Amounts

Number of Units	Basic Ceiling	High-Cost Ceiling
One	$200,160	$362,790
Two	$256,248	$464,449
Three	$309,744	$561,411
Four	$384,936	$697,696

There are two limits that determine the maximum FHA loan amount available for a particular transaction. The first is the local loan ceiling; the second is the loan-to-value ratio limit.

Maximum loan amount for FHA transaction determined by:
- Local loan ceiling
- LTV rules

Local Loan Ceilings

The FHA's local loan ceilings are limits on loan amounts that vary from one area to another based on local median housing costs. An area where housing is expensive has a higher ceiling (a higher maximum loan amount) than a low-cost area. In each area, there are different ceilings for one-, two-, three-, and four-unit residences.

Local loan ceilings:
- Based on local median housing costs
- Change periodically

The FHA's loan ceilings are tied to the conforming loan limits—the maximum loan amounts set annually by Fannie Mae and Freddie Mac for the conventional loans they buy (see Chapter 10).

Under current rules, the basic ceiling for FHA loans is 48% of the conforming loan limit. In 2006, the conforming loan limit for a single-family home is $417,000. That means the FHA's basic maximum loan amount for a single-family home is $200,160 ($417,000 × .48 = $200,160). This is the loan ceiling anywhere in the country that doesn't qualify as a high-cost area.

But housing is expensive in many places, so there are many communities in which the $200,160 limit does not apply. In a high-cost area, the FHA may increase the loan ceiling up to 95% of the median home price in the area. Regardless of housing prices, however, the FHA may not raise the loan ceiling in any area higher than 87% of the conforming loan limit. Thus, when the conforming loan limit for single-family homes is $417,000, the loan ceiling in a high-cost area can't exceed $362,790 ($417,000 × .87 = $362,790).[†]

[†] There's an exception to this rule for Alaska, Hawaii, Guam, and the Virgin Islands. In those places, the 2006 ceiling for single-family homes is $544,185.

Fig. 11.2 Example illustrating the FHA's rules for setting local loan ceilings

Location	Median Home Price	2006 FHA Loan Ceiling
Lowood	$150,000	$200,160 (basic ceiling)
Anytown	$200,000	$200,160 (basic ceiling)
Midville	$250,000	$237,500 (95% of median price)
Highline	$380,000	$361,000 (95% of median price)
Goldenvale	$690,000	$362,790 (ceiling for high-cost areas)

Figure 11.1 shows the FHA's basic and high-cost loan limits for 2006. Figure 11.2 shows how the rules for local loan ceilings would apply to hypothetical places with various median housing costs. In Lowood, where housing prices are comparatively low, the FHA's basic ceiling (48% of the conforming loan limit) would apply. It would also apply in Anytown, where prices are somewhat higher but don't exceed the basic ceiling. Midville and Highline are high-cost areas where the ceiling is set at 95% of the median price in the area. In the most expensive location, Goldenvale, the ceiling is set at the FHA's upper limit for high-cost areas. In Goldenvale, 95% of the median price would be $655,500, far above the FHA's upper limit for single-family loan amounts.

The Expanding American Homeownership Act (the legislation currently pending) would raise the FHA's basic maximum loan amount from 48% to 65% of the conforming loan limit. In a high-cost area, the ceiling could be raised to 100% of the median housing price (not just 95%). For the highest-cost areas, the maximum would be increased from 87% to 100% of the conforming loan limit. How great an effect would those anticipated new rules have? To give you a general idea, here's how they would apply using the current conforming loan limit of $417,000: the basic ceiling would be $271,050 instead of $200,160. The high-cost ceiling would be $417,000 instead of $362,790.

HUD usually sets maximum loan amounts on a county-by-county basis. As a result, if a county includes a large city where housing is expensive, the entire county will be treated as a high-cost area, even though housing in its rural sections is relatively inexpensive. In other cases, HUD treats an extensive metropolitan area (overlapping county lines) as a single high-cost area. To get the loan ceiling for a particular area increased, lenders or other interested parties submit a request to HUD with recent sales price data showing that an increase is justified.

Check with a local lender for the current FHA loan ceiling in your community. Keep in mind that the ceiling will be adjusted periodically to reflect changes in the cost of housing. It will also increase significantly if the Expanding American Homeownership Act becomes law.

Loan-to-Value Ratios

The maximum loan amount for a particular transaction is determined not just by the FHA loan ceiling for the local area, but also by the FHA's rules concerning maximum loan-to-value ratios. The LTV limits that apply depend on whether the FHA has classified the state where the property is located as a low closing cost state or a high closing cost state. (See Figure 11.3.) Low closing cost states include Arizona, California, Colorado, Idaho, Illinois, Indiana, New Mexico, Nevada, Oregon, Utah, Washington, Wisconsin, Wyoming; all other states are high closing cost states.

FHA LTVs range from 97.15% to 98.75%, depending on property value and whether state has low or high closing costs

To calculate the loan amount available for a particular transaction, multiply the appropriate LTV ratio by the property's sales price or appraised value, whichever is less.

Note that when the home being purchased with an FHA loan is less than one year old, special rules apply. Unless the home was

Fig. 11.3 Maximum loan-to-value ratios for FHA loans

FHA Maximum LTV Ratios

Property's Value or Sales Price	Low Closing Cost State	High Closing Cost State
$50,000 or less	98.75%	98.75%
$50,001 to $125,000	97.65%	97.75%
Over $125,000	97.15%	97.75%

New home: LTV can't exceed 90% unless approved prior to construction or covered by construction insurance

FHA- or VA-approved prior to construction, or else is covered by an approved construction insurance program, the loan-to-value ratio can't exceed 90%.

If the builder submits plans and specifications to the FHA for approval before construction and agrees not to discriminate in selling the home, the buyer will be eligible for the full 203(b) loan amount (not just a 90% loan).

Note that the loan-to-value rules are likely to change if the Expanding American Homeownership Act becomes law.

Minimum Cash Investment

Borrower's minimum cash investment must be at least 3%

One other factor that can limit the amount of an FHA loan in a particular transaction is the requirement that the borrower make a minimum cash investment of at least 3% of the sales price. The closing costs paid by the borrower are counted toward this 3% requirement, along with the borrower's downpayment.

> **Example:** Sam is purchasing a home for $100,000; the property has been appraised for the same amount. Sam lives in a low closing cost state, so the applicable LTV ratio is 97.65%. The maximum loan amount is therefore $97,650 ($100,000 × 97.65%) and his minimum downpayment must be $2,350. If Sam is going to pay $1,000 in closing costs, his total cash investment will be $3,350. This fulfills the requirement of a minimum cash investment of at least $3,000.
>
> On the other hand, suppose the seller has agreed to pay Sam's closing costs. A $2,350 downpayment from Sam would not be enough to fulfill the minimum cash investment requirement. As a result, the loan amount would be reduced from $97,650 to $97,000, requiring a $3,000 downpayment from Sam.

Downpayment and closing costs paid by borrower count toward minimum cash investment; discount points and prepaids do not

Note that any discount points the borrower is paying do not count toward the minimum cash investment. Neither do "prepaid expenses," which include interim interest on the loan and impounds for property taxes and hazard insurance.

An FHA borrower is not allowed to use secondary financing from the seller or a lender to come up with the minimum cash investment, but may be allowed to use funds provided by a family member or certain other sources. We'll discuss these rules later in this chapter, in the section on secondary financing.

Note that if the borrower is an eligible military veteran, the 3% minimum cash investment requirement does not apply. A veteran's maximum loan amount is determined only by the loan-to-value ratio rules (see Figure 11.3).

Minimum cash investment requirement doesn't apply to eligible veterans

As we mentioned earlier, if the Expanding American Homeownership Act becomes law, the 3% minimum cash investment requirement will be eliminated for all FHA borrowers.

Exercise No. 1

1. Jerry Fletcher lives in a high closing cost state, in a county where the FHA loan limits are at the ceiling for high-cost areas (see Figure 11.1). Fletcher has agreed to pay $447,000 for a duplex that he and his mother will occupy. He would like to finance the transaction with an FHA loan. The appraisal comes in at $448,100. Fletcher's closing costs would total $9,660.

   a. What's the maximum FHA loan amount for this type of transaction in Fletcher's area?

   b. Apply the appropriate loan-to-value ratio to determine the maximum loan amount for this transaction. (Refer back to Figure 11.3.)

   c. How much is the minimum cash investment required for this transaction?

FHA Insurance Premiums

FHA insurance premiums:
- Up-front (one-time) MIP
- Annual premiums

Mortgage insurance premiums for FHA loans are referred to as MMI (mutual mortgage insurance premiums) or MIP (mortgage insurance premiums). For most programs, an FHA borrower pays an upfront premium and annual premiums, as described below.

The rules concerning FHA insurance premiums will be revised by the Expanding American Homeownership Act, if that legislation passes. The current system, in which all borrowers are charged a standard premium amount, will be replaced with a risk-based system that takes a borrower's credit score into account. Borrowers with poor credit scores will be charged slightly higher premiums.

Upfront MIP

Up-front MIP
- Paid in cash, or financed
- Percentage of base loan amount

The upfront premium (UFMIP) is also called the one-time premium (OTMIP). The UFMIP is currently 1.5% of the base loan amount (the amount determined by the loan-to-value and minimum cash investment rules).

Example: John Rubino is buying a house with a $210,300 FHA loan. His upfront premium will be $3,154.50.

$210,300	Loan amount
× 1.5%	
$3,154.50	UFMIP

Base loan
+ Financed UFMIP
Total amount financed

Paying the UFMIP. Either the borrower or the seller can pay the upfront MIP in cash at closing. Alternatively, the borrower has the option of financing the entire UFMIP amount over the loan term. When the UFMIP is financed, it is simply added to the base loan amount. The monthly payments are then set to pay off the total amount financed by the end of the loan term.

Example: Rubino has chosen to finance his upfront MIP instead of paying it in cash at closing.

$210,300.00	Loan amount
+ 3,154.50	UFMIP
$213,454.50	Total amount financed

Note that the total amount financed (or the base loan amount, if the upfront MIP is paid in cash) is rounded down to the next dollar. So if the base loan and the MIP add up to $213,454.50, the total amount financed will be $213,454.

When applying the maximum loan amount rules to a transaction, keep in mind that the financed upfront MIP is not considered part of the loan amount. The borrower can borrow the maximum loan amount allowed in the community plus the full amount of the upfront MIP.

FHA buyer may borrow maximum loan amount plus UFMIP

The loan origination fee paid by the borrower is based only on the base loan amount, not including the upfront MIP. In the example above, the loan fee would be $2,103 (1% × $210,300 = $2,103). Discount points, however, are based on the total amount financed, including the upfront MIP. If the seller were going to pay two points in the example above, he would pay $4,269 (2% × $213,454 = $4,269.08).

Loan fees for FHA loan:

- Origination fee is percentage of base loan amount
- Discount fee is percentage of total amount financed

UFMIP Refund. If an FHA loan that was made before December 8, 2004 is paid off early (because the borrower is selling the property or refinancing, for example), the borrower may be entitled to a refund of part of the upfront MIP. The refund is prorated based on the number of years that have passed since the loan was made.

UFMIP refunds have been eliminated for loans made on or after December 8, 2004. There's an exception if the borrower refinances the property with another FHA-insured loan within the first three years of the original loan's term. In that case, the borrower will be entitled to receive a prorated refund of part of the UFMIP. Alternatively, the money that would otherwise be refunded may be applied to the UFMIP for the new loan.

Annual Premium

In most FHA programs, the borrower is required to pay annual renewal premiums in addition to the upfront MIP. The annual premium is 0.25% or 0.50% of the loan balance (not including any financed UFMIP), depending on the loan term and the loan-to-value ratio.

Annual premium:

- 0.25% or 0.50% of base loan balance
- Paid during first several years of loan term
- Included in monthly loan payments

For loan terms that exceed 15 years, the annual premium is 0.50% of the loan balance. For loan terms of 15 years or less, the annual premium is 0.25%, as long as the LTV is 90% or higher. If the LTV is less than 90%, no annual premium is charged. The loan-to-value ratio is calculated by dividing the base loan amount (not including the financed upfront MIP) by the sales price or appraised value, whichever is less.

Cancellation of Annual MIP. Previously, an FHA borrower was required to pay the annual MIP for a period ranging from four to 30 years, depending on the loan term and the loan-to-value ratio. (The higher the LTV, the greater the risk and the longer the annual premium had to be paid.) For loans closed on or after January 1, 2001, the annual MIP is canceled automatically once certain conditions are met.

Annual MIP canceled when LTV reaches 78%

Loan term exceeds 15 years. For a mortgage with a loan term longer than 15 years, the annual premium will be canceled once the LTV reaches 78%, as long as the borrower has paid the premium for at least five years.

Loan term of 15 years or less. For a mortgage with a loan term of 15 years or less, the annual MIP will be canceled once the LTV reaches 78%. Cancellation occurs regardless of how many years the borrower has paid the premium.

The FHA determines when a borrower has reached the 78% threshold, based on the scheduled amortization of the loan. However, if the borrower prepays the loan and thus reaches the required threshold ahead of schedule, the borrower can request cancellation of the annual MIP.

Even after the annual premium is canceled, the mortgage insurance policy will remain in force for the full term of the loan.

Exercise No. 2

Diane Skillin is buying a home for $274,000, and she's applying for a 30-year FHA loan. (The home is located in a low closing cost state, in an area where the maximum FHA loan amount for a single-family home is $268,800.) The appraised value of the property is $275,500.

1. Calculate the upfront MIP amount and the annual MIP amount for this transaction.

2. Assume that Skillin is going to finance the upfront MIP. What will the total amount financed be? Does it matter that the total amount financed exceeds the maximum FHA loan amount for the area where the property is located?

Sales Concessions and FHA Loans

As you know, sometimes a seller agrees to pay for a buydown, or pay all or part of the buyer's prepaid expenses, or make a variety of other contributions to help the buyer afford the property. When a transaction is financed with an FHA loan, the FHA places certain restrictions on these sales concessions. The restrictions also apply if an interested party other than the seller—for example, the seller's real estate broker, or the subdivision developer—makes any contribution to help the buyer. The basic purpose of these restrictions is to prevent the parties from using contributions to defeat the FHA's loan-to-value rules.

The FHA classifies contributions either as seller contributions or as inducements to purchase, and treats the two types differently.

Seller Contributions

The FHA considers it to be a seller contribution if the seller (or another interested party) pays for part or all of:

- the buyer's closing costs;
- the buyer's prepaid expenses;
- any discount points;
- a temporary or permanent buydown,
- the buyer's mortgage interest; or
- the upfront MIP.

Seller contributions are limited to 6% of the sales price. Any contributions in excess of 6% are treated as inducements to purchase, and are deducted from the sales price in the loan amount calculations.

If seller contributions exceed 6% of sales price, excess is subtracted from sales price in base loan calculations

> **Example:** The Johanssons are buying a home for $154,000 and financing the purchase with an FHA loan. The seller has agreed to pay the lender $9,600 to buy down the interest rate on the Johanssons' loan. Six percent of the sales price is $9,240, so the buydown is $360 over the 6% limit on seller contributions ($9,600 – $9,240 = $360). The $360 excess seller contribution will be treated as an inducement to purchase.

Keep in mind that the 6% limit applies only to contributions from the seller or another interested party. FHA borrowers are allowed to pay discount points to their lenders to buy down their own interest rates. Points paid by the borrower may exceed 6% of the sales price without making it necessary to deduct the excess from the price.

Inducements to Purchase

Other types of payments besides seller contributions in excess of 6% of the sales price may be deemed inducements to purchase. The FHA considers it to be an inducement to purchase if the seller (or another interested party):

- gives the buyer a decorating allowance;
- gives the buyer a repair allowance;
- pays for the buyer's moving expenses;
- pays the buyer's agent's commission;
- pays the real estate agent's sales commission on the sale of the buyer's current home; or
- gives the buyer items of personal property other than those that are customarily included in the sale of a home.

Inducements to purchase are subtracted from sales price before LTV ratio is applied

The total value of any inducements to purchase is subtracted from the property's sales price, on a dollar-to-dollar basis, before the appropriate LTV ratio is applied. This reduces the amount of the mortgage available to the FHA borrower.

> **Example:** Suppose that the seller has also agreed to give the Johanssons $500 to cover their moving costs. This $500 and the $360 excess in seller contributions are considered inducements to purchase, and are subtracted from the property's sales price before the LTV ratio is applied.

$154,000	Sales price
- 500	Inducement to purchase
- 360	Inducement to purchase
$153,140	Adjusted sales price

The adjusted sales price of $153,140 is used as the basis for calculating the mortgage. If a 97.15% LTV applies, the Johanssons' loan amount will be $148,775. That's $836 less than the loan amount they would have had without the inducement to purchase.

Secondary Financing with FHA Loans

As you'll recall, secondary financing refers to a loan secured by a second mortgage against the property that is being purchased with a first mortgage. The rules concerning secondary financing in conjunction with an FHA loan depend on whether the secondary financing is being used for the minimum cash investment, or simply as a supplement to make up the permitted base loan amount.

Secondary Financing and the Cash Investment. An FHA borrower is generally not allowed to use secondary financing—a second mortgage against the home being purchased with the FHA loan—from the seller, another interested party, or an institutional lender to pay the required minimum cash investment.

FHA may not use secondary financing from the seller or a lender for the minimum cash investment

Fig. 11.4 Secondary financing from seller or lender can't be used for minimum cash investment

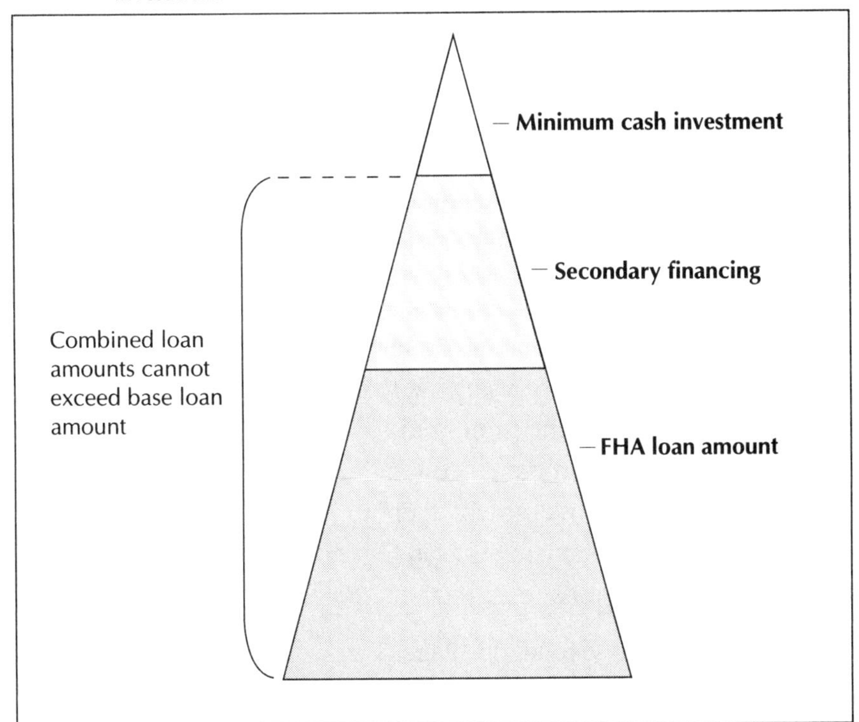

FHA borrower may use secondary financing from a close family member, or from a government or nonprofit agency, for minimum cash investment and other costs

However, secondary financing may be used to cover the minimum cash investment if it is provided by a member of the borrower's family (a child, parent, or grandparent of the borrower or of the borrower's spouse). Closing costs, prepaids, and discount points may also be financed by a family member.

When a family member provides this kind of secondary financing, the total financing (the combined first and second mortgage loans) cannot exceed the property's value or sales price plus closing costs, prepaids, and discount points. If the family member's secondary financing provides for regular installment payments, the combined payments for the FHA loan and the secondary financing can't exceed the borrower's ability to pay. (In other words, the borrower is qualified based on the total of both payments.) And the secondary financing can't call for a balloon payment within five years after closing.

Government agencies (and certain approved nonprofit agencies) may also provide a borrower with secondary financing to cover the minimum cash investment. The secondary lien on the property must be held in the name of the agency. The total financing cannot exceed the property's value plus closing costs, prepaid expenses, and discount points, and the combined payments cannot exceed the borrower's ability to pay.

Older Borrowers. There are fewer restrictions on using secondary financing for the minimum cash investment if the borrower is 60 years old or older. In that case, the secondary financing may be provided by a relative (not necessarily a member of the borrower's immediate family), a close friend with a clearly defined interest in the borrower, the borrower's employer, or a humanitarian or welfare organization. The total financing cannot exceed the property's value plus prepaid expenses.

Secondary Financing for the Base Loan. Any FHA borrower is permitted to use secondary financing to make up part of the base loan amount (as opposed to the minimum cash investment). This type of secondary financing can come from anyone; it doesn't have to be a family member or a government agency.

When secondary financing is used for part of the base loan amount, the following conditions must be met:

1. The first and second mortgages together may not exceed the FHA maximum mortgage amount for the transaction (calculated as if there were no secondary financing involved).

2. The combined total of the payments under the FHA-insured first mortgage and the non-FHA second mortgage may not exceed the borrower's ability to pay.
3. If the second mortgage has periodic installment payments, the payments must be collected on a monthly basis. Each payment must be substantially the same amount as the others.
4. The second mortgage may not have a balloon payment due sooner than ten years after closing (unless the FHA gives special approval).
5. The second mortgage may not impose a prepayment penalty (although the borrower may be required to give the second mortgagee 30 days' notice before prepaying).

FHA rules for secondary financing from seller or lender:
- Not for minimum cash investment
- Combined loans can't exceed FHA base loan amount
- Borrower must qualify for combined payment
- Balloon allowed only after 10 years

Since the borrower will still have to come up with the same cash investment, why would anyone choose this arrangement? When market interest rates are high, a seller might be willing to give a second mortgage at a lower rate than the FHA first mortgage (see Chapter 13). That would make the total payments on the two mortgages less than the payment on an FHA-insured mortgage for the full loan amount. In a marginal case, this might benefit a buyer whose income would otherwise be insufficient to qualify for an FHA loan.

Assumption of FHA Loans

An FHA loan that was originated before December 15, 1989 can be assumed by any buyer. The buyer may be an investor; he or she doesn't have to occupy the property. The buyer also doesn't have to be approved by the lender or the FHA, unless the original borrower wants to be released from liability.

FHA loans closed before 12/15/89 can be assumed:
- Without FHA or lender approval
- By investor (non-occupant)

FHA loans originated on or after December 15, 1989 can be assumed only by buyers who will occupy the property. And if the loan was originated on or after January 27, 1991, the property must be the buyer's primary residence (not a second home).

For FHA loans that were originated on or after December 15, 1989, the lender must review the creditworthiness of the buyer before the property transfer takes place (even if the buyer simply plans to take title subject to the FHA loan instead of assuming it). As a general

For FHA loans closed since 12/15/89, buyer assuming loan must:
- Pass creditworthiness review
- Occupy home

Fig. 11.5 A summary of the rules for assuming an FHA loan

FHA Assumption Rules			
	Date of loan commitment		
	Before 12/15/89	**On or after 12/15/89**	**On or after 1/27/91**
No creditworthiness review unless seller wants release	✓		
Buyer may be investor	✓		
Creditworthiness review required		✓	✓
Buyer must occupy		✓	✓
Buyer must occupy as primary residence			✓

rule, the creditworthiness review for an FHA assumption is very similar to the process of qualifying a buyer for a new FHA loan (see the next section of this chapter).

For loans originated on or after December 15, 1989, if the buyer assuming the loan is creditworthy, the lender is required to release the original borrower from liability automatically. For older loans, the lender must release the original borrower upon written request (if the buyer is creditworthy).

FHA loans closed since 1/27/91: home must be buyer's primary residence

For loans originated between February 5, 1988 and January 27, 1991, if the original borrower was an owner-occupant, and the buyer is purchasing the property as a second home, the loan must be paid down to an 85% loan-to-value ratio.

For loans originated before December 15, 1989, if the original borrower was an owner-occupant and the buyer is an investor (someone who does not intend to occupy the property), the investor must pay the loan down to a 75% LTV if the original borrower requests a release of liability from the lender.

FHA Underwriting

As for any institutional loan, the underwriting for an FHA-insured loan involves analysis of the applicant's income, net worth, and credit history (see Chapter 8). But the FHA's underwriting standards aren't as strict as the Fannie Mae/Freddie Mac standards used for conventional loans. The FHA standards make it easier for low- and middle-income home buyers to qualify for a mortgage.

Income Analysis

When evaluating an application for an FHA-insured loan, an underwriter must determine the applicant's monthly **effective income**. Effective income is the applicant's gross income from all sources that can be expected to continue for the first three years of the loan term. As with a conventional loan, the underwriter will apply two ratios to determine the adequacy of the applicant's effective income: the fixed payment to income ratio and the housing expense to income ratio. As a general rule, an FHA borrower's fixed payment to income ratio should not exceed **43%**. In addition, the housing expense to income ratio should not exceed **31%**. The applicant should qualify under both tests.

FHA maximum income ratios:
- 43% fixed payment to income ratio
- 31% housing expense to income ratio

Fixed payments include the proposed monthly housing expense plus all recurring charges. The housing expense includes principal and interest (based on the total amount financed), property taxes, hazard insurance, one-twelfth of the annual premium for the FHA mortgage insurance (or for a condo, the monthly premium), and any dues owed to a homeowners association or condominium association.

The **recurring charges** are the monthly payments on any debt with ten or more payments remaining. (A debt with fewer payments remaining will also be considered if it is a large debt.) Alimony and child support payments, installment debt payments, and payments on revolving credit accounts are all counted.

> **Example:** Helen Crowder would like to buy a home with an FHA loan. She has a monthly salary of $2,500. Her ex-husband reliably sends her a child support payment each month for their four-year-old daughter. The child support is tax-exempt, so the lender "grosses up" the payment, and concludes that it's the equivalent of $350 in taxable income. Thus, Crowder's effec-

tive income is $2,850, and her total fixed payments should not exceed $1,225:

$2,850	Effective income
× 43%	Fixed payment to income ratio limit
$1,225.50	Maximum fixed payments

Crowder has to pay the following recurring charges:

$223	Car payment (11 payments remaining)
35	Furniture store payment (15 payments remaining)
55	Minimum Visa payment
29	Minimum MasterCard payment
22	Student loan (63 payments remaining)
+ 63	Texaco credit card
$427	Total recurring charges

To determine the maximum housing expense Crowder could qualify for under the 43% fixed payment to income ratio, subtract her recurring charges from the maximum fixed payments figure.

$1,225	Maximum fixed payments
− 427	Recurring charges
$798	Maximum housing expense under the 43% fixed payment ratio

Crowder's housing expense could be as high as $883 without going over the 31% housing expense to income ratio limit ($2,850 × 31% = $883.50). But since Crowder is required to qualify under both ratios, her monthly housing expense probably should not be more than $798.

Compensating factors for an FHA loan:
- 10% downpayment
- Savings and conservative attitude toward credit
- Ability to devote extra income to housing expenses
- Short-term income
- Small increase over current housing expense
- Three months' payments in reserve
- Potential for increased earnings

A loan applicant whose income ratios exceed the 43% and/or 31% limits won't qualify for an FHA loan unless there are compensating factors that reduce the risk of default. The FHA lists the following compensating factors:

- Over the past 12-24 months, the loan applicant has paid housing expenses at least equal to the proposed housing expenses under the new mortgage.
- The applicant plans to make a large downpayment (at least 10%).
- The applicant has demonstrated the ability to accumulate savings and a conservative attitude toward the use of credit.

- The applicant's credit history demonstrates the ability to devote a greater portion of income to housing expenses.
- The applicant receives income that was not counted as effective income (for example, because it will not continue for at least three years), but which directly affects the applicant's ability to pay the mortgage.
- The proposed housing expense represents only a small increase (10% or less) over the applicant's current housing expense.
- The applicant would have substantial reserves after closing (at least three months' mortgage payments).
- The applicant's job training or professional education indicates potential for increased earnings.

This list isn't exclusive—these are only examples. There may be other aspects of the loan applicant's financial situation that the lender and the FHA would accept as compensating factors that justify loan approval in spite of income ratios over 43% and 31%.

Also, when an FHA inspection has determined that the home in question is an energy-efficient home (EEH), the income ratios can be exceeded by 2%. In other words, buyers with a fixed payment to income ratio of 45% and a housing expense to income ratio of 33% can qualify for an FHA loan if they're buying an energy-efficient home.

Temporary buydowns are allowed in connection with FHA loans, but the buyer must qualify at the note rate. So even if a buydown brings the interest rate down from 9% to 7% in the first year, the buyer would still be required to qualify for the loan at 9%.

Exercise No. 3

The Herrons are applying for an FHA loan. Maggie Herron works for the Northshore Boat Company as a bookkeeper, earning $1,700 a month. Her husband, Bob, earns $420 a week as a customer service representative for Garner Industries. They have two personal loans from a local bank. The first loan has a monthly payment of $114 and a balance of $1,254. The second loan calls for monthly payments of

$135, with $1,655 still owing. Their Visa card requires a minimum payment of $47; the balance is $1,460.

1. What is the Herrons' effective income?

2. Applying both the fixed payment ratio and the housing expense ratio (and assuming there are no compensating factors that would allow higher-than-standard ratios), what's the maximum housing expense the Herrons could qualify for under the FHA's rules?

3. How does the answer to question 2 compare to the maximum housing expense the Herrons could qualify for if they were applying for a 95% conventional loan?

Assets for Closing

Cash required for closing:
- Minimum cash investment
- Prepaids
- Discount points
- Closing costs or repair costs that can't be financed
- Difference between sales price and appraised value, if sales price is greater

At closing, an FHA borrower will need to have enough cash to cover:

- the minimum cash investment;
- the prepaids;
- any discount points the borrower has agreed to pay;
- the upfront MIP, if it isn't being financed; and
- any closing costs, repair costs, or other expenses (e.g., all or part of a buyer's agent's fee) that aren't eligible for financing.

FHA generally does not require reserves

If the borrower has agreed to pay a sales price higher than the property's appraised value, then he or she has to come up with the difference in cash, in addition to the minimum cash investment. Ordinarily, no reserves are required for an FHA loan (although reserves may be used as a compensating factor if the borrower's income ratios exceed the FHA limits—see above).

The borrower may use gift funds for part or even all of the cash required for closing. The donor must be the borrower's employer or labor union, a relative, a close friend with a clearly defined interest in the borrower, a charitable organization, or a government agency. The funds must be deposited in the borrower's bank account or with the closing agent, and a gift letter will be required (see Chapter 8).

Sources of cash for closing:
- Gift funds
- Secondary financing from family member
- Unsecured loan from family member
- Loan secured by collateral other than home

There are other possibilities besides gift funds. As we discussed earlier, under certain circumstances a borrower may use secondary financing to cover the minimum cash investment and other funds needed for closing. Alternatively, a close family member may simply loan the funds to the borrower without requiring a second mortgage or any other form of security in return.

Also, the borrower may be permitted to borrow the cash needed for closing from someone other than a close family member, as long as this loan is secured by collateral other than the home being purchased with the FHA mortgage. The borrower must obtain the loan from an independent third party, not from the seller or a real estate agent involved in the transaction. (Of course, a loan requiring more than ten payments will be taken into account in qualifying the borrower.)

Home Inspection Disclosure Form

In an effort to prevent FHA borrowers from purchasing homes with significant defects, the FHA requires lenders to provide a disclosure form titled "For Your Protection: Get a Home Inspection." This form explains to borrowers the importance of obtaining a home inspection, and distinguishes a home inspection from an appraisal. It also provides information on radon gas testing. By signing the form, the borrower acknowledges that the FHA will neither perform a home inspection nor guarantee the price or condition of the property.

This disclosure form may either be incorporated into a standard sales agreement or signed as a separate form, and it must be signed by the buyer on or before the date on which the purchase contract is signed. If necessary, parties must re-execute a sales contract to meet this requirement. The FHA will not insure a loan unless it receives a copy of the signed and dated form.

Chapter Outline: FHA-Insured Loans

I. FHA Mortgage Insurance

   A. The Federal Housing Administration (FHA) is part of the Department of Housing and Urban Development (HUD). The purpose of the FHA is to promote the financing, improvement, and sale of residential real estate.

   B. The primary function of the FHA is insuring mortgage loans. It does not build homes or provide mortgage loans.

      1. A borrower applies to an FHA-approved lender who either underwrites the loan application directly or submits it to the FHA for approval.

      2. The borrower is liable to the federal government for any compensation the FHA must pay a lender as a result of the borrower's default.

II. FHA Loan Characteristics

   A. FHA loans are designed to help people with low and moderate incomes buy homes.

   B. Loan terms are typically 30 years. A 1% origination fee is charged. Prepayment penalties are prohibited.

   C. The FHA sets the maximum loan amount for a county or a metropolitan area based on median home prices. In addition, maximum loan-to-value ratios determine the maximum loan amount allowable for a particular transaction.

   D. An FHA borrower must make a minimum cash investment of 3% of the sales price. The downpayment and closing costs paid by the borrower count toward the minimum cash investment.

   E. A home purchased with an FHA loan is generally required to be an owner-occupied primary residence.

   F. FHA loans have less stringent qualifying standards than conventional loans.

III. FHA Loan Programs

   A. Section 203(b) is the standard FHA loan program. It provides insurance for loans used to purchase or refinance one- to four-unit properties.

   B. Section 203(k) insures mortgages used to purchase (or refinance) and rehabilitate one- to four-unit properties.

      1. All loan proceeds used for the upgrade work must be put into an escrow account and released as the work progresses.

2. Rehabilitation work must meet HUD standards. The work must cost at least $5,000, and cannot include temporary or luxury improvements.

C. Section 223(e) insures loans used to purchase, rehabilitate, or build housing on property in older, declining urban areas that would otherwise be ineligible for FHA mortgage insurance.

D. Section 234(c) insures loans used to purchase or refinance individual units in condominiums that have been approved by the FHA. A 234(c) loan may also be available to buy a unit in a non-approved condominium, if the unit meets certain criteria. This is called a "spot loan."

E. Section 245(a) insures graduated payment mortgages (GPMs) and growing equity mortgages (GEMs).

1. The payments for an FHA GPM increase over the first five or ten years of the loan term. The property may not have more than one dwelling unit.
2. The payments for an FHA GEM increased over the first ten years of the loan term, and the increases are applied to principal, shortening the loan term.

F. Section 251 insures 30-year adjustable rate mortgages (ARMs) used to purchase or refinance owner-occupied properties with up to four units.

1. An FHA ARM can have an initial fixed interest rate period of one, three, five, seven, or ten years. After the initial period, rate increases occur annually.
2. Depending on the length of the initial period, the annual interest rate adjustment is limited to 1% or 2%, and the total rate increase over the life of the loan is limited to 5% or 6%.

G. Section 255 insures home equity conversion mortgages (HECMs), also known as reverse mortgages.

1. Allows older homeowners to convert their equity into either a source of monthly income or a line of credit.
2. Repayment is not required as long as the property remains the owner's principal residence.
3. The homeowner must be at least 62 years old.
4. The property may have up to four units or be a condominium unit.
5. The property must be owned free and clear, or have only a small balance remaining on the existing mortgage.
6. The loan amount depends on the FHA loan ceiling, the home's appraised value, the current interest rate, and the age of the borrower.

7. The lender recovers the amount borrowed, plus interest, when the property is sold. The FHA will make up any shortfall in the sale proceeds.

IV. Maximum Loan Amounts

A. The maximum FHA loan amount for a transaction is determined by the local loan ceiling and a maximum loan-to-value ratio.

B. The local loan ceiling is based on median housing costs in the area. There are different ceilings for one-, two-, three-, and four-unit residences.

C. Maximum loan-to-value ratios range from 97.15% to 98.75%, depending on the property's value and on whether the state where the property is located is classified as a low or high closing cost state.

1. If the loan is used to buy a home that is less than a year old, the LTV cannot exceed 90%.

2. This rule doesn't apply if the home is approved by the FHA or VA before construction or is warranted by a construction insurance program.

V. Minimum Cash Investment

A. The borrower must make a minimum cash investment of at least 3% of the sales price.

1. The downpayment and borrower-paid closing costs count toward the 3% requirement.

2. Discount points and prepaid expenses do not count toward it.

B. The 3% minimum cash investment requirement does not apply to eligible veterans.

VI. FHA Insurance Premiums

A. The mortgage insurance premiums (MIP) for most FHA programs include an upfront premium (UFMIP) and annual renewal premiums.

B. The UFMIP is 1.5% of the base loan amount. It may be paid in cash at closing by the buyer or the seller, or it may be financed.

1. A financed UFMIP is not included in the base loan amount used to calculate the maximum loan amount and loan origination fee.

2. If an FHA loan made before December 8, 2004 is paid off early, the borrower may be eligible for a prorated refund of part of the UFMIP.

C. The annual MIP is 0.25% or 0.50% of the loan balance, depending on the loan term and LTV.

1. No annual premium is charged if the LTV is under 90%.
2. For loans that closed on or after January 1, 2001, the annual premium is canceled once certain conditions are met. The mortgage insurance remains effective for the full loan term.
    a. If the loan term is over 15 years, the annual MIP is automatically canceled when the LTV reaches 78%, as long as the borrower has paid the premium for at least five years.
    b. If the loan term is 15 years or less, the annual MIP is automatically canceled when the LTV reaches 78%, regardless of how long the borrower has paid the premium.
    c. If the 78% threshold is reached early, the borrower may request cancellation.

VII. Sales Concessions and FHA Loans

A. The FHA restricts sales concessions from the seller or other interested parties, to prevent circumvention of the FHA's LTV rules.

B. Sales concessions are classified either as seller contributions or as inducements to purchase.

1. Seller contributions include payments towards the borrower's closing costs, prepaid expenses, mortgage interest, UFMIP, discount points, or a buydown.
    a. Seller contributions are limited to 6% of the sales price.
    b. Contributions in excess of 6% are considered inducements to purchase.
2. Inducements to purchase are deducted from the property's sales price before the LTV is applied, lowering the allowable maximum loan amount.
    a. In addition to seller contributions in excess of 6%, inducements to purchase include funds given to the buyer for decorating, repairs, moving expenses, and buyer's agent fees, as well as personal property.

VIII. FHA Loans and Secondary Financing

A. Secondary financing may be used with an FHA loan, if the primary and secondary loans don't add up to more than the maximum base loan amount for the transaction and the borrower qualifies for the combined payment.

B. As a general rule, secondary financing cannot be used for the borrower's minimum cash investment, but there are significant exceptions.
   1. Secondary financing provided by a close family member or a government agency may be used to cover the minimum cash investment, if the total financing doesn't exceed the property's value or sales price plus closing costs, prepaids, and discount points.
   2. A borrower 60 years or older may cover the minimum cash investment with secondary financing from a relative, a close friend, an employer, or a charitable organization. The total financing cannot exceed the property's value plus prepaid expenses.

IX. Assumption of FHA Loans
   A. A new FHA loan can only be assumed by a creditworthy buyer who intends to occupy the property as a primary residence. Older FHA loans (closed before December 15, 1989) can be assumed by anyone, unless the seller wants to be released from liability.
   B. If the buyer assuming the loan is creditworthy, the lender must release the original borrower from liability automatically. With older loans, the lender must release the original borrower upon written request.
   C. In some circumstances, the loan must be paid down to a 75% or 85% LTV ratio before it is assumed; otherwise the original borrower won't be released from liability.

X. Underwriting an FHA Loan
   A. In FHA loan underwriting, the applicant's monthly effective income is measured against the applicant's fixed payments and proposed housing expense.
   B. Effective income is the total amount of income from all sources that can be expected to continue for the first three years of the loan term.
   C. Fixed payments include the proposed monthly housing expense (principal, interest, property taxes, hazard insurance, one-twelfth of the annual MIP, and any homeowners or condominium association dues), plus recurring charges (monthly payments on any debt with ten or more payments remaining).
   D. A borrower's fixed payment to income ratio should not exceed 43%, and the housing expense to income ratio should not exceed 31%.
   E. An applicant whose income ratios exceed these limits may still qualify for an FHA loan if compensating factors reduce the risk of default.
      1. Compensating factors include a demonstrated ability to save money and meet financial obligations, a large downpayment, good credit history, and substantial reserves left over after closing.

XI. Assets Required for Closing

A. At closing, an FHA borrower must have enough cash to cover the minimum cash investment, the prepaids, any borrower-paid discount points, the upfront MIP (if it isn't being financed), and any other closing costs that are not being financed or paid for by the seller.

B. Allowable sources for the cash required for closing:

1. Gift funds from an employer, labor union, relative, close friend, charitable organization, or government agency may be used to cover these costs.
2. Secondary financing (secured by a lien against the home being purchased) in compliance with the rules explained earlier.
3. An unsecured loan from a family member.
4. A loan from any independent third party (not the seller or a real estate agent involved in the transaction), as long as it is not secured by the home being purchased with the FHA loan.

XII. Home Inspection Disclosure Form

A. The FHA requires that borrowers receive a form titled "For Your Protection: Get a Home Inspection," which explains the importance of a home inspection and provides information on radon testing.

B. The borrower must sign and date the form on or before the date the purchase contract is signed; otherwise the FHA will not insure the loan.

C. By signing, the borrower acknowledges that the FHA will not perform a home inspection and does not guarantee the price or condition of the property.

Key Terms

HUD: The Department of Housing and Urban Development, a cabinet-level department of the federal government.

Federal Housing Administration (FHA): An agency within the Department of Housing and Urban Development that provides mortgage insurance to encourage lenders to make more affordable home loans.

FHA-insured loan: A loan made by an institutional lender with mortgage insurance provided by the Federal Housing Administration, protecting the lender against losses due to borrower default.

MMI: The Mutual Mortgage Insurance program, the formal name of the FHA insurance program.

Direct endorser: A lender authorized to underwrite its own FHA loan applications, rather than having to submit them to the FHA for approval.

Effective income: In FHA underwriting, the loan applicant's gross monthly income from all sources that can be expected to continue; the FHA equivalent of stable monthly income.

MIP: The fee charged for FHA insurance coverage. The initial FHA premium is referred to as the upfront MIP (UFMIP) or the OTMIP (one-time MIP).

Chapter Quiz

1. The FHA:
   a. makes loans
   b. insures loans
   c. buys and sells loans
   d. All of the above

2. Bill Zelinski is buying a duplex. He can finance the transaction with an FHA loan if he intends to:
   a. occupy one of the units as his primary residence
   b. occupy one of the units as a secondary residence
   c. rent out both of the units
   d. Any of the above

3. The appraised value of a single-family home is $365,000, and it's selling for $364,000. The home is located in a low closing cost state, in a very high-cost area where the FHA's local loan ceiling is $362,790. The maximum loan amount available for this transaction is:
   a. $328,500
   b. $346,918
   c. $353,626
   d. $362,790

4. FHA local loan ceilings are based on local:
   a. median income
   b. debt to income ratios
   c. median housing costs
   d. mortgage insurance costs

5. All of the following statements about FHA loans are true *except*:
   a. points must be paid by the borrower
   b. the seller or an institutional lender is not allowed to provide secondary financing for the minimum cash investment
   c. mortgage insurance is required on all loans
   d. the government does not set a maximum interest rate

6. The Howells are buying a house worth $315,000 with a 30-year FHA 203(b) loan. Because of the FHA's local loan ceiling and LTV rules, the maximum loan amount for this transaction is $307,913. If the Howells borrow that amount and also decide to finance the upfront MIP:
   a. the maximum loan amount will be reduced by the amount of the MIP
   b. the total amount financed, including the MIP, cannot exceed $307,913
   c. the total amount financed will be $307,913 minus the MIP
   d. the total amount financed will be $307,913 plus the MIP

7. Returning to the previous question, if the Howells obtain a 30-year loan for $307,913, they will be required to pay an annual premium of:
   a. 0.25% of the loan balance
   b. 0.50% of the loan balance
   c. 0.25% of the upfront MIP
   d. None of the above; an annual premium is not required if the MIP is financed

8. The buyer is obtaining a $187,000 FHA loan. The seller agrees to pay $3,000 toward the buyer's closing costs. The seller also agrees to pay the buyer's upfront MIP. Which of the following statements is correct?
   a. The seller contributions will total $3,935
   b. The seller contributions will total $5,805
   c. The seller contributions will exceed the 6% limit
   d. The $3,000 will be treated as an inducement to purchase

9. Secondary financing may be used to cover the borrower's minimum cash investment:
   a. only if the second loan comes from the seller
   b. only if the second loan comes from an institutional lender
   c. only if the two loans do not add up to more than the property's value
   d. under no circumstances

10. The Munnimans bought their house in 1986 with an FHA loan. Now they're selling it. The loan:
    a. could be assumed by an investor
    b. could only be assumed by a buyer who intends to occupy the property as his or her primary residence
    c. could only be assumed by a buyer who is found creditworthy
    d. cannot be assumed

11. For the purposes of calculating the income ratios, an FHA borrower's housing expense includes:
    a. hazard insurance
    b. principal and interest for the total amount financed
    c. one-twelfth of the annual MIP
    d. All of the above

12. Hannah Graumann's effective income is $3,600 per month. If she wants to qualify for an FHA loan, her monthly fixed payments (including the proposed housing expense) probably should not exceed:
    a. $644
    b. $1,247
    c. $1,302
    d. $1,548

Answer Key

1. b. The FHA insures mortgage loans made by FHA-approved lenders in accordance with FHA rules.

2. a. An FHA loan generally must be used to finance an owner-occupied primary residence.

3. c. Multiply the property's sales price or appraised value (whichever is less) by the appropriate LTV ratio to get the maximum loan amount available under the FHA's LTV rules. In a low closing cost state when the property's value or price is over $125,000, the maximum LTV is 97.15%. $364,000 × 97.15% = $353,626. Since this does not exceed the local loan ceiling ($362,790), $353,626 is the maximum loan amount.

4. c. FHA local maximum loan amounts are based on local median housing costs.

5. a. Discount points may be paid by the borrower or by another party, such as the seller.

6. d. The borrower can obtain a loan for the maximum amount allowed for the area, plus the amount of the upfront MIP.

7. b. For a loan with a term longer than 15 years, the annual premium is 0.50% of the loan balance.

8. b. The upfront MIP is 1.5% of the loan balance, or $2,805. With the upfront MIP added to the $3,000 in closing costs, the seller's contributions come to $5,805.

9. c. Secondary financing may be used to pay the borrower's required minimum cash investment, but it cannot come from the seller, another interested party, or an institutional lender. The total amount financed cannot exceed the property's value.

10. a. FHA loans that were originated before December 15, 1989 may be assumed by any buyer. The buyer may be an investor, and does not need to be approved by the lender or the FHA unless the original borrower wants a release from liability.

11. d. The borrower's housing expense includes principal, interest, property taxes, hazard insurance, one-twelfth of the annual mortgage insurance premium, and any condominium or homeowners association dues.

12. d. An FHA borrower's fixed payment to effective income ratio generally should not exceed 43%. Multiply her effective income ($3,600) by the income ratio (43%) to find the fixed payment amount. $3,600 × .43 = $1,548.

Case Study: Qualifying the Buyer
FHA-Insured Loans

After considering conventional loans, Rick and Teresa Cortina want to know whether an FHA-insured loan might work for them. They live in an area where the maximum FHA loan amount for single-family homes is $227,900, and in a state classified as a high closing cost state. Refer back to the case study at the end of Chapter 10 for the information about the Cortinas' financial situation that you will need to prequalify them for an FHA loan.

Interest rates:

Through your contacts in the mortgage market, you know that the current market interest rates for 30-year FHA loans are approximately as follows:

Fixed rate: 6.75%, 1% origination fee, no discount points

ARM: 5.5%, 1% origination fee, no discount points

Using the worksheets to help you with your calculations, answer the following questions.

1. Calculate the Cortinas' effective income and recurring charges. What is the maximum housing expense that the Cortinas could qualify for under the FHA income ratios?

2. Suppose the Cortinas were to borrow the maximum FHA loan amount for their area ($227,900) and finance the upfront MIP. If the loan term is 30 years, what would the total amount financed be? Round the total amount financed down to the next dollar.

3. If the Cortinas borrowed the maximum FHA loan amount for their area at 6.75% interest (for a fixed-rate loan) and financed the upfront MIP, the required monthly payment of principal and interest would be $1,500.32. If they borrowed the same amount at 5.5% interest (for an ARM), the monthly payment of principal and interest would be $1,313.40. For each loan, add 15% to the principal and interest payment to estimate the property taxes, hazard insurance, and the FHA annual mortgage insurance premium. Could the Cortinas qualify for a 30-year FHA loan for $227,900 (plus the upfront MIP) at each of the interest rates listed above?

4. Suppose the Cortinas want to buy a house for $220,000. Its appraised value is $220,750. What is the maximum FHA loan the Cortinas could obtain to finance this purchase? If the Cortinas financed the upfront MIP, what would the total amount financed be?

5. For the transaction in question 4, how much cash would the Cortinas need at closing? Include the downpayment and the origination fee. Use 2.5% of the sales price as an estimate of the other closing costs. Does this add up to enough to meet the minimum cash investment requirement for this transaction?

6. For the Cortinas, would there be any advantage to getting an FHA loan instead of a conventional loan? (Compare the results of your FHA calculations to your answers to the questions in the case study for conventional financing at the end of Chapter 10.)

Income Qualifying—FHA-Insured Loans

Effective Income

Base salary	
Wage earner 1	________
Wage earner 2	________
Overtime	________
Commissions	________
Bonuses	________
Other	+ ________
Total	________

Recurring Charges

Car loans	________
Credit cards	________
Student loans	________
Other loans	________
Child care	________
Child support	________
Alimony	________
Other	+ ________
Total	________

Fixed Payment to Income Ratio

________	Effective income
x 43%	Maximum ratio
________	Maximum fixed payments
– ________	Recurring charges
________	Maximum mortgage payment (PITI) under fixed payment ratio

Housing Expense to Income Ratio

________	Stable monthly income
x 31%	Maximum ratio
________	Maximum mortgage payment (PITI) under housing expense ratio

Maximum Mortgage Payment (PITI) ________

________	Maximum PITI payment
÷ 115%	(less 15% for taxes and insurance)
________	Maximum principal and interest payment

Chapter 12
VA-Guaranteed Loans

Characteristics of VA Loans

Eligibility for VA Loans

- Service requirements
- Eligibility of spouse

VA Guaranty

- Guaranty amount
- Veteran's liability
  - Liability after assumption
  - Release of liability
- Substitution of entitlement
- Remaining entitlement
- Entitlement and co-ownership
- Refinancing with a VA loan

VA Loan Amounts

- Making a downpayment
- Secondary financing

Underwriting Guidelines

- Income ratio analysis
- Residual income analysis
- Compensating factors
- Income ratio exceptions

Introduction

The VA home loan program was established to help veterans finance the purchase of their homes with affordable loans. For the eligible veteran, a VA-guaranteed loan is an excellent financing choice. VA financing offers many advantages over conventional financing and has few disadvantages. In this chapter, we'll discuss the characteristics of VA loans, eligibility requirements, and the underwriting standards used to qualify loan applicants.

Characteristics of VA Loans

VA-guaranteed loans are made by institutional lenders, just like conventional loans and FHA-insured loans. However, when a VA-guaranteed loan is approved by the lender, a portion of the loan amount is guaranteed by the Department of Veterans Affairs. The loan guaranty works like mortgage insurance—it protects the lender against a large loss if the borrower defaults and the foreclosure sale proceeds fail to cover the full amount owed.

VA guaranty protects lender against losses from default

The term "VA-guaranteed loan" causes some confusion. You may occasionally encounter buyers who believe that, as eligible veterans, they are guaranteed to receive a VA home loan, no matter what their financial circumstances are. But a veteran is required to qualify for a VA loan, just as for any other kind of mortgage loan; there are specific underwriting standards that the veteran has to meet in order for the loan to be approved. The VA guaranty refers only to the lender's protection against loss.

A VA loan can be used to finance the purchase or construction of a single-family residence, or a multi-family residence containing up to four units. The VA does not guarantee investor loans, so the veteran borrower must intend to occupy the home. In the case of a multi-family property, the veteran must occupy one of the units.

VA loans:
- One- to four-unit residences
- Vet must occupy

Here are the key characteristics of VA-guaranteed loans:

- Unlike most home loans, a typical VA loan doesn't require a downpayment. The loan amount can be as large as the appraised value of the property. This is probably the most important advantage of VA financing. It's particularly helpful to first-time home buyers, who usually have less cash available to invest in a home.

- The VA does not set a maximum loan amount, in the way that HUD does for FHA loans.
- There are no maximum income limits. (In other words, VA loans aren't restricted to low- or middle-income buyers.)
- VA underwriting standards are less stringent than either conventional or FHA underwriting standards, so it's easier for a veteran to qualify for a VA loan.
- VA loans have traditionally been 30-year fixed-rate loans, but currently ARMs, hybrid ARMs (3/1, 5/1, 7/1, or 10/1), graduated payment mortgages (GPMs), and growing equity mortgages (GEMs) are also available to VA borrowers.
- VA loans don't require any mortgage insurance (either private mortgage insurance or FHA-style insurance).
- The VA doesn't set a maximum interest rate for VA loans; the interest rate is negotiable between the borrower and lender.
- The lender may charge a VA borrower a flat fee of no more than 1% of the loan amount to cover administrative costs (the equivalent of an origination fee). The lender may also charge reasonable discount points, which can be paid by the borrower, the seller, or a third party.
- The lender is not allowed to impose a prepayment penalty if a VA borrower pays the loan off early.
- Forbearance is extended to homeowners who are experiencing temporary financial difficulties resulting from problems such as unemployment, disability, large medical bills, or the death of a spouse. The VA has loan officers who can help borrowers and lenders negotiate repayment plans for delinquent loans.
- VA loans may be assumed, and the assumptor (the buyer who is assuming the loan) doesn't have to be a veteran. To assume any VA loan made on or after March 1, 1988, the assumptor must pass a complete credit check. The interest rate on a VA loan is not raised when the loan is assumed, but the VA does charge a funding fee of 0.5%.

Characteristics of VA loans:
- No downpayment required
- No maximum loan amount
- No maximum income limits
- Least stringent qualifying standards
- Fixed-rate or ARM
- No mortgage insurance
- Funding fee
- Forbearance for vet in financial difficulties
- Can be assumed by creditworthy buyer, veteran or non-veteran

Funding Fees. While VA borrowers don't have to pay a mortgage insurance premium, they do have to pay the VA a **funding fee**. The funding fee may be paid at closing or financed along with the loan amount.

Funding fee: 2.15% of loan amount, unless vet makes downpayment of 5% or more

For a member of the regular military obtaining a no-downpayment loan, the funding fee is 2.15% of the loan amount. If the borrower makes a downpayment of 5% or more, the funding fee is reduced. When the downpayment is at least 5% but less than 10%, the funding fee is 1.5%. When the downpayment is 10% or more, the funding fee is 1.25%.

For a member of the Reserves or the National Guard obtaining a no-downpayment loan, the funding fee is 2.4%. If the downpayment is between 5% and 10%, the funding fee is 1.75%; if the downpayment is 10% or more, the fee is 1.5%.

In cases where the borrower has had a VA-guaranteed loan before, the funding fee for the second (or subsequent) loan is 3.35% if less than a 5% downpayment is made.

Certain parties are exempt from the funding fee requirement:

- veterans entitled to receive VA compensation for service-related disabilities (including those still on active duty and awaiting discharge);
- veterans who would be entitled to receive compensation for service-related disabilities if they did not receive retirement pay;
- surviving spouses of veterans who died in service or from service-related disabilities.

Eligibility for VA Loans

Eligibility for VA-guaranteed loans is based on the length of continuous active duty service in the U.S. armed forces. The minimum requirement varies depending on when the veteran served, as follows:

90 days of active duty, any part of which occurred:

1. September 16, 1940 through July 25, 1947 (World War II)
2. June 27, 1950 through January 31, 1955 (the Korean War)
3. August 5, 1964 through May 7, 1975 (the Vietnam War)
4. August 2, 1990 to the present (Persian Gulf War*)

* An official termination date for the Persian Gulf War had not yet been established when this book was printed.

181 days of continuous active duty during one of these peacetime periods:

1. July 26, 1947 through June 26, 1950
2. February 1, 1955 through August 4, 1964
3. May 8, 1975 through September 7, 1980

For service that began on or after September 8, 1980 (or for service as an officer that began on or after October 17, 1981):

- **24 months** of continuous active duty, or the full period for which the individual was called to active duty, as long as it was at least 181 days (90 days if it was during the Persian Gulf War, which began on August 2, 1990*);
- except that a shorter period of service (usually 181 days) is sufficient for veterans who are suffering from a compensable service-connected disability, or who were discharged for the convenience of the government, for hardship, or because of certain medical conditions that are not service-connected.

For veterans who were discharged for a service-connected disability, there is no minimum active duty service requirement. They are eligible for VA-guaranteed loans, no matter how brief their period of service was.

If an individual applies for a VA loan while still on active duty, he or she is eligible after serving at least 181 days of continuous active duty (regardless of when the period of service began), or after at least 90 days of continuous active duty service during the Persian Gulf War.

Eligibility for VA loan:
1. Minimum active duty service requirement
2. Other than dishonorable discharge
3. Unremarried spouse may be eligible

Eligibility has also been extended to those who have served in the Reserves or National Guard for at least six years.

Individuals who have served six months of active duty for training purposes only aren't eligible, nor are veterans who received a dishonorable discharge.

The VA determines a veteran's eligibility for a VA loan. If a veteran is eligible, the VA will issue a **Certificate of Eligibility**, which the vet then uses to apply for a VA loan. To get a Certificate of Eligibility, the vet must complete and sign an application form, which is available from VA lenders or on the VA website. The vet must also provide a photocopy of his or her most recent discharge or separation papers (usually form DD-214). If the vet is currently on active duty, a statement of service on military letterhead signed by the appropriate military personnel is required.

In many cases, the lender can now instantly obtain a Certificate of Eligibility for a VA loan applicant through an automated online system.

Eligibility of a Spouse. A veteran's surviving spouse may be eligible for a VA loan if he or she has not remarried and the veteran was killed in action or died of service-related injuries. A veteran's spouse may also be eligible if the veteran is listed as missing in action or is a prisoner of war.

VA Guaranty

VA guaranty amount:
- Depends on loan amount
- Covers only part of loan amount

One of the essential characteristics of VA loans is that they are guaranteed by the U.S. government. Because the government guarantees part of the loan amount, the lender's risk of loss in case of default is significantly reduced. Without the guaranty, lenders would be unwilling to make a no-downpayment loan.

Entitlement: guaranty amount available to particular veteran

The VA guaranty doesn't cover the entire loan amount; only a portion of it is guaranteed. The guaranty amount available to a particular veteran is sometimes called the vet's **entitlement**. VA regulations establish the amount of the guaranty, the vet's personal liability in the event of default, and how the vet's guaranty entitlement can be restored.

Guaranty Amount

The guaranty amount has increased considerably over the years to keep pace with rising housing costs:

The World War II guaranty was $4,000;
it was increased on September 1, 1951, to $7,500;
it was increased on May 7, 1968, to $12,500;
it was increased on December 31, 1974, to $17,500;
it was increased on October 1, 1978, to $25,000;
it was increased on October 1, 1980, to $27,500;
it was increased on February 1, 1988, to $36,000;
it was increased on January 1, 1990, to a maximum of $46,000;
it was increased on August 25, 1995 to a maximum of $50,750; and
it was increased on July 14, 2003 to a maximum of $60,000.

Most recently, the maximum guaranty amount was increased on December 10, 2004. The maximum is no longer a fixed amount; instead, it is equal to 25% of the Freddie Mac conforming loan limit for a single-family residence, as adjusted for the year in question. Freddie Mac's loan limits change regularly; for 2006, the conforming loan limit for a single-family residence is $417,000. Therefore, the maximum VA loan guaranty amount for 2006 is 25% of $417,000—or $104,250.

However, not all borrowers get the maximum guaranty amount. As the following chart indicates, the amount of the guaranty available for a particular loan depends on the loan amount.

Loan Amount	Guaranty Amount
Up to $45,000	50% of loan amount
$45,001 - $56,250	$22,500
$56,251 - $144,000	40% of loan amount, up to a maximum of $36,000
Over $144,000	25% of loan amount, up to a maximum of 25% of the Freddie Mac conforming loan limit for single-family residences

Examples:

1. $75,000 Loan amount between $56,251 and $144,000
   × 40% (Guaranty is 40% of loan amount, up to $36,000)
   $30,000 Guaranty amount

2. $125,000 Loan amount between $56,251 and $144,000
   × 40% (Guaranty is 40% of loan amount, up to $36,000)
   $50,000 40% of loan amount (exceeds $36,000)
   $36,000 Guaranty amount

3. $300,000 Loan amount over $144,000
   × 25% (Guaranty is 25% of loan amount, up to $104,250*)
   $75,000 Guaranty amount

4. $450,000 Loan amount over $144,000
   × 25% (Guaranty is 25% of loan amount, up to $104,250*)
   $112,500 25% of loan amount (exceeds $104,250)
   $104,250 Guaranty amount

---

* 2006 maximum guaranty.

A veteran's guaranty entitlement doesn't expire. The entitlement is available until it is used by the veteran or by his or her surviving spouse.

Full entitlement restored when vet pays off loan

If a veteran borrower sells the property that he or she financed with a VA loan, and is able to repay the loan in full from the proceeds of the sale, full guaranty entitlement is **restored**. (Restoration of entitlement is also referred to as reinstatement.)

VA rules also allow for a one-time restoration of entitlement to a vet who pays off a VA loan without selling the property. So the vet could keep the first property and use his or her restored entitlement to obtain a second VA loan to buy a new home. (The vet would have to occupy the newly purchased home, because of the VA's owner-occupancy requirement.) This is permitted only once, however; after that, if the vet wants to obtain another VA loan, entitlement won't be restored without selling the property.

The Veteran's Liability

The VA guaranty doesn't relieve the borrower of personal liability for the VA loan. If the veteran fails to make the payments, the lender can foreclose on the property and demand reimbursement from the government for the amount of any loss, up to the guaranty amount. In turn, the veteran may be required to repay the VA the amount that the VA paid to the lender. However, for loans closed on or after January 1, 1990, repayment after default is required only if the veteran was guilty of fraud, misrepresentation, or bad faith.

If VA reimburses lender for loss (up to guaranty amount):

- Vet may have to repay VA
- Vet may still be liable to lender for uncovered loss

When the VA requires the veteran to repay the amount that the VA paid the lender, the amount owed constitutes a delinquent federal debt. The veteran's income tax refunds can be applied to it, and any federal pay owed to the veteran can be garnished. The vet isn't eligible for any further federal loans until arrangements to repay the debt are made.

Also, if the lender's foreclosure loss is not fully covered by the guaranty amount, the veteran may still be liable to the lender for the uncovered amount. So in certain cases the vet is liable to the lender as well as the VA after foreclosure.

Liability After Assumption. A VA loan can be assumed by anyone—veteran or non-veteran—as long as he or she is creditworthy. A loan that closed prior to March 1, 1988 may be assumed without approval from the lender or VA. However, if the loan closed on or after March 1, 1988, the original borrower must obtain a release of liability from the VA when the home is sold (see below). Without this release, the original borrower continues to be liable for the rest of the loan term, even though the property has been transferred and the foreclosure occurs because of the default of a subsequent owner.

Unless vet obtains release, liability to VA continues after assumption

> **Example:** Suppose Kirby gets a VA loan. Seven years later, he sells the property and Swanson, the buyer, assumes the loan; Kirby does not obtain a release from the VA. Two years after that, Swanson defaults and the VA reimburses the lender for its losses. Kirby is still liable to the VA for the amount it paid to the lender on default.

Release of Liability. The VA will release the original borrower from liability at the time of a sale and assumption if the following conditions are met:

1. The loan must be current.
2. The purchaser must be an acceptable credit risk.
3. The purchaser must assume the veteran's obligations and liabilities on the loan (including the obligation to repay the VA for any amount paid to the lender upon foreclosure). The assumption of obligations must be evidenced by a written agreement, as specified by the VA.
4. The veteran must request a release of liability from the VA.

Too often these steps are neglected, and a veteran closes a sale without submitting a request for a release of liability to the VA. In that case, it may be difficult or even impossible for the veteran to obtain a release later on.

Substitution of Entitlement

After an assumption, even if the veteran (the original borrower) is released from liability, the veteran's entitlement is not automatically restored. Guaranty entitlement is only restored—making it possible for the vet to obtain another VA loan—under certain conditions. The buyer who assumes the original loan must be an eligible veteran with entitlement equal to (or greater than) the loan's guaranty amount, and must agree to substitute his or her entitlement for the original borrower's. In addition, the loan payments must be current, and the assumptor must be an acceptable credit risk. If these conditions are

Vet's full entitlement restored after assumption only if buyer is also veteran and agrees to substitution of entitlement met, the parties can formally request a substitution of entitlement from the VA.

Remaining Entitlement

After VA loan assumed by non-veteran, veteran may have some remaining entitlement

A veteran who arranges for his or her VA loan to be assumed by a non-veteran can't have full entitlement restored. Even so, the veteran may still have **remaining entitlement** (also called partial entitlement) that can be used to get another VA loan. Someone who obtained a VA loan several years ago is likely to have remaining entitlement now, because the maximum available guaranty has increased.

Amount of remaining entitlement: difference between $36,000 or $104,250 and guaranty amount used on prior loan

The amount of remaining entitlement the vet can use for a new loan depends on the loan amount. If the new loan amount is $144,000 or less, the remaining entitlement is determined by subtracting the amount of entitlement used on the original loan from $36,000. If the new loan amount is over $144,000, then the amount of entitlement used is subtracted from 25% of the conforming loan limit (in 2006, that means it's subtracted from $104,250).

> **Example:** Andrea Jordan obtained a VA loan in 1987 and used the maximum guaranty then available, $27,500. Jordan sold her old home and allowed the non-veteran buyer to assume her VA loan. Now she's ready to buy a new home and wants another VA loan.
>
> If Jordan wants to borrow $144,000 or less, her remaining entitlement is $8,500.
>
> | | |
> |---:|---|
> | $36,000 | Basis for calculation of remaining entitlement |
> | – 27,500 | Guaranty on existing loan |
> | $8,500 | Remaining entitlement to be used for new loan |
>
> If Jordan wants to borrow more than $144,000, her remaining entitlement is $76,750.
>
> | | |
> |---:|---|
> | $104,250 | Basis for calculation of remaining entitlement |
> | – 27,500 | Guaranty on existing loan |
> | $76,750 | Remaining entitlement to be used for new loan |
>
> Keep in mind that even though Jordan has up to $76,750 in remaining entitlement for a loan amount over $144,000, the guaranty for these larger loans can't exceed 25% of the loan amount. (See the guaranty chart earlier in the chapter.) For instance, Jordan's guaranty for a $200,000 loan would be $50,000.

Remaining entitlement is generally used only when the veteran has sold the property for which the earlier loan was obtained without paying that loan off, since VA loans require owner occupancy. A veteran who had a previous VA loan and isn't certain whether he or she has any remaining entitlement should call the local VA office. The veteran will need the VA's identifying numbers for the original loan.

Entitlement and Co-Ownership

If both a husband and wife are veterans with guaranty entitlements, when they buy a home together, they can't combine their entitlements to increase the guaranty amount for their VA loan. For example, if they're buying a $360,000 home, the guaranty is still only $90,000 (25% of $360,000). Either spouse can use his or her entitlement for the loan, or they can each contribute part of their entitlement.

Co-ownership:
- Even if buyers are both eligible veterans, maximum guaranty is not increased
- If veteran buys home with non-veteran other than spouse, guaranty only covers vet's half of the loan

If a veteran uses a VA loan to buy a home with a non-veteran who isn't his or her spouse, the guaranty is based only on the veteran's portion of the loan. The guaranty doesn't cover the non-veteran's portion. For example, suppose two brothers are purchasing a home together. Only one brother is a veteran. If they're borrowing $160,000, the amount of the guaranty will be $36,000—the guaranty amount for an $80,000 loan.

Refinancing with a VA Loan

VA loan can be used to refinance any existing loan

A VA loan can be used to refinance an existing conventional or FHA loan or seller financing, or to refinance another VA loan. If the new VA loan is used to refinance an existing VA loan (to take advantage of lower interest rates, or to replace an ARM with a fixed-rate loan), the loan amount is limited to the balance of the old loan plus the closing costs, up to two discount points, a 0.5% funding fee, and up to $6,000 for energy-efficient improvements. Use of additional entitlement is not required.

If the VA loan is used to refinance an existing loan that is not a VA loan, guaranty entitlement must be used. The VA loan generally can't exceed 90% of the appraised value of the property, plus a 2.15% funding fee (2.4% for Reserves or National Guard) and up to $6,000 for energy-efficient improvements.* In some cases, the veteran may receive cash from the proceeds of the new loan.

> **Example:** Lieutenant Colonel James Nelson owns a house encumbered by a $220,000 conventional mortgage. Nelson applies for a VA loan to refinance the property, and obtains an appraisal

* If the veteran has used his or her entitlement before, the funding fee is 3.3%. This is true for both veterans of the regular military and the Reserves or National Guard.

indicating the property is worth $270,000. Ninety percent of $270,000 is $243,000. The funding fee (2.15% of $243,000) is an additional $5,225. Nelson obtains a VA loan for $248,225 (90% of the appraised value, plus the funding fee) and applies the proceeds as follows:

$248,225	Loan
220,000	Payoff of existing loan
5,225	Funding fee
− 3,725	Closing costs
$19,275	Cash to veteran

Exercise No. 1

John Woods was on active duty in the U.S. Navy from December 2, 1990 until June 2, 1991, the full period for which he was called. He left the Navy with an honorable discharge. It's now 2006, and Woods wants to buy his first home. He has submitted an application for a $325,000 VA-guaranteed loan.

1. Is Woods eligible for a VA-guaranteed loan? If so, based on 2006 guaranty amounts, what is the amount of his entitlement?

2. If Woods gets a $325,000 loan, how much of the loan will the VA guarantee?

VA Loan Amounts

Although there is no maximum VA loan amount, the loan may not exceed the appraised value of the property. A VA-approved appraiser appraises the property, and the VA issues a **Notice of Value** (NOV) (also referred to as a Certificate of Reasonable Value, or CRV) that indicates the appraised value.

The only other restrictions on the loan amount come from the lender, not the VA. Most lenders require the veteran's guaranty entitlement to equal at least 25% of the loan amount. Since the maximum guaranty amount is 25% of the conforming loan limit, most lenders will not loan more than the conforming loan limit ($417,000 in 2006) without a downpayment.

VA loan amount:
- VA does not set maximum
- Lenders require guaranty to equal 25% of loan amount
- No-downpayment loan over $417,000 unlikely

$104,250	Maximum guaranty amount
÷ 25%	Percentage of loan amount
$417,000	Maximum loan amount

Making a Downpayment

A veteran who wants a VA loan larger than $417,000 can make a downpayment. The lender will require the downpayment plus the guaranty amount to equal 25% of the loan amount.

For loan over $417,000, guaranty + downpayment should equal 25% of sales price

Example: Robert Mendez wants to buy a home that has been valued at $450,000. He has the full entitlement of $104,250, but his lender will not make a loan for more than $417,000 unless Mendez makes a downpayment.

$450,000	Sales price
× 25%	Desired ratio of guaranty + downpayment to price
$112,500	25% of loan amount
– 104,250	Maximum guaranty
$8,250	Downpayment required by lender

$450,000	Sales price
– 8,250	Downpayment
$441,750	Loan amount

If the veteran only has partial entitlement left, making a downpayment becomes even more important.

Example: Marcia Riggs wants to buy a home for $215,000; the appraised value is $216,000. Her remaining entitlement is $32,000.

$215,000	Sales price
× 25%	Desired ratio of guaranty + downpayment to price
$53,750	
– 32,000	Remaining entitlement
$21,750	Downpayment required by lender

$215,000	Sales price
– 21,750	Downpayment
$193,250	Loan amount

Secondary Financing

Vet who needs downpayment may use secondary financing
- Combined loans may not exceed NOV
- Buyer must qualify for combined payment
- Interest rate on second can't exceed rate on VA loan

If the veteran doesn't have enough cash for a downpayment, he or she can finance part or all of it if the following conditions are met:

1. the total of all financing does not exceed the appraised value of the property (established by the NOV);
2. the buyer has enough income to qualify based on the payments required for both loans;
3. there are no more stringent conditions connected with the second loan than apply to the VA loan (for example, the second loan must be assumable by a creditworthy buyer); and
4. the interest rate on the second loan may exceed the interest rate on the VA loan, but cannot exceed industry standards for second mortgage interest rates.

Secondary financing is useful as a means of generating enough cash for the downpayment or closing costs, or when the interest rate on the secondary financing is lower than the interest rate on the VA loan.

Exercise No. 2

In each of the following cases, assume that it's 2006, the prospective borrower is an eligible veteran, and the lender follows the 25% rule explained above.

1. Jeffrey Bates has never had a VA loan before. He wants to buy a home with an appraised value of $259,000. What is the largest loan the lender will offer him? How much of a downpayment would he be required to make for that loan? How much would the guaranty be?

2. Helena Moreau wants to buy a home for $425,000 (the appraised value is $426,500). What is the largest loan the lender will offer

her? How much of a downpayment would she be required to make for that loan? How much would the guaranty be?

3. Ben Jessell bought a home with a VA loan in 1987. He recently sold the home, and the non-veteran buyer assumed the loan. The guaranty on that loan is $36,000. Now Jessell wants to buy a new home for $382,000. How much remaining entitlement does he have if he chooses to finance this transaction with a VA loan? How much of a downpayment will the lender require Jessell to make?

Underwriting Guidelines

Lenders use the guidelines established by the Department of Veterans Affairs when analyzing a veteran's creditworthiness. Many of the net worth and credit guidelines are identical to the general qualifying principles discussed in Chapter 8. However, the guidelines for analyzing income are quite different from those used for conventional or FHA loans.

A VA loan applicant's income is analyzed using two different methods: the income ratio method and the residual income method. The vet must qualify under both methods.

Two methods of income analysis for VA loans:
- Income ratio
- Residual income (cash flow)

Income Ratio Analysis

Like conventional and FHA underwriting, underwriting for VA loans involves an income ratio method of analysis. But instead of using both a housing expense to income ratio and total obligations to income ratio, the VA uses only a total obligations to income ratio. As a general rule, a VA borrower's total obligations to income ratio should not exceed **41%**. Installment debts with 10 or more payments

Total obligations to income ratio generally should not exceed 41%

remaining are taken into account in calculating the ratio, along with the borrower's other recurring obligations.

> **Example:** Robin Young is eligible for a VA loan. She and her husband, Mike Appleton, have a combined income of $6,000 per month. Their monthly obligations, not including housing expense, add up to $1,030.
>
> | | |
> |---:|---|
> | $6,000 | Monthly income |
> | × 41% | Maximum total obligations to income ratio |
> | $2,460 | |
> | − 1,030 | Monthly recurring obligations |
> | $1,430 | Maximum housing expense (PITI) |
>
> Young and Appleton could qualify for a $1,430 monthly housing expense under the total obligations to income ratio.

Residual Income Analysis

Residual income = gross monthly income minus taxes, recurring obligations & housing expense

The second method used to qualify a VA loan applicant is residual income analysis, which is also called cash flow analysis. For this analysis, the proposed housing expense, all other recurring obligations, and certain taxes are subtracted from the veteran's gross monthly income to determine his or her **residual income**. (The taxes include federal income tax, any state or local income tax, social security tax, Medicare tax, and any other taxes deducted from the veteran's paychecks.) The vet's residual income usually should be at least one dollar more than the VA's minimum requirement. The minimum requirement varies based on the region of the country where the veteran lives, family size, and the size of the proposed loan, as shown in Figure 12.1.

> **Example:** Continuing with the previous example, suppose Robin Young and Mike Appleton have two children and live in the VA's Midwest region. They're planning to buy a home that costs more than $80,000. To meet the VA's guidelines, they should have at least $1,003 in residual income (see Figure 12.1).
>
> | | |
> |---:|---|
> | $6,000 | Gross monthly income |
> | 1,100 | Federal income tax withheld |
> | 250 | State income tax withheld |
> | 460 | Social security and Medicare withheld |
> | 1,030 | Recurring obligations |
> | − 1,430 | Maximum housing expense (from 41% ratio) |
> | $1,730 | Residual income |

Fig. 12.1 Minimum residual income requirements for VA loan applicants

Table of Residual Incomes by Region
For loan amounts of $79,999 and below

Family Size	Northeast	Midwest	South	West
1	$390	$382	$382	$425
2	$654	$641	$641	$713
3	$788	$772	$772	$859
4	$888	$868	$868	$967
5	$921	$902	$902	$1,004

Over 5: Add $75 for each additional member up to a family of 7.

Table of Residual Incomes by Region
For loan amounts of $80,000 and above

Family Size	Northeast	Midwest	South	West
1	$450	$441	$441	$491
2	$755	$738	$738	$823
3	$909	$889	$889	$990
4	$1,025	$1,003	$1,003	$1,117
5	$1,062	$1,039	$1,039	$1,158

Over 5: Add $80 for each additional member up to a family of 7.

Since Young and Appleton's residual income is well above the $1,003 requirement, they can easily qualify for a VA loan with a $1,430 monthly payment (PITI). In fact, because their residual income exceeds the required minimum by so much, they may be able to qualify for a larger payment than that (see below).

Compensating Factors

The VA emphasizes that the 41% income ratio and the figures on the residual income chart are only guidelines, and failure to meet them shouldn't automatically result in rejection of the loan application. For instance, although residual income is a very important factor in evaluating a VA loan application, the loan may still be approved even if the applicant's residual income is less than the minimum shown on the chart, if there are compensating factors. The chart merely helps the underwriter judge the applicant's relative strength or weakness in regard to residual income.

VA underwriting standards are merely guidelines, not hard and fast rules

Compensating factors may allow loan approval in spite of marginal income or other weakness

The VA lists all of the following as examples of compensating factors which can help a loan application that is weak in certain respects:

1. an excellent long-term credit history;
2. conservative use of consumer credit;
3. minimal consumer debt;
4. long-term employment;
5. significant liquid assets;
6. a downpayment;
7. little or no increase in the housing expense;
8. military benefits;
9. satisfactory previous experience with home ownership;
10. high residual income;
11. a low total obligations to income ratio.

The VA points out that a particular compensating factor helps only if it's relevant to the particular weakness in the loan application. For example, if the applicant's residual income is slightly below the VA's minimum, significant liquid assets are a relevant compensating factor, because the family could draw on the liquid assets to supplement their income. On the other hand, long-term employment isn't relevant. The fact that the applicant has an exceptionally stable employment history strengthens the application in a general sense, but it doesn't specifically address the issue of marginal residual income—whether the applicant's family will have enough money to live on after paying all the bills. Without any compensating factors that are relevant to marginal income, the underwriter will probably reject the application, in spite of the applicant's good employment history.

If residual income exceeds minimum by 20% or more, loan can be approved even though vet's income ratio is over 41%, without any other compensating factors

Income Ratio Exceptions. The VA has specific rules for approving a loan to an applicant whose income ratio is above 41%. The lender is generally required to submit a detailed statement to the VA listing the relevant compensating factors that justify loan approval in spite of the high income ratio, such as significant liquid assets, a substantial downpayment, or more residual income than the minimum requirement.

Extra residual income is especially helpful. If the applicant's residual income is at least 20% over the required minimum, the lender can approve the loan (in spite of a high income ratio) without any other compensating factors, and without submitting a statement of justification to the VA.

Example: Refer back to the previous example. With a $1.430 proposed housing expense (based on the 41% income ratio), Young and Appleton have residual income of $1,730. This is $727 more than the VA's required minimum of $1,003 for a family of four in the Midwest region.

$1,730	Residual income (with $1,430 housing expense)
– 1,003	Required minimum residual income
$727	Residual income in excess of required minimum

Since Young and Appleton's residual income exceeds the minimum, the next step is to apply the 20% rule—to determine if their residual income exceeds the required minimum by 20% or more.

$1,003	Required minimum residual income
× 20%	
$201	20% of required minimum

Young and Appleton's extra $727 in residual income exceeds the minimum by much more than 20%. So a lender would probably be willing to qualify Young and Appleton for a larger monthly housing expense than the $1,430 maximum calculated with the 41% total obligations to income ratio. For example, if the lender were willing to accept a 45% income ratio, then the couple could qualify for a $1,670 monthly payment:

$6,000	Monthly income
× 45%	Total obligations to income ratio
$2,700	
– 1,030	Recurring obligations
$1,670	Maximum housing expense (PITI)

By qualifying for a $1,670 mortgage payment with the 45% income ratio, Young and Appleton would be able to buy a more expensive home than they could have if the 41% income ratio had limited them to a $1,430 payment.

Overall, the VA's qualifying rules are much more liberal than the Fannie Mae/Freddie Mac rules. A borrower who would be considered marginal for a conventional loan might easily qualify for a VA-guaranteed loan. Eligible veterans should always keep VA financing in mind.

Exercise No. 3

Vince Martin, a former marine, is eligible for a VA loan; he hasn't used any of his entitlement yet. He and his wife, Cheryl, have four children, and they live in the VA's Western region. They have found a home that they would like to buy.

The Martins apply for a VA loan, and the NOV establishes the appraised value of the home as $187,000. The Martins' gross monthly income is $5,200. The withheld taxes come to $1,325 per month. Their recurring obligations (not counting housing expenses) come to $807 per month.

If the Martins don't make a downpayment, and if the lender is charging 7% interest, the monthly housing expense for this transaction would be approximately $1,393. (That includes a principal and interest payment of $1,244, plus 12% for estimated property taxes and hazard insurance. Mortgage insurance is not required.)

Could the Martins qualify for this housing expense?

Outline: VA-Guaranteed Loans

I. Characteristics of VA Loans
   A. VA loan is made by institutional lender, but a portion of loan amount is guaranteed by the Department of Veterans Affairs.
      1. Loan guaranty functions like mortgage insurance, protecting the lender against a loss in the event of buyer default.
   B. VA loan can be used for purchase or construction of residence with up to four units.
      1. Veteran must occupy the home (or one of the units in a multi-family residence).
   C. Key characteristics of a VA loan:
      1. No downpayment required, as long as loan does not exceed home's appraised value.
      2. No maximum loan amount; no maximum income limits.
      3. No mortgage insurance required.
      4. No prepayment penalty allowed.
      5. Forbearance extended to borrowers with temporary financial difficulties.
      6. May be assumed by a veteran or a non-veteran.
   D. VA borrowers pay a funding fee ranging from 1.25% to 3.3% of the loan amount, depending on the downpayment, the type of service, and whether the veteran is a first-time VA borrower.

II. Eligibility for VA Loans
   A. Eligibility depends on the length of continuous active duty in the U.S. armed forces.
   B. Minimum requirements:
      1. 90 days of active duty during WWII, Korean War, or Vietnam War; *or*
      2. 181 days of active duty during peacetime periods following WWII, Korean War, or Vietnam War; *or*
      3. either two years or the full period of time called to active duty (at least 90 days during wartime and 181 days during peacetime), if service began after Sept. 7, 1980 (enlisted) or after October 16, 1981 (officers); *or*
      4. six years of service in the Reserves or National Guard.

C. Shorter period of service required for disabled veterans or veterans discharged early for government, hardship, or medical reasons.

D. An eligible veteran is issued a Certificate of Eligibility, which the vet uses to apply for a VA loan.

E. The spouse of a veteran who was killed in action, died of service-related injuries, or is listed as missing in action or as a prisoner of war, may be eligible for a VA loan.

III. VA Guaranty

A. Guaranty available to a particular veteran is known as the veteran's "entitlement."

1. Guaranty available for a particular loan depends on the size of the loan.

2. Maximum guaranty (for loan amounts over $144,000) is 25% of the current Freddie Mac conforming loan limit; current maximum guaranty is $104,250.

B. Entitlement may be restored (and then reused) if veteran pays off loan in full.

C. VA loan may be assumed by a veteran or non-veteran.

1. If loan closed on or after March 1, 1988, original borrower must request and obtain a release of liability from the VA; otherwise the original borrower remains liable on the loan.

2. Generally, VA will issue release as long as loan is current and buyer is acceptable credit risk.

3. If loan is assumed by a veteran, the original borrower's entitlement is restored.

D. If spouses are both veterans, they cannot combine their entitlements to increase the guaranty amount for a single VA loan.

E. If a veteran buys a home with a non-veteran, the guaranty only applies to the veteran's portion of the loan.

F. VA loan may be used to refinance an existing VA loan without using additional entitlement.

1. If used to refinance a non-VA loan, entitlement must be used. Veteran may receive cash from the proceeds of the new loan.

IV. VA Loan Amounts

A. No maximum VA loan amount, but the loan may not exceed the property's appraised value.

1. VA-approved appraiser appraises the property; VA issues a Notice of Value (NOV).

B. Most lenders require guaranty to equal 25% of the loan amount.
   1. With a current maximum guaranty amount of $104,250, most lenders won't lend more than $417,000 without a downpayment.
C. If VA loan is larger than $417,000, borrower must make a downpayment to make up the difference between the maximum guaranty amount and 25% of the loan amount.
D. Borrower can finance part or all of a downpayment, as long as:
   1. total financing doesn't exceed property's appraised value;
   2. buyer's income is enough to qualify based on payments for both loans;
   3. conditions attached to the second loan are no more stringent than the conditions on the VA loan; and
   4. the interest rate on the second loan doesn't exceed industry standards for second mortgage interest rates.

V. Underwriting Guidelines
   A. Applicant must qualify under both methods of income analysis: income ratio and residual income.
   B. In the income ratio method, the borrower's total obligations are measured against income. The total obligations to income ratio should be 41% or less.
   C. In the residual income method, the borrower's proposed housing expense, recurring obligations, and certain taxes are subtracted from the gross monthly income to determine the residual income. The residual income should exceed the VA's minimum requirement, which is determined by the borrower's location, family size, and proposed loan size.
   D. The income ratio and residual income methods of analysis are only guidelines; if a borrower does not qualify under one of them, the loan may still be approved.
      1. Compensating factors include: good credit history, minimal debt, long-term employment, significant liquid assets, downpayment, high residual income, and a low income ratio.
      2. If the applicant's income ratio exceeds 41% but the residual income is at least 20% over the required minimum, the lender may approve the loan without any compensating factors.

Key Terms

VA: The U.S. Department of Veterans Affairs.

VA-guaranteed loan: A home loan to an eligible veteran made by an institutional lender and guaranteed by the Department of Veterans Affairs, protecting the lender against losses resulting from default.

VA guaranty: The portion of a VA loan guaranteed by the Department of Veterans Affairs; the maximum amount that the VA will pay the lender for a loss resulting from the borrower's default.

Funding fee: A charge paid by a VA borrower at closing, which the lender submits to the VA.

Certificate of Eligibility: A document issued by the Department of Veterans Affairs, indicating a veteran's eligibility for a VA-guaranteed loan.

VA entitlement: The guaranty amount to which a particular veteran is entitled.

Substitution of entitlement: When a VA borrower sells the security property to another eligible veteran, who agrees to substitute his or her guaranty entitlement for the seller's, so that the seller's entitlement is restored.

Notice of Value (NOV): A document issued by the Department of Veterans Affairs, setting forth a property's current market value, based on a VA-approved appraisal. Previously referred to as a Certificate of Reasonable Value.

Residual income: The amount of income that an applicant for a VA loan has left over after taxes, recurring obligations, and the proposed housing expense have been deducted from his or her gross monthly income.

Chapter Quiz

1. Because the VA guarantees the loan:
   a. the veteran borrower is not obligated to repay it
   b. lenders are willing to make no-downpayment loans
   c. a VA loan cannot be assumed by a non-veteran
   d. the veteran is entitled to at least two such loans

2. If a veteran allows his or her VA loan to be assumed, the vet's entitlement can be restored only if:
   a. the assumptor is a veteran with entitlement
   b. the loan payments are current
   c. the original borrower formally requests a substitution of entitlement
   d. All of the above

3. Which of the following is *not* true of a VA loan?
   a. A small prepayment penalty is allowed
   b. Owner occupancy is required
   c. The loan amount can't exceed the appraised value of the property
   d. No mortgage insurance is required

4. If a veteran with full entitlement wanted to obtain a $325,000 loan, how much would the required downpayment be?
   a. No downpayment is required
   b. $3,250
   c. $2,479
   d. $1,112

5. A veteran may obtain a VA-guaranteed loan on a:
   a. single-family residence only
   b. four-plex, as long as all units are rented out
   c. residence with up to two units, as long as the veteran occupies one unit
   d. one- to four-unit residence, as long as the veteran occupies one unit

6. Martha Jones served in the army on active duty for 120 days in 1989. Jones is:

   a. eligible for full VA entitlement
   b. eligible for partial VA entitlement
   c. eligible for a VA loan only if she meets the underwriting standards
   d. not eligible for a VA loan

7. If Ryan Spar gets a $132,000 VA loan, how much of the loan will the VA guaranty?

   a. $24,800
   b. $32,800
   c. $36,000
   d. $5,500

8. The VA allows secondary financing to be used in conjunction with a VA-guaranteed loan if:

   a. the total amount financed does not exceed the appraised value
   b. the buyer's income is sufficient to qualify for the payments on both loans
   c. the interest rate on the second does not exceed the industry standards for second mortgage interest rates
   d. All of the above

9. In 1992, Sam Walters obtained a VA loan with a $46,000 guaranty. A few years ago he sold his house and allowed a non-veteran to assume the VA loan. Now it's 2006 and Sam wants to borrow $260,000 to buy a new home. How much remaining entitlement does he have?

   a. None
   b. $58,250
   c. $65,000
   d. $104,250

10. Unless there are compensating factors, a VA loan applicant's total obligations to income ratio usually should not exceed:

    a. 36%
    b. 33%
    c. 41%
    d. 53%

Answer Key

1. b. The government's guaranty reduces the lender's risk of loss in case of default by the buyer. Because of this, lenders are willing to make loans without a downpayment from the buyer.

2. d. If a VA loan is assumed by another veteran, the new borrower may agree to substitute his or her entitlement for the original borrower's entitlement. If the loan's payments are current, the new borrower is qualified, and the parties obtain a substitution of entitlement from the VA, the original borrower's entitlement will be restored.

3. a. No prepayment penalties are allowed with VA loans.

4. a. Currently, most lenders will lend up to $417,000 without a downpayment. As long as the loan doesn't exceed the property's appraised value, the veteran won't need to make a downpayment.

5. d. A VA loan must be used for a one- to four-unit residence, and the veteran must occupy one of the units.

6. d. For service that began after September 8, 1980 but before August 2, 1990 (when the Persian Gulf War period began), eligibility requires a minimum of 181 days of continuous active duty. Since Jones only served 120 days in 1989, she isn't eligible for a VA loan, even if that was the full period she was required on active duty.

7. c. For a loan amount between $56,251 and $144,000, the VA guaranty amount is 40% of the loan amount, up to a maximum of $36,000. Forty percent of $132,000 is $52,800, so the guaranty amount would be $36,000.

8. d. A VA borrower may finance a downpayment if the total amount financed doesn't exceed the property's appraised value, the buyer's income is enough to qualify for payments on both loans, the conditions on the second aren't more stringent than those attached to the VA loan, and the interest rate on the second doesn't exceed industry standards.

9. b. Sam's remaining entitlement is calculated by subtracting the previously used entitlement, $46,000, from $104,250 (25% of the conforming loan limit). Sam's remaining entitlement is $58,250.

10. c. A VA loan applicant's total obligations to income ratio generally should not exceed 41% unless there are compensating factors, such as a large residual income amount.

Case Study: Qualifying the Buyer
VA-Guaranteed Loans

Once again, let's return to Rick and Teresa Cortina. This time we'll assume that they're thinking of buying their first home with a VA loan. (Rick served in the Army for three years, from 1999 to 2001, and his service included more than 24 months' continuous active duty. He received an honorable discharge.) Refer back to the case study at the end of Chapter 10 for the information you will need about the Cortinas' financial situation.

Interest rates:

Lenders in your area are generally charging the following interest rates on VA loans:

Fixed rate: 6.75% interest, 1% origination fee, no discount points
ARM: 5.5% interest, 1% origination fee, no discount points

Using the worksheet to help you with the calculations, answer the following questions. The Cortinas live in the VA's Southern region, and they have no children.

1. Apply the standard VA income ratio to the Cortinas' monthly income to determine a maximum mortgage payment figure (PITI).

2. Calculate how much residual income the Cortinas would have if they had the monthly housing expense you arrived at in question 1.

3. Compare the Cortinas' residual income to the VA's required minimum. Could they qualify for a larger mortgage payment than the payment you arrived at in question 1? What's the largest payment they could qualify for if they were allowed a 45% total obligations ratio? If approximately 12% of that payment would go toward property taxes and insurance, calculate the maximum principal and interest payment.

4. Based on the principal and interest payment that you calculated in question 3, the maximum VA loan that the Cortinas could qualify for at 6.75% interest is approximately $292,556. Using 2005 guaranty amounts, how much would the VA guaranty be for this loan amount?

5. How much cash would the Cortinas need at closing for this loan? They would have to pay the origination fee and the funding fee. Assume that they'd also have to pay other closing costs adding up to about 2% of the loan amount.

6. Are the Cortinas likely to choose a VA loan over a conventional loan or an FHA loan? Why or why not?

Income Qualifying—VA-Guaranteed Loans

Taxes (per month)

________	Federal income tax
________	
________	State income tax
________	Social security/Medicare
+ ________	Other
________	Total

Recurring Charges

Car loans	________
Credit cards	________
Student loans	________
Other loans	________
Child care	________
Child support	________
Alimony	________
Other	+ ________
Total	________

Gross Monthly Income

Base salary	
Wage earner 1	________
Wage earner 2	________
Overtime	________
Commissions	________
Bonuses	________
Other	+ ________
Total	________

Obligations to Income Ratio

________	Gross monthly income
x 41%	Standard maximum ratio
________	Maximum obligations
– ________	Recurring obligations
________	Maximum mortgage payment (PITI) under the 41% income ratio

Income Qualifying—VA-Guaranteed Loans

Residual Income Analysis

________	Gross monthly income
________	Taxes
________	Recurring obligations
– ________	Proposed housing expense (from 41% ratio)
________	**Residual Income**
– ________	Minimum residual income*
________	Residual income in excess of minimum

________	Minimum residual income
x 20%	
________	20% of minimum residual income

If applicant's residual income exceeds the minimum by more than 20%, a larger mortgage payment amount may be approved (exceeding 41% income ratio), even without any compensating factors.

Maximum Mortgage Payment (PITI) ________

________	Maximum PITI payment
÷ 112%	(less 12% for property taxes and hazard insurance)
________	Maximum principal and interest payment

Interest rate ________

Maximum Loan Amount ________

Loan amount is sales price, unless downpayment required.

* See Figure 12.1 for minimum residual income requirements.

Chapter 13
Seller Financing

How Seller Financing Works

When and Why Seller Financing is Used

Seller Seconds

- Supplementing a new loan
- Supplementing an assumption

Seller Financing as Primary Financing

- Unencumbered property
  - Protecting seller's security
  - Seller financing plus institutional second
  - Land contracts
- Encumbered property: wraparound financing
  - Wraparound vs. assumption plus seller second
  - Protecting a wraparound buyer

Alternatives to Seller Financing

- Buydowns
- Contributions to closing costs
- Equity exchanges
- Lease arrangements

Agent's Responsibilities in Seller-Financed Transactions

- Disclosures
- Liability

Introduction

Institutional lenders are not the only source of residential financing; home sellers are another important source. The wide variety of ways in which a seller can finance a buyer's purchase is the subject of this chapter.

We will begin with a basic explanation of how seller financing works and why it is used. Then we'll examine the forms seller financing can take, looking first at how it can function as secondary financing, and then at how it can function as primary financing. After that, we will briefly consider a few alternatives to seller financing—ways a seller can help the buyer without actually financing the purchase. In the last section of the chapter, we'll discuss the real estate agent's responsibilities in a seller-financed transaction.

How Seller Financing Works

Purchase money loan:
- Seller extends credit to buyer
- Buyer gives seller mortgage or deed of trust

Just like a bank or a savings and loan, a seller can use a promissory note accompanied by a mortgage or deed of trust to finance the buyer's purchase. The buyer takes title to the property and makes regular payments to the seller; the seller is the mortgagee or beneficiary, with the right to foreclose if the buyer defaults. A mortgage or deed of trust given by a buyer to a seller (instead of a third-party lender) is commonly called a **purchase money loan**.

A purchase money loan differs from an institutional loan in that the seller is simply extending credit to the buyer, rather than actually supplying loan funds. The seller finances the purchase by allowing the buyer to pay the price in installments over time, instead of requiring payment in full at closing

Land contract: alternative to purchase money loan in certain situations

For certain transactions, a seller has an alternative that institutional lenders do not have: the land contract. With a **land contract**, the buyer (vendee) takes possession of the property, but the seller (vendor) retains title until the contract price has been paid in full. Like a purchase money loan, a land contract represents an extension of credit from the seller to the buyer. We'll discuss land contracts in more detail later in this chapter.

In some transactions, seller financing is secondary financing: a "seller second" that supplements an institutional first mortgage. In other cases, the seller provides primary financing, serving as the buyer's main source or only source of financing for the purchase.

Seller financing can be secondary financing or primary financing

In a transaction that involves both institutional financing and seller financing, the seller probably will not be allowed to use a land contract. As a general rule, an institutional lender is not willing to make a loan to someone who does not have title to the security property (which is the case with the vendee in a land contract).

Aside from that consideration, a seller will usually decide which type of finance instrument to use based on the various remedies each type allows in the event of default (see Chapter 5). For instance, in most states if the seller wants to be able to foreclose without going to court, he or she would choose a deed of trust. Foreclosure laws are generally the same for a purchase money mortgage or deed of trust as for any other mortgage or deed of trust, but there may be important exceptions. For example, in some states a seller cannot obtain a deficiency judgment after foreclosure of a purchase money loan, even if it was a judicial foreclosure.

The finance instruments used in a seller-financed transaction should be prepared by a real estate lawyer, or at least reviewed by a lawyer before the parties sign them. If the seller uses a deed of trust, he or she will have to appoint a trustee when the loan documents are executed. Institutional lenders, title insurance companies, and lawyers often serve as trustees.

When and Why Seller Financing Is Used

Seller financing can:
- Attract buyers when interest rates are high
- Help buyer qualify for institutional loan
- Enable seller to charge higher price
- Provide tax benefits to seller

What's the point of seller financing? In a tight money market, somtimes the only way a seller can get the property sold is to finance part of the purchase price him or herself. When prevailing market interest rates are very high, many potential home buyers cannot qualify for institutional financing. Others decide not to buy because they aren't willing to take on an expensive institutional loan. In this situation, a seller can attract buyers by offering financing at an interest rate significantly below the market rate. Even if the seller isn't in a position to finance the entire transaction, a seller second at a lower interest rate can offset the high rate charged on the institutional loan and enable the buyer to qualify.

Although seller financing is most important when interest rates are high, it can also be used as a marketing tool at other times. In some cases, buyers are willing to pay more for a home if the seller offers financing. It may allow the buyers to avoid or reduce certain loan costs (such as the origination fee and discount fee), enabling them to close with less cash. A seller could set up a payment plan that might not be available from local lenders: graduated payments, bi-weekly payments, partial amortization with a balloon payment, or an interest-only loan with a balloon. Or the seller might be willing to extend credit to buyers who can't qualify for a conventional loan even though market interest rates are low.

> **Example:** Grandma Perkins owns her house free and clear. She has decided to move to her sister's farm, so she wants to sell her house. The Jarrells, a young couple from Grandma's church, are interested in buying it. They couldn't qualify for conventional financing, but Grandma believes they are honest and reliable people who can be trusted to pay off a loan.
>
> She offers them the following deal: a sales price of $70,000, with $2,500 down and the balance in the form of a purchase money loan, secured by a deed of trust with Grandma as the beneficiary. Interest will accrue at the rate of 5% for the first year, and increase 0.5% per year until it reaches 7%, where it will stay for the balance of the 30-year loan term. Payments are to be interest-only for the first five years, with the principal then fully amortized over the balance of the term.

Seller must evaluate risks, but is not bound by institutional lending rules

Flexibility is the keynote; the seller isn't bound by institutional policies regarding yields, loan-to-value ratios, or qualifying standards. There are risks involved in setting those standards aside, and these risks should be carefully weighed. (The unusual financing arrangement in the example above could turn out badly for both parties. See the "Agent's Responsibilities" section at the end of this chapter.) But a little extra risk may be justified if the financing arrangement allows the sale to proceed or enables the seller to get a higher price for the home.

In addition to making it easier to sell the home, seller financing can have tax benefits for the seller. Because the buyer is paying in installments over a period of years, the seller is not required to report the full profit from the sale on his or her federal income tax return in the year of the sale. Only the amount of profit actually received in a given year is considered taxable income for that year. Not only is the seller allowed to defer payment of part of the taxes, the profit from the sale may be taxed at a lower rate. (If it had been received in one lump sum, it could have pushed the seller into a higher tax bracket.)

Fig. 13.1 Summary of secondary financing rules

Secondary Financing with a Conventional First Loan

1. Total financing (the combined LTV) may not exceed 95%.
2. The second loan must have regularly scheduled payments.
3. The second loan can't require a balloon payment less than five years after closing.
4. If the first loan has variable payments, the second loan may be required to have fixed payments.
5. The second loan can't permit negative amortization.

Of course, seller financing is not an option for a seller who needs to be fully cashed out right away—for example, a seller who is planning to use all of his or her net equity from this home to buy a new one. But in many circumstances a downpayment is enough to satisfy the seller's need for cash at closing.

Now that you have a general understanding of how seller financing works and why it is used, we'll look more closely at the different forms it can take. First we'll focus on secondary financing from the seller, used in conjunction with an institutional loan. Then we'll discuss seller financing as primary financing.

Seller Seconds

Seller financing is often secondary financing. The buyer is paying most of the purchase price with an institutional loan—either by taking out a new loan, or by assuming the seller's existing loan. But instead of requiring the buyer to pay the difference between the loan amount and the purchase price in cash, the seller accepts a second mortgage for part of the remainder.

Seller second can supplement new institutional loan or assumption

In this section of the chapter, we will show how a seller second can help a buyer qualify for an institutional loan. We'll also discuss the factors that shape a seller second for a particular transaction—how much of the price the seller will finance, and on what terms. At the end of this section, we'll look at how a seller second can supplement an assumption.

Supplementing a New Loan

Seller second supplementing new loan must comply with lender's rules

When it supplements a new institutional loan, a seller second has to meet certain standards applied by the lender. If the new loan is conventional, the lender will usually apply the secondary financing rules that were explained in Chapter 6, and which are summarized in Figure 13.1. There are also specific rules for secondary financing in conjunction with FHA and VA loans (see Chapters 11 and 12).

Although the secondary financing rules impose significant limitations, many different kinds of seller seconds can comply with them. The seller second in the following example meets the requirements for secondary financing with a conventional loan on a single-family home. In the example, the institutional loan combined with a seller second is compared to an institutional loan without seller financing. This comparison demonstrates how a seller second can help a buyer qualify for an institutional loan.

> **Example:** The Bukowskis are selling their home; its appraised value is $101,000. The Fulbrights have offered to buy the house for $100,000. Setting aside enough cash for closing costs and reserves, they have about $10,000 left over for a downpayment. Market interest rates are high; the Fulbrights will have to pay 10.5% interest for a fixed-rate mortgage.
>
> If the Fulbrights applied for a 30-year, 90% conventional loan from an institutional lender, they would have to qualify for a monthly payment of approximately $945. That includes principal, interest, taxes, and hazard insurance, and also private mortgage insurance, since the LTV is over 80%.
>
> However, the Fulbrights' stable monthly income is only $3,600, and their monthly debt payments (other than their housing expenses) add up to $400. There aren't any compensating factors in their financial situation that would lead the lender to accept income ratios higher than the standard 36% and 28%. That means the highest monthly mortgage payment the Fulbrights can qualify for is $896.

$3,600	Stable monthly income
× 36%	Maximum total obligations ratio
$1,296	
– 400	Monthly debt payments
$896	Maximum allowable monthly housing expense

Thus, the 90% conventional loan is out of the Fulbrights' reach at current market rates. But suppose the Bukowskis are willing to finance part of the purchase price in order to close the sale. They agree to finance $15,000 at 8% interest; there will be monthly interest-only payments, with a balloon payment of $15,000 (the entire principal amount) due in seven years. Now the Fulbrights will only need to borrow $75,000 from an institutional lender, instead of $90,000. Here's how the transaction would work:

Downpayment: $10,000

Conventional first mortgage:
$75,000, 30-year term, 10.5% fixed interest rate
$768 monthly payment (PITI, but no mortgage insurance)

Seller second mortgage:
$15,000, 7-year term (no amortization)
8% fixed interest rate
$100 monthly interest payment
$15,000 balloon payment due after 7 years

Total monthly payment for both loans: $868

The total monthly payment for both loans will be $868, which is $77 a month less than the payment on the $90,000 conventional loan. That's enough of a difference so that the Fulbrights should be able to qualify for this combination of an institutional loan and a seller second.

The $15,000, 8%, interest-only second in the example is by no means the only one that would comply with the rules for secondary financing in conjunction with a conventional loan. The sellers could have financed a larger share of the price, charged a different interest rate, partially amortized the loan, provided for interest rate adjustments, and so on. In combining a conventional loan with a seller second (a process sometimes called "loan structuring"), several different elements can be manipulated: the relative amounts of the two loans; the downpayment amount; the amortization, term, payment schedule, and interest rate of the seller second. Taken altogether, there are dozens of combinations for financing a $100,000 single-family home with a conventional first mortgage and a seller second.

Loan structuring: combining a first mortgage with secondary financing

Of course, all combinations are not created equal. Only certain combinations will fit the financial circumstances of a particular buyer and a particular seller.

The Buyer's Situation. As the previous example suggests, two factors in a prospective buyer's financial situation shape the design of a seller second. The first is how much money the buyer has for a downpayment (after setting aside enough cash for the closing costs and the required reserves). The second factor is the total monthly payment that the buyer can qualify for.

Buyer's evaluation of first loan + seller second:
- Downpayment amount
- Combined monthly payment for both loans
- Balloon payment

In evaluating a seller second, the buyer will naturally focus on these two factors. But many seller seconds have another feature that the buyer should consider carefully: the balloon payment.

Look at the example again. This interest-only second has a low monthly payment. However, after seven years the buyers will have to come up with $15,000 to pay off the sellers. If the buyers aren't planning to keep the house that long, the balloon payment doesn't present much of a problem; they will pay it when they sell the property. Otherwise, the buyers will have to save up the amount of the balloon payment, or else refinance the property when the time comes.

> **Example:** Nearly seven years have passed, and it's almost time for the Fulbrights to make their $15,000 balloon payment to the Bukowskis. The house the Fulbrights bought is now worth about $121,000, and their equity in the property is about $34,000.
>
> The Fulbrights apply to an institutional lender for refinancing. The lender loans them $86,000 and accepts a new mortgage against the home. The Fulbrights use part of this refinance loan to make the balloon payment on the seller second, and they pay off their old conventional loan with the rest.

In many situations, it's easy to refinance, especially when the property has appreciated substantially. (In the example, the LTV for the refinance loan is only 71%.) And if interest rates have fallen, refinancing can result in lower mortgage payments. Under other circumstances, however, refinancing may be difficult to obtain or may increase the mortgage payments. Also, refinancing usually costs a few thousand dollars (for loan fees, an appraisal, and so forth).

Seller financing arrangements that require a large balloon payment often work out fine, so a buyer should not be frightened away from them. But the buyer should give some thought to where the money for the balloon payment will come from.

The Seller's Situation. When a seller evaluates different possible secondary financing arrangements, he or she has to think about cash flow and yield. How much cash is needed at closing? Will the monthly payment on the seller second be an adequate addition to his or her income? How soon does he or she need the balloon payment (if any)? Does the interest rate on the second represent a reasonable return?

The seller also has to consider the tax consequences of each possible arrangement, preferably with expert advice. Although seller financing often has tax benefits for the seller, some arrangements will backfire. For instance, a seller who offers financing at an exceptionally low interest rate may run up against the "imputed interest" rules in the federal tax code. Under those rules, if the stated interest rate on seller financing is below a specified minimum, the Internal Revenue Service will treat a portion of the principal received each year as if it were interest. In effect, the IRS treats the sale as if the seller had charged a lower price for the home, but a higher interest rate on the financing. This can have an impact on the seller's income taxes, since all of the interest on an installment sale is taxed, while only part of the principal payments are taxed. (In fact, if the seller took a loss on the sale, the principal wouldn't be taxed at all.)

Seller's evaluation of second:
- Cash at closing
- Monthly income
- Timing of payoff (balloon payment)
- Yield on investment
- Tax consequences
- Lien priority

Lien priority is another important consideration for a seller who offers secondary financing. Purchase money mortgages are subject to the same priority rules as institutional mortgages. In the event of foreclosure, the first mortgage must be paid in full from the sale proceeds before any proceeds are allocated to the second mortgage (see Chapter 5). The seller should keep this in mind when negotiating the amount of a seller second. Is the property worth enough so that the proceeds of a foreclosure sale would be likely to cover both the first and second mortgages? The seller should be especially careful when there is a possibility that property values will decline in the next few years.

Supplementing an Assumption

In some cases, a seller second can supplement the buyer's assumption of an existing mortgage on the property. The buyer will make a monthly payment to the seller, and also take over responsibility for the monthly payment the seller has been making to the lender.

> **Example:** The current market interest rate for a fixed-rate loan is 9%. The Rainwaters' property has an existing mortgage with a $125,500 balance and an 6% interest rate. The mortgage has 240 payments of $899.12 remaining.
>
> Ray McCarthy is interested in buying the Rainwaters' property and assuming their mortgage, but he does not have the $36,500 cash needed to meet the $162,000 sales price. McCarthy can make a $10,000 downpayment if the Rainwaters will take back a second deed of trust for the remaining $26,500. The Rainwaters agree to accept the second deed of trust at 8% interest (partially

amortized, with a balloon payment due in ten years), and the sale closes. Each month, McCarthy sends $899.12 to the Rainwaters' lender for the first loan, and $194.45 to the Rainwaters themselves for the second loan.

Assumption + seller second: when existing mortgage has low interest rate and no due-on-sale clause

Assumption is attractive to buyers whenever the interest rate on the seller's existing mortgage is significantly lower than market rates at the time of the sale. But an assumption is only possible if the existing mortgage does not include a due-on-sale clause, or if the lender agrees to the assumption (see Chapter 5).

Whether or not there is a due-on-sale clause, the lender's consent is always necessary if the seller wants to be released from liability on the existing mortgage. When the assumption is going to be supplemented by a seller second, the lender will scrutinize the second loan before releasing the seller from the first loan. The lender will generally apply the same standards to a seller second supplementing an assumption as it would to a seller second supplementing a new loan (see above). For example, the lender will make sure that the buyer can afford the payments on both loans before agreeing to the release—or, if therc is a due-on-sale clause, before agreeing to the assumption at all.

Exercise No. 1

The Pengs have listed their house for $179,000; it's been on the market for quite awhile. Mary Underwood and Joe Schirmer have offered to buy the property for $174,000, its appraised value. The current market interest rate for a fixed-rate mortgage is 7.5%. Underwood and Schirmer have $15,000 in cash; they will need approximately $4,700 for closing costs and reserves, and will be able to use the remainder ($10,300) as a downpayment. Their combined stable monthly income is $5,200, and their debt payments (not including housing expenses) total $560 per month.

Suppose that the Pengs accept the $174,000 offer and are willing to finance 5% of the purchase price at 6% interest. This seller second would be amortized over 30 years, so the monthly principal and interest payment would be only $52.16, but a balloon payment of the remaining principal balance would be due after five years. (The remaining principal balance after five years would be approximately $8,136.) Underwood and Schirmer apply to an institutional lender for a conventional loan at 7.5% interest, with a monthly principal and interest payment of $1,083.78.

1. What percentage of the purchase price would a $10,300 downpayment represent? With that downpayment and a 5% seller second, what would the loan-to-value ratio of the institutional loan be?

2. Calculate the loan amounts for the institutional loan and the seller second. What is the combined loan amount?

3. Does this loan arrangement comply with the general rules for secondary financing in conjunction with a conventional loan?

4. Will Underwood and Schirmer be able to qualify for this conventional loan combined with the seller second? First calculate their maximum total debt to income ratio using a 36% limit, and then use a 33% limit. Add 15% to the principal and interest payment for the institutional loan to estimate the monthly payments toward taxes, hazard insurance, and mortgage insurance.

Seller Financing as Primary Financing

Seller financing is most flexible when it is the buyer's main source or only source of financing. We'll look first at financing arrangements for unencumbered property, including land contracts, and then at wraparound financing, a technique used for property that is subject to an existing mortgage.

Unencumbered Property

Seller financing is very flexible when property is not encumbered by an existing loan

When the seller has clear title to the property, free of any mortgages or other liens, seller financing is straightforward. The buyer and seller simply negotiate the sales price and the terms of their financing arrangement and have the appropriate documents drawn up. Of course, they still have to consider how much of a downpayment the buyer can make, how much cash the seller needs, and whether the buyer can afford the monthly payments; but they are not constrained by any institutional rules.

Even if the seller requires a substantial downpayment, the buyer is likely to need less cash for seller financing than for a comparable institutional loan. The buyer won't have to pay discount points or an origination fee, and in some cases other closing costs will be lower.

Protecting the Seller's Security. Lien priority does not present the same problem here that it does with a seller second. As long as the finance instruments are recorded at closing, the seller is assured of first lien position. Then the seller's security interest will not be threatened by the foreclosure of most other liens. If a junior lienholder were to foreclose, the foreclosure sale purchaser would take title subject to the seller's lien.

However, the seller should still be concerned about protecting his or her security interest. Even a mortgage in first lien position has lower lien priority than the lien for general property taxes and any special assessment liens. If the buyer fails to pay the taxes or assessments, the government can foreclose, and the seller may take a loss at the foreclosure sale. Also, if the buyer fails to keep the property insured, the seller's security interest could become worthless if the property is damaged or destroyed.

Of course, failure to pay the taxes or insure the property is a default under the terms of virtually all finance instruments (see Chapter

5). But the seller can help prevent this type of default by setting up an impound account for taxes and hazard insurance, just as many institutional lenders do (see Chapter 8). The seller may choose to have a loan servicer handle the buyer's payments, in exchange for a servicing fee. Many banks, savings and loans, and mortgage companies service loans on behalf of private parties; so do many certified public accountants. Each month, the servicer will deposit part of the buyer's payment into the impound account and pass the remainder on to the seller.

Seller can require impound account to protect security interest

Seller Financing Plus an Institutional Second. Sometimes a seller is willing to finance a good part of the purchase price, but also needs a substantial amount of cash at closing. For example, the seller may need enough to make a downpayment for another property. If the buyer does not have that much cash, it may be possible to bridge the gap between the seller financing and the downpayment with a second mortgage from an institutional lender.

Institutional second can supplement seller financing if seller needs cash

> **Example:** Linda Stanford has agreed to buy Charlotte Halvorsen's house for $160,000. Halvorsen is willing to accept a purchase money mortgage for $141,000 (at 7% interest, partially amortized with a balloon payment due in ten years), but she needs at least $19,000 at closing.
>
> Stanford can only afford an $11,000 downpayment, so she applies to an institutional lender for an $8,000 loan. The lender agrees to make the loan at 9% interest (fully amortized over a ten-year term), accepting second lien position for its mortgage. Stanford will pay $938 per month to Halvorsen and $101 per month to the institutional lender.

This is the mirror image of the financing arrangements we looked at earlier, where a seller second made up the difference between an institutional loan and the downpayment. Like an institutional lender, a seller offering primary financing should find out where the buyer is going to get the rest of the purchase price. If a second mortgage is involved, the seller should investigate the terms of the proposed second before agreeing to the transaction. Can the buyer afford the monthly payment on both loans? Does the second have any provisions that make default likely? For example, a second that requires a large balloon payment 18 months after closing is quite risky; the buyer could end up defaulting on the seller's loan as well as the second.

Land contract: when seller is financing whole transaction, or for wraparound

Land Contracts. A seller who is providing primary financing for the buyer might choose to use a land contract instead of a mortgage or deed of trust. Land contracts are still a popular form of seller financing in some parts of the country, especially rural areas. They are known by several different names in different states; they may be called contracts for deed, bonds for deed, conditional sales contracts, installment sales contracts, installment land contracts, or real estate contracts.

Like a mortgage or deed of trust, a land contract is used to secure repayment of a debt. But while either a seller or a third-party lender can finance a buyer's purchase with a mortgage or deed of trust, only a seller can use a land contract. And a land contract works in quite a different way than those other instruments.

When the purchase of property is financed with either a mortgage or a deed of trust, the buyer takes title to the property immediately. Under a land contract, however, the seller (referred to as the **vendor**), retains legal title to the property until the buyer (the **vendee**) pays off the entire purchase price in installments. While paying off the contract—which may take many years—the vendee has the right to possess and enjoy the property, but is not the legal owner. (The vendee's interest in the property is sometimes called equitable title, in contrast to the vendor's legal title.) The vendor typically delivers the deed to the vendee only after the contract price has been paid in full.

A land contract should always be recorded. A mortgage or a deed of trust is recorded to protect the lender by establishing lien priority, but a land contract is recorded to protect the vendee. It gives public notice of the vendee's interest in the property and establishes the priority of his interest.

Unlike a mortgage or a deed of trust, a land contract is generally not accompanied by a promissory note. The contract states all of the terms of the sale and the financing arrangement between the vendor and vendee: the price, the interest rate, and the monthly payment amount; when the vendee can take possession; when the vendor will be required to deliver the deed to the vendee; and what action the vendor can take if the vendee breaches the contract by failing to pay as agreed.

Remedies for breach of contract. Land contracts sometimes provide that if the vendee defaults on the contract obligation, all of the vendee's rights in the property are terminated, all payments made may be retained by the vendor as liquidated damages, and the vendor may retake possession of the property immediately. This severe penalty for breach of a land contract is called **forfeiture**. Unfortunately for vendors and fortunately for vendees, courts do not always enforce land contracts exactly the way they are written.

If the contract has been recorded, or if the vendee is in possession and refuses to leave, the vendor will usually have to undertake some legal action to clear title and/or remove the vendee from possession. As with a judicial foreclosure, the delay in reaching trial may be a matter of months or years, depending on court congestion in the county where the property is located. Once the case finally goes to trial, the judge may have a wide range of discretion in fashioning a remedy for the vendor. Depending on state law and on the circumstances of the case, a judge may:

- enforce the contract as written, allowing the seller to retain all payments received, terminating the vendee's rights, and ordering the vendee to vacate the property;
- give the vendee a certain amount of time (anywhere from one month to one year) to pay off the entire contract balance;
- allow the vendee to simply reinstate the contract by paying delinquent payments plus interest; or
- order a sheriff's sale of the property with any surplus to go to the vendee, as would occur with a mortgage foreclosure.

In some states, the vendee's rights depend on how far along in the contract term it is when the vendee defaults. If the vendee has been making payments to the vendor for a long time, forfeiture would be especially harsh. In that situation, the law might not allow a forfeiture.

Advantages and disadvantages. For the vendor, one advantage of a contract sale may be the sense of security that can come from remaining the legal owner and not giving the vendee a deed until the entire purchase price has been paid. As our discussion of the forfeiture remedy suggests, however, this feeling of security may be largely illusory.

When forfeiture is allowed, the vendor may reacquire the property—which may have appreciated in value—instead of having to sell it and give any surplus to the debtor (as would be required in a mortgage or deed of trust foreclosure). This can be a substantial advantage for the vendor.

The main disadvantage for the vendor under a land contract is the delay and expense involved in court proceedings, which are frequently necessary in the event of breach. In many states, this disadvantage is increased by the uncertainty concerning the result after the case gets to trial.

For the vendee, the slow court proceedings can be an advantage, although the uncertainty is undesirable. A serious disadvantage for the vendee under a land contract (one that is not a problem with a mortgage or deed of trust) is that the vendor remains the legal owner of the property. This could create a variety of problems for the vendee. For example, in some states, a court judgment entered against the vendor might cloud the vendee's interest in the property, since the vendor is still the legal owner. And it might be difficult or even impossible for the vendee to obtain bank financing for construction or improvements. As we're about to discuss, banks are very reluctant to lend to someone who does not have legal title.

Using a land contract. A seller who is financing the entire transaction is free to use a land contract if she prefers it to a mortgage or deed of trust. But if the buyer wants to combine primary financing from the seller with institutional secondary financing, it will be hard to find a lender to make the second loan if the seller is using a land contract.

> **Example:** In an earlier example, Linda Stanford agreed to buy Charlotte Halvorsen's house for $160,000. Halvorsen was willing to accept a purchase money mortgage for $141,000, but she needed at least $19,000 at closing. Stanford could only afford an $11,000 downpayment, so she applied to an institutional lender for an $8,000 second mortgage.
>
> Now suppose Halvorsen offers to sell Stanford the property on those same terms, but she wants to use a land contract instead of a purchase money mortgage. Stanford still needs to pay Halvorsen $19,000 at closing, and she still has only $11,000 in cash. When she applies to a lender for an $8,000 mortgage, the lender turns her down.
>
> The problem is that under the contract, Stanford will not have legal title to the property. For that reason, she cannot use the property as security for the loan.

In theory, there are two possible solutions to this dilemma. Halvorsen (the vendor, who still has title) could agree to let the property stand as security for a loan to Stanford, without assuming personal responsibility for repayment. If Stanford were to default on the institutional second, the lender could foreclose on the property, but could not sue Halvorsen for a deficiency judgment. This might be acceptable to the lender, but it would present an additional risk for the vendor.

The other solution would be for Stanford to mortgage her equitable interest in the property. In a foreclosure, the lender would merely acquire Stanford's contract rights; the lender could not force the sale of the property. To obtain title, the lender would still have to pay Halvorsen the remainder of the contract price. Very few lenders regard a vendee's equitable interest as an acceptable form of collateral.

Neither of these solutions is particularly serviceable. So as a practical matter, a land contract only works in three situations. It works when the seller is able to provide all the financing the buyer needs. It works when the seller is supplementing an assumption, as long as the mortgagee's consent is not required; then the seller can use a contract for the secondary financing. And a land contract can also work for wraparound financing, which is our next topic.

Encumbered Property: Wraparound Financing

It's relatively rare to find a seller whose property is not encumbered by some form of mortgage lien. The seller of encumbered property generally cannot afford to offer primary financing to the buyer and also pay off the existing mortgage at closing.

> **Example:** Hank Ellison is selling his home for $202,000. For tax reasons, Ellison would prefer to sell the property on an installment basis, receiving payments over a long period. But there is a mortgage against the property that has a 6.25% interest rate and a $152,600 balance. With an installment sale, Ellison would not have enough money at closing to pay off that balance.

As you saw earlier in the chapter, Ellison might be able to arrange for the buyer to assume the existing mortgage, then finance the rest of the purchase price himself with a seller second. But there is another alternative that might appeal to Ellison: wraparound financing.

Wraparound:
- Seller accepts mortgage for most of purchase price
- Property remains subject to underlying loan

With a wraparound, the property remains subject to the seller's existing mortgage after the sale. The amount of the seller financing is larger than the balance owed on the existing mortgage, so the seller financing "wraps around" the existing mortgage. The buyer does not take on responsibility for the existing mortgage, which is usually referred to as the **underlying loan** after the wrap. The seller remains responsible for making the payments on the underlying loan. Each month, the buyer makes a payment to the seller on the wraparound loan, and the seller uses a portion of that payment to make the payment on the underlying loan.

> **Example:** Continuing with the example above, suppose Ellison sells his house to Janet Kingman for $202,000, accepting $20,000 down and financing the balance of the purchase price ($182,000) with a deed of trust at 8.5%.
>
> Kingman takes title to the property subject to the $152,600 underlying mortgage, but she does not assume that loan. Her monthly payment to Ellison is $1,400. Out of that amount, $1,115 goes to the underlying mortgagee and Ellison gets to keep $285. The underlying mortgage will be paid off in 20 years, and at that point Kingman will be required to make a balloon payment to Ellison for the remaining balance on the wraparound loan.

For a wraparound, the seller can use a mortgage, a deed of trust, or a land contract. When a deed of trust is used for a wrap, it is often referred to as an **all-inclusive trust deed**.

Wraparound works only if underlying loan does not have due-on-sale clause

A wrap only works when the underlying loan does not have a due-on-sale clause. Occasionally a seller will try to get around a due-on-sale clause by using a wraparound land contract and failing to notify the lender of the transaction; this is called a "silent wrap." But even though a contract sale does not involve an immediate transfer of title, it still gives the lender the right to accelerate the underlying loan pursuant to the due-on-sale clause. So if the lender finds out about the secret transaction, both the seller and the buyer will be in jeopardy. A real estate agent should never get involved in a silent wrap.

Wraparound financing is attractive because it enables the buyer to finance the purchase at a below-market interest rate while still providing a market rate of return (or better) for the seller. To clarify this apparent contradiction, let's continue with the example given above.

> **Example:** Although Ellison has received a $182,000 deed of trust from Kingman, he has actually extended only $29,400 in credit to her:

$202,000	Sales price
20,000	Downpayment
–152,600	Underlying mortgage balance
$29,400	Credit extended — net owed to seller

> Yet Ellison will receive 8.5% interest on the entire $182,000 wraparound, while paying only 6.25% interest on the $152,600 underlying loan balance. This means that in the first year he will

pay out $9,538 in interest on the underlying mortgage, but will receive $15,470 in interest on the wrap from the buyer. That gives him a net gain of $5,932. Since he extended only $29,400 in credit, he is earning $5,932 on $29,400, which represents a 20% annual return.

Here are the steps for determining the seller's yield in the first year of the loan term:

1. Calculate the interest the seller will receive in the first year on the wraparound loan.

   $182,000 × 8.5% = $15,470

2. Calculate the interest the seller will pay the same year on the underlying loan.

   $152,600 × 6.25% = $9,538

3. Determine the net interest to the seller in the first year.

   $15,470 − 9,538 = $5,932

4. Divide the net interest by the amount of credit actually extended.

   $5,932 ÷ $29,400 = 20%

If the market interest rate is currently 9.5%, the seller is receiving more than double the market rate, while the buyer is paying 1% below the market rate.

Calculating seller's yield on wraparound:

Interest seller will receive
– Interest seller will pay
Net interest to seller

Seller's yield = Net interest to seller ÷ Credit extended

Even when the interest rate that the seller charges on the wrap is not below the market rate, the arrangement may still be attractive to the buyer because of the greater flexibility of seller financing and lower closing costs. The seller's yield on the transaction depends in part on the difference between the interest rate on the wrap and the rate on the underlying loan, and in part on the amount of credit extended. The more credit extended by the seller, the lower the return.

Exercise No. 2

Compute the seller's first-year yield in the following situations. You may want to use the worksheet below.

1. Sales price $75,000; $8,000 downpayment; all-inclusive trust deed at 9% interest; underlying mortgage with a $39,700 balance at 7% interest.

Wraparound Worksheet

Sales price	________				
– Downpayment	________				
Wraparound	________	x	____% =	________	Interest received
– Underlying loan	________	x	____% =	________	– Interest paid
Credit extended	________ →			________	Net interest
				________	÷ Credit extended
				________	Seller's yield

2. Sales price $187,000; $28,000 downpayment; wraparound contract at 10% interest; underlying deed of trust with a $142,000 balance at 8% interest.

Wraparound vs. Assumption plus Seller Second. When the seller's existing loan has no due-on-sale clause, the parties can choose between a wraparound and an assumption plus a seller second. In either case, the actual amount of credit extended by the seller is the same; but the two arrangements have different benefits for the parties.

In an assumption, the buyer receives the benefit of an existing loan with a low interest rate. On the other hand, if the transaction is structured with a wraparound loan at the market rate, the seller receives the benefit of the existing low interest rate loan and a very attractive rate of return on the portion of the financing actually extended to the buyer.

> **Example:** A home is sold for $100,000, with the buyer making a $20,000 downpayment. The seller's existing loan with a balance of $60,000 carries an interest rate of 6%. The prevailing market interest rate at the time of the sale is approximately 9%.

	Wraparound	Assumption + Second
Sales price:	$100,000	$100,000
Downpayment:	$20,000	$20,000
Balance financed:	$80,000 @ 9% Wrap	$60,000 @ 6% Assumption $20,000 @ 9% Second
Credit extended by seller:	$20,000	$20,000
Yield to seller on credit extended:	18%	9%
Overall interest rate to buyer on $80,000 financed:	9%	6.75%

As you can see from this example, if a wraparound loan is made at the market rate, the seller enjoys a high yield on the credit he or she extends to the buyer. If the transaction is structured with an assumption and a second mortgage to the seller at the market rate, the buyer enjoys financing at a very low overall rate.

A wraparound can also be structured so that the seller receives an above-market rate on the credit actually extended and, at the same time, the buyer pays a below-market rate on the total amount financed. Then both of them are getting a good deal. In the example just given, if the wraparound loan were made at an interest rate of 7.5%, the buyer would be paying an overall rate 1.5% less than the prevailing market rate of 9%. The seller would be receiving a yield of approximately 12% on the $20,000 of credit that he or she extended to the buyer.

Wrap can offer:
- Below-market rate for buyer
- Above-market yield for seller
- In some cases, both of the above

Protecting a Wraparound Buyer. From the buyer's point of view, the obvious problem with a wraparound is how to make sure that the seller makes the payments on the underlying loan. The buyer may have made every wrap payment to the seller on time, yet if the seller defaults on the underlying loan and the underlying lender forecloses, the buyer will lose the property.

One solution is to include in the finance instruments a provision requiring the seller to make timely payments on the underlying loan, and allowing the buyer to make those payments directly to the lender if the seller fails to do so.

> Seller shall maintain the existing mortgage in good standing; in the event that Seller fails to make any payment when due, or in any other way causes or allows the loan to go into default, Buyer shall be entitled to cure the default, and deduct all costs from the amounts next falling due to Seller on this note [or, this contract].

In order for a provision like this to be effective in preventing foreclosure, the buyer needs some way of finding out when the seller has fallen behind in the payments on the underlying loan. In most states, the buyer can send the lender a "Request for Notice of Delinquency" when the wraparound transaction closes. (The seller's consent is usually necessary.) Then if the seller stops paying the lender, the lender will notify the buyer, and the buyer can take the necessary steps to cure the default.

Protection for wrap buyer:
- Request for Notice of Delinquency
- Escrow account

Even with these safeguards in place, the best protection for the wraparound buyer is an escrow account for the loan payments, with a third party appointed to manage the wrap. Each month, the buyer will make the wrap payment into the escrow account, and the escrow agent will send part of the payment to the underlying lender and the remainder to the seller. Property taxes and hazard insurance can also be handled through this account (see the discussion of impound accounts, earlier in this chapter). The parties may appoint a certified

Escrow Instructions

1. The buyer shall make all payments into an escrow account to be maintained by the escrow agent.
2. Upon receipt of each monthly payment, the escrow agent shall immediately make all payments due on the seller's underlying mortgage.
3. The escrow agent shall maintain a balance in the account equal to two monthly mortgage payments; all funds in excess of this minimum balance shall be disbursed to the seller, after compliance with provision 2 of these instructions.

public accountant or some other qualified person to manage their wrap; in some cases, they'll find that the loan servicer for the underlying loan is willing to take on this task.

Exercise No. 3

In one of the examples given earlier in this chapter, the Rainwaters sold their house to Ray McCarthy for $162,000. They allowed McCarthy to assume their mortgage and accepted a second deed of trust for part of the remainder of the price. The existing mortgage had a balance of $125,500, a 6% interest rate, and 240 payments remaining. The seller second was for $26,500, at 8% interest (compared to the market rate of 9%); it was amortized over 30 years, with a balloon payment due in 10 years. McCarthy was going to make a $10,000 downpayment, and each month he would pay $899.12 to the lender on the assumed mortgage, and $194.45 to the Rainwaters on the seller second.

Now suppose that instead of that arrangement, the Rainwaters offered McCarthy a $152,000 wraparound mortgage at 7% interest, amortized over 30 years, with a balloon payment due after 20 years. (McCarthy would still make a $10,000 downpayment.) McCarthy's monthly payment on the wraparound would be $1,011.26.

1. Compare McCarthy's monthly payment on the wraparound to the total monthly payment for the assumption plus seller second.

2. What would the Rainwaters' yield on the wraparound loan be during the first year? Compare this to their yield on the seller second.

3. With the assumption plus second, what overall interest rate would McCarthy pay on the total amount financed? To determine the approximate overall rate, calculate the annual interest paid on each of the two loans, add those two figures together, and then divide that result by the total amount of financing. Compare this answer to the interest rate McCarthy would pay on the wraparound, and compare both of those rates to the market rate.

Alternatives to Seller Financing

Short of financing purchase, seller can help buyer with:
- Buydown
- Contribution to closing costs
- Equity exchange
- Lease/option

As you have seen, with a mortgage, deed of trust, or land contract, the seller can play the role of a lender by extending credit to the buyer. But in these seller financing arrangements, the seller often has to wait several years to collect the full profit from the sale. Not every seller is in a position to do that. In this section of the chapter, we will discuss some ways that a seller can help a buyer purchase his property without financing the transaction.

Buydowns

One popular way for a seller to assist a buyer is a buydown. Buydowns were explained in detail in Chapter 10. To buy down the interest rate on the buyer's institutional loan, the seller does not actually have to pay the lender a lump sum at closing. However, the seller's proceeds from the sale will be reduced by the amount of the buydown. From the seller's point of view, it's as if he or she had agreed to lower the sales price; but the buydown can have greater benefits for the buyer than a straight price reduction would have (see Chapter 10).

Contributions to Closing Costs

Occasionally, after coming up with the required downpayment and reserves for an institutional loan, the buyer doesn't have quite enough cash left over to pay for closing costs. The seller may be willing to make up the shortfall. Depending on the circumstances, this type of cash contribution from the seller may be more helpful than a price reduction for the same amount.

However, there are limits on how much a seller can contribute to the buyer's closing costs for a conventional loan. If the seller's contribution exceeds those limits, the loan amount will be reduced (see Chapter 10). Seller contributions also affect the maximum loan amount calculations for an FHA loan (see Chapter 11). Because of these rules, in some cases a large contribution from the seller doesn't really help the buyer.

Equity Exchanges

When a buyer can't come up with enough cash for a purchase, the seller may be willing to accept other assets and reduce the cash sales price. Maybe the buyer has equity in some vacant land, or in personal property such as a recreational vehicle or a yacht. If the seller wants the property and the buyer is ready to part with it, they can work out an exchange.

> **Example:** Ellen Jarvis has decided to sell a rental house she owns. She lists the house for $225,000.
>
> Frank Tillman would like to buy the house. He has $22,000 for a downpayment, which would be enough if he could obtain an institutional loan for $203,000. But Tillman could not qualify for a loan that large.
>
> Tillman meticulously restored a vintage sports car and has been planning to sell it. The appraised value of the car is $27,500. In the course of a conversation with Jarvis, Tillman discovers that she happens to be a sports car buff. He shows her the car he restored, and after long negotiations, Jarvis agrees to reduce the sales price on her house to $200,000 if Tillman will give her the car.
>
> With the sales price reduced to $200,000, Tillman applies for an 80% conventional loan ($160,000). He easily qualifies for this smaller loan, and the transaction closes.

Lease Arrangements

In some cases, a prospective buyer is interested in leasing a home before actually buying it. The buyer may need additional time to acquire enough cash for a downpayment or closing costs—by saving, or by selling other property, for instance. Or perhaps the buyer is currently unable to qualify for a large enough loan, but has reason to believe that circumstances will change before long.

If the seller is willing, the property can be leased to the prospective buyer in one of two ways: with a lease/option (a lease agreement that includes an option to purchase) or with a lease/purchase contract (a purchase contract that allows the buyer to lease the property for an extended period before closing). Although the two arrangements are related, there are important differences between them.

Lease/Options. A lease/option is made up of a lease and an option to purchase. A seller leases his or her property to a prospective buyer for a specific term (often six months or one year), and grants the buyer an option to purchase the leased property at a specified price during the term of the lease. The seller is the landlord and optionor, and the prospective buyer is the tenant and optionee. The tenant/optionee is

Lease/option:
- Lease with option to buy
- Limited time period
- Option money
- Rent credit

under no obligation to buy the property, but the landlord/optionor is not supposed to sell the property to anyone else during the option period.

A lease/option is by no means the equivalent of a sale. A seller considering this type of arrangement should be warned that in the majority of cases, the tenant/optionee decides not to buy. However, a carefully structured lease/option may keep a possible sale alive until the buyer is in a position to close.

Because the failure rate is high, a seller generally only grants a lease/option when it seems unlikely that other offers will be forthcoming in the near future, or when the arrangement allows the seller to ask a higher price for the property. Of course, a lease/option won't work for residential property unless the seller has somewhere else to live. But the lease provides the seller with some income from the property, which can be used to make mortgage payments on a new house until the old house is sold, or to cover payments on an existing mortgage on the old house.

Option money:
- Consideration for option
- Non-refundable
- Applied to purchase

How a lease/option works. The prospective buyer pays the seller a sum of money in exchange for the option. This **option money** is the consideration that makes the option binding on the seller. Once paid, the option money is not refundable, whether or not the optionee goes through with the purchase. Many lease/option agreements provide that the option money will be applied to the purchase price, much like the good faith deposit (earnest money) in an ordinary purchase and sale agreement.

A lease/option may also provide that part of the rental payments will be applied to the purchase if the tenant/optionee decides to buy. This is called a **rent credit** provision.

> **Example:** John Caldwell is selling a house for $315,000. Mark Bettelheim is interested in the property, but he will not be able to qualify for a loan until he receives a raise that he's expecting this year. The parties execute a lease/option, and Bettelheim pays Caldwell $6,000 as option money.
>
> Under the terms of their agreement, Bettelheim will lease the house for six months, paying $2,200 per month in rent. Bettelheim has the right to purchase the property at the agreed price at any time until the lease expires. If Bettelheim exercises his option, the option money and $1,100 out of each rental payment will be applied to the sales price.

> So if Bettelheim decides to buy at the end of six months, he will pay $302,400, the amount owed after deducting the option money and $6,600 in rental payments from the original price. If Bettelheim decides not to buy, Caldwell will keep the option money and all of the rent.

The rent charged in a lease/option is often considerably higher than the rent that would be charged for the property under an ordinary lease. This gives the optionee an incentive to exercise the option as soon as possible, and also provides additional compensation to the seller for the uncertainty and inconvenience of the option.

Lease/option rent:
- Often higher than market rent
- Rent credit applied to purchase

There are two ways a rent credit can be applied toward the purchase: the amount of the credit can be deducted from the sales price (as it was in the example above), or the credit can be treated as part of the downpayment. A buyer who is short of cash might prefer to treat the credit as part of the downpayment. However, most institutional lenders will only accept a rent credit as part of the downpayment to the extent that the credit represents an extra amount paid above the fair market rent for the property. For instance, if the fair market rent was $1,500 and the lease/option rent was $1,800, no more than $300 out of each month's rent could be applied to the downpayment.

Provisions of a lease/option agreement. A lease/option should include all the terms of the lease, and in addition, all the terms of the potential purchase contract. That way, a binding purchase contract will be formed immediately if the optionee exercises the option to purchase.

Lease/option includes:
- All terms of lease
- All terms of potential purchase contract

The lease/option agreement should state that if the tenant/optionee defaults in connection with the lease (by failing to pay the rent, for example), the option rights will be forfeited.

The agreement should also make it clear that the option money is not a security deposit. (In most states, a tenant's security deposit must be kept in a trust account and refunded at the end of the lease. The seller can require a security deposit in a lease/option arrangement, but the deposit must be separate from the option money.) The agreement should specify that the option money may be disbursed to the seller/optionor as soon as the tenant/optionee moves in to the home.

The amount of option money is negotiable, but it should be at least enough to pay the real estate brokerage fee. In some cases, the broker arranges to collect part of his or her fee out of the option money, and the remainder if the optionee goes through with the purchase. Keep in mind that the more option money the prospective buyer pays, the more likely it is that the option will be exercised.

Before signing the lease/option, the seller—like any other landlord—should review a copy of the prospective tenant's credit report, to make sure that he or she is a good credit risk.

Lease/purchase contract:
- Parties sign purchase agreement, not option
- Closing date far off
- Eventual sale more likely than with lease/option

Lease/Purchase Contract. A number of variations on the lease/option have been tried, as sellers and their real estate agents attempt to improve the chances that a sale will eventually take place. One of these variations is the lease/purchase contract.

For a lease/purchase contract, instead of signing an option, the seller and the prospective buyer actually sign a purchase contract along with the lease. The buyer usually gives the seller a substantial earnest money deposit, and the closing date is set quite far off—six months or a year away. In the meantime, the buyer leases the property.

The practical effect of a lease/purchase contract is very similar to that of a lease/option. If the tenant/buyer decides not to buy the property, he or she simply forfeits the earnest money deposit—which isn't very different from losing option money, in practical terms. But there is a significant psychological difference; the buyer tends to feel more committed with a lease/purchase contract. Deciding not to go through with the purchase means breaching a contract (as opposed to merely choosing not to exercise an option). Many real estate agents believe a lease/purchase contract is much more likely to result in a sale than a lease/option is.

A lease/purchase contract should have many of the same provisions as a lease/option. There may be a rent credit provision, and the contract should make clear that the earnest money deposit is not a security deposit. Again, the seller should be sure the buyer has a satisfactory credit history before signing the contract.

The Agent's Responsibilities in Seller-Financed Transactions

The old saying "Where there's a will, there's a way" could be used as a slogan for seller financing. Open-minded negotiation between buyer, seller, and lender closes many transactions that otherwise would not make it. An imaginative real estate agent can be the catalyst, showing the parties that they have many alternatives.

However, there are risks in any seller financing arrangement, even if it's straightforward and carefully planned. An extension of credit always involves the risk of default. In a badly planned transaction without adequate safeguards, default may be more likely than repayment, and may result in a devastating financial loss for the seller. The risks affect the buyer, too. Suppose a seller offers graduated payment financing with very low initial payments; if the buyer can't afford the payment increases when the time comes, he may lose the home and everything he's put into it.

A real estate agent negotiating a seller-financed transaction should make sure that both the seller and the buyer understand all the terms and implications of their agreement. The agent should always suggest—and in most cases should strongly recommend—that they get legal and tax advice from real estate lawyers and/or certified public accountants. At the very least, the finance instruments should be prepared or reviewed by a lawyer. The real estate agent should not prepare these documents, even using standard forms; in most states that would be considered the unauthorized practice of law.

Real estate agent should:
- make sure both parties understand seller financing arrangement
- encourage both parties to consult lawyers or CPAs

Disclosures

Some states require special disclosure forms to be used when a third party (such as a real estate agent) helps arrange seller financing. The agent is usually supposed to fill out the disclosure form and give a copy to both the seller and the buyer before they commit themselves. As an example, a form that meets the requirements of California's seller financing disclosure law is shown in Figure 13.2, on the following pages. The form details all the terms of the financing agreement, from the interest rate to the late payment charge.

Notice that the form also has a section for information concerning the buyer's creditworthiness. In a seller-financed transaction, the seller should always check into the buyer's financial situation—income, net worth, and credit history. After obtaining this information, the seller doesn't have to apply the same standards to it that an institutional lender would. For example, a seller might decide to finance the transaction even though the buyers have a 45% debt to income ratio. But the seller should at least have a clear picture of the buyers' circumstances.

Seller financing disclosure statement:
- Discloses all financing terms
- Informs seller of buyer's financial situation
- Required in some states

Even in states that don't require it, a real estate agent handling a seller-financed transaction is always well advised to prepare a disclosure statement. A local real estate organization (such as a multiple listing association or a Board of Realtors®) might have a form available for this purpose. Otherwise, an agent could have a local real estate lawyer draw up a form that accurately reflects state law concerning the rights of the parties.

Liability

A disclosure statement protects the parties by helping them understand the financing transaction. It can also protect the real estate agent, by documenting that certain information was provided to the parties. However, the agent should not regard the disclosure statement as a shield against liability. With or without disclosures, an agent who suggests or encourages a financing arrangement that is plainly imprudent could be held liable for breach of fiduciary duty if the seller later suffers a loss. This is especially true when an unsophisticated seller relies on the real estate agent alone instead of consulting another professional (such as a lawyer or a CPA).

In a seller-financed transaction, a court could hold that the seller's agent also had fiduciary duties to the buyer. An inadvertent dual agency may arise if the buyer believes the agent is representing his or her interests in negotiating the financing arrangement with the seller. In that case, the agent could be held liable for breach of duties owed to the buyer/debtor as well as to the seller/creditor. And even without a finding of dual agency, a seller's agent who persuaded a buyer to enter into an extremely unwise transaction might be held liable for fraud.

So use your imagination, but don't lose touch with reality. While seller financing can close a sale, what happens after closing matters too. The buyer must be able to pay as agreed, and the seller must be well protected in case of default. Make sure both parties get good professional advice and understand every aspect of their transaction.

Fig. 13.2 Seller financing disclosure statement

CALIFORNIA ASSOCIATION OF REALTORS®

SELLER FINANCING ADDENDUM AND DISCLOSURE
(California Civil Code §§2956-2967)
(C.A.R. Form SFA, Revised 10/02)

This is an addendum to the ☐ California Residential Purchase Agreement, ☐ Counter Offer, or ☐ Other ______________________, ("Agreement"), dated ______________

On property known as ______________________ ("Property"),
between ______________________ ("Buyer"),
and ______________________ ("Seller").

Seller agrees to extend credit to Buyer as follows:

1. **PRINCIPAL; INTEREST; PAYMENT; MATURITY TERMS:** ☐ Principal amount $ __________, interest at ______% per annum, payable at approximately $ __________ per ☐ month, ☐ year, or ☐ other __________, remaining principal balance due in ______ years.
2. **LOAN APPLICATION; CREDIT REPORT:** Within 5 (or ☐ ______) **Days** After Acceptance: **(a)** Buyer shall provide Seller a completed loan application on a form acceptable to Seller (such as a FNMA/FHLMC Uniform Residential Loan Application for residential one to four unit properties); and **(b)** Buyer authorizes Seller and/or Agent to obtain, at Buyer's expense, a copy of Buyer's credit report. Buyer shall provide any supporting documentation reasonably requested by Seller. Seller, after first giving Buyer a Notice to Buyer to Perform, may cancel this Agreement in writing and authorize return of Buyer's deposit if Buyer fails to provide such documents within that time, or if Seller disapproves any above item within **5 (or ☐ ______) Days** After receipt of each item.
3. **CREDIT DOCUMENTS:** This extension of credit by Seller will be evidenced by: ☐ Note and deed of trust; ☐ All-inclusive note and deed of trust; ☐ Installment land sale contract; ☐ Lease/option (when parties intend transfer of equitable title); OR ☐ Other (specify) ______________________

THE FOLLOWING TERMS APPLY ONLY IF CHECKED. SELLER IS ADVISED TO READ ALL TERMS, EVEN THOSE NOT CHECKED, TO UNDERSTAND WHAT IS OR IS NOT INCLUDED, AND, IF NOT INCLUDED, THE CONSEQUENCES THEREOF.

4. ☐ **LATE CHARGE:** If any payment is not made within ____ **Days** After it is due, a late charge of either $ __________, or ____% of the installment due, may be charged to Buyer. **NOTE:** On single family residences that Buyer intends to occupy, California Civil Code §2954.4(a) limits the late charge to no more than 6% of the total installment payment due and requires a grace period of no less than 10 days.
5. ☐ **BALLOON PAYMENT:** The extension of credit will provide for a balloon payment, in the amount of $ __________, plus any accrued interest, which is due on __________ (date).
6. ☐ **PREPAYMENT:** If all or part of this extension of credit is paid early, Seller may charge a prepayment penalty as follows (if applicable): __________. Caution: California Civil Code §2954.9 contains limitations on prepayment penalties for residential one-to-four unit properties.
7. ☐ **DUE ON SALE:** If any interest in the Property is sold or otherwise transferred, Seller has the option to require immediate payment of the entire unpaid principal balance, plus any accrued interest.

8.* ☐ **REQUEST FOR COPY OF NOTICE OF DEFAULT:** A request for a copy of Notice of Default as defined in California Civil Code §2924b will be recorded. **If Not**, Seller is advised to consider recording a Request for Notice of Default.

9.* ☐ **REQUEST FOR NOTICE OF DELINQUENCY:** A request for Notice of Delinquency, as defined in California Civil Code §2924e, to be signed and paid for by Buyer, will be made to senior lienholders. **If not**, Seller is advised to consider making a Request for Notice of Delinquency. Seller is advised to check with senior lienholders to verify whether they will honor this request.

10.* ☐ **TAX SERVICE:**
   A. If property taxes on the Property become delinquent, tax service will be arranged to report to Seller. **If not**, Seller is advised to consider retaining a tax service, or to otherwise determine that property taxes are paid.
   B. ☐ Buyer, ☐ Seller, shall be responsible for the initial and continued retention of, and payment for, such tax service.

11. ☐ **TITLE INSURANCE:** Title insurance coverage will be provided to **both** Seller and Buyer, insuring their respective interests in the Property. **If not,** Buyer and Seller are advised to consider securing such title insurance coverage.
12. ☐ **HAZARD INSURANCE:**
   A. The parties' escrow holder or insurance carrier will be directed to include a loss payee endorsement, adding Seller to the Property insurance policy. **If not**, Seller is advised to secure such an endorsement, or acquire a separate insurance policy.
   B. Property insurance **does not** include earthquake or flood insurance coverage, unless checked:
   ☐ Earthquake insurance will be obtained; ☐ Flood insurance will be obtained.
13. ☐ **PROCEEDS TO BUYER:** Buyer will receive cash proceeds at the close of the sale transaction. The amount received will be approximately $ __________, from __________ (indicate source of proceeds). Buyer represents that the purpose of such disbursement is as follows: __________.
14. ☐ **NEGATIVE AMORTIZATION; DEFERRED INTEREST:** Negative amortization results when Buyer's periodic payments are less than the amount of interest earned on the obligation. Deferred interest also results when the obligation does not require periodic payments for a period of time. In either case, interest is not payable as it accrues. This accrued interest will have to be paid by Buyer at a later time, and may result in Buyer owing more on the obligation than at its origination. The credit being extended to Buyer by Seller will provide for negative amortization or deferred interest as indicated below. (Check A, B, or C. CHECK ONE ONLY.)
   ☐ **A.** All negative amortization or deferred interest shall be added to the principal __________ (e.g., annually, monthly, etc.), and thereafter shall bear interest at the rate specified in the credit documents (compound interest);
   OR ☐ **B.** All deferred interest shall be due and payable, along with principal, at maturity;
   OR ☐ **C.** Other __________.

*(For Paragraphs 8-10) In order to receive timely and continued notification, Seller is advised to record appropriate notices and/or to notify appropriate parties of any change in Seller's address.

SFA REVISED 10/02 (PAGE 1 OF 3) Print Date

Buyer's Initials (______)(______)
Seller's Initials (______)(______)

Reviewed by ______ Date ______

EQUAL HOUSING OPPORTUNITY

SELLER FINANCING ADDENDUM AND DISCLOSURE (SFA PAGE 1 OF 3)

Property Address: ______________________ Date: ____________

15. ☐ **ALL-INCLUSIVE DEED OF TRUST; INSTALLMENT LAND SALE CONTRACT:** This transaction involves the use of an all-inclusive (or wraparound) deed of trust or an installment land sale contract. That deed of trust or contract shall provide as follows:

A. In the event of an acceleration of any senior encumbrance, the responsibility for payment, or for legal defense is: ______________________ ; OR ☐ **Is not** specified in the credit or security documents.

B. In the event of the prepayment of a senior encumbrance, the responsibilities and rights of Buyer and Seller regarding refinancing, prepayment penalties, and any prepayment discounts are: ______________________; OR ☐ **Are not** specified in the documents evidencing credit.

C. Buyer will make periodic payments to ______________________ (Seller, collection agent, or any neutral third party), who will be responsible for disbursing payments to the payee(s) on the senior encumbrance(s) and to Seller. **NOTE:** The Parties are advised to designate a neutral third party for these purposes.

16. ☐ **TAX IDENTIFICATION NUMBERS:** Buyer and Seller shall each provide to each other their Social Security Numbers or Taxpayer Identification Numbers.

17. ☐ **OTHER CREDIT TERMS** ______________________

18. ☐ **RECORDING:** The documents evidencing credit (paragraph 3) will be recorded with the county recorder where the Property is located. **If not**, Buyer and Seller are advised that their respective interests in the Property may be jeopardized by intervening liens, judgments, encumbrances, or subsequent transfers.

19. ☐ **JUNIOR FINANCING:** There will be additional financing, secured by the Property, junior to this Seller financing. Explain: ______________________

20. SENIOR LOANS AND ENCUMBRANCES: The following information is provided on loans and/or encumbrances that will be **senior** to Seller financing. **NOTE:** The following are estimates, unless otherwise marked with an asterisk (*). If checked: ☐ A separate sheet with information on additional senior loans/encumbrances is attached

	1st	2nd
A. Original Balance	$	$
B. Current Balance	$	$
C. Periodic Payment (e.g. $100/month):	$	$ /
Including Impounds of:	$	$ /
D. Interest Rate (per annum)	%	%
E. Fixed or Variable Rate:		
If Variable Rate: Lifetime Cap (Ceiling)		
Indicator (Underlying Index)		
Margins		
F. Maturity Date		
G. Amount of Balloon Payment	$	$
H. Date Balloon Payment Due		
I. Potential for Negative Amortization? (Yes, No, or Unknown)		
J. Due on Sale? (Yes, No, or Unknown)		
K. Pre-payment penalty? (Yes, No, or Unknown)		
L. Are payments current? (Yes, No, or Unknown)		

21. BUYER'S CREDITWORTHINESS: (CHECK EITHER A OR B. Do not check both.) In addition to the loan application, credit report and other information requested under paragraph 2:

A. ☐ No other disclosure concerning Buyer's creditworthiness has been made to Seller;

OR B. ☐ The following representations concerning Buyer's creditworthiness are made by Buyer(s) to Seller:

Borrower ____________	**Co-Borrower** ____________
1. Occupation ____________	1. Occupation ____________
2. Employer ____________	2. Employer ____________
3. Length of Employment ____________	3. Length of Employment ____________
4. Monthly Gross Income ____________	4. Monthly Gross Income ____________
5. Other ____________	5. Other ____________

22. ADDED, DELETED OR SUBSTITUTED BUYERS: The addition, deletion or substitution of any person or entity under this Agreement or to title prior to close of escrow shall require Seller's written consent. Seller may grant or withhold consent in Seller's sole discretion. Any additional or substituted person or entity shall, if requested by Seller, submit to Seller the same documentation as required for the original named Buyer. Seller and/or Brokers may obtain a credit report, at Buyer's expense, on any such person or entity.

Buyer's Initials (________)(________)
Seller's Initials (________)(________)

SFA REVISED 10/02 (PAGE 2 OF 3)

Reviewed by ______ Date ______

EQUAL HOUSING OPPORTUNITY

SELLER FINANCING ADDENDUM AND DISCLOSURE (SFA PAGE 2 OF 3)

Property Address: ______________________________ Date: ______________

23. CAUTION:

A. If the Seller financing requires a balloon payment, Seller shall give Buyer written notice, according to the terms of Civil Code §2966, at least 90 and not more than 150 days before the balloon payment is due if the transaction is for the purchase of a dwelling for not more than four families.

B. If **any** obligation secured by the Property calls for a balloon payment, Seller and Buyer are aware that refinancing of the balloon payment at maturity may be difficult or impossible, depending on conditions in the conventional mortgage marketplace at that time. There are no assurances that new financing or a loan extension will be available when the balloon prepayment, or any prepayment, is due.

C. If **any** of the existing or proposed loans or extensions of credit would require refinancing as a result of a lack of full amortization, such refinancing might be difficult or impossible in the conventional mortgage marketplace.

D. In the event of default by Buyer: (1) Seller may have to reinstate and/or make monthly payments on any and all senior encumbrances (including real property taxes) in order to protect Seller's secured interest; (2) Seller's rights are generally limited to foreclosure on the Property, pursuant to California Code of Civil Procedure §580b; and (3) the Property may lack sufficient equity to protect Seller's interests if the Property decreases in value.

If this three-page Addendum and Disclosure is used in a transaction for the purchase of a dwelling for not more than four families, it shall be prepared by an Arranger of Credit as defined in California Civil Code §2957(a). (The Arranger of Credit is usually the agent who obtained the offer.)

____

Arranger of Credit - (Print Firm Name) By Date

Address ______________ City ______________ State ______ Zip ______

Phone ______________ Fax ______________

BUYER AND SELLER ACKNOWLEDGE AND AGREE THAT BROKERS: (A) WILL NOT PROVIDE LEGAL OR TAX ADVICE; (B) WILL NOT PROVIDE OTHER ADVICE OR INFORMATION THAT EXCEEDS THE KNOWLEDGE, EDUCATION AND EXPERIENCE REQUIRED TO OBTAIN A REAL ESTATE LICENSE; OR (C) HAVE NOT AND WILL NOT VERIFY ANY INFORMATION PROVIDED BY EITHER BUYER OR SELLER. BUYER AND SELLER AGREE THAT THEY WILL SEEK LEGAL, TAX AND OTHER DESIRED ASSISTANCE FROM APPROPRIATE PROFESSIONALS. BUYER AND SELLER ACKNOWLEDGE THAT THE INFORMATION EACH HAS PROVIDED TO THE ARRANGER OF CREDIT FOR INCLUSION IN THIS DISCLOSURE FORM IS ACCURATE. BUYER AND SELLER FURTHER ACKNOWLEDGE THAT EACH HAS RECEIVED A COMPLETED COPY OF THIS DISCLOSURE FORM.

Buyer ______________________________ Date ______________
(signature)

Address ______________ City ______________ State ______ Zip ______

Phone ______________ Fax ______________ E-mail ______________

Buyer ______________________________ Date ______________
(signature)

Address ______________ City ______________ State ______ Zip ______

Phone ______________ Fax ______________ E-mail ______________

Seller ______________________________ Date ______________
(signature)

Address ______________ City ______________ State ______ Zip ______

Phone ______________ Fax ______________ E-mail ______________

Seller ______________________________ Date ______________
(signature)

Address ______________ City ______________ State ______ Zip ______

Phone ______________ Fax ______________ E-mail ______________

Reviewed by ________ Date ________

SFA REVISED 10/02 (PAGE 3 OF 3)

SELLER FINANCING ADDENDUM AND DISCLOSURE (SFA PAGE 3 OF 3)

Outline: Seller Financing

I. How Seller Financing Works
   A. A seller can use a promissory note and security instrument to finance the buyer's purchase; such a loan is known as a purchase money loan.
   B. A seller may also use a land contract, where the buyer takes possession of the property but the seller retains title until the price has been paid in full.
   C. Seller financing is usually secondary financing, where a "seller second" supplements an institutional first mortgage.

II. When and Why Seller Financing is Used
   A. If interest rates are high and buyers have difficulty qualifying for loans, the only way a seller may be able to sell the property is by financing part of the purchase price.
   B. Sellers may use seller financing as a marketing tool; buyers may pay more for a house if they can get favorable seller financing terms.
   C. Seller financing may have tax advantages: if payments are made over a period of years, the seller doesn't have to report the full profit from the sale in the first year.

III. Seller Seconds
   A. Often, seller financing is secondary financing, where the seller accepts a second mortgage (a "seller second") for the difference between the loan amount and the purchase price.
   B. Supplementing a new loan
      1. The seller second must meet lender requirements; for instance, for a conventional loan, the total financing may not exceed 95% of the sales price, and the second loan may not require a balloon payment within less than five years after closing.
      2. A buyer considering a seller second needs to consider how much he has for a downpayment, the total monthly payment he can qualify for, and how large the balloon payment for the seller second will be.
      3. A seller considering a seller second needs to think about whether cash flow and yield will be adequate, possible negative tax consequences (such as the imputed interest rule), and lien priority.
   C. Supplementing an assumption
      1. A seller second can supplement a buyer's assumption of an existing loan; the buyer will make a monthly payment to the seller as well as making the monthly payment the seller has been making to the lender.

2. If the loan has a due-on-sale clause, an assumption isn't possible unless the lender agrees to it.
3. Regardless of whether there is a due-on-sale clause, the lender's consent is necessary for the seller to be released from liability.

IV. Seller Financing as Primary Financing

A. Unencumbered property

1. Seller financing is straightforward if the seller owns the property free and clear.
2. While lien priority is not as much of a concern with primary seller financing, the seller must make sure that taxes and special assessment liens are paid *so that the government doesn't foreclose.
3. Escrow account can be set up to handle the buyer's tax payments.
4. If a seller is willing to provide substantial financing but needs cash at closing, a possibility is seller financing with an institutional second mortgage.

B. Land contracts

1. A seller providing primary financing might choose to use a land contract (also known as a conditional sales contract or installment sales contract) instead of a mortgage.
2. Under a land contract, the seller (or vendor) retains legal title to the property until the buyer (or vendee) pays off the entire purchase price in installments.
3. A land contract is not accompanied by a promissory note; the contract describes the terms of sale and the financing arrangements.
4. For some land contracts, if a vendee defaults on the contract obligation, the vendee's rights in the property are terminated and the vendor retains all payments made so far; this remedy is known as forfeiture.
5. Courts won't necessarily allow forfeiture, depending on how long the vendee has been making payments.
6. The expense and delay of court proceedings in the event of breach of a land contract is the main disadvantage.
7. Lenders are not likely to offer institutional secondary financing if the primary financing is through a land contract.

C. Encumbered property: Wraparound financing

1. With a wraparound, the property remains subject to the existing mortgage (or underlying loan), and the seller continues to make payments.

2. Each month, the buyer makes a payment to the seller, and the seller uses a portion of that payment to make the payment on the underlying loan.
3. A wraparound can use a mortgage, deed of trust (called an all-inclusive deed of trust), or land contract.
4. The underlying loan cannot have a due-on-sale clause. It is never a good idea to use a "silent wrap," where the lender isn't informed of the sale of the property.
5. Wraparound financing can be attractive since it allows the buyer to finance a purchase at a below-market rate on the total amount financed while the seller receives an above-market rate on the credit extended.
6. The buyer's concern with a wraparound is to make sure that the seller makes payments on the underlying loan. The buyer may request a provision where the buyer can make the payment directly to the lender if the seller fails to do so, or make payments directly to an escrow account.

V. Alternatives to Seller Financing

A. Buydowns: The seller may assist a buyer with a buydown, by paying discount points to reduce the buyer's interest rate.

B. Contributions to closing costs: The seller may pay some of the buyer's closing costs, which can be more helpful than a price reduction for the same amount.

C. Equity exchanges: A seller may accept other assets from a buyer as well as cash, and reduce the cash sales price.

D. Lease arrangements: A seller may lease a property to a buyer for a time before the buyer purchases it, either through a lease/option or a lease/purchase.

1. A lease/option involves a lease for a specific term and then the option to purchase the property at a specified price.
2. The rental payments may be applied toward the purchase price in a lease/option, either deducted from the sales price or treated as part of the downpayment.
3. In a lease/purchase, buyer and seller sign a purchase contract along with the lease, so that deciding not to purchase at lease's end means a breach of the contract.

VI. Agent's Responsibilities in Seller-Financed Transactions

A. An agent should recommend that both parties get legal and tax advice, and have documents reviewed by a lawyer, before proceeding with seller financing.

B. A real estate agent should not prepare seller financing documents, which would be considered the unauthorized practice of law.

C. Disclosures: Some states require disclosure forms when a third party (such as a real estate agent) helps arrange seller financing.

D. Liability: A disclosure statement does not limit an agent's liability.

1. An agent who encourages an unwise financial arrangement might be liable for breach of fiduciary duties.

2. An agent who arranges seller financing might create an inadvertent dual agency.

Key Terms

Purchase money loan: A mortgage or deed of trust given by a buyer to a seller.

Seller financing: When a seller extends credit to a buyer to finance the purchase of the property, as opposed to having the buyer obtain a loan from a third party, such as an institutional lender.

Secondary financing: Money borrowed to pay part of the required downpayment or closing costs for a first loan, when the second loan is secured by the same property that secures the first loan.

Seller second: Secondary financing from the seller, when a purchase money loan is used to supplement an institutional first mortgage.

Land contract: A contract for the sale of property in which the buyer (vendee) pays the seller (vendor) in installments, taking possession of the property immediately but not taking title until the purchase price has been paid in full. Also called a contract for deed, conditional sales contract, installment sales contract, or real estate contract.

Wraparound financing: A seller financing arrangement in which the seller uses part of the buyer's payments to make the payments on an existing loan (called the underlying loan); the buyer takes title subject to the underlying loan, but does not assume it.

Buydown: When the seller or a third party pays the lender a lump sum at closing to lower the interest rate charged to the buyer, either for the life of the loan or during the first years of the loan term.

Equity exchange: When a buyer gives a seller real or personal property in addition to or instead of cash for the purchase price.

Lease/option: A lease that includes the option to purchase the leased property during the term of the lease.

Lease/purchase: A variation on the lease/option, in which the parties sign a purchase contract (instead of an option) and the prospective buyer leases the property for an extended period before closing.

Chapter Quiz

1. A seller can finance a buyer's purchase with:
   a. an all-inclusive trust deed
   b. a purchase money mortgage
   c. a land contract
   d. Any of the above

2. A seller second is most likely to be used to supplement a new institutional loan when:
   a. market interest rates are high
   b. the seller needs an exceptionally high yield on his or her investment
   c. the buyer has no cash for a downpayment
   d. negative amortization is a possibility

3. The Kramers are applying for a conventional loan that would be combined with a seller second. The monthly payment (PITI) on the institutional loan would be $1,838, and the payment on the seller financing would be $520; the Kramers' other debts add up to $490 per month. Applying a 36% maximum debt service to income ratio, the lender will make the loan if the Kramers' stable monthly income is at least:
   a. $5,106
   b. $6,467
   c. $6,550
   d. $7,911

4. Which of the following statements regarding balloon payments is true?
   a. A large balloon payment usually results in default
   b. In some cases, the buyer raises the cash for the balloon payment by refinancing
   c. A real estate agent should never suggest a seller financing arrangement that involves a balloon payment
   d. A new conventional loan cannot be combined with a seller second that requires a balloon payment

5. Which of the following instruments generally couldn't be used for a seller second supplementing a new institutional loan?
   a. Deed of trust
   b. Mortgage
   c. Land contract
   d. None of these could be used

6. The buyer made a downpayment, assumed the seller's mortgage, and gave the seller a deed of trust for the balance of the purchase price. The buyer defaults and the mortgagee forecloses on the assumed loan. If the foreclosure sale proceeds are not sufficient to cover the outstanding balance on the assumed mortgage:
   a. the seller will not be paid
   b. the mortgagee will not be paid
   c. the seller will be paid before the mortgagee is paid
   d. the mortgagee and the seller will each receive a prorated share of the sale proceeds

7. With wraparound financing:
   a. the buyer assumes the underlying loan
   b. the balance owed on the underlying loan is larger than the wrap-around loan amount
   c. the seller remains responsible for making the payments on the underlying loan
   d. the more credit the seller extends to the buyer, the higher the seller's yield

8. The chief advantage of wraparound financing is that:
   a. it complies with the secondary financing rules that institutional lenders apply
   b. the seller can get an exceptionally high yield on the credit extended
   c. the due-on-sale clause on the underlying loan is not triggered, as it would be by an assumption
   d. the seller retains title to the property until the buyer has paid the full price

9. The remaining balance on the underlying loan is $230,000, and the interest rate is 8%. The seller offers a $260,000 wraparound at 10% interest. What would the seller's approximate yield be?
   a. 8%
   b. 12%
   c. 17%
   d. 25%

10. In a lease/option arrangement, the rent charged:
    a. is usually refunded if the tenant exercises the option to buy
    b. cannot be applied toward the purchase price
    c. cannot exceed the fair market rent for the property
    d. is often higher than the fair market rent for the property

Answer Key

1. d. A seller may use an all-inclusive trust deed, a purchase money mortgage, or a land contract to finance a buyer's purchase.

2. a. A seller second is likely to be used when market interest rates are high. If interest rates are high, few buyers may be able to qualify for a loan large enough to afford the full purchase price, so a seller may offer secondary financing as an incentive.

3. d. To calculate the required stable monthly income, add all of the monthly debt payments ($1,838 + $520 + $490 = $2,848) and then divide that figure by the maximum debt to income ratio ($2,848 ÷ .36 = $7,911).

4. b. When a balloon payment comes due, a borrower may be able to refinance the amount due rather than having to pay the full amount in cash.

5. c. A land contract generally cannot be used for a seller second that supplements an institutional loan.

6. a. If a lender forecloses on an assumed loan, and the foreclosure sale proceeds are not sufficient to cover the balance on the assumed loan, then the seller will not be paid any of the proceeds.

7. c. A seller who uses wraparound financing will remain responsible for making payments on the underlying loan.

8. b. With wraparound financing, a seller can get an above-market yield on the credit extended.

9. d. To determine the seller's yield, first calculate the amount of credit extended ($260,000 – $230,000 = $30,000). Calculate the interest received on the wraparound ($260,000 × .1 = $26,000) and the interest received on the underlying loan ($230,000 × .08 = $18,400). Subtract the interest received on the underlying loan from the interest received on the wraparound, in order to calculate the net interest received by the seller ($26,000 – $18,400 = $7,600). Finally, divide the net interest by the total amount of credit extended to find the seller's yield ($7,600 ÷ $30,000 = .25, or 25%).

10. d. The rent in a lease/option arrangement is usually higher than the market rate, since the tenant is receiving an additional benefit in having the possibility of purchase.

Case Study: Qualifying the Buyer
Seller Financing

In the case study at the end of Chapter 10, the market interest rate for a 90% fixed-rate loan was 6.75%. Now suppose interest rates are much higher than that (see the rates listed below), and as a result the Cortinas have mainly been looking at homes priced below $180,000.

Although the Cortinas have seen several properties that would meet their needs, they haven't felt enthusiastic about any of them—until now. This afternoon they looked at a home they really want. Unfortunately, because interest rates for institutional loans are so high, the property is a little out of the Cortinas' price range.

The seller, Bonnie Wellman, was recently widowed and is about to retire. She plans to use part of the sale proceeds as a downpayment on a condominium, and to invest the rest to supplement her income. She'll have to pay off her mortgage, which has a due-on-sale clause; the current balance is about $67,500.

Wellman's home has been listed for more than three months. Quite a few people have looked at the property, but the only offer so far was for $176,000—$9,000 less than the appraised value, $185,000—and Wellman turned it down. She would accept $185,000 for the property, but she's not willing to go any lower than that.

You tell Wellman how much the Cortinas like her house, and explain that they probably could not qualify for an institutional loan large enough to enable them to buy it. You ask if she would consider accepting a second deed of trust for part of the price. Wellman says she's willing to discuss it with you. She needs at least $25,000 in cash at closing. She would like to be paid at least 9% interest on any financing she provides, since that's approximately the rate of return she could expect to get on a secure investment.

You sit down to design a seller second to supplement a conventional loan that the Cortinas could qualify for. Refer back to the case study at the end of Chapter 10 for the information you will need about the Cortinas' financial situation.

Interest rates for 30-year conventional loans:

Fixed rate, 90% or 95% LTV: 12% interest, 2% origination fee, 1 point discount
ARM (1% annual rate cap), 90% LTV: 10%, 1.75% origination fee, 1 point discount
Fixed rate, LTV 80% or less: 11.75%, 2% origination fee, 1 point discount
ARM (1% rate cap), LTV 80% or less: 9.75%, 1.75% origination fee, 1 point discount

1. Assume that the Cortinas will obtain their primary financing from a lender with strict secondary financing rules; the primary loan may not exceed 75% of the property's value, and the buyer must make at least a 10% downpayment. If the Cortinas buy Wellman's home for $185,000, what is the largest conventional loan they could supplement with a seller second? If they obtain a conventional loan for that amount, what is the largest amount Wellman could finance?

2. Suppose that the Cortinas obtain a 30-year ARM for the maximum amount (determined in question 1) at the market rate, and Wellman finances her maximum share at 9% interest. If both the conventional loan and the seller second are amortized over a 30-year term, the monthly principal and interest payment for the conventional loan would be $1,192.08, and the monthly principal and interest payment for the seller second would be $223.28. To find the monthly housing expense, add 15% to the combined principal and interest payment to cover taxes and insurance, but then subtract $50 from that figure, since no mortgage insurance will be required. Could the Cortinas qualify for this combination of an institutional loan and a seller second?

3. If the Cortinas have to pay the origination fee and the discount fee for the conventional loan, plus other closing costs estimated at 2% of the sales price, how much cash would they need at closing for this transaction? Also calculate how much two months' combined loan payments (PITI) would be, because the lender will require the Cortinas to have two months of reserves.

4. Wellman isn't willing to wait 30 years to collect her full profit from the sale; she would like it in five years. How could this be arranged, without preventing the Cortinas from qualifying for the institutional loan?

5. If her selling costs came to 10% of the sales price, how much cash would Wellman receive at closing in this transaction? Remember that she would have to pay off her mortgage.

Chapter 14
Fair Lending and Consumer Protection

Fair Lending Laws

- Equal Credit Opportunity Act
- Fair Housing Act
- Home Mortgage Disclosure Act

Consumer Protection Laws

- Truth in Lending Act
- Real Estate Settlement Procedures Act

Predatory Lending

- Predatory lending practices
- Targeted victims
- Predatory lending laws
  - Home Ownership and Equity Protection Act
  - State laws
- Other efforts to stop predatory lending

Introduction

In this chapter we'll cover several federal laws that are intended to promote fairness, clarity, and honesty in residential mortgage lending. Some of these are fair lending laws, which make it illegal for lenders to discriminate when they evaluate loan applications and make loan approval decisions. Consumer protection laws also apply to mortgage lending. These laws are designed to help buyers understand the lending process and make wise financing decisions. In spite of these laws, unscrupulous lenders and mortgage brokers often manipulate vulnerable and unsophisticated borrowers into taking out loans that are not in their own interests. The problem of predatory lending is discussed at the end of this chapter.

Fair Lending Laws

Residential mortgage loan transactions are subject to federal antidiscrimination laws, including the Equal Credit Opportunity Act, the Fair Housing Act, and the Home Mortgage Disclosure Act.

Equal Credit Opportunity Act

The Equal Credit Opportunity Act (ECOA), which became law in 1974, applies to all consumer credit, including residential mortgage loans. Consumer credit is credit that is extended to an individual (not a corporation or other business) for personal, family, or household purposes.

Equal Credit Opportunity Act prohibits discrimination based on:

- Race
- Color
- Religion
- National origin
- Sex
- Marital status
- Age
- Public assistance

ECOA prohibits discrimination against loan applicants based on race, color, religion, national origin, sex, marital status, or age (as long as an applicant is old enough to have contractual capacity under the laws of his or her state). The act also prohibits discrimination against applicants because all or part of their income is from a public assistance program, such as welfare. And it prohibits discrimination against applicants who have exercised their rights under federal credit laws (for example, by requesting corrections to a credit report).

Lenders have to comply with ECOA in interviewing and communicating with loan applicants, in analyzing applicants' finances, and in the credit terms they offer applicants. They must not discourage anyone from applying for a loan, and they must apply their credit guidelines to every loan applicant in the same manner, based on amount and stability of income, net worth, and credit history. Under ECOA, it's illegal for lenders to base lending decisions on assumptions about the creditworthiness of members of particular racial, ethnic, and religious groups; women or men; unmarried couples, divorced people, or single people; or elderly people or young adults.

Note that the law permits lenders to ask about a loan applicant's age or marital status, as long as the information isn't used as a basis for discrimination. Inquiries about marital status must be limited to asking whether an applicant is married, unmarried, or separated (divorced, widowed, and single people are all categorized as unmarried) and whether the applicant prefers to be addressed as Mr., Ms., Mrs., or Miss.

Applicants may be asked about the number and age of their dependents and about expenses related to the dependents. However, lenders aren't allowed to ask whether loan applicants are planning to bear, adopt, or raise children (or more children in addition to the ones they already have). It's also illegal for a lender to assume that applicants who belong to certain groups are more likely to bear or raise children, and therefore will probably have diminished or interrupted income.

Lenders aren't allowed to ask loan applicants about their childbearing plans

Fair Housing Act

The Federal Fair Housing Act, a 1968 law, includes provisions that address lending discrimination. The act applies to transactions involving residential properties with one to four dwelling units, and it prohibits discrimination based on race, color, national origin, religion, sex, disability, or familial status (a term used in the law to refer to families with children).

Under the Fair Housing Act, lenders may not do any of the following for discriminatory reasons:

- refuse to provide information about mortgage loans,
- refuse to make a mortgage loan, or
- impose different terms or conditions on a loan.

Fair Housing Act prohibits discrimination based on:

- Race
- Color
- National origin
- Religion
- Sex
- Disability
- Familial status

The Fair Housing Act also prohibits **redlining**. Redlining is the refusal to make loans secured by property located in a certain neighborhood because the people who live there belong to a particular racial or ethnic group. At one time lenders routinely refused to make loans in minority neighborhoods and newly integrated neighborhoods

Redlining: refusing to make loans in certain neighborhoods based on the race or ethnic background of the residents

because it was assumed that property values in those areas were declining. (The term "redlining" originates from the practice of using red ink to mark off these neighborhoods on a map of the community; mortgages weren't available for properties inside the red lines.) Redlining can turn discriminatory assumptions into self-fulfilling prophecies. Because it isn't possible to obtain purchase or renovation loans in a redlined neighborhood, it's difficult to sell, maintain, or improve homes there, and property values decline as a result. While redlining is not as widespread as it once was, the problem has not been eliminated.

It is legal for a lender to refuse to make a loan because property values in the neighborhood are in fact declining. But the refusal has to be based on objective economic criteria about the condition and value of the neighborhood surrounding the property, without regard to the neighborhood's racial or ethnic composition. Lenders may not automatically assume that minority or integrated neighborhoods have declining property values.

Home Mortgage Disclosure Act

Home Mortgage Disclosure Act helps the government spot redlining and predatory lending

The Home Mortgage Disclosure Act (HMDA) was enacted in 1975. It provides a way for the government to monitor whether lenders are fulfilling their obligation to serve the housing needs of the communities where they are located. The act also facilitates enforcement of the Fair Housing Act's prohibition of lending discrimination and redlining.

HMDA applies to large institutional lenders located in metropolitan areas. These lenders each must submit an annual report to the government on the residential mortgage loans—purchase loans, home equity loans, and refinancings—that they originated or purchased from other lenders during the fiscal year. The report must also include applications that did not result in loans.

Among other information, a lender has to furnish all of the following for each loan or loan application:

- the dollar amount of the loan;
- the type of loan (FHA, VA, or other);
- the purpose of the loan;
- whether the application was a request for preapproval and whether it was denied or approved;

- the race, ethnicity, sex, and gross annual income of the borrower;
- the type of property; and
- the geographic location of the property.

The geographic information is used to detect redlining. If a lender's report reveals areas where few or no home loans have been made, government investigators are alerted that there may be a problem.

HMDA is implemented by the Federal Reserve Board's Regulation C. Amendments to Regulation C that went into effect in 2004 require lenders to report additional information that may help the government address predatory lending issues. For example, a lender's report now must provide information concerning the cost of a loan and whether it is subject to the Home Ownership and Equity Protection Act, discussed below.

Consumer Protection Laws

The consumer protection laws that apply to mortgage loan transactions include the Truth in Lending Act, the Home Ownership and Equity Protection Act, and the Real Estate Settlement Procedures Act.

Truth in Lending Act

The Truth in Lending Act (TILA) was passed in 1968. It's implemented by the Federal Reserve Board's **Regulation Z**. Regulation Z does not set limits on interest rates or other finance charges, but it does regulate the disclosure of these charges.

Truth in Lending Act is implemented by Regulation Z

Loans Covered by TILA. A loan is a consumer loan if it is used for personal, family, or household purposes. A consumer loan is covered by the Truth in Lending Act if it is to be repaid in more than four installments, or is subject to finance charges, and is either:

- for $25,000 or less, or
- secured by real property.

Thus, any mortgage loan is covered by TILA as long as the proceeds are used for personal, family, or household purposes (such as buying or remodeling a home, consolidating personal debt, or sending children to college).

TILA applies to any mortgage loan used for personal, family, or household purposes

Loans Exempt from TILA. The Truth in Lending Act applies only to loans made to natural persons, so loans made to corporations or organizations aren't covered. Loans for business, commercial, or agricultural purposes are also exempt. So are loans in excess of $25,000, unless the loan is secured by real property. (Mortgage loans for personal, family, or household purposes are covered regardless of the loan amount.) Most seller financing is exempt, because extending credit isn't in the seller's ordinary course of business.

Disclosure Requirements. TILA's disclosure requirements apply to lenders and **credit arrangers**, a term that includes mortgage brokers. As we discussed in Chapter 7, a lender (or credit arranger) is required to give a loan applicant a disclosure statement with estimates of the loan costs within three business days after receiving the written application.

As you'll recall from Chapter 7, the two most important disclosures required under TILA are the total finance charge and the annual percentage rate. All of the required disclosures are supposed to be presented "clearly and conspicuously in writing, in a form that the consumer may keep." However, the total finance charge and the annual percentage rate, along with the lender's name, must be presented even more conspicuously than the rest of the information. The total finance charge should be labeled "the dollar amount your credit will cost you," and the APR should be labeled "the cost of your credit as a yearly rate."

APR shows relationship of total finance charge to total amount financed

Lenders are expected to use the best information reasonably available to them in preparing a TILA disclosure statement and calculating the total finance charge and annual percentage rate. They are allowed to use "banker's months" with 30 days, rather than the exact number of days in each month in the calculations. The disclosures are considered adequate if the total finance charge is accurate to within $100 and the APR is accurate to within one-eighth of one percent.

Total finance charge may include:

- Interest
- Origination fee
- Points paid by borrower
- Finder's fee
- Service charge
- Mortgage insurance premium or guaranty fee
- Mortgage broker's compensation

Total finance charge. Let's take a slightly more detailed look at the finance charge. The total finance charge is the sum of all fees and charges the borrower will pay in connection with the loan. It includes the interest, and it also may include an origination fee, discount points, a finder's fee, service charges, mortgage insurance premiums or guaranty fees, and a mortgage broker's fee or commission.

Fig. 14.1 Truth in Lending Act disclosure statement form

TRUTH-IN-LENDING DISCLOSURE STATEMENT
REQUIRED BY FEDERAL RESERVE REGULATIONS Z

BORROWER(S)

DATE 19

LOAN NUMBER

TYPE OF LOAN

LOAN TERM YEARS

PROPERTY LOCATION

ANNUAL PERCENTAGE RATE The cost of your credit as a yearly rate	**FINANCE CHARGE** The dollar amount your credit will cost you	AMOUNT FINANCED The amount of credit provided to you or on your behalf	TOTAL OF PAYMENTS The amount you will have paid after you have paid all payments as scheduled
%	$	$	$

Notice to Borrower(s): In compliance with Truth-In-Lending Law you are receiving a Good Faith Estimate of Settlement Charges in lieu of an itemization statement.

Your Payment Schedule will be:

Monthly Beginning

Date

Number of Payments	Amount of Payments	When Payments Are Due	Number of Payments	Amount of Payments	When Payments Are Due
	$			$	
	$			$	
	$			$	
	$			$	

☐ This loan has a **Demand Feature.**

☐ Your loan contains a **Variable Rate Feature.** Disclosures about the Variable Rate have been provided to you earlier.
Your ARM Loan ☐ has ☐ does not have a **Conversion Feature.** (The option to convert your ARM loan to a Fixed Rate Mortgage loan.) If choose to convert to a Fixed Rate mortgage loan, your new interest rate will not be higher than ______ %, which is the Maximum Rate.

☐ **Variable Rate not applicable.**

☐ **Insurance:** The following insurance is required: ☐ Property Insurance ☐ Flood Insurance
You may obtain insurance from an agent of your choice, provided they are acceptable to this lender.
- ☐ Property Insurance is available through the lender at a cost of $__________ for a one year term.
- ☐ Flood Insurance is available through the lender at a cost of $__________ for a one year term.
- ☐ Credit Life Insurance or Disability Insurance are not required.
- ☐ Credit Life Insurance and/or Disability Insurance are not provided.
- ☐ Credit Life Insurance and/or Disability Insurance are not available through this lender.
- ☐ Credit Life is available at a cost of $______ for a ______ term. (X __________)
- ☐ Disability Insurance is available at a cost of $______ for a ______ term. (X __________)

Security: You are giving a Security Interest ☐ in the property being purchased ☐ other accounts you have with us
other (describe) __________

Late Charge: If your payment is ______ days late, you will be required to pay a Penalty charge of ______% of your payment.

Prepayment: If you pay this loan early, you ☐ will ☐ will not have to pay a penalty
and you ☐ may ☐ will not be entitled to a refund of a part of the finance charge.

Assumption: Someone buying your property ☐ may, subject to conditions ☐ may not assume the remainder of your loan on the Original terms.

☐ This is an assumption of an existing loan. The interest rate for the term of the loan will not exceed ______%, which is the maximum rate.

☐ Filing Fees $__________

☐ This is an **Early Disclosure** and all dates and numerical disclosures are estimates except for late payment disclosures.

☐ This is your **Final Disclosure**

NOTE: See your contract documents for any additional information about nonpayment, default, any required repayment in full before the scheduled date and prepayment refunds and penalties.

(e) means an-estimate

I/we acknowledge receipt of a completed copy of this disclosure statement.

X __________ Date ______ 19 ___ X __________
Borrower *Co-Borrower*

Jiffy Prints

However, none of the following costs are included in the total finance charge for a mortgage loan transaction:

- application fee,
- appraisal fee,
- document preparation or notary fee,
- credit report fee,
- title report fee,
- title insurance premium,
- survey fee,
- pest inspection fee,
- flood hazard inspection fee,
- impounds for taxes and insurance,
- any points paid by the seller,
- late payment fees, or
- fees charged in the event of default.

Also, the total finance charge doesn't include any charges that would be incurred anyway if the transaction were being carried out entirely in cash.

An escrow or closing agent's fee and the borrower's hazard insurance premiums may be included in the total finance charge if the lender requires a particular closing agent or insurance company to be used, rather than letting the borrower choose. In most transactions, however, the closing agent's fee and hazard insurance premiums are not part of the total finance charge.

In addition to APR and total finance charge, TILA disclosure statement must also show:

- Lender's identity
- Total amount financed
- Payment schedule
- Prepayment fee
- Late charges
- Assumption policy

Other disclosures. In addition to the total finance charge and annual percentage rate, all of the following must appear on a TILA disclosure statement: the identity of the lender; the amount financed; a payment schedule, with the number, amounts, and timing of payments; the total amount those payments will add up to; the prepayment fee (if any); late charges; and whether and under what terms the loan can be assumed by another person if the property is sold.

ARM disclosures. In addition to the disclosures already listed, the Truth in Lending Act requires a number of special disclosures for adjustable-rate mortgages.

Lenders must give applicants a general brochure about ARMs (the "Consumer Handbook on Adjustable-Rate Mortgages," prepared by the Federal Reserve), establish guidelines for calculating and disclosing the annual percentage rate, and make specific disclosures relevant to the particular ARM program applied for. The disclosures must be made at the time the loan application is submitted to the lender, or before the applicant pays any nonrefundable fee, whichever occurs first.

For each ARM program a prospective loan applicant expresses interest in, the lender is required to provide the following disclosures, if appropriate for the program:

TILA requires detailed additional disclosures for ARM programs

1. the fact that the interest rate, payment, or term of the loan may change;
2. the index used to determine the interest rate;
3. where the borrower can find the index;
4. how the interest rate and payment will be determined;
5. a statement that the applicant should ask the lender about the loan's margin and the current interest rate;
6. if the initial interest rate is discounted (lower than the rate indicated by the index), a disclosure of that fact and a statement that the applicant should inquire as to the amount of the discount;
7. the rate and payment adjustment periods;
8. any rules regarding changes in the index, interest rate, payment amount, or loan balance (including an explanation of any caps, a conversion option, or the possibility of negative amortization);
9. an explanation of how to calculate the monthly payments for the loan;
10. a statement that the loan has an acceleration clause;
11. a description of the information that will be included in the adjustment notices and how often the lender will send those notices to the borrower; and
12. a statement that disclosure forms are available for the lender's other ARM programs.

In addition, the lender is required to give the loan applicant a historical example illustrating how the monthly payments on a $10,000 adjustable-rate loan (with the same features as the ARM that the applicant is considering) would have been affected by actual interest rate changes over the past 15 years, or an example of how the maximum potential interest rate and payment amount would be calculated for such a $10,000 loan.

When calculating the annual percentage rate for an ARM, a lender is allowed to base the APR on the loan's initial interest rate. At closing this is usually the only interest rate for the loan that the lender can be sure of; the rates that will apply later on are uncertain, since they depend on changes in the index. However, the lender is required to state that the APR may increase ("6.41% APR, subject to increase after closing").

ARM's APR is subject to increase after closing

Once the loan has been made, Regulation Z requires the lender to give the borrower advance notice of any change in the payment, the interest rate, or (in case of negative amortization) the loan balance. These disclosures must be provided to the borrower at least 25 days, but not more than 120 days, before a new payment level takes effect, and at least once in each year in which the interest rate on the loan changes without a payment adjustment.

TILA's three-day right of rescission applies only to home equity loans

Rescission of Home Equity Loans. TILA has a special rule for home equity loans. When the security property is the borrower's existing principal residence, the law gives the borrower a right of rescission. The borrower may rescind the loan agreement any time within three days after signing it, receiving a disclosure statement, or receiving notice of the right of rescission, whichever comes latest. If the borrower never receives the statement or the notice, the right of rescission does not expire for three years. (Remember that this applies only to home equity loans. There is no right of rescission for a loan financing the purchase or construction of the borrower's principal residence.)

Advertising Under TILA. In addition to its disclosure requirements, the Truth in Lending Act has rules that govern the advertising of credit terms. Its advertising rules apply to anyone who advertises consumer credit, not just lenders and credit arrangers. For example, a real estate broker advertising financing terms for a listed home has to comply with TILA and Regulation Z.

APR and cash price can be advertised without triggering TILA's full disclosure requirement

It's always legal to state the cash price or the annual percentage rate in an ad. But if any other particular loan terms (such as the downpayment, the interest rate, or the monthly payment amount) are stated in the ad, then all of the rest of the terms must also be stated.

> **Example:** A newspaper ad says, "Assume VA loan at 5% interest." Because it mentions the interest rate, the ad will violate the Truth in Lending Act if it doesn't go on to reveal the APR, the downpayment, and all the other terms of repayment.

In the example, the reference to the interest rate triggered the full disclosure requirement. However, general statements such as "low downpayment," "easy terms," or "affordable interest rate" would not trigger the full disclosure requirement.

An example of a flyer that violates the Truth in Lending Act is shown in Figure 14.2.

Real Estate Settlement Procedures Act

The Real Estate Settlement Procedures Act (RESPA), a 1974 law, affects how closing is handled in most residential transactions financed with institutional loans. The law has two main goals:

- to provide borrowers with information about their closing costs; and
- to eliminate kickbacks and referral fees that unnecessarily increase the costs of settlement.

RESPA's main goals:
- Informing borrowers about closing costs
- Eliminating kickbacks

Transactions Covered by RESPA. RESPA applies to "federally related" loan transactions. A loan is federally related if:

1. it will be secured by a mortgage or deed of trust against:
   - property on which there is (or on which the loan proceeds will be used to build) a dwelling with four or fewer units;
   - a condominium unit or a cooperative apartment;
   - a lot with (or on which the loan proceeds will be used to place) a mobile home; and
2. the lender is federally regulated, has federally insured accounts, is assisted by the federal government, makes loans in connection with a federal program, sells loans to Fannie Mae, Ginnie Mae, or Freddie Mac, or makes real estate loans that total more than $1,000,000 per year.

RESPA applies to federally related loans, which includes most mortgage loans made by institutional lenders

In short, the act applies to almost all institutional lenders and to most residential loans.

Exemptions. RESPA doesn't apply to the following transactions:

- a loan used to purchase 25 acres or more;
- a loan primarily for a business, commercial, or agricultural purpose;

Fig. 14.2 Example of an actual flyer that violates the Truth in Lending Act's advertising rules

GET THAT
DREAM HOME...

...NOW!!!

$400,000 HOME LOAN FOR
$958/MONTH

PURCHASE/REFINANCE

1-800-555-4321

FREE $400 APPRAISAL

- a loan used to purchase vacant land, unless there will be a one- to four-unit dwelling built on it or a mobile home placed on it;
- temporary financing, such as a construction loan;
- an assumption for which the lender's approval is neither required nor obtained.

Note that RESPA also does not apply to seller-financed transactions, since they are not federally regulated.

RESPA Requirements. RESPA has these requirements for federally related loan transactions:

1. Within three days after receiving a written loan application, the lender must give all loan applicants:
   - a copy of a **booklet about settlement procedures**, prepared by HUD, which explains RESPA, closing costs, and the settlement statement;
   - a **good faith estimate of closing costs** (see Figure 14.3), which must also include information about any provider of settlement services (such as a particular title insurance company or escrow agent) that the lender requires the borrower to use; and
   - a **mortgage servicing disclosure statement**, which discloses whether the lender intends to service the loan or transfer it to another lender.

RESPA requires lender to give loan applicant:
- HUD booklet
- Good faith estimate of closing costs
- Mortgage servicing disclosure statement
- Uniform Settlement Statement

2. The closing agent must itemize all loan settlement charges on a **Uniform Settlement Statement** form (see below).
3. If the borrower will have to make deposits into an impound account to cover taxes, insurance, and other recurring costs, the lender cannot require **excessive deposits**—more than necessary to cover the expenses when they come due.
4. A lender or a provider of settlement services (such as a title company) may not:
   - pay **kickbacks** or **referral fees** to anyone for referring customers;
   - accept **unearned fees**—that is, fees for settlement services that were not actually provided; or

Fig. 14.3 Good faith estimate of closing costs form

GOOD FAITH ESTIMATE

Date: ______________________

Borrower: ______________________

Property Address: ______________________

This gives an **ESTIMATE** of most of the charges you will have to pay at the settlement of your loan. The figures shown **AS ESTIMATES**, are subject to change. The figures are computed on an estimated value of $____________, a loan amount of $ ____________ an interest rate of __________%, a term of ____________ and a LTV of __________%.

______ owner occupied ______ non-owner occupied Loan Type ______________

Unless otherwise discussed rates and fees are not locked in.

ESTIMATED CLOSING COSTS

801 Loan Origination Fee __________% ______________
802 Discount __________ ______________
803 Appraisal Fee ______________
804 Borrower Credit Report(s) ______________
808 Document Preparation Fee/Underwriting Fee ______________
810 Tax Registration ______________
812 Processing Fee ______________
1101 Escrow Fee ______________
1106 Flood Determination Letter/Courier/Fed. Express ______________
1108 Title Insurance Premium ______________
1201 Recording Fees ______________
Total Closing Costs $ ______________

PREPAID ITEMS AND RESERVES

901 Interim Interest ______ Days @ $ ________ ______________
902 Mortgage Insurance Premium ______________
902 Hazard Insurance Premium (12 months to be prepaid) ______________
1001 Hazard Insurance Reserve _______ mos. @ $_______ ______________
1002 Mortgage Insurance Reserve ________ mos. @ $ ______________
1004 Property Tax Reserve for _______mos. @ $ ______ ______________
Total Prepaids and Reserves to be paid at closing $ ______________

ESTIMATED MONTHLY PAYMENT

Principal & Interest $______________
Property Tax $______________
Hazard Insurance $______________
Mortgage Insurance $______________
Total Estimated Monthly Payment $______________

ESTIMATED CASH REQUIRED AT CLOSING

Sales Price/Cost to Build/Payoff $______________
Closing Costs $______________
Prepaid Items & Reserves $______________
Sub-Total $______________
Less Earnest Money $______________
Less Good Faith Deposit $______________
Less Standby Takeout Fee $______________
Less Seller Contributions $______________
Less Loan Amount $______________
Est. Cash Req. at Closing $______________

The above is for information only and is not a loan commitment.

The information provided below reflects estimates of the charges which you are likely to incur at the settlement of your loan. The fees listed are estimate - the actual charges may be more or less. Your transaction may not involve a fee for every item listed. The numbers listed beside the estimates generally correspond to the numbered lines contained in the HUD-1 settlement statement which you will be receving at settlement. The HUD-1 settlement statement will show you the actual cost for items paid at settlement.

An applicant, by signing this Good Faith Estimate, acknowledges receipt of HUD Booklet outlining settlement costs.

An applicant for an Adjustable Rate Mortgage, by signing this Good Faith Estimate, acknowledges receipt of the booklet entitled, "Consumer Handbook on Adjustable Rate Mortgages".

______________________ ______________ DATE

______________________ ______________ DATE

Prepared by: ______________________ ______________ DATE

- charge a **document preparation fee** for the Uniform Settlement Statement, an impound account statement, or the disclosure statement required by the Truth in Lending Act.

5. The property seller may not require the buyer to use a particular **title company**.

RESPA prohibits lenders and service providers from:
- requiring excessive impound deposits
- paying kickbacks or referral fees
- collecting unearned fees
- charging for preparation of Uniform Settlement Statement, impound account statement, or TILA disclosure

RESPA's prohibition on referral fees (number 4 above) helped to curb practices that were once widespread and that generally benefited real estate agents, lenders, and settlement service providers at the expense of home buyers.

Uniform Settlement Statement. The closing agent must provide completed Uniform Settlement Statement forms to the buyer, the seller, and the lender on or before the closing date. Although the same form is used for both the buyer and the seller, in most cases a separate statement is prepared for each party. The one given to the buyer presents only the buyer's closing information, and the one given to the seller presents only the seller's closing information.

A copy of the Uniform Settlement Statement form is shown in Figure 14.4. The back of the form (that is, the second page shown here) is used to itemize each party's closing costs. The buyer's statement will show the buyer's costs in the left column. The seller's statement will show the seller's costs in the right column. On each statement, the costs are added up and the total is transferred to the front of the form. On the buyer's statement, the buyer's total costs are entered on line 103. On the seller's statement, the seller's total costs are entered on line 502.

On the front of the buyer's statement, lines 101 through 120 list the buyer's debits, and 201 through 301 list the buyer's credits. On the front of the seller's statement, lines 401 through 420 list the seller's credits, and 501 through 601 list the seller's debits. The amount of cash the buyer must bring to closing appears on line 303, and the amount of cash the seller will receive at closing is shown on line 603.

Predatory Lending

In the 1990s, during the same years that the subprime mortgage market expanded dramatically, the attention of the public and public policy makers was drawn to the problem of predatory lending.

Fig. 14.4 Uniform Settlement Statement form

A. **Settlement Statement** | **U.S. Department of Housing and Urban Development** | OMB Approval No. 2502-0265

B. Type of Loan

1. ☐ FHA 2. ☐ FmHA 3. ☐ Conv. Unins. 4. ☐ VA 5. ☐ Conv. Ins.	6. File Number:	7. Loan Number:	8. Mortgage Insurance Case Number:

C. Note: This form is furnished to give you a statement of actual settlement costs. Amounts paid to and by the settlement agent are shown. Items marked "(p.o.c.)" were paid outside the closing; they are shown here for informational purposes and are not included in the totals.

D. Name & Address of Borrower:	E. Name & Address of Seller:	F. Name & Address of Lender:

G. Property Location:	H. Settlement Agent:	
	Place of Settlement:	I. Settlement Date:

J. Summary of Borrower's Transaction		K. Summary of Seller's Transaction	
100. Gross Amount Due From Borrower		**400. Gross Amount Due To Seller**	
101. Contract sales price		401. Contract sales price	
102. Personal property		402. Personal property	
103. Settlement charges to borrower (line 1400)		403.	
104.		404.	
105.		405.	
Adjustments for items paid by seller in advance		**Adjustments for items paid by seller in advance**	
106. City/town taxes to		406. City/town taxes to	
107. County taxes to		407. County taxes to	
108. Assessments to		408. Assessments to	
109.		409.	
110.		410.	
111.		411.	
112.		412.	
120. Gross Amount Due From Borrower		**420. Gross Amount Due To Seller**	
200. Amounts Paid By Or In Behalf Of Borrower		**500. Reductions In Amount Due To Seller**	
201. Deposit or earnest money		501. Excess deposit (see instructions)	
202. Principal amount of new loan(s)		502. Settlement charges to seller (line 1400)	
203. Existing loan(s) taken subject to		503. Existing loan(s) taken subject to	
204.		504. Payoff of first mortgage loan	
205.		505. Payoff of second mortgage loan	
206.		506.	
207.		507.	
208.		508.	
209.		509.	
Adjustments for items unpaid by seller		**Adjustments for items unpaid by seller**	
210. City/town taxes to		510. City/town taxes to	
211. County taxes to		511. County taxes to	
212. Assessments to		512. Assessments to	
213.		513.	
214.		514.	
215.		515.	
216.		516.	
217.		517.	
218.		518.	
219.		519.	
220. Total Paid By/For Borrower		**520. Total Reduction Amount Due Seller**	
300. Cash At Settlement From/To Borrower		**600. Cash At Settlement To/From Seller**	
301. Gross Amount due from borrower (line 120)		601. Gross amount due to seller (line 420)	
302. Less amounts paid by/for borrower (line 220)	( )	602. Less reductions in amt. due seller (line 520)	( )
303. Cash ☐ From ☐ To Borrower		**603. Cash ☐ To ☐ From Seller**	

Section 5 of the Real Estate Settlement Procedures Act (RESPA) requires the following: • HUD must develop a Special Information Booklet to help persons borrowing money to finance the purchase of residential real estate to better understand the nature and costs of real estate settlement services; • Each lender must provide the booklet to all applicants from whom it receives or for whom it prepares a written application to borrow money to finance the purchase of residential real estate; • Lenders must prepare and distribute with the Booklet a Good Faith Estimate of the settlement costs that the borrower is likely to incur in connection with the settlement. These disclosures are manadatory.

Section 4(a) of RESPA mandates that HUD develop and prescribe this standard form to be used at the time of loan settlement to provide full disclosure of all charges imposed upon the borrower and seller. These are third party disclosures that are designed to provide the borrower with pertinent information during the settlement process in order to be a better shopper.

The Public Reporting Burden for this collection of information is estimated to average one hour per response, including the time for reviewing instructions, searching existing data sources, gathering and maintaining the data needed, and completing and reviewing the collection of information.

This agency may not collect this information, and you are not required to complete this form, unless it displays a currently valid OMB control number.

The information requested does not lend itself to confidentiality.

Previous editions are obsolete | Page 1 of 2 | form **HUD-1** (3/86) ref Handbook 4305.2

L. Settlement Charges

	Paid From Borrowers Funds at Settlement	Paid From Seller's Funds at Settlement
700. Total Sales/Broker's Commission based on price $ @ % =		
Division of Commission (line 700) as follows:		
701. $ to		
702. $ to		
703. Commission paid at Settlement		
704.		
800. Items Payable In Connection With Loan		
801. Loan Origination Fee %		
802. Loan Discount %		
803. Appraisal Fee to		
804. Credit Report to		
805. Lender's Inspection Fee		
806. Mortgage Insurance Application Fee to		
807. Assumption Fee		
808.		
809.		
810.		
811.		
900. Items Required By Lender To Be Paid In Advance		
901. Interest from to @$ /day		
902. Mortgage Insurance Premium for months to		
903. Hazard Insurance Premium for years to		
904. years to		
905.		
1000. Reserves Deposited With Lender		
1001. Hazard insurance months@$ per month		
1002. Mortgage insurance months@$ per month		
1003. City property taxes months@$ per month		
1004. County property taxes months@$ per month		
1005. Annual assessments months@$ per month		
1006. months@$ per month		
1007. months@$ per month		
1008. months@$ per month		
1100. Title Charges		
1101. Settlement or closing fee to		
1102. Abstract or title search to		
1103. Title examination to		
1104. Title insurance binder to		
1105. Document preparation to		
1106. Notary fees to		
1107. Attorney's fees to		
(includes above items numbers:)		
1108. Title insurance to		
(includes above items numbers:)		
1109. Lender's coverage $		
1110. Owner's coverage $		
1111.		
1112.		
1113.		
1200. Government Recording and Transfer Charges		
1201. Recording fees: Deed $; Mortgage $; Releases $		
1202. City/county tax/stamps: Deed $; Mortgage $		
1203. State tax/stamps: Deed $; Mortgage $		
1204.		
1205.		
1300. Additional Settlement Charges		
1301. Survey to		
1302. Pest inspection to		
1303.		
1304.		
1305.		
1400. Total Settlement Charges (enter on lines 103, Section J and 502, Section K)		

Previous editions are obsolete — Page 2 of 2 — form **HUD-1** (3/86) ref Handbook 4305.2

Predatory lending became a widespread problem during the subprime boom in the 1990s

Predatory lending refers to practices that unscrupulous mortgage lenders and mortgage brokers use to take advantage of (prey upon) unsophisticated borrowers for their own profit. Real estate agents, appraisers, and home improvement contractors sometimes participate in predatory lending schemes, and in some cases a buyer or seller may play a role in deceiving the other party.

For a variety of reasons, predatory lending is especially likely to occur in the subprime market. It tends to be more common in refinancing and home equity lending, but home purchase loans are also affected.

We'll examine some of the tactics and loan terms predatory lenders use, describe the buyers they tend to target, and consider the laws and regulatory efforts that are intended to address the problem.

Predatory Lending Practices

Some predatory lending practices involve tactics that are always abusive; others involve ordinary lending practices and loan terms that can be misused for a predatory purpose. The following list doesn't separate those two categories, but you should keep the distinction in mind.

Predatory Steering. Steering a buyer toward a more expensive loan (one with a higher interest rate and/or fees) when the buyer could qualify for a less expensive loan.

Fee Packing. Charging interest rates, points, or processing fees that far exceed the norm and are not justified by the cost of the services provided.

Loan Flipping. Encouraging a home owner to refinance repeatedly in a short period, when there's no real benefit in doing so.

Equity Stripping. "Stripping away" a home owner's equity by charging high fees on repeated refinancings.

Property Flipping. Purchasing property at a discount (because the seller needs a quick sale) and then rapidly reselling it to an unsophisticated buyer for an inflated price. This isn't illegal in and of itself, but it is illegal when a real estate agent, appraiser, and/or lender commit fraud to make the buyer believe the property is worth substantially more than it's actually worth.

Disregarding Buyer's Capacity to Pay. Making a loan based only on the property's value, without considering the borrower's ability to afford the loan payments. The borrower will default and the lender will profit from the foreclosure.

Unaffordable Payments. Making loans to borrowers without using appropriate qualifying standards, so that they can't afford the payments and will probably default and lose their homes. In this situation, the predator doesn't care whether the borrower will eventually default, because the predator is either making the loan on behalf of another lender or intends to sell the loan immediately.

According to HUD, many foreclosures that occur within the first two years of owning a home result from predatory lending practices.

Impound Waivers. Not requiring a borrower to make monthly deposits for property taxes and insurance into an impound account, even though the borrower is unlikely to be able to pay the taxes and insurance when they're due. Waiving the impound requirement encourages a home buyer or owner to borrow more because it reduces the monthly payment. Once again, predatory brokers or lenders use this tactic when they won't be affected by an eventual default and foreclosure.

Loan in Excess of Value. Loaning a home buyer or owner more than the appraised value of the property. This usually involves a fraudulent appraisal. It may occur when a lender and an appraiser collude in a property flipping scheme, or when a mortgage broker and an appraiser collude to deceive a lender, victimizing both the lender and the borrower.

Negative Amortization Schemes. Deliberately making a loan with payments that don't cover the interest. The unpaid interest will be added to the outstanding principal balance and the loan will become very difficult to pay off. When adjustable-rate mortgages were a new type of loan, negative amortization was an unfortunate side effect of the way some ARMs were structured. Legitimate lenders now generally structure loans to avoid negative amortization, but predatory lenders profit from it.

Balloon Payment Abuses. Making a partially amortized or interest-only loan that has low monthly payments, without properly disclosing to the borrowers that a large balloon payment will be required after a short period. When the time comes, the borrowers will be told that their only alternative to foreclosure is an expensive refinancing loan from the same lender.

Predatory lending practices and loan provisions:
- Steering
- Fee packing
- Loan flipping
- Equity stripping
- Property flipping
- Disregarding buyer's capacity to repay
- Unaffordable payments
- Impound waivers
- Loans in excess of value
- Negative amortization
- Balloon payment abuses
- Fraud
- High-pressure sales tactics
- Advance payments from loan proceeds
- Excessive prepayment penalties
- Unfair default interest rates
- Discretionary call provisions
- Single-premium credit life insurance

Fraud. Misrepresenting or concealing unfavorable loan terms or excessive fees, falsifying documents, or using other fraudulent means to induce a prospective borrower to enter into a loan agreement.

High-pressure Sales Tactics. Telling prospective borrowers that they must decide immediately, that no other lender will loan them the money they need, and so on.

Advance Payments from Loan Proceeds. Requiring a series of the borrower's mortgage payments to be paid at closing, out of the loan proceeds.

Excessive or Unfair Prepayment Penalties. Imposing an unusually large penalty, failing to limit the penalty period to the first few years of the loan term, and/or charging the penalty even if the loan is prepaid because the property is being sold. Prepayment penalties can also be used to prevent refinancing by borrowers who were steered to an expensive loan.

Unfair Default Interest Rate. Increasing a loan's interest rate by an excessive amount when the borrower defaults, in a way that isn't justified by the additional risk involved in the situation.

Discretionary Call Provision. Including in loan documents a call provision (acceleration clause) that allows the lender to accelerate the loan at any time, not just because the payments are delinquent or the property is being sold.

Single-premium Credit Life Insurance. A credit life insurance policy will pay off a mortgage if the borrower dies. Some borrowers choose to purchase credit life insurance with reasonable premiums that are paid in installments, but predatory lenders often require their victims to purchase a credit life policy with a single large premium due at closing.

In addition to predatory lenders and brokers, there are predatory loan servicers. They charge improper late fees, fail to credit payments the borrower has made, and sometimes even institute foreclosure proceedings against borrowers who are not in default.

Targeted Victims

Targeted victims of predatory lending tend to be unsophisticated and in vulnerable circumstances

As you read through the list of predatory practices, you may have wondered how borrowers can possibly be persuaded to agree to some of the arrangements and terms described. The unfortunate explanation is that predatory lenders and brokers deliberately target prospective borrowers who:

- aren't able to understand the transaction they're entering into, and/or
- don't know that better alternatives are available to them.

Potential borrowers are especially likely to be targeted if they:

- are elderly,
- have a limited education,
- speak limited English,
- have a low income,
- are deeply in debt,
- have a poor credit history or no credit history, or
- live in redlined neighborhoods.

Predatory lending concerns overlap with fair lending issues, because racial and ethnic minority groups are disproportionately represented in the ranks of predatory lending victims.

Elderly people who are cognitively impaired and who have a lot of equity in their homes are the most frequent victims of predatory refinancing and equity stripping schemes.

Elderly people with lots of equity are frequently targeted by predatory lenders

Here is some of the advice that experts offer borrowers to help them avoid being victimized by predatory lenders:

1. Don't let a real estate agent, a mortgage broker, or anyone else steer you to one particular lender.
2. Don't assume that you won't be able to qualify for a loan on reasonable terms from a legitimate lender.
3. Don't let anyone persuade you to make false statements on a loan application or in other aspects of the transaction.
4. Don't let anyone persuade you to borrow more money than you can afford to repay.
5. Don't let anyone convince you that you've committed yourself to a transaction before you actually have. For example, signing a disclosure form does not obligate you to proceed with the loan.
6. Don't sign documents that have blanks that haven't been filled in. In provisions that don't apply in the current transaction, the blank lines should have "N/A" (for "not applicable") written in them.

7. Don't sign documents without reading them first and asking questions about provisions you don't understand.
8. If you don't speak English fluently, try to arrange for a translator to accompany you to the loan interview and help you review documents before signing.
9. Even if you are fluent in English, get the assistance of a lawyer, a housing counselor, a trusted real estate agent, or even a trusted friend or relative who has some experience in financial matters. Two pairs of eyes are better than one.

Many borrowers believe they can't afford to have a lawyer review their loan documents before they sign them. However, it's a precaution that typically costs only a few hundred dollars, and it could save borrowers thousands of dollars by helping them avoid a predatory lending scheme. Also, by calling the local bar association, low-income loan applicants may be able to find a free legal services clinic where an attorney will help them.

Predatory Lending Laws

Legal efforts to put a stop to predatory lending include one federal law and a growing number of state laws.

Home Ownership and Equity Protection Act. Although it's usually discussed as a separate law, the Home Ownership and Equity Protection Act (HOEPA) is actually a series of provisions that were added to the Truth in Lending Act in 1994.

HOEPA is limited in scope. It applies only to high-cost home equity loans. It doesn't apply to residential purchase mortgages or to reverse mortgages.

HOEPA's restrictions on predatory lending:
- Apply to high-cost home equity loans
- Don't apply to home purchase loans or reverse mortgages

To be covered by HOEPA, a home equity loan must be secured by the loan applicant's principal residence and meet at least one of these criteria:

1. the initial APR exceeds the yield on certain Treasury securities by more than 8% for first lien loans, or by more than 10% for junior loans; or
2. the total points and fees that the borrower will pay at or before closing will exceed 8% of the total loan amount, or $528, whichever is greater.

The dollar threshold for points and fees is adjusted annually to reflect inflation; $528 is the 2006 limit. It will increase to $547 in 2007.

When a home equity loan is covered by HOEPA, the lender must make certain disclosures, may not engage in certain practices, and may not include certain types of provisions in the loan agreement. Here are some examples of HOEPA's rules:

- the lender may not make the loan without regard to the applicant's repayment ability;
- a prepayment penalty can't be charged if the applicant's debt-to-income ratio is over 50%;
- the prepayment penalty period may not exceed five years;
- if the loan term is less than five years, the loan can't be structured so that a balloon payment will be necessary;
- negative amortization is not allowed;
- the interest rate can't be raised because of default; and
- the disclosure statement must explain that the applicant could lose his or her home if the loan obligations aren't met.

If a lender violates HOEPA, the loan applicant has the same three-year right of rescission available under the Truth in Lending Act when the required disclosures aren't provided. (Again, this right of rescission applies only to home equity loan applicants, not to purchase loan applicants.)

State Predatory Lending Laws. HOEPA is the only federal consumer protection law that specifically addresses the problem of predatory lending. However, a majority of the states now have their own predatory lending laws, and other states are in the process of adopting similar laws.

Of course, the coverage and the provisions of these state laws vary, but at least some of them apply to high-cost home purchase loans as well as home equity loans. To take the California predatory lending statute as an example, it applies if these criteria are met:

1. the loan is secured by a one- to four-unit property that's used as the loan applicant's principal residence;
2. the loan amount doesn't exceed Fannie Mae's conforming loan limit; and
3. either:
   a. the APR exceeds the yield on Treasury securities by more than 8% at the time the loan is made, or
   b. the total points and loan fees payable by the borrower at or before closing will exceed 6% of the total loan amount.

Like HOEPA, the California law requires certain disclosures and prohibits a number of predatory provisions in the loans that it covers. Some of its rules match HOEPA, but there are also significant differences. For example, under the California law, a prepayment penalty can't extend beyond the first three years of the loan term, compared to the five-year limit in HOEPA.

Other Efforts to Stop Predatory Lending

In addition to the statutes we've discussed, predatory lending is also being addressed in other ways.

For example, federal regulators have imposed new rules on the financial institutions that they regulate, although those institutions are already much less likely to engage in predatory lending than unregulated subprime mortgage lenders and brokers. Fannie Mae and Freddie Mac, the secondary market agencies, have informed lenders that they won't purchase high-cost loans with certain provisions that are considered predatory.

State license laws that regulate mortgage brokers, appraisers, and real estate agents are sometimes applied to suspend or revoke the licenses of those who participate in predatory lending schemes.

Some wholesale lenders are considering changing the way that they compensate mortgage brokers, to reduce brokers' incentives to push loan applicants toward more expensive loans.

There are also public education campaigns to put people on their guard against predatory lenders and brokers. Unfortunately, the people most vulnerable to predatory lending are the most difficult to reach.

While all of these efforts are worthwhile, there's probably a limit to how much can be done to stop predatory lending. No matter what the laws and rules are, unscrupulous people will still take advantage of uneducated and vulnerable people, and they can often do so without getting caught.

Outline: Fair Lending and Consumer Protection

I. Fair Lending Laws

A. Equal Credit Opportunity Act

1. The Equal Credit Opportunity Act applies to all consumer credit, including residential mortgages.
2. ECOA prohibits discrimination against loan applicants based on race, color, religion, national origin, sex, marital status, age, or whether income comes from public assistance.
3. Lenders may not base lending decisions on assumptions about creditworthiness of racial, ethnic, or religious groups.

B. Fair Housing Act

1. The Fair Housing Act applies to transactions involving residential properties and prohibits discrimination based on race, color, national origin, religion, sex, disability, or familial status.
2. Under the act, a lender may not refuse to provide information about loans, refuse to make a loan, or impose different terms or conditions on a loan for discriminatory reasons.
3. The act also prohibits redlining: refusing to make loans secured by property in particular neighborhoods because persons of a particular racial or ethnic group live there.
4. A lender may refuse to make a loan in a neighborhood where property values are declining, but the decision must be based on objective economic criteria.

C. Home Mortgage Disclosure Act

1. The Home Mortgage Disclosure Act requires large lenders in metropolitan areas to make disclosures to the federal government regarding all loans they originate or purchase.
2. The intent is for the government to monitor whether lenders are engaging in redlining or other illegal lending practices.

II. Consumer Protection Laws

A. Truth in Lending Act

1. The Truth in Lending Act requires disclosure of interest rates and other finance charges; it is implemented through the Federal Reserve Board's Regulation Z.
2. TILA covers many consumer loans, including those secured by real property.

3. TILA applies only to loans made to natural persons (not corporations), and excludes loans made for business or agricultural purposes; seller financing is also exempt, since it doesn't originate with a commercial lender.
4. The two most important TILA disclosures are the total finance charge and the annual percentage rate (i.e., the cost of credit as a yearly rate).
5. The total finance charge may include interest, origination fee, borrower-paid points, finder's fee, service charges, and mortgage insurance; it doesn't include appraisal, credit report, or inspection fees, title insurance, or seller-paid points.
6. TILA disclosures must also include the lender's identity, the total amount financed, the payment schedule, any prepayment fee, late charges, and the assumption policy.
7. Additional disclosures are required for ARMs, including a general brochure; the APR may be based on the initial interest rate but must state that it is subject to change.
8. Home equity loan borrowers have a right of rescission for the first three days following signing the loan agreement or receiving the disclosure statement.
9. If certain loan terms are stated in an advertisement, then TILA requires that all loan terms must be stated; APR and cash price can be stated without triggering the requirement.

B. Real Estate Settlement Procedures Act

1. The Real Estate Settlement Procedures Act provides borrowers with information about closing costs and prohibits kickbacks that increase settlement costs.
2. RESPA applies to federally related loan transactions, which entails almost all residential loans made by institutional lenders.
3. RESPA doesn't apply to loans used to purchase 25 acres or more, loans for business or agricultural purposes, loans to purchase vacant land, temporary financing, or assumptions where lender's approval isn't required.
4. Within three days of a loan application, a lender must provide a copy of a booklet about settlement procedures, a good faith estimate of closing costs, and a mortgage servicing disclosure statement.
5. The closing agent must itemize all closing costs on a Uniform Settlement Statement.

6. The lender cannot require excessive deposits, accept unearned fees, charge a document preparation fee, or pay kickbacks to anyone for referring customers.

III. Predatory Lending

A. Predatory lending refers to practices in the lending business that take advantage of unsophisticated borrowers for profit.

B. Predatory lending practices include predatory steering, fee packing, loan flipping, equity stripping, property flipping, disregarding buyer's capacity to pay, requiring unaffordable payments, issuing loans in excess of value, waiving impound accounts, negative amortization schemes, and balloon payment abuses.

C. Predatory lenders tend to target persons who aren't able to understand the transaction they're entering into and aren't aware of better alternatives.

D. Home Ownership and Equity Protection Act

1. The Home Ownership and Equity Protection Act applies to high-cost home equity loans secured by a primary residence.
2. A lender making a loan covered by HOEPA must make certain disclosures and may not engage in certain practices.

E. Many states also have predatory lending laws that require disclosures and prohibit predatory practices.

F. States may revoke or suspend the licenses of mortgage brokers, appraisers, and real estate agents who participate in predatory lending schemes.

Key Terms

Equal Credit Opportunity Act: A federal law prohibiting discrimination by lenders against loan applicants on the basis of race, color, religion, national origin, sex, marital status, age, or whether income comes from public assistance.

Fair Housing Act: A federal law prohibiting discrimination in residential property transactions, including lending, on the basis of race, color, national origin, religion, sex, disability, or familial status.

Redlining: Refusing to make loans for the purchase or rehabilitation of property in a certain neighborhood because of its racial or ethnic composition.

Home Mortgage Disclosure Act: A federal law requiring institutional lenders to report on residential loans they originated or purchased from other lenders; the law's intent is to detect redlining and other unlawful lending practices.

Truth in Lending Act (TILA): A federal law that requires lenders and credit arrangers to make disclosures concerning loan costs (including the total finance charge and the annual percentage rate) to consumer loan applicants.

Total finance charge: Under the Truth in Lending Act, the total finance charge on a mortgage loan includes the interest, any discount points paid by the borrower, the loan origination fee, and mortgage insurance costs.

Annual percentage rate (APR): Under the Truth in Lending Act, the relationship between a loan's total finance charge and the total amount financed, expressed as an annual percentage.

Real Estate Settlement Procedures Act (RESPA): A federal law that requires lenders to disclose certain information about closing costs to loan applicants.

Uniform Settlement Statement: A settlement statement required for any transaction involving a loan that is subject to the Real Estate Settlement Procedures Act.

Predatory lending: Lending practices where lenders or mortgage brokers take advantage of unsophisticated borrowers for their own profit.

Fee packing: Charging points or processing fees that are higher than usual and not justified by the services provided.

Equity stripping: Stripping away a home owner's equity by charging high fees for repeated refinancings.

Home Ownership and Equity Protection Act: A federal law applicable to high-cost home equity loans that requires certain disclosures and prohibits certain predatory lending practices.

Chapter Quiz

1. The federal legislation that prevents discrimination against loan applicants on the basis of race is:
   a. RESPA
   b. the Truth in Lending Act
   c. the Equal Credit Opportunity Act
   d. Regulation Z

2. All of the charges payable by or to a party in a real estate transaction show up on the:
   a. settlement statement
   b. financial statement
   c. TILA disclosure statement
   d. impound account statement

3. Under the Real Estate Settlement Procedures Act, lenders:
   a. may pay real estate agents a fee for referring loan applicants to them
   b. are prohibited from paying kickbacks or referral fees
   c. must require borrowers to use a particular title insurance company
   d. must disclose the APR of the loan they are offering to make

4. RESPA requires a lender to give the loan applicant a good faith estimate of the closing costs:
   a. at the time of application
   b. within three days of application
   c. within seven days of application
   d. before closing

5. The purpose of the Home Mortgage Disclosure Act is to:
   a. require that lenders provide good faith estimates of all closing costs
   b. require that lenders disclose the total finance charge and annual percentage rate
   c. require that lenders disclose information that may provide evidence of redlining
   d. prohibit discrimination against individuals whose income is derived from public assistance

6. Which of the following phrases in an advertisement would NOT trigger the requirement, under TILA, that the annual percentage rate and total finance charge must be disclosed?
   a. "Low monthly payments of $1,200"
   b. "Great financing terms for borrowers with good credit"
   c. "Own with a downpayment of just $10,000"
   d. "Act now and get a 6% interest rate"

7. Which of the following practices is prohibited under the Real Estate Settlement Procedures Act?
   a. Kickbacks
   b. Redlining
   c. Equity stripping
   d. Loan flipping

8. Which of the following predatory lending practices involves charging processing fees or points that are higher than normal and not justified by the services provided?
   a. Property flipping
   b. Predatory steering
   c. Impound waivers
   d. Fee packing

9. Which federal law requires certain disclosures and prohibits predatory practices by lenders making high-cost home equity loans?
   a. Equal Credit Opportunity Act
   b. Home Mortgage Disclosure Act
   c. Real Estate Settlement Procedures Act
   d. Home Ownership and Equity Protection Act

10. Which of the following loans would be covered by the Truth in Lending Act?
    a. An unsecured loan for $35,000
    b. A loan secured by a farm property used to purchase farm equipment
    c. A loan issued by a savings and loan to purchase a four-unit residential property
    d. A second mortgage offered by a seller to cover part of the downpayment

Answer Key

1. c. The Equal Credit Opportunity Act prevents discrimination against loan applicants on the basis of race, color, religion, national origin, sex, marital status, age, or whether income is received from public assistance.

2. a. A Uniform Settlement Statement is used to show all closing costs payable by or to a party in a real estate transaction.

3. b. Lenders may not receive pay kickbacks or referral fees to anyone for referring customers, under the Real Estate Settlement Procedures Act.

4. b. Under RESPA, a lender must provide a good faith estimate of closing costs to an applicant within three days of receiving the loan application.

5. c. The Home Mortgage Disclosure Act requires large lenders to disclose information about all loans that they purchase or originate so that patterns suggesting redlining or other prohibited lending practices may be observed.

6. b. If an advertisement doesn't specifically disclose any loan terms but contains only general statements, it does not trigger the TILA requirement of disclosure of the total finance charge and annual percentage rate.

7. a. Kickbacks and other referral fees paid by lenders are prohibited under the Real Estate Settlement Procedures Act.

8. d. Fee packing is a predatory practice involving points or processing fees that are much higher than usual and not justified by the services provided.

9. d. The Home Ownership and Equity Protection Act applies to high-cost home equity loans and prohibits certain predatory practices.

10. c. The Truth in Lending Act excludes consumer loans for over $25,000 that aren't secured by real property; loans made for business or agricultural purposes; and seller financing.

Answer Key for Exercises

Chapter 8, Qualifying the Buyer

Chapter 8, Exercise No. 1

1.

$26	Roy's hourly wage
× 40	Hours in a work week
$1,040	Weekly income
× 52	Weeks in a year
$54,080	Annual income
÷ 12	Months in a year
$4,507	Roy's monthly income

Shortcut:

$26	Roy's hourly wage
× 173.33	(Result of 40 × 52 ÷ 12)
$4,507	Roy's monthly income

$685	Judy's weekly income
× 52	Weeks in a year
$35,620	Annual income
÷ 12	Months in a year
$2,968	Judy's monthly income
+ 4,507	Roy's monthly income
$7,475	Total stable monthly income

2. Yes, there are special circumstances in this case that may persuade the lender to approve the loan. Roy had special training in the Air Force, and Judy is a vocational nurse, which implies special training. They've been at their jobs for only a short time because they are new to the area. The lender will want to know whether Judy was employed as a nurse while Roy was in the Air Force.

Chapter 8, Exercise No. 2

1.

$1,400	Received every two weeks
× 26	Number of paychecks per year
$36,400	Annual income
÷ 12	Months in a year
$3,033	Able's stable monthly income

2.

$162,500	Sales price for old home
– 133,250	Mortgage to be paid off
$29,250	Gross equity
– 14,500	Estimated selling expenses
$14,750	Net equity in old home

3. Yes, Able will have problems closing the transaction. He doesn't even have enough cash and other liquid assets to cover the downpayment and closing costs, much less the required reserves.

$3,600	In savings account
200	In checking account
+ 14,750	Net equity in old home
$18,550	Liquid assets available

$17,000	Required downpayment
+ 3,400	Closing costs
$20,400	Needed at closing
+ 2,615	Required reserves
$23,015	Total liquid assets needed
– 18,550	Liquid assets available
$4,465	Shortfall

4. The savings account was opened quite recently, and the current balance in the account is significantly higher than its average balance. These facts would lead an underwriter to wonder where the money in the account came from: Did Able borrow it?

5. Able might be able to sell some personal property to raise more cash, or his relatives might be willing to give him some money with a gift letter. If he has a life insurance policy, he might consider tapping into its cash value. Or perhaps the seller would be willing to pay part of Able's closing costs.

   Able will also have to explain where the money in his savings account came from. Maybe he recently sold his old car, or received a bonus at work, or closed an account at another bank and transferred the funds. (Of course, if the money was in fact borrowed, it won't count as money available to close the transaction, which will make Able's cash problem even worse.)

Chapter 10, Conventional Financing

Chapter 10, Exercise No. 1

1. Maynard's LTV would be 92%. To determine this, first divide the downpayment by the sales price to find out what percentage of the sales price the downpayment represents. (Remember that the LTV is based on the sales price or the appraised value, whichever is less. In this problem, the sales price, $318,750, is less than the appraised value, $321,000.)

   $$\$25{,}500 \div \$318{,}750 = 8\%$$

   Since the downpayment is 8% of the sales price, a loan for the remainder would be 92% of the sales price:

   $$100\% - 8\% = 92\%$$

2. Maynard's loan would be treated as a 95% loan, since its LTV is over 90%.

Chapter 10, Exercise No. 2

1.

$289,500	Sales price (less than appraised value)
× 80%	LTV for first mortgage
$231,600	First mortgage loan amount
$289,500	Sales price
× 15%	LTV for second mortgage
$43,425	Second mortgage loan amount

2.

$289,500	Sales price
× 5%	
$14,475	Downpayment
$231,600	Amount of first mortgage
× 1.5%	
$3,474	Loan origination fee

3. The total monthly payment for both loans would be $2,141.15.

$1,540.84	Principal and interest for first loan
274.48	Principal and interest for second loan
265.83	Share of property taxes ($3,190 ÷ 12)
+ 60.00	Share of insurance premium ($720 ÷ 12)
$2,141.15	Total monthly payment for both loans

Chapter 10, Exercise No. 3

1. For a 90% loan, the Tanakas could qualify for a $2,477 payment.

Stable monthly income: $9,917

$62,000	Mike's annual salary
÷ 12	Months in a year
$5,167	Mike's monthly income
+ 4,750	Barbara's monthly income
$9,917	Stable monthly income

Recurring obligations: $1,093

$317	Car payment
375	Car payment
250	Payment on personal loan
55	Store charge card payment
42	Visa payment
+ 54	MasterCard payment
$1,093	Total recurring obligations

Total obligations to income ratio calculation:

$9,917	Stable monthly income
× 36%	
$3,570	Maximum total obligations
– 1,093	Recurring obligations
$2,477	Maximum housing expense under total obligations ratio

Housing expense to income ratio calculation:

$9,917	Stable monthly income
× 28%	
$2,777	Maximum housing expense under housing expense ratio

The result of the total obligations ratio calculation will be the maximum housing expense for the Tanakas (since that's less than the result of the housing expense ratio calculation). Thus, the maximum mortgage payment they could qualify for would be $2,477.

2. The Tanakas might be able to qualify for a larger payment if they have excellent credit scores, if their current housing expense represents an unusually large share of their income (demonstrating that they can devote a greater portion of their income to basic needs than most people can), or if either of them has a strong potential for increased earnings, or if they have a substantial net worth. They could also qualify for a larger payment if the home they choose is energy-efficient.

3. If the Tanakas can afford to pay off their personal loan, or pay off one or more of their charge accounts, that would enable them to qualify for a larger mortgage payment. (Remember that in order to have a charge account payment excluded from the total obligations ratio calculation, the Tanakas might be required to close the account altogether.)

Chapter 10, Exercise No. 4

1.

$110,000	Sales price
× 90%	LTV
$99,000	Loan amount
× 6%	Six points (= 1% interest)
$5,940	Approximate cost of buydown

2. The buydown could save Johnson as much as $27,061. (The savings would be less if he paid the loan off before the end of the 30-year term.)

$999.32	Monthly P&I payment at 11.75% (without buydown)
– 924.15	Monthly P&I payment at 10.75% (with buydown)
$75.17	Monthly savings
× 360	Months (30 years)
$27,061	Savings over 30 years

Chapter 11, FHA-Insured Loans

Chapter 11, Exercise No. 1

1a. In 2006, for a two-unit residence, the maximum FHA loan amount in a high-cost area can't exceed $464,449.

1b. The LTV ratio for a property with a sales price over $125,000 located in a high closing cost state is 97.75%.

Use the property's sales price for the calculation, since it's lower than the appraised value.

$447,000	Sales price
× 97.75%	
$436,943	Maximum loan amount

Fletcher's maximum loan amount is $436,943, so he'll have to make a downpayment of $10,057 ($447,000 – $436,943 = $10,057).

1c. The borrower must make a minimum cash investment of 3% of the sales price. So Fletcher's minimum cash investment for this transaction is $13,410.

$447,000	Sales price
× 3%	
$13,410	Minimum cash investment

Chapter 11, Exercise No. 2

1. The base loan will be $266,191, based on a maximum LTV of 97.15% for a sales price over $125,000 in a low closing cost state. (The loan amount will be based on the sales price rather than the appraised value, since the sales price is lower.) The upfront MIP, which is 1.5% of the base loan amount, will be $1,339.18.

$274,000	Sales price
× .9715	LTV
$266,191	Loan amount
× .015	
$3,992.87	Upfront MIP

The annual MIP is .50% of the loan balance, since the loan term exceeds 15 years. The annual MIP is $1,330.96.

$266,191	Loan amount
× .005	
$1,330.96	Annual MIP

2. If Skillin were to finance the upfront MIP, the total amount financed would be $270,183. It doesn't matter that the total amount financed exceeds the maximum loan amount for the community, as long as the base loan is under the limit (which it is in this case).

$266,191.00	Base loan
+ 3,992.87	Upfront MIP
$270,183.87	Total amount financed

The total amount financed will be rounded down to the next dollar, or $270,183.

Chapter 11, Exercise No. 3

1. The Herrons' effective income is $3,520.

$420	Bob's weekly income
× 52	Weeks in a year
$21,840	Bob's annual income
÷ 12	Months in a year
$1,820	Bob's monthly income
+ 1,700	Maggie's monthly income
$3,520	Effective income

2. With an FHA loan, the Herrons could qualify for a maximum housing expense of $1,091.

$114	Personal loan payment
135	Personal loan payment
+ 47	Visa payment
$296	Total recurring charges

$3,520	Effective income
× 43%	
$1,514	Maximum fixed payments
− 296	Recurring charges
$1,218	Maximum housing expense under the fixed payment ratio

$3,520	Effective income
× 31%	
$1,091	Maximum housing expense under the housing expense ratio

The maximum housing expense would be $1,091, the result of the housing expense to income ratio calculation, since that's less than the result of the fixed payment to income ratio calculation.

3. If the Herrons were applying for a 95% conventional loan, the lender might apply either the standard 36% total obligations ratio, or the stricter 33% total obligations ratio. If the lender used the 36% ratio, the Herrons could only qualify for a mortgage payment of $971. That's $120 less than the FHA payment they could qualify for. If the lender would accept a total obligations ratio no higher than 33% for a 95% conventional loan, the Herrons' maximum mortgage payment would be only $865, which is $226 less than their FHA payment.

$3,520	Stable monthly income
× 28%	Conventional housing expense ratio
$985	Maximum housing expense under housing expense ratio

$3,520	Stable monthly income
× 36%	Standard total obligations ratio for conventional loans
$1,267	Maximum total obligations
– 296	Monthly obligations
$971	Max. housing expense with 36% total obligations ratio

$3,520	Stable monthly income
× 33%	Lower total obligations ratio for 95% loans
$1,161	Maximum total obligations
– 296	Monthly obligations
$865	Max. housing expense with 33% total obligations ratio

Chapter 12, VA-Guaranteed Loans

Chapter 12, Exercise No. 1

1. Yes, Woods is eligible for a VA-guaranteed loan, since his active duty service lasted longer than 90 days, and he served for the full period he was called to serve. That is the applicable minimum requirement, because he served during the Persian Gulf War.

   It's clear that Woods hasn't used up any of his entitlement; he's buying his first home. So Woods's entitlement is $104,250, the 2006 maximum.

2. The VA guaranty will cover $81,250. The 2006 maximum guaranty for loans over $144,000 is 25% of the loan amount, up to a maximum of $104,250. $325,000 × .25 is $81,250.

Chapter 12, Exercise No. 2

1. The lender would offer Bates a loan for as much as $259,000, the full price of the home, with no downpayment necessary. Since the guaranty is 25% of the loan amount for a loan over $144,000, the guaranty amount would be $64,750.

$259,000	Loan amount
× 25%	
$64,750	Guaranty for $259,000 loan

2. The lender would be willing to loan Moreau up to $423,000 and require a $2,000 downpayment. The downpayment plus the guaranty amount would cover 25% of the cost of the home.

$425,000	Sales price (less than appraised value)
× 25%	
$106,250	
– 104,250	Maximum guaranty
$2,000	Downpayment required by lender

3. Since the loan amount is going to be over $144,000, the lender will use $104,250 (25% of the 2006 conforming loan limit) as the basis for calculating Jessell's remaining entitlement. His remaining entitlement for this transaction will be $68,250.

$104,250	Basis for calculating remaining entitlement
– 36,000	Guaranty on existing loan
$68,250	Remaining entitlement

Applying the 25% rule, the lender will require a $27,250 downpayment. The loan amount will be $354,750.

$382,000	Sales price
× 25%	Ratio of guaranty + downpayment to price
$95,500	25% of sales price
– $68,250	Remaining entitlement
$27,250	Downpayment required by lender

$382,000	Sales price
– $27,250	Downpayment
$354,750	Loan amount

Chapter 12, Exercise No. 3

The Martins could probably qualify for the $1,393 payment, even though their total obligations to income ratio would be over 41%.

$5,200	Monthly income
× 41%	Standard obligations to income ratio
$2,132	
– 807	Recurring obligations
$1,325	(Less than proposed housing expense)

To see how the Martins could qualify, first calculate how much residual income they would have with the proposed housing expense.

$5,200	Monthly income
1,325	Taxes withheld
807	Recurring obligations
– 1,393	Proposed housing expense
$1,675	Residual income

Next, check to see if the amount of residual income exceeds the VA's minimum required residual income by at least 20%. The minimum residual income for a family of six in the Western region is $1,238 if they're borrowing $80,000 or more (see Figure 12.1 in Chapter 12).

$1,238	Minimum residual income
× 20%	
$248	20% of the required minimum

Add $248 to $1,238 to find that the Martins need a residual income of $1,486 in order to be at least 20% over the minimum. Their residual income of $1,675 exceeds $1,486, so a lender could accept an income ratio over 41% without other compensating factors.

Calculate what the Martins' total obligations to income ratio would be if their housing expense were $1,393.

$1,393	Housing expense
+ 807	Other recurring obligations
$2,200	Total obligations
÷ 5,200	Monthly income
42.3%	Total obligations to income ratio

With the $1,393 housing expense, the Martins' income ratio would be slightly over 42%. It's very likely that the lender would approve a no-downpayment, $187,000 loan for the Martins.

Chapter 13, Seller Financing

Chapter 13, Exercise No. 1

1. A $10,300 downpayment would be 5.92% of the purchase price.

   $10,300 (downpayment) ÷ $174,000 (purchase price) = 0.592 = 5.92%

   The 5.92% downpayment plus the 5% seller second would make up about 11% of the price, so Underwood and Schirmer would need an institutional loan with a 89% loan-to-value ratio.

2. The loan amount for the seller second would be $8,700. To determine the amount of the institutional loan, subtract the amount of the seller second and the amount of the downpayment ($10,300) from the purchase price. The amount of the institutional loan would be $155,000. The combined loan amount would be $163,700.

$174,000	Purchase price
× 5%	Loan-to-value ratio for seller second
$8,700	Loan amount for seller second

$174,000	Purchase price
8,700	Seller second
– 10,300	Downpayment
$155,000	Loan amount for institutional loan

$155,000	Institutional loan
+ 8,700	Seller second
$163,700	Combined loan amount

3. Yes, this arrangement complies with the general rules for secondary financing in conjunction with a conventional loan. The combined LTV for the first and second loans does not exceed 95%; the second loan does not require a balloon payment in less than five years; and there is no possibility of negative amortization on the second.

   $155,000 (first loan) + $8,700 (seller second) = $163,700 (total financing)

   $163,700 (financing) ÷ $174,000 (purchase price) = 94%

4. First calculate the proposed monthly housing expense for this transaction.

$1,083.78	Principal and interest for institutional loan
× 15%	
$162.57	Estimated taxes and insurance

$1,083.78	Principal and interest for institutional loan
52.16	Principal and interest for seller second
+ 162.57	Estimated taxes and insurance
$1,298.51	Proposed monthly housing expense

Next, use the income ratios to calculate the housing expense that Underwood and Schirmer can qualify for.

$5,200	Stable monthly income
× 28%	Housing expense to income ratio
$1,456	Maximum housing expense under the 28% housing expense ratio

$5,200	Stable monthly income
× 36%	Total obligations ratio
$1,872	Maximum total obligations
– 560	Monthly debt payments
$1,312	Maximum housing expense under the 36% total obligations ratio

$5,200	Stable monthly income
× 33%	Total obligations ratio
$1,716	Maximum total obligations
– 560	Monthly debt payments
$1,156	Maximum housing expense under the 33% total obligations ratio

The proposed monthly housing expense (approximately $1,300) is less than the buyers' maximum housing expense figure ($1,312) if the lender uses a 36% total obligations ratio. But if the lender uses a 33% ratio, the proposed expense is much more than their maximum housing expense figure ($1,156). Thus, whether the buyers can qualify for this combination of an institutional loan and a seller second depends on which figure the lender uses as its maximum total obligations ratio for a 95% loan.

Chapter 13, Exercise No. 2

1. The seller's first-year yield will be approximately 12%.

Wraparound Worksheet

Sales price	$75,000					
– Downpayment	$8,000					
Wraparound	$67,000	x	9%	=	$6,030	Interest received
– Underlying loan	$39,700	x	7%	=	– 2,779	– Interest paid
Credit extended	$27,300				$3,251	Net interest
	→				$27,300	÷ Credit extended
					12%	Seller's yield

2. The seller's first-year yield would be about 26.7%.

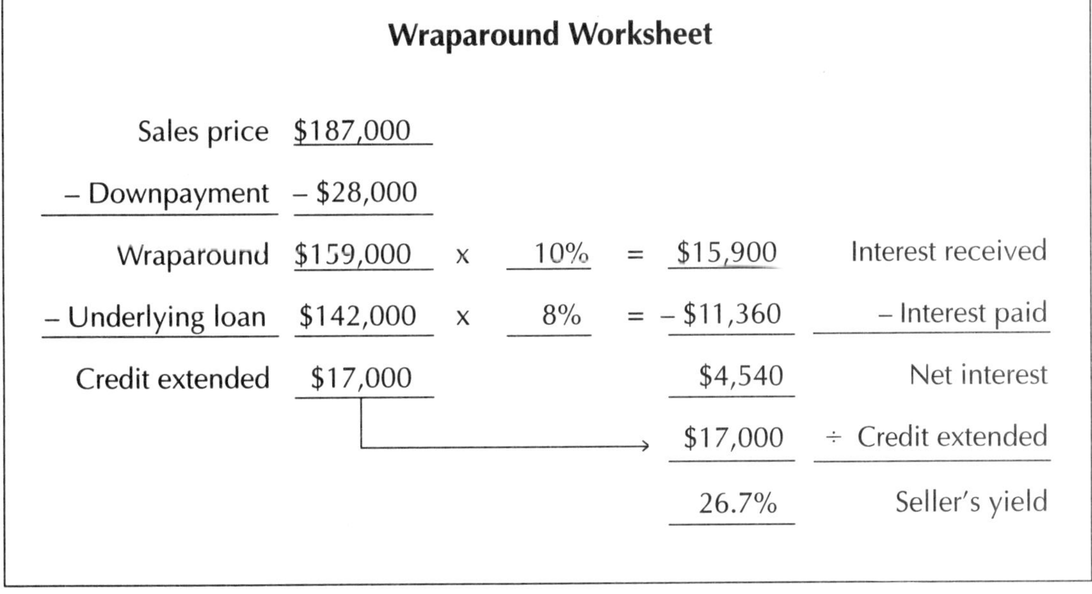

Wraparound Worksheet

Sales price	$187,000					
– Downpayment	– $28,000					
Wraparound	$159,000	x	10%	=	$15,900	Interest received
– Underlying loan	$142,000	x	8%	=	– $11,360	– Interest paid
Credit extended	$17,000				$4,540	Net interest
	→				$17,000	÷ Credit extended
					26.7%	Seller's yield

Chapter 13, Exercise No. 3

1. The total monthly payment for the assumption plus seller second would be $1,093.57. The monthly payment for the wraparound ($1,011.26) is significantly less.

$899.12	Payment on assumed loan
+ 194.45	Payment on seller second
$1,093.57	Total monthly payment for assumption plus seller second

2. The Rainwaters' yield on the wraparound would be approximately 11.7%, compared to their 8% yield on the seller second.

$152,000	Wraparound loan
– 125,500	Underlying loan
$26,500	Credit extended

$152,000	Wraparound
× 7%	Interest rate
$10,640	Annual interest received

$125,500	Underlying loan
× 6%	Interest rate
$7,530	Annual interest paid

$10,640	Interest received on wraparound
– 7,530	Interest paid on underlying loan
$3,110	Net interest earned

Divide the net interest by the credit extended to find the yield.

$3,110 ÷ $26,500 = 11.7% yield

The Rainwaters would have an 11.7% yield on the wraparound arrangement, compared to an 8% yield on the seller second.

3. With the assumption plus seller second, McCarthy would pay approximately 6.35% interest on the total amount financed, which is 2.65% below the current market rate of 9%. On the wraparound, he would pay 7% interest, which is higher than the rate on the assumption plus seller second, but still below the market rate.

\$125,500	Assumed loan
× 6%	Interest rate
\$7,530	Annual interest paid
\$26,500	Seller second
× 8%	Interest rate
\$2,120	Annual interest paid
\$7,530	Interest on assumed loan
+ 2,120	Interest on seller second
\$9,650	Total annual interest paid
\$125,500	Assumed loan
+ 26,500	Seller second
\$152,000	Total amount financed

Divide the total annual interest paid by the total amount financed to find the approximate overall interest rate on the assumption plus seller second.

\$9,650 ÷ \$152,000 = 6.35% overall interest rate

Case Study Answers

Chapter 10, Conventional Financing

Question 1

The Cortinas' stable monthly income is $5,971.61.

$18.50	Teresa's hourly wage
× 173.33	Factor for translating hourly wage into monthly income
$3,206.61	Teresa's monthly income
1,300.00	Rick's monthly salary
+ 1,465.00	Rick's average commission
$5,971.61	Stable monthly income

(Rick's $1,500 bonus probably won't count toward their stable monthly income, since he has received the bonus only once.)

Question 2

If they apply for a conventional loan with a 90% LTV, the Cortinas could qualify for a maximum principal and interest payment of approximately $1,380.68. They could qualify for that same payment amount for a 95% loan, if the lender uses the standard 36% total obligations ratio. If the lender won't accept a total obligations ratio over 33% for 95% loans, however, then their maximum principal and interest payment would be $1,224.90.

First calculate their monthly recurring liabilities (aside from their housing expense).

$265	Car payment
142	Installment contract payment
105	Credit card payments
+ 50	Student loan payment
$562	Recurring liabilities

(The $215 car payment should not be counted, since only eight payments remain to be made.)

Next, calculate their maximum housing expense using the standard 36% and 28% income ratios.

$5,971.61	Stable monthly income
× 36%	Maximum total obligations ratio
$2,149.78	Maximum total obligations
– 562.00	Recurring liabilities
$1,587.78	Maximum housing expense under the 36% total obligations ratio

$5,971.61	Stable monthly income
× 28%	Maximum housing expense to income ratio
$1,672.05	Maximum housing expense under the 28% housing expense ratio

Using the 36% and 28% ratios, their maximum housing expense would be $1,587.78, the result of the total obligations ratio calculation, since that's less than the result of the housing expense to income ratio calculation. The next step is to set aside 15% for taxes and insurance, to determine their maximum principal and interest payment.

$1,587.78	Maximum housing expense
÷ 115%	15% for taxes and insurance
$1,380.68	Maximum principal & interest payment (using the 36% ratio)

Now go through the same process using the 33% total obligations to income ratio that some lenders apply for 95% loans. The maximum housing expense to income ratio will still be 28% of their stable monthly income ($1,672.05).

$5,971.61	Stable monthly income
× 33%	Maximum total obligations ratio
$1,970.63	Maximum total obligations
− 562.00	Recurring liabilities
$1,408.63	Maximum housing expense under the 33% total obligations ratio

$1,408.63	Maximum housing expense
÷ 115%	15% for taxes and insurance
$1,224.90	Maximum principal and interest payment (using the 33% ratio)

Question 3

a) A 90% fixed-rate loan for $212,871 could buy a $236,523 home, with a minimum downpayment of $23,652.

$212,871	Loan amount
÷ 90%	LTV
$236,523	Sales price
− 212,871	Loan amount
$23,652	Minimum downpayment

b) A 90% ARM for $243,168 could buy a $270,187 home, with a minimum downpayment of $27,019.

$243,168	Loan amount
÷ 90%	LTV
$270,187	Sales price
− 243,168	Loan amount
$27,019	Minimum downpayment

c) A 95% fixed-rate loan for $210,172 could buy a $221,234 home, with a minimum downpayment of $11,062.

$210,172	Loan amount
÷ 95%	LTV
$221,234	Sales price
– 210,172	Loan amount
$11,062	Minimum downpayment

d) A 95% fixed-rate loan for $186,459 could buy a $196,273 home, with a minimum downpayment of $9,814.

$186,459	Loan amount
÷ 95%	LTV
$196,273	Sales price
– 186,459	Loan amount
$9,814	Minimum downpayment

Question 4

For the 90% fixed-rate loan, the Cortinas would need approximately $38,181 in cash. For the 90% ARM, they'd need approximately $42,556 in cash. For the 95% fixed-rate loan with a $1,587.78 PITI payment (using the 36% income ratio for qualifying), they'd need approximately $25,078 in cash. And for the 95% fixed-rate loan with a $1,408.63 PITI payment (using the 33% income ratio), they'd need approximately $22,249 in cash.

a) 90% fixed-rate loan at 6.75% interest, with a 2% origination fee

Sales price: $236,523
Loan amount: $212,871
Downpayment: $23,652
Monthly mortgage payment (PITI): $1,587.78

$212,871	Loan amount
× 2%	
$4,257.42	Origination fee
$236,523	Sales price
× 3%	
$7,095.69	Estimated closing costs
$1,587.78	PITI
× 2	Months
$3,175.56	Reserves

$23,652.00	Downpayment
4,257.42	Origination fee
+ 7,095.69	Closing costs
$35,005.11	Cash for closing
+ 3,175.56	Reserves
$38,180.67	Total cash requirement

b) 90% ARM at 5.5% interest, with a 1.75% origination fee

Sales price: $270,187
Loan amount: $243,168
Downpayment: $27,019
Monthly mortgage payment (PITI): $1,587.78

$243,168	Loan amount
× 1.75%	
$4,255.44	Origination fee

$270,187	Sales price
× 3%	
$8,105.61	Closing costs

$1,587.78	PITI
× 2	Months
$3,175.56	Reserves

$27,019	Downpayment
4,255.44	Origination fee
+ 8,105.61	Closing costs
$39,380.05	Cash for closing
+ 3,175.56	Reserves
$42,555.61	Total cash requirement

c) 95% loan at 6.875% interest (36% income ratio), with a 2% origination fee

Sales price: $221,234
Loan amount: $210,172
Downpayment: $11,062
Monthly mortgage payment (PITI): $1,587.78

$210,172	Loan amount
× 2%	
$4,203.44	Origination fee

$221,234	Sales price
× 3%	
$6,637.02	Closing costs

$1,587.78	PITI
× 2	Months
$3,175.56	Reserves

(Note: For a 95% loan, some lenders require a borrower to have three months' mortgage payments in reserve, not just two. If that rule applied in this case, it would add another $1,587.78 to the Cortinas' total cash requirement.)

$11,062.00	Downpayment
4,203.44	Origination fee
+ 6,637.02	Closing costs
$21,902.46	Cash for closing
+ 3,175.56	Reserves
$25,078.02	Total cash requirement

d) 95% at 6.875% interest (33% income ratio), with a 2% origination fee

Sales price: $196,273
Loan amount: $186,459
Downpayment: $9,814
Monthly mortgage payment (PITI): $1,408.63

$186,459	Loan amount
× 2%	
$3,729.18	Origination fee

$196,273	Sales price
× 3%	
$5,888.19	Closing costs

$1,408.63	PITI
× 2	Months
$2,817.26	Reserves

$9,814.00	Downpayment
3,729.18	Origination fee
+ 5,888.19	Closing costs
$19,431.37	Cash for closing
+ 2,817.26	Reserves
$22,248.63	Total cash requirement

Since the Cortinas have $39,500 in savings, they have enough cash for any of the fixed-rate loans (though it would be a fairly close call for the 90% fixed-rate loan). But their savings fall $3,056 short of the cash required for an ARM as large as $243,168. They have enough cash for a smaller ARM, however. For example, if they bought a $250,000 home with a 90% ARM (loan amount $225,000), their payment (PITI) would be approximately $1,469.16, and they'd need about $39,376 in cash. So, in contrast to the 90% fixed-rate loan, an ARM would enable them to buy a somewhat more expensive home, and the monthly payment would be considerably lower—at least at first.

Question 5

If the Cortinas are willing to consider an ARM, it seems appropriate for them to look at homes priced anywhere from $195,000 to $250,000. If they want a fixed-rate loan, however, it will be difficult for them to qualify for a loan large enough to buy a home at the high end of that price range. In that case, they probably shouldn't look at homes priced much over $235,000.

But these calculations only provide a rough idea of the buyers' price range; it shouldn't be used to rule out too many possibilities too soon. Consider whether there are compensating factors in the Cortinas' financial situation that would make a total obligations ratio over 36% acceptable to the lender. If so, they might be able to qualify for a larger monthly payment, so that they could buy a more expensive home. If they are interested in relatively new homes, energy efficiency could make a difference for them. Fannie Mae and Freddie Mac allow higher income ratios for borrowers who purchase energy-efficient homes.

Chapter 11, FHA-Insured Loans

Question 1

The Cortinas' effective income is $5,971.61 (just the same as the stable monthly income you calculated for conventional loans). Their recurring charges add up to $562. So the maximum housing expense they could qualify for under the FHA's 43% and 31% income ratios is $1,851.20.

$265	Car payment
142	Installment contract payment
105	Credit card payments
+ 50	Student loan payment
$562	Recurring charges

$5,971.61	Effective income
× 43%	Maximum fixed payment to income ratio
$2,567.79	Maximum fixed payments
– 562.00	Recurring charges
$2,005.79	Maximum housing expense under the fixed payment ratio

$5,971.61	Effective income
× 31%	Maximum housing expense to income ratio
$1,851.20	Maximum housing expense under the housing expense ratio

The Cortinas' maximum housing expense for an FHA loan would be $1,851.20, the result of the housing expense to income ratio calculation.

Question 2

With a base loan amount of $227,900 and the upfront MIP (1.5% of the base loan amount) financed, the total amount financed would be $231,318.

$227,900	Loan amount
× 1.5%	MIP percentage
$3,418.50	Upfront MIP

$227,900.00	Loan amount
+ 3,418.50	Upfront MIP
$231,318.50	Total amount financed

Question 3

Yes, they should be able to qualify for a $227,900 FHA loan (either fixed-rate or adjustable-rate) with the upfront MIP financed. The payment (PITI) for a fixed-rate loan at 6.75% interest would be approximately $1,725.37. The PITI payment for an ARM at 5.5% interest would be approximately $1,510.41. Both of these figures are under their $1,851 limit.

$1,500.32	Principal and interest payment for loan at 6.75% interest
× 15%	
$225.05	Estimated taxes, insurance, and annual MIP
+ 1,500.32	
$1,725.37	PITI payment for fixed-rate FHA loan with financed upfront MIP

$1,313.40	Principal and interest payment for loan at 5.5% interest
× 15%	
$197.01	Estimated taxes, insurance, and annual MIP
+ 1,313.40	
$1,510.41	PITI payment for FHA ARM with financed upfront MIP

Question 4

For a $220,000 home, the Cortinas' loan (not including the upfront MIP) could be as much as $215,050.

$220,000	Sales price (since less than appraised value)
× 97.75%	LTV for high closing cost state
$215,050	Loan amount

The loan amount would be $215,050. With financed upfront MIP, the total amount financed would be $218,275.

$215,050	Base loan amount
× 1.5%	MIP percentage
$3,225.75	Upfront MIP
+ 215,050.00	
$218,275.75	Total amount financed

Question 5

The Cortinas would need approximately $12,600 at closing for this transaction.

$220,000	Sales price
– 215,050	Loan amount
$4,950	Downpayment

$215,050	Loan amount
× 1%	
$2,150	Origination fee

$220,000	Sales price
× 2.5%	
$5,500	Closing costs

$4,950	Downpayment
2,150	Origination fee
+ 5,500	Closing costs
$12,600	Total cash needed at closing

For this transaction, the minimum cash investment (3% of the sales price) would be $6,600 ($220,000 × .03 = $6,600). The Cortinas will easily fulfill that requirement. The minimum cash investment generally isn't an issue unless someone other than the borrowers (the seller, a family member, or another party) is providing some of the funds the borrowers need to close the transaction.

Question 6

The Cortinas might very well choose an FHA loan in the current market. The chief advantage of an FHA loan is that they could close with much less cash than they'd need for a comparable conventional loan. As we saw in Chapter 10, with a conventional 95% fixed-rate loan, they could probably qualify for a loan large enough to buy a home worth $221,234, and they'd need $25,078 in cash for that transaction. An FHA loan would enable them to buy the same house with only about $12,600 in cash (and they'd qualify for the loan more easily, too). Although they have enough savings to buy a $220,000 home with a fixed-rate 95% conventional loan, they might prefer to hold on to more of their savings.

However, the Cortinas need to consider that their monthly payment would be higher for the FHA loan. That's because the FHA downpayment is less—so the loan amount is greater—and because the FHA monthly payment includes the financed upfront MIP.

Chapter 12, VA-Guaranteed Loans

Question 1

Under the VA's standard 41% total obligations to income ratio, the Cortinas could have a maximum housing expense of $1,886.36.

$5,971.61	Monthly income
× 41%	Maximum total obligations to income ratio
$2,448.36	
– 562.00	Recurring obligations
$1,886.36	Maximum housing expense

Question 2

With a $1,886.36 housing expense, the Cortinas' residual income would be $2,552. To simplify the residual income calculations, first add up all of the taxes that are withheld from their paychecks.

$259	Federal income tax (Rick)
73	State income tax (Rick)
185	Social security & Medicare (Rick)
223	Federal income tax (Teresa)
65	State income tax (Teresa)
+ 166	Social security & Medicare (Teresa)
$971	Total taxes

$5,971.61	Monthly income
971.00	Taxes
562.00	Recurring obligations
– 1,886.36	Proposed housing expense
$2,552.25	Residual income

Question 3

The Cortinas' residual income is clearly far more than 20% above the $738 minimum required for a two-person family in the Southern region borrowing $80,000 or more.

$737	Minimum residual income
× 20%	
$147.40	20% of required minimum

Because the Cortinas have so much residual income, it is very likely that a lender would allow them a total obligations to income ratio over 41%. If they were allowed to have a 45% ratio, they could qualify for a mortgage payment up to $2,125.22.

$5,971.61	Monthly income
× 45%	
$2,687.22	Maximum total obligations
− 562.00	Recurring obligations
$2,125.22	Maximum housing expense (PITI)

With 12% of the payment going toward taxes and insurance, a $2,125.22 PITI payment translates into a maximum principal and interest payment of $1,897.52.

$2,125.22	Maximum housing expense
÷ 112%	For property taxes and insurance
$1,897.52	Maximum principal and interest payment

Question 4

The VA guaranty for a $292,556 loan would be approximately $73,139.

$292,556	Loan amount
× 25%	
$73,139	Guaranty amount

Question 5

The 1% origination fee, 2.15% funding fee, and 2% closing costs add up to 5.15% of the loan amount. The Cortinas would only need about $15,066 in cash to close this VA loan. (Note that the lender would require no downpayment, since the loan amount is under $417,000.)

$292,556	Loan amount
× 5.15%	
$15,066.63	Cash needed for closing

Question 6

The Cortinas would be very likely to choose a VA loan over a conventional loan or an FHA loan, because it would allow them to buy a much more expensive home with a smaller amount of cash.

Of course, they'd be taking on a larger monthly mortgage payment in order to buy a $292,000 home. But even if they chose a home in the price range they were considering for a conventional loan (for example, around $235,000), so that the monthly payment would be less, a VA loan could save them lots of money.

Chapter 13, Seller Financing

Question 1

This lender doesn't allow a conventional loan that's supplemented with a seller second to exceed 75% of the sales price or appraised value, whichever is less. In this case, that's $185,000.

$185,000	Sales price/appraised value
× 75%	Maximum LTV
$138,750	Maximum conventional loan amount

Also, according to this lender's secondary financing rules, the Cortinas must make at least a 10% downpayment, so the LTV of Wellman's seller second can't exceed 15%. That means she can finance no more than $27,750 of the price.

$185,000	Sales price/appraised value
× 15%	Maximum LTV
$27,750	Maximum seller second

Question 2

The monthly housing expense for this combination of a conventional loan and a seller second would be approximately $1,577.66.

$1,192.08	Principal and interest for first loan
+ 223.28	Principal and interest for seller second
$1,415.36	Combined principal and interest payment
× 15%	
$212.30	Estimated taxes and insurance

$1,415.36	Combined principal and interest payment
+ 212.30	Estimated taxes and insurance
$1,627.66	
− 50.00	(Because mortgage insurance is not required)
$1,577.66	Total monthly housing expense

As you determined in the case study for Chapter 10, with the 36% total debt to income ratio the Cortinas can qualify for a monthly housing expense (PITI) of up to $1,587. So they should be able to qualify for this combination of a conventional loan and a seller second.

Question 3

The Cortinas would need about \$26,015.63 to close, plus \$3,155.32 in reserve, for a total cash requirement of approximately \$29,171.

\$185,000	Sales price
× 10%	LTV
\$18,500	Downpayment

\$138,750	Conventional loan amount
× 1.75%	
\$2,428.13	Origination fee

\$138,750	Conventional loan amount
× 1%	One point
\$1,387.50	Discount fee

\$185,000	Sales price
× 2%	
\$3,700	Other closing costs

\$1,577.66	Combined loan payment
× 2	Months
\$3,155.32	Reserves

\$18,500.00	Downpayment
2,428.13	Origination fee
1,387.50	Discount fee
+ 3,700.00	Other closing costs
\$26,015.63	Cash for closing
+ 3,155.32	Reserves
\$29,170.95	Total cash requirement

Question 4

The seller second can be amortized over 30 years (so that the monthly payment is only \$223.28), but require a balloon payment of the entire unpaid principal balance after five years. At that point, the balloon payment of principal would be approximately \$26,607.

Question 5

Wellman would receive approximately \$71,250 at closing.

\$185,000	Sales price
× 10%	
\$18,500	Selling costs

$185,000	Sales price
18,500	Selling costs
67,500	Mortgage payoff
– 27,750	Credit extended to the buyers
$71,250	Cash to seller at closing

Income Qualifying—Conventional Loans
FIXED RATE, LTV 90%

Stable Monthly Income

Base salary	
Wage earner 1	$3,206.61
Wage earner 2	1,300.00
Overtime	
Commissions	1,465.00
Bonuses	
Other	+
Total	$5,971.61

Recurring Liabilities

Car loans	$265.00
Credit cards	105.00
Student loans	50.00
Other loans	
Child support	
Alimony	
Other	+ 142.00
Total	$562.00

Total Obligations to Income Ratio

$5,971.61	Stable monthly income
x 36%	Maximum ratio
2,149.78	Maximum obligations
– 562.00	Recurring liabilities
$1,587.78	Maximum mortgage payment (PITI) under total obligations ratio

Housing Expense to Income Ratio

$5,971.61	Stable monthly income
x 28%	Maximum ratio
$1,672.05	Maximum mortgage payment (PITI) under housing expense ratio

Maximum Mortgage Payment (PITI) $1,587.78

$1,587.78	Maximum PITI payment
÷ 115%	(less 15% for taxes and insurance)
$1,380.68	Maximum principal and interest payment

Interest rate 6.75%

Maximum Loan Amount $212,871

$212,871	Maximum loan amount
÷ 90%	Loan-to-value ratio
$236,523	Sales price

Sales Price $236,523

Income Qualifying—Conventional Loans
ADJUSTABLE RATE, LTV 90%

Stable Monthly Income

Base salary	
Wage earner 1	$3,206.61
Wage earner 2	1,300.00
Overtime	
Commissions	1,465.00
Bonuses	
Other	+
Total	$5,971.61

Recurring Liabilities

Car loans	$265.00
Credit cards	105.00
Student loans	50.00
Other loans	
Child support	
Alimony	
Other	+ 142.00
Total	$562.00

Total Obligations to Income Ratio

$5,971.61	Stable monthly income
x 36%	Maximum ratio
2,149.78	Maximum obligations
– 562.00	Recurring liabilities
$1,587.78	Maximum mortgage payment (PITI) under total obligations ratio

Housing Expense to Income Ratio

$5,971.61	Stable monthly income
x 28%	Maximum ratio
$1,672.05	Maximum mortgage payment (PITI) under housing expense ratio

Maximum Mortgage Payment (PITI) $1,587.78

$1,587.78	Maximum PITI payment
÷ 115%	(less 15% for taxes and insurance)
$1,380.68	Maximum principal and interest payment

Interest rate 4.75%

Maximum Loan Amount $243,168

$243,168	Maximum loan amount
÷ 90%	Loan-to-value ratio
$270,187	Sales price

Sales Price $270,187

Income Qualifying—Conventional Loans
FIXED RATE, LTV 95%
Using 36% total obligations to income ratio

Stable Monthly Income

Base salary	
Wage earner 1	$3,206.61
Wage earner 2	1,300.00
Overtime	
Commissions	1,465.00
Bonuses	
Other	+
Total	$5,971.61

Recurring Liabilities

Car loans	$265.00
Credit cards	105.00
Student loans	50.00
Other loans	
Child support	
Alimony	
Other	+ 142.00
Total	$562.00

Total Obligations to Income Ratio

$5,971.61	Stable monthly income
x 36%	Maximum ratio
2,149.78	Maximum obligations
– 562.00	Recurring liabilities
$1,587.78	Maximum mortgage payment (PITI) under total obligations ratio

Housing Expense to Income Ratio

$5,971.61	Stable monthly income
x 28%	Maximum ratio
$1,672.05	Maximum mortgage payment (PITI) under housing expense ratio

Maximum Mortgage Payment (PITI) $1,587.78

$1,587.78	Maximum PITI payment
÷ 115%	(less 15% for taxes and insurance)
$1,380.68	Maximum principal and interest payment

Interest rate 6.875%

Maximum Loan Amount $210,172

$210,172	Maximum loan amount
÷ 95%	Loan-to-value ratio
$221,234	Sales price

Sales Price $221,234

Income Qualifying—Conventional Loans
FIXED RATE, LTV 95%
Using 33% total obligations to income ratio

Stable Monthly Income

Base salary	
Wage earner 1	$3,206.61
Wage earner 2	1,300.00
Overtime	
Commissions	1,465.00
Bonuses	
Other	+
Total	$5,971.61

Recurring Liabilities

Car loans	$265.00
Credit cards	105.00
Student loans	50.00
Other loans	
Child support	
Alimony	
Other	+ 142.00
Total	$562.00

Total Obligations to Income Ratio

$5,971.61	Stable monthly income
x 33%	Maximum ratio
1,970.63	Maximum obligations
– 562.00	Recurring liabilities
$1,408.63	Maximum mortgage payment (PITI) under total obligations ratio

Housing Expense to Income Ratio

$5,971.61	Stable monthly income
x 28%	Maximum ratio
$1,672.05	Maximum mortgage payment (PITI) under housing expense ratio

Maximum Mortgage Payment (PITI) $1,408.63

$1,408.63	Maximum PITI payment
÷ 115%	(less 15% for taxes and insurance)
$1,224.90	Maximum principal and interest payment

Interest rate 6.875%

Maximum Loan Amount $186,459

$186,459	Maximum loan amount
÷ 95%	Loan-to-value ratio
$196,273	Sales price

Sales Price $196,273

Income Qualifying—FHA-Insured Loans

Effective Income

Base salary	
Wage earner 1	$3,206.61
Wage earner 2	1,300.00
Overtime	
Commissions	1,465.00
Bonuses	
Other	+
Total	$5,971.61

Recurring Charges

Car loans	$265.00
Credit cards	105.00
Student loans	50.00
Other loans	
Child care	
Child support	
Alimony	
Other	+ 142.00
Total	$562.00

Fixed Payment to Income Ratio

$5,971.61	Effective income
x 43%	Maximum ratio
2,567.79	Maximum fixed payments
– 562.00	Recurring charges
$2,005.79	Maximum mortgage payment (PITI) under fixed payment ratio

Housing Expense to Income Ratio

$5,971.61	Stable monthly income
x 31%	Maximum ratio
$1,851.20	Maximum mortgage payment (PITI) under housing expense ratio

Maximum Mortgage Payment (PITI) $1,851.20

$1,851.20	Maximum PITI payment
÷ 115%	(less 15% for taxes and insurance)
$1,609.74	Maximum principal and interest payment

Income Qualifying—VA-Guaranteed Loans

Taxes (per month)

$259.00, 223.00	Federal income tax
73.00, 65.00	State income tax
185.00, 166.00	Social security/Medicare
+	Other
$971.00	Total

Recurring Charges

Car loans	$265.00
Credit cards	105.00
Student loans	50.00
Other loans	
Child care	
Child support	
Alimony	
Other	+ 142.00
Total	$562.00

Gross Monthly Income

Base salary	
Wage earner 1	$3,206.61
Wage earner 2	1,300.00
Overtime	
Commissions	1,465.00
Bonuses	
Other	+
Total	$5,971.61

Obligations to Income Ratio

$5,971.61	Gross monthly income
x 41%	Standard maximum ratio
2,448.36	Maximum obligations
– 562.00	Recurring obligations
$1,886.36	Maximum mortgage payment (PITI) under the 41% income ratio

Income Qualifying—VA-Guaranteed Loans

Residual Income Analysis

$5,971.61	Gross monthly income
971.00	Taxes
562.00	Recurring obligations
– 1,886.36	Proposed housing expense (from 41% ratio)
$2,552.25	**Residual Income**
– 738.00	Minimum residual income*
1,814.25	Residual income in excess of minimum
738.00	Minimum residual income
x 20%	
$147.60	20% of minimum residual income

If applicant's residual income exceeds the minimum by more than 20%, a larger mortgage payment amount may be approved (exceeding 41% income ratio), even without any compensating factors.

Maximum Mortgage Payment (PITI) $2,125.22

$2,125.22	Maximum PITI payment
÷ 112%	(less 12% for property taxes and hazard insurance)
$1,897.52	Maximum principal and interest payment

Interest rate 6.75%

Maximum Loan Amount $292,556

Loan amount is sales price, unless downpayment required.

* See Figure 12.1 for minimum residual income requirements.

Glossary

The definitions given here explain how the listed terms are used in the field of real estate finance. Some of the terms have additional meanings, which can be found in a standard dictionary.

Acceleration—Declaring a loan's entire balance immediately due and payable, either because the borrower has defaulted or (if the loan includes an alienation clause) has sold the security property without the lender's approval.

Acceleration Clause—A provision in a security instrument that allows the lender to declare the entire debt due immediately if the borrower breaches one or more provisions of the agreement. Also called a call provision.

Accrued Items of Expense—Expenses that have been incurred but are not yet due or payable; in a settlement statement, the seller's accrued expenses are credited to the buyer.

Acknowledgment—When a person who has signed a document formally declares to an authorized official (usually a notary public) that he or she signed voluntarily. The official can then attest that the signature is voluntary and genuine.

Acquisition Cost—The amount of money a buyer was required to expend in order to acquire title to a piece of property; in addition to the purchase price, this ordinarily includes a variety of closing costs, and may also include other expenses.

Adjustable-Rate Mortgage (ARM)—A loan in which the interest rate is periodically increased or decreased to reflect changes in the cost of money. *Compare:* Fixed-Rate Loan.

Age, Actual—The age of a structure from a chronological standpoint (as opposed to its effective age); how many years it has actually been in existence.

Age, Effective—The age of a structure indicated by its condition and remaining usefulness (as opposed to its actual age).

Alienation—The transfer of ownership or an interest in property from one person to another, by any means.

Alienation Clause—A provision in a security instrument that gives the lender the right to accelerate the loan if the borrower sells the property or transfers a significant interest in it without the lender's approval. Also called a due-on-sale clause.

All-Inclusive Trust Deed—A deed of trust used for wraparound financing.

AML—Adjustable mortgage loan; essentially the same thing as an ARM. (Savings and loans initially referred to their ARMs as AMLs, but the term is no longer in common use.)

Amortization—Gradually paying off a loan through installment payments that include both principal and interest.

Annual Percentage Rate (APR)—Under the Truth in Lending Act, the relationship between a loan's total finance charge and the total amount financed, expressed as an annual percentage.

Anticipation, Principle of—An appraisal principle which holds that value is created by the expectation of benefits to be received in the future.

Anti-Deficiency Rules—Laws that prohibit a secured lender from suing the borrower for a deficiency judgment after foreclosure, in certain circumstances.

Appraisal—An expert's estimate of the value of a piece of real estate as of a particular date, based on a documented analysis of the property's features. Also called a valuation.

Appraiser—One who estimates the value of property, especially an expert qualified to do so by training and experience.

Appreciation—An increase in the value of an asset; the opposite of depreciation.

APR—*See:* Annual Percentage Rate.

ARM—*See:* Adjustable-Rate Mortgage.

Arm's Length Transaction—A sale in which both the buyer and seller are fully informed of the property's attributes and deficiencies, neither is acting under unusual pressure, and the property has been offered for sale on the open market for a reasonable length of time.

Asset—Anything of value that an individual owns.

Assets, Liquid—Cash or other assets that can be readily turned into cash (liquidated), such as stock.

Assign—To transfer rights (especially contract rights) or interests to another.

Assignee—One to whom rights or interests have been assigned.

Assignment—A transfer of contract rights from one person to another.

Assignment of Contract and Deed—The instrument used to substitute a new vendor for the original vendor in a land contract.

Assignor—One who has assigned his or her rights or interests to another.

Assumption—When a buyer takes on personal responsibility for repayment of the seller's existing mortgage loan, becoming liable to the lender. The seller remains secondarily liable unless released by the lender.

Assumption Fee—A fee charged by the lender when a buyer assumes a seller's loan; usually paid by the buyer.

Assumptor—One who assumes a mortgage or deed of trust (usually a buyer).

Audit—A verification and examination of records, particularly the financial accounts of a business or other organization.

Automated Underwriting (AU)—*See:* Underwriting, Automated.

Bad Debt/Vacancy Factor—In the income approach to appraisal, a percentage deducted from a property's potential gross income, estimating the income that's likely to be lost because of vacancies and tenants who don't pay.

Balance Sheet—*See:* Financial Statement.

Balloon Mortgage—A mortgage loan (partially amortized or interest-only) that requires the borrower to make a balloon payment.

Balloon Payment—1. The payment of the remaining principal balance due at the end of the term of a partially amortized or interest-only loan; so called because it is much larger than the regular payments made during the loan term. 2. Any loan payment that is larger than the regular payments.

Basis—A figure used in calculating a gain on the sale of real estate for federal income tax purposes. Also called cost basis.

Basis, Adjusted—A property owner's initial basis in the property, plus capital expenditures for improvements, and minus any allowable cost recovery (depreciation) deductions.

Basis, Initial—The amount of a property owner's original investment in the property; what it cost to acquire the property, which may include closing costs and certain other expenses, as well as the purchase price.

Bearer—Whoever has possession of a negotiable instrument.

Beneficiary—In a deed of trust transaction, the lender. *Compare:* Mortgagee.

Bill of Sale—A document used to transfer title to personal property from one person to another.

Bi-Weekly Loan—A fixed-rate loan that requires a payment every two weeks instead of once a month, so that the borrower makes 26 half payments per year, the equivalent of 13 monthly payments.

Blanket Mortgage—A mortgage that encumbers more than one parcel of real property.

Bond—A certificate of indebtedness issued by a governmental body or a corporation; the bondholder receives a return in the form of periodic payments of interest until the principal is repaid in a lump sum.

Bonus—An extra payment, over and above what is strictly due; especially an extra payment an employer gives to an employee, as an incentive or in recognition of good performance.

Breach—Violation of an obligation, duty, or law; especially an unexcused failure to perform a contractual obligation.

Brokerage Fee—The commission or other compensation charged for a real estate broker's services.

Budget Mortgage—A mortgage where monthly payments include a share of the property taxes and insurance, in addition to principal and interest. The amounts for taxes and insurance are placed in the borrower's impound account.

Buydown—When the seller or a third party pays the lender a lump sum at closing to lower the interest rate charged to the buyer, either for the life of the loan (permanent buydown) or during the first years of the loan term (temporary buydown).

Call Provision—*See:* Acceleration Clause.

Capital Expenditures—Money spent on property improvements and modifications that add to the property's value or prolong its life.

Capital Improvement—Any improvement to real property that is designed to become a permanent part of the property or that will have the effect of significantly prolonging the property's life.

Capitalization Method—*See:* Income Method.

Carryback Loan—*See:* Purchase Money Loan.

Cash Flow Analysis—*See:* Residual Income Analysis.

Certificate of Deposit (CD)—A savings arrangement in which a depositor agrees to leave money on deposit for a specified period, or pay a penalty for early withdrawal.

Certificate of Eligibility—A document issued by the Department of Veterans Affairs, indicating a veteran's eligibility for a VA-guaranteed loan.

Certificate of Reasonable Value (CRV)—*See:* Notice of Value.

Certificate of Veteran Status—A document issued by the Department of Veterans Affairs, indicating a veteran's eligibility for an FHA-insured loan.

Certificate of Sale—The document given to the purchaser at a sheriff's sale instead of a deed, and which is replaced with a sheriff's deed only after the statutory redemption period expires.

Charter—A written instrument granting a power or a right of franchise.

Chattel Mortgage—An instrument that makes personal property (chattels) security for a loan. In states that have adopted the Uniform Commercial Code, the chattel mortgage has been replaced by the security agreement.

Closed Mortgage—A loan that cannot be paid off early.

Closing—The final stage in a real estate transaction, when the loan funds are disbursed, the seller is paid the purchase price, and the buyer receives the deed; also called settlement.

Closing Costs—Expenses incurred in the transfer of real estate, aside from the purchase price; for example, the appraisal fee, title insurance premiums, brokerage fee, and transfer taxes. Also called settlement costs.

Closing Statement—*See:* Settlement Statement.

CMA—*See:* Competitive Market Analysis.

Co-Borrower—Someone (often a member of the borrower's family) who accepts responsibility for the repayment of a mortgage loan along with the primary borrower, to help the borrower qualify for the loan. Also called a co-mortgagor or cosigner.

Collateral—Property (personal or real) accepted by a lender as security for a loan. If the borrower fails to repay the loan, the lender has the right to keep or sell the collateral.

Commercial Bank—A type of financial institution that traditionally has emphasized commercial lending, but which also makes many residential mortgage loans.

Commission—The compensation paid to a real estate broker for services in connection with a real estate transaction; usually a percentage of the sales price.

Commitment—A lender's promise to make a loan. A loan commitment may be either firm or conditional.

Commitment, Conditional—A conditional approval of a loan that requires fulfillment of certain conditions.

Commitment, Firm—A lender's approval of a loan without any conditions.

Co-Mortgagor—*See:* Co-Borrower.

Comparables—In a sales comparison appraisal, properties similar to the subject property that have recently been sold; the appraiser uses the sales prices of the comparables as an indication of the value of the subject property.

Competition, Principle of—An appraisal principle which holds that profits tend to encourage competition, and excess profits tend to result in ruinous competition.

Competitive Market Analysis (CMA)—A real estate agent's estimate of the value of a listed home, based on the sales prices or listing prices of comparable homes.

Compound Interest—*See:* Interest, Compound.

Condition—A provision in an agreement that makes the parties' rights and obligations depend on the occurrence (or nonoccurrence) of a particular event. Also called a contingency clause.

Conditional Commitment—A conditional approval of a loan that requires fulfillment of certain conditions.

Conforming Loan—A loan made in accordance with the standardized underwriting criteria of the major secondary market agencies, Fannie Mae and Freddie Mac, and which therefore can be sold to those agencies. A loan that does not meet the Fannie Mae/Freddie Mac standards is called a nonconforming loan.

Conformity, Principle of—An appraisal principle which holds that property achieves its maximum value when there is a reasonable degree of social and economic homogeneity in the neighborhood.

Consideration—Something of value given to induce another to enter into a contract. An agreement is not a legally binding contract unless the parties exchange consideration.

Construction Loan—A loan to finance the construction of a building, which remains in place only until construction is completed, at which point it is replaced by a take-out loan. Also called an interim loan.

Consumer Price Index—An index that tracks changes in the cost of goods and services for a typical consumer. Formerly called the cost of living index.

Contingency Clause—*See:* Condition.

Contract Rate—*See:* Note Rate.

Contract Rent—The rent an owner is currently receiving from a property. *Compare:* Economic Rent.

Contribution, Principle of—An appraisal principle which holds that the value of real property is greatest when the improvements produce the highest return commensurate with their cost. Some improvements add more to the property's value than they cost, and others cost more than they add.

Conventional Loan—An institutional loan that is not insured or guaranteed by a government agency.

Convertible ARM—An adjustable-rate mortgage that gives the borrower the option of converting to a fixed interest rate at certain times during the first years of the loan term.

Conversion Option—A provision in an adjustable-rate mortgage allowing the borrower to convert the loan to a fixed rate at certain points in the loan term.

Cosigner—*See:* Co-Borrower.

Cost, Replacement—In appraisal, the current cost of constructing a building with the same utility as the subject property, using modern materials and construction methods.

Cost, Reproduction—In appraisal, the cost of constructing a replica (an exact duplicate) of the subject property, using the same materials and construction methods that were originally used, but at current prices.

Cost Approach to Value—One of the three main methods of appraisal (along with the income approach and the sales comparison approach), in which an estimate of the subject property's value is arrived at by estimating the cost of replacing the improvements, then deducting the estimated accrued depreciation and adding the estimated market value of the land.

Cost Basis—*See:* Basis.

Cost Recovery Deductions—Real estate investors may take other deductions from their income taxes, such as deducting depreciation of investment property.

Coupon Rate—*See:* Note Rate.

Credit—On a settlement statement, a payment receivable (owed to one of the parties), as opposed to a debit, which is a payment due (owed by one of the parties).

Creditor—One who is owed a debt.

Creditor, Secured—A creditor with a lien on specific property, which enables him or her to foreclose and collect the debt from the sale proceeds if the debtor does not pay.

Credit Report—A report prepared by a credit reporting agency outlining the credit history of an individual, showing the amount of debt and a record of repayment.

Credit Score—A figure used in underwriting to evaluate a loan applicant's credit history, which is calculated by a credit reporting agency.

Credit Union—A type of financial institution that serves only the members of a particular group, such as a professional organization or a labor union. Credit unions have traditionally emphasized consumer loans, and now also make residential mortgage loans.

CRV—*See:* Notice of Value.

Cure—To remedy a default, by paying money that is overdue or by fulfilling other obligations.

Debit—On a settlement statement, a payment owed by one of the parties.

Debtor—One who owes money to another.

Debt Investment—*See:* Investment, Debt.

Debt Service—The amount of money required to make the periodic payments of principal and interest on an amortized debt, such as a mortgage.

Debt Service Ratio—*See:* Debt to Income Ratio.

Debt to Housing Gap Ratio—The difference between a loan applicant's debt to income ratio and housing expense to income ratio.

Debt to Income Ratio—A ratio describing the maximum percentage of total monthly income that may be taken up by a proposed housing expense plus all other installment debt payments and liabilities. Also called a total obligations to income ratio or total debt service ratio.

Deduction—An amount a taxpayer is allowed to subtract from his or her income before the tax on the income is calculated.

Deed in Lieu of Foreclosure—A deed given by a borrower to a lender, transferring title to the security property to the lender to satisfy the debt and avoid foreclosure.

Deed of Reconveyance—A document which acknowledges that a deed of trust has been paid in full, releasing the security property from the lien. *Compare:* Satisfaction of Mortgage.

Deed of Trust—A security instrument similar to a mortgage giving the power of sale to a third party. The parties are the grantor or trustor (the borrower), the beneficiary (the lender), and the trustee (a neutral third party).

Default—Failure to fulfill an obligation, duty, or promise, as when a borrower fails to make payments, or a tenant fails to pay rent.

Deferred Interest—*See:* Interest, Deferred.

Deferred Maintenance—Depreciation resulting from physical wear and tear.

Deficiency Judgment—A court judgment against a debtor requiring the debtor to pay the creditor the shortfall between the amount of the debt and the proceeds of the foreclosure sale.

Demand—Desire to own, coupled with the ability to afford; this is one of the four elements of value, along with scarcity, utility, and transferability.

Demand Deposit—A deposit in a financial institution that the depositor can withdraw at any time, without notice, such as a deposit in a checking account. *Compare:* Time Deposit.

Department of Housing and Urban Development (HUD)—*See:* HUD.

Deposit—Money offered as an indication of commitment or as a protection, and which may be refunded under certain circumstances, such as an earnest money deposit or a tenant's security deposit.

Depreciation—A loss in value due to any cause.

Depreciation, Curable—Depreciation (resulting from deferred maintenance or functional obsolescence) that a prudent property owner would ordinarily correct, because the cost of correction could be recovered in the sales price when the property is sold.

Depreciation, Incurable—Depreciation that is either impossible to correct, or not economically feasible to correct, because the cost could not be recovered in the sales price when the property is sold.

Direct Endorser—A lender authorized to underwrite its own FHA loan applications, rather than having to submit them to the FHA for approval.

Discount—1. In the origination of a loan, to charge a discount fee. 2. In the purchase of a loan, to pay less than the face value of the promissory note.

Discount Points—A fee a lender may charge at closing to increase its profit on the loan above the interest rate.

Discount Rate—The interest rate a Federal Reserve Bank charges on loans to member banks that borrow funds on a short-term basis. *Compare:* Federal Funds Rate.

Disintegration—In a property's life cycle, the period of decline when the property's present economic usefulness is near an end and constant upkeep is necessary.

Disintermediation—When depositors withdraw their savings from financial institutions and put the money into other types of investments with higher yields.

Diversification—The practice of investing in a variety of different sectors of the economy, to make a portfolio safer.

Dividend—A share of a company's profits paid to a stockholder as a return on the investment.

Double-Entry Bookkeeping—An accounting technique in which an item is entered in the ledger twice, once as a credit and once as a debit; used for settlement statements.

Downpayment—The part of the purchase price of property that the buyer is not borrowing; the difference between the purchase price and the financing.

Due-on-Sale Clause—*See:* Alienation Clause.

Earnest Money—A deposit that a prospective buyer gives the seller when the purchase and sale agreement is signed, as evidence of his or her good faith intention to complete the transaction. Also called a good faith deposit.

Economic Life—The period during which improved property yields a return over and above the rent due to the land itself; also called the useful life. *Compare:* Physical Life.

Economic Obsolescence—*See:* External Obsolescence.

Economic Rent—The rent a property could command in the current marketplace if it were available for lease today. Also called market rent. *Compare:* Contract Rent.

Effective Income—In FHA underwriting, the loan applicant's gross monthly income from all sources that can be expected to continue; the FHA equivalent of stable monthly income.

Elements of Comparison—In the sales comparison approach to appraisal, considerations taken into account in selecting comparables and comparing them to the subject property; they include the date of sale, location, physical characteristics, and terms of sale.

Encumber—To place a lien or other encumbrance against the title to a property.

Encumbrance—A nonpossessory interest in real property; a right or interest held by someone other than the property owner; it may be a lien, an easement, or a restrictive covenant.

Endorsement—When the payee of a negotiable instrument (such as a check or a promissory note) assigns the right to payment to another, usually by signing the back or the face of the instrument.

Entitlement—*See:* VA Entitlement.

Equal Credit Opportunity Act (ECOA)—A federal law prohibiting discrimination by lenders against loan applicants on the basis of race, color, religion, national origin, sex, marital status, age, or whether income comes from public assistance.

Equilibrium—In the life cycle of a property, a period of stability, during which the property undergoes little, if any, change.

Equitable Title—*See:* Title, Equitable.

Equity—1. The difference between a property's value and the outstanding liens against it; an owner's unencumbered interest in his or her property. 2. Fairness.

Equity Exchange—When a buyer gives a seller real or personal property in addition to or instead of cash for the purchase price.

Equity Stripping—A predatory loan practice where a lender charges high fees for repeat refinancing that eat into a homeowner's equity.

Escalation Clause—A clause in a contract or mortgage that provides for payment or interest increases if specified events occur, such as a change in the property taxes or in the prime interest rate. Also called an escalator clause.

Escrow—A system in which parties to a transaction can have a disinterested third party hold things of value (such as money or documents) until the specified conditions have been fulfilled.

Escrow Agent—A third party who holds things of value (such as money or documents) on behalf of parties to a transaction until specified conditions have been fulfilled.

Estoppel—A legal doctrine that prevents a person from asserting rights or facts that are inconsistent with his or her earlier conduct or statements, when someone else has taken action in reliance on that earlier conduct.

Estoppel Letter—A document signed by a lender when property is sold subject to an existing mortgage. It either acknowledges the transfer and waives the right to accelerate the loan pursuant to a due-on-sale clause, or else merely states the balance due and the status of the loan.

Exclusion of Gain on Sale of Home—A taxpayer may exclude from taxation any gain on the sale of a principal residence, up to a limit of $250,000 (or $500,000 if filing jointly).

Execute—1. To sign an instrument and take any other steps (such as acknowledgment) that may be necessary to its validity. 2. To perform or complete.

Execution, Order of—A court order directing a public officer (such as the sheriff) to seize and sell property to satisfy a debt; also called a writ of execution.

Expenses, Fixed—Recurring property expenses, such as general real estate taxes and hazard insurance.

Expenses, Maintenance—Cleaning, supplies, utilities, tenant services, and administrative costs for income-producing property.

Expenses, Operating—For income-producing property, the fixed expenses, maintenance expenses, and reserves for replacement; does not include debt service.

Expenses, Variable—Expenses incurred in connection with property that do not occur on a set schedule, such as the cost of repairing a roof damaged in a storm.

External Obsolescence—Depreciation resulting from factors outside the property itself and outside the owner's control. Also called economic obsolescence.

Fair Housing Act—A federal law prohibiting discrimination in residential property transactions, including lending, on the basis of race, color, national origin, religion, sex, disability, or familial status.

Fannie Mae—The Federal National Mortgage Association (FNMA), a private corporation supervised by HUD; one of the three major secondary market agencies, along with Freddie Mac and Ginnie Mae.

Farmers Home Administration (FmHA)—*See:* Rural Housing Service.

Federal Deficit—A shortfall in funds that occurs when the federal government spends more money than it collects in a particular year.

Federal Funds Rate—The interest rate that banks charge one another for overnight loans; set by the Federal Reserve. *See:* Discount Rate.

Federal Home Loan Mortgage Corporation (FHLMC)—*See:* Freddie Mac.

Federal Housing Administration (FHA)—An agency within the Department of Housing and Urban Development that provides mortgage insurance to encourage lenders to make more affordable home loans.

Federal National Mortgage Association (FNMA)—*See:* Fannie Mae.

Federal Open Market Committee—The Federal Open Market Committee is a board that makes decisions regarding open market operations by the Federal Reserve.

Federal Reserve Bank—There are twelve Federal Reserve Banks, one for each Federal Reserve District, owned by the commercial banks within that district.

Federal Reserve Board—The Federal Reserve System is controlled by a seven-member Board of Governors, known as the Federal Reserve Board. Each member is appointed from a different district to a 14-year term.

Federal Reserve System—The Federal Reserve System regulates commercial banks, and that implements monetary policy. Commonly referred to as "the Fed."

Fee Packing—A predatory loan practice where a lender charges points or processing fees that are higher than usual and not justified by the services provided.

FHA—*See:* Federal Housing Administration.

FHA-Insured Loan—A loan made by an institutional lender with mortgage insurance provided by the Federal Housing Administration, protecting the lender against losses due to borrower default.

FHLMC—*See:* Freddie Mac.

Finance Charge—Any charge a borrower is assessed, directly or indirectly, in connection with a loan. *See also:* Total Finance Charge.

Financial Institutions Reform, Recovery & Enforcement Act (FIRREA)—A federal law enacted in 1989 in response to the savings and loan crisis; it reorganized the federal agencies that oversee financial institutions.

Financial Statement—A summary of facts showing the financial condition of an individual or a business, including a detailed list of assets and liabilities. Also called a balance sheet.

Financing Statement—A brief instrument that is recorded to establish and give public notice of a creditor's security interest in an item of personal property.

FIRREA—*See:* Financial Institutions Reform, Recovery, & Enforcement Act.

First Lien Position—The position of lien priority held by a mortgage or deed of trust that has higher priority than any other mortgage or deed of trust against the property.

First Mortgage—The mortgage (or deed of trust) against a property that has first lien position; the one with higher lien priority than any other mortgage against that property.

Fiscal Policy—The government's actions in raising revenue through taxation, spending money, and financing budget deficits.

Fiscal Year—Any twelve-month period used as a business year for accounting, tax, and other financial purposes, as opposed to a calendar year. For example, the federal government's fiscal year runs from October 1 through September 30.

Fixed-Rate Loan—A mortgage loan in which the lender charges an unchanging interest rate throughout the loan term. *Compare:* Adjustable-Rate Mortgage.

Fixture—An item that was originally personal property, but which has been attached to or closely associated with real property in such a way that it has legally become part of the real property.

FmHA—*See:* Rural Housing Service.

Foreclosure—When a lienholder forces property to be sold, so the unpaid debt secured by the lien can be satisfied from the sale proceeds.

Foreclosure, Judicial—A court-supervised foreclosure, beginning with a lawsuit filed by a mortgagee or beneficiary to foreclose on property on which a borrower has defaulted.

Foreclosure, Nonjudicial—Foreclosure by a trustee under the power of sale in a deed of trust.

Forfeiture—Loss of a right or something of value as a result of failure to perform an obligation or condition.

FNMA—*See:* Fannie Mae.

Freddie Mac—The Federal Home Loan Mortgage Corporation (FHLMC), a private corporation supervised by HUD; one of the major secondary market agencies, along with Fannie Mae and Ginnie Mae.

Free and Clear Ownership—Ownership of real property completely free of any mortgage liens.

Fully Amortized Loan—A loan structured so that the loan balance is paid off at the end of the loan term.

Functional Obsolescence—Depreciation resulting from functional inadequacies, such as those caused by poor or outmoded design.

Funding Fee—A charge paid by a VA borrower at closing, which the lender submits to the VA.

Garnishment—A legal process by which a creditor gains access to the funds or personal property of a debtor that are in the hands of a third party. For example, if the debtor's wages are garnished, the employer is required to turn over part of each paycheck to the creditor.

Gift Funds—Money given to a buyer who otherwise would not have enough cash to close the transaction.

Gift Letter—A document in which a donor of gift funds states that the money given is not a loan and does not have to be repaid; required by the lender when the borrower intends to use gift funds as part of the downpayment or closing costs.

GI Loan—*See:* VA-Guaranteed Loan.

Ginnie Mae—The Government National Mortgage Association (GNMA), a government agency within HUD; one of the major secondary market agencies, along with Fannie Mae and Freddie Mac.

GNMA—*See:* Ginnie Mae.

Good Faith Deposit—*See:* Earnest Money.

Government-Sponsored Enterprise (GSE)—An entity that is privately owned and functions as a private corporation, but is created, chartered, and supervised by the government.

Graduated Payment Mortgage (GPM)—A loan in which the payments are increased periodically during the first years of the loan term, usually according to a fixed schedule.

Grantor—In a deed of trust transaction, the borrower. Also called the trustor.

Gross Income—An individual's income before income taxes have been deducted.

Gross Income Multiplier (GIM)—A figure used to estimate the value of residential rental property, determined by dividing the sales price by the rental income. Also called a gross rent multiplier.

Growing Equity Mortgage (GEM)—A fixed-rate loan with annual payment increases that are used to reduce the principal balance, so that the loan is paid off much more quickly than it would be with ordinary level payments.

Guaranty—An arrangement in which one party accepts liability to another party for the payment of a third party's obligations, if the third party fails to pay them. *See also:* VA Guaranty.

Hard Money Mortgage—A mortgage given to a lender in exchange for cash, as opposed to one given in exchange for credit.

Hazard Insurance—Insurance against damage to real property caused by fire, flood, or other mishaps. Also called casualty insurance.

HECM—*See:* Reverse Equity Mortgage.

Highest and Best Use—The use which, at the time of appraisal, is most likely to produce the greatest net return from the property over a given period of time.

Holder in Due Course (HDC)—A third party purchaser of a promissory note who purchased the note for value and in good faith. An HDC is entitled to payment by the maker or drawer of the check or note.

Home Equity Conversion Mortgage—*See:* Reverse Equity Mortgage.

Home Equity Loan—A loan obtained by the borrower using property he already owns as collateral.

Home Mortgage Disclosure Act—A federal law requiring institutional lenders to report on residential loans originated or purchased from other lenders; the intent of the law is to detect redlining and other unlawful lending practices.

Home Mortgage Interest Deduction—Taxpayers may deduct from their taxable income interest paid on home mortgages, up to a limit of $500,000 (or $1,000,000 for married couples filing jointly).

Homeowners Association—A nonprofit association made up of homeowners in a subdivision, responsible for enforcing the restrictive covenants and managing other community affairs.

Home Ownership and Equity Protection Act—A federal law applicable to high-cost home equity loans that requires certain disclosures and prohibits certain predatory lending practices.

Homeowner's Insurance—Insurance against damage to the homeowner's personal property as well as the real property.

Housing Expense to Income Ratio—A ratio describing the maximum percentage of total monthly income that may be taken up by a proposed housing expense.

HUD—The Department of Housing and Urban Development, a cabinet-level department of the federal government.

Hypothecation—Making property security for a loan by transferring title to the lender without surrendering. *Compare:* Pledge.

Impound Account—An escrow account maintained by a lender for paying property taxes and insurance premiums for the security property; the lender requires the borrower to make regular deposits, and pays the expenses out of the account when they come due. Also called a reserve account.

Improvements—Manmade additions to real property.

Income Method—A method of appraisal in which an estimate of the subject property's value is based on the net income it produces. Also called the capitalization method.

Income Property—Property that generates rent or other income for the owner, such as an apartment building.

Income Ratio—A test applied in qualifying a buyer for a loan, to determine whether he or she has sufficient income; the buyer's proposed housing expense and other debt should not exceed a specified percentage of his stable monthly income.

Index—A published statistical report that indicates changes in the cost of money (market interest rates), used as the basis for interest rate adjustments in an ARM.

Inflation—Inflation is a period of price increases which occur as a result of too-rapid economic growth. The Fed seeks to limit inflation by using monetary policy to control growth.

Installment Land Contract—*See:* Land Contract.

Installment Note—*See:* Note, Installment.

Institutional Lender—A bank, savings and loan, or similar regulated lending institution; in some contexts, the term also includes private companies that are in the business of loaning money, such as mortgage companies.

Instrument—A legal document; usually one that transfers title, creates a lien, or establishes a right to payment.

Integration—In a property's life cycle, the earliest stage, when the property is being developed. Also called the development stage.

Interest—A periodic charge a lender requires a borrower to pay in exchange for the loan, usually expressed as a percentage of the remaining principal balance. *Compare:* Principal.

Interest, Compound—Interest calculated as a percentage of both the principal and any accumulated unpaid interest. *Compare:* Interest, Simple.

Interest, Deferred—Interest that accumulates over the course of one or more payment periods but is not payable until some later time; a feature of some adjustable-rate loans.

Interest, Interim—*See:* Interest, Prepaid.

Interest, Prepaid—Interest on a new loan that must be paid at closing; it covers the interest due for the first month of the loan term. Also called interim interest.

Interest, Simple—Interest calculated as a percentage of the principal balance only. *Compare:* Interest, Compound.

Interest-Only Loan—A loan where payments of only the interest due (with no principal) are made during the loan term, or during a specified period at the beginning of the loan term.

Interest Rates—The Fed has control over two key interest rates, the federal discount rate and the federal funds rate. Lenders tend to adjust their own short-term interest rates in response to changes in these rates.

Interest Rate Cap—A provision in an ARM that limits the amount that the interest rate may be increased (and in some cases, decreased).

Interest Rate Risk—The risk that, after a loan is made for a specified term at a fixed interest rate, market interest rates will rise and the lender will miss the opportunity to invest the loaned funds at a higher rate.

Interest Shortfall—When more interest accrues on a loan than the lender collects during a particular period; this can occur with adjustable-rate mortgages that have certain features.

Interim Loan—*See:* Construction Loan.

Intermediary—An individual or entity who originates and/or services loans on behalf of another.

Investment—When someone makes a sum of money (investment capital) available for use by another person or entity, in the expectation that it will generate a return (profit) for the investor.

Investment, Debt—An investment where temporary use of an investor's funds is exchanged for interest payments, in accordance with an agreement requiring repayment of the funds or allowing withdrawal of the funds.

Investment, Liquid—An investment that can be quickly and easily converted into cash.

Investment, Ownership—An investment where an investor's funds are used to purchase an asset or a property interest in an asset.

Investment Capital—A sum of money made available to fund business enterprises or other ventures.

Investment, Return of—*See:* Return of Investment.

Investment, Return on—*See:* Return on Investment.

Judicial Foreclosure—*See:* Foreclosure, Nonjudicial.

Junior Lienholder—A secured creditor whose lien is lower in priority than another's lien against the same property.

Junior Mortgage—A mortgage that has lower lien priority than another mortgage against the same property. Also called a second mortgage or secondary mortgage.

Land Contract—A contract for the sale of property in which the buyer (vendee) pays the seller (vendor) in installments, taking possession of the property immediately but not taking title until the purchase price has been paid in full. Also called a contract for deed, conditional sales contract, installment sales contract, or real estate contract.

Law of Supply and Demand—*See:* Supply and Demand, Law of.

Lease—A contract in which one party (the tenant) pays the other (the landlord) rent in exchange for the possession of real estate.

Lease/Option—A lease that includes an option to purchase the leased property during the term of the lease.

Lease/Purchase—A variation on the lease/option, in which the parties sign a purchase contract (instead of an option) and the prospective buyer leases the property for an extended period before closing.

Legal Title—*See:* Title, Legal.

Level Payment Loan—A loan that is repaid with equal periodic (usually monthly) payments; the payment amount does not change over the entire term. *Compare:* Graduated Payment Mortgage; Growing Equity Mortgage.

Leverage—The effective use of borrowed money to finance an investment, such as a real estate purchase.

Liability—1. A debt or obligation. 2. Legal responsibility.

Liable—Legally responsible.

Lien—A nonpossessory interest in real property giving the lienholder the right to foreclose if the owner does not pay a debt owed to the lienholder. A financial encumbrance on the owner's title.

Lienholder—A secured creditor who has a lien against a debtor's real property.

Lien Priority—The order in which liens will be paid off out of the proceeds of a foreclosure sale.

Lien Theory—The legal theory holding that a mortgage or a deed of trust does not involve a transfer of title to the lender, but merely creates a lien against the borrower's property in the lender's favor. *Compare:* Title Theory.

Liquid Investment—*See:* Investment, Liquid.

Listing—A contract between a real estate broker and a seller, by which the seller makes the broker his or her agent in order to put the property up for sale.

Loan Correspondent—An intermediary who arranges loans of an investor's money to borrowers and then services the loans.

Loan Fee—Any one-time fee that a lender charges at closing for a loan or an assumption, including origination fees, discount fees, or assumption fees.

Loan Guaranty—An arrangement where a third party guarantor accepts secondary liability for a loan and will reimburse a lender for any losses from a borrower's default.

Loan Servicing—*See:* Servicing.

Loan Term—*See:* Repayment Period.

Loan-to-Value Ratio (LTV)—The relationship between the loan amount and either the sales price or the appraised value of the property (whichever is less), expressed as a percentage.

Local Market—*See:* Primary Market.

Lock-In—When a lender guarantees a loan applicant a particular interest rate if the transaction closes within a specified period.

Lock-In Clause—A clause in a promissory note or land contract that prohibits prepayment before a specified date, or prohibits it altogether.

LTV—*See:* Loan-to-Value Ratio.

Low Appraisal—An appraisal where the appraised value is lower than the agreed-upon sales price, which may affect financing and terminate the transaction.

Maker—In a promissory note, the party who promises to pay; the debtor or borrower. *Compare:* Payee.

Margin—The difference between the index rate and the interest rate charged on an ARM.

Market Data Approach—*See:* Sales Comparison Approach.

Market Interest Rates—The rates that are paid on particular types of investments or charge for particular types of loans under current economic conditions.

Market Price—The price for which a property actually sold; the final sales price.

Market Value—The most probable price a property should bring if sold in an arm's length transaction; also called objective value.

Minimum Property Requirements (MPRs)—A lender's requirements concerning the physical condition of a building, which must be met before a loan can be approved.

MIP—Mortgage insurance premium. Most often used to refer to the fee charged for FHA insurance coverage. The initial FHA premium is referred to as the UFMIP (upfront MIP) or the OTMIP (one-time MIP).

MMI—The Mutual Mortgage Insurance program, the formal name of the FHA insurance program. The FHA MIP is also sometimes called the MMI.

Monetary Policy—Government action in controlling the supply and cost of borrowing money.

Mortgage—An instrument creating a voluntary lien on a property to secure repayment of a debt. The two parties involved are the mortgagor (borrower) and mortgagee (lender).

Mortgage-Backed Securities (MBS)—*See:* Securities, Mortgage-Backed.

Mortgage Banker—An intermediary who originates and services real estate loans on behalf of investors.

Mortgage Broker—An intermediary who brings real estate lenders and borrowers together and negotiates loan agreements between them.

Mortgage Company—A type of real estate lender that originates and services loans on behalf of large investors (acting as a mortgage banker) or for immediate resale on the secondary market; not a depository financial institution.

Mortgagee—The one who receives a mortgage from the mortgagor; the lender.

Mortgage Insurance—Insurance against losses resulting from mortgage default in which an insurer will reimburse a lender for all or part of a loss.

Mortgage Loan—A loan secured by a mortgage or a deed of trust that creates a lien against real property.

Mortgage Payment Cap—A provision in an ARM that limits the amount the monthly payment can be increased, either during a given year, or over the entire life of the loan.

Mortgaging Clause—A clause in a mortgage that describes the security interest given to the mortgagee.

Mortgagor—A property owner (usually a borrower) who gives a mortgage against the property to another (usually a lender) as security for payment of an obligation.

MPRs—*See:* Minimum Property Requirements.

Mutual Fund—A company that invests its capital in a diversified portfolio of securities on behalf of its investors, who own shares in the fund.

Mutual Savings Bank—A savings bank originally organized as a mutual company, owned by and operated for the benefit of its depositors (as opposed to stockholders).

National Market—*See:* Secondary Market.

Negative Amortization—When deferred interest on an adjustable-rate loan is added to the principal balance, increasing the amount owed.

Negative Amortization Cap—In an ARM, a limit on the amount of deferred interest that can be added to the principal balance.

Negotiable Instrument—An instrument establishing a right to payment, which is freely transferable from one person to another. It can be a check, promissory note, bond, draft, or stock.

Net Equity—The market value of a property, minus any liens against the property and all anticipated selling expenses.

Net Worth—An individual's personal financial assets, minus total personal liabilities.

Nonconforming Loan—A loan that does not meet the underwriting guidelines set by Fannie Mae and Freddie Mac, and therefore can't be sold to those agencies, except by special arrangement.

Nonjudicial Foreclosure—*See:* Foreclosure, Nonjudicial.

Note—*See:* Note, Promissory.

Note, Demand—A promissory note that is due whenever the holder of the note demands payment.

Note, Installment—A promissory note that calls for regular payments of principal and interest until the debt is paid off, as used for an amortized loan.

Note, Joint—A promissory note signed by two or more persons with equal liability for payment.

Note, Promissory—A written, legally binding promise to repay a debt; may or may not be a negotiable instrument.

Note, Straight—A promissory note that calls for regular payments of interest only.

Note Rate—The interest rate specified in the loan's promissory note. Also called the coupon rate or contract rate.

Notice of Default—A notice sent by a lender (mortgagee or deed of trust beneficiary) to the borrower, informing the borrower that he or she has breached the terms of the loan agreement and warning that the lender is going to begin the foreclosure process.

Notice of Sale—A notice stating that foreclosure proceedings have been commenced against a property.

Notice of Value (NOV)—A document issued by the Department of Veterans Affairs, setting forth a property's current market value, based on a VA-approved appraisal. Previously referred to as a Certificate of Reasonable Value (CRV).

NOV—*See:* Notice of Value.

Obligatory Advances—Disbursements of construction loan funds that the lender is obliged to make (by prior agreement with the borrower) when the borrower has completed certain phases of construction.

Obsolescence—*See:* External Obsolescence; Functional Obsolescence.

Open End Loan—A loan that permits the borrower to reborrow the money he or she has repaid on the principal, usually up to the original loan amount, without executing a new loan agreement; similar to a line of credit.

Open Market Operations—The Federal Reserve adjusts the money supply by engaged in open market operations, buying and selling government securities and therefore changing the amount of money available in circulation.

Option—A contract that gives one party the right to do something (such as purchase a piece of property), without obligating him or her to do it.

Optionee—The person to whom an option is given.

Option Money—The consideration paid by a buyer/optionee that makes an option to purchase binding on the seller/optionor.

Optionor—The person who gives an option to the optionee.

Option to Purchase—An option giving the optionee the right to buy property owned by the optionor at an agreed price during a specified period.

Origination—The process of approving and funding a new loan.

Origination Fee—A fee charged by a lender upon making a new loan, intended to cover the administrative cost of making the loan. Also called a loan fee.

OTMIP—*See:* MIP.

Overimprovement—An improvement that is more expensive than the value of the land justifies.

Ownership Investment—*See:* Investment, Ownership.

Package Mortgage—A mortgage secured by items of personal property (such as appliances) in addition to the real property.

Partial Reconveyance—*See:* Partial Release.

Partial Release Clause—A clause in a security instrument allowing one or more of the parcels of property under a blanket lien to be released from the lien while other parcels remain subject to it.

Partial Satisfaction—*See:* Partial Release.

Partially Amortized Loan—A loan where monthly payments include both principal and interest but where the loan balance is not fully paid off at the end of the loan term.

Participation Loan—A loan made in exchange for a share of the borrower's equity in the property.

Payee—In a promissory note, the party who is entitled to be paid; the creditor or lender. *Compare:* Maker.

Payment Adjustment Period—The minimum interval between adjustments of the monthly payment amount on an ARM.

Personal Property—Any property that is not real property; movable property not affixed to land. Also called chattels or personalty.

Physical Life—An estimate of the time a building will remain structurally sound and capable of being used. *Compare:* Economic Life.

PITI Payment—The full monthly mortgage payment, including property taxes and hazard insurance as well as principal and interest.

Pledge—When a debtor transfers possession of property to the creditor as security for repayment of the debt, as when an item of personal property is pawned. *Compare:* Hypothecation.

PMI—Private mortgage insurance, used to insure high-LTV conventional loans; provided by a private insurance company (instead of a government agency).

Point—One point is one percent of the loan amount.

Points—1. The discount fee paid to a lender at closing. 2. Any loan fee paid to the lender at closing, including both the origination fee and the discount fee.

Portfolio—The collection of investments and cash reserves that are held by an investor.

Portfolio Loan—A mortgage loan that the lender keeps in its own investment portfolio until the loan is repaid (as opposed to selling it on the secondary market).

Power of Sale—A provision in a deed of trust that gives the trustee the right to foreclose nonjudicially (sell the property without court supervision) in the event of default.

Preapproval—Formal loan approval from a lender stating a maximum loan amount that the lender is willing to issue, based on the borrower's income and assets.

Predatory Lending—Lending practices where lenders or mortgage brokers take advantage of unsophisticated borrowers for their own profit.

Prepayment—Paying off part or all of a loan before payment is due.

Prepayment Penalty—A penalty some lenders charge a borrower who prepays a loan, to compensate for the lost interest that the lender would have received if the borrower had continued paying off the loan over its entire term.

Prepayment Provision—A clause allowing a lender to charge borrowers for prepaying on a loan, to compensate the lender for lost interest.

Prepayment Risk—The risk that a loan will be paid off sooner than expected, reducing the lender's anticipated yield.

Prequalification—Informal approval from a lender or real estate agent suggesting the maximum amount a buyer could afford to spend on a home.

Primary Market—The market in which real estate loans are originated, where lenders make loans to borrowers; also called the local market. *Compare:* Secondary Market.

Prime Rate—The interest rate a bank charges its largest and most desirable customers.

Principal—1. The original amount of a loan, or the remainder of that amount after part of it has been paid. *Compare:* Interest. 2. One of the parties to a transaction (such as a buyer or seller), as opposed to those who are involved in the transaction as agents or employees (such as a real estate broker or escrow agent).

Principal Residence Property—Real property that is the owner's main dwelling. Under the federal income tax laws, a taxpayer can only have one principal residence at a time.

Priority—*See:* Lien Priority.

Private Mortgage Insurance—*See:* PMI.

Progression, Principle of—An appraisal principle which holds that a property of lesser value tends to be worth more when it is located in an area with properties of greater value than it would be if located elsewhere. The opposite of the principle of regression.

Promissory Note—*See:* Note, Promissory.

Proration—The process of dividing or allocating something (especially a sum of money or an expense) proportionately, according to time, interest, or benefit.

Purchase and Sale Agreement—A contract in which a seller promises to convey title to real property to a buyer in exchange for the purchase price. Also called an earnest money agreement, deposit receipt, sales contract, purchase contract, or contract of sale.

Purchase Money Loan—1. Generally, any loan used to purchase the property that secures the loan. 2. More narrowly, a loan given to a buyer by a seller in a seller-financed transaction.

Purchaser's Assignment of Contract and Deed—The instrument used to assign the vendee's equitable interest in a contract to another.

Qualifying—*See:* Underwriting.

Qualifying Standards—The rules (concerning income, net worth, credit history, loan-to-value ratios, etc.) that an underwriter applies in deciding whether or not to approve a loan application. Also called underwriting standards.

Rate Adjustment Period—The minimum interval between adjustments of an ARM's interest rate.

Real Estate Contract—*See:* Land Contract.

Real Estate Investment Trust (REIT)—A real estate investment business with at least 100 investors, organized as a trust and receiving tax benefits in exchange for compliance with certain rules.

Real Estate Settlement Procedures Act (RESPA)—A federal law that requires lenders to disclose certain information about closing costs to loan applicants.

Reamortize—To recalculate level payments for a loan, either because the loan term has been changed or because the loan balance has increased (due to negative amortization).

Recast—To reamortize a loan.

Reconciliation—The final step in an appraisal, when the appraiser assembles and interprets the data in order to arrive at a final value estimate. Also called correlation.

Reconsideration of Value—A request by an agent to a lender to increase the appraised value of a property, based on evidence provided by comparables other than those selected by the appraiser.

Reconveyance—*See:* Deed of Reconveyance.

Redemption—The right of a defaulting borrower to prevent foreclosure by paying the full amount of the debt, plus costs.

Redemption, Equitable Right of—The period prior to a sheriff's sale when a defaulting mortgagor has the right to redeem the property by paying the debt plus costs.

Redemption, Statutory Right of—The period following the sheriff's sale in which a defaulting mortgagor has the right to redeem the property by paying off the loan balance, plus costs.

Redlining—When a lender refuses to make loans secured by property in a certain neighborhood because of the racial or ethnic composition of the neighborhood, in violation of fair lending laws.

Refinance Mortgage—A mortgage loan used to pay off an existing mortgage on the same property.

Regression, Principle of—An appraisal principle which holds that a valuable property surrounded by properties of lesser value tends to be worth less than it would be worth in a different location; the opposite of the principle of progression.

Regulation Z—The Federal Reserve Board's regulation that implements the Truth in Lending Act.

Reinstatement—The right of a defaulting borrower to prevent foreclosure by curing the default and costs. The loan is reinstated and repayment resumes.

Release—1. To give up a legal right. 2. A document in which a legal right is given up.

Rent—Compensation paid by a tenant to a landlord in exchange for the possession and use of the leased property.

Rent Credit Provision—A provision in a lease/option or lease/purchase contract that allows part of the rent paid by the tenant to be applied to the purchase of the property.

Repayment Period—The number of years over which a borrower will make payments on a loan. Also called the loan term.

Replacement Cost—The current cost of constructing a building with the same utility as the subject property, using modern materials and construction methods.

Replacement Cost Method—A method of appraisal in which an estimate of the subject property's value is arrived at by estimating the cost of replacing the improvements, then deducting estimated depreciation, and adding the estimated market value of the land.

Reproduction Cost—The current cost of constructing a replica of the subject property using the same materials and methods as originally used but at current prices.

Reserve Account—*See:* Impound Account.

Reserve Requirements—The Fed requires commercial banks to hold a certain portion of their deposits on reserve for immediate withdrawal by depositors.

Reserves for Replacement—For income-producing property, regular allowances set aside to pay for the replacement of structures and equipment that can be expected to wear out.

Residual Income—The amount of income that an applicant for a VA loan has left over after taxes, recurring obligations, and the proposed housing expense have been deducted from his or her gross monthly income.

Residual Income Analysis—A method used in qualifying VA loan applicants; the underwriter calculates the amount of residual income left over after deducting the proposed housing expense, recurring obligations, and taxes from the applicant's gross monthly income. Also called cash flow analysis.

RESPA—*See:* Real Estate Settlement Procedures Act.

Return of Investment—When an investment generates enough money to replace the amount originally invested in it. Also called recapture.

Return on Investment—The profit an investment generates for an investor, over and above the amount of money originally invested in it.

Reverse Equity Mortgage—An arrangement in which a homeowner mortgages a home to a lender in exchange for a monthly payment from the lender. Also called a home equity conversion mortgage (HECM).

RHS—*See:* Rural Housing Service.

Risk Analysis—*See:* Underwriting.

Rural Housing Service—A federal agency within the Department of Agriculture that subsidizes or guarantees loans for the purchase, development, or rehabilitation of property located in rural areas.

Sale-Leaseback—A financing arrangement in which the owner of industrial or commercial property sells the property and leases it back from the buyer. In addition to certain tax advantages, the seller/lessee obtains more cash through the sale than would normally be possible by borrowing and mortgaging the property, since lenders will not often lend 100% of a property's value.

Sales Comparison Approach—A method of appraisal in which the sales prices of comparable properties are used to estimate the value of the subject property. Also called the market data approach.

Satisfaction of Mortgage—A document which acknowledges that a mortgage has been paid in full, releasing the security property from the mortgage lien. *Compare:* Deed of Reconveyance.

Savings and Loan Association—A type of financial institution that has traditionally specialized in home mortgage loans; also called a savings association.

Savings Bank—A type of financial institution that has traditionally emphasized consumer loans and accounts for small depositors, but is now know for making home mortgage loans. Also called a mutual savings bank or thrift.

Scarcity—When there is a limited or inadequate supply of something; one of the four elements of value (along with utility, demand, and transferability).

Seasoned Loan—A loan with an established record of timely payment by the borrower.

Second Mortgage—A mortgage that does not have first lien position. Also called a junior mortgage.

Secondary Financing—Money borrowed to pay part of the required downpayment or closing costs for a first loan, which is secured by the same property that secures the first loan.

Secondary Liability—Liability that arises only in the event that the person who has primary liability for a debt fails to pay it.

Secondary Market—The market in which investors (including Fannie Mae, Freddie Mac, and Ginnie Mae) purchase real estate loans from lenders; also called the national market. *Compare:* Primary Market.

Secondary Market Agency—One of the three government-created entities that purchase loans and issue mortgage-backed securities: Fannie Mae, Freddie Mac, and Ginnie Mae.

Securities—Investment instruments, such as stocks and bonds, that confer an interest or a right to payment, without allowing direct managerial control over the enterprise invested in.

Securities, Mortgage-Backed (MBS)—Investment instruments that have pools of real estate loans as collateral; issued and sold to investors by the major secondary market agencies (Fannie Mae, Freddie Mac, and Ginnie Mae) and other companies.

Security Agreement—Under the Uniform Commercial Code, a document that creates a lien on personal property that is being used to secure a loan.

Security Instrument—A document that creates a voluntary lien against real property, to secure repayment of a loan; either a mortgage or a deed of trust.

Security Interest—A secured creditor's interest in property owned by the debtor, which entitles the creditor to have the property seized and sold if the debtor does not pay as agreed.

Security Property—Property owned by a borrower that is serving as collateral (the lender's security) for a loan.

Seller Financing—When a seller extends credit to a buyer to finance the purchase of the property; as opposed to having the buyer obtain a loan from a third party, such as an institutional lender.

Seller Second—Secondary financing from the seller, when a purchase money loan is used to supplement an institutional first mortgage.

Servicing—The process of collecting loan payments, keeping the records associated with loans, and handling defaults.

Servicing Fee—A fee paid by a secondary market agency or other investor to the lender that is servicing the mortgage loan.

Settlement—Closing, the final stage in a real estate transaction.

Settlement Statement—A document that presents a final, detailed accounting for a real estate transaction, listing each party's debits and credits and the amount each will receive or be required to pay at closing. Also called a closing statement.

Sheriff's Deed—The deed that is given to someone who purchases property at a foreclosure sale, after the statutory redemption period has expired.

Sheriff's Sale—A public auction of property after judicial foreclosure.

Stable Monthly Income—Gross monthly income (from primary and secondary sources) that meets the lender's tests of quality and durability.

Stock—A share of a corporation's stock represents a fractional ownership interest in the corporation; a shareholder may receive a return on the investment in the form of dividends and/or appreciation of the share's value.

Straight Note—*See:* Note, Straight.

Subject Property—In an appraisal, the property that is being appraised.

Subject To—When a borrower sells the security property without paying off the mortgage or deed of trust, and the purchaser takes title "subject to" the lien, but does not assume the loan.

Subordination—When a mortgagee or trust deed beneficiary agrees to accept lower lien priority than he or she is entitled to, allowing a lender with a lien recorded later to have higher priority.

Subordination Clause—A provision in a security instrument that permits a later security instrument to have higher lien priority than the one in which the clause appears.

Subprime Lending—Making riskier loans to persons who might otherwise be unable to qualify for a loan, often requiring higher interest rates and fees to make up for the increased risk of default.

Substitution, Principle of—A principle of appraisal holding that the maximum value of a property is set by how much it would cost to obtain another property that is equally desirable, assuming that there would not be a long delay or significant incidental expenses involved in obtaining the substitute.

Substitution of Entitlement—When a VA borrower sells the security property to another eligible veteran, who agrees to substitute his or her guaranty entitlement for the seller's, so that the seller's entitlement is restored.

Supply and Demand, Law of—A basic rule of economics holding that prices rise when supply decreases or demand increases, and that prices fall when supply increases or demand decreases.

Take-Out Loan—Long-term financing used to replace a construction loan (an interim loan) when construction has been completed. Also called a permanent loan.

Taxation—The federal government collects revenue through taxation. The rates at which people are taxed affects the amount of money taxpayers have available to invest.

Term—A prescribed period of time; especially the length of time allotted to a borrower in which to pay off a loan.

Thrift Industry—Term referring to savings banks together with savings and loan associations.

Tight Money Market—When loan funds are scarce, leading lenders to charge high interest rates and discount points.

TILA—*See:* Truth in Lending Act.

Time Deposit—A deposit in a financial institution that is not supposed to be withdrawn until a certain period has elapsed, unless the depositor pays a penalty. A certificate of deposit is an example. *Compare:* Demand Deposit.

Title Theory—The legal theory holding that a mortgage or deed of trust gives the lender legal title to the security property while the debt is being repaid. *Compare:* Lien Theory.

Title, Equitable—The interest of the vendee under a land contract, including the right to possession of the property and the right to acquire legal title by paying off the contract according to its terms. *Compare:* Legal Title.

Title, Legal—Title held as security, without the right to possess the property. *Compare:* Equitable Title.

Total Finance Charge—Under the Truth in Lending Act, the total finance charge on a loan includes the interest, any discount points paid by the borrower, the loan origination fee, and mortgage insurance costs. *See also:* Annual Percentage Rate.

Total Obligations to Income Ratio—*See:* Debt to Income Ratio.

Transferability—If an object is transferable, then ownership and possession of that object can be conveyed from one person to another. Transferability is one of the four elements of value, along with utility, scarcity, and demand.

Trust Account—A bank account in which funds held in trust on behalf of another person are kept separate from the holder's own money.

Trust Deed—*See:* Deed of Trust.

Trustee—In a deed of trust transaction, a neutral third party appointed by the lender to handle nonjudicial foreclosure (if necessary) or reconveyance after the loan has been repaid.

Trustee's Deed—The deed given to the purchaser at a trustee's sale.

Trustee's Sale—A nonjudicial foreclosure sale conducted by a trustee under the power of sale clause in a deed of trust.

Trustor—In a deed of trust transaction, the borrower. Also called the grantor.

Truth in Lending Act (TILA)—A federal law that requires lenders and credit arrangers to make disclosures concerning loan costs (including the total finance charge and the annual percentage rate) to consumer loan applicants.

UCC—*See:* Uniform Commercial Code.

UFMIP—*See:* MIP.

Underimprovement—An improvement that is not the most profitable use of the land.

Underlying Loan—*See:* Wraparound Financing.

Underwriter—The employee of an institutional lender who evaluates loan applications, deciding which loans to approve.

Underwriting—The process of evaluating the financial status of a loan applicant and the value of the property he or she hopes to buy, to determine the risk of default and the risk of loss in the event of default and foreclosure. Also called risk analysis or qualifying.

Underwriting, Automated (AU)—Underwriting using software that makes a preliminary analysis of a loan application and makes a recommendation for approval or additional scrutiny.

Underwriting Standards—*See:* Qualifying Standards.

Uniform Commercial Code (UCC)—A body of law that has been adopted in slightly varying versions in most states, which attempts to standardize commercial law dealing with such matters as negotiable instruments and sales of personal property.

Uniform Settlement Statement—A settlement statement required for any transaction involving a loan that is subject to the Real Estate Settlement Procedures Act (RESPA).

Uniform Standards of Appraisal Practice—Guidelines for appraisers adopted by the Appraisal Foundation, a nonprofit organization of professional appraiser associations.

Usury—Charging an interest rate that exceeds legal limits.

Utility—The ability of an object to satisfy some need or arouse a desire for possession; one of the four elements of value, along with scarcity, demand, and transferability.

VA—Department of Veterans Affairs.

VA Entitlement—The VA guaranty amount that a particular veteran is entitled to.

VA-Guaranteed Loan—A home loan to an eligible veteran made by an institutional lender and guaranteed by the Department of Veterans Affairs, protecting the lender against losses resulting from default.

VA Guaranty—The portion of a VA loan guaranteed by the Department of Veterans Affairs; the maximum amount that the VA will pay the lender for a loss resulting from the borrower's default.

Valuation—*See:* Appraisal.

Vendee—The buyer in a land contract.

Vendor—The seller in a land contract.

Verification of Deposit—A form a lender sends to a financial institution for confirmation that a loan applicant has the funds on deposit that he or she claims to have.

Verification of Employment—A form a lender sends to a loan applicant's employer, for confirmation that the applicant is actually employed as claimed, and to verify the amount of the applicant's salary.

Wholesale Lending—Lending by a large investor through a loan correspondent who originates and services loans.

Wraparound Financing—A seller financing arrangement in which the seller uses part of the buyer's payments to make the payments on an existing loan (called the underlying loan); the buyer takes title subject to the underlying loan, but does not assume it.

Writ of Execution—*See:* Execution, Order of.

Index

D

J

K

L

V

W

Y